Basic processes in
ADULT DEVELOPMENTAL PSYCHOLOGY

Basic processes in ADULT DEVELOPMENTAL PSYCHOLOGY

Merrill F. Elias, Ph.D.

Department of Psychology
University of Maine at Orono

Penelope Kelly Elias, Ph.D.

Department of Psychology
University of Maine at Orono

Jeffrey W. Elias, Ph.D.

Department of Psychology
Texas Tech University

with 119 *illustrations*

The C. V. Mosby Company

Saint Louis 1977

Cover photograph by Beverly Wood

Printed in the United States of America

Distributed in Great Britain by Henry Kimpton, London

The C. V. Mosby Company
11830 Westline Industrial Drive, St. Louis, Missouri 63141

Library of Congress Cataloging in Publication Data

Elias, Merrill F 1938-
Basic processes in adult developmental psychology.
Bibliography: p.
Includes index.

1. Adulthood. 2. Developmental psychology.
I. Elias, Penelope Kelly, joint author. II. Elias, Jeffrey W., 1946- joint author. III. Title.
BF724.5.E38 155.6 76-57941
ISBN 0-8016-1519-4

CB/CB/B 9 8 7 6 5 4 3 2 1

To our favorite cross-sectional sample:

EARL
MARY

MERRILL
RUTH
MARGE

"BIG" SUSAN

"LITTLE" SUSAN

ERIC

MIKE

BEN

PREFACE

This book was written to help fill a growing need for textbooks dealing with basic behavioral processes in adult development. Historically, developmental psychology curricula have concentrated on children. As late as 1970 a review of the literature on developmental psychology that appeared in the *Annual Review of Psychology* included major discussions on infancy, childhood, and adolescence, but no major section was devoted to either adult development or aging. Until recently only a few developmental textbooks have covered more than the lower end of the life span.

Sidney Pressey, an innovator in many fields of psychology, was one of the first authors dealing with adult development psychology. In collaboration with Janney and Kuhlen (1939) he wrote *Life: A Psychological Survey*. The literature on adult developmental psychology and aging has increased appreciably since Pressey and his colleagues wrote their life-span book, although texts in this area are few in number compared to the many texts that deal exclusively with the years from birth to young adulthood. Many new texts in adult psychology will emerge as behavioral scientists become increasingly aware that psychological development continues well past the time that biological growth has ceased. This year one of the first, if not the first book, in introductory psychology that includes a chapter on aging will be published (Weiner and Rundquist, 1977).

The present text is written with a life-span developmental perspective, although there is an emphasis on the latter portion of the human life span that is dictated by the paucity of literature for the middle years. Philosophically, we embrace the idea that developmental psychology does not constitute the study of infants, children, college students, or retired persons at a particular stage of their life. Rather, behavioral processes must be studied for the entire life span and for many species. If psychology is to qualify as one of the *life* sciences, it must deal with the phyletic and historical antecedents of behavior for the human species and it must be dynamic; that is, it must deal with a growing, developing, and ever-changing organism.

Our emphasis on what has been commonly referred to as "the aging literature" may seem a contradiction to the life-span philosophy we so strongly endorse. It has been forced by the sheer impossibility of adequately reviewing the literature relevant to the entire life span in a book designed for a semester course. In the last ten years the research literature on adult developmental psychology and gerontology has grown immensely. Thus texts are, of necessity, becoming increasingly specialized and must become increasingly selective with regard to the literature they cover.

Practical limitations on emphasis and scope present no major problem with regard to the learning of critical concepts. Critical concepts can be structured around a variety of emphases. In this book there is more of an experimental or research emphasis than that found in many of the early books on adult developmental psychology and aging. Many were oriented toward social gerontology. Others were collections of generalizations with little reference to experimental methodology or specific experiments. Some dealt with life-span methodology in depth but provided little in the way of content in terms of specific studies. Nevertheless, they all furthered an understanding of adult development and aging because the authors approached the subject with a point of view that reflected their background and interests.

Our backgrounds include experimental and life-span developmental psychology, and we approach this book with that frame of reference. Experimental psychology is not a subdiscipline within psychology. Many areas of psychology are experimental in nature if one accepts a broad definition of experimentation as a systematic approach to the solution of a problem that embraces the concept of control. Experimental psychology is no more animal psychology or the psychology of perception than developmental psychology is the psychology of children. The experimental method is a tool for research. Development is a process. Aging is a natural consequence of growth, differentiation, and development.

Chapters 9 and 10 were prepared by Jeffrey W. Elias with final editing by M. F. Elias for length and style consistency with other chapters in the book. Penelope K. Elias and M. F. Elias collaborated on the other chapters.

We would especially like to acknowledge certain people who directly contributed to this book: Mrs. Beverly J. Wood, who did most of the original artwork and cartoons and whose talent enabled her to execute these drawings, a task far beyond the limitations imposed by the right parietal areas of our respective right cerebral hemispheres; Dr. W. Gibson Wood for his help in the coordination of artwork: Drs. Jack Botwinick, Thomas Roderick, Kathleen Light, and Richard Sprott and many others who provided us with copies of their figures and permission to use them. We also thank those kind authors and publishers who gave us permission to use illustrations and quotes, and George and his friends who posed for the cartoons. Many thanks also go to Mrs. Nicole Maier for the endless hours spent typing the manuscript.

Merrill F. Elias
Penelope Kelly Elias
Jeffrey W. Elias

A WORD TO THE STUDENT

In many areas of adult developmental psychology, behavioral scientists simply do not have firm answers to important questions. Adult developmental psychology and aging research are relatively new in comparison with other areas of emphasis and interest within psychology. There are special problems with regard to control and research methodology. Thus many of the most important findings have to do with the way in which research should be conducted rather than with firm generalizations about behavior.

Sometimes data do not support generalizations and conclusions that all scientists would like to be true. There is always a danger of selecting data that support personally or socially popular generalizations. If researchers have a genuine desire to use their knowledge to improve the quality of life, they must avoid that trap. It is wise to be most suspicious of the popular generalizations because they are rarely subjected to the same rigorous tests that are applied to unpopular generalizations.

The important thing is to avoid being blinded by belief or logic. Both help scientists to generate and pursue important hypotheses; neither guarantees truth. In the final analysis, truth is dictated by facts on hand. Facts are derived from scientific information. Science is not truth. It merely provides a set of useful rules for collecting facts.

As behavioral scientists and teachers, we have examined some of the many facts, and we have reached conclusions. We are human, and thus our conclusions are unavoidably influenced by our perspectives and personal philosophies; they are affected by our experiences with significant persons and events. You may not agree with some conclusions. Good. A healthy disrespect for the weight of authority, even scientific authority, is important if we are to continue to learn more about changes in behavior across the life span. There is nothing final about a conclusion. It represents a stepping-stone to further research. Therefore if you disagree with one or more conclusions reached in this book, go into the laboratory, into the field, to the library, and examine the issues with as much care and objectivity as is humanly possible. If you will do this and thus generate more valid conclusions, we have accomplished our objectives.

CONTENTS

CHAPTER 1

SCOPE AND ORIENTATION

To many students a book with an "experimental emphasis" promises endless summaries of experiments. This is neither the objective nor the format of this text. Rather, our objective is to impart knowledge of important methods for the study of adult developmental processes and important generalizations that have resulted from the application of experimental methods. We choose to build this knowledge within the concept of a topical organization that is familiar to the experimental psychologist. However, there is no neglect of the social aspect of adult development. New avenues of social-experimental research are suggested in hopes that they may complement research in naturalistic settings.

There is a greater emphasis on the animal literature than that which may be found in many adult development texts. This emphasis is not based on the intimate association of animals with experimental psychology. Rather, it is based on the potential value in allowing psychologists to study behavioral change over the entire life span of the animal in a very short time. One may do so in the context of designs that allow the manipulation of genetic factors and environment. However, the human literature remains the critical focus of discussion. The animal model serves when human data cannot be collected for ethical and moral reasons or when answers are not forthcoming from the human literature because manipulative strategies cannot be carried out or important life history variables cannot be controlled.

The second chapter deals with the history of psychology, not for the sake of history per se, but to prepare the way for a better understanding of contemporary issues and attitudes toward older persons and aging research. When you read this chapter, you should get a better understanding of why developmental psychology was, and still is, used by many psychologists as a term that is synonymous with child psychology.

The third chapter discusses methods for life-span research. Research designs become much more complex when one studies changes in behavior over time or differences among persons of different ages. Adult developmental psychology is not merely the study of different age groups. Many of the acceptable designs for the study of behavior at a single time period are not acceptable for developmental research.

The most studied area of adult development, intelligence, is discussed in Chapter 4. Does it decline with age or is decline a methodological artifact? Do healthy persons show the same changes over time as do unhealthy persons? How do definitions of intelligence influence our thinking about decline as opposed to growth?

Chapter 5 examines the many factors that influence intelligence test scores and measures of learning ability. Here we grapple with the many factors that prevent us from obtaining a true picture of the intellectual capacity of persons at different stages of the life span.

Chapters 6 and 7 deal with perception, mental processing, and motor response in the context of experimental studies designed to answer which specific mental processes decline and which remain stable or improve with increasing age. Here we focus on *input-throughput-output* concepts of information processing.

Chapter 8 discusses learning. There is considerable emphasis on the animal literature as it relates to learning across the life span. Limitations and advantages of animal models for life-span psychology are discussed. The literature on human learning is not neglected, since humans think and learn differently from animals by virtue of the ability to speak and communicate with words.

Motivational changes with advancing age are so important with respect to personal adjustment and the ability to survive and adapt to the environment that we devote Chapters 9 and 10 to this topic. Chapter 9 deals with motivation from the perspective provided by the experimental literature. Chapter 10 considers motivation in the social-molar sense, that is, it integrates the theme of "motivation" with studies of work, retirement, and leisure. It emphasizes the fact that important motivational variables at the human level are social in nature.

Chapter 11 deals with the emerging new field of behavioral endocrinology and aging. There is increasing evidence that changing patterns of hormone interaction with advancing age influence the behaviors of men and women. They can play a dramatic role in the onset of age-associated mental illnesses. Although the fountain of youth has not yet been discovered through the study of hormones, potential ways to improve the quality of life by alleviating symptoms of mental illness that accompany age-associated hormone imbalance have been discovered.

Chapter 12 considers the effect of physical health and the biological systems on behavior. Nothing has emerged as a more critical topic in the literature on aging. It may well be that much of the decline in human abilities with age may be related to sickness, mental or physical, rather than decrements in the functioning of the brains of healthy persons with advancing age. This promises a brighter future as psychologists learn more about how to fight debilitating diseases of middle and old age.

Genetic and environmental interactions, as they influence behavior at various stages in the life span, are discussed in Chapter 13. This chapter does not presume that genetic factors control behavior. Genotype has no direct influence on behavior. It influences behavioral changes at various periods of the life cycle by virtue of its influence on the physiology of the organism. Paradoxically, the study of behavior genetics provides one of the most convincing arguments for the importance of environment. A truly life-span developmental psychology cannot ignore the influence of genotype on behavior across the life span. Development does not begin at birth; it begins at conception.

In Chapter 14 we introduce some of the behavior genetic methods available to comparative psychologists who may wish to make maximal use of animals and animal models in the study of *how* genotype influences behavior over the life span. A number of genetic tools are reviewed, and suggestions are made with regard to necessary genetic controls and manipulations for the investigation that utilizes genetic methods to create a physiological phenotype for purposes of study in a developmental context.

CHAPTER 2

HISTORICAL PERSPECTIVE
from decline to development

It is tempting to skip a chapter on history. It would be a mistake to do so. This chapter sets the stage for the chapters that follow, and it establishes a historical framework for the student of adult development. A discipline can never be fully understood and appreciated unless one understands its history. In short, it is difficult to know where you are unless you know where you have been.

The history of adult development parallels the development of psychology in general. In some areas it has lagged behind, for example, language and cognitive development (see Riegel, 1973a). In other respects it has developed far ahead of other areas, for example, research designs that better enable measures of age changes as distinct from age differences (Riegel, 1973a). This is in part related to the fact that adult developmental psychology has not grown as a natural extension of child psychology.

Historically, the child psychologists have ignored the adult years as if they assume that development terminates at the end of adolescence (see Goulet and Baltes, 1970). Brackbill's (1971) survey of ninety-six four-year graduate training programs in developmental psychology revealed that only ten offered training in adulthood. On the other hand, many investigators who advocate a life-span approach to aging have neglected the early years of development in all but theoretical and methodological discussions. Ransom (1956) has provided data which indicate that one of the problems in establishing a truly life-span approach to developmental psychology is related to the fact that the same investigators have not traditionally been involved in both child and adult developmental research. It is probably because of the different research interests of the child development and adult developmental psychologists that there have been so few developmental psychology texts that cover more than the periods of infancy, childhood, and adolescence.

Why have adult psychology and child psychology grown up in different ways and with different research emphases if adult and child psychology are both concerned with "developmental" processes? Why did child psychology develop first, more rapidly, and more fully in the United States than adult developmental psychology? Why has aging been described as a process of decline rather than development? To answer these questions, it is helpful to examine the influence of persons who helped create and promote these two areas of developmental psychology. It is also important to examine the social and political attitudes that existed during the various points in history when child psychology and adult psychology were developing.

Where does one begin such an examination? The obvious answer is to begin at the beginning, but it is really very difficult to know where the beginning is. In part, difficulty in marking the beginning of adult developmental psychology is related to the problems involved in establishing individuals who may be credited with the first conception of an idea, a methodology, or data collection in a particular area of inquiry. Sometimes original ideas and concepts failed to gain recognition. In some instances they were not promoted. In others they were promoted at a time when society was not ready, for a variety of economic and ideological reasons, to accept or recognize them. Thus it is difficult to find agreement with regard to the criteria for describing who is a father or founder of a subject area. How did adult developmental psychology begin? Did it start with research in aging, with an official program, or with descriptions of the aging phenomenon?

THE BEGINNING

Groffman (1970) traces the origins of adult developmental psychology descriptions and theories of adult development and aging in philosophy and literature in Europe, extending as far back as the Greeks and Romans. Apparently, the Greeks' concept of development was provided by Aristotle. Aristotle's concept was *teleological.* He conceived of development as movement from a lower to a higher level from birth *through the adult years.* Other references to adult development have been traced to the German philosophy of the eighteenth century as reflected in the novels and other literature of the time (Groffman, 1970).

Tetens and life-span psychology

If science may be broadly defined as *a systematic approach to knowledge building,* the distinction of "father of adult developmental psychology and aging research" may well belong to J. N. Tetens (1736-1807). It was Tetens who first attempted to organize the European literature of his time into a publication that described the process of human development and change over the entire life span (Groffman, 1970).

Teten's book was philosophically oriented, and thus many of the propositions and generalizations put forth were not subject to experimentation and empirical test. Nevertheless, the book was of considerable value for two reasons. First, it represented one of the first, if not the first, comprehensive reviews of the current status of thinking about development across the life span. Second and more important, it anticipated the current emphasis on the life-span approach to the understanding of adult development and behavioral change.

The life-span approach assumes that an understanding of behavior of any stage of development can be more fully appreciated by an understanding of the historical antecedents of that behavior. Comparisons of behaviors at two different age groups provide a valuable description of age differences, but a complete understanding of how the behavior evolved can only result from the exploration of factors that contribute to age-related behavioral differences from the moment of conception. Although no single investigator can accomplish the enormous research task implied by the life-span approach, researchers working together to synthesize existing data and theories can provide a life-span account of behavioral processes. Tetens (1777) employed this strategy. However, his approach was historical and philosophical rather than empirical, in the sense of data collection.

Quetelet: creativity and cross-sectional data collection

Adolph Quetelet (1796-1874), a Belgian statistician, is recognized as one of the first investigators to approach adult development and aging in a scientific manner (Birren, 1961). This distinction may well be deserved if science is defined in the conventional sense of data collection. Quetelet was clearly and unmistakably a scientist. He received the first doctorate in science from the University of Ghent in 1819 in mathematics, but like many of the early scientists, his interests extended far beyond one field. He was also a statistician, an astronomer, and had there been a discipline called psychology in the early nineteenth century, a social psychologist.

Quetelet was one of the first scientists to formulate quantitative methods for investigation of social phenomena as well as physical phenomena (Hankins, 1908, cited in Birren, 1961a). Most important, he combined his interest in social science with an interest in quantifying the changes that occur with advancing age. For example, he presented data relating the author's age to creativity in French and English drama (Birren, 1961a). This study was of great importance for two reasons: (1) it anticipated a later and more comprehensive study of creativity by Lehman in 1953; (2) its results emphasized the *developmental* aspect of adult aging rather than the *stagnation* view, which came to be popularized and perpetuated by misunderstanding and misuse of early testing results with adults. Quetelet presented evidence that dramatic talent in England and France began to develop after the twenty-first year, manifested itself between the ages of 25 and 35 years, and continued to increase vigorously until the age of 55 years. Only then is it characterized by gradual decline. In this early presentation of data, Quetelet makes an important point, which was emphasized many years later by Lorge (1936) and others (Riegel, 1973b)—whether one views adulthood as mental stagnation and the later years as abrupt mental decline depends partly on one's definition of mental ability and the choice of behaviors that are evaluated.

Quetelet was probably the first investigator to employ the *cross-sectional* method for empirical data collection, although Stern, an American statistician, has been credited as the first to actually use the term *cross-sectional* (Baltes and Goulet, 1970). Extensive use of the cross-sectional method has been forced on developmental psychologists by the inconvenient, but unavoidable, fact that investigators grow old at the same rate and sometimes faster than their human subjects. Of necessity, it has become an important tool in developmental psychology, particularly life-span developmental psychology, and thus it will be discussed in detail in the following chapters. Briefly, in the *cross-sectional design, data are collected from persons of different ages rather than following the same individual over a number of years,* that is, the longitudinal approach. Cross-sectional data collection strategies are compromised because they deal with individuals who were born and reared at different points in history and thus differ in a variety of ways; for example, educational experiences, prenatal care, and diet. The *longitudinal approach, or the collecting of data for the same persons over time,* is confounded by educational, political, ideological, cultural, and other environmental changes as one grows older. Thus the cross-sectional approach attempts to measure *age differences,* whereas the longitudinal approach attempts to measure *age changes.* Neither approach does so in an absolute sense. Alternate designs and the methodological solutions will be discussed in detail in Chapter 3. Fortunately, Quetelet was aware of the fact that his cross-sectional data were influenced by sampling characteristics such as sex, geographical location, and socioeconomic status.

It is obvious from the foregoing material that Quetelet contributed significantly to the empirical science of adult development. In addition to his own contributions with regard to data collection across the life span, he had considerable influence on the work of quantitative social scientists who were to follow. Boring (1950:446-447) discusses this influence as it affected Francis Galton, another early social scientist.

Galton: the index of correlation and eugenics

Galton (1822-1911) was a truly versatile scientist. He began his training in medicine in Birmingham as a result of his parents' wishes, and he received training in mathematics at Cambridge. When his father died, releasing him from his obligation to medicine, he traveled extensively and established such a reputation as a geographer that he was awarded a gold medal by the Royal Geographic Society in 1854. From an interest in geography, he moved into anthropology and the social sciences. Utilizing principles from Quetelet's earlier statistical work, he invented the index of correlation as a method of mathematically describing the relationship between two variables. Galton was not merely satisfied to develop statistical concepts. He was concerned with social conditions that existed in England, and he began to apply statistical concepts, measurement techniques, and experimental apparatus to the study of the aging process.

In 1879 he established the experimental psychology of adult development in Great Britain with the use of a whistle, which was placed on one end of a walking stick with a rubber bulb on the other end for its operation (Boring, 1950:485). Using this whistle, Galton made what is most likely the first report of decline in sensitivity to high-frequency tones in the elderly. As shall be seen in later chapters, experiments on hearing loss in the elderly have not, unfortunately, advanced much beyond this early psychophysical experiment.

In 1884 Galton opened a demonstrational Anthropometric Laboratory at the International Health Exhibition. The laboratory was utilized to collect cross-sectional data on 9,377 males and females ranging in age from 5 to 80 years. It is important to note that although Galton was concerned with mental functioning, he did not use paper-and-pencil tests. He believed strongly that "apparatus-tests" of sensory discrimination were a valid measure of intellectual functioning. Consequently, he used methods from the psychophysical laboratory for the collecting of data on individual differences in mental functioning. He was particularly ingenious with regard to the invention of psychophysical apparatus. He developed a pendulum device for measuring reaction time, an apparatus that measured speed of a blow struck with the arm, an instrument for measuring discrimination of color depth, visual acuity testing cards, a set of tools that were used for color discrimination, a bar that could be extended at variable distances to estimate visual extension, a disc to test judgments of perpendicular, and a set of three weights, each to test muscular sense. Originally the weights were made of cartridge cases, but later they were placed on the market finished beautifully in brass. Perhaps this is why the term *brass instruments* came to be used to describe the apparatus used by experimental psychologists. It is important to remember that the early testing of individual differences in adults was done with brass instruments. When child psychology began to flourish in America, these techniques were inadequate and inappropriate for testing the kind of mental ability that was of interest to educators—ability that predicts success in school.

Galton's interest in the collecting of anthropometric and psychophysical data over a wide age range may not have been necessarily related to an interest in developmental processes, per se. A review of Galton's contribution in Boring's *A History of Experimental Psychology* (1950:482-484) leads us to believe that Galton's cross-sectional data collection was stimulated by his concept of eugenics. *Eugenics* was viewed as *a scientific means of improving the quality and fitness of the human race by artificial selection for superior persons.* This goal was to be accomplished by discouraging, or even forbidding, persons of inferior strength and ability to marry or copulate. Ever since its introduction by Galton, eugenics has been repugnant to most, but not all, social and natural scientists. The fundamental problem in Galton's time and now is that there is by no means agreement with regard to the appropriate array of characteristics possessed by the superior person (Elias, 1973). Galton's selection of physical and mental strength as qualities that the "fit" person must possess may have reflected the strong emphasis on competition that was stressed in the British philosophy, ideology, and economics of his time (see Riegel, 1973a). These philosophies may still have an influence on society's current attitudes toward the worth of elderly adults. Unfortunately, the early association of genetics with eugenics may have slowed the growth of behavior genetics, particularly the behavior genetics of life-span development (Elias, 1973). Nevertheless, data collection across the life span was undertaken to document a *hypothesized* deterioration in mental and physical strength with successive generations. To gather baseline data against which to compare the results of his proposed "genetic" selection procedure, it was necessary to collect cross-sectional data across the life span. He did, indeed, collect such data. The information that he amassed at the International Health Exhibition, and later in his laboratory in the South Kensington Museum in London, which was maintained for six years, was still being analyzed forty years after the laboratory closed (Birren, 1961a). Many of these data were reported in his book entitled *Inquiries Into Human Faculty and Its Development* (1883).

THE EARLY YEARS: 1875-1920

Before discussing the series of events following Galton, it will be helpful to discuss two approaches to the interpretation of history: (1) the *personalistic* and (2) the *naturalistic*. Boring (1950: 3-5) distinguishes between the two views. *The personalistic interpretation of history emphasizes the contribution of great persons. The opposing conception, the naturalistic interpretation, emphasizes the preparedness of society to accept certain changes.* Social attitudes and cultural conditions must be in a state of readiness in order to be receptive to ideas of great persons. Taken to an extreme, the naturalistic view of history sees persons as inflexible agents or symptoms of historical change. On the other hand, the personalistic view ignores the antecedents of great persons. Many times a long chain of research is begun and carried out by a great number of persons. Then one individual, capitalizing on groundwork by predecessors, puts the pieces together and takes credit for the ultimate scientific discovery. Nevertheless, the work of the persons before him and the readiness of the times to accept the findings or theoretical formulation are essential to its success.

Galton's influence

A strictly personalistic approach might predict that Galton's extensive collection of cross-sectional data would have stimulated further work in aging in British universities and ultimately the rapid growth of adult developmental psychology in America. However, Galton's emphasis on data collection for all age groups did not stimulate an emphasis on adult development in either British or American universities in the early 1900s.

It may be helpful to adapt a naturalistic view to explain the sequence of events that retarded the growth of adult developmental psychology. First, at the turn of the century, Great Britain gave little support to the development of psychology within universities. Applied psychology in industry received far more support in Great Britain than academic psychology. Boring (1950:48) has commented that at the Oxford International Congress of Psychology in 1923 it was easier to find a British psychologist affiliated with a coal mine than with a psychological laboratory. Second, the slow growth of academic psychology meant that there were few university-based psychologists in Great Britain who would carry on Galton's interest in adult development and influence students. Galton did not educate graduate students who could continue his work with its emphasis on laboratory experimentation and cross-sectional data collection over the life span. In contrast, Willhelm Wundt, a German psychologist with a strong belief in general laws of behavior, provided formal training for many American psychologists, and his thinking had an immediate influence on their early expression of ideas about what psychology should be.

Wundt

Many American students traveled to Wundt's laboratory in Leipzig (formally founded in 1879). The movement to Leipzig did not reflect a desire to study abroad as much as a need for formal graduate research training in experimental psychology. Aside from William James' single room for psychological experimentation at Harvard University in 1875, there were no formal psychology laboratories or departments in the United States until 1881, when one was established at Johns Hopkins University (Boring, 1950: 324). Thus an American student who wanted to take his Ph.D. in a viable laboratory had to travel to Germany to take it under "Professor Wundt." Many of the American psychologists who turned out to be the most highly influential in American psychology in the early 1900s (e.g., G. Stanley Hall, J. McKeen Cattell, E. W. Scripture, Frank Angell) took advantage of this opportunity.

How fortunate it might have been for the early advancement of adult developmental psychology if Wundt, like Galton, had been concerned with the study of individual differences. Wundt, however, considered them an annoyance. Boring (1950:533-539) tells us that Wundt wanted to study what were referred to as general laws of behavior in the adult. Galton's data revealed individual differences which varied in magnitude depending on age, but Wundt argued that both the aging phenomenon and individual differences phenomenon did not reflect the *normal* state of affairs, which was demonstrated only by using highly practiced subjects. In contrast, his American student, J. McKeen Cattell, took the position that individual differences were the normal state of affairs. Boring (1950:505) states that despite Cattell's interest in studying individual differences and his disagreement with Wundt over what constituted "normal behavior," the American psychologists, including Cattell, came back from Leipzig with a high degree of motivation to infuse Wundt's "new" experimental psychology into the American university system.

Thus at the beginning of the century the stage was set for the development of an American version of Wundt's brand of academic psychology, which was concentrated on experimentation at one time period of adult life and thus was episodic rather than developmental in nature. The mature adult would be the prototype for infants, children, adolescents, and the elderly. This prediction is very reasonable within the context of a personalistic view of historical events. This is not what transpired, at least not for long.

To be sure, Wundt-like laboratories of "psychophysiology," concentrating on the "normal" adult, were established in American universities, but in a short time the psychology of children, spreading like wildfire in the United States, brought the laboratory psychologist into the field and the child into the laboratory. Furthermore, it fanned the flames of interest in individual differences, but with a new brand of mental measurement, which in a short period of time rejected the "brass instruments" of the psychophysiology laboratory for the paper-and-pencil tests. Child psychology continued to dominate American psychology through two world wars and to such an extent that one could only conclude from examining textbooks and published materials, as well as course curricula in American colleges and universities, that development ceases to occur after adolescence.

How could child psychology have had such an influence that it moved the laboratory psychologists away from the study of the "average" adult to the study of individual differences in children? One possible answer is that children made an excellent captive subject pool, once they were made available in the public school system. One cannot deny the tendency of the pragmatic American psychologist to fit the problem to the available subject population. Nevertheless, the convenience hypothesis is not entirely sufficient to explain the rapid development of child psychology laboratories in the early 1900s.

Functionalism and G. Stanley Hall

Both Boring (1950:533-539) and Charles (1970:35) provide an interesting account of the interacting social and ideological forces, that is, the *Zeitgeist,* which potentiated the growth of child development laboratories. It seems that education, children, and psychology were closely related from the beginning. This close relationship was made explicit by the work of William James, an American educator, who is also given credit for being the first experimental psychologist in the United States. He did not experiment himself, which led some to refer to him as an "armchair psychologist," but he was a strong advocate of experimental psychology as well as a *functional* psychology in which the public school system was viewed as a vehicle for preparing children to cope in an active manner with a competitive society. James' student, G. Stanley Hall, was the founder of child psychology, but he was an experimental psychologist as well. He developed the experimental psychology laboratories at Johns Hopkins University and later Clark University. His books, *Adolescence* (1904) and *Educational Problems* (1911), focused attention on the child's developmental needs and emphasized the application of psychological tools of inquiry and findings to these needs. In short, Hall advocated an applied or functional psychology. Since American educator-psychologists like James and John Dewey led the functionalist movement in education, they were easily convinced of the need for research evidence that had bearing on the development of children.

Developmental child psychology flourished in response to these needs (Charles, 1970). Thus shortly after Wundt's American students, including Cattell, returned to the United States, there was a growing emphasis on the creation of applied programs that would improve the quality of schooling for children, and hence the quality of life (see Looft, 1973).

Why was the emphasis on education for children alone, rather than on educational opportunities for both children and adults? Education for children made good sense in terms of the nation's needs. In the early 1900s the public school system was still relatively new in most parts of the country, and the United States was a young nation. Adults of all ages were desperately needed in the labor market or on the farm. In the early 1900s the industrial revolution had just begun, and the country had not yet moved entirely away from an agrarian economy. Large numbers of adults were playing an important and necessary role in society up until the point when they died. Not only was attention directed more to the needs of children as opposed to adults, but nursery schools and grade schools did, indeed, provide captive subject pools.

Zeitgeist

It is important to remember, however, that it was not merely the intense interest in public education for children, the fact that children were readily available subjects, or functional psychology per se that dictated the move from the "average" adult to child developmental psychology. Rather, it was because all of these influences were consistent with and, in fact, a symptom of the American *Zeitgeist.* Boring (1950:507-508) expresses it better than anyone.

> America was a new pioneer country. Land was free—to the strong pioneer who was ready to take it and wrest a living from nature. Survival by adaptation to environment was the key to the culture of the New World. America's success-philosophy, based on individual opportunity and ambition, is responsible for the shirt sleeves democracy ("every man a king"), for pragmatism ("the philosophy of a dollar-grubbing nation"), and functionalism of all kinds, within psychology and without.*

Wundt's brand of "new" psychology just could not survive in the context of this American *Zeitgeist.* It rejected individual differences, it ignored children as subjects, and it placed too little emphasis on the environment. In short, it was not develop-

*From Boring, E. G. *A history of experimental psychology.* © 1950. Englewood Cliffs, N.J.: Prentice-Hall, Inc.

mental in emphasis and thus did not fit in with national, political, and ideological values that emphasized individual development rather than position by virtue of birth.

Thorndike and the chickens

The demise of Wundt's psychology was hastened by another movement in American psychology that was consistent with the American *Zeitgeist,* behaviorism. With its emphasis on environment, behaviorism emerged in America almost simultaneously with the increasing interest in educating children. This "new" American psychology not only hastened the end of Wundt's "new" psychology, but it was a major factor stimulating the growth of child developmental psychology.

Connectionism and the *law of effect* anticipated behaviorism. Connectionism may have begun in William James' basement. At least this is where E. L. Thorndike, father of the concept, began his behavioral experiments with chickens (Charles, 1970:35). He completed this research with Cattell at Columbia and published *Animal Intelligence* in 1898 (Thorndike, 1898). Out of these early experiments came his concept of *connectionism.* The basic idea was that learning reflected the association of stimuli and responses through neural conditioning, which was "stamped in" by reward. This process was termed the *law of effect.* The law of effect was highly consistent with a view of behavior as dependent on the environment, an environment that could be modified by teachers and parents. Thus it quickly became a major force in educational and developmental psychology. It turned the attention of researchers in child psychology to the identification of experiences antecedent to knowledge and skills. Thus Thorndike's work is viewed by many (e.g., Charles, 1970) as the beginning of experimental child psychology. Connectionism is not entirely consistent with many contemporary views of development because it emphasized a concept of the developing child as a passive, rather than an active, organism. Nevertheless, Thorndike's work had an important long-term influence on developmental child psychology.

J. B. Watson: rats and babies

The next important indirect influence on adult developmental psychology was *behaviorism.* J. B. Watson, a laboratory psychologist, promoted behaviorism first in 1908 and more fully in 1913. Similar to connectionism, behaviorism, because of its extreme emphasis on the environment, had both a positive and negative impact on developmental psychology. Basically, the behaviorists objected to Wundt's heavy reliance on introspection in his psychophysics laboratory. Wundt relied not only on behavioral responses but on the comments of highly trained subjects in order to develop his laws that were to describe the relationship between physical properties of stimulation and perception. Watson (1919), and other behaviorists who followed, believed that psychology should be scientific and that it should develop a unified methodological approach which emulated the natural sciences. They needed a model for the "science of psychology," and they turned to the early concept of physics, one of the oldest and most respected of the natural sciences, to fund that model. Once the model was adapted, only observable events were the proper data for the psychologist-scientist. His role was to explore stimulus-response contingencies that governed these observable events rather than to speculate about the inner workings of the mind. Having "freed" psychology both from the mind and from the necessity of dealing with verbal responses, it was possible to study the behavior of animals as well as humans. Thus at the same time that mammalian geneticists were building a discipline based on the mouse, behaviorists were beginning to build a science of psychology with the rat.

Fortunately, some of the "laws" of learning in rats and humans were similar, and out of the rat laboratory came a multitude of techniques that were useful not only in the classroom but have continued to be useful in the formulation of behavior modification techniques. These techniques have become an important part of adult developmental psychology in recent years.

It would be incorrect to leave the impression that Watson confined himself to the rat laboratory. As Charles (1970) points out, most of Watson's work of interest to the developmental psychologists was done at the Phipps Clinic at Johns Hopkins University. In 1916 he was given a small sum of money to study the behavior of human infants. His research in conditioning of Albert's fear response has become a classical example of early developmental research (Watson and Raynor, 1920).

As previously mentioned, some developmental psychologists believe that the learning models and the insistence on empirical data collection made a vital contribution to developmental psychology. Others believe that it has limited the scope of developmental psychology by overemphasizing the role of the environment at the expense of the organism (Riegel, 1973b) and genetic influences on behavior (Elias, 1973). Regardless of the side that one wishes to take in this issue, Americans were ready for environmentalism by the 1930s, and behaviorism filled the bill. Charles (1970) argues that the impact of behaviorism was to provide a feeling that scientific explanations were forthcoming, or available, for most aspects of behavior. He points out that the volume of research increased sharply and that public confidence in the quality of scientific work by psychologists was reflected in the establishment of a number of child-study institutes, both tax supported and private, between 1920 and 1930. Although this enormous amount of attention to child psychology and child clinics initially detracted from public interest in aging and adult developmental research, many of these early child institutes eventually extended their studies to the adult.

The testing movement

Perhaps one of the most important contributions of behaviorism to child developmental psychology was indirect; that is, behaviorism was *not* incompatible with the testing movement. Test data were observable and empirical. Thus the *testing movement,* which also made an important contribution to developmental psychology, could develop side by side with behaviorism without conflict. As might be expected, the earliest research with tests in the United States was done with children and young persons. Again, this may have been partly because children were captive subjects. For the most part, however, it seems to have reflected the demand for diagnostic techniques that could aid in determining students' abilities and progress in school.

In 1890 F. Boas at Clark University made anthropological measurements on 1,500 children in addition to testing vision, hearing, and memory. But the major stimulus for mental testing in the United States came from James McKeen Cattell. As noted before, Cattell was trained by Wundt, but he was heavily influenced by Galton's concept of individual differences. Thus, when he returned from Wundt's Leipzig laboratory to become Professor of Psychology at the University of Pennsylvania, he was convinced that psychology should be concerned with measurement of individual differences. In 1890 he introduced the term "mental test" in a paper entitled *Mental Tests and Measurements* (1890). Cattell's tests were given to 100 freshmen at Columbia University. It is important to note that these tests were all of the "brass instrument" variety. In keeping with their origins in Galton's and Wundt's laboratories of psychophysics, they were basically tests of sensory capacity, precision of discrimination, and reaction time (Boring, 1950:572). In 1893, J. A. Gilbert (1894) gave the same general kinds of tests to 1,200 New Haven schoolchildren. The tests included height, weight, lung capacity, and tests of sensation, tapping, reaction time, memory for tones, and suggestibility. The basic problem with these tests was that they were extremely poor predictors of success in school with its heavy demands on the processing of verbal materials. For example,

Clark Wissler's (1901) review of Cattell's Columbia study revealed that the correlation of class standing with reaction time was only –0.02. In contrast, the correlation of performance in Latin with performance in Greek was 0.75. Thus the early pioneers in mental measurement were learning that the best predictor of success in school was success in school, or at least a mental test which approximated the kinds of materials students were required to handle.

Binet to the rescue

Fortunately, better tests of school abilities were developed in France. Binet was commissioned to study students who were having difficulties in the Paris schools in 1904. He and Simon produced the first version of the Binet and Simon (1905, 1908) test in 1905. It turned out to be a much better predictor of school success than the psychophysical measurements, chiefly because test items made heavy demands on the kinds of abilities required of schoolchildren. Most important, the scoring system was "developmental"; that is, it was scaled in terms of item difficulty and scored in terms of mental and chronological age.

It did not take long for the pragmatic American psychologists to acquire the Binet test and to translate it into English (Goddard, 1910). However, it was not used on children to any great extent until Terman published his revision of Binet's test in 1916 and provided normative information based on 1,000 subjects, ranging in age from 3 to 18 years. Terman used the mental age concept developed by Stern in 1914. Binet had subtracted mental age from chronological age to estimate abnormality. Stern developed the concept of IQ as a ratio of mental age divided by chronological age. Terman established 16 years of age as normal adult achievement and 18 years of age as performance at the superior adult level.

Development, stagnation, decline?

Clearly, the earliest tests and norms were designed for children, not for adults, and particularly not for elderly adults. Apparently, one of the big controversies generated by the testing movement was the question of when mental maturity was reached (Charles, 1970). Doll (1919) argued that it peaked at 13 years of age. Yerkes' (1921) group agreed, and Thorndike (1923) suggested that the peak was at 18 years or shortly after. By the 1930s the literature emphasized decline in mental test performance with advancing age (Jones and Conrad, 1933; Miles and Miles, 1932). Botwinick (1967) points to a statement by Wechsler that sums up the state of the mental functioning of adults as seen by one prominent psychometrician. Wechsler (1958:135) wrote:

> Beginning with the investigation by Galton in 1883 and continuing up to and including the most recent studies of Pacaud, nearly all studies dealing with the age factor in adult performance have shown that most human abilities, in so far as they are measurable, decline progressively after reaching a peak somewhere between age 18 and 25. The peak age varies with the ability in question, but the decline occurs in all mental measures of ability, including those employed in tests of intelligence.*

It is not surprising that between the years of 1900 and 1914, aging was viewed as decline or reverse development. Data reported from psychometric tests made it difficult to conceive of the study of adults in a developmental context. It appears possible that the early psychometricians, in their haste to respond to the need for testing children or in their use of children as convenient subjects, inadvertently defined development only in terms of children. Thus, in the earliest days of testing, adults were compared against test norms designed for schoolchildren. The Wechsler Adult Intelligence Scale (WAIS) was designed to correct this misuse of the Stanford-Binet test. However, the normative data were cross-sectional, and thus they did not take into account differences in educational and social opportunities for persons

---

*From Wechsler, D. *The measurement and appraisal of adult intelligence.* © 1958. The Williams & Wilkins Co., Baltimore, p. 193.

born at different times. Furthermore, it is difficult to determine the extent to which persons in poor health were included in the samples. As shall be seen later, the incidence of certain health problems increases with age, and often these health problems are associated with poor performance on some psychological tests.

These health and methodology factors confound interpretations of decline in performance in terms of declining intellective ability and have prompted many contemporary developmental psychologists to argue that the standardized intelligence tests do not validly measure the ability of the aging adult. Riegel (1973b:3) summarizes this position very well.

> Early in the thirties, Lorge (1936) carried convincingly the infamous statement that "intelligence is what the intelligence measures." He demonstrated that such a test, when specifically designed for old people would test the intelligence of old people, and would, therefore, show a continuing rise in scores with age and would make many young examinees appear as inferior. Only nowadays, and only as a result of massive social pressure, do students of individual differences admit that tests designed for Women, Chicanos, or Blacks are likely to place the other groups into inferior positions.

Thus, as far back as 1936, Lorge appreciated the extent to which the choice of tests determined the inferences that could be made regarding adult intelligence. When he used materials that were very familiar to the everyday existence and survival of adults, he found that performance actually improved with advancing age. Demming and Pressey (1957) demonstrated the same principle in a later study in which problems on the tests were indigenous to adult life rather than child life. These conclusions are criticized by those who argued that the speed with which one solves a novel problem is a valid measure of intelligence and that adults, particularly older adults, exhibit a growth of performance only in tests which do not measure speed of problem solving. The controversy would require considerable space to describe in detail, and it will be considered in later chapters. However, it becomes clear that whether or not the healthy, aging person exhibits a decline in intellectual functioning is related to one's definition of intelligence to begin with and that Lorge realized this important fact as early as 1936.

The point to be made here is not that tests have been useless to the adult developmental psychologists. The psychological test, when used ethically and thoughtfully, has been one of the most useful scientific tools in the study of adult development. It is the misinterpretation of decline in performance as reflecting decline in innate mental ability that has worked against the concept of adult development by suggesting that no further cognitive development occurs in adulthood. Chapter 5 reviews a number of studies which indicate that such a generalization is premature when it is applied to healthy, aging adults and when one takes into consideration modifiers of performance such as choice of tests, motivation, anxiety, cooperation, education, socioeconomic status, loss of speed, and cultural influences. The modifiers of intelligence concept is not new. Wechsler (1958) and others were well aware of the limitations of the cross-sectional design as well as the confusion between intelligence and the estimates of intelligence. In the early 1900s Stern, one of the foremost persons in test development, argued that adulthood is not a state of stagnation, and both he and Thorndike promoted the study of the adult with psychological tests. Thus misuses of tests and misunderstandings of generalizations that were possible from available test data, rather than the designers of tests, contributed to a view of aging as stagnation followed by decline. Furthermore, it is clear that development of the individual may entail growth in many traits other than intellective ability.

SUMMARY: QUETELET TO THE TESTING MOVEMENT

The major historical events and persons discussed in the preceding sections are summarized in Fig. 2-1.

Up to this point in the chapter we have

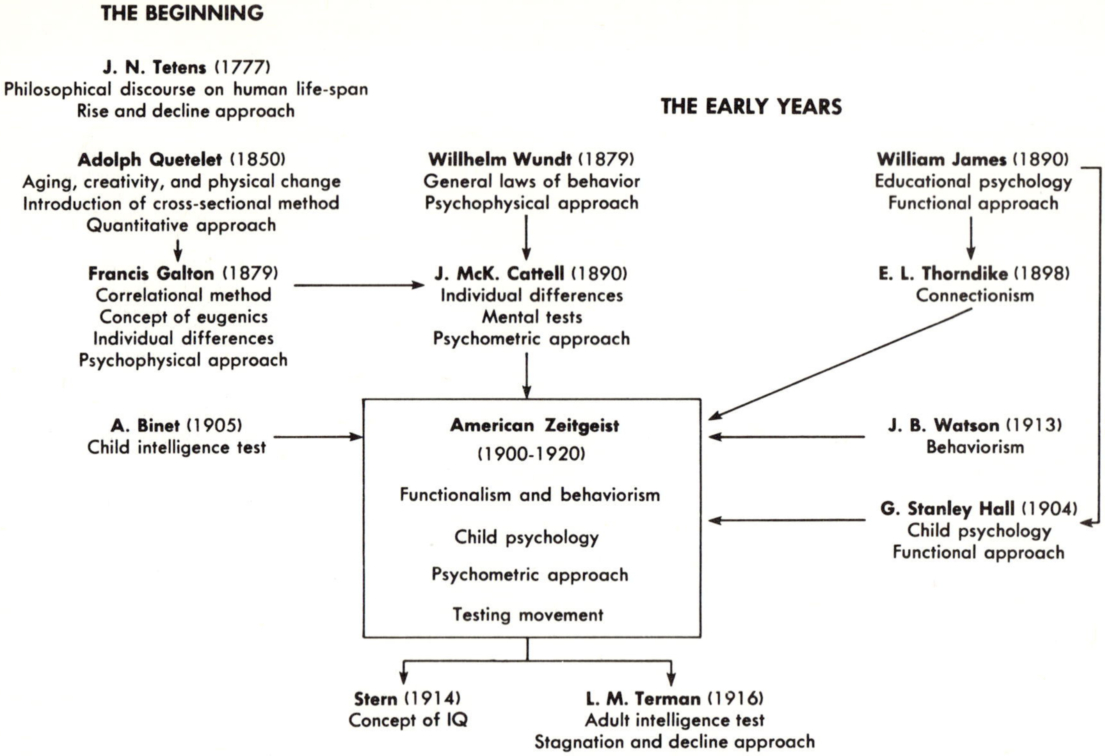

Fig. 2-1. Summary of major persons and events during the beginning and early years of adult developmental psychology. Dates approximate time of strongest influence. Arrows indicate direct lines of influence.

considered the growth of adult developmental psychology in the context of the events taking place in psychology, in general, and the American *Zeitgeist*. The relatively rapid growth of child psychology relative to adult psychology has been emphasized. It has been pointed out that the popular conception of the adult years in terms of stagnation and then decline made it difficult to conceive of the adult years in terms of development. However, it should by no means be concluded that (1) all psychologists, particularly those in the testing movement, viewed the adult years in terms of stagnation and decline; (2) the only area of psychology was child psychology; and (3) after the turn of the twentieth century nothing much at all was accomplished in the area of adult development and aging. These generalizations are clearly *not* true.

It is true that the years between 1920 and 1945 were lean. More studies were conducted in adult development and aging in the decade of 1950 to 1959 than in the entire preceding 115 years (Birren, 1961b). However, a thread of research was maintained through the lean years. By and large, however, this thread was maintained through the efforts of individuals rather than in response to social pressure for adult developmental and aging research.

LEAN YEARS: 1920-1945

Developmental physiological psychology with animals

In 1920 the Russians ventured into aging research with animals. The Russians were interested in understanding the way in which *connections* were established between stimuli and responses (learning). Unlike many

American psychologists of this time period, they were concerned with the physiological bases of these connections. In the 1920s Pavlov and his students found that old animals conditioned in a different way from young animals and that their responses extinguished differently (Birren, 1961a). Furthermore, they provided evidence that differences in learning between old and young animals were related, in part, to structural changes in the central nervous system, particularly the cerebral cortex (Petrova, quoted from Nitkin, 1958, cited in Birren, 1961a).

The emphasis on the underlying neurochemical and physiological bases for learning and other kinds of behavior has continued to develop in Russia. A parallel emphasis on physiological psychology in the context of developmental processes did not develop in the United States between 1920 and 1945. Geographical and ideological barriers may have been responsible for this lack of parallel development by limiting the exchange of scientific literature regarding Russian experiments. Perhaps more important to the lack of growth of the physiological psychology of developmental processes was the strong deemphasis by American behaviorists on exploration of the physiological links between stimulus and response.

Testing

The testing movement continued to develop in its own right in the early 1900s. The Army Alpha (Yerkes, 1921) became a popular instrument for testing and "placing" men entering the armed forces in World War I. The test was specifically designed for young adults. Thus it is not surprising that peak performance was established at about 20 years (Jones and Conrad, 1933) rather than 13 or 18 years of age, as revealed by earlier tests designed for children.

In 1928 Thorndike, who was already well known for his research on intelligence and learning in humans and animals, published *Adult Learning,* a summary of studies concerned with the influence of age on ability and achievement of mature persons (Charles, 1970). Later (1935) he published *Adult Interests,* a book that described the changes in intensity of interest with age as well as the possibility of modifying and improving personality characteristics at various ages. Wechsler (1939) introduced the Wechsler Adult Intelligence Scale (WAIS) to compensate for the inadequacies of the Stanford-Binet test for testing the abilities of adults.

Adult psychophysiology

Scattered research in the area of adult psychophysiology was done from 1920 to 1945. In one of the earliest American studies, Kogan and Morant (1923) examined both the auditory and visual systems of elderly subjects, and established the fact that slower performance in the reaction times of older subjects was *not* correlated with decreased sensory input caused by a lack of acuity. Birren (1961a) has commented that this important finding went unnoticed by adult developmental psychologists because of its markedly sophisticated statistical techniques and the fact that it was published in *Biometrika,* a journal much more familiar to statisticians than psychologists of the early 1900s.

Social psychology

Although the mainstream of social psychology in the 1920s and 1930s was not concerned with aging, several social psychologists departed from investigations involving psychophysics and mental testing and moved toward the study of social aspects of adult development. In 1922 G. Stanley Hall, father of child psychology and the questionnaire method, published what has been referred to as the first book of importance to adult psychology published in the United States: *Senescence, the Last Half of Life.* In this book Hall expressed the idea that the psychology of the elderly adult was qualitatively different from that of younger persons and, as such, should be studied in its own right. Charles (1970) notes that the most in-

Fig. 2-2. Sidney L. Pressey, Ph.D. (Harvard University, 1917). Dr. Pressey was one of the earliest researchers and teachers in life-span developmental psychology. He has been the "academic father" to many outstanding researchers on the psychology of aging, including Dr. Raymond Kuhlen. He authored and taught what were among the first books and courses in the psychology of aging. He has been honored many times over the years, receiving the first E. L. Thorndike Award from the Division of Educational Psychology of the American Psychological Association. He was also the first President of the Division of Maturity and Old Age of the American Psychological Association (now Division 20).

teresting chapter concerned data resulting from a questionnaire administered to the elderly asking them about their self-perceptions, problems, and attitudes. Hall disagreed with a popular view that older persons are more religious than younger persons because they are closer to death. He gathered questionnaire data which indicated that the reverse was true. It should be noted that, despite the reference to questionnaire data in various parts of the book, *Senescence, the Last Half of Life* was largely subjective impressions written in retrospect. Hall wrote the book when he was 78 years old.

Sidney Pressey introduced one of the first books in adult development that summarized the experimental literature of the early 1900s. As noted in Chapter 1, the book, *Life: A Psychological Survey* (Pressey et al., 1939) employed a life-span approach to developmental psychology. Pressey alone had a profound influence on the stimulation and maintenance of interest in adult development during the lean years. During his tenure as Chairman of Psychology, Ohio State University produced more Ph.D.s in aging than any other department in the United States (Birren, 1961a). One of his students, Raymond Kuhlen, carried on Pressey's interests to the Department of Psychology at Syracuse University.

The first major research project dealing with the social psychological aspects of aging involved a committee organized under Terman in 1928 to study difficulties in acquiring jobs for California workers over the age of 40 years (Charles, 1970). The significance of the Terman project lies both in the research publications it produced during the 1930s, such as Miles' *Age and Human Ability* (1933) and Strong's *Change of Interests with Age* (1931), and the eight doctoral dissertations that it supported. These dissertations and those by Pressey's students at Ohio State University were probably the first doctoral dissertations in the United States that dealt with the psychological aspects of aging.

Government support

By the mid-1930s many adult psychologists were beginning to see the need for an integration of the accumulated knowledge on the physiological aspects of aging. The need was met by a comprehensive volume edited by E. V. Cowdry (1939), called *Problems of Aging*. Chapters were contributed by many well-known pioneers in adult development and aging from both the biological and social sciences. The book was financed by the Macy Foundation, which simultaneously was supporting The Club for Research on Aging, the membership of which was made up largely of contributors to the volume. In the late 1930s, one of the contributors, L. K. Frank, urged the United States Public Health Service to subsidize a section on aging, and for the first time aging research was incorporated into a governmental agency. The section became known as the National Advisory Committee on Gerontology, and funds were made available by the USPHS for projects reviewed and recommended for support by the advisory group (Birren, 1961a).

Governmental support for aging research continued. In 1941 the USPHS organized a conference on the mental health aspects of later life. Unfortunately, the psychiatry of aging was slow to develop because there were almost no trained psychiatrists and clinical psychologists who could be induced to enter this relatively unexplored field. Furthermore, many whose interest might have been maintained became permanently involved in other projects at the start of World War II (Birren, 1961a).

Developmental psychology matures

Undoubtedly, many investigators who contributed to the literature in adult development and aging during the lean years were intrinsically interested in the aging process. Others may have been sufficiently farsighted to see that they would be considered pioneers in a research area that was bound to grow in size and importance as a result of the shift in the population of the United States toward the older end of the age scale. However, one of the most important elements in the continued growth of the study of adults was a developmental phenomenon taking place in the well-funded and well-established child development research centers. The original subjects recruited for longitudinal studies were growing up. Faced with this change in the age of their samples, and inspired by a curiosity to investigate the outcomes of their earlier efforts, many child developmental psychologists became life-span psychologists (see Charles, 1970). The investigators associated with the Stanford Studies of Gifted Children, originated by Terman in 1921, are now collecting data on the children of the original subjects. In 1958, the name of the Institute of Child Welfare at Berkeley, established in 1927, was changed to the Institute of Human Development to reflect the fact that its subjects had matured. The Fels Research Institute at Yellow Springs, Ohio, founded in 1929, supported data collection on subjects from birth to maturity (Kagan and Moss, 1962).

The child development research institutes of the 1920s and 1930s anticipated the current research programs in adult psychology and aging in several respects. First, they were multidisciplinary in nature. Their staffs included biochemists, geneticists, physicians, sociologists, psychologists, and anthropologists. Second, they offered supportive services for children, such as nursery schools and day care centers. Third, many of the researchers trained at the various institutes became teachers and researchers in American universities. As will be seen in the next section, with a few exceptions adult development and aging research followed the path from federally funded programs and multidisciplinary institutes to the universities in almost the same manner.

THE LEAP FROM ADOLESCENCE TO SENESCENCE: 1945-1970

During the postwar years, the study of child development was becoming substantially entrenched within the university system. Federal grants supported both research projects and training programs for child psychologists. The interests of many of the new child psychologists were moving from purely empirical descriptions of growth in the early years of childhood to theoretical discussions and controversies concerning the concept of development itself. For example, Heinz Werner (1948) borrowed his orthogenetic principle from biological conceptions of development, based on the expectation that there is a correspondence between physical and mental growth. The *orthogenetic principle* states that *development involves increasing differentiation and simultaneous subordination of parts to a whole; that is, the living organism is characterized as an ever-increasingly complex hierarchy.* Werner (1957) also believed that a broad conception of development should not apply only to the study of child growth but to all areas of life science and that it was "potentially useful in interrelating the many fields of psychology." Certainly the stage was set for the theoretical, if not empirical, view of life-span development. But such a view failed to materialize. Child psychology programs within universities simply were not funded to extend either their research or training efforts into the adult years. Perhaps the postwar baby boom, the middle-class child-centered family structure, and the emphasis on youth culture contributed to the lack of both private and governmental support for the psychology of adult development. So although there existed a theoretical concept of development that logically should have been reflected in research on the adult years, developmental research continued to be largely restricted to infants, children, and adolescents.

Nevertheless, during the years following World War II, interest was beginning to develop, both in public and private institutions, for research dealing with the aged. The number of older persons in the United States was steadily increasing (Brotman, 1970), and thus it is tempting to speculate that the increased interest in, and attention to, the elderly person was the result of an American *Zeitgeist,* which demanded an increased attention to the social, educational, emotional, nutritional, and medical needs of the elderly and to the consequences of the shift in the population. Such speculation reflects wishful thinking rather than fact. Certainly there were those who described the plight of the elderly as well as the need for adult education and pre-retirement and retirement programs (e.g., Beattie, 1961, 1967, 1970). The efforts of Beattie and other pioneers in the sociology of aging were not rewarded by resources for elderly adults. Rather, increasing public attention to aging was largely due to the specific contributions of significant persons. Through the efforts of these persons, research organizations and centers for the study of aging came into existence, many of which followed in the multidisciplinary tradition of the earlier child research institutes.

Journals and professional organizations

In 1945 a multidisciplinary organization for the study of the aged, The Gerontological Society, was founded, which immediately decided to sponsor the *Journal of Gerontology* to reflect its multidisciplinary efforts. The first issue appeared in 1946.

In 1947 the newly formed Division 20 on Maturity and Old Age, now the Division of Adult Development and Aging, of the American Psychological Association held its first meeting. In his Division 20 presidential address, Sidney Pressey stressed a life-span approach to adult developmental psychology. He argued that the initial efforts of the new division should be to promote a psychology of adulthood with an emphasis on development and change throughout maturity but that the ultimate goal should be a union with the firmly established Division on Developmental Psychology, which was devoted almost exclusively to the study of childhood (Pressey, 1948).

Centers

The growth of professional organizations in the early years was accompanied by a modest increase in federal support for aging

Fig. 2-3. Ewald W. Busse, M.D. (Washington University, 1942). Dr. Busse, pictured here at his desk in Duke University School of Medicine, is presently J. P. Gibbons Professor of Psychiatry and Associate Provost and Director, Medical and Allied Health Education. He is a pioneer researcher and teacher in gerontology, human development, and aging. A former, and first, Director of the Center for the Study of Aging and Human Development at Duke University, Dr. Busse has served as President of the Gerontological and American Geriatric Societies. He has been honored many times for his contributions to aging and psychiatry, receiving the Robert W. Kleemeier Award, the William C. Menninger Award, and the Modern Medicine Award. He is presently a member of the Institute of Medicine of the National Academy of Sciences.

research that was undertaken by special programs and centers within the university system. The new aging research centers were not typically housed in psychology departments, and they clearly did *not* reflect a petitioning by psychology departments for federal funds for the development of training and research capacities in the area of adult development. The interaction of adult and child psychologists within psychology departments simply was not promoted to any significant extent in the 1940s.

When federal support became available in the early 1950s, it was directed primarily toward the study of the elderly adult (gerontology) rather than research on developmental change across the adult years. Research programs expanded rapidly. Their multidisciplinary nature probably contributed significantly to their support by the public.

Similar to the child development centers, aging centers tended to be oriented either toward social problems or health problems. There was a real need for special attention to psychiatric teaching and research that was specifically directed toward the needs of the elderly adult. Ewald Busse, Chairman of the Department of Psychiatry at Duke University and a pioneer in aging research in psychiatry, responded to this need by developing one of the first research and training programs in the mental health aspects of aging. The program was located in the Department

Fig. 2-4. James E. Birren, Ph.D. (Northwestern University, 1947). A pioneer in the development of the psychology of aging as a subspecialty field within psychology, Dr. Birren is presently Dean of the Davis School of Gerontology and Director of the Ethel Percy Andrus Gerontology Center (University of Southern California). He has trained and influenced the lives of many students. Among other honors he has received the American Psychological Association Distinguished Scientific Contribution Award and the Gerontological Society Award (Robert W. Kleemeier Award) for meritorious research.

of Psychiatry at Duke University Medical Center, and thus much of the early research was biomedical in nature, but it was also directed toward applied psychiatric practice and the sociology of aging. Because of the efforts of Busse, and later Carl Eisdorfer and George Maddox, the program matured into one of the most significant multidisciplinary aging research programs in the United States, the Duke University Center for the Study of Aging and Human Development.

In 1965 James Birren, who had previously organized and headed the Section on Aging in the National Institute of Mental Health, assumed the directorship of what is now the Ethel Percy Andrus Gerontology Center at the University of Southern California and built it into another highly productive training and research center in adult development.

Both the Duke University Center and the Ethel Percy Andrus Gerontology Center were interdisciplinary, with a rather heavy concentration on the psychobiology and psychophysiology of the middle and later adult years. However, the social psychology of aging was not neglected. Even before Busse received his grant to study aging at Duke University, R. J. Havighurst, at the University of Chicago, was provided with USPHS funds to develop an interdisciplinary program related to the social aspects of aging. Since then, the University of Chicago has made outstanding progress in the social psychology of adult development through its interdisciplinary program in human development.

From gerontology to adult development

The university-based and multidisciplinary programs in psychobiology, psychophysiology, geropsychiatry, and the social psychology of aging were beginning by 1960 to make an impact on the published literature in psychology. However, there were problems with experimental designs and statistical procedures used to make generalizations about changes in behavior and underlying processes with advancing age. The cross-sectional designs were plagued by the cohort (generational) differences that were discussed previously. The longitudinal designs were compromised by the fact that sample size not only became smaller but, because of increasing mortality with advancing age, sample characteristics as well as behavior changed with increasing years. A methodological solution was needed, and it was provided by K. Warner Schaie, Paul Baltes, John Nesselroade, Larry Goulet (Goulet and Baltes, 1970; Nesselroade, 1970; Schaie, 1965, 1967), and others, who were in the process of building a life-span psychology program at West Virginia University. These methodologically sophisticated psychologists developed statistical and methodological models that were addressed to the problems of longitudinal and cross-sectional research as well

Fig. 2-5. Raymond G. Kuhlen, Ph.D. (1913-1967); Ohio State University, 1940. Dr. Kuhlen promoted and initiated many successful educational and research projects in the area of aging and adult development throughout his distinguished career at Syracuse University. He stimulated a number of graduate students to achieve significant careers in adult developmental psychology, including his friend, colleague, and former student Dr. Rolf Monge (Chairman, Department of Psychology, Syracuse University). Dr. Kuhlen coauthored one of the first textbooks in life-span developmental psychology (Pressey, Janney, and Kuhlen, 1939) and continued to publish books and articles on many aspects of the life cycle. Dr. Kuhlen was a Fellow in the Gerontological Society and the American Psychological Association and served as President of the Division of Maturity and Old Age. He is deeply missed by his many friends and colleagues at Syracuse University and across the United States.

as the problems of fair and valid evaluation of the skills of elderly persons.

In parallel with the development of more refined methodological approaches, the aging centers and special programs exerted an increasing influence on the growth of adult development programs within psychology departments. They did so in a variety of ways. Directors of the early aging programs and centers were behavioral scientists, psychiatrists, and psychologists. They influenced psychology departments to make joint appointments or adjunct appointments in psychology for members of research teams. Thus there was a common communication that facilitated the merging of multidisciplinary programs and psychology programs. Eventually, many senior research staff of the aging centers and programs moved into psychology departments as faculty members and heavily influenced the growth of adult development programs. By 1973 half the faculty in developmental psychology at Syracuse University had been trained in the life-span program at West Virginia University, the Duke University Center for the Study of Aging and Human Development, or the Ethel Percy Andrus Gerontology Center. Furthermore, the growth of adult developmental psychology at Syracuse was significantly enhanced by the founding (1972) and rapid growth of the multidisciplinary All-University Gerontology Center at Syracuse University. Because of the interdisciplinary nature of adult developmental and aging research, adult developmental psychology programs are strengthened by the presence of centers that act to promote and coordinate interdisciplinary interactions that are problem oriented rather than discipline limited.

Space does not allow the discussion of other names and programs, although most certainly many important contributions and contributors have not been mentioned. The important point is that the characteristics of aging research changed as it became more firmly entrenched in the field of psychology and related academic disciplines. It moved from description to explanation and the application of sophisticated research methodology. Furthermore, it changed from a concern for the aged to a concern for *aging as a developmental process.*

One must not conclude that psychology programs became instantly well balanced with regard to their offerings in child and adult psychology. It will be recalled that Brackbill, in her survey of four-year graduate programs in developmental psychology, reported that only ten out of ninety-six offered a program in the psychology of adulthood. However, a more recent survey sponsored by the newly formed (1973) Association for Educators in Gerontology shows that many individual courses and research programs are being developed and have been developed within the various academic disciplines in colleges and universities across the United States. Approximately 300 colleges and universities indicated that they offered some form of course work in adult development or aging or that they sponsored research in this area. Similarly, new journals have been developed to deal with an increasingly sophisticated and diverse literature in adult development and aging, for example, *Experimental Aging Research, Aging and Human Development, Human Development, Gerontologia.*

Thus there is a rapidly growing literature and a growing trend toward interaction of child and adult developmental psychologists as they are brought together within developmental psychology programs. This is fortunate. It is difficult to see how a true life-span program can be fully developed in the absence of the interface of child and adult developmental psychologists within developmental psychology programs.

SUMMARY AND FUTURE DIRECTIONS

Table 2-1 summarizes the flow of events in the lean years.

The evolution of adult psychology as an area within psychology has been described in previous sections. In the years between 1900 and 1950, interest and research in adult development was maintained largely as the result of individual efforts and natural extensions of child studies to adults when the child subjects grew up. Growth of adult developmental psychology was retarded by the competition from child psychology for institutional and federal resources. However, the slow development of adult developmental psychology may have been even more a result of the difficulties in conceiving of the adult years in any terms other than mental stagnation followed by decline.

In recent years this view has been challenged by an increased sophistication in developmental methodology and by an examination of the value systems leading to the stagnation and decrement view. It would be comforting to think that these new directions were dictated by spontaneous concern on the part of the lay public and the federal government with the decreasing birthrate and the rising number of older persons. Unfortunately, this explanation is both misleading and inadequate. Programs of research in adult development were started in response to the availability of federal funds in the 1950s. However, these funds materialized only as the result of intense efforts of individuals who not only argued the case for funding but actually organized sections of government institutes that controlled and distributed funds.

The emphasis of early research efforts was on the elderly (1950 to 1960). Later (1960 to 1973), more and more students and senior staff from aging programs and centers be-

Table 2-1. Summary of the major events contributing to the continuation of the study of adult development during the lean years*

	Landmarks in academic community	The testing movement	Federal support for aging
1920	Russians establish a psychophysiological approach to aging		
1921		R. M. Yerkes publishes Army Alpha test	
1922	G. Stanley Hall establishes a social psychological approach to aging with his attitude survey of the elderly		
1928	L. M. Terman conducts a social psychological survey of work force over 40 years of age	E. L. Thorndike publishes his studies on relationship of age to ability and achievement	
1939	S. Pressey, J. E. Janney, and R. Kuhlen summarize early experimental literature on adult development and propose a life-span approach	D. Wechsler publishes his adult intelligence scale (WAIS)	USPHS establishes a National Advisory Committee on Gerontology and provides funds for research projects approved by committee
	E. V. Cowdry edits a comprehensive volume on biological, psychological, and social aspects of adult development		
1941			USPHS organizes a conference on the Mental Health Problems of the Elderly
1945	The Gerontological Society is founded		
1947	The American Psychological Association Division of Maturity and Old Age is founded		
1948	Psychological concepts of development move from description to theory (e.g., H. Werner's orthogenetic principle)		
1950-		Multidisciplinary aging research centers are founded Emphasis is placed on study of the elderly Major founders and their institutional affiliations included R. J. Havighurst (University of Chicago), E. Busse (Duke University Medical Center), J. Birren (University of Southern California)	

*In the 1920s and 1930s support for aging research was on a scattered individual basis. Federal funds were not available until the 1940s. A concentrated government support program did not materialize until the 1950s and 1960s, when the earlier pioneering efforts of the academic community, the testing movement, and the federal government became consolidated in multidisciplinary research centers.

came integrated into academic institutions, and the emphasis shifted to a life-span approach. The increased presence of aging researchers in academic institutions marked a turn from the collection of social and biomedical data to a serious questioning of theoretical models for adult development and research methodology.

Current trends

The economic and political aspects of adult development are beginning to receive increased attention because Riegel (1973a,b) and others (e.g., Looft, 1973; Weiner, 1973) have demonstrated the influence of these factors on psychological functioning as well as voicing concern for a societal value that emphasizes mental competition rather than the quality of life and individual growth. Furthermore there is a movement toward philosophical and historical interpretations and approaches to the understanding of adult development as well as the traditional scientific approach. Such a movement may lead to a synthesis of existing data into new theories and models of development.

SELECTED READINGS

Birren, J. E. A brief history of the psychology of aging. I. *Gerontologist,* 1961, **1,** 69-77.

Birren, J. E. A brief history of the psychology of aging. II. *Gerontologist,* 1961, **1,** 127-134.

Charles, D. C. Historical antecedents of life-span developmental psychology. In L. R. Goulet and P. B. Baltes (Eds.), *Life-span developmental psychology: research and theory.* New York: Academic Press, Inc., 1970.

Demming, J. A., and Pressey, S. L. Tests "indigenous" to the adult and older years. *Journal of Counseling Psychology,* 1957, **4,** 144-148.

Elias, M. F. Disciplinary barriers to progress in behavior genetics: defensive reactions to bits and pieces. *Human Development,* 1973, **16** (1-2), 119-132.

Groffman, K. J. Life-span developmental psychology in Europe: past and present. In L. R. Goulet and P. B. Baltes (Eds.), *Life-span developmental psychology: research and theory.* New York: Academic Press, Inc., 1970.

Riegel, K. F. On the history of psychological gerontology. In C. Eisdorfer and M. P. Lawton (Eds.), *Psychology of adult development and aging.* Washington, D.C.: American Psychological Association, 1973.

CHAPTER 3

DEVELOPMENTAL/EXPERIMENTAL RESEARCH METHODOLOGY

How do psychologists proceed to carry out research once they have decided to focus their interests in the area of adult development? For the most part they proceed in much the same manner as the child developmental psychologist. In fact, it is becoming increasingly popular to speak in terms of "life-span developmental research methodology," and much of the material discussed in this chapter is equally applicable to investigations at all segments of the life span.

Throughout this book we describe the manner in which studies are conducted as well as providing generalizations resulting from various studies. We do this so that you may critically evaluate the conclusions reached by an investigator and may form an opinion concerning the usefulness of his data for expanding knowledge of developmental processes. However, at the outset it is important to have a firm grasp of what are, and what are not, appropriate methodological and statistical procedures. Thus the purpose of this chapter is to acquaint you with the process of carrying out adult developmental research, the problems in designing aging experiments, and the kinds of qualifications that must be attached to generalizations based on data from current research studies. Many readers, especially those who have taken child development courses, will recognize many of the following topics. We hope this chapter will serve the additional purpose of pointing out the potential for a *life-span* experimental approach to developmental research.

WORLD VIEWS: METAPHYSICAL FRAMEWORKS FOR RESEARCH

Sooner or later most students of developmental psychology begin to feel that certain aspects of the material which they are required to learn simply "aren't important"; that a particular problem, such as how younger and older persons associate nonsense syllables, is trivial; or that their professor seems to hold biased opinions which just do not make sense in view of what the world is really like. Often these same students find that not everyone in the class agrees with them. In contrast, other students may believe that the professor has an outstanding grasp of what is really important. Like the professor, they may believe that once we understand how older and younger persons differ with regard to how they associate nonsense syllables, we will be on the verge of discovering a general principle which will explain developmental changes in the learning process.

It may come as no surprise to many readers that psychology professors also disagree among themselves about what is trivial and what is important as a research problem. Why is this so? The answer lies in the metaphysical orientation of individual researchers. This orientation substantially determines what they choose as a significant topic for research, the kind of theory they espouse, the types of methods that they use in seeking answers to their research questions, and sometimes the conclusions they draw from their data. Recently there has been an upsurge of interest among developmental psychologists with regard to the importance of distinguishing between different metaphysical orientations and of specifying how each orientation influences researchers as they go about their business of scientific investigation. Reese and Overton have written two excellent papers (Overton and Reese, 1973; Reese and Overton, 1970) on this "unscientific" aspect of the scientific process. The following discussion leans heavily on the insights presented in their papers.

MECHANISTIC AND ORGANISMIC MODELS OF DEVELOPMENT

All researchers (whether they admit to it or not) hold certain beliefs about the nature of the universe which extend all the way down to characteristics attributed to the phenomena that they study. Kuhn (1962) has called these beliefs "world views." Reese and Overton (1970) have noted that world views or models of reality are expressed as *metaphors.* The two most important metaphors for today's developmental psychologists are the machine and the biological organism. The machine metaphor is called the *mechanistic model,* and it is borrowed from the scientific field of physics. Basically, this metaphor implies that the universe and all the phenomena that occur within it behave *as if* they were a machine or parts of a machine. Thus psychologists whose world views fit this model construct theories and carry out research as if their subjects behaved like machines. The biological organism metaphor is called the *organismic model.* It is borrowed from the field of biology. Psychologists who hold an organismic view of the universe construct theories and carry out research *as if* their subjects behaved like a biological organism. The reader should keep in mind that metaphors are always *as if* statements. Even though the human being may be classified as a biological organism, it is perfectly acceptable, on a metaphysical level, to state that he behaves *as if* he were a machine. Because metaphors (models) are only *as if* statements, they cannot be demonstrated to be true or false. Models must be evaluated only on the basis of their usefulness, that is, their capacity to act as a framework for coherent and concise theories, which, in turn, provide general laws and principles for the explanation of scientific data.

Reese and Overton (1970) have defined the major issues and implications of the organismic and mechanistic models within the context of developmental psychology, which are summarized as follows:

Mechanistic model
- Reactive organism
- Types of causality
  - Material
  - Efficient
- Quantitative change
  - Elementarism
  - Antecedent-consequent relationships
  - Continuity of development

Organismic model
- Active organism
- Types of causality
  - Material
  - Efficient
  - Formal
  - Final
- Qualitative change
  - Holism
  - Structure-function relationships
  - Discontinuity of development

Perhaps the most important issue involves the contrasting views of the organism as *active* or *reactive.* Within the mechanistic model, the human being is assumed to be a reactive, passive organism, whose natural state, like that of the machine, is to be at rest. All activity (behavior) is the result of external forces originating in the environment. In contrast, the organismic model includes the assumption that the human being is *spontaneously* active. Thus man himself is considered to be a source of change. In the mechanistic model, change is brought about only by external forces.

Are there other ways in which the two models differ with regard to explanations for developmental change? Overton and

Reese (1973) have suggested that the differences are very clear if one thinks in terms of the four types of causality originally proposed by Aristotle: material, efficient, formal, and final causes. The mechanistic model assumes two types of causality, *material* and *efficient* cause. *Material cause is related to the physical constitution of the organism.* In terms of the psychological aspects of man, Overton and Reese (1973:75) refer to material cause as "the physiological, neurological, and genetic substrate that is a necessary condition for behavior." *Efficient cause is any external force imposed by the environment that produces a change in the organism's behavior.* For many developmental psychologists it is the *S* in an S-R sequence. Efficient cause is explored in the laboratory by the manipulating of independent variables. Within the framework of the mechanistic model, all developmental processes can be explained by reference to material and efficient causes.

The organismic model also includes the assumptions of material and efficient causes, but two additional types of causes are postulated: *formal* and *final* causes. *Formal cause* is difficult to explain. Overton and Reese (1973:75) refer to it as "the pattern, organization, or form of the object." Some good examples of formal causes are the psychological structures postulated by Piaget, for example, sensorimotor structures, concrete, and formal operations. Formal causes are not observable. Rather, they are *inferred* from observables, such as patterns of behavior. *Final cause is the end point of development.* For example, Piaget has proposed that the end point of intellectual development is adaptation to the environment. Intellectual adaptation is a state in which the organism's psychological structures are capable of maintaining the stability of their organization in the face of internal and external disturbances (e.g., discrepant perceptions). Psychologists who accept the organismic model use all four causes to explain developmental processes. Their additional assumptions of formal and final causes make a great deal of difference in the types of research questions that they formulate and the methods they choose in attempting to answer these questions.

Reese and Overton (1970) have identified some further issues that are implicit in the mechanistic and organismic models. The models differ with respect to whether change is described as *quantitative* (the mechanistic point of view) or *qualitative* (the organismic point of view). The statement that change is quantitative implies that "Change occurs only in the quantity of behavioral content (impressions, associations, and responses) that the person acquires in the course of life and the strength with which he maintains these impressions, associations, and responses once he has acquired them [Langer, 1969: 159]." If change is to be described as quantitative, three additional assumptions are necessary. First, it must be assumed that there are quantifiable, basic units of analysis (behaviors) available for study. Ultimately, all more complex behaviors may be reduced to these more basic units. In other words, the whole is equal to the sum of its parts. This assumption is referred to as *elementarism.* Second, all present behaviors are assumed to be subject to explanation and prediction solely by reference to antecedent conditions, that is, a knowledge of past S-R sequences and present external forces acting on the organism. Consequently, specific *antecedent-consequent relationships* become the focus of research. Third, changes are assumed to occur in a continuous sequence made up of discrete (S-R) events. Thus the *continuity* assumption implies that more global antecedent-consequent relationships can be broken down into units, such as basic S-R chains.

In summary, developmental psychologists, working within the mechanistic framework, will attempt to analyze behaviors in terms of past S-R sequences. They will be particularly interested in explaining how a specific series of S-R events may lead to a predictable behavioral outcome.

As Reese and Overton (1970) have pointed out, the situation is different for the psychologist working within an organismic framework, one of whose major assumptions is that developmental processes involve qualitative change; that is, the present state of the organism (in terms of psychological organization) is qualitatively different from past states. New psychological structures emerge, and past relationships among old structures change. Three additional assumptions, paralleling those derived within the mechanistic framework, are necessary if change is to be viewed as qualitative. First, specific behaviors of the organism are assumed to be meaningless unless they are put into context with the "whole." There are no basic elements that can be analyzed as discrete units, or "building blocks," for more complex behaviors. This assumption is called *holism.* It implies that the whole is *not* equal to the sum of its parts. However, the holism assumption does not imply that the organismic psychologist must study the "whole" organism. Such an implication would be too much of a challenge for the most ingenious psychologist. For example, it is considered perfectly acceptable to study perceptual processes during the adult portion of the life span. However, in doing so, it is important to be aware that these processes take place within the context of other cognitive structures and overall cognitive organization.

A second, more complex assumption involves the nature of *structure-function relationships.* Instead of attempting to identify specific S-R sequences, the organismic psychologist examines *patterns* of behavior and attempts to infer the underlying psychological structures that serve a particular function. Piaget did just this when he inferred sensorimotor structures as the first step to intellectual adaptation from his observations of infant behavior. Thus the organismic psychologist makes inferences about a formal cause, given the fact that he has defined a final cause and has observed material and efficient causes.

Third, the organismic psychologist assumes that developmental changes are intrinsically discontinuous. The *discontinuity* assumption implies that new psychological structures and organization have qualitatively different attributes from old ones. Furthermore, the new structures are not predictable solely from a knowledge of antecedent-consequent relations. For example, in Piaget's theory a child who has reached the stage of concrete operations has a qualitatively different knowledge of the world than he did when he was in the sensorimotor stage. This knowledge is a product of all four types of causality rather than simply material and efficient causes. On the other hand, the organismic psychologist is interested in both material and efficient causes, viewing them as facilitating or inhibiting factors in development. For example, inherited forms of mental retardation (material cause) or lack of educational opportunity (efficient cause) certainly can inhibit structural changes, such as the acquisition of concrete operations (formal cause), which serve to achieve a specific end, such as intellectual adaptation (final cause).

Research implications

There are a number of major implications for adult development psychology, given the fact that researchers in this area differ among themselves with regard to their acceptance of the mechanistic or organismic models. It is obvious that there will be definite communication problems between psychologists who hold different world views. A mechanistic researcher cannot be expected to provide answers to questions that he considers are meaningless. The same is true of the organismic researcher. Overton and Reese (1973) have provided a convincing example of the communication problem as originally presented by Kessel (1969). He noted that behaviorists tend to choose both methods and areas of study which are "safe" in the sense that no data will emerge to refute their basic position. For example, Kessel (1969:1003) suggested that "It is hardly likely that the human being will reveal 'higher-order' activities when his eye blink or knee jerk are being conditioned, or when he is learning to associate pairs of nonsense syllables." Furthermore, Kessel noted that, should a subject display a "higher-order" activity during a typical conditioning experiment (e.g., a verbal report of how he is learning), the behaviorist's presuppositions would fail to allow him to recognize the event as either interesting or important.

Overton and Reese (1973) further reported that Kessel provided an excellent example of how higher-order activities may be "handled" within the mechanistic framework. K. W. Spence (1964), a renowned psychologist in the S-R tradition, acknowledged that "higher mental processes" do affect the conditioning procedure; however, Spence preferred to treat them as confounding variables that *interfered* with identification of the more important processes in learning theory! The opposite situation might occur for the organismic psychologist. His theories lead to a search for *patterns* of behavior that might reveal underlying psychological structures and organization. Thus it is unlikely that a knee jerk or eye blink, should it occur in this context, will be considered very meaningful data.

If organismic and mechanistic psychologists differ with regard to what they consider either a problem or a solution, it is obvious that they will also differ with regard to how they define the concept of development and the concept of age. Overton and Reese (1973) have discussed the major aspects of these differences. From the mechanistic point of view, development consists of changes in *responses* (i.e., behaviors). For the most part, age is treated as an index of time along which changes in behavior are measured. From the organismic point of view, development consists of changes in *structures* and their *organization.* Age is sometimes treated as an index of time in the sense that certain structures are more likely to occur within particular age ranges. However, the organismic psychologist may also treat age as part of the dependent variable (see Wohlwill, 1970). Some good examples of this kind of treatment of the age variable are current notions of biological, psychological, and social ages (see Birren, 1968). For example, "psychological age" is defined by Birren (1968:547) as the "adaptive capacities of the individual." Presumably, these adaptive capacities might be represented by the qualitative type of psychological structures (e.g., concrete as opposed to formal operations) characterizing an individual rather than by his membership in a certain chronological age group.

It is also inevitable that organismic and mechanistic developmental psychologists will choose different research strategies and statistical methods of analyses. However, American psychology traditionally has been influenced to a greater extent by the mechanistic world view. Consequently, most of the methodological and statistical techniques that have been developed (and that are discussed throughout this book) are based on a mechanistic analysis of behavior. A number of researchers currently are exploring new techniques based on an organismic research strategy. Unfortunately, these techniques (e.g., certain applications of factor analysis) require a discussion of sophisticated methodological and statistical concepts that are beyond the scope of this book. Those readers who are well versed in research methodology and statistics may find it profitable to consult Nesselroade (1970), Overton and Reese (1973), and Wohlwill (1970).

At the beginning of this section we commented on the varying attitudes of students toward different aspects of the material that they are required to learn in typical developmental psychology courses. We fully expect that most readers will develop similar attitudes towards the different topics presented in this text. You may find yourself questioning the rationale for including certain areas of research in a textbook on adult development, or you may think that we have presented a rather biased view of certain topics. If so, it might be interesting, and personally enlightening, to examine your own "world view" in relation to the conclusions you reach with regard to important research issues and questions raised in this book.

ADULT DEVELOPMENTAL RESEARCH DESIGNS

Compared with child developmental psychologists, adult developmental psychologists have been somewhat more progressive in terms of methodological tools designed to study behavior over time. Perhaps the major reason for this sophistication lies in the fact that the adult portion of the life span is much longer than the childhood portion. Thus psychologists, who wish to study adult subjects from a developmental perspective, have been forced to devise techniques that take into account this larger age range. Furthermore, examination of data covering a large age range often leads to "discoveries" that are less apparent when child subjects are the focus of study. For example, current researchers have become aware that many of the differences between groups of younger (e.g., 30 years) and older (e.g., 70 years) subjects may not reflect an *age* effect but rather a *cohort* effect. In other words, 30- and 70-year-old persons may differ solely because they were born in different generations and, consequently, have had very different life experiences (e.g., the Great Depression, World Wars I and II). K. W. Schaie and his colleagues have been particularly active in calling attention to the need for methodological techniques that separate effects such as those due to age and cohort. Unfortunately, few researchers have taken advantage of the solutions offered by Schaie and his associates. However, many researchers are beginning to call attention to the portions of their data that involve confounded effects; this recognition of the problem has helped considerably in producing more correct interpretations.

In the sections that follow we discuss both the traditional and the newer developmental designs. The reader should keep in mind that all these designs involve either the age variable, the cohort variable, or both; that is, they are aimed at the investigation of *developmental* phenomena. We have included a special section on the "experimental approach," which involves more general designs that may be used in combination with developmental designs. These combinations are very important for the researcher who is interested in manipulating independent variables and measuring dependent variables rather than simply collecting descriptive data.

Traditional developmental designs

Many readers will already be familiar with the two most popular developmental research designs: the cross-sectional and longitudinal methods. In spite of the many problems inherent in these designs, they are still the most commonly employed for studying age trends among both children and adults. Furthermore, many areas of adult research are limited only to the cross-sectional method because it is considered more difficult and costly to apply the longitudinal method over a wide age range.

Cross-sectional method. The cross-sectional design involves the selection of two or more independent age groups that are each measured at one point in time. Schaie (1967) has noted that *age differences* are the focus of concern in a cross-sectional study; that is, comparisons are made for age groups composed of *different* subjects. The major disadvantage of the cross-sectional study is that it involves an inherent confounding of *age* and *cohort;* that is, it is impossible to determine if group differences are a product of age, per se, or the specific experiences of each group of subjects which occurred because they were born into a particular generation (cohort). Of course, it is entirely possible that group differences may be exaggerated or cancelled out by joint age and cohort effects. The major advantage of the cross-sectional method is that random groups of subjects who are representative of particular age ranges within the current population are obtained easily. It is also possible to collect data on specific segments of the population, such as 30-, 50-, and 70-year-old subjects who received a college education and are in good health.

Longitudinal method. The longitudinal method involves the selection of one age group of subjects (e.g., 30 years) who are measured successively at different points in time. Schaie (1967) has pointed out that the focus of concern in a longitudinal study is *age changes;* that is, the *same* group of subjects is measured repeatedly and comparisons are made to determine how this particular group has changed over the years. The major disadvantage of the longitudinal design is that it is impossible to separate the effects of *age* and *time of measurement.* Thus researchers do not know if changes should be attributed to age, per se, or to the unique set of circumstances surrounding a particular time of measurement. For example, it is intuitively obvious that a subject who receives an aptitude test several times will become progressively more familiar with the test and that his performance may improve solely as a consequence of this acquired familiarity. College students often experience a similar type of phenomenon: most seniors are considerably more confident than freshmen when presented with a computer-score multiple choice examination by virtue of the fact that they have spent four years "practicing" with this type of examination.

The longitudinal design suffers from a number of further difficulties. Botwinick (1973) has pointed out that cultural effects, similar to the cohort effects present in cross-sectional studies, may occur under certain circumstances, although these effects may not be readily apparent. He cited several studies in which age and cultural effects were confounded; the investigators were able to identify the confounding effects because they measured both longitudinal and cross-sectional samples. Two of these studies may be summarized as follows (Botwinick, 1973: 292).

> Nelson (1954) tested college students and then, 14 years later, tested them again. He noted a marked trend in liberalism. Fortunately, Nelson tested a new sample at the time he retested the initial sample. He found that the scores of the new college students and those retest scores of the older subjects were about the same. The cultural influences had their impact, confounding the maturational effects, all in the course of a single lifetime.
>
> In another study (Bender, 1958), college students were given a test of values and then retested fifteen years later. A trend in greater religious interest was seen. Again, however, a sample of new college students tested for the first time when the older sample was tested the second time, showed similarity of values.

Botwinick (1973) has suggested that few researchers have recognized the possibility of confounded age and cultural effects in longitudinal studies. However, Botwinick (1973: 292) has expressed concern that this problem might become more severe in future studies because, "As the tempo or rate of cultural change increases, the potential for cultural confounding within a lifetime increases."

One additional major problem occurs in the use of longitudinal designs. Because the same subjects are measured repeatedly, the experimenter must deal with some degree of subject attrition; that is, subjects may "drop out" prior to the time the investigation is completed, or if the subjects are studied well into old age, progressively larger numbers may be expected to die. At any rate, the investigator who uses a longitudinal design almost always will find that he is dealing with a smaller and smaller subject pool as his study nears completion. Moreover, there is a related problem. Several researchers have shown that, in addition to smaller sample size, the terminal sample will differ considerably from the initial sample with regard to characteristics such as intelligence, social class, and health (see Siegler, 1975). It appears that dropouts take with them many of the characteristics that were needed to make the original sample representative of the general population. Thus the investigator may find that the sample he chose at the beginning of his study is no longer available to be used for making inferences about population characteristics.

Rusin and Siegler (1975:1-2) have summarized the most recent research that has been directed toward the identification of subject characteristics which differ for continuing participants in, as opposed to dropouts from, longitudinal aging studies.

> Studies of cognitive and attitudinal variables have shown that those who refuse to continue as research subjects tend to be less intelligent and more rigid than those who do continue to participate (Riegel, Riegel, and Meyer, 1968; Baltes, Schaie and Nardi, 1971). Riegel and Riegel (1972) observed that refusers were more likely to die within the following five-year period when compared to continuing participants.
>
> When sociological dimensions are examined, it is found that refusers from longitudinal aging studies are less likely to be married (Maddox, 1962), members of the lower social class (Streib, 1966; Atchley, 1969), in poorer health (Maddox, 1962; Atchley, 1969), and more socially isolated (Cumming and Henry, 1961; Atchley, 1969) than continuing participants. A high self-esteem accompanied by a denial of old age is also noted among refusers. Siegler (1971) found that refusers were similar to participants on measures of life satisfaction, morale, and health but that refusers were low on measures of social interaction.

Rusin and Siegler (1975) also reported recent personality data from the Duke Adaptation Study: subjects (age range = 45 to 69 years) were first tested in 1968 and then retested twice more over a six-year period. Compared with continuing participants, male dropouts were found to be "anxious and aloofly independent." Female dropouts could be described as "anxious, dull, and inflexible."

Although several studies have attempted to characterize differences between dropouts who refuse to participate at some point during a longitudinal study and subjects who die prior to completion of the study (e.g., Powers and Bultena, 1972; Riegel et al., 1967), Rusin and Siegler (1975) reported that they could not distinguish between these two groups in terms of personality characteristics. The issue of subjects who live to complete the experiment as opposed to subjects who die is treated at length in Chapter 12. Basically, the issue centers around the "terminal drop" hypothesis; that is, subjects who are very near to death will exhibit characteristics (e.g., a sharp decline in IQ scores) significantly different from subjects who are far from death.

We have seen that both the cross-sectional and longitudinal methods involve a considerable number of difficulties in terms of interpretations of age changes and age differences. In the next section we will examine some of the newer methods that have been developed to isolate effects due to age, cohort, and time of measurement.

New developmental designs

The research designs discussed in this section are applicable, in theory, to all segments of the life span. However, they originated within the framework of adult developmental psychology because the study of adults involved longer time periods than the study of children, and thus generation and cohort effects were recognized more readily. These newer designs do not eliminate the fact that researchers who are conducting adult developmental studies must be prepared to spend a considerable amount of time and effort if they are interested in age *changes* rather than age *differences*. On the other hand, the designs do provide a methodology that allows the investigator to analyze the effects of confounding variables (e.g., cohort differences) that might compromise the results of major concern (e.g., age differences).

Time lag method. In the previous section three dimensions of developmental research designs were introduced: age, cohort (time of birth), and time of measurement. These dimensions are illustrated in Fig. 3-1. Age of subjects is represented by the cells A_1, B_1, C_1, etc. Cross-sectional designs are represented by individual columns, for example, the column including cells B_1, C_2, and D_1. Longitudinal designs are represented by individual rows, for example, the row including cells C_1, C_2, and C_3. You may recall that cohort differ-

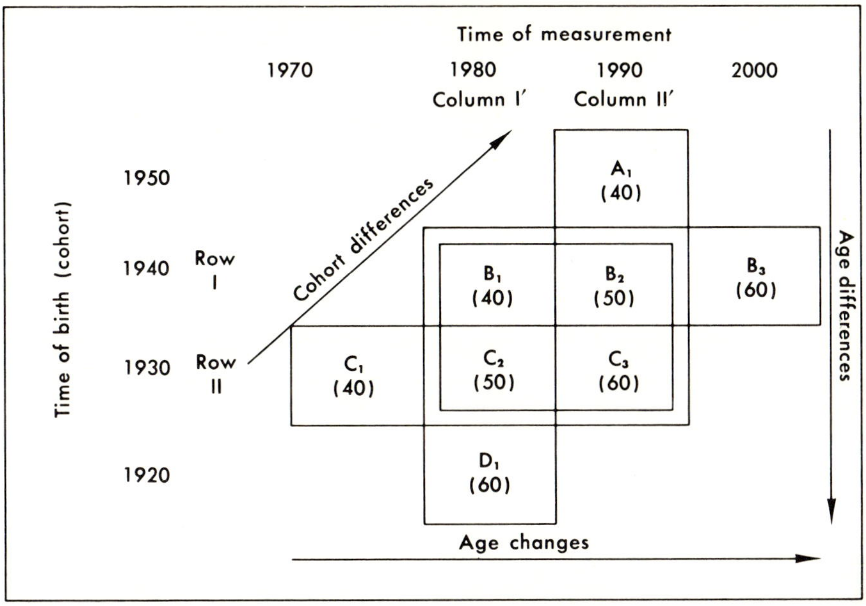

Fig. 3-1. A comparison of developmental research designs based on age, cohort, and time of measurement. Cross-sectional studies are represented by columns; longitudinal studies by rows. Time lag studies are represented by diagonals. Cohort sequential studies involve at least two rows (e.g., I and II). Time-sequential studies involve at least two columns (e.g., I′ and II′). Cross-sequential studies are represented by the large square bordered by double lines.

ences were a major confounding factor in cross-sectional studies and were also of potential concern in longitudinal studies because of rapidly changing cultural milieus. How can one evaluate the effects of cohort independently of age? Schaie (1967) has proposed the possible use of a *time lag* design. In Fig. 3-1 time lag designs are represented by individual diagonals; that is, a time lag design employing 40-year-old subjects would include cells C_1, B_1, and A_1. Similarly, a time lag design employing 60-year-old subjects would include cells D_1, C_3, and B_3. The major disadvantage of the time lag design is that one cannot separate the effects of time of measurement (which necessarily must be different for each cohort) from the effects of cohort, per se. Thus we now have three types of research designs: each involves two variables that are intrinsically confounded. The cross-sectional design measures age differences, but age and cohort are confounded. The longitudinal design measures age changes, but age and time of measurement are confounded. The time lag design measures cohort differences, but cohort and time of measurement are confounded. Is there any way out of this dilemma? Schaie (1970) has suggested three additional designs that permit separation of the effects of the confounded variables, provided one can make certain assumptions. We will present only a general description of these designs; a detailed discussion of the statistical methods that are necessary to isolate confounded effects is beyond the scope of this chapter.

Sequential designs. The investigator who is interested in separating the effects of age and cohort might consider Schaie's *cohort-sequential* design, which basically involves two or more longitudinal studies of different cohorts. In Fig. 3-1 a cohort-sequential study is represented by the cells in rows *I* and *II*. The cohort-sequential method is most

Fig. 3-2. K. Warner Schaie, Ph.D. (University of Washington, 1956). Dr. Schaie is best known for his methodological innovations with respect to experimental designs used in aging studies. He is largely responsible for operationalizing the concepts of life-span psychology in research and training. A former Chairman of the Department of Psychology at West Virginia University, he is presently Professor of Psychology and Director of the Gerontology Research Institute of the Andrus Gerontology Center at the University of Southern California. Dr. Schaie has authored many books and articles in psychological gerontology and many other areas of psychology. He has, among many other contributions, served as the Chairman of the Developmental Behavioral Sciences Study Section of the National Institutes of Health.

useful if the investigator knows or can assume that time of measurement effects are trivial. This is true because time of measurement cannot be separated from cohort effects; both necessarily begin at different intervals (Schaie, 1975).

Often an aging experiment involves some type of measurement technique that may be expected to produce varying results, depending on the time of data collection. The studies by Botwinick (1973), noted in the section on traditional developmental designs, are prime examples. In this case the investigator would be concerned with separating the effects of age and time of measurement. Schaie's *time-sequential* design provides a useful strategy for isolating these effects. This design includes two or more cross-sectional samples obtained at two or more times of measurement. For example, a time-sequential study might include the cells in columns *I′* and *II′* in Fig. 3-1. You may have noticed that cohort differences are the confounding factor in a time-sequential design because obviously *one cannot obtain two cross-sectional samples of the same age groups that belong to the same cohort* (Schaie, 1975).

Finally, it is possible that the major concern of an investigator may be to isolate the effects of cohort and time of measurement under conditions in which he can assume trivial age differences. For example, scores on verbal intelligence tests have been shown to be fairly stable between the ages of 30 and 60 years for highly educated subjects, and thus the age of subjects may be of little interest for many researchers who are concerned with verbal behavior. However, the experimenter

Table 3-1. Summary of potential confounded effects and isolated effects in developmental research designs

Design	Confounded effects: Age	Confounded effects: Cohort	Confounded effects: Time of measurement	Isolated effects: Age	Isolated effects: Cohort	Isolated effects: Time of measurement
Cross-sectional	X	X				
Longitudinal	X		X			
Time lag		X	X			
Cohort-sequential*			X	X	X	
Time-sequential†		X		X		X
Cross-sequential‡	X				X	X

*Most useful if it can be assumed that time-of-measurement effects are nonsignificant.
†Most useful if it can be assumed that cohort effects are nonsignificant.
‡Most useful if it can be assumed that age effects are nonsignificant.

who is interested in verbal tests of slang usage might be very concerned with both cohort and time-of-measurement effects. To separate these effects he might use Schaie's *cross-sequential* design, which is represented in Fig. 3-1 by the large square enclosed in double lines. Table 3-1 summarizes the six developmental research designs that we have discussed; it shows the potential confounded effects and the isolated effects obtained by using each design.

In addition to the two-component cohort-sequential, time-sequential, and cross-sequential designs, Schaie (1965, 1967, 1970) has provided a three-component *general developmental model,* which includes a statistical analysis for establishing the approximate proportions of variance contributed by age, cohort, and time of measurement effects. As Botwinick (1973) has noted, the three-component model is the best method currently available for adult developmental researchers. We must point out that researchers who use animal subjects might also profit from the use of Schaie's method. For example, it has been shown that time of measurement may make a great deal of difference in the results obtained in many animal studies (see Elias and Elias, 1975, for a discussion of varying periods of different housing conditions prior to the time of testing and their effects on age data in animal studies). If age is also an important variable, a time-sequential experiment would be useful in isolating time-of-measurement and age effects. Recently, Schaie (1975) has pointed out the unique applications of his model for human behavior genetic studies. The model is equally useful for behavior genetic studies employing inbred strains or selected lines (see Elias and Elias, 1975:423-425). In this type of study, age, cohort, and time-of-measurement effects all are likely to be important. As researchers become more aware of the potential uses of the new developmental designs, it may be expected that their contributions will become increasingly valuable for expanding knowledge of aging processes.

EXPERIMENTAL APPROACH

Most readers probably are aware that psychologists make a distinction between studies that are basically descriptive (e.g., correlational or demographic studies) and studies that are based on an experimental design. All experimental designs involve independent variables (i.e., those manipulated by the investigator) and dependent variables (i.e., those measured by the investigator). Researchers use experimental designs when they wish to manipulate treatment conditions (independent variables) while holding all other conditions constant. In this way they are able to determine the direction of

Table 3-2. A factorial design (4 × 3 × 2) with four levels of a drug dosage factor, three levels of an age factor, and two levels of a hospital factor*

Mean age (years)	Hospital A				Hospital B			
	Drug dosage level				Drug dosage level			
	0 mg	40 mg	80 mg	120 mg	0 mg	40 mg	80 mg	120 mg
30	S_1	S_{31}	S_{61}	S_{91}	S_{121}	S_{151}	S_{181}	S_{211}
	.	.	.	.	.	.	.	.
	.	.	.	.	.	.	.	.
	.	.	.	.	.	.	.	.
	S_{10}	S_{40}	S_{70}	S_{100}	S_{130}	S_{160}	S_{190}	S_{220}
50	S_{11}	S_{41}	S_{71}	S_{101}	S_{131}	S_{161}	S_{191}	S_{221}
	.	.	.	.	.	.	.	.
	.	.	.	.	.	.	.	.
	.	.	.	.	.	.	.	.
	S_{20}	S_{50}	S_{80}	S_{110}	S_{140}	S_{170}	S_{200}	S_{230}
70	S_{21}	S_{51}	S_{81}	S_{111}	S_{141}	S_{171}	S_{201}	S_{231}
	.	.	.	.	.	.	.	.
	.	.	.	.	.	.	.	.
	.	.	.	.	.	.	.	.
	S_{30}	S_{60}	S_{90}	S_{120}	S_{150}	S_{180}	S_{210}	S_{240}

*Si represents a single subject. There are ten subjects in each cell and a total of 240 subjects. Each subject contributes a single score (e.g., IQ) to the data analysis.

causality because any change in the dependent variable may be attributed to the treatment conditions. Sometimes extraneous variables cannot be held constant so they are randomized or counterbalanced by the use of special designs. However, the manipulative, experimental design is still the most powerful tool currently available in terms of identifying cause-and-effect relationships. The reader should keep in mind that experimental designs are *not* alternatives to the developmental research designs that we discussed in the previous section. Rather, they are the specific methodological designs necessary for establishing cause-and-effect relationships between variables. Of course, they may be used within the general framework of developmental designs.

Factorial designs

Experimental research designs that involve only one independent variable are called *single factor designs*. Usually, they are not very useful for adult developmental studies because researchers most often are interested in manipulating at least two variables. If a research design involves more than one kind of independent variable or treatment, it is called a *factorial or multifactor design*. Table 3-2 illustrates a typical factorial design in which the investigator chose four dosages of a drug, three age groups, and two different hospitals to systematically evaluate the drug's effect on intelligence test scores. Note that the drug-dosage level of 0 mg represents a control group and a baseline for comparison with groups who receive the drug. Given the design shown in Table 3-2, one may say that there are four levels of a drug dosage factor, three levels of an age factor, and two levels of a hospital factor; that is, it is 4 × 3 × 2 factorial design.

Factorial designs involve both *main effects* and *interaction effects*. A significant main effect for a particular factor means that factor has an effect on the dependent variable when one ignores the presence of all other factors. For example, if drug dosage has an effect on

Table 3-3. Partially repeated measurements design with six levels of a drug dosage factor and two age groups, that is, a 6 (within subjects) × 2 (between subjects) design*

Mean age (years)	Subjects	Drug dosage level					
		0 mg	20 mg	40 mg	60 mg	80 mg	100 mg
30	S_1	X_1	X_2	X_3	X_4	X_5	X_6
	S_2	X_1	X_2	X_3	X_4	X_5	X_6
	.						
	.						
	.						
	.						
	S_{29}	X_1	X_2	X_3	X_4	X_5	X_6
	S_{30}	X_1	X_2	X_3	X_4	X_5	X_6
50	S_{31}	X_1	X_2	X_3	X_4	X_5	X_6
	S_{32}	X_1	X_2	X_3	X_4	X_5	X_6
	.						
	.						
	.						
	.						
	S_{59}	X_1	X_2	X_3	X_4	X_5	X_6
	S_{60}	X_1	X_2	X_3	X_4	X_5	X_6

*Each subject (Si) receives six scores (e.g., IQ), one for each drug dosage level. If only one age group were used, the design would involve *all* repeated measurements.

intelligence test scores, regardless of the age of the subjects and the hospital in which they were tested, it can be said that there is a significant main effect for drug dosage.

Interactions are more difficult to explain. It is probably sufficient to say that they reflect circumstances in which the treatment conditions of one factor do not have the same effect under all treatment conditions or levels of another factor. For example, the effects of four drug dosages may vary considerably for different age groups. Fig. 3-3 shows how a simple two-way interaction (drug dosage × age) might appear when the data are graphed. Of course, it is also possible to have a three-way interaction (e.g., drug dosage × age × hospital) when the entire experimental design involves three factors.

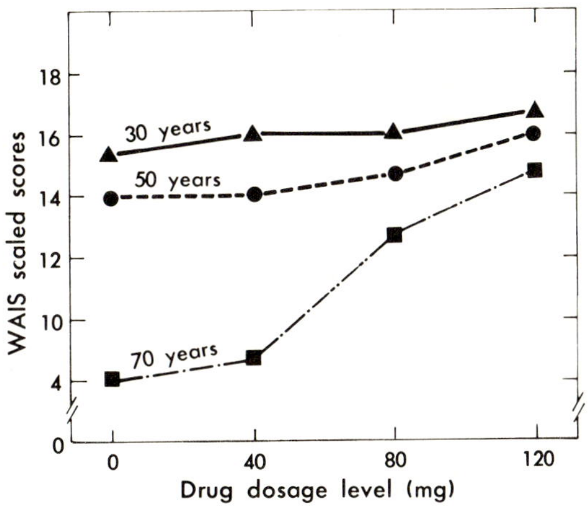

Fig. 3-3. Hypothetical age × drug dose level interaction. The drug had little effect on the scaled scores of 30- and 50-year-old subjects on the similarities subtest, but it substantially improved the scaled scores of 70-year-old subjects who received the 80 and 120 mg doses.

Repeated measurements designs

Many of the studies discussed throughout this book involve repeated measurements designs. A *repeated measurements* design sometimes is called a "within subjects" design, and it simply involves one or more treatments that are repeated over time for the same subjects. Table 3-3 presents an example of a *partially* repeated measurements design in which the same subjects receive different dosages of a drug. Any design that involves components of a repeated measurements design and components of a nonrepeated measurements design naturally is called a *partially repeated measurements design*. For example, in Table 3-3 drug dosage involves repeated measurements, but age does not; that is, different subjects comprise each age group. Actually, all longitudinal studies involve a broad repeated measurements design because the same subjects are tested at successive points in time. Other examples of the use of repeated measurements designs include learning experiments in which many trials are given to each subject and social psychological experiments in which anxiety or aggression are measured in a group of subjects who are presented with various social situations.

Multivariate designs

The multivariate design always involves more than one *dependent* variable. For example, the investigator who is interested in drug dosage effects on different age groups may wish to measure more than one standardized test score. He may also be concerned with the subjects' reaction times and anxiety test scores and may wish to monitor a physiological variable, such as heart rate, when subjects are under the influence of the drug. This particular multivariate design is illustrated in Table 3-4.

Frequently two or more of the experimental designs that we have discussed are

Table 3-4. Multivariate design with four dependent variables and two drug dosage levels*

Drug dosage level	Subjects	Variables			
		IQ	Reaction time	Anxiety score	Average heart rate
0 mg	S_1	W_1	X_1	Y_1	Z_1
	S_2	W_1	X_1	Y_1	Z_1
	.				
	.				
	.				
	.				
	S_{29}	W_1	X_1	Y_1	Z_1
	S_{30}	W_1	X_1	Y_1	Z_1
60 mg	S_{31}	W_1	X_1	Y_1	Z_1
	S_{32}	W_1	X_1	Y_1	Z_1
	.				
	.				
	.				
	.				
	S_{59}	W_1	X_1	Y_1	Z_1
	S_{60}	W_1	X_1	Y_1	Z_1

*Each subject (Si) receives a single score for each dependent variable for a total of four scores (W, X, Y, and Z). Compare this design with the repeated measurements design shown in Table 3-1, where each subject received six IQ scores (dependent variable), one for each level of the *same* independent variable (drug dosage level). The designs in Tables 3-1 and 3-2 could be combined so that multiple response measures (IQ, reaction time, anxiety, and heart rate) could be obtained for different age groups at each drug dosage level.

combined. For example, dependent variables are always repeated measures in a longitudinal design. Usually more than one dependent variable is measured because longitudinal studies often involve the collaborative efforts of many investigators who are interested in different aspects of their subjects' behavior. If the experimental, rather than descriptive, approach is used, the longitudinal study may include more than one independent variable or "factor" (e.g., drug dosage and hospital). Thus the longitudinal study is most often of the repeated measurements, multivariate, factorial variety.

Do not be concerned if you cannot understand the statistical bases for these designs. The important thing is to distinguish between them in terms of when they are applied and how they relate to the developmental designs that we discussed in the previous section. Close examination of Tables 3-2, 3-3, and 3-4 should help you understand the basic strategy of factorial, repeated measurements, and multivariate research designs.

BLOCKING VARIABLES: THE AGE FACTOR

Although many experimental variables may be manipulated by the experimenter, there are variables that are not manipulated. For example, the age factor in developmental research is rarely manipulated by the investigator. He does not "create" three different age groups and observe the resulting changes in behavior. Rather, he chooses subjects falling within defined age ranges (i.e., cohorts) if he has a cross-sectional design, or he follows the same individuals over a period of time if he has a longitudinal design. In both cases the investigator has nothing directly to do with the manipulation of the age factor. This kind of factor is sometimes called a *blocking factor,* sometimes a classification factor, and sometimes a "subject factor." For example, the investigator may "block" on age because he is interested in how four drug dosage levels affect behavior at two or three widely different ages. Some examples of blocking factors and manipulated variables commonly used in adult developmental research follow.

Blocking variables
- Age
- Sex
- Weight
- Occupational status
- Health status

Manipulated variables
- Drug dosage
- Days of deprivation
- Level of shock
- Type of instructions
- Number of choice points in a maze
- Massed versus spaced practice

It is important to remember that a blocking factor does not have the same power as a manipulated factor in terms of drawing cause-and-effect relationships, even though both factors may be used in an *experimental* design. In this case it is better to refer to the design as "quasi-experimental" because age is not manipulated. For example, even though anxiety scores may be different for different age groups, one cannot say that age *caused* the change in anxiety scores any more than one could say that there is a causal relationship if age and anxiety were highly correlated. Many students fail to realize this important point and thus assume that an experimental design is somehow more powerful than the correlational approach in those circumstances in which a blocking factor, such as age, is used. We will discuss the concept of correlation in the section on statistical terms. For the present it is important to understand that the experimental design only provides information regarding cause-and-effect relationships when it involves *manipulated* treatments (e.g., drug dosage levels).

Sometimes, for a factor such as age, the correlational approach is more meaningful and provides more information. This is especially true when a wide range of ages is available. For example, if there are 100 subjects ranging in age at rather even intervals from 25 to 50 years, it would be better to employ a correlational approach than to artificially divide the subjects into three age groups because such divisions do not provide any more information about causation. It is easier to understand this point if an extreme example is used. In some instances experimenters attempt to evaluate the effects of age by performing a *median split*. Subjects whose age falls below the median for the entire group are placed in one category (younger), whereas those whose ages fall above the median are placed in another category (older). Differences between these two groups may allow one to infer that age is influencing the dependent variables; but they do not tell much about *how* age is influencing the results. Persons in the two different groups may be very close to the median and thus resemble each other in age (and scores on the dependent variables) much more than those of extreme ages. A correlational approach at least would have given information about the strength of the relationship between age and the dependent variable. Thus, given a large enough sample of subjects with a wide, evenly distributed age range, it is often better to obtain a correlation for age and the dependent variable(s) of interest.

There are some instances when age group blocking is justified. Sometimes subjects may be grouped on the basis of a meaningful age-correlated variable, such as preretirement as opposed to postretirement status. In other instances the groups may have age means that are widely divergent and the range of ages within each group may be narrow (e.g., 20 to 25, 40 to 45, 60 to 65, 80 to 85 years). In this case it may make more sense to treat age as a factor with four blocks or "age classifications." Nevertheless, significant differences between these age groups do not allow one to infer causation, and information about intermediate age groups is missed. Often a design that includes blocks of age groups is necessary because large numbers of subjects are not available. However, when age means are close and age ranges are uneven within groups (e.g., 20 to 35, 45 to 50, 60 to 90 years), it is probably unwise to use either the correlational or the factorial approach.

One age group

Sometimes adult developmental researchers obtain data for a single age group because they are interested in the effect of one or more treatments on subjects in "older" cohorts. These studies may be useful for the gathering of preliminary data, but they are not developmental studies because the results cannot be compared with those for a younger group tested under the same conditions. For example, if a certain drug improves performance in the elderly adult, one may conclude that it is a useful drug as applied to elderly adults; but the drug also may improve performance in a younger person to the same extent. Thus, although this is a useful drug, the age factor is irrelevant because the investigator knows that the drug "works" for persons of different ages to the same extent. However, if the drug does not affect the performance of younger persons, the age factor becomes relevant; that is, this is an age-by-drug interaction. No conclusion about age relevance can be drawn if a young age group is not included in the study. Try to keep this in mind as you evaluate the studies considered in the following chapters because some of them include only one group of older subjects.

Two age groups

Two is better than one, but more than two is better than two. As you read the material in the following chapters, you will see that the use of more than two age groups is highly desirable because often the relationship between age and the dependent variable is not a simple positive or negative one. For example, adult development investigators may find an increase, then a decrease, in scores on a dependent variable as age increases. The choice of only two age groups (e.g., young and old) may lead to the conclusion that age is associated with a decline in performance, but choice of another age group (e.g., middle age) may indicate improvement prior to decline. Thus at least three and, if possible, multiple age groups representative of the life span are recommended when age is used as a blocking factor.

SOME STATISTICAL TERMS

Throughout this book we discuss numerous studies in which statistical terms are used. Many readers may be familiar with most of these terms. They may wish to use this section for a short review. Although it is helpful to have had a course in statistics and experimental design, it is not essential if you read and digest the following information carefully.

Sample size

Sample size and the extent to which a sample is representative of a larger population are very important considerations for any study. They are particularly critical aspects of aging research. For complex statistical reasons it is absolutely imperative that the number of subjects be greater than the number of variables in a multivariate study. Earlier in this chapter we discussed the fact that in a longitudinal study large sample size may be easily achieved for younger groups; but as individuals get older, they are eliminated from the sample by virtue of death, geographical mobility, and other factors contributing to attrition. Furthermore, the sample characteristics change in such a way that data collected later in the study may produce biased results.

The problem of shrinking sample size is less critical in cross-sectional designs, since given numbers of subjects may be selected from different cohorts. However, in this case of the cross-sectional study, samples are chosen from populations (cohorts) that are influenced not only by age but by many other factors, such as health and education. The influence of these factors will be different within each cohort. For example, "healthy" 70-year-old subjects are a more highly select group than "healthy" 20-year-old subjects. Consequently, the healthy older sample may not be as representative of the cohort from which it was drawn as the healthy young sample is. The point to remember is that many of the studies we discuss throughout this book involve biased older samples. Findings based on these samples may not be applicable to the general population of older persons.

Replication

A major question that arises when one does an experiment is whether the results are replicable. This is a natural question to ask because psychologists often must use small numbers of subjects (samples), which may or may not be representative of larger numbers of individuals (populations). If samples deviate from "randomness," or if some kind of experimental error slips into one or more treatment conditions, it may not be possible to generalize the findings to an entire population. Furthermore, the results may not be repeatable. The best way to discover if an initial finding has occurred as a result of biased samples or experimental error is to see if it can be replicated; that is, the experiment is done several times in the same manner to see if the same results are obtained. Russian psychologists often use this approach, but American psychologists generally elect to use tests of statistical significance.

Statistical significance

When investigators report that their findings are statistically significant, they refer to the fact that their experimental treatments produced different results based on a given probability of error in making that statement. Basically, a statistically significant finding has a higher probability of replicating with the same results than one that is statistically nonsignificant. However, it is wise to evaluate carefully *statistically significant* results in terms of their importance to the literature on aging; that is, one must evaluate the *practical significance* of all findings with regard to whether or not they increase knowledge of adult developmental processes, and whether differences observed are meaningful in terms of the percentage of behavioral variance accounted for by the variables included in the study.

Correlations

Correlation coefficients provide an index of the degree to which two variables, such as age and IQ, are related (co-vary). They also indicate the extent to which knowing a score on one measure allows the investigator to predict a score on another. Correlations range from 0.00 to +1.00 (positive) and 0.00 to −1.00 (negative). A high positive correlation means that two variables are related in such a way that an increase in one is accompanied by an increase in the other. A high negative correlation means that two variables are related in such a way that an increase in one is accompanied by a decrease in the other.

The significance of a correlation may be tested. In other words, one may determine the probability that it occurred by chance. A statistically significant correlation has a low probability of occurring by chance. However, statistically significant correlations may be relatively insignificant in terms of their importance. With an *important* correlation a high proportion of the variance in one measure is accounted for by the variance in the other, and thus the investigator can predict a subject's score on the second measure accurately if he knows his score on the first measure. The "percent variance accounted for" is calculated by squaring the correlation coefficient. Thus the common variance accounted for with a correlation of 0.50 is 0.25 or 25%. In many cases a correlation of 0.50 is statistically significant, but because the common variance is only 25%, one cannot make very precise predictions. There is no ironclad rule with regard to an acceptable level of "percent variance accounted for." The important thing to remember is that a statistically significant correlation may not be significant in terms of its importance to the literature on aging if it does not produce highly accurate predictions.

Analysis of variance

Analysis of variance is merely the term applied to the analytic procedure that permits the investigator to determine whether or not he has obtained statistically significant main effects and/or interactions. In a single factor design only the main effect can be evaluated; that is, the experimenter determines if his treatment conditions for a single factor (e.g., drug dosage levels) produced significantly different results. You may recall that a factorial or multifactor design includes more than one factor (e.g., drug dosage levels and age). With a factorial design it is also possible to determine the statistical significance of interaction effects (e.g., drug dosage × age).

Multivariate analysis of variance

As multivariate designs, that is, those with more than one dependent variable, increase in popularity among adult developmental researchers, multivariate analysis of variance is becoming a common statistical technique in the literature on aging. Multivariate statistics are based on the commonsense notions that (1) more than one behavioral measure is relevant to the performance of different age groups, and (2) a composite measure may be a better indicator of age changes or age differences when more than one performance measure is available. Stated somewhat differently, multivariate analysis of variance helps researchers to add apples and oranges in a legitimate manner.

Suppose you design an experiment with three dependent variables: reaction time, anxiety scores, and heart rate. Of course you are interested in how each of these dependent variables relates to age and treatment conditions, but you may also be interested in how they "trade off" with one another to influence a composite of behavior represented by the interaction of all three measures. It is obvious that you simply cannot add the scores for all three variables because the proper weights for each variable are not known. In the absence of such knowledge, the multivariate analysis of variance allows researchers to form a meaningful composite based on the "best possible set of weights." The actual statistical procedure involves the concept of canonical correlation and thus is not easily explained; the basic idea is that correlations among the variables dictate the weights to be used to construct the composite score.

Of course, one does not need a multivariate analysis of variance simply to examine correlations between dependent variables. For example, it may be found that anxiety scores and heart rate are negatively related to reaction time for older subjects but positively related for younger and middle-aged subjects. Even when an overall multivariate analysis is performed, individual correlations should be examined because they provide important information as to why certain results are obtained with a given set of dependent variables.

Multivariate analysis of variance also serves as a "protection procedure" in those situations where the investigator must perform multiple univariate analyses of variance because he has several dependent variables. The rationale for this procedure requires more space than can be provided here, but the interested reader may consult papers by Elias (1975b), McCall (1970), and McCall and Appelbaum (1973).

Basically, the probability of obtaining a statistically significant univariate result by chance alone increases as the number of dependent variables in an experiment increases. However, if the overall multivariate analysis of variance is statistically significant, the investigator can assume that his univariate analyses are not significant simply by chance. If this procedure is not familiar to you, do not be concerned. The important thing is that you do not confuse the terms *multifactor* univariate analysis of variance and *multivariate* analysis of variance. A multifactor analysis of variance merely involves a factorial design with more than one *independent* variable (e.g., drug dosage levels and age). A multivariate analysis of variance always involves a design with more than one *dependent* variable (e.g., reaction time, anxiety scores, and heart rate). However, it may include more than one independent variable as well; that is, a multivariate analysis of variance may be performed if an experiment is based on a combination multivariate and factorial design (e.g., Tables 3-1 and 3-2).

Covariance adjustments

Analysis of covariance techniques often have been applied in aging studies. Generally, an analysis of covariance is used when the experimenter cannot control a relevant variable that might be influencing the results to a significant extent. For example, we may wish to compare the standardized intelligence test scores for three different age groups, but we may find that the educational levels are different for each group. In this case we will be unable to determine if group differences in test scores are related to age, per se, or to varying educational levels for each cohort. However, we may adjust the test scores for the influence of educational level by means of covariance analysis. Stated in somewhat oversimplified terms, the test score for each of the subjects in the three age groups is adjusted on the basis of the correlation between age and education. If the correlation is low, the adjustment will have little effect on the results. If the correlation is high, the adjustment may make a great deal of difference; that is, a statistically significant relationship between age and test scores may disappear altogether, or a nonsignificant relationship may become statistically significant.

Covariance analysis can be useful in a number of contexts where experimental control over a potentially confounding variable cannot be achieved. However, there are many statistical assumptions that must be met before it can be *correctly applied*. These assumptions are difficult to meet because the relationship between the dependent variable (e.g., test scores) and the "covariate" (e.g., educational level) may not be the same for different age groups. Analysis of covariance often is used in aging studies when it should not be used because the necessary assumptions have not been met. Recently, a number of researchers have written methodological papers on this issue that may be of interest to the reader who is sophisticated in statistical techniques (see Storandt and Hudson, 1975).

Because of the difficulty of meeting many of the necessary assumptions, *blocking* on relevant variables is preferred to covariance analysis whenever it is possible. For example, if the subjects in each age group can be blocked or classified on the basis of educational level, it is often wise to use this procedure rather than to adjust test scores for educational level by means of covariance analysis. As you read the chapters that follow, it will be helpful to distinguish between studies in which analysis of covariance is used and those in which relevant variables are blocked.

Factor analysis

Factor analysis is basically a multivariate technique that may be applied to descriptive data when large numbers of variables have been included in a study. The major objective of the factor analytic technique is to reduce these large numbers of variables to a smaller number of "factors" or "components" to obtain a clearer picture of the relationship among the original variables. Factor analysis is particularly useful when applied to developmental data because often the relationships among a set of variables will not be the same for different age groups. Currently, it is a popular statistical approach for researchers who are interested in patterns of intellectual and personality change over the life span (e.g., Horn, 1970, 1975; Livson, 1973; Reinert, 1970). In addition to producing more concise descriptions of specific behavior patterns, factor analysis permits the construction of new scores (factor scores) that are based on the composite variables (factors). These scores may be analyzed further with statistical techniques, such as multivariate analysis of variance. For example, one may ask whether the factor scores obtained for a young group of subjects are statistically different from those obtained for an older group. Those readers who are familiar with factor analytic techniques may wish to consult Nesselroade (1970) for an excellent discussion of the many potential applications of factor analysis in developmental research.

GENETIC CONTROL AND GENETIC MANIPULATION

Throughout the remaining chapters of this book, the terms *inbred strain* and *stock* will be used. They will be particularly important when behavioral data for animals are discussed and when behavior genetics and aging are discussed in the final chapter. Experimenters use inbred strains of rats or mice to obtain genetic control in experiments in which they vary environmental conditions. This unique advantage of rodent models for research allows the investigator to use many genetically identical subjects in a study in which environmental parameters are manipulated. Thus he may determine the extent to which changes in behavior with age, or changes that are a function of the interaction of age and treatment conditions, may be attributed to environmental, maturational, or generational factors. He can do this because inbred animals are genetically homozygous and, consequently, genetic variability is eliminated. Except for an extremely small amount of "heterozygous residual," animals from inbred strains all carry the same "genetic baggage."

Although genetic control is advantageous,

it also has its limitations. Generalizing from an animal study in which a single inbred strain was used is like generalizing from a human study in which genetically identical individuals (identical twins) were used; that is, any generalizations must be limited to that unique genotype. Human subjects are heterozygous (genetically dissimilar), and consequently, genetic control is not possible, but results may be generalized to the entire heterozygous population. Using a single strain of inbred mice or rats results in genetic control at the expense of inferences concerning the species as a whole. Some researchers have suggested that, in instances where generalizability to an entire animal species is of concern, mice or rats in a wild state (presumably random-bred animals) should be used. This solution is not too practical. Thus behavior geneticists (e.g., Henderson, 1969) have suggested systems of breeding that result in the mixing of genes to produce random-bred animals for research. The procedure is time-consuming and tedious and seldom has been used in aging research.

You should be careful to note that occasionally the term *stock* rather than *strain* is used. Basically, a strain is derived from brother and sister matings for a minimum of twenty to twenty-five generations (Russell, 1972). Animals that have not been inbred for this period of time are called stocks. Stocks have heterozygous gene pools; that is, all animals of the stock are not genetically identical. However, stocks may not be *randomly* bred. Random breeding is difficult to achieve, and it should be distinguished from haphazard breeding. In other words, the absence of strict inbreeding procedures does not necessarily produce a randomly bred group of animals.

It is important to remember the distinctions between randomly bred animals, inbred animals, and stocks when reading the literature dealing with animals. One further term, *selected stocks,* is sometimes used; selected stocks are genetically heterozygous. They have been deliberately selected by genetic procedures for a specific trait, such as behavioral aggressiveness or hypertension. We will discuss some of these procedures in Chapter 14.

You will find that some researchers do not specify whether they have used inbred strains, randomly bred stocks, or haphazardly bred stocks in their studies. This lack of attention to a very important subject characteristic is as serious as forgetting to specify how old the subjects are in an aging study. You will also find that frequently experimenters attempt to replicate a study (perform it exactly as it was done before), but they do so with a different strain of mice or rats. Thus no one knows whether a failure to replicate a certain result is because data from the first study were unreliable or specific to the unique genotype (strain) employed. Since strain differences in behavior are more the rule than the exception, the experimenter who uses a different strain in an attempt to replicate previous findings is making things extremely difficult for himself. The obvious solution to this dilemma is to employ more than one strain in the initial study so that the interaction between genotype and behavior clearly may be assessed.

SUMMARY

A complete discussion of developmental/experimental research methodology easily could fill several volumes. Scientific research has many facets, ranging from the metaphysical world views that influence the behavioral scientist's choice of problems and solutions to sophisticated statistical tools that allow him to draw accurate conclusions from his data. It is difficult to do justice to this many-faceted topic in only one chapter. It is even more difficult to summarize the most important aspects of research methodology. Nevertheless, there are a number of specific points that you will find helpful to recall as you study the remaining chapters of this book.

The mechanistic and organismic models of development are based on the machine metaphor and the biological organism metaphor, respectively. The mechanistic model includes a view of man as a reactive, passive organism. Development is considered to be a product of material cause (the biological prerequisites for behavior) and efficient cause (the external, environmental forces that impinge on the organism). In addition, the mechanistic model implies that developmental change is quantitative; it may be measured as continuous, successive increments in the elementary units of behavior. Psychologists who work within the mechanistic framework focus their research on antecedent-consequent relationships (e.g., S-R sequences).

In contrast, the organismic model includes a view of man as a spontaneously active organism. Thus, man, himself, is a primary force in developmental change. Material and efficient causes are considered important because they may facilitate or inhibit developmental processes. However, formal cause (i.e., psychological structures and their organization) and final cause (the end point or function of development) are thought to be equally important determinants of change. Within the organismic framework, development is best described as discontinuous, qualitative change in structures and their functions. Thus research is directed primarily toward the discovery of structure-function relationships from the observation of behavior in different contexts throughout the life span. Because the whole is assumed to be more than the sum of its parts, organismic researchers believe that the search for elementary units of behavior is meaningless.

There can be no reconciliation between the mechanistic and organismic models of development because they are based on metaphors (as if statements), and thus they cannot be demonstrated to be true or false. Researchers who differ with respect to their world views also differ with respect to how they define the concepts of development and age, what they consider meaningful developmental data, and which statistical tools they choose for data analysis.

Traditional developmental research designs include the cross-sectional and longitudinal methods. The cross-sectional method measures age differences, but it involves an inherent confounding of age and cohort. The longitudinal method measures age changes, but it involves an inherent confounding of age and time of measurement, as well as cultural effects that may occur within a single lifetime. Time lag designs allow researchers to evaluate cohort or generational change, but they cannot separate the effects of cohort and time of measurement. Schaie and his colleagues have advocated the use of three "sequential" designs (cohort-sequential, time-sequential, and cross-sequential), as well as a three-component model, which permit researchers to isolate the effects of age, cohort, and time of measurement. Although these newer designs are the best methods currently available to developmental researchers, they have not been used extensively in the current literature on aging.

Many researchers are beginning to recognize the advantages offered by a combined developmental/experimental approach. Traditional experimental methods include factorial designs, repeated measurements designs, and multivariate designs. Factorial or multifactor designs are used when more than one independent variable is studied; they allow researchers to evaluate both main effects and interaction effects. Repeated measurements designs are familiar to developmental researchers who have conducted longitudinal studies in which the same subjects are measured over successive points in time. Multivariate designs are based on research strategies that involve two or more dependent variables. They are particularly useful to the researcher who believes that a composite of many behaviors may be a better indicator of developmental change than individual, isolated behaviors.

Adult developmental researchers necessarily have many concerns when they design a study. If they wish to conduct a longitudinal investigation, they must be aware that subject attrition will be an important factor in the extent to which they can generalize their findings, especially to the population of older adults. If they choose the cross-sectional approach, they must decide whether to match subjects on variables, such as health and education, at the risk of limiting the generalizability of their results, or to select random samples from each cohort, at the risk of losing experimental control over many confounding variables. Furthermore, they must decide whether to "block" on the age variable or to use the correlational approach, a decision that often is dictated by subject availability. Investigators who employ animal subjects must be extremely careful with regard to choice of strain or stock, as well as with regard to their evaluation of genotype by age interactions. Finally, all developmental researchers must have a thorough knowledge of the appropriate statistical techniques for their data analyses.

We hope that this short introduction to developmental/experimental research methodology has provided a stimulus and has laid the foundation for a critical evaluation of the current adult developmental and aging literature.

SELECTED READINGS

Kuhn, T. S. *The structure of scientific revolutions.* Chicago: University of Chicago Press, 1962.

McCall, R. B. The use of multivariate procedures in developmental psychology. In P. H. Mussen (Ed.), *Carmichael's manual of child psychology* (Vol. I). New York: John Wiley & Sons, Inc., 1970.

Nesselroade, J. R. Application of multivariate strategies to problems of measuring and structuring long-term change. In L. R. Goulet and P. B. Baltes (Eds.), *Life-span developmental psychology: research and theory.* New York: Academic Press, Inc., 1970.

Overton, W. F., and Reese, H. W. Models of development: methodological implications. In J. R. Nesselroade and H. W. Reese (Eds.), *Life-span developmental psychology: methodological issues.* New York: Academic Press, Inc., 1973.

Reese, H. W., and Overton, W. F. Models of development and theories of development. In L. R. Goulet and P. B. Baltes (Eds.), *Life-span developmental psychology: research and theory.* New York: Academic Press, Inc., 1970.

Riegel, K. F., and Riegel, R. M. *Development, drop, and death. Developmental Psychology,* 1972, **6**, 306-309.

Schaie, K. W. Age changes and age differences. *Gerontologist,* 1967, **7**, 128-132.

Schaie, K. W. A general model for the study of developmental problems. *Psychological Bulletin,* 1965, **64**, 92-107.

Wohlwill, J. F. Methodology and research strategy in the study of developmental change. In L. R. Goulet and P. B. Baltes (Eds.), *Life-span developmental psychology: research and theory.* New York: Academic Press, Inc., 1970.

CHAPTER 4

INTELLIGENCE

Wisdom and experience are necessary to make the world go round; creative ability to make it go forward.

DAVID WECHSLER (1958)

Intellectual performance is of particular concern to most persons who live in the highly competitive society of the United States. Recently, some educators and psychologists have challenged this emphasis on competition in view of the fact that other personal qualities are important to individual growth and happiness. Clearly, self-actualization and working together cooperatively to build a better life for all are important personal and societal objectives. Nevertheless, the current educational and cultural milieu does emphasize competition, and an important aspect of successful competition is intellectual competence.

For this reason almost everyone is concerned about the possibility that their own level of intellectual performance will decline as they grow older. Does intelligence decline with advancing age? If so, can anything be done about it? No problem in the literature on the psychology of adult development has received greater attention. Paradoxically, there are no final answers to these basic questions. A number of prominent researchers argue that there is little, if any, decline in intellectual functioning with advancing age with the exception of a sudden drop in performance shortly before death. They point out that data suggesting a progressive decline may be accounted for by such factors as level of education, poor health, and generational differences. Other psychologists believe strongly that even when these factors are accounted for, there is a decline in intellectual ability with increasing age. Still others believe that whether or not intelligence declines is a less important question than the extent to which specific abilities remain at a functionally high level in later years.

As you read this chapter you will formulate your own opinions on these issues. You will find that whatever generalizations you select as those you prefer will have to be qualified in terms of the conditions under which the data were collected, the type of test used, and the subject sample. Moreover, you will find that those who advocate the decline hypothesis and those who advocate little decline may have different definitions of intelligence. One question you should ask again and again as you read through the chapter is: how important are these intellectual changes with regard to the everyday life of the elderly person? As we pointed out in Chapter 3, there is a difference between a statistically significant finding and a finding that is significant in terms of the lives of older persons.

WHAT DO INTELLIGENCE TESTS MEASURE?

One reason that there are no final answers with regard to the question of intellectual decline with age is that intelligence tests do not measure intelligence. *Intelligence tests sample performance.* Researchers make inferences

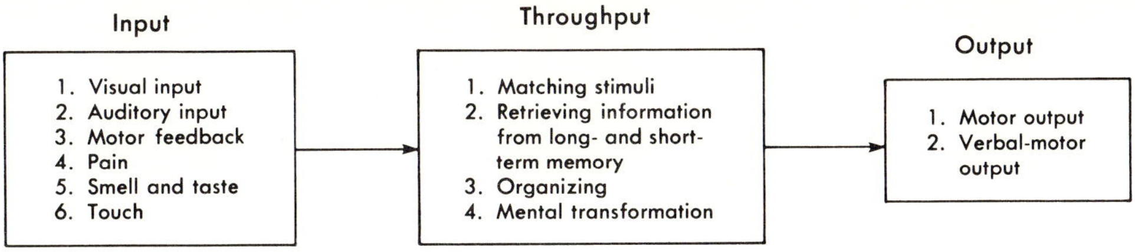

Fig. 4-1. Hypothetical model for the "processing" of information from the environment. *Input* involves the perception of events in the world. *Throughput* involves thinking, remembering, and other cognitive activities. *Output* involves a motor or verbal response; that is, it involves an act on the environment.

about intellectual ability from these samples. They attempt to select samples of performance that allow the best possible estimates of intellectual capacity rather than learned abilities; but ultimately the behaviors that must be used to answer questions on the test are learned behaviors that become more efficient with practice and familiarity. Moreover, execution of a response rather than mental processing of information may be a *limiting factor* with regard to performance.

A good example is provided by a test on the Wechsler Adult Intelligence Scale (WAIS), which requires persons to solve problems and execute a rapid manipulative response, that is, the block design test. Blocks are to be ordered into patterns as quickly as possible. Generally, older persons do not perform this task as rapidly as younger persons. Does this imply that they cannot solve the problem rapidly? Is it possible that the processing of information required to solve the problem is unaltered but speed of manipulative responses is reduced? If so, speed is a *limiting factor.* If a very old person does not perceive the patterns to be copied because of altered visual capacity, *input* is a limiting factor. It is possible for input, mental processing, and output to be impaired, but it is difficult to determine which factor is actually impaired because the researcher can only make inferences based on output.

Limiting factors

The concept of limiting factors may be easily understood if the researcher makes use of a simple model for intellectual functioning that breaks the processing of information from the external world into three major components: *input-throughput-output.* This simple model is illustrated in Fig. 4-1. Since all the researcher can observe is *output,* he cannot be absolutely sure that the limitation on efficient performance is not related to motor response rather than decreased ability to process information in the throughput stage, unless, of course, the researcher performs experimental manipulations of input variables that allow him to make educated guesses. Ways of disentangling the *input-throughput-output* aspects of information processing will be discussed in Chapters 9 and 10. For now it is important to remember that impaired performance does not necessarily imply defective processing at the *throughput* stage.

Power

The problems with regard to inferences about age-associated differences in intelligence that result from timed tests requiring manipulative skills or rapid motor responses have induced some psychologists to emphasize *power tests* as the only fair way to measure intellectual ability in older persons. *Power* is a term generally used when one wants to refer to a test that allows a person to take as much time as necessary to answer a question or solve a problem. Power tests allow the person being tested to use long-term skills and learned abilities to solve the problem. They do get around the problem of time limitations and speed of response, but many psychologists argue that both speed and power are important. After all, they argue, if person A can accomplish the same amount of mental work as person B in half the time, person B must be intellectually more capable with respect to the work in question. Moreover, power tests often place a greater emphasis on acquired skills (achievement) than problem solving. Problem solving is a component of ability that many psychologists believe is very important to intellectual competence.

Later on you will see that whether or not one places emphasis on power tests or speed tests is largely related to one's definition of intelligence, and furthermore, that one's definition of intelligence influences whether or not decline in intellectual functioning with advancing age is viewed as a reasonable conclusion.

Logic and assumptions of testing

Whether or not one emphasizes power or speed, *intelligence tests are ultimately measures of achievement that are designed to permit inferences about capacity to achieve.* This makes some sense because a person who has achieved a certain amount certainly had the capacity to achieve that amount. The basic assumption that has to be met is *equal opportunity.* This is best explained by turning to the "bucket analogy" first introduced to the senior author of this text by E. J. Asher.*

Assume for the moment that water is analogous to acquired skills and that the capacity of the bucket is analogous to intelligence. Furthermore, assume that we have no way of inferring how much capacity each bucket has unless we pour the water out and measure its volume. It may be seen in Fig. 4-2 that there are three buckets. The smallest bucket and the middle-sized bucket are filled to capacity. Thus we correctly infer that bucket *B* has a greater capacity than bucket *A*. It has to have more capacity because it holds more water. The problem enters when we try to make the inference that buckets *B* and *C* have the same capacity. Bucket *C* was not filled up all the way, and thus we cannot make an accurate comparison with bucket *B*.

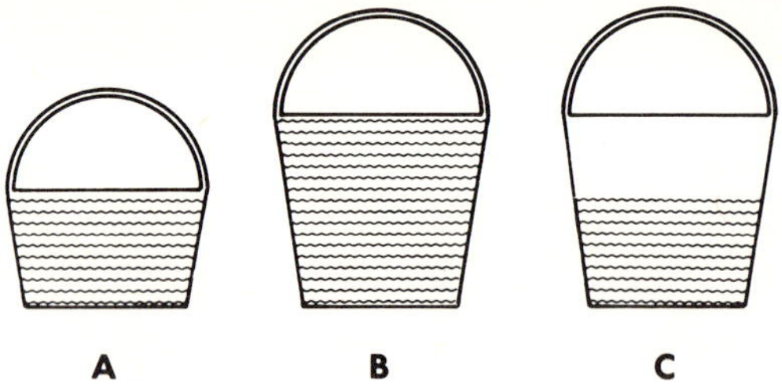

Fig. 4-2. The "bucket analogy." In this analogy to intellectual capacity and achievement, volume of water in the bucket represents achievement, whereas volume capacity of the bucket represents intellectual capacity. Bucket *B* and bucket *C* have similar capacities, but bucket *C* is only filled part way. Bucket *A* has less capacity than bucket *C*, but it has been filled to the top and thus has the same volume of water as bucket *C*. An intelligence test attempts to measure capacity but can only measure capacity adequately if achievement (the volume of knowledge and skills) matches capacity closely. The analogy to the buckets is that one cannot adequately estimate the capacity of bucket *C* from a knowledge of the volume of water it contains. On the other hand, the capacity of buckets *A* and *B* may be inferred accurately from the volume of water in these buckets.

In a very general sense, intelligence tests measure how much is in the bucket, particularly power tests that emphasize acquired skills and overlearned abilities such as vocabulary and information. They are only valid measures of how much is in the bucket if the bucket has had an opportunity to be filled to capacity. Just as bucket *C* did not have a chance to be filled to capacity, some individuals, because of their environment, do not have the same opportunity to develop fully certain aspects of potential intellectual ability. The person who drops out of school

*We would like to give credit where credit is due for the bucket analogy, but we have no idea where it originated. Merrill Elias first heard the bucket analogy in a graduate class. It was presented by Professor E. J. Asher, now deceased, who was an outspoken advocate for culture-fair intelligence tests.

at an early age and the person who grows up in an impoverished environment are two examples. Persons born at different points in time do not have the same opportunities to "fill the bucket." Educational opportunities have increased significantly over the years, and thus today's children, all other things being equal, will have an even greater opportunity than their parents have. As positive as this situation may be, it poses problems in research designed to measure *age changes* in intelligence from comparisons of persons of different ages who were born at different times. In fact, *only age differences* may be inferred if persons born at different points in time *(age-cohorts)* are compared. K. Warner Schaie and his associates have provided a detailed description of the problems involved in making inferences about age changes from cross-sectional designs. Later in this chapter you will see that the longitudinal designs are not without their own unique difficulties.

The chicken-or-the-egg problem

Another difficulty in inferring intellectual capacity from intelligence tests is the fact that capacity and achievement are so intimately interwoven. Persons with a higher level of education perform better on formal tests of intelligence. Is this because they are more capable than persons with less education, or are persons with more education better able to perform on tests of intelligence by virtue of their education? Is it a combination of both factors? Hopefully, you will be better able to answer these questions when you finish this chapter, but two facts must be very clear at this point: (1) *IQ and intelligence are not synonymous terms;* and (2) *IQ values reflect a person's score relative to persons of a homogeneous age group.*

The IQ

The IQ concept was originally developed for children and was designed as a ratio of chronological age (CA) to mental age (MA) (MA/CA × 100). When applied to adults, the MA/CA concept is rather meaningless because the highest MA an adult may achieve on the Stanford-Binet test is 16 years. A 60-year-old adult with an MA of 16 years would thus appear quite retarded. For this reason the CA/MA formula was discarded in favor of deviation scores, which could be converted to IQ points. Thus an adult with an average level of performance relative to other adults his age would have an IQ of 100.

Handicap system

The Stanford-Binet test, although developed for children, was "extended upward" for adults. The Wechsler tests were specifically designed for adults and later "extended downward" to children. One basic stimulus for the Wechsler tests was test content that was appropriate for adults. When Wechsler developed his adult intelligence test, he intended IQ to be expressed relative to one's age-cohort rather than in absolute terms. Handicaps for golfers are designed to give the poorer golfer a chance to compete on an equal basis with a good golfer. However, a golfer's handicap is based on his own performance. An older person's handicap is based on the average performance of persons in his age cohort.

Botwinick (1973:183) provides a clear description of the age correction (age handicap) procedure.

> In the Wechsler scoring system, for example, if a 25-year-old man and a 75-year-old man each makes the same I.Q. score, the actual performance of the older man is poorer than that of the younger one. The reason is that the I.Q. has an age correction as part of its definition. It is average (i.e., "normal") for old people to perform less well than young people on this test, and the I.Q. is constructed to reflect this "normal" process. If in one man's lifetime there is neither decline nor improvement in his test performance, his measured I.Q. will go up as he gets older.

The reason that his IQ will go up is because average scores by persons in *each* age group used to construct WAIS norms were converted to an IQ of 100. Botwinick has provided a useful graphic illustration of the age correction procedure (Fig. 4-3). If the reader

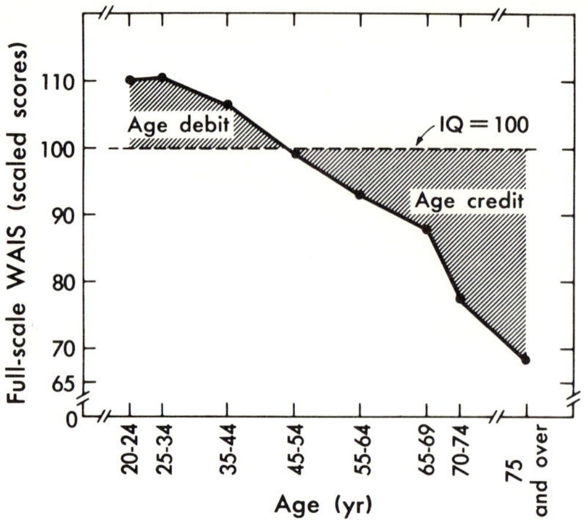

Fig. 4-3. Full-scale WAIS scores plotted against age. Data were obtained from Table 18 of the *WAIS Manual* (1955:82-97) by culling scaled scores of IQs of 100. Broken line indicates the conversion of scaled scores to IQs of 100. (From Botwinick, J. *Cognitive processes in maturity and old age*. New York: Springer Publishing Co., Inc., 1967.)

considers Fig. 4-3 in light of Botwinick's (1973:184) description of the correction procedure, it should become clear.

> The curve was constructed on the basis of the scores made by people in various age groups, each group having an I.Q. of 100 (Wechsler, 1955). The scaled scores were arbitrarily set at approximately 110 with the group aged 20-34 years, and the scores of the other age groups scaled from this reference point. These scores were then converted to I.Q.s of 100, the average. This conversion means that the youngest group in Figure [4-3] had 10 points subtracted, and the oldest group had approximately 32 points added, in order to result in "normal" I.Q.s of 100 (Wechsler, 1955, pp. 82-97).

It is important to note that age correction for IQ scores does not imply that all age groups must be expected to meet a standard for intelligence established by one age group (in this case 20 to 34 years). To the contrary. Wechsler emphasizes that intelligence itself is not synonymous with IQ but could change at different ages because different factors in the composite of abilities making up intelligence become of greater or lesser relevance as one grows older. It is for this reason that *"WAIS" IQ was intended to be a measure of a person's ability relative to his own age group.*

From a research standpoint one must be aware that the matching of older and younger subjects on IQ for purposes of control of intellective factors is inappropriate. They should be matched on an absolute basis (scaled scores). Furthermore, studies designed to address the question of "absolute" level of intellectual functioning for different age groups should use scaled scores, not IQ.

WHAT IS INTELLIGENCE?

Despite the fact that we have emphasized the dangers in thinking of IQ and intelligence as isomorphic terms, we have not defined intelligence.

Catch 22: The circular definition

At one time, not long ago, some textbooks defined intelligence as that which intelligence tests measure. It is obvious that the definition is circular and therefore dangerous. Many abuses of intelligence tests with children stemmed from the foolish notion that a test designed to measure intelligence actually measured intelligence in the same way that a ruler measures inches. From a practical standpoint the important consideration is how well an individual adapts to his environment. Intelligence tests provide only one kind of information regarding the potential for adaptation. Wechsler (1958:7) was very clear in his precautionary comments regarding the measurement of "intelligence."

> Although intelligence is not a mere sum of intellectual abilities the only way we can evaluate it quantitatively is by the measurement of the various aspects of these abilities. There is no contradiction here unless we insist upon the identity of general intelligence and intellectual ability. We do not, for example, identify electricity with our modes of measuring it. Our measurements of electricity consist of quantitative records of its chemical, thermal and magnetic effects. But these effects are not identical with the "stuff" which produced

them. We do not know what the ultimate nature of the "stuff" is which constitutes intelligence, but as in the case of electricity, we know it by the "things" it enables us to do.*

Operational definitions

Wechsler (1958:7) defined intelligence as "the aggregate of total capacity of the individual to act purposefully, to think rationally, to deal effectively with his environment." Baldwin's *Directory of Philosophy and Psychology* (1901, cited by Wechsler, 1968) defined intellect (intelligence) as the "faculty or capacity of knowing." The term *capacity* emphasizes the idea that intelligence reflects how much can be learned rather than how much has been learned (achievement). Wechsler (1968:8) noted that E. L. Thorndike subdivided intelligence into three main types and, in so doing, provided an operational definition of each. Abstract or verbal intelligence was seen as involving facility in using symbols; practical intelligence, as involving the manipulation of objects; and social intelligence, as facility in dealing with human beings. Wechsler points out that the important thing about this classification is that it not only emphasizes the kinds of abilities involved in various classifications of intelligence but *how* the person would behave to demonstrate these abilities.

"Neurophysiologizing"

It is logical to think of intelligence as a behavioral manifestation of the organization and activities of the central nervous system. Clearly, intelligent behavior is affected by the structural and functional integrity of the brain, but is it isomorphic with brain structure and function? Wechsler's (1958:17) answer to this question is not outdated, even though today there are more sophisticated techniques to examine correlations between brain function and behavior that existed when he summed up the situation in 1958.

*From Wechsler, D. *The measurement and appraisal of adult intelligence.* © 1958. The Williams & Wilkins Co., Baltimore, p. 7.

In dealing with the brain as an "organ of the mind," its investigators have been concerned chiefly with two questions: (1) the manner and the degree to which brain structure is related to mental activity, and (2) assuming that mental activity is dependent upon brain structure, which parts of the brain are associated with which mental functions. More progress has been made on the latter, but no satisfactory answer can be given to either of these questions. Particularly vague is our knowledge as to where and how intelligence is mediated.

Like all mental functions, general intelligence may be said to depend upon the condition and structure of the brain, in the broad sense that no intelligent behavior is possible without at least partially intact cerebral hemispheres. But in this broad sense, the statement does not explain very much. In particular, it does not distinguish the possible role of the brain in the mediation of intelligence from the part it plays in sensory, motor, perceptual and other processes, since injury or removal of various parts of the cortex can involve one without the other. Especially challenging is the fact that except in cases of injuries involving the speech area, human beings can apparently continue to function intellectually after considerable loss of brain substance, whereas much less damage area wise is sufficient to impair severely or destroy entirely specific sensory functions. In general, measures of global intelligence are less affected by local injuries than are measures of specific ability.*

In Chapter 12 we will return to an interesting hypothesis about how the brain may work to influence intellectual behavior. However, brain-intelligence theories, interesting as they may be, do not help psychologists much when they want to study changes in global intelligence with age because these theories are in their infancy, and as yet no set of physiological measurements has been demonstrated to be isomorphic with intellectual activity.

Intelligence as a composite: a logical construct

Even the best operational definitions and neurophysiological theories fall short of de-

*From Wechsler, D. *The measurement and appraisal of adult intelligence.* © 1958. The Williams & Wilkins Co., Baltimore, p. 17.

fining intelligence. Wechsler (1958:143) sums up the problem neatly.

> What we are proposing is that generally intelligence is a multivariate construct, the differentiae of which may and do alter with successive periods in the individual's life. There will be differences in how we define intelligence at different ages, and these differences will depend in a great measure on which of the elements entering into the construct one wishes to emphasize and how consistent an evaluation one wishes to maintain. One cannot, operationally, attach a unique or fixed meaning to the term intelligence because at different times and under different circumstances we are compelled to appraise it from different points of view. In the case of older people, it seems that the one thing we wish most to include under the term intelligence is what William James long ago referred to as *sagacity,* a trait which may be broadly defined as the ability to deal with life's situations in terms of past experience.*

One thing that becomes clear as we read Wechsler's description of intelligence is that he views it as a composite of many different abilities which may be brought to bear on the solution of a problem. If one views intelligence in this manner, it really does not matter whether one specific ability is greater than another. What matters is how the individual taps into his array of abilities and weighs them in such a way as to deal effectively with the environment. We will refer to this global ability as *composite intelligence.*

Specific intelligence

Despite the fact that persons display composite intelligence, psychologists have found it useful to examine the decline with age in specific abilities that make up composite intelligence. This has been done by examining scores on the various subtests of the WAIS or by factor analytic techniques designed to uncover "primary mental abilities." These studies will be discussed in this chapter. One of the most important questions asked in these studies is: Which skills hold up best with age and with decline? The difficulty with this kind of research in terms of understanding composite intelligence is that it assumes a mechanistic model. In reality, an organismic model is probably more realistic, since it views the composite of abilities, not as additive but interactive such that the sum of intelligence is more than its parts, and each individual organizes his abilities in a unique hierarchy, which may be different at different stages in his development.

The organismic view of intelligence is not new. Wechsler (1958:7) effectively expresses his view and the definition of intelligence that we prefer.

> Intelligence, operationally defined, is the aggregate or global capacity of the individual to act purposefully, to think rationally and to deal effectively with his environment. It is aggregate or global because it is composed of elements or abilities which, though not entirely independent, are qualitatively differentiable. By measurement of these abilities, we ultimately evaluate intelligence. But intelligence is not identical with the mere sum of these abilities, however inclusive. There are three important reasons for this: (1) The ultimate products of intelligent behavior are a function not only of the number of abilities or their quality but also of the way in which they are combined, that is, their configuration. (2) Factors other than intellectual ability, for example, those of drive and incentive, are involved in intellectual behavior. (3) Finally, while different orders of intelligent behavior may require varying degrees of intellectual ability, an excess of any given ability may add relatively little to the effectiveness of the behavior as a whole. It would seem that, so far as general intelligence is concerned, intellectual ability, per se, merely enters as a necessary minimum. Thus to act intelligently one must be able to recall numerous items, i.e., have a retentive memory. But beyond a certain point this ability will not help much in coping with life situations successfully.*

Individual differences

One last word of caution is necessary before we consider the literature on aging and intelligence. The data we discuss will describe

*From Wechsler, D. *The measurement and appraisal of adult intelligence.* © 1958. The Williams & Wilkins Co., Baltimore, p. 143.

*From Wechsler, D. *The measurement and appraisal of adult intelligence.* © 1958. The Williams & Wilkins Co., Baltimore, p. 7.

statistical trends not individual trends. In other words, intellectual functioning will be discussed in terms of means and standard deviations. As psychologists, we know that individual differences in intellectual functioning are not reflected in statistics describing average performance and, in many cases, unique personal aspects of intellectual functioning which are not measured on tests of intelligence. Many persons who are 60, 70, 80, and even 90 years of age can run "intellectual circles" around middle-aged and younger persons. Many very healthy older persons show little if any decline until near the end of life.

Fig. 4-4. David Wechsler, Ph.D. (Columbia University, 1925). Dr. Wechsler is best known for his original and outstanding contributions to the measurement of adult intelligence. He has published many books and articles on intelligence and mental measurement.

OVERALL DECLINE?

Classical patterns

The earliest tests of intelligence such as the Otis Self Administering Test and the Army Alpha Test indicated a decline in intelligence from young adulthood to late middle age (Jones and Conrad, 1933; Miles and Miles, 1932). Jones and Conrad, for example, found that adults who were 45 to 59 years of age scored more poorly than did young persons ranging in age from 17 to 21 years of age. However, these tests were generally designed with content that was more appropriate for young adults than for middle-aged and elderly adults. Moreover, they did not allow for testing of the upper limits of capacity. The Otis and the Army Alpha are paper-and-pencil tests. Thus they provide no opportunity for "testing the limits."

The Stanford-Binet test allowed for testing the limits, but its content was more appropriate for children and young adults than for older adults. Moreover, adequate normative samples were not available for adults. The Wechsler-Bellevue Scale (W-B) represented an improvement in terms of test content, but adequate normative data were lacking for older persons. Botwinick (1967) points out that the age credits extrapolated to persons over 80 years were so large that an average IQ score could be obtained if any response was given. The WAIS was more adequate with regard to norms for adults, but all persons beyond 75 years of age were grouped together.

Data collected with the WAIS were widely published, and for many years they have been considered to be reflective of the general trend in intellectual functioning from early adulthood to late life. Fig. 4-3 may be considered as a "classical curve" relating total WAIS scaled scores and age. Similar versions of this curve have been published in many textbooks on psychology. We know that these data have limitations because they were cross-sectional in nature, and samples may well have included persons with subclinical pathology of a kind that would not affect performance in healthy persons. For now, however, the reader should assume that the data shown in Fig. 4-3 really reflect what happens to intellectual functioning with age, keeping in mind that Wechsler pointed out the limitations of his test and never implied that either scaled scores or IQs were intelligence. What does it mean in a practical sense if intellectual functioning does, in fact, decline with age? First, one is dealing with averages in this curve. It has already been noted that any given older person may have extraordinarily high intelligence compared with anyone else of any age. Botwinick (1967:4) calls attention to some important correlational data, which emphasize how significant individual differences are.

> The individual differences are so great that the extent of correlation between chronological age and intelligence is low. It is only of the order of –0.416 with the newer Wechsler test (Wechsler, 1958, p. 139), –0.50 with the 15-minute Otis Self-Administering Examination (Miles, 1934) and –0.53 or less with a variety of other tests (Weisenberg, Roe, and McBride, 1936, pp. 82-83). Thus, predictions of I.Q. on the basis of age alone, are hardly useful for any but the grossest purposes.

A second important point regarding practical implications of the curve in Fig. 4-3 is that performance on the WAIS is only one indicator of effective mental performance (Wechsler, 1958:142).

> The problem may be summed up as follows. General intelligence as evaluated by pragmatic criteria appears to maintain itself unimpaired over a much greater portion of adult life, and to decline at a much slower rate than do the mental abilities by which it is inevitably measured. Our general answers have been that sheer ability enters as only one of several factors of intelligence, that factors like drive, interest and motivation also operate in varying degrees as determinants and that learned responses, stored information and general experience may substitute for, or better serve, the individual than original aptitude. To these may be added the fact that at different ages different skills or abilities contribute varying amounts of whatever is needed for effective performance.*

Why bother? One logical question is why psychologists bother at all to study age trends on intelligence tests when they know that intelligence tests do not measure many intellectual abilities and personal qualities which are critical to efficient mental performance. One reason is that it is important to know which specific intellectual abilities do, in fact, remain at a high level as one grows older and to do so with tests that have standardized content. The WAIS *subtests* have been helpful in this respect, particularly with regard to comparisons of healthy persons with those who are in generally poor health or who fall in diagnostic categories most likely to influence mental performance, for example, stroke or heart attack patients. Patterns of subtest performance that emerge from such comparisons can lead to the development of psychoneurological diagnostic techniques that may be useful in the monitoring of recovery from disease as well as detection of brain impairment.

Pattern analyses. The idea of "patterns" of subtest performance is related to the fact that intelligence is not necessarily a unitary factor, even though composite capacity is important. Are there specific abilities? Do they decline at the same rate? Are there some abilities that do not decline at all or perhaps improve with age?

At the present time there is general agreement that there are specific intellectual abilities that are partially independent of other intellectual abilities. Many studies of specific abilities have been done with the subtests of the WAIS. The boxed material shows a summary of the WAIS subtests and provides a brief summary of the kinds of mental processes that Wechsler was attempting to measure. Very generally, the verbal subtests tap stored information that is acquired over a lifetime of experience, whereas performance tests place heavier demands on the solution of novel problems of a perceptual-motor nature and do so under time constraints. Performance tests are generally of the speed variety, whereas the verbal tests place more emphasis on power.

Botwinick (1967:7-8) has provided a detailed description of the relationship between verbal and performance scores with advancing age. Up to 60 years of age, verbal scaled scores on the WAIS exhibit relatively little decline with age. Performance scores, par-

---

*From Wechsler, D. *The measurement and appraisal of adult intelligence.* © 1958. The Williams & Wilkins Co., Baltimore, p. 142.

A BRIEF DESCRIPTION OF THE KINDS OF ABILITIES MEASURED BY THE WAIS SUBTESTS*

Verbal tests

Information: The information questions are formulated to tap the person's range of information. The test items call for knowledge that an average individual with an average opportunity may be able to acquire.

Comprehension: A test of common sense. Success on the test seems to depend on possession of a certain amount of practical information and a general ability to evaluate past experience. Presumaby the questions are of the type that the "average adult" may have had occasion to answer for himself at some time or has heard discussed in some form or another.

Arithmetic reasoning: The ability to solve arithmetic problems. The problems deal with commonplace situations or involve calculations of a practical nature. They have been constructed so as to avoid verbalization or reading difficulties, and the computation skills required to solve the problems are not beyond those taught in grade school or used in day-to-day computations. (The test is influenced by education and occupation, and individual scores are affected by fluctuations of attention and transient emotional responses.)

Digit span: A simple test for the rather immediate retention of material. (This test correlates poorly with other tests of intelligence; low scores when not associated with brain disease can be related to inattention or anxiety.)

Similarities: One of the most reliable indices of intellectual ability. It taps a person's ability to perceive the common elements of the terms he is asked to compare and his ability to bring them together under a single concept. A certain degree of verbal comprehension seems necessary for minimal performance, but "sheer word knowledge need only be a minor factor."

Vocabulary: The title of the test is self explanatory. "Contrary to lay opinion, the size of a man's vocabulary is not only an index of his schooling, but also an excellent measure of his general intelligence. Its excellence as a test of intelligence may stem from the fact that the number of words a man knows is at once a measure of his learning ability, his fund of verbal information and of the general range of his ideas. The one serious objection that could be raised against it was that a man's vocabulary is necessarily influenced by his education and cultural opportunities."

Performance tests

Digit symbol test: This test requires the subject to associate certain symbols with other symbols and to do so quickly and accurately. Motor speed definitely enters into performance on this test, and may account for some of the decrement seen for older persons. Subjects with visual defects and specific motor disabilities are also penalized. ("Neurotic and unstable individuals also tend to do rather poorly on the Digit Symbol. . . . Tendler suggested that this was due to some sort of associative inflexibility in the subject, and a tendency toward mental confusion. More obviously neurotic subjects do badly because they have difficulty in concentrating and applying themselves for any length of time and because of their emotional reactivity to any tasks requiring persistent efforts.")

Picture completion test: This test requires the person being tested to discover and name

*Information from Wechsler, D. *The measurement and appraisal of adult intelligence.* © 1958. The Williams & Wilkins Co., Baltimore, pp. 61-85.

Continued.

A BRIEF DESCRIPTION OF THE KINDS OF ABILITIES MEASURED BY THE WAIS SUBTESTS—cont'd

the missing part of an incompletely drawn picture. It is particularly valuable for the testing of intelligence at lower levels. "Ostensibly it measures the individual's basic perceptual and conceptual abilities as far as these are involved in the visual recognition and identification of familiar objects and forms. To be able to see what is missing from any particular picture, the subject must first know what the picture represents. But, in addition, he must be able to appreciate that the missing part is in some way essential either to the form or to the function of the object or picture. In a broad sense the test measures the ability of the individual to differentiate essential from non-essential details. But one must note, again, that the ability of an individual to do this depends in a large measure upon his relative familiarity with the object with which he is presented, that is to say, upon the content of the picture."

Block design: This test was first offered by Cohs as a comprehensive measure of non-verbal intelligence. Many examiners feel that the test involves the ability to perceive and to analyze forms and the ability to perceive pattern. Basically the subject constructs the blocks (different sides painted red or white) in such a way as to reproduce a pattern which is shown to him/her on a test card. The examination is timed, and generally elderly adults do less well on it than younger persons. "Oddly enough, individuals who do best on the test are not necessarily those who see, or at least follow, the pattern as a whole, but more often those who are able to break it up into small portions. In this connection, an early study by Nadel (375) on intellectual disturbances following certain (frontal lobe) brain lesions is of interest. As between 'following the figure' and breaking up the design into its component parts, patients with frontal lobe lesions in contrast to the control group used the former method almost exclusively."

Picture arrangement: A series of pictures which tell a story when placed in the right sequence. The pictures are presented out of order and the person being tested is asked to place them in their correct order so that they will make a sensible story. The test appears to test a person's ability to comprehend and "size up a total situation." "The subject must understand the whole, must get the 'idea' of the story, before he is able to set himself effectively to the task." There is trial and error experimentation, but the subject is called upon to attempt an appraisal of the total situation more than in most other tests. The subject matter of the test most always involves a human or practical situation. "The understanding of these situations more nearly corresponds to what other writers have referred to as 'social intelligence.' "

Object assembly: This test requires assembling objects into a familiar configuration. Generally, examiners feel that the test gets at the ability to deal with part-whole relationships. "The subjects' 'approach' to the task may be one of several kinds. The first is an immediate perception of the whole, accompanied by a critical understanding of the relation of the individual parts."

ticularly those that emphasize speed, show a more accelerated decline than verbal scores. Stated another way, an examination of Fig. 4-5 reveals that performance and verbal scores on the WAIS become increasingly divergent with increasing age. This general pattern has been reported in many different studies summarized by Botwinick (1967) and others. It seems to hold across race, sex, socioeconomic level, and it holds for health status for persons of superior and inferior levels of ability. A number of researchers have attempted to understand why this pattern exists for the verbal tasks as opposed to perform-

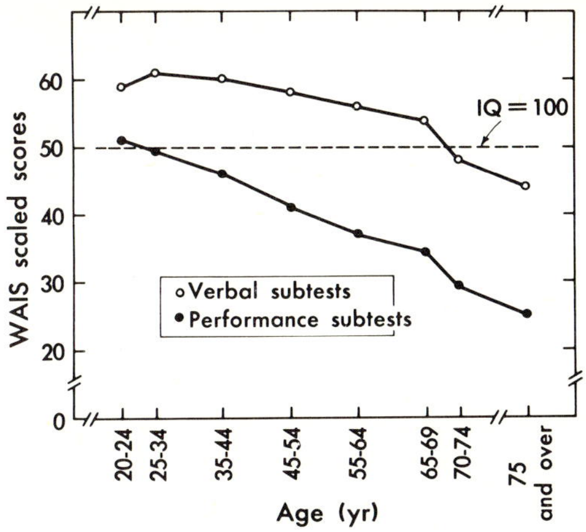

Fig. 4-5. Scaled scores on the verbal and performance portion of the WAIS as a function of age-cohort grouping. Data were obtained from Table 18 of the *WAIS Manual* (1955:82-98) by culling scaled scores, which result in IQs of 100. Remember that the broken line represents the data that are obtained when scaled scores are converted to IQs of 100. (From Botwinick, J. *Cognitive processes in maturity and old age.* New York: Springer Publishing Co., Inc., 1967.)

Table 4-1. Rank orders obtained on an analysis of sensitivity of the various subtests of the WAIS or Wechsler-Bellevue Scale as reported in ten studies and calculated by Botwinick (1967)*

Subtests	Mean ranks
Information	1.85 (least)
Vocabulary	2.33
Comprehension	2.75
Arithmetic	4.40
Similarities	5.60
Digit span	6.50
Picture completion	6.65
Object assembly	7.00
Block design	8.55
Picture assembly	9.85
Digit symbol	10.85 (most)

*These rankings were taken from Botwinick, J. *Cognitive processes in maturity and old age.* New York: Springer Publishing Co., Inc., 1967. He provides references to the ten studies and describes how the rankings were derived. Some of the studies used the WAIS and others used the Wechsler-Bellevue Scale.

ance tasks. One way to address these questions is to examine each of the verbal and performance subtests. Another approach has been to examine decline on other tests that measure different aspects of mental abilities.

One of the earliest studies of "differential decline" in intellectual ability with age was done by Willoughby (1927). He found that analytic reasoning showed a more rapid decline than arithmetic reasoning. Other studies have been done with Thurstone's Primary Mental Abilities Test (PMA). The PMA is based upon factor analytic techniques and is constructed so that scores representing different abilities are relatively unrelated to each other. There are five subtests: word fluency, number, reasoning, space, and verbal meaning. The space test deals with problems that demand shifting of the spatial positions of two-dimensional geometric forms. In one experiment, space and reasoning abilities decline more rapidly with age than the other abilities measured (Schaie et al., 1953). Strother and colleagues (1957) obtained similar results with the PMA and found that the earliest and largest decrements occurred for memory, speed, reasoning, and spatial abilities. Kamin (1957) reported that the most severe losses were in spatial and reasoning abilities. In a later study, Bilash and Zubek (1960) reported that for the King Factored Aptitude Test, reasoning, memory, perception, and dexterity factors declined gradually from the teenage years to the seventies. In contrast, comprehension, verbal fluency, numerical, and spatial abilities were maintained until the mid-forties and showed decline thereafter.

In general, these studies are consistent with the classical subtest aging patterns revealed on WAIS analyses. Botwinick (1973:185) has summarized analyses based on ten aging studies with the WAIS. In so doing, he ranked subtests from various studies in order of sensitivity with respect to age differences. The bottom-ranked subtests in Table 4-1 are those that are more sensitive to age differences (age sensitive). Block design, picture, arrangement, and digit symbol tests are the lowest ranked tests, whereas information, vocabulary, and comprehension tests are the three highest ranked tests. Results of the ten experiments that were used to construct these rankings were highly similar, and they usually confirmed the generalization that those abilities labeled "verbal" on the WAIS tend to be maintained with advancing age, whereas those labeled "performance" tend to decline. However, these data do not answer the question as to which *specific* mental processes hold up well and which deteriorate with the passage of time.

It is particularly difficult to answer this question by examination of the WAIS subtests. The bottom-ranked tests are performance tests that involved speed of responding, but they also place heavy demands on perceptual-integrative and perceptual-motor skills. The least sensitive tests place heavy demands on acquired experience and emphasize the use of long-stored information, but at least one of the tests, comprehension, involves problem solving. In short, *input-throughput-output* aspects of performance are confounded.

Reed and Reitan (1963) approached the question of differential decline in specific abilities by developing a battery of twenty-nine tests, which included the eleven subtests of the Wechsler-Bellevue Scale (W-B) and various tests found to be sensitive to brain damage. They predicted that differences between age groups should be minimal on tests of stored information, like vocabulary, and maximal on problem-solving tests that did not allow extensive use of prior experience. Thus they had three judges rank the twenty-nine tests on a "stored information" as opposed to adaptive intelligence dimension. Twenty of the ranked tests were given to young adults (mean = 28 years) and older adults (mean = 52.6 years). Results were consistent with predictions. The three W-B subtests that had the highest ranks (age insensitive) in terms of mean age differences in test scores were information, vocabulary, and comprehension. A number of other studies are not summarized, but they are all consistent with the following generalization: *the stability of information, vocabulary, and comprehension subtests over time has been well documented, but those subtests placing demands on solving novel problems under time constraints show age-related decline.* Later we will see evidence suggesting that it is the problem-solving processes *(throughput)* that may be more impaired than speed of response *(output)*. In general, the small but significant differences in speed of responding among age groups do not account for large differences in performance on problem-solving tasks involving time (see Horn, 1975).

GROUP DIFFERENCES IN PERFORMANCE PATTERNS

Normal as opposed to psychotic groups

We discussed the fact that one of the most important uses of psychometric data was to make comparisons between persons who may be defined as "normal" or well and those who may be defined as mentally or physically ill. Furthermore, such studies may lead to better diagnosis and prediction. A classical study by Botwinick and Birren (1951a) provides an important principle for those who would use the WAIS in a geriatric-diagnostic context. Fig. 4-6 summarizes the results of their investigation of WAIS subtest scores for nonpsychotic and institutionalized psychotic elderly subjects. As might be expected, scores were all lower for psychotic subjects. Nonpsychotic and psychotic subjects show similar patterns of decline on the verbal and nonverbal subtests, with the exception of vocabulary. Most important, however, is the fact that *the subtests that are sensitive to age differences for normal subjects and institutionalized psychotic subjects are not the same tests that are sensitive to differences between these two groups.* For example, information shows little decline with age for both groups but maximum sensitivity to differences between the normal and the psychotic groups. On the other hand, vocabulary and digit symbol were poor discriminators between the

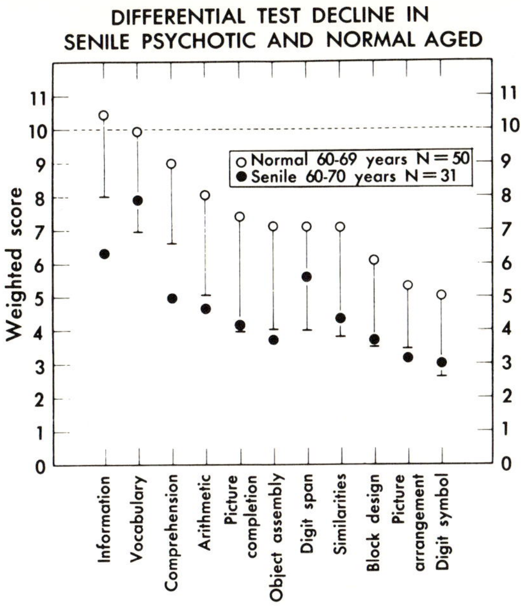

Fig. 4-6. Mean W-B scores for psychotic and nonpsychotic elderly persons. "Vertical lines represent minus one standard deviation from the control mean. Dashed line represents mean level expected in all subtests for a young adult population [Botwinick, 1973]." (From Botwinick, J., and Birren, J. E. *Journal of Gerontology,* 1951, **6,** 365.)

two groups. Generally, the best discriminators were information and comprehension, followed by arithmetic and object assembly.

It must be kept in mind that these are group statistics and that individual patterns can be different. The psychotic patients were institutionalized; the same pattern of results may not have been obtained with noninstitutionalized psychotic patients. One may be able to make discriminations between institutionalized psychotic patients and normals without the use of the WAIS. The latter may be particularly true in those instances in which psychosis is severe and/or institutionalization has been prolonged. Nevertheless, the study by Botwinick and Birren (1951) does illustrate the potential usefulness of pattern analysis as a diagnostic tool and prevents researchers from assuming that those subtests most sensitive to age differences are necessarily sensitive to differences between defined groups at different ages.

Survivors as opposed to nonsurvivors

Performance differences for survivors as opposed to nonsurvivors are discussed at some length in the following chapters. These data further emphasize the principle that age-sensitive tests are not the best discriminators between samples of like-aged subjects with different characteristics. For example, Birren (1968) compared test scores for elderly men (60 to 70 years of age) who lived five years beyond the testing period and those who did not. The tests that discriminated best between survivors and nonsurvivors were those that contained verbal information. The subtests involving response speed, although sensitive to differences among age groups, did not discriminate significantly between those who survived five years and those who did not.

ORGANIZATION OF ABILITIES

You will recall from Chapter 3 that factor analytic techniques can be used to identify groupings of tests, or test items, which are relatively independent of each other and fewer in number than the original number of tests (or test items). These groupings, or constellations, are called factors. Factors are named by examining the items, or tests, that comprise the factor to determine what kind of common ability they seem to be measuring. For example, if the test items that cluster together and are relatively independent of other test items *seem* to be measuring memory, the factor is called a memory factor. Using correlational techniques, these factors may then be related to other factors or tests measuring one or more specific abilities.

In general, factor analytic studies reported by Botwinick (1973) tend to support the notion that a "general ability factor" and a "memory factor" are among the most important factors with respect to the *organization* of specific abilities. Moreover, memory seems to account for success on a variety of tasks to a much greater extent for elderly than for younger persons. This does not indicate that memory is unimportant for young adults. Rather, it reflects the fact that younger persons are more similar to each other in memory, and thus differences among them are too small to account for a high percentage of the variance in performance on any given task (Botwinick, 1973).

Theoretical framework

Whereas factor analytic techniques are promising in terms of the identification of "constellations" of abilities that are more critical at different ages, the technique is used most effectively within a theoretical framework. Recently, Horn (1975) presented a theoretical framework for the study of intellectual ability and, in so doing, demonstrated the usefulness of the factor analytic method (1) for determining those aspects of specific ability that decline and those that remain stable across the life span, and (2) for understanding better how specific aspects of intelligence are organized for different age groups.

Horn views intelligence as a composite of multiple abilities that are more or less independent of one another on a behavioral level. He notes that, for each individual, the mixture of these abilities may be different even though they receive the same overall score on an intelligence test. The various abilities making up the composite of abilities for any given individual may be derived from different neurological bases, and they may have different relationships to biological, social, and psychological variables. For example, one specific component of intelligence may be more susceptible to educational modification than another component.

To determine which components of intelligence change during development, one must rely on *operational* definitions. These definitions are inherent in specific tests of intelligence (e.g., WAIS, Stanford-Binet); that is, they derive from the particular scales or subtests that make up these tests. These operational definitions are different for each test because the subtests or scales themselves are different. This is true even though the test may be designed to measure the same attribute, "overall intelligence."

At this point in Horn's description of intelligence as multiple abilities, individual differences, and operational definitions, one is reminded very much of Wechsler's concept of intelligence. However, Wechsler approached the "measurement" of intelligence using subtests of the W-B or the WAIS. The subtests themselves were important as operational definitions of specific abilities. Horn emphasizes multivariate factor analysis as a method for exploring the major abilities that comprise intelligence. The basic idea is to identify those scales, from sets of tests, that measure a relative *distinct and independent ability* and to describe that ability with reference to the kind of content contained in the scales (subtests). Thus, rather than examine subtests from a single test such as the WAIS, many scales and subtests are used to define primary abilities.

Horn (1975) states that current factor analytic studies have identified twenty-five to thirty abilities labeled as *primary mental abilities*. He notes that one possible interpretation of factor analytic studies is to view each of these abilities as a *distinct intelligence*. Horn disagrees with this view for several reasons. First, there are often trivial distinctions between some of the abilities tested, for example, copying a sentence as many times as possible within a given time period as opposed to printing a set of words as quickly as possible. Second, primary mental abilities often are poor predictors of such criteria as on-the-job success. Third, many primary mental abilities correlate positively with each other. This implies a higher level of organization among these abilities. This higher level of organization may be more useful to the individual than specific abilities from a practical and theoretical standpoint.

Higher levels of organizations. Just as factor analytic techniques can be used to identify primary abilities, they can be used to identify higher levels of organization. Here the basic objective is to determine what interrelationships exist among the primary mental abilities. The products of these so-called "second order" factor analyses are re-

HORN'S (1975) MEASUREMENT AND PROCESS DESCRIPTIONS OF TWO MAJOR DIMENSIONS OF INTELLIGENCE (FLUID AND CRYSTALLIZED) AS INDICATED BY SECOND ORDER FACTORING AMONG PRIMARY MENTAL ABILITIES* †

I. Gf, *Fluid intelligence*. Involving processes of perceiving relationships, educing correlates, maintaining span of immediate awareness in reasoning, abstracting, concept formation, and problem solving, as measured in unspeeded as well as speeded tasks involving figural, symbolic, or semantic content but in which relatively little advantage accrues from intensive or extended education and acculturation. Good measures of the dimension include the following primary mental abilities.

A. I, Inductive reasoning, as measured in:
   1. Letter grouping: Find the rule which relates three of four sets of letters and mark the one set that does not fit.
   2. Number series: Select the number which should appear next in a progression.

B. CRF, Figural relations, as measured in:
   1. Matrices: Choose a figure to fill in an empty cell in a matrix in such a way that it maintains a relationship extant among the figures of the other cells of the matrix.
   2. Dominoes: Insert a domino into a pattern of dominoes in accordance with the rules of the game and in such a way as to extend the pattern.

C. Ma, Associative memory, as measured in:
   1. Recall paired associates: Picture-number. Recall a number that had been paired with a picture.
   2. Recognition paired associates: Landmarks-names. Match (recognize) names with landmarks as previously paired.

D. Ms, Span memory, as measured in the tests indicated for factor M below.

II. Gc, *Crystallized intelligence:* Involving processes of perceiving relationships, educing correlates, reasoning, abstracting, concept of attainment, and problem solving, as measured primarily in unspeeded tasks involving various kinds of content (semantic, figural, symbolic), but content which clearly represents relatively advanced education and acculturation either in the fundaments of the problems or in the operations which must be performed on the fundaments. Good measures of the dimension include the following primary mental abilities.

A. V, Verbal comprehension, as measured in:
   1. Synonyms vocabulary: Select the best synonym for a word among five choices.
   2. Information recall: Provide the correct answers to a wide range of questions pertaining to matters of fact as reported through the mass media.

B. Rs, Syllogistic reasoning, as measured in:
   1. Nonsense syllogisms: Indicate which conclusion follows from stated premises which, however, are nonsensical.
   2. Inference: Select the most justifiable conclusion to be drawn from a set of statements.

C. R, General reasoning, as measured in:
   1. Arithmetical reasoning: Solve word problems of a kind similar to those presented in elementary algebra courses.
   2. Ship destination: Use rules of a game and information about wind direction and velocity, ocean current direction and velocity to calculate time to port.

D. Mk, Mechanical knowledge (when a sample is all male), as measured in:
   1. Tools: Indicate use intended for a wide range of tools.
   2. Mechanical principles: Choose correct answer to indicate knowledge about mechanics, use of tools, etc.

*From Horn, J. L. Psychometric studies of aging and intelligence. In S. Gershon and A. Raskind (Eds.), *Aging* (Vol. 2). *Genesis and treatment of psychologic disorders in the elderly.* New York: Raven Press, 1975, p. 23.

†All major dimensions indicated by second order factoring shown in this material are not included. Horn points out that the information is not reflective of a single study, but represents his attempt to summarize and make sense out of results from many studies.

ferred to as *dimensions or components* of intelligence. Horn reports that current studies have identified six to ten major components. The boxed material presents a description of each of the major components identified and a sample of the primary mental abilities from which the components are derived. You may wish to examine this material carefully because it will be helpful later when we discuss *fluid* and *crystallized* intelligence.

The important question with regard to adult development is whether these major components of intelligence, as inferred from factor analytic statistical techniques, exhibit age-related patterns of change. The bulk of the research relative to this important question has involved comparisons of fluid and crystallized intelligence (see boxed material). The reader should keep in mind that fluid and crystallized intelligence are defined operationally as being composed of certain primary mental abilities, which are constructed, in turn, from scales and subtests that correlate highly and seem to measure a unique ability that is relatively distinct from other abilities. Now, Horn points out that *if* fluid and crystallized intelligence represent distinct and unitary intellectual functions, it follows that the scales (or subtests) from which the fluid and crystallized components are derived should show similar age-associated trends. He states that most evidence seems to indicate that *those scales measuring crystallized intelligence exhibit a pattern of no change with age or slight improvement between the ages of 20 and 50 years. Those scales measuring fluid intelligence exhibit a pattern of age-related decline.* At this point you should carefully examine the primary mental abilities listed under crystallized and fluid intelligence in the boxed material. If you do this, you will see that it is somewhat an oversimplification to say that verbal skills hold up well with age whereas nonverbal skills decline. Moreover, the simple distinction between speed and power in terms of decline as opposed to stability does not seem to hold.

What is particularly important to note is that a number of scales and subtests correlate significantly with both crystallized and fluid measures. These scales exhibit relatively little change during the adult years. Horn offers an interesting explanation for this finding. He suggests that performance on scales that tap both fluid and crystallized intelligence may be determined by either or both types of abilities, depending on the age of the person being tested. Thus a young person with high fluid intelligence will receive a higher score on those scales that tap both fluid and crystallized intelligence than a person with low fluid intelligence, but so will an older person with high crystallized intelligence. In fact, the shift in composition of these two hypothetical kinds of intelligence with increasing age would leave the composite unaffected if increase in one is accompanied by decrease in the other. How does this notion, not unlike that expressed by Wechsler, agree with tests of "general" intelligence?

Horn points out that studies of tests designed to measure general intelligence can lead to very different conclusions, depending on whether the sets of primary mental abilities sampled are biased more in the direction of fluid or crystallized intelligence. He argues that most intelligence tests are biased in the direction of fluid intelligence. Thus the investigators using these tests often reported decline over the life span. This reasoning led to a logical hypothesis and some interesting data. The hypothesis was that an intelligence test designed with a balanced mixture of scales sampling both crystallized and fluid intelligence would show no age-associated differences. Horn and Cattell (1967) designed just such a test of "omnibus intelligence" and gave it to different age groups. The results are shown in Fig. 4-7. Note that crystallized and fluid intelligence exhibited age-related trends in the hypothesized directions: fluid intelligence declined; crystallized intelligence improved. However, *omnibus* intelligence, what we refer to as composite intelligence in this book, remained substantially the same for all age groups.

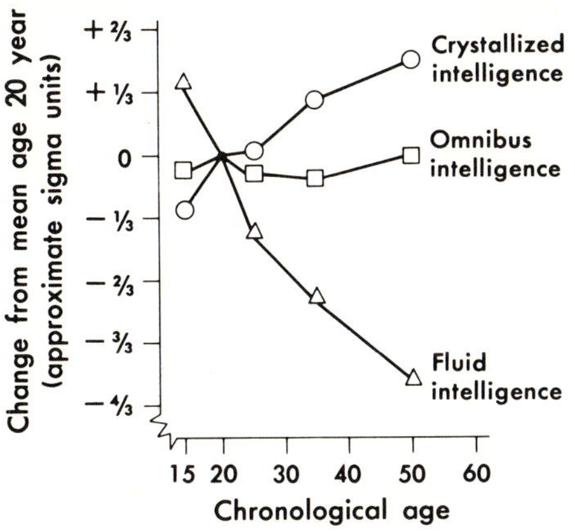

Fig. 4-7. Age-cohort differences for three different operational definitions of intelligence: crystallized, fluid, and omnibus. The test of omnibus intelligence contained a balanced group of tests measuring both fluid and crystallized intelligence. (From Horn, J. L. Psychometric studies of aging and intelligence. In S. Gershon and A. Raskind [Eds.], *Aging* [Vol. 2]. *Genesis and treatment of psychologic disorders in the elderly.* New York: Raven Press, 1975.)

No doubt you will challenge the Horn and Cattell (1967) data on the basis of the cross-sectional design employed. Horn (1975) acknowledged the legitimacy of many criticisms lodged against cross-sectional studies. Of course the most important criticism is that cross-sectional studies may reflect generational differences to a significant extent (Schaie, 1970). He argues, however, that the majority of longitudinal studies support the findings of cross-sectional studies. This point might be debatable, but it is clear that longitudinal studies often err in the direction of overestimating intellectual functioning in the elderly persons. Horn's most important argument in defense of his data is that the "generational differences hypothesis" may be used to predict essentially the opposite results from those indicated by most current studies. Specifically, if one assumes that younger persons are exposed to better and more extensive educational opportunities than their elders and, furthermore, that crystallized intelligence is more susceptible to cultural and educational modification, the age-related trend for crystallized intelligence should be in the direction of decline. On the other hand, if one assumes that fluid intelligence is relatively independent of cultural and educational influences, one would expect it to change little during the adult years. Since data do not seem to be consistent with this hypothesis (Horn, 1975), Horn argues that age-cohort effects, at least in terms of educational differences, are not substantially related to the "usual" patterns found for adult intellectual change with age. Of course it is clear to the reader by now that many more factors influence age-cohort effects than simply educational differences.

Speed as opposed to power. The reader will recall that researchers in aging have debated as to whether or not decline in speed of response with advancing age accounts for poor performance on many scales and subtests. The question revolves around whether *output* or *throughput* (Fig. 4-1) is the *limiting factor* in performance. Horn (1975) points out that older adults perform as well as younger adults on some speeded tasks (e.g., verbal fluency and numerical skill) and that, even though older adults do perform more slowly on many tasks subsumed under fluid intelligence, they also do not perform as well as younger adults on untimed (power) tests using the same tasks. This generalization has been substantiated by a number of studies, including a classical study by Doppelt and Wallace (1955), which revealed no differences in the pattern of scores when the WAIS was given with and without time limits. Furthermore, young persons who receive low scores on fluid intelligence scales tend to perform problem-solving tasks more slowly, that is, in a manner characteristic of many elderly adults. Based on this evidence, Horn (1975:34) draws the following conclusion:

> It appears that we do not score less well on a complex intellectual task because we think slowly, but instead, we think slowly because we have difficulty in resolving complexities, i.e., because we lack sufficient Gf (fluid intelligence). The capacity which enables a person to resolve difficult complexities under conditions in which there is no press for speed is also the capacity which en-

ables the person to quickly solve less difficult problems when a test is speeded.*

Memory. We have already presented data indicating the importance of memory to general intellectual functioning. Horn employs "memory" and "attention" as an explanation of the decline in fluid intelligence with age. He argues that the decline in fluid intelligence is related to the fact that older adults have greater difficulty than younger adults in maintaining a set of relationships in mind while using those relationships to solve a problem. This ability is required for many of the scales that are assumed to measure fluid intelligence and is a necessary factor in achieving high scores regardless of whether the test is timed or untimed; however, the ability to hold relationships in mind may facilitate performance considerably if, in fact, the test is timed.

Horn provides examples to support his argument. For a simple decoding task, the test participant may either hold certain symbol-letter codes in mind or may refer back to a sheet of paper listing the symbol codes for each letter. Assuming the task is timed, the subject who is able to remember and recall codes without spending time to search for them in the list will receive a higher score. Horn (1975) reminds us of the extensive studies by Welford (1958), which indicate that younger persons perform much more rapidly than older persons on tests that demand the maintenance of information in awareness while solving a problem. Thus, Horn argues, loss of speed is not a cause of decline; rather, the loss of a specific mental ability may cause the older person to perform more slowly on certain types of tests, and this loss is primarily revealed in scores that measure fluid intelligence. Evidence from many sources (see Botwinick, 1967: 107-130) suggests that important elements in terms of this loss are memory and attention.

Many of Horn's views about intelligence are similar to those of Wechsler. The difference is that Horn, Cattell, and others with similar views employed factor analyses of many tests in their quest for understanding of intellectual changes with age, whereas Wechsler concentrated on one test. Moreover, the work of Horn, Cattell, and others has provided more information about the specific abilities that are sustained, improved, or lost as an individual grows older because the research technique is not limited to examination of only a few tests.

Role of education

Factor analytic studies have contributed in areas other than theory construction. They have provided a substantial amount of evidence that education is an extremely important correlate of intelligence, possibly more important than the "age factor" between the twenties and sixties. In a classical study using factor analytic techniques, Birren and Morrison (1961) analyzed the WAIS data gathered during its standardization. They used scores for persons ranging in age from 25 to 64 years. Rather than treat age and education as classification (blocking) variables, they treated them as dependent variables and thus correlated age and education scores with WAIS. As would be expected, a general (composite) intelligence component accounted for about one half of the total variance in scores. Age accounted for only 11% of the total variance. Education contributed as much as any one of the eleven subtests of the WAIS to the general intelligence component. Clearly, the education component is a potential source of confounding of "age" effects in cross-sectional studies.

The issues of educational level and age-associated differences in specific abilities are intimately related. Factor analytic and correlational approaches have been useful in constructing theories of intellectual functioning, but they have also been useful in an-

*From Horn, J. L. Aging and intelligence. In S. Gershon and A. Raskind (Eds.), *Aging.* Vol. 2. *Genesis and treatment of psychologic disorders in the elderly,* New York: Raven Press, p. 34.

swering some practical questions related to education and intelligence.

PRACTICAL CONSIDERATIONS

Psychologists know relatively little about "practical" abilities of older adults because, traditionally, studies of specific abilities have been oriented toward abilities more relevant to children and young adults. Analyses of WAIS subtests and use of such tests as the PMA provide limited information with regard to abilities that are directly relevant to the everyday life of the senior adult and are not of much practical use in terms of understanding strengths and weaknesses in skills relevant to adult education, for example, reading, spelling, vocabulary, word fluency, etc. However, most of the tests in this area have been designed for children and young adults and thus do not contain test content most directly relevant to older adults. Standardized IQ tests of general intelligence have not been very useful in the selection of adults for occupations (Hoyt, 1965), nor have they been particularly useful in the design of adult education curricula and teaching methods.

In response to a need for examination of "adult relevant skills," Monge and Gardner (1972) conducted an extensive study involving participants from Syracuse, New York, and Dade County, Florida. These investigators raised the question as to whether the well-established generalization regarding the stability of functions measured by vocabulary and information (e.g., WAIS and W-B vocabulary and information) might reflect an oversimplification. Test items were designed with the objective of developing test content that reflected both the new and the static aspects of culture. Most important, test items were selected so as to represent interest areas that are not normally measured on the WAIS or other more "generally" and/or scholastically oriented tests of intelligence. Twenty-eight tests were developed to measure interest domains such as finances, sports, art, transportation, death, disease, and religion as well as items employed in conventional tests of ability. The study was too extensive to allow us to summarize all the findings, but a brief summary of the highlights is possible.

Monge and Gardner (1972), and their associate Kuhlen, elected to use a cross-sectional design, although they were aware of the limitations of cross-sectional data collection strategies. They did so because they wished to focus on differences within *existing* age groups. It is these differences with which the adult educator must cope, in terms of either general education or retraining (Monge and Gardner, 1976). Here, they make an important point that cannot be stressed too often: *Decisions to elect either cross-sectional or longitudinal designs for research should be based on the use to which the data are to be put, not on the absolute merit of one or the other design.*

The sample of subjects was drawn from adults in social and church organizations, Parent-Teacher Associations, local organizations, and industrial establishments. All participants came from New York except for some individuals 60 years of age and over who were sampled from Dade County, Florida, senior centers. This was necessary to obtain a large sample over 60 years of age. There were at least 100 males and females from each of the decades from the twenties through the seventies. Since education varied considerably for persons of different age groups, raw performance scores were adjusted for age by covariance analyses or data were blocked into two discrete age groups. In general, test items were selected for suitability for the entire age range.

General knowledge

Results for the word familiarity test are summarized in Fig. 4-8. It may be seen that the same general pattern was observed when subjects were placed in "high" and "low" education groups. The high education group contained those individuals who had graduated from high schools and had some formal posthigh school education. The low educa-

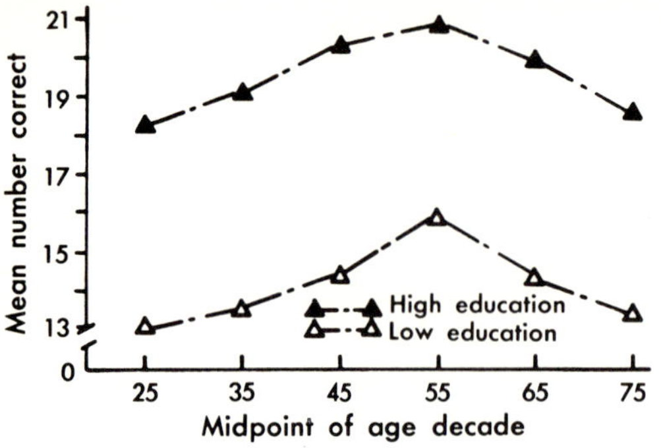

Fig. 4-8. Performance on the word familiarity survey as a function of age-cohort and education. (From Monge, R. H., and Gardner, E. F. *A program of research in adult differences in cognitive performance and learning.* Final report. [Project No. 6-1963, Grant No. OEG 1-706193-0149], 1972.)

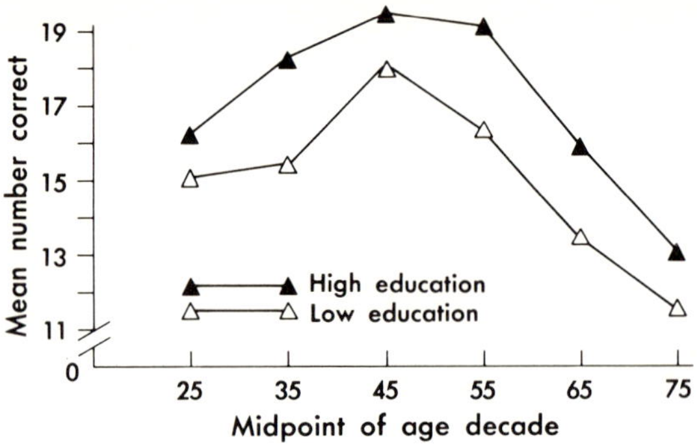

Fig. 4-9. Performance on the test of current slang as a function of age-cohort and education. (From Monge, R. H., and Gardner, E. F. *A program of research in adult differences in cognitive performance and learning.* Final report [Project No. 6-1963, Grant No. OEG 1-706193-0149], 1972.)

tion group consisted of participants who had obtained a high school education or less. Increasing age was associated with higher levels of performance, with maximum scores for the 50- to 59-year-old group (plotted as *55* in the graph) and then a decrease for the next two older age-decade groups. The low education group performed at a generally lower level, but the age trends are remarkably similar. Also note that education is as powerful a variable as age in terms of discriminating between good and poor performances.

Results for the old and current slang test show a similar curve (Fig. 4-9), but the peak of performance occurred for the 49- to 50-year-old group (*45* in the graph), and differences between educational groups were diminished.

For the modes of transportation test, the level of performance increased from the twenties to a peak in the fifties and then declined slightly thereafter *to a level similar to that of the twenties and thirties.* For tests concerning matters related to disease and death, interesting sex differences were obtained. Females performed at a higher level at all ages than did males. Males improved from the twenties to the seventies; females exhibited increased scores up to the fifties and then declined thereafter with means for the sixties and seventies similar to those observed for the forties and thirties respectively.

Results for the finance test were more complicated. Generally, mean scores (adjusted for education) increased in a similar manner for both sexes until the thirties; by the decade representing the fifties, females scored considerably better than males. Then scores for males and females converged again in the sixties, only to diverge in the seventies with males increasing to a point above their performance in the thirties.

Although the specific details and all the results of these studies cannot be summarized, there are important generalizations that may be gleaned from them. *First, on tests with adult-relevant items, adults in mid-life exhibited a greater fund of knowledge than younger subjects. Second, in some cases the decline beyond the middle years brought them to a level of performance which was similar to that of the young adults. Third, education differences and sex differences were, in some instances, as important or almost as important as age-cohort differences.*

It is neither surprising to find that the fund of experience and knowledge available to individuals increases with the passage of time, nor is it surprising to find that those abilities most relevant for successful environmental adaptation in old age hold up better than those more relevant to children. We did, however, note a downward trend from the mid-adult years to the seventies. Monge and Gardner (1972) do not offer an explanation for these downward trends, but they do provide evidence that they are not related to age-cohort differences in general education. Whenever scores were not shown in terms of two educational groups, scores were adjusted for education by means of covariance analysis. It is possible that the mid-fifties and mid-forties represent the years when practical knowledge is most actively employed.

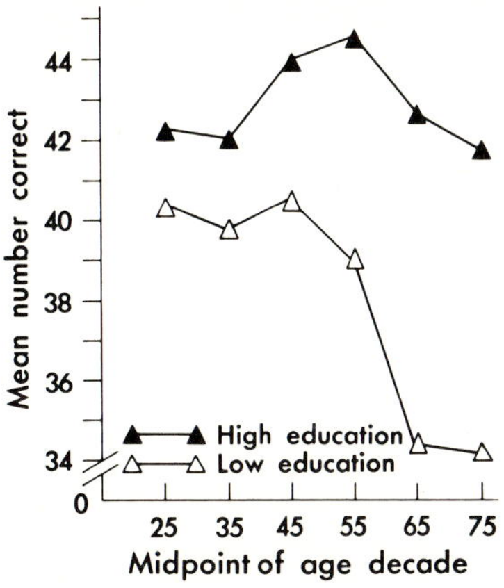

Fig. 4-10. Performance on the test of spelling as a function of age-cohort and education. (From Monge, R. H., and Gardner, E. F. *A program of research in adult differences in cognitive performance and learning.* Final report [Project No. 6-1963, Grant No. OEG 1-706193-0149], 1972.)

Educational skills

A second battery of tests was directed toward the assessment of educational skills important to adults. The following tests from the *Adult Basic Learning Examination* (ABLE) were used: spelling, reading comprehension, reading retention, arithmetic computation, and arithmetic problem solving.

For the spelling test (adjusted for education), females were superior to males at every age and showed relatively minor age-associated differences. Males declined from the twenties to the thirties and then increased again to the fifties. The peak in the fifties was followed by a decline to age 70 years, but at this age, performance was similar to that seen at age 35 years. Fig. 4-10 shows mean spelling scores for males and females combined but separated into "high" and "low" education groups. Persons with higher levels of education exhibited an increase in scores up to the fifties and then a decline that does not really fall too much below the level of performance that was characteristic of the twenties. In contrast, participants classified as falling in the low educational group showed a rather progressive and significant decline from the mid-twenties to the seventies. One is tempted to postulate *disuse* as an explanation of these findings in view of the fact that curves diverge with increasing age after the forties. It is likely that the more educated persons would continue to have exposure to professions demanding spelling skills for a more extended time than less educated persons. Although this is a logical hypothesis and an almost intuitively obvious conclusion, it awaits confirmation by the weight of empirical data.*

For the reading retention test, the part of the battery of tests that involved the reading of a simulated newspaper for a predetermined interval and then answering questions about the material, males improved slightly up to the sixties and then showed decline, whereas females declined from the twenties to the fifties and then remained at that level through the seventies. The decline for the "high" education group was later and less steep than that for the "low" education group. Moreover, the low education group

*One of our professors defined logic as "a systematic way of going wrong with reason" (G. E. Buckingham, Professor Emeritus, Allegheny College); a colleague is fond of reminding us that, after all, it was at one time intuitively obvious that the world is flat (J. R. Florini, Professor of Biology, Syracuse University).

exhibited reading retention scores in the seventies that were significantly poorer than those observed for the twenties. In contrast, the high education group exhibited similar scores in the twenties and seventies. This same group showed a notable increase in reading comprehension from the twenties to the thirties and then a progressive decline to a level similar to that of the twenties. The low education group showed a steady and more accelerated decline from the twenties to the seventies, but for some unexplained reason they performed at a higher level in the twenties than the high education group.

For the arithmetic computation test males were superior to females for every age-cohort tested. However, sex differences decreased with increasing age and males and females were highly similar in the seventieth decade. For both sexes there was a progressive and notable decline from the twenties to the seventies, and this was observed for both high and low educational groups, although participants in the high education group performed at a generally higher level. Similar results were obtained for the arithmetic problem-solving test, although persons with higher levels of education were considerably superior to those with lower education levels. The rate of decline was much less steep for persons with lower education levels; however, the twenties cohort had lower scores to begin with. This brings out an important point that cannot be stressed too much: one must always take initial levels of performance into account when evaluating the *rate* of decline or improvement across time or for different age-cohorts. Persons starting out at a higher level may show a greater rate of decline because they have further to decline. To put it another way, persons starting out at a lower level may not decline beyond a particular point because of a lower limit of performance (floor effect). The reader should be aware of the influence of floor and ceiling effects (upper limits) when evaluating age by treatment interactions with respect to rate of change.

With the exception of scores on the reading retention test, which were not associated with age in a major way, and the spelling test, which held up relatively well for persons of higher education levels, the general conclusion which must be drawn is that performance on basic educational skills was generally poorer for older persons when compared with persons in the twenties and thirties. Monge and Gardner (1972) turn to the disuse model to explain these findings; that is, The further a person is in time from early formal schooling, the poorer is performance on school-learned abilities (Monge and Gardner, 1976). Indirect evidence for this is provided by inspection of differences between persons with higher and lower levels of education. For all tests the higher the level of education the higher the level of performance in general, and these differences were exaggerated with age for many tests. Moreover, the pattern of differences between males and females suggests that sex differences reflect opportunity for males to practice some skills at some ages more than females and vice versa. It will be interesting to see how this pattern changes as females have increasingly, and long deservedly, equal opportunities to participate in a variety of professions and trades. That the patterns of sex differences for different age groups may change in the future is suggested by the fact that age-cohort by sex interactions were obtained in the Syracuse–Dade County sample.

One might argue that psychologists have learned nothing new. It is logical to assume that specific educational skills decline with distance from formal schooling. Psychologists have learned a number of things from the Syracuse–Dade County studies and have identified some exceptions to this rule. They have seen that trends in decline are dissimilar for men and women at the same temporal distance from schooling and that factors other than distance from schooling influence basic skills. Such information is invaluable to designers of adult education courses. Here the emphasis is on the development of curricula best suited for the cognitive functioning and learning of different age groups rather than the "age-old" argument about whether general levels of capacity, or composite intelligence, decline with age.

SUMMARY

One of the basic questions raised in the literature on aging and by the lay person is whether intellectual capacity declines with age. Perhaps no other question has received greater attention in terms of research; yet there is still disagreement among researchers as to the answer. In part, the disagreement is related to the fact that intelligence must be defined operationally, that is, in terms of the tests used to measure it or in terms of general characteristics of these tests, and investigators simply do not agree on the appropriate operational definitions. Sometimes disagreement is not overt but rather implicit in the way they design their experiments and interpret their data.

Biological definitions of intelligence offer no solution because biological measurements do not allow psychologists to estimate intelligent behavior in normal, healthy persons. Moreover, brain structure and intelligent behavior are not isomorphic, although clearly brain damage influences specific skills and/or general intellectual ability, depending on its location, nature, and rate of progression. On the other hand, intelligence is clearly not "that which is measured by intelligence tests." The solution seems to have been to measure intelligence in terms of the sets of responses that demonstrate intelligent behavior. The problem is that there is disagreement as to what these sets of behaviors are or, more specifically, how they should be assigned weights in terms of their contributions to overall intelligence. With regard to aging, there is the additional problem that some behaviors may be more important in terms of adaptation and survival at one age than at another. In other words, the criteria for intelligent behavior may change as one grows older.

If intelligence is defined in terms of those abilities which require long-term memory and the use of acquired skills, there appears to be relatively little decline in intellectual ability in "normal," healthy persons; at least this is true up to 65 years of age for most adults. In fact, acquired skills in certain areas can increase with age and experience and compensate for losses in other areas. Often, psychologists ignore the value of experience and knowledge when they judge the intellectual competence of older persons. It is clear that if one defines intelligence in terms of a set of behaviors that reflect rapid responding and competency with visual-spatial problem-solving ability, persons in elderly adult cohorts do not do as well as persons in younger cohorts. However, these skills may be less important to the elderly adult than to the younger adult.

One question that has been raised is whether or not slowed speed of responding (decreased *output* speed), rather than decline in speed of processing material (*throughput* speed), might not be responsible for the decrements in performance exhibited by elderly adults on timed tests of cognitive functioning. However, when time constraints are relaxed or eliminated, elderly adults improve, but they still do not perform at the same level as younger persons for tasks demanding problem solving with an emphasis on visual-motor skills.

It is important to remember that we are describing group trends and that there are individual differences in intellectual functioning. You should remember that the age variable accounts for only about 25% of the variance in IQ test scores and that highly educated, healthy persons often perform better at a very old age than younger persons of lesser opportunity and/or in poor health. Moreover, persons with higher levels of education tend to retain the capacity to perform well intellectually longer than do persons with lower levels of education. Of course, one does not know if this phenomenon reflects the fact that basic capacity holds up better in more highly educated persons or whether these persons have more opportunity, by virtue of professional associations and responsibilities, to maintain familiarity with the kind of scholastic type of activities that are heavily emphasized by intelligence tests.

Although it is useful to think of overall intelligence as reflecting a composite of abilities that can be brought to bear on the solution of a problem, it is also useful to examine the specific abilities that make up the composite and to ask which show decline and which hold up well with age or improve. On the WAIS, performance abilities seem to decline more rapidly with age than do verbal abilities, although examination of verbal and performance portions of the WAIS as entities presents a somewhat oversimplified picture. When one examines the subtests of the verbal and performance scales, it becomes clear that some subtests decline more rapidly than others, whereas some (e.g., vocabulary and information) hold up rather well. Usually tests involving problem solving in the visual modality, and an emphasis on rapid response with time constraints, exhibit age-related decline. However, psychologists should keep in mind that those subtests on the WAIS that are most sensitive to age differences are not the most sensitive tests for differences between groups *within* age categories, for example, psychotic as opposed to nonpsychotic groups, brain-damaged as opposed to nonbrain-damaged groups. Factor analytic studies represent another approach to the generation of profiles of specific abilities with advancing age. In general, those abilities referred to as "crystallized" tend to hold up well, whereas those referred to as "fluid" seem to decline with age. However, one may compensate for the other so that overall capacity to function intellectually is maintained fairly well in normal, healthy, elderly persons.

Several classical studies have demonstrated that tests can be designed that will reveal *improvement* in performance with advancing age. This should not come as a surprise because psychologists know that older adults do better on some kinds of test content than others. Selecting test content in which older persons should do well leads to the reasonable prediction that they will, in fact, do well. The real question is whether these tests actually represent those sets of behaviors that one could logically agree were indicative of intellectual capacity. Often the items are informational in nature and thus place demands on acquired skills. Yet older adults also must function in a world where rapid response and novel problem solving are important, although these parameters may vary in importance depending on the demands of each person's occupation. Perhaps it is better to design tests that have items relevant to a wide range of ages across the life span, to extend age norms upward on standardized tests of intelligence, and to concentrate more on the measurement of skills and abilities that are relevant to persons within occupations.

A much more important question than the issue of decline as opposed to no decline is: Which sets of specific abilities and skills decline more rapidly with age than others and which skills are spared? The factor analytic studies and information about performance on subtests of the WAIS are useful in this respect, but psychometric tests often combine demands on visual, motor, and memory processes within a single task. The result is that *input, output,* and *throughput* processes are confounded, and it is not possible to determine precisely which aspects of information processing are improving, declining, or remaining stable. As shall be seen later in this text, experimental studies of perception and information processing are useful in teasing out factors (e.g., perceptual as opposed to motor) that are often confounded in standardized psychometric tests because these tests were orginally designed to measure abilities or overall capacity rather than to separate stages of information processing.

Use of experimental paradigms to study "information processing" does not deny the usefulness of tests that are designed to measure specific academic skills relevant to adult education and technical training, for example, spelling, arithmetic, word finding. Much of the work that has been done with elderly adults has been done with global tests of intelligence, such as the WAIS. Those studies which have been done on specific scholastic abilities indicate that the picture of decline from young to old adulthood is an overgeneralization.

The most important consideration in the assessment of overall ability or specific abilities is how the data were collected. Was sampling representative? Were modifiers of performance, such as health, education, occupation, culture, motivation, and personality taken into consideration in the procedure and design? Was a cross-sectional or longitudinal design employed? In other words, were the studies done properly in terms of life-span methodology? These considerations will be discussed in detail in the next chapter.

SELECTED READINGS

Baltes, P. B., and Schaie, K. W. Aging and IQ: the myth of the twilight years. *Psychology Today,* 1974, **70,** 419-425.

Botwinick, J. *Does intelligence decline in old age?* In J. E. Birren and K. W. Schaie. *Handbook on the psychology of aging.* New York: Von Nostrand-Reinhold Co., in press.

Botwinick, J., and Birren, J. E. Differential decline in the Wechsler-Bellevue subtests in the senile psychoses. *Journal of Gerontology,* 1951, **4,** 365-368.

Botwinick, J., and Birren, J. E. The measurement of intellectual decline in the senile psychoses. *Journal of Consulting Psychology,* 1951, **6,** 365-368.

Eisdorfer, C., and Wilkie, F. Intellectual changes with advancing age. In L. F. Jarvik, C. Eisdorfer, and J. E. Blum (Eds.), *Intellectual functioning in adults.* New York: Springer Publishing Co., Inc., 1973.

Horn, J. L. Psychometric studies of aging and intelligence. In S. Gershon and A. Raskind (Eds.), *Aging* (Vol. 2). *Genesis and treatment of psychologic disorders in the elderly.* New York: Raven Press, 1975.

Horn, J. L., and Cattell, R. B. Age differences in fluid and crystallized intelligence. *Acta Psychologica,* 1967, **26,** 107-219.

Schaie, K. W. A reinterpretation of age related changes in cognitive structure and function. In L. R. Goulet, and P. B. Baltes (Eds.), *Life-span developmental psychology,* New York: Academic Press, Inc., 1970.

Wechsler, D. *The measurement and appraisal of adult intelligence* (4th ed.). Baltimore: The Williams & Wilkins Co., 1958.

CHAPTER 5

MODIFIERS OF INTELLECTUAL PERFORMANCE

The phrase "modifiers of intelligence" was used by Botwinick (1967:28) in his review of the literature on intelligence and aging. It refers to variables that influence performance on tests of intelligence but are not thought of as being directly related to the true capacity of the individual. These modifier variables limit the extent to which inferences about intellectual capacity can be made with accuracy.

EDUCATION AND OCCUPATION

In Birren and Morrison's (1961) factor analytic study, level of education was a critical factor in general intellectual performance. In the Syracuse–Dade County study, performance on tests measuring educational skills and informational areas was higher for more highly educated persons. In some instances the pattern of intelligence test performance decline was different for the "high" and "low" education groups. Furthermore, it has long been known that cross-sectional data are compromised by the fact that persons in different age-cohorts have had different educational opportunities.

Educational and occupational influences on test performance are intimately related to the question of whether or not persons with initially high intellectual ability show patterns of change over time that are similar to those with initially low levels of ability. This is true because education and/or occupation are often used as indicators of initial ability when test scores are not available. The generally high correlations among occupation, education, and general ability are used as a rationale for the use of occupation and education as indices of initial ability. The questions raised in studies of initial and later ability are (1) do initially more capable persons come to the end of their lives as more capable persons, and (2) is the magnitude of the difference between a person of high and low ability the same at the beginning and the end of the life span.

In general, studies using education and occupation as indices of initial ability have reported greater declines in general intelligence test performance for persons of lesser initial education and for persons in what were defined as the least intelligent occupations (Botwinick, 1967). However, the dangers of inferring that persons of lesser initial intellectual capacity decline more rapidly than those with greater initial intellectual capacity are obvious. Estimates of initial capacity based on education and occupation assume equal opportunity for jobs and training. Moreover, estimates of initial ability based on occupation require value judgments with regard to less intelligent occupations. In some cases these judgments may have clear face validity, but in other instances they may not. Generally, tests of scholastic types of abilities have been used, for example, the Primary Mental Abilities Test (PMA), and the Wechsler Adult Intelligence Scale (WAIS). Some occupations place heavy demands on scholastic types of abilities (e.g., teachers or lawyers), whereas others demand a qualitatively different kind of intelligence. Moreover, attitudes about acceptable occupations for persons with a given level of intelligence may change with successive generations. Young persons today find that what used to be considered less intelligent occupations are particularly worthwhile in terms of self-actualization. This trend may become increasingly apparent for middle-aged and aged persons as mid- and late-career changes in jobs become more acceptable and possible. Thus it has become increasingly difficult to infer intelligence from occupational choice.

Pressey and Kuhlen (1957) reported that scores on general ability tests were significantly different for men of different occupations, but they point out that it must not be concluded that most persons in the United States rise to the occupation for which they are capable. They cite the fact that 10% of the machine operators they tested scored above the median for lawyers. This generalization correctly emphasizes problems associated with occupation as an index of initial level of ability. However, the student should not infer that the implication is that machine operators are less intelligent than lawyers. Again it should be noted that tests of general ability are scholastically oriented, and thus persons in the professions are more likely to perform well on them than persons in the trades. The bias in general intelligence test measures toward the professions complicates matters if one uses such a test to compare elderly machinists and elderly lawyers in a study that estimates initial level of ability based on occupation. Mr. Jones may elect to become a machinist because of interest and a desire to capitalize on specific abilities of a nonscholastic nature. At the time he makes this choice (after high school), he may not be as disadvantaged (relative to the future lawyer) in scholastic abilities as he is many years later when he is further from formal schooling. Attorney Williams not only remains in school for a longer period of time, but his occupation demands an everyday practice of scholastic abilities, for example, reading, comprehension, writing, verbal fluency, and spelling. Thus the machinist's initial level of ability may be underestimated, and in later years his actual IQ scores may be lowered by disuse of scholastic skills.

The best way to answer the question of the relationship of initial ability to later ability is to use the same tests of that ability. Botwinick (1973:192) states that cross-sectional studies have generally supported the notion that,

> In later life, high level elderly people are characterized by very high verbal ability, independent of age; they are characterized by high non-verbal intelligence, however, only when compared to others of the same age. With low ability people, both functions decrease in later life and are low by any comparison. People of average ability maintain verbal ability with only slight decrease, if any, but they show appreciable decrements in non-verbal intelligence.

These generalizations are consistent with longitudinal studies, but even in this instance, performance at time 2 may be lowered more for persons with lower time 1 performance scores by virtue of disuse of particular skills. In general, tests of the relationship between initial and later ability should be done *within occupations* and/or education levels.

Adult development is increasingly characterized in terms of professional and trade specialization. For this reason it would seem more practical and profitable to spend less effort on the question of initial as opposed to later levels of general intellectual ability and more effort on the identification of strengths and weaknesses of adults of different ages with respect to skills that are important in their everyday lives.

TEST CONTENT

It has been noted already that the relationship between IQ and school performance is extremely important for children and adolescents but that IQ does not predict success in adult occupations other than in a very general manner. This is not surprising, since test content is often not relevant to specific occupations. When occupation-relevant tests are given, some skills show decline, others show improvement, and others remain stable from youth through the middle years.

In a study by Thumin (1970), male job applicants were relatively well matched in terms of education and placed in four age-cohort groups; mean ages were 24.8, 31.4, 37.7, and 45.1 years. Numerical reasoning ability showed a slight decline with age, but no statistically significant age differences were obtained for verbal fluency, vocabulary, reading speed, and reading comprehension. Of course, you will note that these are verbal skills and that verbal skills hold up well with age on general tests of intelligence. Furthermore, the subjects were all professionals and businessmen, and thus one would not expect a decline in these skills over the age range studied. In an earlier study with females 17 to 57 years of age, Thumin and Boernke (1966) found that numerical ability remained approximately at the same level between 19 and 32 years, increased up to the early forties, and then decreased in the early fifties. Clerical ability declined in the late forties after remaining constant between 19 and 42 years. Typing accuracy improved up to 32 years and remained constant thereafter. Verbal comprehension and typing speed improved progressively across the age range studied.

The importance of test content and age-relevant questions was also emphasized by the Syracuse–Dade County study. Depending on test content, participants exhibited no decline until the seventies, and even then they performed better than 20-year-old subjects on some tests (Monge and Gardner, 1972). The Syracuse–Dade County study, reviewed in Chapter 4, was influenced by the earlier work of Demming and Pressey (1957). They argued that tests used to measure the intelligence of older persons should deal with problems which are meaningful to their daily lives. To test this hypothesis they constructed a test with questions that were practical in nature and related to the needs of adults. It was based on the yellow pages of the telephone directory, common legal terms, and how to get services necessary for daily life. Test scores exhibited a rise through the middle and late years, and this was true for individuals who exhibited decline on conventional tests of intelligence. The important question psychologists must deal with is whether results such as these indicate that an "age-fair" test of intelligence will not reveal decline. Such a conclusion is not justified on the basis of this study. First, many psychologists would not agree that the test designed by Demming and Pressey was a test of general ability. The items selected were of the information and comprehension variety, which do not show much decline on the WAIS for relatively healthy persons. Second, the items were less difficult for older persons than for younger persons because they were deliberately selected for older persons. In the Syracuse–Dade County study, items were selected to reflect interests and knowledge relevant to a number of different age-cohorts. Thus their findings of improvement well into old age for some measures of ability are more impressive.

It is obvious that one may produce a variety of different results by shifting test content. Thus the important principle to be learned from the literature on test content is that *test content should not be biased toward a particular age-cohort.* It is not a simple matter to select test questions that are fair for many different age groups. One solution to this problem is to use a large number of tests or test questions (items) with content that is believed to be appropriate for a wide range of age groups. Once a test made up of this content has been given, item analyses may be performed on the resulting data. The objective of the item analysis is to determine the proportion of persons in each age group that obtains the correct answer on a given test question. Items can be characterized in terms of the age group obtaining the largest number of correct answers.

The usefulness of this kind of data analysis is that it allows the construction of a test with items selected on the basis of their suitability for given age groups. Suitability is based on empirical evidence rather than a guess based on the face validity (apparent validity) of the questions for different age groups. Monge and Gardner (1972) used this "item analysis" approach in the Syracuse–Dade County study. The results are too extensive to review here, but it is important to take note of item analysis as a valid approach to the development of tests that contain content that is fair to a wide range of age groups.

HEALTH STATUS

There is no question that health status influences performance on tests of ability and achievement. Recently, Abrahams (1976) called attention to the fact that few investigators either identify the health status of their subjects or bother to determine their health status prior to experimentation. It is often impossible for a researcher with limited resources to specify health status to any significant extent. Often hospital records are unavailable, or appropriate tests have not been performed. Nevertheless, some inquiry into health status or a statement that health status is unknown seems to be an important aspect of designing and reporting data from developmental studies. We review the literature on mental and physical health as it relates to performance and learning in later chapters. Thus it is sufficient to say here that psychoses, depression, brain damage, severe cardiovascular and cerebrovascular disease do influence performance on tests of ability. Often these factors are interrelated. Physical injury or prolonged physical illness can lead to depression, which serves to exaggerate performance decrements related to the injury. Poor performance leads to further depression, which, in turn, results in a further impairment in performance.

In many instances depression is a realistic response of elderly adults to their life situation. Many retired elderly adults are facing increased costs of living on fixed incomes, the loss of status and pleasure derived from work-related activities, and the loss of life-long friends and loved ones. These economic and social factors may be further complicated by decreasing physical mobility, deteriorating health, impaired taste, hearing, and vision, and altered physical appearance. Not all elderly persons face all of these problems, and some face only a few. They tend to be exaggerated for persons on very low incomes and in poor health. In those instances where poor health forces early retirement, economic deprivation may become a factor in late or even early middle age. In this instance the combined effects of poor health and depression may exert an adverse effect on performance.

SOCIETAL CHANGE

Environmental limitations on the expression of "true potential" exist in a broad cultural sense as well as an individual sense. Societal changes within a lifetime influence longitudinal data just as differences in educational opportunity influence cross-sectional data. As one grows older, the environment is constantly changing, and thus test performance reflects the interaction of developmental processes and environment.

LOSS OF SPEED

In the last chapter we made note of Horn's argument against the possibility that speed of motor response is an important limiting factor with regard to performance on tests of intelligence. One of the earliest arguments regarding the limiting aspects of decline in speed of response was offered by Lorge (1936). He believed that the decline in speed of response was largely responsible for the poor performance of older adults but that speed was not an important factor in intelligence. He reanalyzed data by Jones and Conrad (1933) with a statistical adjustment for the speed factor. You will recall that Jones and Conrad reported a decline in Army Alpha test performance for older (45 to 59 years) as opposed to younger (17 to 24 years) persons. No age differences were found when these scores were adjusted for speed differences.

Not all studies agree with the Lorge (1936) study. Miles (1934) reported an age decrement on the Otis Self Administering Test, despite the elimination of the time factor. Doppelt and Wallace (1955) found that, with the exception of a slight improvement in block design performance, performance for a group of WAIS subtests did not improve when the speed factor was eliminated. Klodin (1976) reevaluated the Doppelt and Wallace study because it did not include a group of young subjects as controls.

Using Doppelt and Wallace's timed as opposed to untimed conditions, Klodin compared young men (mean = 22 years) and old men (mean = 73 years). He found no improvement in the object assembly subtest of the WAIS for the young group and slight improvement for the old group without timing. Failure of the young men to show improvement in the absence of timing was probably because they did relatively well under the timed conditions and really could not improve much.

Klodin's study illustrates an important methodological point. A young group (or young groups) is necessary if the effectiveness of a treatment for older adults is to be evaluated, but relative amounts of improvement for younger and older groups are difficult to interpret if baseline levels (pretreatment or nontreatment levels) of performance are not the same. Young subjects may improve less because they operate close to a ceiling level without the treatment. One solution to the problem is to match older and younger groups on the basis of a measure of pretreatment performance.

Klodin (1976) calls attention to the fact that Doppelt and Wallace altered an important aspect of the standardized WAIS scoring procedure under their timed scoring condition. They did not provide bonus points for rapid solutions. Klodin suggests that this procedure may contribute to major differences in time scores for older and younger adults. If this is true, older adults may be doubly penalized by timing and the bonus point system. To test this hypothesis, he compared the standardized procedure (timing and bonus points for rapid response) with timed (no bonus) and untimed procedures. The standardized procedure was associated with better object assembly performance for the young subjects than the timed (no bonus) and untimed conditions. For the older subjects the standard procedure was associated with poorer performance on the object assembly test than was the untimed procedure, but bonus points made little difference.

For the block design scores, timing plus bonus and timing plus no bonus procedures did not differ for old subjects, but young subjects performed better under the timing plus bonus condition. The critical feature for improvement in older subjects was the removing of time requirements, and the critical feature for improvement in younger subjects was the addition of bonus points. Improvement was observed relative to timed conditions for both block design and object assembly tests for older subjects, but the absolute level of performance did not reach the level achieved by younger subjects under untimed conditions.

Many other studies could be summarized. However, it is sufficient to say that elimination of the speed factor often brings mean scores for older and younger age groups closer together, but it seldom eliminates age differences if they existed under timed testing procedures. Disagreements in findings are difficult to resolve because different tests and subtests are used in studies, which also differ with respect to critical aspects of procedure, design, and subject samples.

PERSONALITY

Schaie (1958), Chown (1961), and many others have provided data with regard to personality variables and performance. Schaie's work indicates that PMA scores and rigidity scores are affected by age and correlated at every age. Chown's data indicate that, when problem-solving ability is lowered for older persons, these older persons seem to be more rigid. However, Botwinick (1967) cautions against inferring that the reason for poor performance is rigidity rather than the other way around. Moreover, Chown (1961) cautions against the idea of the rigid person and notes that five kinds of rigidity can be identified. It is probably best to talk about rigid behavior with specific references to a specific situation rather than think of it as a general personality characteristic with identical origins for persons of all ages.

In summary, it is safe to say that personality factors influence intelligence test performance, but it is also true that the shaping of one's personality through childhood and the adult years is influenced by intellectual functioning. Intellectual functioning is an intimate part of one's personality.

PRACTICE

Recently, there has been some attention paid to the idea that deficits in intellectual performance of older persons are present because of the lack of environmental supports necessary for high levels of performance. If this is true, the manipulation of environmental factors should result in better performance.

Hoyer and associates (1973:233) call attention to the fact that, "most attempts at explaining intellectual change phenomena in later adulthood have focused on biological and neurophysiological antecedents," and that "explanations of age-related decline have deemphasized the importance of experientially determined changes in intellectual performance." They point to research demonstrating the existence of cohort or generational differences as suggesting that "intellectual ontogeny during adulthood and old age is to a large extent controlled by both historical and environmental events." Furthermore, they (1973:234) emphasize data which suggest that intellectual decline in old age is attributable to "poor environmental conditions for the acquisition and maintenance of intellectual behaviors . . ." In the context of this emphasis on supportive environments, Hoyer and colleagues (1973:234) hypothesize that "response slowing reflects the lack of appropriate practice and reinforcement schedules in the elderly person's environment." They designed an experiment to (1) examine the possibility of increasing speed of performance on paper-and-pencil tests by using training and reinforcement procedures, and (2) examine whether improvement in speed of response transfers to tests of intellectual ability that feature a speed component.

These authors' training materials consisted of tests of cancellation, marking, and writing, which were administered to reinforced and nonreinforced practice groups in two separate sessions. For the reinforcement condition, participants were positively reinforced whenever they exhibited response speeds in excess of a baseline level. For the nonreinforcement condition, no feedback with regard to response speed was given. Results indicated no significant differences between the reinforced and nonreinforced groups, and the "reinforcement factor" did not interact significantly with the session or trial factors. However, the investigators point out that all three tasks used revealed performance superiority for the reinforced as opposed to the nonreinforced groups.

No convincing evidence was obtained for the notion that increase in speed for the reinforced group would transfer to the "intellectual, verbal and speeded perceptual tests" used, although there was evidence for greater improvement on these tests for subjects who were practiced. Based on these data Hoyer and colleagues concluded that these data did provide convincing evidence for the modifiableness of response speed in the aged but that they were far less persuasive with regard to transfer to various measures of intellectual functioning. These authors (1973:238) also comment on the interpretation of their data in light of previous interpretations of response speed deficits as reflecting neurophysiological processes.

> In contrast to neurophysiological interpretations, the fairly strong specific training effects obtained demonstrated the heuristic value of considering decrements in response speed as being experientially based and modifiable by environmental intervention.

The word *heuristic* places an emphasis on

the value of considering alternatives to traditional interpretations that emphasize neurophysiological bases for decline. It would be erroneous to conclude that a study in which environment and experience are important to response speed eliminates the importance of neurophysiological factors or, more specifically, that improvement in response time by reinforcement or practice casts doubt on neurophysiological interpretations of loss of speed with age. Neurophysiological explanations, correct or incorrect, neither stand in contrast to the notion of modifiability of response speed nor are refuted by demonstrations that practice and reinforcement improve response speed. Response speed may decline as a result of alterations in structure or biochemistry, and yet it may show improvement with practice and/or reinforcement.

Environmental manipulations not only influence performance, but they can actually have feedback effects on the size and chemistry of the brain (e.g., Bennett et al., 1964; Rosenzweig et al., 1964). Thus experiments on the modifiableness of response speed by Hoyer and associates and others sharpen the researcher's awareness of experiential factors and emphasize the desirability of considering factors other than neurophysiological decline as explanations of age-associated decrements in response speed. Nevertheless, the student must not conclude that data with regard to the importance of experience and training refute neurophysiological hypotheses or vice versa. It is best to think of experiential and neurophysiological factors as interacting in a dynamic manner.

Failure of the increased speed of responding, exhibited by Hoyer and associates' reinforced group, to transfer to the set of intellectual performance tests may well have resulted from the fact that too few training trials were given. On the other hand, it may well have been related to the fact that improvement in speed of response was less important on the tests of intellectual performance than other factors. The latter interpretation is consistent with Horn's (1975) argument that speed decrements in motor response in the elderly are too small to account for rather large decrements in some timed tasks.

CAUTION AND RISK TAKING

A number of studies indicate that older persons tend to take no course of action if that is a permissible alternative (Botwinick, 1966a; Wallach and Kogan, 1961). However, if risk taking is required, older persons do not seem to be more cautious than younger persons (Botwinick, 1966a). Birkhill and Schaie (1975) have also presented data which indicate that some older persons do less well when they fear that task involvement will lead to embarrassment but that careful control of instructional set may induce the older person to consider alternatives that he might otherwise not consider.

Psychologists must not forget the "chicken-and-the-egg" dilemma posed by these kind of studies: are the elderly subjects performing less well because they are reluctant to risk embarrassment or are they reluctant to risk embarrassment because they have performed less well in the past and thus fear that they will perform less well in the present? To answer this question psychologists need to know much more about the "learning or task performance orientation" of the older adult and about the past history of successes and failures for different individuals.

LEARNING ORIENTATION

Learning orientation comes under the general heading of motivation. Motivational factors are such important modifiers of test performance that we have devoted two chapters to the discussion of motivational processes. The Syracuse–Dade County study (Monge and Gardner, 1972) was concerned with the relationship between motivational factors and the specific age-relevant abilities that were tested. For this reason we devote some space to the discussion of findings with regard to the relationship between motivational factors and test performance in this chapter.

Monge and Gardner (1972) pointed out that the extent to which older adults are either positively oriented toward new learning experiences or negatively react to these experiences is of greater importance, in a practical sense, than the specific abilities that they bring to a learning situation. They identified a number of important motivational factors that they believed contributed to learning orientation for different age groups: (1) achievement motivation (motivation to learn); (2) learning apprehension (anxiety); (3) life-style (learning set); and (4) dogmatism (rigidity).

Achievement motivation was defined as the desire to achieve and accomplish with respect to several standards: (1) competition with one's own self; (2) competition with others; and (3) absolute standards of competence. *Learning apprehension* was defined as the degree of apprehension, uneasiness, or nervousness generated by learning situations or various cognitive task situations. *Dogmatism* (used interchangeably with the term *rigidity*) was defined as a need for structure. It is perhaps best to use the term *dogmatism* in this instance. Hollander and Hunt (1967: 160) point out that both rigidity and dogmatism refer to resistance to change but that dogmatism is a "higher order" and more "complexly organized form of resistance to change." Thus dogmatism is more general and can lead to rigidity, but rigidity does not lead to dogmatism. Rigidity is more task specific than dogmatism. Monge and Gardner (1972) point to the literature indicating that dogmatism poses handicaps to effective learning which result from the incorporation of irrelevant elements into the solution of a problem or the reaching of premature decisions. *Style of life* was broadly defined in terms of learning set or learning orientation; for example, a person who is aware that he has not participated in new learning situations for some years may not have the same test-taking orientation as a person who has consistently participated in new learning experiences.

Sarason's Demand for Achievement test was used as a measure of achievement motivation. You will recall from the last chapter that Monge and Gardner used a cross-sectional sample ranging in age from the twenties to the seventies. Demand for Achievement scores showed a decline from the twenties to the thirties and then a relatively steady increase up to the sixties for females and the seventies for males.

There were several tests of general anxiety. The trend was decline from the twenties to the thirties and then increasing and decreasing trends thereafter. Most important, there was no highly significant and progressive rise of anxiety scores with age. Generally, women exhibited higher anxiety scores than men. However, it should be remembered that these were self-ratings of anxiety, and it is possible that women were more willing to admit to anxiety symptoms than men.

The most striking finding was the dramatic increase across successively older age-cohort groups for scores on the test designed to measure dogmatism (items from the short form of the Rokeach dogmatism scale). These curves are shown in Fig. 5-1 for males and females.

Style of life (educational set) was inferred from prior educational participation scores taken from the leisure activity survey. Results for persons falling into the high and low education level classifications are shown in Fig. 5-2. It is not surprising to find that educational participation was higher for persons with higher levels of education. What is particularly interesting is the U-shaped curve for the higher educational group and the variable trends across age for the group with the lower levels of education. At 25 and 65 years of age the low and high education groups converge, but they are furthest apart when one compares the 35-, 55-, and 75-year-old groups. If nothing else, these data emphasize *the dangers of age comparisons using only two extreme groups,* or two groups

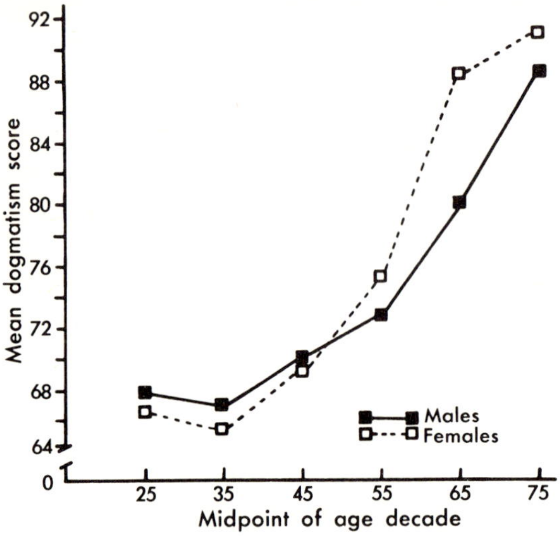

Fig. 5-1. Influence of age and sex on the short form of the dogmatism scale used by Monge and Gardner (1972) in the Syracuse–Dade County study. (From Monge, R. H., and Gardner, E. F. *A program of research in adult differences in cognitive performance and learning.* Final report [Project No. 6-1963, Grant No. OEG 1-706193-0149], 1972.)

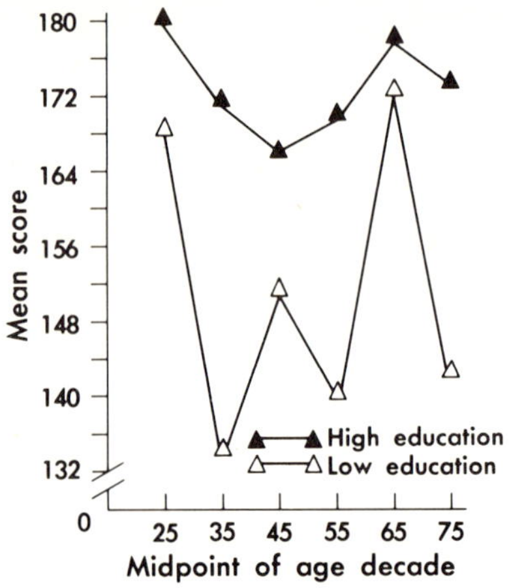

Fig. 5-2. Mean educational participation score (Syracuse–Dade County study) by age, sex, and education. (From Monge, R. H., and Gardner, E. F. *A program of research in adult differences in cognitive performance and learning.* Final report [Project No. 6-1963, Grant No. OEG 1-706193-0149], 1972.)

of any age. What would we be tempted to conclude had only the 35-, 55-, and 65-year-olds been tested for the low education group? Educational participation increases with age? Obviously this is the conclusion one might reach based on comparison of these three groups, but it is invalidated when one compares additional age-cohorts and compares both high and low education groups.

The most important implications of these interesting findings relate to their correlations, or lack of correlations, with tests of ability. The relationship between age-cohort groupings and measures of anxiety is complex, although it is fairly clear that women rated themselves more highly with respect to anxiety. Principal component analyses indicated that all the anxiety measures used tended to cluster together and were positively associated with the sex factor but were independent of age, education, dogmatism, and vocabulary measures, which were all gathered at the same time.

Can we conclude from these data that men are generally less anxious than women at all ages? We cannot, and Monge and Gardner do not, reach this conclusion. Just as intelligence tests do not measure intelligence in the same way that rulers measure inches, anxiety tests do not measure all of the elements that make up the hypothetical construct referred to as anxiety. Anxiety can be task specific just as rigidity can be task specific; and of all constructs, anxiety is one of the most difficult to define operationally. Note, also, that the anxiety scales called for self-rating. Thus the apparent difference in anxiety level may reflect differences in how men and women rate themselves on self-rating scales or other factors relating to feelings about the social desirability of responding one way or the other on specific questions.

Kuhlen (1964) hypothesized that dogmatism serves as a means of controlling anxiety. The increase in dogmatism scores in the Syracuse–Dade County study (Fig. 5-1) was clear cut, but dogmatism scores were not positively correlated with anxiety.

It is important to note that dogmatism

increased with age, but dogmatism and education were inversely related. In other words, older subjects tended to receive higher dogmatism scores but so did less educated subjects. Thus a question was raised as to whether age and dogmatism would be related if the correlation was adjusted for the influence of education. Without adjustment the correlation between age and dogmatism was 0.50; with adjustment for age it was 0.43. Thus lower education scores for older persons cannot provide the major explanation for the positive correlation between age and dogmatism.

These data on dogmatism point to interesting directions for future research and are generally consistent with the notion that older age-cohorts exhibit higher levels of dogmatism. However, it is not safe at this point to say that increasing age brings with it increasing dogmatism. The reader should remember that a cross-sectional design was used. Moreover, dogmatism, like rigidity, takes many different forms; some are age related and some are not (see Botwinick, 1973:70-79). For example, there are data which suggest that dogmatism which is related to anxiety and insecurity does not increase with age, whereas a more general type of "stereotypic dogmatism" does (Riegel and Riegel, 1960). Botwinick (1973:79) describes stereotypic dogmatism as beliefs such as, "It is a sign of weak character to give up one's earlier convictions." More data need to be gathered before psychologists can say with conviction that "stereotypic dogmatism" increases with older age. At best, they can safely say that older age-cohorts achieve higher scores for dogmatism on some tests of dogmatism and that it seems questionable that dogmatism is used to control anxiety. Also, one must keep in mind that the correlation of 0.43 between dogmatism and age (education adjusted) was statistically significant but that only a small percentage of the variance in dogmatism (about 18%) can be predicted from an individual's age. Many other variables influence dogmatism.

Psychologists must question the practical implications in terms of efficiency of mental performance if it could be clearly shown that older persons exhibit more rigidity of the stereotypic nature than younger persons. Is it bad? Monge and Gardner (1972:49) make some interesting observations in this respect.

> One possible explanation for the increase with age in rigidity or dogmatism is that ready-made, stereotyped responses are energy-conserving. Little or no thought is required, and there is little wasted action. And, more often than not, such responses are adaptive. They have, after all, been learned through oft-repeated experience and in a variety of circumstances through a long life. Some of the older subjects in this study, for example, betrayed something of this in their arguments with the proctors over how to treat the task of rating the "bounced check" and the "supermarket over-run" situation. Many of the older people assured us that they would never let such things occur, and how in the world could they imagine how they might feel in such a situation? This unwillingness to experience, even vicariously, might certainly be construed as rigid behavior—but it is also symptomatic of an unremitting caution in important matters that has been translated into an iron-clad routine to avoid both trouble and expenditure of energy that would be required to put things right.

Clearly, what young persons call rigid behavior might be cautious behavior born of experience. No individual has not, at some time or other, formed an iron-clad rule in some area of conduct that is based on an unfortunate past experience. Is it not possible that versatility and flexibility to the young man may be seen as "rashness" to the older person? Conversely, a well-thought-out, cautious approach to the solution of a problem may be seen as slow, ponderous, and indecisive to a younger adult. Psychologists need to know much more about these dimensions of "age-associated value systems" before they advance much further with regard to their understanding of personality and motivational correlates of intellectual performance.

Neither anxiety nor dogmatism was related to performance on the vocabulary test. Correlations of anxiety with the other tests of special abilities given by Monge and Gardner

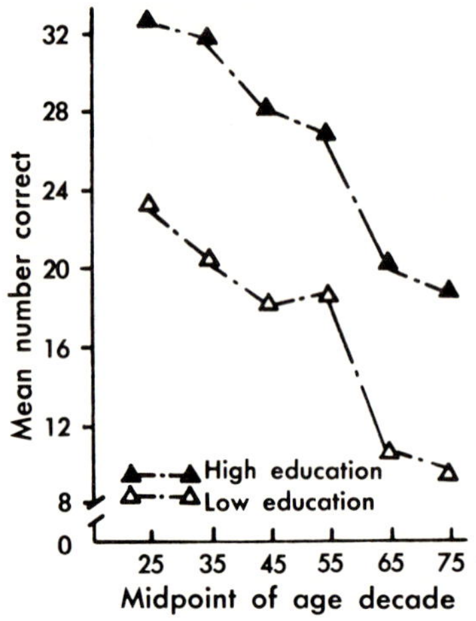

Fig. 5-3. Mean scores on the arithmetic computation portion of ABLE (Syracuse–Dade County study) by age, sex, and education. (From Monge, R. H., and Gardner, E. F. *A program of research in adult differences in cognitive performance and learning.* Final report [Project No. 6-1963, Grant No. OEG 1-706193-0149], 1972.)

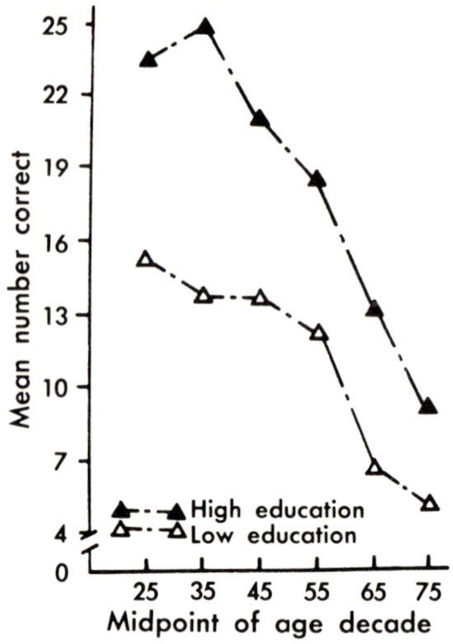

Fig. 5-4. Mean score on the arithmetic problem-solving portion of ABLE (Syracuse–Dade County study) by age, sex, and education. (From Monge, R. H., and Gardner, E. F. *A program of research in adult differences in cognitive performance and learning.* Final report [Project No. 6-1963, Grant No. OEG 1-706193-0149], 1972.)

(1972) are not reported. Figs. 5-3 and 5-4 summarize results from the Adult Basic Learning Examination (ABLE) for the two tests of specific abilities, which did show a notable and progressive decline from the twenties to the seventies. Compare these curves with the dogmatism curve in Fig. 5-1. Can one conclude that increasing dogmatism across age-cohort groups was responsible for the decline in performance scores for the two arithmetic tests? Obviously, no, although these findings are not inconsistent with data which indicate that lowered problem solving for older adults is related to increased rigidity (Chown, 1961) and that rigidity scores and problem-solving ability are negatively correlated at every age (Schaie, 1958). One approach to analysis of the Monge and Gardner data would be to correlate measures of arithmetic problem solving and computation with dogmatism for each age group in their study. However, the presence of high correlations for all age groups would not indicate that lowered problem-solving ability is *caused* by increased dogmatism. As Botwinick (1973) points out, the reverse could be true. Moreover, the two phenomena (poor problem solving and dogmatism) could be correlated with each other only by virtue of the fact that they are correlated with as yet unknown variables, which are, in turn, correlated with age. These variables may be related to maturation and adult socialization, or they may be artifacts of the manner in which the samples were drawn and the data collected.

Aside from the many problems associated with making sense out of correlations between personality traits and performance scores, there is the major problem that the content validity of "nonintellective" measures is often low and they are often situation specific. Thus, whereas it is appropriate to challenge the reliability and validity of tests of intelligence and specific ability for older persons, one must approach tests of personality and motivation with equal, if not greater, skepticism.

SCORING PROCEDURES

Strictly speaking, if an investigator wishes to examine patterns of change on the subtests of the WAIS with advancing age, the subtests should be given in a standardized order and the complete set should be given. Dramatic alterations in the sequence of tests or in scoring procedures utimately means that the investigator is not presenting the subject with a standardized version of the WAIS. As long as one keeps this important fact in mind, alterations in the order of tests, the number of tests given, and scoring systems can provide useful information about effects of set, fatigue, and the sensitivity of scoring procedures to age differences. Data resulting from altered testing procedures do not challenge age-cohort differences reported for the WAIS. Rather, they represent "aging patterns" based on whatever new operational definitions of ability are introduced by the new procedures.

Altered methods of scoring were central to the debate over the importance of age-related decline in speed of response to intelligence test scores. In this context the bulk of the studies were designed as a challenge to the "decline hypothesis." Recently, Botwinick and Storandt (1974b) examined the opposite side of the coin. They questioned whether the stability in WAIS vocabulary subtest performance might not possibly reflect lack of age sensitivity in the standardized ("quantitative") scoring method, that is, 2, 1, or 0 point responses (good, poor, wrong). Consequently, they administered the verbal test but scored responses on a nine-point scale, ranging from superior synonyms to totally incorrect. Before they administered the test they matched their older and younger groups (mean ages = 18 and 71 years, respectively) on scores obtained using the standardized scoring procedure.

The older group obtained significantly lower mean scores than the younger group, mainly because they used fewer superior synonyms. The authors concluded that their study casts doubt on the widely held notion of the maintenance of vocabulary ability with increasing age, although they add an important qualification. It is impossible to state whether the findings are a result of maturational changes or generational factors (e.g., education) because the study was cross-sectional.

Essentially the same results were obtained in a second study in which subjects ranged in age from 20 to 79 years (Botwinick, West, and Storandt, 1975). The subjects in this study were divided into age-cohorts by decades, and age-associated trends for the standardized and qualitative scoring methods were compared. A slight increase in scores was seen up to 50 years of age and a decline after 60 years with the standardized scoring system. However, the differences among means were not statistically significant. With the "qualitative" (nine-point) scoring system, performance showed a decline between the ages of 20 and 30 years and an even greater decline after 60 years. These differences were statistically significant, and thus they provide additional support for the hypothesis that age differences are observed for some aspects of verbal ability and that more sensitive scoring techniques are successful in identifying this trend. Again, the reader should keep in mind that psychologists cannot speak of age changes in vocabulary skills because a cross-sectional data collection design was employed.

Another difficulty in interpreting the Botwinick, West, and Storandt (1975) data is introduced by the fact that the age by scoring system interaction was not statistically significant when the standard and qualitative scores were analyzed together. Thus, from a conservative viewpoint, the curves describing the results for the standard and the qualitative scoring systems must be considered as parallel to each other. However, the trends shown by the curves for the two measures were similar to those obtained in the first study, in which age-associated decrements in vocabulary performance were observed for the qualitative scoring system. Further studies seem necessary before psychologists can determine whether more sensitive scoring techniques will reveal decrements on the vocabulary subtest of the WAIS with advancing age, and if so, whether these trends are observed with cross-sectional designs because of educational differences among cohorts or other factors influencing performance of persons born at different times.

MODE OF ADMINISTRATION

The effects of the way in which tests are administered are considered in some detail in Chapter 6. One study is particularly worth mentioning here because of its practical implications in terms of research methodology. As technological sophistication increases, computers are becoming increasingly popular as a means of stimulus presentation. They allow the investigator to manipulate the rate at which stimuli are presented and automatically record responses in terms of latency and errors. In some instances "on-line" facilities permit data to be reduced and analyzed as they are being collected.

White and Johnson (1975) report some interesting data with regard to the effects of computer as opposed to noncomputer test presentation on the performance of younger and older adults. Subjects were given a group test (the Wonderlic Personnel Test), which is widely utilized for employment counseling and screening of applicants. Two studies were done but with slightly different age ranges for young and old groups: young (18 to 26 years) and old (60 to 90 years); young (18 to 24 years) and old (60 to 86 years). Under one experimental condition, form A of the test was administered with the standardized paper-and-pencil format. In another condition, form F was adapted for computer presentation. Education levels were high for both groups, and both conditions of stimulus presentation allowed unlimited time to respond.

Results were essentially the same for both experiments. There were no significant differences between the two age groups for the standard paper-and-pencil presentation procedure, but the older subjects were inferior to the younger subjects with regard to computer test performance.

The authors of this study point to the interesting possibility that differences in familiarity with computer testing procedures may explain the differences between the two age groups when the computer was used. This is a plausible explanation, since older adults tend to have less experience with computer terminal testing. However, the investigators did not report the level of computer experience for their subjects. It would be interesting to repeat the study with young and old subjects who are computer familiar and noncomputer familiar and, in so doing, to examine the effect of familiarity.

The computer testing as opposed to standard testing study was stimulated by a previous investigation (Johnson and Mihal, 1973), in which no differences were obtained between the performance of blacks and whites on a computer-administered paper-and-pencil test of intelligence, although differences were found with standard test procedures. It seems important to extend the Johnson-Mihal study so that it includes different age groups. Comparisons of persons with different ethnic backgrounds and technical as opposed to nontechnical backgrounds would be particularly interesting. The increasing use of computers in instruction and testing provides a practical stimulus for other studies dealing with age-cohort differences in computer-administered test performance.

DATA COLLECTION STRATEGIES

One of the most persistent arguments regarding the decline or nondecline of intellectual ability centers on the issue of whether decline for healthy persons might not be an artifact of cross-sectional data collection. We have already discussed the fact that the WAIS data and many factor analytic studies which suggest decline in fluid intelligence with increasing age are based on cross-sectional comparisons.

Confounding of maturational and generational effects has been a long-standing criticism of cross-sectional data collection strategies. Schaie and his associates have provided much of the data that support the validity of this criticism (e.g., Schaie et al., 1973). Schaie and his associates compared cross-

Fig. 5-5. Jack Botwinick, Ph.D. (New York University, 1953). Dr. Botwinick is Director of the Aging Program and Professor of Psychology at Washington University, St. Louis. He has contributed significantly to the "experimental psychology of aging" in terms of research and teaching. He is best known for his research in cognitive processes and intelligence, but he has published research articles on many areas of psychology and aging. He has been honored frequently and is a Fellow of the American Psychological Association and the Gerontological Society. He has served psychology well in many professional capacities.

sectional and longitudinal analyses for the same subjects and found that age effects were greater for the former than for the latter design. Based on these data and other studies which support this finding, they suggest that there is little or no decline with age in the intellective performance of healthy persons. This conclusion is reported in a recent article (Baltes and Schaie, 1974), entitled "Aging and IQ: myth of the twilight years." The general thesis is highly attractive to those individuals who wish to maintain their intellectual prowess well into old age.

Botwinick (1975) has provided an analysis of the basic data that support the "nondecline hypothesis." He points out that Schaie and his colleagues (1973) reported three important findings with the Primary Mental Abilities Test (PMA) and notes that these three points have not been adequately emphasized. First, longitudinal data collection occurred at three time periods that were seven years apart; thus the age span was fourteen years. In contrast, several age groups, the youngest in their twenties and the oldest in their sixties or seventies, were used in the cross-sectional analysis; thus the period covered in the cross-sectional analysis was forty to fifty years. Botwinick argues that one would expect greater age-associated differences for the cross-sectional than the longitudinal design because of the wider range of ages.

Second, Schaie and his associates (1973) obtained evidence for a longitudinal age decrement in PMA scores after about 50 years of age. Botwinick argues that to minimize the decrement after 50 years of age, or to ignore it, is to discard important information.

Third, and the most important point made by Botwinick (1975:10), is the fact that *just as cross-sectional analyses may unduly emphasize age deficit, longitudinal studies may unduly minimize age deficit.*

In just about all longitudinal studies that are carried out over several years, there is a biased subject attrition, especially in the upper age brackets. Those scoring poorly at test-time 1 tend to drop out, leaving mainly the intellectually superior subjects for subsequent retest. Such a biased dropout was seen in the data of Schaie et al. (1973). In fact, the bias was so severe with one of the PMA tests (Word Fluency) that an original age decrement at test-time 1 was seen as an age increment during the same period of time when only the data analyzed were of subjects who were tested three times over the longitudinal course of 14 years.

To Botwinick's comments on the influence of subject attrition in longitudinal designs, we would add a second point. Not only does subject attrition bias the sample toward superior adults but the sample becomes smaller than that which entered into data collection at the beginning of the study. Thus the sample is less representative, and in some cases the number of dependent variables (performance measures) becomes larger than the number of subjects in the experiment. The latter problem is most likely to occur when many investigators are collecting data for the same longitudinal study and the study is carried on into very old age. The existence of fewer subjects than variables is a factor that seriously compromises the validity of statistical analyses, although the problem is often overlooked.

The important point to remember is that neither the cross-sectional nor the longitudinal design is without methodological difficulties. One must use the strategy that makes the most sense in terms of the applications of the resulting data. The cross-sectional design may be the design of choice if one wishes to apply data to the development of educational curricula for today's older person who coexists with today's youth. It is not the design of choice if one wishes to make assumptions concerning age changes over time.

Botwinick's points with regard to the limitations of the longitudinal design are well taken and suggest that psychologists should not be too hasty to accept a notion of nondecline no matter how appealing it may be. On the other hand, Schaie, Baltes, Labovie and their colleagues have challenged traditional notions of decline and, in so doing, have forced a close examination of the nature of the methodological factors that limit psychologists in terms of their ability to gain a true picture of intellectual change with advancing age. Perhaps what is more important than the issue of decline as opposed to no decline is that psychologists (1) understand more fully the factors that contribute to decline (e.g., methodological artifact, poor health, diffuse organic damage, nonsupportive environment); and (2) begin to examine more closely the specific cognitive abilities which remain stable (or improve) and those which decline during various segments of the life span.

SUMMARY

There is some disagreement as to whether or not intelligence declines, remains stable, or improves with age. There are conflicting findings with regard to the patterns of change on tests of specific ability. These disagreements arise because psychologists are forced to make inferences about intelligence from samples of behavior called tests. These samples of behavior may be modified or influenced by a variety of factors that are not directly related to intellectual capacity per se, such as level of education, occupation, test content, methods of scoring, health status (physical and mental), personality factors, practice, learning orientation (motivation), caution, and data collection strategies.

In a broad sense persons with higher educational attainment and higher levels of "occupational status" tend to perform better on tests of general intelligence and, barring disease and disability, tend to sustain relatively high levels of general intelligence across the life span. This may be related to the fact that highly educated persons remain mentally active and are thus familiar with the kind of content that is presented on tests. On the other hand, initial levels of capacity do determine, to some extent, the highest levels of education and occupation that can be obtained. For this reason, level of education and occupational status are sometimes used to estimate levels of initial ability when test data are missing for earlier and later years. This practice can lead to an underestimation of initial ability because all persons in American society do not achieve the levels of education or occupation that are consistent with their intellectual ability. This practice may also underestimate later ability because some occupations do not involve the repeated use of the kinds of scholastic abilities that are measured on standardized tests of intelligence. Nevertheless, studies in which the same test materials have been used in young and old age do suggest that persons with initially higher levels of ability exhibit less age-related loss than those with lower initial levels of ability. Here again, however, this phenomenon may be related in no small part to disuse of scholastic skills by those of lower educational attainment or persons who go into occupations that place minimal demands on scholastic types of activities.

By manipulating test content one may demonstrate that general intelligence (1) does not decline, (2) remains stable, or (3) shows a steady rise through the adult years. Whether one accepts the results of a study with a particular type of content as representative of general intellectual ability depends on one's operational definitions of intelligence. Many tests that show a rise in performance with increasing age are characterized by test items that are indigenous to the everyday lives of older persons. Generally, these materials place considerable emphasis on what may be termed *crystallized intelligence.* Conversely, tests that show decline place demands on abilities such as those subsumed under the concept of *fluid intelligence.* Tests that contain a balance of items that tap both crystallized and fluid intelligence show generally stable patterns of performance up to 70 years of age for healthy persons. The fact that different trends in intellectual functioning can be demonstrated by manipulating test content does not demonstrate that intelligence does or does not decline with increasing age. Rather, it emphasizes how important one's operational definition of intelligence is in terms of interpretation of test data.

Methods of scoring influence patterns of age change and age differences on tests of intelligence. Generally, elderly persons do not do as well as middle-aged and younger adults on tests that emphasize rapid responding under time limits. Removal of time limits often brings the performance of older and younger persons closer together, although equal levels of performance are seldom achieved.

Scoring of vocabulary measures seems to influence age trends. Whereas standardized scoring techniques reveal rather stable vocabulary subtest scores (WAIS) up to 70 years, more stringent scoring techniques reveal age differences. Again, these studies of vocabulary skills demonstrate that the operational definition of intelligence, which is modified by scoring procedure, is particularly important to the age pattern obtained.

Some psychologists argue that speed is not an important dimension of intellectual performance, and thus tests with an emphasis on speed are not fair to elderly persons. One cannot really refute this argument because it is based on the acceptance of an operational definition of intelligence that emphasizes the importance of power. However, it has been noted that older and younger persons who do most poorly on tests involving speed also do more poorly on tests emphasizing power.

The question has been raised as to whether reaction time for elderly persons represents a "limiting" performance factor on tests involving motor response. In general, the small but significant decreases in reaction time with advancing age do not seem to account for rather large decrements that are observed on tests that demand problem solving under time constraints. Thus some investigators argue that elderly adults respond more slowly because they think more slowly. Obviously, it is difficult to resolve the question concerning whether the limiting factor in test performance with advancing age is *throughput* (thinking) or *output* (responding) because researchers must make inferences from a behavioral end point. Clearly, speed of motor response remains a potentially important limiting factor with regard to test performance for elderly persons who move and react slowly because of disability and poor health.

It is not surprising to find that practice improves response times for older persons, but improved speed of response does not appear to transfer to timed tasks which are demanding of intellectual ability and perceptual-integrative skills. Possibly this is related to the fact that practice has not been maintained for sufficiently long periods of time, but it is also possible that speed is far less important to intellectual and perceptual integrative abilities than are *throughput* processes.

Improvement in test scores with practice or manipulation of environmental variables, for example, mode of test presentation or reinforcement, is sometimes cited as evidence for the greater importance of environmental factors than neurophysiological factors. In general, these studies do support the importance of environmental supports for sustained performance well into old age, but they do not offer convincing evidence that neurophysiological factors do not play a very important role in intellectual functioning across the life span. Environmental supports may compensate for decline related to neurophysiological factors. This does not denigrate the importance of the latter. Moreover, environmental factors may have positive feedback effects on neurophysiological factors within defined limits.

The extent to which so-called "normal" changes in the brain with advancing age play a role in intellectual functioning is questionable and subject to further research. Certainly, any change in physiology must influence behavior, but practice and redundancy in neural mechanisms may serve to sustain high levels of intellectual performance in the healthy person. Clearly, diseases affecting the brain, heart, and other important parts of the nervous system do result in decreased efficiency of test performance and may directly influence intellectual capacity by way of brain damage or impaired oxygenation of the brain. Mental health factors (e.g., depression or psychosis) have a profound effect on test performance. Thus it is important to assess the life situation of individuals in different age-cohorts when evaluations of mental status are performed.

In a broad sense, personality variables influence performance on tests of ability, but psychologists should be extremely cautious about labeling persons as rigid or even dogmatic. Most likely these are situation-specific traits that can be brought out in testing situations. Older persons tend to be more cautious, and in some cases they behave in a more rigid manner, than younger persons. There is also evidence that rigidity and poor performance are correlated at every age. The question remains as to whether increased rigidity causes poor performance or is the result of poor performance. Rigidity and/or caution may serve to compensate for decreased competency. Alternatively, caution and rigidity may cause decreased performance efficiency, particularly for tests placing demands on rapid decision making and versatility. Dogmatism appears to be a more general phenomenon than rigidity. It has been argued that dogmatism leads to rigidity, but the reverse is not true. Some tests of dogmatism show a rather dramatic increase in scores with advancing age, but psychologists still do not know to what extent correlations between dogmatism and impaired problem-solving ability are the result of a causal relationship between these variables. Basically, personality and "response-style" variables influence patterns of change with advancing age, but causal relationships between performance and these variables are difficult to demonstrate. One reason for this is that intellectual performance, personality traits, and response style are really all part of one's personality. Psychologists artificially separate these dimensions to study them. They all determine whether adjustment will be successful or unsuccessful at any age.

Learning orientation influences test performance. Those who are used to being in learning, and hence testing, situations may perform better than those who are not. Many older persons have not been in school for many years and thus believe that they will perform inadequately on tests. Others perform inadequately because they have not used test-taking skills for many years and they have not practiced relevant scholastic skills. Decreased "learning" orientation may lead to test anxiety.

Test anxiety is not conducive to maximal levels of performance at any age. It does not appear that older persons are more or less anxious than younger persons in a general sense. However, older persons may be more susceptible to test-induced anxiety. This issue is not yet resolved.

Conclusions regarding improvement, decline, or stability are influenced by experimental designs. Longitudinal studies may *underestimate* age-related deficits in mental ability because of subject attrition and sampling factors, which bias samples toward more intelligent participants at the upper age levels. Cross-sectional studies often *overestimate* intellectual decline because they are based on comparisons of persons born at different points of time, and different age-cohorts do not always have the same opportunities to develop this potential fully. Moreover, modifiers of intelligence may be present to a greater or lesser degree for different age-cohorts.

In Chapter 12 it will be seen that longitudinal biases can be partially eliminated by studying only those persons who survive at several different points in time. However, changes in intellectual behavior over time for surviving persons are not simply due to intellectual factors but are influenced by an ever-changing environment created by the interaction of individuals with their culture.

If nothing else, we now know how highly complex the question of intellectual capacity at different ages really is. Thus it is wise to be skeptical about such statements as: "Psychologists have shown that intelligence (does) does not decline with age." It is obvious that this statement has to be qualified in many ways. Psychologists need to ask: Under what circumstances and by what definition of intelligence?

SELECTED READINGS

Abrahams, J. P. Health status as a variable in aging research. *Experimental Aging Research,* 1976, **2,** 63-71.

Baltes, P. B., and Labouvie, G. V. Adult development of intellectual performance: description, explanation, modification. In C. Eisdorfer and P. Lawton (Eds.), *APA task force on aging.* Washington, D. C.: American Psychological Association, 1972.

Bennett, E. L., Diamond, M., Krech, D., and Rosenzweig, M. R. Chemical and anatomical plasticity of the brain. *Science,* 1964, **146,** 610-619.

Birren, J. E., and Morrison, D. F. Analysis of the WAIS subtests in relation to age and education. *Journal of Gerontology,* 1961, **16,** 363-369.

Botwinick, J., West, R., and Storandt, M. Qualitative vocabulary test responses and age. *Journal of Gerontology,* 1975, **30,** 574-577.

Chown, S. M. Age and the rigidities. *Journal of Gerontology,* 1961, **16,** 353-362.

Demming, J. A., and Pressey, S. L. Tests "indigenous" to adult and older years. *Journal of Counseling Psychology,* 1957, **2,** 144-148.

Doppelt, J. E., and Wallace, W. L. Standardization of the Wechsler Adult Intelligence Scale for older persons. *Journal of Abnormal and Social Psychology,* 1955, **51,** 312-320.

Edwards, A. E., and Wine, D. B. Personality changes with age: their dependency on concomitant intellectual decline. *Journal of Gerontology,* 1963, **2,** 182-184.

Fisher, J. Competence, effectiveness, intellectual functioning, and aging. *Gerontologist,* 1973, **13,** 61-68.

Foulds, G. A. Variations in the intellectual activities of adults. *American Journal of Psychology,* 1949, **62,** 238-246.

Kamin, L. J. Differential changes in mental abilities in old age. *Journal of Gerontology,* 1957, **12,** 66-70.

Kuhlen, R. G. Age and intelligence: the significance of cultural change in longitudinal vs. cross-sectional findings. *Vita Humana,* 1963, **6,** 113-124.

Lorge, I. The influence of test upon the nature of mental decline as a function of age. *Journal of Educational Psychology,* 1936, **27,** 100-110.

Miles, C. C. The influence of speed and age on intelligence scores of adults. *Journal of General Psychology,* 1934, **10,** 208-210.

Monge, R. H., and Gardner, E. F. Education as an aid to adaptation in the adult years. In K. F. Riegel and J. A. Meacham (Eds.), The developing individual in a changing world (Vol. II). *Social and environmental issues.* The Hague: Mouton & Co., Publishers, 1976.

Schaie, K. W. A reinterpretation of age related changes in cognitive structure and function. In L. R. Goulet and P. B. Baltes (Eds.), Life-span developmental psychology, New York: Academic Press, Inc., 1970.

Veronon, P. E. The variation of intelligence with occupation, age, and locality. *British Journal of Psychology,* 1947, **1,** 52-63.

CHAPTER 6

MOTIVATION—DRIVE, GENERAL ACTIVITY, AND INCENTIVE

Motivation makes one demand
The things in life
One needs at hand
MARTHA J. NEWTON

Changes in motivation and activity through the adult years have been research topics of considerable interest to students of aging and human development. There appears to be no succinct generalization with regard to changes in motivation across the adult years because motivation is a very general concept that includes many complex processes. Clearly, discussions of changes in motivation must include references to other related processes such as learning and test performance.

A number of major advances have been made in the identification of age-related motivational differences that affect learning, cognition, and social interaction. To this end, both descriptive and experimental designs have been employed. Although both human and animal subjects have been used in investigations of motivational change, these studies have not focused on analogous motivational states. Animal studies have been primarily concerned with the basic needs for food and water or escape from pain (Elias and Elias, in press), whereas human studies have been concerned with complex social needs. As yet, no major theories of motivational change across the life span have been entirely successful in explaining the data that presently exist. Furthermore, little is known with regard to the underlying physiological mechanisms involved in age-related motivational change.

Perhaps the most difficult task faced when one attempts to arrive at generalizations regarding aging and motivation is deciding on an appropriate definition of motivation. One reason that much of the literature is contradictory and lacking in integration is that different investigators have offered very different definitions of motivation based on their own intuitive biases. Consequently, many of the same terms and constructs take on different meanings in the literature that are dependent on a specific investigator's theoretical notions. For example, the concept of *drive* is frequently used to describe the extent of a person's motivation to engage in an experimental laboratory task. For the investigator doing research based on traditional Hull-Spence theories of learning, drive refers to an intervening variable that generally activates behavior. It cannot be measured directly, although it can be assessed by duration of deprivation (e.g., hours of food deprivation) and the intensity of the behavior that it produces. In contrast, a Freudian psychoanalyst's concept of drive is based on his ideas about instinctual energies that, in turn, arise from bodily needs. Thus there are similarities and dissimilarities with regard to drive as defined in a Hull-Spence context and drive as interpreted from a Freudian psychoanalytical view. Psychologists who subscribe to Lewin's "topological psychology" view drive as a tension state that arises from needs unique to each individual. Finally, a Skinnerian researcher refers to drive as a hypothetical state that is not necessary for a full and valid explanation of changes in specific behaviors.

Although many similarities and differences may be noted in these definitions, each dictates a slightly different experimental approach. Thus it is often difficult to discuss the concept of drive with regard to age-related motivational changes. The same difficulty is inherent in attempts to focus on many of the other terms used in describing motivational processes (e.g., *need, goal*).

For the purposes of this chapter, *motivation* is defined as a general term that includes more specific terms such as *drive, incentive,* and *need.* Fig. 6-1 summarizes the relationships among these specific terms. Drive will refer to a hypothetical state that "pushes" or "activates" behavior. Because it is a purely hypothetical state, it cannot be directly manipulated or measured. Drive is the result of psychogenic or biogenic needs that are brought about by either internal or external stimulation. These needs can be manipulated by the experimenter. For example, food deprivation results in a biological need that produces a "hunger drive." The first consequence of any type of drive is a heightened state of arousal, which is frequently accompanied by an increase in general activity. As shall be seen later, arousal can sometimes be directly manipulated through procedures such as the administration of certain types of drugs. A general increase in arousal and activity is usually accompanied by an increase in specific behaviors directed toward the attainment of a specific goal. *Incentives* act to direct behavior toward *specific goals.* Many incentives are learned; that is, they are products of past interactions of the individual with his environment. For example, it is learned very early in life that proximity to the mother (incentive) by way of specific behaviors involved in crawling results in satisfaction of a psychogenic need for security and a biogenic need for food. Later in life a person may learn that money (incentive) results from working longer hours (specific behavior), which results in higher status (psychogenic need) and food for the table (biogenic need). Thus incentives are tied to specific behaviors because a specific relationship between the incentive and the behavior has been learned.

Incentives may be intrinsically tied to be-

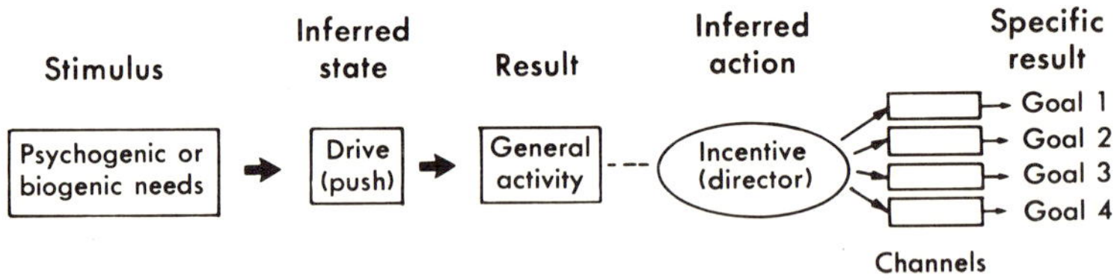

Fig. 6-1. The authors' "push" and direction notion of motivation. The push notion of drive is strongly influenced by Spence's (1958) concept of drive. The concept of incentive is not the same as that of Spence. Incentive, as defined here, directs responses to specific goals. Incentive stimuli gain incentive value by way of past reinforcement history or by virtue of the fact that they evoke reflexive responses in some instances, for example, withdrawal of the hand from shock. The broken line between general activity and incentive (director) indicates that the latter does *not* necessarily follow the former. If no incentive is available, the specific behavior necessary for goal achievement will not be performed. (From Elias, M. F., and Elias, P. K. Motivation and activity. In J. E. Birren and K. W. Schaie [Eds.], *Handbook of the psychology of aging.* New York: Littore Educational Publishing, Inc. Reproduced by permission of Van Nostrand-Reinhold Co., 1976.)

havior on a more elementary level. For example, shock (incentive) results in a withdrawal response (specific behavior) and consequent escape from pain (satisfaction of a biogenic need). Often these relationships are reflexive, but they can be learned as well. Because of their external or tangible nature, incentives can be manipulated by laboratory investigators, and any observable behavior that they direct can be measured. It is an easy matter to vary the strength of shock in an avoidance learning task or to increase the amount of money provided for a perfect performance on a laboratory task.

The final end point of the chain of events involving drive and incentive is *goal achievement.* A goal is the tangible outcome that results in satisfaction of a need (e.g., status, food). In some cases it is difficult to distinguish between incentives and goals. Often incentives constitute intermediate goals, and sometimes these goals become so important that they become final goals in themselves. Many investigators have attempted to determine whether or not specific goals change with age or whether or not persons are more or less successful in achieving goals as they approach old age.

You may not agree completely with the definitions of drives, incentives, and goals provided in this chapter, but it should be helpful to know how we define these terms. It is easily seen that these terms are difficult to define, and many investigators disagree concerning their definition.

We mentioned earlier that both animal and human research studies in motivation have been done. For the most part, animal studies have focused on basic and primary needs, such as hunger and thirst. Human research has been more concerned with complex motivational processes, such as those related to personal relationships, work, satisfaction, leisure, and retirement. A few investigations have been focused on analogous animal and human motivational processes such as the effects of stress and changes in general activity levels for different age groups. Our discussion of aging and motivation concentrates primarily on human motivational processes, but animal studies of importance to the understanding of motivational changes across all species are discussed.

CHANGES IN BASIC NEEDS

Hunger

It is easy to understand why studies concerned with hunger-induced drive have used animal subjects. It is not ethical or morally proper to manipulate hunger drive in humans to the extent that it has been manipulated in animals, although many would point out that in some instances it seems to be particularly cruel to starve animals. One must decide this issue on the basis of one's individual beliefs regarding the merit of scientific findings for human welfare as opposed to the risks to animal subjects.

Generally, hunger drive is produced by food deprivation for a period of time prior to testing or until the animal dies (terminal food deprivation). Hunger drive is associated with a specific goal, food, but it also has a diffuse and generalized effect on activity level.

Studies summarized by Botwinick (1959) and Elias and Elias (in press) suggest that deprivation in excess of a single day produces unequal motivational strength (drive for food) in different age groups. A study by Jakubczak (1967) sheds considerable light on why this may be true.

Five age groups of albino rats (2, 3, 6, 11, and 26 months) were observed for the effects of food deprivation on (1) maximum levels of running activity, (2) number of days required to reach maximum levels of activity, and (3) the increase in activity each day to maximum activity. The 2- and 3-month-old groups had significantly greater scores for each of these performance measures than did the 6-, 11-, and 26-month-old groups. The two youngest age groups also lost relative body weight at a significantly greater rate and survived for a significantly shorter time than did the older group. However, there were no age differences in the percentage body weight loss at death (approximately 43%). Moreover, maximum activity for all age groups occurred with approximately equal values of percent weight loss. It would appear that energy stores deplete much more rapidly in the younger animal following a given number of days of deprivation. This makes sense if one considers the fact that metabolic rate per unit of body weight decreases between 2 and 6 months of age in rats (Kleiber et al., 1956). These findings have important implications for animal research on motivational processes across the life span because they indicate that *hunger motivation is largely a function of relative weight loss rather than a given period of deprivation.*

An analogous situation probably exists for humans. Energy stores are utilized for three types of metabolic activity (growth, basal metabolism, and physical activity). After the adult years are reached, energy stores are needed for only two types of activity: basal metabolism and physical activity. Therefore the amount of necessary caloric intake in relation to body weight drops substantially and continues to drop gradually throughout the adult life span (Timiras, 1972:218). Consequently, it might be expected that food deprivation would result in more rapid weight loss and greater hunger-induced drive during pubescence and young adulthood than later in adulthood.

Activity level does indeed play an important role in the degree of motivation induced by given hunger states. Age differences may also affect the rate at which bodily energy stores are utilized and thus influence hunger motivation. This finding has important implications for studies that use general measures of activity as a behavioral index of deprivation-induced drive.

Jakubczak (1969) found that age differences in wheel-running activity in response to food deprivation contribute to age-related differences in weight loss for the rat. Male albino rats of 2.2, 3.5, and 6.2 months of age were confined in the living compartment of a wheel-running apparatus or permitted free access to an activity drum. A 2-month-old group given free access to the activity wheel differed significantly from the two older groups in the direction of increased activity. This active 2-month-old group also exhibited greater weight loss per day compared with the confined 2-month-old group. They also took significantly fewer days to lose 35% of their predeprivation weight. However, when comparisons were made for confined and nonconfined animals in the older groups, no weight differences were observed.

The important implication of Jakubczak's findings is that *wheel-running activity may itself increase drive by depleting energy stores at a higher rate than would normally be the case* if the animal were confined to the home cage. Moreover, it would seem that utilization of change in activity resulting from a given amount of food deprivation as an index of age differences in drive level is a practice which could actually lead to an overestimation of age differences in drive level when young and old animals are compared.

A similar relationship may hold for humans, but it is more difficult to establish a relationship between activity level and drive level in terms of energy stores because activity in humans may be related to a greater extent to psychogenic needs than to biogenic needs. The evidence for a decrease in general activity level for humans is reviewed in Chapter 7. Generally, a decline in activity occurs for some persons but not for others, depending on a myriad of factors such as attitudes, health, and physical and social opportunities. One study suggests that active older persons are more psychologically and socially motivated and may live longer than less active older persons (Bartko et al., 1971). However, further studies are needed to confirm this generalization.

A digression concerning comparisons between animals and humans is appropriate at this point. It is extremely important that a laboratory researcher, who is utilizing an animal model to investigate aging, be aware of the biological age of his subjects. One strain of rats at 6 months of age may not be the same distance from death as another strain at 6 months, and thus the portion of life span lived for the two strains is not the same. Biological age depends on the average life span of a particular strain, which is partially related to the susceptibilities of that strain (or stock) to various diseases that are correlated with aging. Inbred strains differ from each other in terms of genotype, but within inbred strains, for all practical purposes, animals are genetically alike. For humans who are not the product of brother-sister matings or parent-offspring matings, which characterize inbred strains of mice, the gene pool is homozygous. Nevertheless, the question of what proportion of the life span has been lived is no less important. An individual who is 50 years old and will live another ten years may be psychologically, socially, and biologically different from one who is 50 years old and will live another twenty years. Activity level and motivation may provide a useful index of "functional age." However, one must always examine the lifelong activity pattern of an individual before making generalizations about decrease in activity level in the later years.

Thirst

In many respects the literature on thirst-induced drive is similar to that for hunger-induced drive. Most of the work has been done with laboratory animals. For water deprivation as for food deprivation, weight loss appears to be a more precise index of drive state (Campbell and Cicala, 1962; Elias and Elias, in press; Jakubczak, 1970).

It is important to note that relatively few studies have been concerned with the underlying mechanisms of hunger and thirst. Studies have mainly concentrated on (1) characterization of the relationship between hunger or thirst and behavior and (2) appropriate operational definitions of hunger and thirst motivation. These more basic questions had to be answered before more detailed studies could be designed to explore the physiological basis of hunger/thirst and behavior relationships.

Sex

Sexual activity is unnecessary for the survival of an individual. It is essential for survival of a species. Thus it is not considered a basic need in the sense that one dies without it. It is a biogenic need and a psychogenic need only to the extent that it is necessary for survival of the species. Moreover, the sexual activity of the aged organism is not a primary issue for species survival, since the childbearing years are *usually* over by middle adulthood. However, since sexual interest and needs are often maintained well into late middle age and frequently into old age (Verwoerdt et al., 1969b), it may be assumed that psychogenic sexual needs are an important aspect of developmental change throughout the life span.

The human literature on sexual activity and aging suggests that many changes are related to psychogenic rather than biogenic needs. The same may be true for some other species, although little research has been directed to this issue. Despite the increasing recognition of the role of social factors in the change of sexual activities of humans with advancing age, one must consider the effects of sex hormones on sexual drive and sexual behaviors. Infrahuman animals have provided a convenient model for the study of hormonal changes as they relate to sexual activity.

Behavioral manifestations of sexual activity involved in mating consist of a number of partially independent components; for example, frequency of mounts, intromissions, frequency and latency of ejaculations, and intercopulatory and postejaculatory intervals. These components are organized into temporal and spatial patterns that are characteristic of a given sex and species. The rate of decline varies with age for these different components. For example, in the male albino rat the number of ejaculates per unit time exhibits an increase from puberty to the first year, a gradual decrease during the second year, and a rapid decline in the third year. On the other hand, the intercopulatory and postejaculatory intervals decrease from puberty to adulthood but actually show an increase in aged rats (Larsson, 1956; Larsson and Esslerg, 1962).

Much of the animal research directed toward an understanding of the factors affecting a reduction in sexual activities with advancing age for infrahuman mammals has concentrated on the identification of the physiological bases for decline. For males, sexual activity and mating are under control of the testes, and onset of mating behavior at puberty is correlated with maximal androgen secretion of the testes. It is also well known that androgens of adrenal origin influence sexual behavior of females as well as males (Tepperman, 1973). Indirect evidence for the role of androgens in declining sexual activity in old age has been provided by the observation that a decrease in the production of androgen also occurs with increasing age (Young, 1961). The androgen-deficiency hypothesis has been supported by findings of increased sexual activity in response to injections of testosterone and anteron, a pituitary-like hormone produced from pregnant mares' serum (Minnick et al., 1946).

Androgen deficiencies also produce changes in the accessory sex glands, which may be related to decreased sexual activities. However, androgen deficiencies with increasing age affect a wide range of biological systems other than those involved in reproductive behavior (Timiras and Meisami, 1972). Moreover, despite the important role of androgens in reproductive activity, there are age-associated changes in accessory sex glands that are not necessarily related to decreases in androgen levels.

Neither androgen deficiency nor aging of the accessory sex glands is a necessary condition for a decrease of all types of sexual activity. Jakubczak (1964) found that older (30 months) guinea pigs performed as well as younger (6 months) guinea pigs in terms of nuzzling, abortive mounting, and successful mounting. However, older males exhibited lower intromission and ejaculation scores. Large doses of exogenous testosterone for 4 weeks failed to increase these activities. Jakubczak concluded that old and young animals were equally sexually aroused and that decreased mating behaviors were related to factors other than lowered levels of androgen. Moreover, other studies have indicated that age changes in mating behavior occur prior to demonstrable deficit in androgen. When animals reach an age where androgen deficit is observed, the level of mating behavior decreases further.

The important question in a life-span developmental context is the nature of the hormonal events prior to androgen deficiency that are related to decreased copulatory behavior. There is a good deal of evidence that age decrements in the mechanisms which mediate the temporal summation of excitatory neuronal impulses from the central nervous system, which lead to ejaculation, occur earlier in the life of the animal than do changes in androgen levels. Thus the decline in sexual activity that occurs in old age may have its origins in more subtle central nervous system changes that begin during the middle adult years.

Levels of the female sex hormone estrogen invariably exhibit a significant decrease at the time of menopause and continue to decline through the sixth decade of life (Eisdorfer and Raskind, 1975). It is clear that much more research needs to be done on the relationship between estrogen and sexual motivation and activity after menopause. Interesting research possibilities have been brought about by the use of oral contraceptives in a significant proportion of today's younger women, who will reach menopause with a "hormonal" history that is different from elderly women of today.

Although the role of changing androgen levels in human males of advanced age is presently unclear, it is well established that older men show a wide range of individual differences in the male sex hormone. Testosterone levels range from low levels, equal to those of women, to high levels, similar to those of young adult men (Eisdorfer and Raskind, 1975).

Recent studies suggest some interesting hypotheses with regard to the role of androgens in elderly persons. It is possible that social and psychological restrictions on sexual intercourse among aging persons may be a cause rather than a consequence of declining testosterone levels in men (Eisdorfer and Raskind, 1975). Testosterone levels may actually rise when coitus is resumed after a period of abstinence (Fox et al., 1972; Ismail and Harkness, 1967), but masturbation does not seem to effect changes in testosterone levels (Fox et al., 1972). It is possible that there is some truth in the old wives' tale that both social contact and coitus with young women renews the strength of elderly men (Comfort, 1956).

As far fetched as this possibility seems, evidence from animals a few steps down the phylogenetic scale from man is consistent with human studies on coitus and testosterone level. Male rhesus monkeys who were presented with a group of females displayed significant elevations in testosterone levels. These same males exhibited declining testosterone levels when they were subjected to submissive roles by other males (Rose et al., 1972).

Obviously, many more studies of the relationship between sexual activity and testosterone levels need to be done before final conclusions can be reached regarding the benefits of coitus. These studies do seem important in view of the rather dramatic changes in social contacts and relationships that must be tolerated by many elderly persons in American society. Hopefully, research over the next ten years will help investigators to understand better the interplay of social-psychological factors and hormones as they influence sexual activity and motivation.

Although much of the literature on sexual decline in humans deals with psychosocial factors, such as lack of privacy and reduced numbers of available sexual partners for aging women, there are a number of research findings indicating that changes in biological capabilities affect sexual behavior in elderly persons. Certainly the increased incidence of physical and psychological illnesses, for example, myocardial infarctions and depression, with increasing age place temporary or permanent restrictions on the amount of sexual behavior (Pfeiffer, 1974).

Men over 70 years of age appear to be capable of both sexual arousal and erection, although studies of the erection cycle during sleep indicate an inverse relationship between age and proportion of full erections (Kahn and Fisher, 1969). The existence of physical changes in the male pattern of sexual responses with advancing age has been well documented. Changes include increased time to arousal, erection, and ejaculation (Masters and Johnson, 1966).

Analogous changes take place in older women, for example, increased time to nipple erection and clitoral engorgement, although the capacity to reach orgasm does not appear to diminish, especially for women who have sources of regular sexual stimulation (Masters and Johnson, 1966). It is heartening to find that many researchers agree that healthy males and females are *capable* of sexual activity, including intercourse, well into the seventh decade and, not infrequently, the ninth decade.

Capabilities tell only part of the story. One must consider the interaction of sexual capabilities and sexual interests. This interaction may be influenced by psychological needs and complex social factors. Studies of sexual interest and activity among the elderly indicate that there is a decline in both. However, the range of sexual activity is probably just as great as the range for any other age group. Based on current research reports regarding sexuality in older adults, a number of generalizations may be advanced. First, frequency of sexual activity declines with advancing age for both sexes (Christenson and Gagon, 1965; Finkle et al., 1959), although the sharpest drop occurs earlier for women (late sixties) than for men (late seventies) (Verwoerdt et al., 1969b). Second, men maintain higher levels of interest and activity than women at all ages up to the ninth decade (Cameron and Biber, 1973; Newman and Nichols, 1960; Verwoerdt et al., 1969a,b). Third, aging men exhibit a relatively large discrepancy between expressed interest in sex, which tends to be sustained well into the eighties, and actual sexual performance. Women do not exhibit as large a discrepancy. Both interest and behavior tend to decline at approximately the same rate (Verwoerdt et al., 1969a,b). Fourth, marital status affects the frequency of sexual activity and interest for women but is of less significance for men (Verwoerdt et al., 1969a,b).

A few investigators have attempted to determine the factors that may account for the overall decrease in sexuality with advancing age. Generally, these factors differ for men and women. For men the determinants of sexual behavior appear to be highly complex. For example, between 45 and 69 years of age, present health status, past and present life satisfaction, and social class correlated positively with sexual functioning, whereas concern over physical well-being and taking of antihypertensive drugs correlate negatively with sexual functioning (Pfeiffer and Davis, 1972). For women the overwhelming determinant of sexual expression in the middle and later years is marital status. Although both single and married men report approximately the same levels of sexual interest and activity, single women report much lower levels of interest and activity than married women (Pfeiffer and Davis, 1972; Verwoerdt et al., 1969a,b). The fact that many elderly women are widowed or divorced may account for their extensive decrease in sexual behavior and interest. Pfeiffer and Davis (1972) note that the decline in sexual interest per se may be a result of a defensive reaction; that is, adaptation is to some extent dependent on the ability to inhibit sexual strivings when no socially sanctioned partners are available.

Perhaps the most significant finding in the current literature is that amounts of *past sexual activity and enjoyment are excellent predictors of sexual activity and enjoyment in old age* (Christenson and Gagon, 1965; Pfeiffer and Davis, 1972; Verwoerdt et al., 1969a,b). The critical implication of this finding is that those persons who failed to enjoy sex in their younger years, for whatever reason, may retreat into the myth of sexless old age (Berezin, 1969), thus taking advantage of the taboo against sexual behavior among the elderly. However, those who previously derived pleasure from sexual experiences may find the taboo a considerable hindrance.

Evidence for cohort differences in attitudes toward the taboo against sexual behavior has been gathered by Wood (1971). Wood performed a questionnaire study to determine whether older persons are less self-accepting of "unconventional" behaviors, such as remarriage of a 70-year-old widower in the face of objections from his children. Results indicated that they were less accepting of unconventional behavior in themselves than were young persons. The latter appeared to be better able to accept unconventional behavior in older persons. Furthermore, the elderly group perceived the young group as far less accepting than they actually were. Thus, although it may be possible to alleviate some of the problems associated with a decrease in sexual behavior among persons by providing incentives such as the opportunity for privacy, it is likely that the central problem is related to attitudes held by many elderly persons.

Social taboos against sexual interests and behavior in the elderly affect physicians and behavioral scientists as well as relatives of the elderly and the elderly themselves. Pfeiffer (1969) notes that many physicians believe that sex is a private matter and a potentially upsetting subject for their patients. This view may not be entirely unrealistic. Elderly patients belong to an age-cohort group that was reared in a tradition where these attitudes prevailed. It is thus not surprising that many elderly persons cannot engage in liberal sexual discussions and behavior.

Perhaps in some instances these attitudes

are adaptive. For example, the number of single women over 65 years of age far exceeds the number of men available as sexual partners. Many of these single women adopt an attitude of waning sexual interest. Although some solutions, such as polygamous marriages, have been advanced (Berezin, 1969), it appears more realistic to concentrate efforts on prolonging the life-span of older men (Pfeiffer and Davis, 1972) and on modifying attitudes toward sexual expression among elderly persons. Attitude modification may provide increased incentive for acting out sexual urges dictated by sex drive.

Finally, it should be noted that loss of sexual interest and decline of sexual behavior with advancing age are not isolated biological and psychological phenomena that can be reduced to simple questions of motivation and attitude. Rather, they are related to the whole life social-psychological situation. For example, Butler (1967) reported that many elderly persons are involved in deteriorating marriages, which may be the result of many factors including rejection, fear or anger concerning physical and mental changes in self and spouse, fear that sexual relations will bring on injury such as heart attacks or strokes, and resentment of the social admonition to "grow old gracefully." *All of these psychological factors represent a severe withdrawal of the personal incentives to engage in sexual relations. Attempts to restore incentives can only be accomplished on an individual basis, which includes a consideration of the aging person's entire life situation.* Investigations in this area may be most fruitfully done in the context of social theories of motivation that emphasize complex life forces and social value systems.

Exploratory behavior

Berlyne (1960) was one of the first researchers to emphasize the notion of curiosity and exploratory behavior as basic drives. Since that time, a great amount of research has been devoted to the investigation of variables affecting these behaviors.

Animal studies have focused on the open-field behavior of rats and mice, although other species such as the monkey have been studied. The open field consists of a large arena in which the animal may move about freely. Various techniques have been devised to measure activity, emotionality, and exploratory behavior in the open field. For many studies, valid measures of exploratory behavior have not been obtained because exploratory behavior is often inferred from locomotion scores (number of squares crossed in a given time). Locomotion may actually be *inversely* related to exploratory behavior under some circumstances, particularly those that elicit fear. This important finding was provided by Goodrick (1966) because he was able to obtain a measure of exploratory behavior that was to a great extent independent of activity level. Basically, the animal was free to enter and leave a darkened portion of the open field. Activities in the bright portion of the field should consist mainly of nonfear responses, since fear may be alleviated by entering the darkened and enclosed area.

Goodrick used two conditions of food intake. Some animals were food deprived and others were permitted food at any time (controls). For the control group, exploration was a decreasing function of increasing age. This phenomenon was largely related to the higher mean exploratory (sniffing in the bright portion of the field) scores and lower mean nonexploratory (lying and grooming) scores for the youngest animals (3 months) in comparison with the two older groups (11 and 24 months). No age-related differences were found between deprived animals of the three age groups for exploratory behavior or nonexploratory behavior. *The effect of food deprivation was to increase exploratory behavior across all age groups and to reduce the magnitude of differences among age groups.*

In a later experiment, again with male albino rats, Goodrick (1967) examined a wider range of young animals for comparison with old animals. Age groups were 1, 1.7, 2.4, 3.0, 12, and 24.3 months. Exploration was low at 1 month of age, increased to a maximum at 1.7 months, decreased at 2 months, and reached a level comparable with the 1-month level of activity at 3 months. The bright area of the field was explored more frequently by the 12- than by the 24-month-old rats. These findings suggest that *exploration does not drop to very low levels until old age*. Nonexploratory responses were inversely related to exploratory responses under all conditions. One important point made in this study is that, *even for young animals, levels of exploration may not always be constant across ages*. The drop in activity for the 2-month-old rats suggests that one should be careful in interpreting age differences which result from selection of only a few young groups for comparison with old groups.

Goodrick's studies of exploratory changes with age involved subjects from inbred strains of male albino rats. The generality of data drawn from a single inbred strain is limited because, genetically, all subjects in the sample represent a single "individual." Moreover, it has been shown that *genotype and age differences do interact* for exploratory behavior. This point is illustrated by a recent study comparing the open-field performance of two strains of mice, C57BL/6J and DBA/2J, of four age groups: 2.5, 6, 12, and 22 months of age (Elias, Elias, and Eleftheriou, 1975). The measure of exploratory behavior was the number of crossings from an illuminated area to a dark area and back. For the C57BL/6J mice there was a drop in exploratory behavior between 2.5 and 6 months of age and no age-related differences thereafter. In contrast, strain DBA/2J exhibited no differences in exploratory scores as a function of age. Consequently, the generalization that *exploratory behavior decreases with advancing age may apply only to specific strains and for specific periods of the life span.*

Goodrick (1971) investigated environmental test factors that influence exploratory behavior with increasing age: testing during the light or dark cycle (time of day or night): individual testing or testing in pairs: testing of gentled as opposed to nongentled animals. Subjects were albino male and female rats of six age groups: 1, 1.7, 2.4, 3, 12, and 24 months. The most important results of this study were as follows. Exploratory behavior was increased dramatically when testing was done in the dark cycle as opposed to the light cycle for adolescent rats (1.7 and 2.4 months), although there were no light/dark cycle effects for the older rats (12 and 24 months). Compared with individually tested controls, adolescent male rats (1.7 months of age) that were tested in pairs increased exploration scores. No differences between individuals and pairs were observed for older adolescent (2.4 months) and old males. These results are interpreted by Goodrick in terms of changing dominance-subordination behavior for the adolescent animals. Gentling (handling the animals prior to testing) did not result in changes of exploration scores relative to controls for older rats (12 and 24 months), but it increased the exploratory scores of adolescent rats (1.7 and 2.4 months). Goodrick concludes that these data are compatible with the hypothesis that general behavior rigidity was greater for old than young animals because of a failure of environmental manipulation to initiate changes in exploration in the older rats.

In an earlier study, Goodrick (1965) found that group as opposed to isolated housing, by itself, did not affect the decrease in exploratory behavior with age that was observed for individually tested rats which were subjected to isolation. Isolation *and* paired testing increased the exploration scores for 24-month-old rats and decreased the exploration scores for 3-month-old rats. Examination of dominance-submissive relationships indicated that the young group of isolated animals, paired during testing, evidenced a decrease in mean exploratory activity because of an increase in dominance-subordination behavior; that is, one member of the pair lay quietly while the other engaged in sniffing and other activities directed toward the submissive rat. Presumably, older rats, when subjected to isolated housing conditions and tested in pairs, showed an increase in exploration because they are less subject to the immediate formation of dominance-submissive hierarchies.

It seems clear that exploratory behavior is an exceedingly complex phenomenon, even for mice and rats. It is influenced by a variety of factors, including time of measurement, genotype, dominance-submissive hierarchies established by caging conditions, paired as opposed to nonpaired testing, sex, and the measure of exploration used.

Caution

It is difficult to find experimental analogs for exploration studies in humans, although one might look to studies of activity in nursing homes or other institutions that house groups of elderly persons. However, movements in the natural setting may be much more goal directed and determined by specific incentives rather than general exploratory drive.

One might draw a parallel between caution in human subjects and decreased tendency to explore on the part of animals. In a sense, caution reflects the tendency to withhold a specific response. There is by no means universal agreement that older persons are more cautious than younger persons (Davies, 1968), although many examples of cautious behavior on the part of older persons, particularly in unfamiliar situations, may be found in the literature on aging. For example, Craik (1965) and Rees and Botwinick (1971) found that older persons established more conservative criteria in reporting the presence or absence of faint auditory stimuli than did younger subjects. Older persons tended to avoid the risk involved in reporting the presence of a tone if they were uncertain: "The instructions to the old subjects to be more free and reckless often met with strong vocalized resistance." (Rees and Botwinick, 1971:135).

It is unreasonable to expect that all older persons are more cautious than all younger persons. One might expect that educational background and other factors leading to confidence and positive self-concepts would affect the extent to which an older person would display cautiousness behavior in a testing situation. A study by Kogan and Wallach (1961) provides evidence that a positive relationship exists between subjective feelings of "elderliness" and caution in decision making. Sixty-nine women (mean age = 69.3 years) were given a questionnaire designed to measure caution and several situational tests of cautiousness behavior. *Subjective age* and caution scores were significantly correlated ($r = .33$), although subjective age and chronological age were also significantly correlated ($r = .40$). Statistical adjustment of subjective age scores for chronological age reduced the correlation between subjective age and caution scores, but it remained significant ($r = .24$).

Taken at face value, these data appear to provide support for the notion that motivation, rather than underlying neurophysiological factors affecting attention and information-processing capacity, may be responsible for cautious behavior. However, it is difficult to determine the extent to which subjective feelings of elderliness were based on relatively accurate estimations of "functional" age as assessed by reliable internal criteria. Nevertheless, the Kogan and Wallach study is consistent with the notion that *indices of functional age, subjective and nonsubjective, may provide a more useful classificatory scheme for examining the relation of age and caution than that provided by chronological age, per se.* This also may be true for the study of the relationship between aging and changes in other behaviors.

Emotion

Emotions are related to motivation in a highly complex manner. Emotional behavior may result from the frustration of not being able to attain a goal when motivation to reach the goal is high. Emotion may also serve as a drive that energizes behavior, which is in turn directed to a goal by way of specific incentives. Because of the complexity of emotional responses, many researchers have attempted to identify their most basic elements by utilizing various animal models. In general, this is what is termed a *reductionistic* approach. The assumption is that by understanding the mechanisms of emotion as found in lower order animals, one may eventually progress to higher order animals with hypothesis for research and better insight into the way in which to study more complex mechanisms. The assumption that emotions in animals are less complex is based on the premise that they possess a less complex nervous system than a higher order animal such as the human being. Of course, animals are used as genetic models as well as models for a more elementary nervous system. In this context inbred strains are used as genetic units in studies designed to determine genotype by environment interactions.

Many animal researchers have been interested in the relationship between emotionality and open-field behavior. Werboff and Havlena (1962), for example, found a *decrease* in emotionality level (defecation, urination, rearing, crouching) with increasing age beyond 6 months but an *increase* from 3 to 6 months. Their data were based on repeated testing of the same animals. Thus their results may be explained in terms of adaptation to the testing situation. The increase in emotionality at 6 months of age may have been related to a stressful testing procedure that was introduced after animals reached 3 months. In general, it is difficult to draw conclusions regarding age changes in activity level from Werboff and Havlena's longitudinal data because subjects were exposed to a variety of experiences, such as water-maze learning between 3 and 6 months of age and attempts at mating at 12 months. A cross-sectional study may have produced different results. For example, Elias, Elias, and Eleftheriou (1975) found no age differences in emotionality between 2 and 24 months for either C57BL/6J or DBA/2J mice.

One of the difficulties in studying the relationship among emotionality, exploratory behavior, and locomotion, is that locomotion, per se, has been used to infer all three phenomena. Generally, decreased exploratory behavior is inferred from decreased locomotion and decreased locomotion is attributed to increased fear responses. However, in some strains of rats, separate measures of emotionality (defecation, crouching, urinating, rearing) and locomotor activity (quadrants entered in the open field) are positively related rather than inversely related (Broadhurst, 1961; Werboff, 1962), and in some cases they are unrelated. Thus, as Werboff (1962) and Goodrick (1966) suggest, it is important to have separate measures of each.

The primate has received relatively little attention in the context of motivation and aging, despite the fact that it provides an excellent model for curiosity, emotional behaviors, and sexual behavior in humans. This is true because of the primate's diversity of behavioral responses and the advanced level of social interaction relative to species lower on the phylogenetic scale. Studies by Bernstein and Mason (1962) illustrate the usefulness of the primate model and provide hypotheses for research with old and senile primates. They point out that, in the course of the ontological evolution of primates, emotional responses develop a degree of functional specificity and that the same environmental conditions may be expected to elicit different emotional patterns in different age groups because one set of environmental conditions which is highly adaptive for the mature animal is often maladaptive for the immature animal. In an examination of responses to fear stimuli and frustration (food out of reach) with male and female rhesus monkeys, aged 3, 7, 16, and 25 months, they found that, with increasing age, directed responses become tied to these stimuli and that the contrast between the characteristics of fear and frustration increased. Frustration in the 25-month-old animals was associated with response patterns indicative of a less mature level of emotional adaptation. These data raise the possibility that the "apparent" decrease in emotionality with increasing age for some strains of rats and mice does not reflect increased behavioral rigidity, but they indicate that general stress responses (defecation) are reduced relative to a diversity of learned responses specifically directed to particular objects. Bernstein and Mason's studies were not extended to elderly or senile primates. Such studies may be particularly important in view of the unproved suggestion by some theorists that the emotional and motivational behavior of the *senile* organism represents a retrogression to infantile, or less mature, developmental stages.

The emotional responsiveness of the primate and its relationship to complex social interactions and stimuli seems to be a potentially useful model for the relationship of emotionality and drive in the human. It is thus unfortunate that more in the way of a formal aging motivation literature does not exist for primates. In most instances, factors that serve to be important motivational variables in the natural or laboratory environment of rodents (for example, noxious stimulation, hunger- and thirst-induced drive, and general locomotor activity) tend to be relegated to a more basic level (Maslow, 1954) in the hierarchy of human needs. Although mice and rats do provide a rich source of genetic material and a short life span, motivational research with these species is more clearly relevant to primary human needs. It is important that these needs be met, since they are basic to survival, but they are probably relatively less important than complex social needs to well-fed humans who are above the poverty level.

Animal studies of age-related emotional change, including those few with primate subjects, have been concerned primarily with fear responses. Similarly, emotionality and aging research with humans has been largely restricted to negative emotions, although a few attempts have been made to explore a broader range of emotions.

For many years it was believed that older persons showed a general decline in their emotional responsivity. This view was supported by research from the Kansas City Study of Adult Life (Dean, 1962). Two hundred men and women were interviewed over a six-year period. The major findings were as follows: (1) Between 50 and 80 years of age there was a steady decline in feelings of irritation; (2) during the sixties there was an abrupt decline in feelings of anger; (3) feelings of boredom remained fairly constant between 50 and 80 years; and (4) feelings of loneliness increased after 80 years. Perhaps the most interesting finding was that the meaning of loneliness changed with increasing age. Specifically, middle-aged persons defined loneliness as an absence of interaction, whereas older persons defined it as an absence of activity.

A different approach to the study of emotionality and aging was used by Rosen and Neugarten (1960). These investigators administered the Thematic Apperception Test (TAT) to subjects aged 40 to 71 years. Each subject was presented with a series of TAT pictures and asked to make up a story about the character or characters depicted. Rosen and Neugarten found a consistent decline with age in the complexity, conflict, activity-energy level, and affective intensity of themes elicited by the TAT. This finding was interpreted in terms of a reduction in "drive level" and ego involvement with advancing age. However, Cameron (1971) has taken issue with the use of projective tests, such as the TAT, as measures of a generalized notion of affective energy. He interviewed younger (mean age = 30.1 years) and older (mean age = 75.8 years) subjects regarding their moods, intensity of affect, and kinds of cognitions. A series of direct questions were asked: for example, "If you were to characterize the last half hour, would you say that you were 'happy,' 'neutral,' or 'sad'?" Participants' responses indicated no age differences in frequency of thoughts with biological or affective content, although the older persons did not think about sex as often as younger persons. Furthermore, there were no apparent differences for quality of affect or intensity of affect for the two age groups. Based on these data, Cameron concluded that affectivity remains constant throughout life. Among other factors, differences in results for Rosen and Neugarten's study and for Cameron's study may be related to the fact that specific methodologies used, in part, influence the results and interpretations of data. It may well be that older persons find it difficult or less comfortable to respond to projective techniques and prefer a more direct approach.

At this point it seems premature to make any generalizations concerning age-related changes or age-cohort differences in emotionality. Both the animal and human research data present contradictory results. One of the most immediate concerns should be for increasing the numbers of investigations that compare the effects of different methodological approaches to the study of emotions during the adult years.

Locomotion

A number of investigators have been concerned with age-associated differences in open-field activity. Locomotor activity, per se, has been more reliably associated with age than have emotionality and exploratory behavior. To some extent, changes in locomotor activity reflect emotional and exploratory factors. Locomotor activity in the open field is measured by counting the number of squares entered or crossed on the grid floor. At least one study indicated that females are generally more active than males; many studies indicated that elderly male and female mice and rats are less active than young adults (Elias and Elias, in press).

Hereditary factors influence activity levels in rats and mice. You will recall from preceding sections that an inbred strain contains, for all practical purposes, genetically identical individuals but that two different inbred strains differ genetically. In a sense, they carry their own unique genetic baggage.

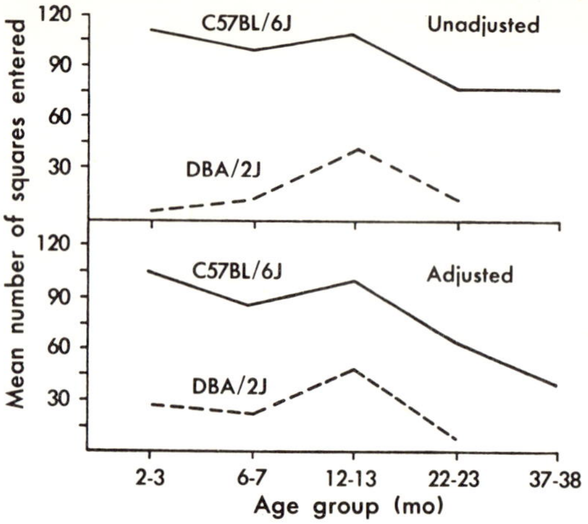

Fig. 6-2. Mean number of squares entered (crossed) in an open-field test. For the C57BL/6J strain of mice, locomotor activity (number of squares entered) decreases with increasing age from 12-13 to 37-38 months. Generally the amount of decline is greater for strain C57BL/6J, but this may be related to initial differences between the two strains in activity level. The experiment was carried out for a longer period of time with the C57BL/6J mice because they live longer and are available for testing over a longer period of the life span. (From Elias, P. K., Elias, M. F., and Eleftheriou, B. E., *Gerontologia,* 1975, **21,** 46.)

If environment is held constant and two inbred strains are compared, behavioral differences related to hereditary differences between the strains may be examined. It may be seen in Fig. 6-2, which summarizes a study by Elias, Elias, and Eleftheriou (1975), that activity levels are generally higher for inbred mouse strain C57BL/6J than they are for inbred mouse strain DBA/2J and that for this reason the difference between activity level for the youngest and oldest animals in each group is greatest for the C57BL/6J strain. Thus initial levels of activity determine, in part, the magnitude of age-associated differences in activity. Another important point should be made with reference to Fig. 6-2. It is very important that a large range of ages be used in any aging study. Use of animals that are 2 to 3, 6 to 7, and 22 to 23 years of age (excluding the 12- to 13-month group of animals) would have sug-

Table 6-1. Mean and standard error of the mean for open field activity scores (squares crossed) for mice of two strains and two ages tested in different laboratory environments*†

Age (months)	C57BL/6J		DBA/2J	
	Environment A	Environment B	Environment A	Environment B
2	151.5 ± 6.3	157.4 ± 17.7	82.1 ± 5.0	79.8 ± 14.0
18	61.8 ± 10.6	147.6 ± 23.9	37.7 ± 5.5	79.2 ± 25.7

*Intermediate age groups were tested in laboratory A (Hamilton Station, The Jackson Laboratory) as well as the 2- and 18-month-old groups. The 2- and 18-month-old data were compared with those obtained from laboratory B (main laboratory, The Jackson Laboratory). The greatest variability was observed in the most protected of the two laboratory environments. These data are taken from a published paper by Sprott and Eleftheriou (1974).

†Only trial 1 activity scores are shown for the two laboratory environments and only two age groups are shown in the table because these conditions were the only conditions that were identical for the two experiments, although all other procedures were identical for trial 1 and the age groups shown.

gested little in the way of age-associated differences for strain DBA/2J. However, it is clear that activity *increases* somewhat from 6 to 7 months to 12 to 13 months of age and decreases from 12 to 13 months to 22 to 23 months of age.

The fact that hereditary factors *influence* activity does not mean that environmental factors play no role in activity level differences among age groups. Quite the contrary is true. *Environment, in interaction with hereditary factors, plays a very important role in activity level at different ages.* This interaction is well illustrated in an experiment conducted by Sprott and Eleftheriou (1974). These investigators were concerned about the effect of laboratory environment on the behaviors of inbred strains. Two mouse strains, C57BL/6J and DBA/2J, were obtained from a common breeding source but were housed and tested in laboratories ten miles apart. Housing conditions, day-night cycle, and temperature conditions in the two colony rooms were the same. However, a number of laboratory routines varied, such as the playing of a radio for 18 hours a day in the colony room of one laboratory.

Two age groups (2 and 18 months) were compared. They were chosen based on a previous study by these investigators in which a wide range of ages were used. Table 6-1 summarizes their findings.

If one looks at the average crossing scores for the C57BL/6J mice, one sees that there was a drop in activity from 2 to 18 months of age in laboratory environment A but only a slight nonsignificant drop in environment B. For the DBA/2J mice there was a drop in activity from 2 to 18 months of age in environment A but none in environment B. Differences between the two mouse strains (genotypes) were exaggerated in environment B. Variability in performance, as measured by the standard errors of the mean, was much greater for the older animals housed in environment B. The greater variability for this age group makes sense when one considers the fact that the younger animals were housed in separate laboratory environments for a considerably shorter span of time prior to testing than were the older animals (1.5 as opposed to 8 to 10 months). Not only does this study demonstrate that environment can influence behavioral differences related to genetic makeup, but it emphasizes that *environmental factors may, in some cases, be more pronounced for older organisms because they have experienced cumulative environmental influences for a longer period of time.*

DRIVE: ANXIETY AND AROUSAL

In the conceptual framework provided at the beginning of the chapter, increased levels of anxiety and arousal were viewed as indicators of increased drive level. Studies which have been concerned with overall levels of anxiety in adult subjects generally suggest that there is an increase in anxiety with age. Gurin and associates (1960) conducted a national mental health survey in which the interview schedule included twenty items dealing with psychological stress. A factor analysis was performed on the data, and four factors relating to anxiety emerged: (1) psychological anxiety, (2) physical health, (3) immobilization, and (4) physical anxiety. The percentage of subjects receiving high factor scores for physical and psychological anxiety increased significantly for subjects between 45 and 65 years of age. Two other studies revealed that reaction times to generalized-anxiety-stimulus words, for example, "worry" and "restless," increased with age (Olsen and Elder, 1958; Powell and Ferraro, 1960). However, these studies do not provide data regarding the *behavioral effects* of diffuse general anxiety or arousal.

Perhaps the most significant contribution to the systematic laboratory study of arousal in older persons has been made by Eisdorfer and his colleagues. Their work can be loosely placed in the context of the general anxiety or arousal concepts of drive as put forth by Spence (1958) and Duffy (1964), respectively. Generally, anxiety-arousal concepts of drive suggest that a general level of anxiety typical of an individual under all or most circumstances (state anxiety) can interact with situational anxiety to produce a heightened drive level. However, drive and performance are related in a positive manner only up to a point that is determined by a number of variables, including task difficulty. Beyond this point, performance efficiency declines in response to further increases in drive level. Thus anxiety and/or arousal are related to performance in a manner that is characterized by an inverted U-shaped curve. Eisdorfer and his colleagues did not design their experimental programs to specifically test the validity of these concepts. Rather,

Fig. 6-3. Carl Eisdorfer, Ph.D., M.D. (New York University, 1951; Duke University School of Medicine, 1964). Dr. Eisdorfer may be best known to psychologists for his work on motivation, psychophysiology, and aging, but he has contributed to a wide range of literature. He has also contributed to aging as a developer of training and research programs and as an advocate on the national level. He is presently Professor and Chairman, Department of Psychiatry and Behavioral Sciences, School of Medicine, University of Washington. He served as Director, Center for the Study of Aging and Human Development at Duke University for a number of years and is a Past President of the Gerontological Society and Division 20 of the American Psychological Association. Dr. Eisdorfer has been honored many times for his professional services to aging, psychology, and medicine, and he is presently a member of the Institute of Medicine, National Academy of Sciences.

they employed them to characterize the relationship of anxiety or arousal or as defined here, drive, to age-related performance decrements on verbal learning tasks.

Explorations of the relationship between anxiety or arousal and learning were precipitated by observations of (1) the nature of performance decrements for elderly persons in verbal learning experiments and (2) the specific circumstances under which these decrements were observed. *Errors of omission* (failure to respond to a stimulus) *exceed errors of commission* (responding incorrectly to a stimulus), *and both kinds of errors are exaggerated when the rate of task pacing* (interstimulus intervals) *is high* (Eisdorfer, 1968; Troyer et al., 1967). Troyer and colleagues (1967) hypothesized that omission errors represented response inhibition related to heightened situational anxiety. Evidence in favor of this hypothesis was provided by the observation that performance of elderly persons improved appreciably when task pacing was reduced; that is, the length of interstimulus intervals was increased. Most important, *the improvement was generally larger for omission than for commission errors.* When longer intervals between stimuli were used as a means for decreasing task pacing, mean response times fell well within a time period required for responding under rapidly paced stimulus presentation conditions (Arenberg, 1965; Eisdorfer et al., 1963; Troyer et al., 1967).

Rapid task pacing may be difficult for older adults to contend with because of a decline in information-processing ability. However, to reach this conclusion the possibility that anxiety and concomitant reduction in performance efficiency are associated with a departure from optimal drive levels must be ruled out. It is difficult to test the anxiety hypothesis because anxiety is difficult to measure. However, Eisdorfer and his colleagues provide data on *arousal* and performance that shed some light on the relationship between performance efficiency and departure from optimal levels of drive. One must assume, however, that increased arousal, as measured by physiological indices, reflects increased drive. There are those who might quarrel with measures of physiological arousal as indices of drive level. However, it is an index of drive that is independent of changes in performance and thus seems to be a reasonable *operational* definition of drive level.

Eisdorfer and his group employed free fatty acid (FFA) levels and measures of heart rate and galvanic skin responses as indices of arousal. Plasma levels of FFA are thought by some investigators to reflect level of autonomic arousal because FFA mobilization constitutes one of the metabolic processes associated with release of catecholamines from the adrenal medulla in response to stress. Using FFA levels as an indicator of arousal, Powell and associates (1964) conducted a serial verbal learning study with older (60+ years) and younger (20 to 48 years) male subjects. The older group exhibited higher FFA levels than the younger group and performed more poorly. After the experiment the younger subjects exhibited a decrease in FFA level, but the older subjects continued to exhibit an increase in FFA levels. In a second study, limited only to older subjects (mean age = 68 years), degree of arousal as inferred from FFA levels was related to performance in a curvilinear manner (Troyer et al., 1966).

These data provide additional support for the hypothesis that older subjects are more stressed by task demands than younger subjects, but they do not provide evidence for a cause-and-effect relationship between poor performance and arousal. To do this, one must demonstrate that experimental lowering of arousal level results in an improvement of performance. To achieve this objective, Eisdorfer and his colleagues (1970) selected a drug that purportedly blocks autonomic nervous system arousal but does not interfere with cognitive functioning. The drug propranolol (Inderal) produces a partial blockade of autonomic adrenergic receptor sites in the peripheral end organs, but it does not seem to influence central nervous system activation or deactivation directly.

Older men (60 to 70 years) were given propranolol during performance of a rote verbal learning task. Their FFA levels, performance, heart rate, and galvanic skin responses were compared with those obtained for an elderly placebo control group. Drug and control groups were given the Weschler Adult Intelligence Scale (Weschler, 1958), the Taylor Anxiety Scale (Taylor, 1953), and a test for organic brain impairment as preliminary measures. There were no differences between the propranolol group and

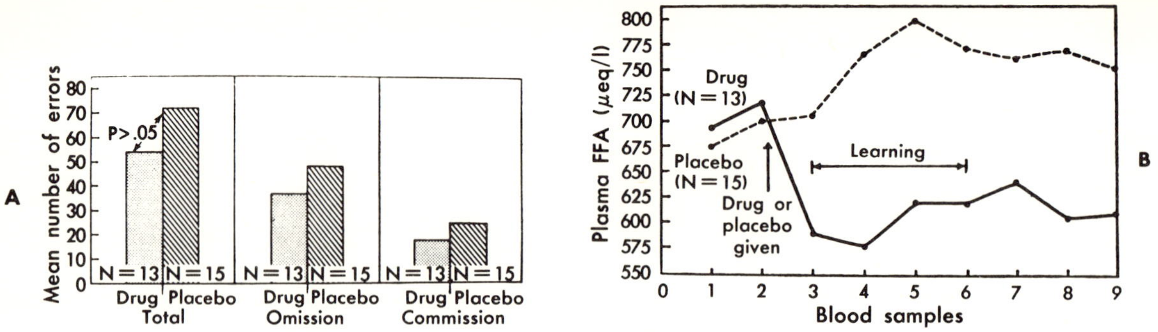

Fig. 6-4. A, "The mean number of errors on a verbal learning task among aged men while under the influence of either 10.0 mg intravenous propranolol hydrochloride (drug) or an equivalent amount of intravenous isotonic saline (placebo)." **B,** "Plasma free fatty acid (FFA) levels among aged men exposed to a verbal learning task after having been given either 10.0 mg intravenous propranolol hydrochloride (drug) or an equivalent amount of intravenous isotonic saline (placebo)." Mean number of errors decreased under the drug condition (right-hand side). FFA levels increased for the placebo, but older adult men given the drug exhibited decreased FFA levels. (From Eisdorfer, C., Nowlin, J., and Wilkie, F. *Science* 1970, **170,** 1327. Copyright 1970 by the American Association for the Advancement of Science.)

the control group for these measures. Consequently, results of the study may not be explained in terms of differences in intelligence, anxiety, or brain integrity between the propranolol group and the control group.

Fig. 6-4 summarizes the most important results of the study. There was a decrease in total number of errors (Fig. 6-4, *A*) for the older men given propranolol. FFA levels (Fig. 6-4, *B*) showed a decrease for the subjects in the drug group *after* propranolol was administered. In contrast, FFA levels for control (placebo) subjects rose during the experiment and remained at a comparatively high level. Heart rate and galvanic skin response exhibited a response pattern similar to FFA levels, but propranolol group as opposed to control group differences were not significant for galvanic skin response.

These data support the contention that arousal induced by threat of task demands may contribute to performance decrements, although a finding that errors of omission were even more favorably affected by drug treatment than were errors of commission would have provided even stronger evidence in support of the anxiety-arousal interpretation. Moreover, it is unfortunate that groups of younger subjects were not tested under drug and placebo conditions. It is important to know whether they would have responded positively under the drug condition.

Data provided by Eisdorfer and his coworkers did not exclude the possible influence of nonmotivational factors on performance differences between old and young subjects. However, they did point out the following: (1) contrary to the notion that decrements in performance are only due to cognitive factors or to decreased motivation to perform, older subjects may be experiencing such a high level of arousal that they perform less well than they are actually *capable* of performing; and (2) failure in task performance may further increase anxiety-induced arousal (drive) in a vicious cycle (Troyer et al., 1966). Most important, the work by Eisdorfer's group provides a stimulus for further comparisons, with both animals and humans, of drug effects on anxiety and arousal at various periods of the life span. One problem encountered in the measurement of arousal is related to the necessity of using obtrusive and stressful measurement techniques. It is clear that the techniques themselves have a differential effect on arousal level in young and old subjects (Eisdorfer, 1968; Troyer et al., 1967), although arousal responses to blood collection and psychophysiological procedures do diminish through adaptation (Eisdorfer, 1968).

A second problem in connection with the concept of general arousal involves the fact that different measures of arousal may not lead to the same conclusions (Jarvik and Cohen, 1973). Different autonomic nervous mechanisms may age at different rates, and they interact at every age. Powell and associates (1975) point to several studies that they believe support the hypothesis of lower arousal in older adults. Botwinick and Kornetsky (1960) found that electrodermal responses were less easily conditioned in old than young subjects. Obrist and Henry (1958) reported less low-voltage, fast activity in the electroencephalogram of older subjects. These data might be interpreted as reflecting underarousal if one assumes that activity and arousal are synonymous terms and that activity in one system provides information regarding general arousal patterns. Perhaps it is best to think of arousal as *reactivity* rather than activity. Levels of central or autonomic nervous system activity may be lower and less easily conditioned for older adults, but this does not mean that their reactivity in certain test or laboratory task situations may not be greater.

It is probably unwise to base inferences about arousal on a single psychophysiological measure because physiological systems work in concert. Increases in one index of autonomic or central nervous system reactivity may be compensated for by decreases in another index. Thus arousal is best inferred from simultaneous measurements of as many indices of nervous system reactivity as are possible, for example, cortisol levels, neuroamine changes, blood pressure, respiration, electroencephalogram, electrodermal response, and heart rate.

A study by Powell and co-workers (1975) provides an admirable illustration of the need to obtain multiple psychophysiological measures if inferences about arousal are to be made. These investigators obtained measures of blood pressure before and after the completion of reaction time and serial learning tasks. Heart rate and electrodermal responses were recorded during the performance of these tasks. Task performance was generally poorer for older subjects (50 to 70 years) than for younger subjects (25 to 35 years). Consistent with the age-arousal hypothesis, a significantly greater number of older subjects exhibited increased blood pressure during task performance. However, *higher blood pressure levels were associated with better task performance* for the older subjects, a finding that is inconsistent with the FFA studies that lead to the prediction of poorer performance. Furthermore, in apparent contradiction with the age-arousal hypothesis, the elderly group showed significantly slower heart rates than younger subjects during performance of the tasks. This might be interpreted as being supportive of the hypothesis of lower arousal for older subjects if it were proper to talk about arousal in terms of one system or to infer general arousal from an examination of one index of autonomic nervous system response. Neither approach seems wise. One must examine how interrelated arousal indices "interreact." Powell and colleagues did just this. They noted the inverse relationship between increased blood pressure and decreased heart rate during task performance and explained these findings in terms of the physiological mechanisms that operate to lower heart rate in response to increased blood pressure.

Thus, if one examines the interaction of heart rate and blood pressure in the Powell and co-workers' study, findings are consistent with the hypothesis of greater task-induced arousal for older subjects, and the arousal interpretation gains support from the observations that (1) baseline levels of electrodermal conductance were greater for the elderly subjects than for the young subjects, and (2) elderly subjects exhibited a higher level of spontaneous fluctuations in electrodermal response. However, the latter data become important because they help researchers to determine whether increased blood pressure and decreased heart rate represent increased or decreased arousal.

An interesting feature of the study by Powell's group was related to their attempt to understand the relationship between levels of social activity and physiological indices of reactivity. Social activity ratings were constructed from periodic observations of the elderly subjects and correlated with physiological indices. Subjects who were defined physiologically as "more aroused" (increased blood pressure, lowered heart rate, increased electrodermal response) performed better and were more highly active socially.

The basic difference in the findings in the study by Powell's group and that by Eisdorfer's group is that higher "arousal" for older subjects did not result in poorer performance in the study by Powell and coworkers. It is difficult to resolve this conflict in findings because, among other procedural differences, different indices of arousal were used. It is impossible to compare absolute levels of arousal for different measures. Levels of arousal in the FFA study by Eisdorfer and associates may have been so high that they were suboptimal for performance of older persons. A question may be raised with regard to the value of FFA level as an index of arousal. However, it is important that studies with psychophysiological indices of arousal include measures of FFA levels if comparisons with the work by Eisdorfer's group are to be made.

The most important point to be remembered is that if one plans to use arousal as an explanatory concept, more than a single index of arousal must be employed. Furthermore, it is important to note that the use of psychophysiological indices as measures of general arousal has been challenged. The basic problem is that unique autonomic response patterns may emerge in response to stress for different individuals (Lacey and Van Lehn, 1952). Factors such as genetic predisposition and unique life experiences contribute to unique individual response patterns. Variance in individual response patterns may be greater than variance as a function of age. Thus *mean* values for various psychophysiological measures may be deceptive.

Increased arousal may or may not be the result of increased anxiety as is suggested by Troyer and colleagues (1966). Moreover, arousal need not be interpreted in the context of drive theories (Duffy, 1964; Spence, 1958). *Regardless of the theoretical framework used to interpret the studies of Eisdorfer and his colleagues, their data illustrate the very important point that performance decrements do not necessarily reflect decline in mental proficiency or learning ability for older persons.*

CHANGES IN THE EFFECTIVENESS OF INCENTIVES

Task involvement and meaningfulness

One of the most obvious problems with a large number of psychological studies is that they employ tasks that are essentially boring and/or meaningless to subjects who are asked to perform them. It is possible that task incentive may be even more important for the performance of older subjects than younger subjects. Many were not exposed to the large-scale psychological testing that takes place in high schools and colleges today. Thus they may not automatically accept the validity or the importance of a laboratory test.

Indirect evidence for the task meaningfulness hypothesis is provided by studies of problem solving (Arenberg, 1968) and learning (Hulicka, 1967a). However, neither investigator obtained a measure of involvement or drive, which was independent of changes in task performance. Arenberg's study required the identification of concepts by logical analysis based on abstract dimensions of form, color, and number. Older subjects had so much difficulty with the task that they could not understand it. When abstract information was translated into concrete terms, older subjects (60 to 77 years) not only understood the task but were able to solve many of the problems, although their performance levels did not reach those achieved by the younger subjects (17 to 22 years). Hulicka (1967a) obtained a similar improvement in the understanding and performance of her older subjects (65 to 85 years) when letter stimuli were replaced with meaningful words in a paired-associates task.

Not all studies of stimulus familiarity obtained better performance for older subjects when familiarity was increased. In studies by Heron and Craik (1964) the reverse was true. Young (20 to 35 years) and older (60+ years) English subjects were presented with either Finnish or English digits. The performance measure was the maximum number of digits correctly repeated following presentation in serial order. Both age groups performed at an equal level of proficiency for Finnish digits. For English digits the younger group was superior to the older group. The authors explained this interaction in terms of decreased efficiency of "coding" stimuli with increasing age. They reasoned that meaningful stimuli lent themselves to organization (coding) much more rapidly than did nonmeaningful stimuli. Thus decreased level of efficiency in the organizing process would be more apparent with the more meaningful stimuli.

Further support for a larger performance decrement with meaningful material was provided in a later study of memory span by Craik and Masani (1967). In this experiment, subjects ranged in "decade" age groups from 20 to 79 years. Three types of stimuli were presented: (1) meaningful sentences, (2) color names, and (3) proverbs in scrambled word order. The hypothesis was that aged subjects would do relatively well with color names because they lend themselves *less* to organization based on familiarity. The hypothesis was confirmed by their findings.

Generally, *it appears that improvement in performance for older subjects is sometimes observed when material is more meaningful, but in some instances the reverse is true, particularly when the more meaningful material lends itself to organization.* The major problem with regard to interpretation of these findings in terms of increased motivation induced by incentives of meaningfulness or involvement is that task difficulty covaries with meaningfulness. Increases in concreteness of stimulus content and less rapid pacing or the opportunity to self-pace may involve decreased demands on abstract reasoning processes and attention. On the other hand, when task difficulty does not exceed a certain level, increased opportunity to organize or encode material may actually result in greater age differences, even though overall performance level is enhanced for both young and old. At best, then, *these studies indicate that motivational factors related to stimulus meaningfulness may influence performance decrements in the elderly, but they do not eliminate alternate explanations involving age-associated changes in central nervous system structure and function which are reflected in cognitive abilities, per se.*

The ideal experimental paradigm would maintain constant task difficulty while manipulating task meaningfulness. An experiment by Wittels (1972) was designed to maintain task difficulty and, at the same time, vary stimulus meaningfulness for older and younger subjects. Word meanings change over time, and the typical stimulus materials for paired-associates tasks were designed for young subjects. Thus Wittels questioned whether the difficulty observed for older persons with paired-associate learning is because they deal with less meaningful materials than younger subjects in the typical paired-associate task.

Word lists were obtained in a manner designed to ensure familiarity. Each person in the old (60 to 82 years) and the young (18 to 24 years) age groups was given fifteen meaningful words and asked to provide his own response associations. The fifth response association to each word was taken as the paired associate to that word. Each person had a different list with stimuli that were common to every other list but response associates that were peculiar to the responder. The assumption was that lists were different from person to person but similar with regard to their strength of associations. When the person was given his own list, it was called a personal list; when it was given to a different person in the same generation (age group), it was called a generational list; and when it was given to persons of a different age, it was called a cross-generational list.

Wittels expected that the elderly persons would perform poorly on the cross-generational list, better on the generational list, and in a superior manner on the personal list. This hypothesis was not confirmed. Elderly subjects performed more poorly than younger subjects with each of the lists. These data provide evidence which is not consistent with the hypothesis that poor performance of the elderly on paired-associate learning tasks is related to stimulus meaningfulness. This is not to say that increased meaningfulness does not result in increased motivation for older subjects. Rather, it seems to improve performance to an equal extent in younger subjects. However, too few systematic studies have been conducted to allow firm generalizations. It is important that more studies include separate parameters of task meaningfulness and task difficulty. Moreover, the meaningfulness dimension of laboratory stimuli may be varied over a wide range, but laboratory tasks themselves may have relatively less meaning to older subjects who have not grown up in the milieu of psychological testing and laboratory experimentation that characterizes the childhood and early adult life experiences of many subjects in younger cohorts.

Aversive stimulation

Aversive stimulation has been a relatively popular method of incentive manipulation, although there is little information available concerning its relationship with age. Two studies involving older subjects have employed eyelid conditioning (Braun and Geiselhart, 1959; Kimble and Pennypacker, 1963). These studies involved a classical avoidance paradigm. A puff of air to the pupil of the eye (unconditional stimulus) could be avoided (conditional response) or escaped (unconditional response) by blinking the eye. The results of both studies indicated that elderly subjects did not acquire a conditional response to the same level as that observed for the younger subjects; that is, the percentage of conditional responses was lower for the older subjects than for the younger subjects. Kimble and Pennypacker (1963) suggest that the unconditional response habituates more rapidly for older subjects. In other words, the eye-blink reflex becomes more susceptible to adaptation, and the result is a lower level of conditioning.

It should be noted that neither the Braun and Geiselhart (1959) nor the Kimble and Pennypacker (1963) experiment was planned as a study of motivation. Consequently, strength of the unconditional stimulus (air puff) was not varied over a wide range of values, and a measure of anxiety level was not obtained prior to the experiments. Additional studies in which several age groups are used and unconditional stimulus intensity is varied over a wide range would provide further information regarding the relationship between incentive and drive. These studies could be done in the context of Spence's (1958) theory of motivation, which views stimulus intensity as an incentive to avoid and views anxiety level as contributing to a generalized drive state. Avoidance conditioning, anxiety measures, and manipulation of unconditional stimulus strength (incentive) represent important tools in the investigation of motivation for younger subjects, but they have not been employed to any significant extent in aging studies.

A study by Botwinick and co-workers (1958) provides a more direct test of the relationship between incentive, in this case shock, and the performance of different age groups. Young (18 to 37 years) and old (65 to 79 years) subjects were required to press their fingers on a response key after hearing a warning signal. The key press set off a warning light, which was followed by a preparatory interval and an auditory stimulus, which terminated with the lifting of the finger. After a series of trials, shock was applied to the subject's wrist at a time after the warning light that was equal to the participant's median reaction time during preliminary trials. Shock reduced reaction times but did not affect young and old subjects differently. Older persons were slower, and the shock "incentive" did not reduce reaction times to a disproportionately greater extent for old than for young persons. This result was repeated in a later study under the same conditions of irregular preparatory intervals and with a new set of irregular preparatory intervals (Botwinick et al., 1958). However, when constant intervals were used, the older group reduced reaction times more than the younger group. The investigators did not comment on the implications of their study for motivation and aging. Presumably, older persons are capable of responding more rapidly under proper conditions of incentive, but only under circumstances in which preparatory intervals are presented in a regular series.

A greater number of studies using aversive stimulation as an incentive have been done with animal subjects than with human participants. Paré (1969) designed an experiment to evaluate the relative effect of two shock intensities on the learning of a discrimination bar-press response for Sprague-Dawley rats. His animals were 1.3, 3.0, and 11.8 months of age. Thus old animals were not used, and results are relevant to age differences between adult and adolescent rats.

All Paré's experimental animals were placed on a deprivation schedule, which resulted in loss of 20% of body weight relative to control animals that were not tested and were permitted to eat freely. The stimuli to be discriminated were beeping tones of 2,000 and 850 cps, respectively. For both shock intensities, speed of acquisition of the discriminated bar-press response was inversely related to age. However, *discrimination* performance was poorer under the high shock than under the low shock conditions for the oldest group but not for the youngest group of rats. This finding led Paré to question whether the incentive value of shock was the same for young and old animals. In another study, Doty and O'Hare (1966) obtained data which suggest that the aversive threshold is higher in 12-month-old rats than in 2-month-old rats.

Decreased threshold for shock in older animals may explain the generally poorer performance of the oldest animals under high as opposed to low shock. It is possible that the oldest subjects in Paré's study were operating under a generally higher drive or arousal state. Thus, consistent with findings for human subjects (Eisdorfer et al., 1970), increased motivation (incentive), beyond an optimum level for most efficient performance, resulted in a performance decrement. Furthermore, as for human subjects, *optimal incentive levels and task complexity appear to interact.* When Paré decreased the complexity of the discrimination task, no age differences were observed.

Stimulation with light

A number of interesting studies have been done with light as an incentive for performance. Stimulation with light is far less aversive than stimulation with shock, yet light stimulation can act as an incentive for performance in albino mice (Lochard, 1963). The albino eye is highly sensitive to light. It has been repeatedly shown that albino rats and mice will learn a bar-press response or simple escape-avoidance response to escape from or avoid, light (Elias and Elias, in press). The interesting question is whether the incentive value for light of a given intensity diminishes with advancing age. Studies of "light-contingent," bar-press activity in aging rats and mice have been inconclusive. In some studies, young animals show a higher light-contingent, bar-press response than do older animals. Other investigators have found no age differences. However, different age groups were compared in various studies and different strains and stocks of albino rats were used, thus introducing differences in genotype as a potential source of variability.

Recently, Goodrick (1970) found that light *onset* had an incentive value that was similar to that of light offset. His results suggest that *stimulus change,* as well as light aversion, may be an incentive for bar-press activity. This hypothesis is entirely consistent with the notion that drive level increases when mean level of environmental stimulation falls below a threshold level. In humans, this threshold level may be different from individual to individual and vary as a function of temperament and past experience. In animals (rats), light- and dark-contingent, bar-press activity was invariant with age when 6- and 26-month-old Wistar albino rats were compared (Goodrick, 1970). Further studies need to be done with older animals. Moreover, the strength of the light stimulus (intensity) needs to be varied over a wider range to determine whether threshold to stimulation is diminished in older animals. Human studies could make good use of the *stimulus change* paradigm to study changes in the "mean levels" of optimal "environmental stimulation" across the life span.

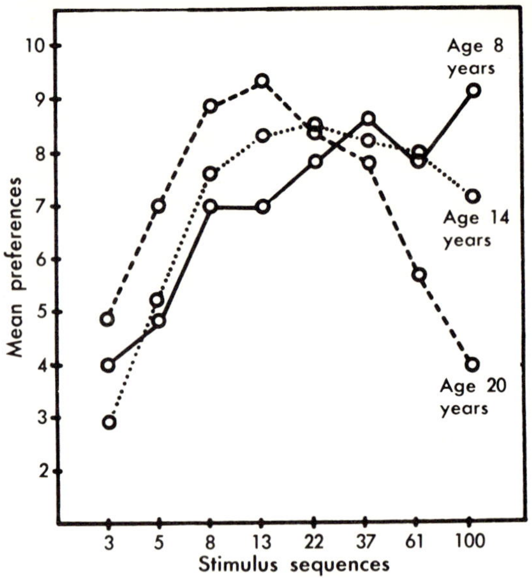

Fig. 6-5. Mean preference of three age groups for eight stimulus sequences. Each stimulus pair was rated relative to each other stimulus pair in terms of preference. The preference profile for the 8-year-old children increases progressively. The profiles for the 14- and 20-year-old participants of the experiment are curvilinear, with the highest preferences falling in the middle range of values. These data point to the possibility that preference for high rates of stimulus input (high levels of environmental activity) decreases with increasing age. It would be interesting to extend data collection across the entire life span. (From Boesch, E. E., Baltes, P. B., and Schmidt, L. R. *Psychonomic Science,* 1968, **10,** 205.)

Stimulus change

There is some interesting, although indirect, evidence that stimulus change may be differentially motivating for different age groups. At least it appears that different age groups do not exhibit preferences for the same *rate* of stimulation. In a cross-sectional study by Boesch and co-workers (1968), male subjects with mean ages of approximately 8, 10, 12, 14, and 20 years were presented with all possible pairs of eight auditory stimulus sequences in a paired-comparisons design; that is, each pair was compared with each other pair with the order of the pairs defined by chance. It may be seen in Fig. 6-5 that the young adults (20 years) showed an increasing preference for higher stimulus sequences (tone units/10 sec interval) up to about 13 tones/10 sec and then a decline in preference. Fourteen-year-olds exhibited lower mean preferences than the young adults up to about 13 tones/10 sec and a maximum preference at 22 tones/10 sec, and they did *not* show the same sharp drop from the maximum level exhibited by the young adults. In contrast to both older groups, the 8-year-old children exhibited a progressive increase in preference for stimulus sequences

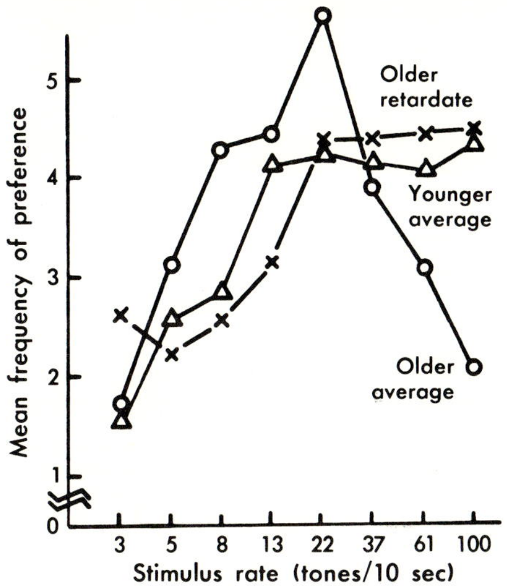

Fig. 6-6. Mean frequency of preference as a function of stimulus rate (sequence) for older retarded, older average, and younger average subjects. Adolescents aged 16.11 to 20.11 years, but with mental ages in the retarded range, were compared with young children (7.8 to 8.5 years) with the same mental age as the retarded adolescents. Adolescents with average mental ages showed an inverted U-shaped preference curve similar to that reported by Boesch and colleagues (Fig. 6-5), but retarded adolescents exhibited preference curves very similar to those exhibited by the children who were of average intelligence. It would seem that functional age (mental age) may be a more critical determinant of preference for varying rates of stimulation than chronological age, per se. (From Leri, J. E., Lesswing, N. J., and Elias, M. F. *Psychonomic Science,* 1969, **17,** 80.)

or *rates* of presentation. Similar findings for visual stimuli were obtained in a later study by Baltes and colleagues (1968).

Leri and co-workers (1969) provide data which indicate that functional age may be an even more critical determinant of stimulus preference than chronological age. Results of this study are shown in Fig. 6-6. When retarded adolescents were compared with young children of the *same mental age,* their stimulus rate preference curves were similar; both showed a relatively progressive increase in preference for higher rates of stimulation. However, curves for adolescents of average intelligence exhibited an inverted U-shaped relationship for preference and stimulus rate which was similar to that reported by Boesch and colleagues (Fig. 6-5) for adolescents. It is possible that the retarded adolescent's level of internal stimulation is lower than that of the adolescent with normal average intellectual ability. Unfortunately there seems to be little agreement concerning possible causes of internal stimulation. Nevertheless, it would be interesting to extend these experiments to include age groups across the entire life span and to make comparisons between longitudinal and cross-sectional data. From a motivation standpoint it would be important to see to what extent varying rates of stimulation would be differentially reinforcing *(serve as incentives)* for various behaviors for subjects of different ages. Does preference for stimulation continue to decline from early adulthood to old age? If so, is chronological age more important that functional age? Is decreased preference for stimulation correlated with the increased incidence of disease? How are individual patterns of preference, revealed on simple laboratory tasks using tone and light sequences, correlated with general social activity and well-being? These seem to be important avenues for future research and may well help psychologists to determine whether some simple laboratory tasks, such as tone-preference studies, will permit predictions concerning complex social activities.

Water escape

Water-escape studies have been popular for the study of incentive with mice and rats. Studies of swimming speed in animals provide an opportunity to examine psychomotor activity of a somewhat different nature than that which is involved in measures of open-field locomotion behavior and wheel-running activity. Similar to open-field and wheel-running activity, swimming involves a prolonged sequence of psychomotor movements, rather than quick and limited responses to aversive stimulation (e.g., jumping to avoid electric shock). However, for water-escape behavior, motor performance is

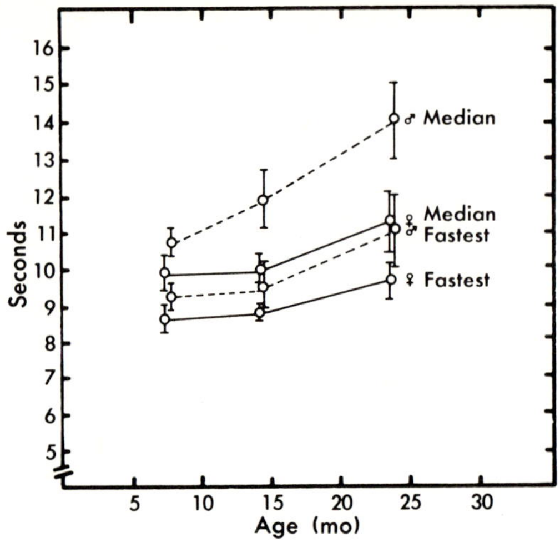

Fig. 6-7. Swimming times for male Sprague-Dawley rats divided into six age groups. Swimming time was greater for the older age groups, but the most notable difference was obtained for old males. (From Birren, J. E., and Kay, H. *Journal of Gerontology,* 1958, **13,** 374.)

Down by the old T-maze

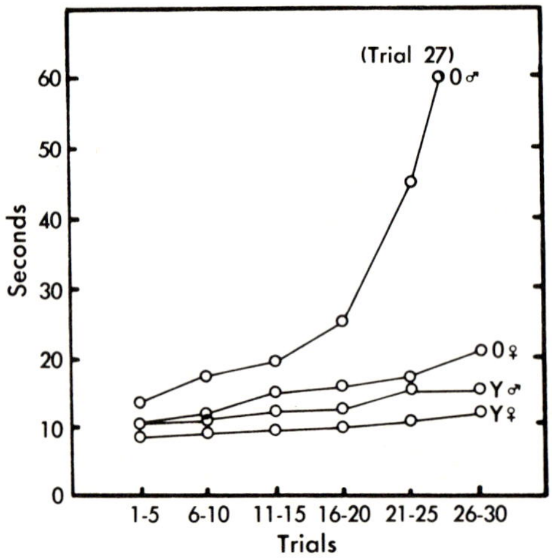

Fig. 6-8. The effects of fatigue on swimming times for male and female rats in two age groups: old (23 to 28 months) and young (7 to 8 months). Curves were constructed using the median values. There is a slight increase in time to escape for the older females relative to the older males with an increasing number of trials, but the most notable difference is observed for the old males. Fatigue effects such as these could affect performance adversely in learning studies where water escape is used as an incentive to perform. (From Kay, H., and Birren, J. E. *Journal of Gerontology,* 1958, **13,** 378.)

closely tied to the survival of the animal. If it fails to swim, it sinks and dies. If it fatigues more readily than another animal, it dies sooner. Thus water escape represents an intensely motivating incentive for performance, which is intimately tied to survival and limited by fatigue. Both changes in incentive value of water escape and fatigue may change with age. Thus changes in swim-escape learning and discrimination learning in water mazes as a function of increasing age may be related to changes in incentive value or extent of fatigue rather than learning ability, per se. Data by Birren and Kay (1958) and Kay and Birren (1958) indicate that older animals do fatigue more quickly than younger animals.

In the first experiment (Birren and Kay, 1958), male Sprague-Dawley rats of six age groups ranging from 5 to 30 months were given five swimming trials (1 minute apart) for 2 days. They were placed at one end of a long metal trough and the time to escape was measured. Maximum (fastest) and median swimming times were reported. It may be seen in Fig. 6-7 that females were generally faster swimmers and that the greatest differences between males and females occurred for the oldest group. Old rats of both sexes were slower than young rats, and this was true for both maximum and median swimming times, although differences were more exaggerated for the latter scores. The

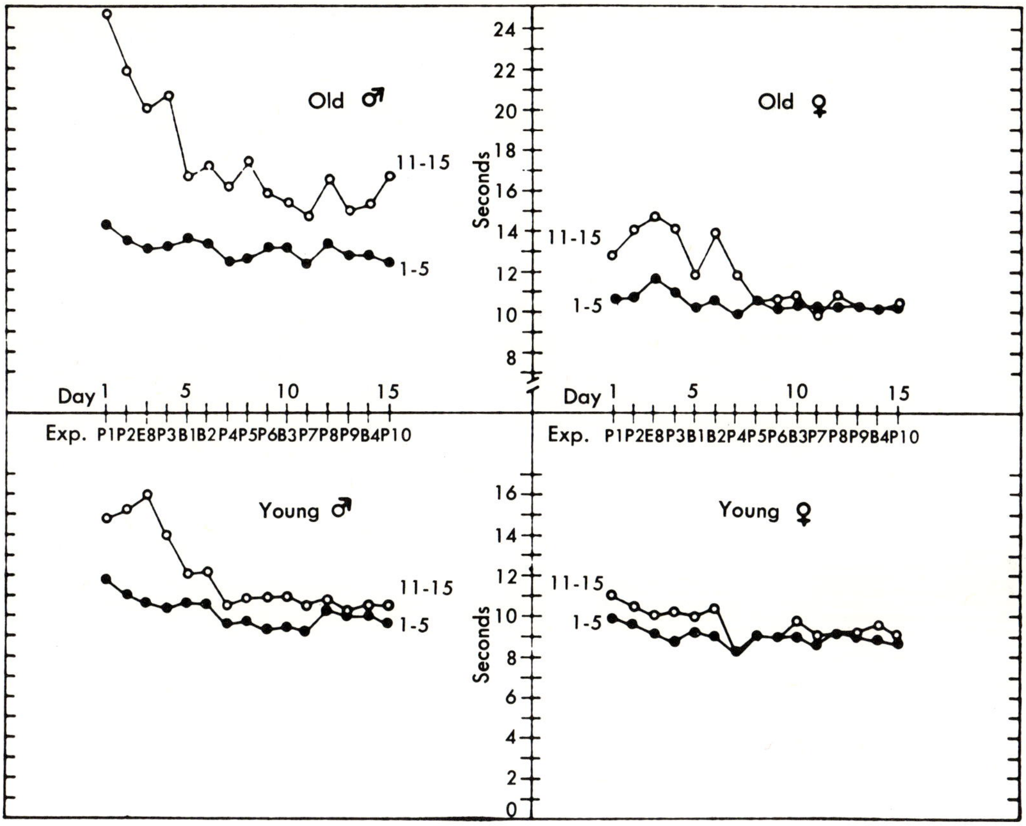

Fig. 6-9. Effects of practice on swimming time for old (23 to 24 months) and young (11 months) rats. Curves are constructed from median values obtained for the first and last blocks of trials on successive practice days. Performance for days 1 to 5 is shown in the bottom curve and for days 11 to 15 on the top curve of each of the four panels. Practice facilitated the performance of old males, but the relationships among swimming times for old and young and for males and females were not altered. Old males were still slower than young males and females despite practice. (From Kay, H., and Birren, J. E., *Journal of Gerontology*, 1958, **13**, 378.)

greatest age difference was observed between 15 and 27 months for both sexes.

In a second study, using the same apparatus and rat strains, Kay and Birren (1958) examined the effects of practice and fatigue. Is slower swimming a compensatory response which conserves the strength of older animals so that they fatigue less quickly than younger animals? Does practice eliminate or reduce age differences? These were the two important questions raised in this experiment.

Two age groups of males and females, 7 to 8 months and 23 to 27 months, were given "fatigue" and "recovery" trials after initial habituation to the task. For the fatigue task each rat was given 30 consecutive trials but was removed from the apparatus prior to 30 trials if it was no longer able to swim or swimming exceeded 60 seconds during a trial. After fatigue trials, animal subjects were rested for 5 minutes and then given 5 additional trials, which were referred to as recovery trials.

Results of this study are shown in Fig. 6-8. Old male rats were more susceptible to fatigue than young males, but old males also were considerably more susceptible than old females. The same relationships were observed for recovery trials, but the differences were even more exaggerated. Kay and Birren (1958:380) concluded that it does not appear that the older organism's slower swimming speed results from conservation of resources "in the nature of an adaptive strategy to meet continuous environmental demands." Even though the old males swam at an initially slower rate, they became easily exhausted. Most important, the effects of fatigue accentuated differences between groups. Kay and Birren attributed the superiority of the old females to differences in vigor between the two sexes and a longer average life span for females. The phase of the Kay and Birren study that considered practice effects used two age groups of females and males, 11 months and 23 to 24 months. Old and young animals of the same sex were matched for body weight and given 15 trials a day for 15 days. It is very important to equate animals for body weight because this may influence swimming ability and swimming speed. Results of this study are summarized in Fig. 6-9. It may be seen that practice effected a reduction in escape times for old males, although the rank order of age and sex groups remained the same.

It is important to note that for some species and strains the relationships between fatigue and age may be positive and linear only after a certain age is reached. A study by Wright and associates (1971) provides a good example. These investigators forced mice of inbred strain C57BL/6J to swim continuously until they submerged in water. The relationship between age and time to submersion is shown in Fig. 6-10. Age and increased susceptibility to fatigue were not positively related until the animals reached 615 days of age. From 615 to 845 days of age the curve shows a steadily downward trend, with the oldest animals fatiguing most rapidly as evidenced by shorter swimming times prior to submersion. The oldest animals fatigued most easily, but the animals in the middle age range showed more resistance to fatigue

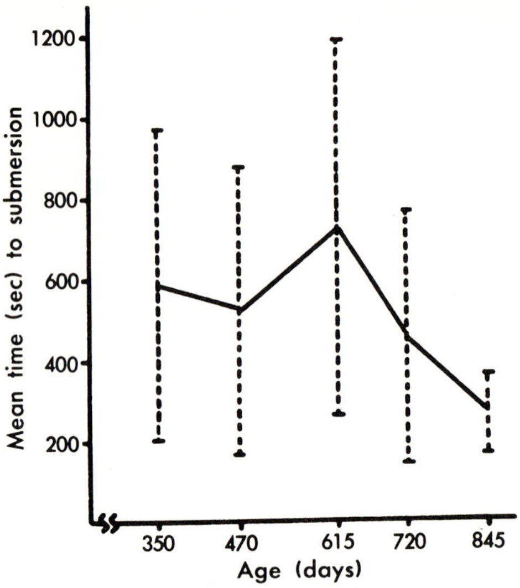

Fig. 6-10. "Mean time in seconds to submersion of C57BL/6J mice at various ages. Vertical line represents standard deviations." Note that the age group in the middle range exhibited the greatest resistance to fatigue, whereas the elderly group exhibited the least. Note also that the submersion times *do not* increase or decrease in a linear manner from the youngest to the oldest groups tested. Thus it seems important that a range of age groups be tested in life-span studies of behavior. (Reprinted from Wright, W. E., Werboff, J., and Haggett, B. N. *Developmental Psychobiology,* 1971, **4,** 363.)

than the younger animals. Why did the middle-aged animals show the *least* resistance to fatigue? Wright and his colleagues (1971:368) offer an interesting hypothesis in explanation of their findings.

> These observations may be explained by the hypothesis that the age threshold after which one may expect to see evidence of debilitation occurring is after the mean life span age (676) for this strain. Prior to this age, there is a selective factor operating so that animals that survive after 50% of their life span are more resistant to severe experiences. This selective factor operates also at the older end of the life span scale but the debilitating effects of age are now so severe as to mask the selective factor.

Under ideal laboratory conditions, mean life span for the C57BL/6J mouse may be greater than the 676 days cited by Wright and his associates. Nevertheless, these investigators make a particularly important point, which has considerable validity for all aging studies with animals or humans. Essentially, they point out that *changes in sample characteristics with age may influence results of aging studies.* Results might have been somewhat different if curves had been plotted for individual mice that were followed from birth until death. Those mice that *died* shortly after 615 days of age may have showed a pronounced decrease in swimming time to submersion relative to those that continued to live to 845 days.

In a second phase of their experiment, Wright and his co-investigators varied water temperature to explore the relationship between incentive to swim and time to submersion. Time to submerge decreased with increased incentive to swim, provided by colder temperatures. However, the oldest animals showed the *least* notable effects of temperature variation. Wright and his colleagues concluded that because of the decreased physical capacity of the old group (i.e., decreased strength, resistance to fatigue, and diminished energy reserves), the differential demands of different water temperature conditions were minimal.

Age differences in reactivity

One of the problems involved in the manipulation of incentive by the use of shock intensity or temperature extremes is that the "effective" level of stimulation produced by *equal* values of temperature and electric current (Elias and Elias, in press) may not be the same for all age groups. Thus 10° C may be more motivating to an animal of one age than to an animal of another age. Moreover, as was learned from the studies by Birren and Kay (1968), Kay and Birren (1968), and Wright and his associates, fatigue and practice may interact with the motivational or incentive characteristics of water temperature extremes.

Human studies have the advantage that they may utilize incentives which are less fatiguing and physiologically stressful to the subjects such as social, financial, or token incentives to perform. Nevertheless, the testing situation and experimental laboratory task may be more fatiguing for elderly than for young persons. There seems to be little doubt that, in general, elderly subjects show a significant reduction in fatigue resistance (Birren, 1959).

Fatigue and boredom in humans

Studies of effects of fatigue and boredom on the performance of younger and older persons indicate that performance on tests of intelligence and mental ability are adversely affected by these "ability-extraneous performance variables." For example, Kamin (1957) hypothesized that fatigue or boredom might be a contributing factor in the observed age decrements in performance for a battery of intelligence tests widely used in adult developmental studies, Thurstone's Primary Mental Abilities Test (PMA). To test this hypothesis, Kamin gave the five PMA subtests to fifty aged subjects and a control group of young volunteers in a Latin square design. He concluded that neither the sequence of presentation nor the order of the subtests resulted in significant effects on performance. Furry and Baltes (1973) criticized this conclusion. They thought that Kamin's design did not allow generalizations to be made with regard to the usual method of presentation of the PMA. Furthermore, they pointed out that one half of the aged subjects in Kamin's study were senile.

In a study designed to correct some of the methodological problems associated with Kamin's (1957) study, Furry and Baltes (1973) manipulated fatigue and boredom by varying the position of the various PMA tests and whether or not a boring pretest designed to fatigue subjects was administered prior to the PMA. Three age groups of females were used: 11 to 14, 30 to 50, and 51 to 80 years. All age groups of participants were obtained in the community. Varying the position of the subtests did not, by itself, result in signifi-

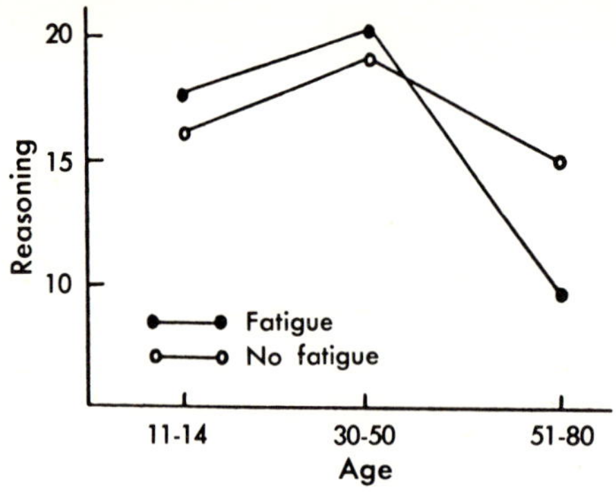

Fig. 6-11. The age-by-fatigue interaction for the reasoning task. Adolescents and adults exhibited a similar level of performance under fatigue and no-fatigue conditions. In contrast, elderly subjects exhibited a significant performance decrement when exposed to a pretest designed to produce fatigue. (From Furry, C. A., and Baltes, P. B. *Journal of Gerontology,* 1973, **28,** 73.)

cant age differences in performance. However, for verbal meaning and reasoning tests the preexperimental fatigue condition produced magnified age differences. Fig. 6-11 shows performance of the three age groups on the reasoning test. Adolescents and adults exhibit similar performances under fatigue and no fatigue, whereas elderly subjects who were exposed to pretest fatigue condition exhibited a pronounced decrement in performance. For the word fluency test, age-fatigue relationships were influenced by position of the tests. Fig. 6-12 summarizes these findings. It may be seen that middle-aged adults and older adults performed better under the no-fatigue (no pretest condition) than fatigue conditions when the test was positioned later in the series of tests, but

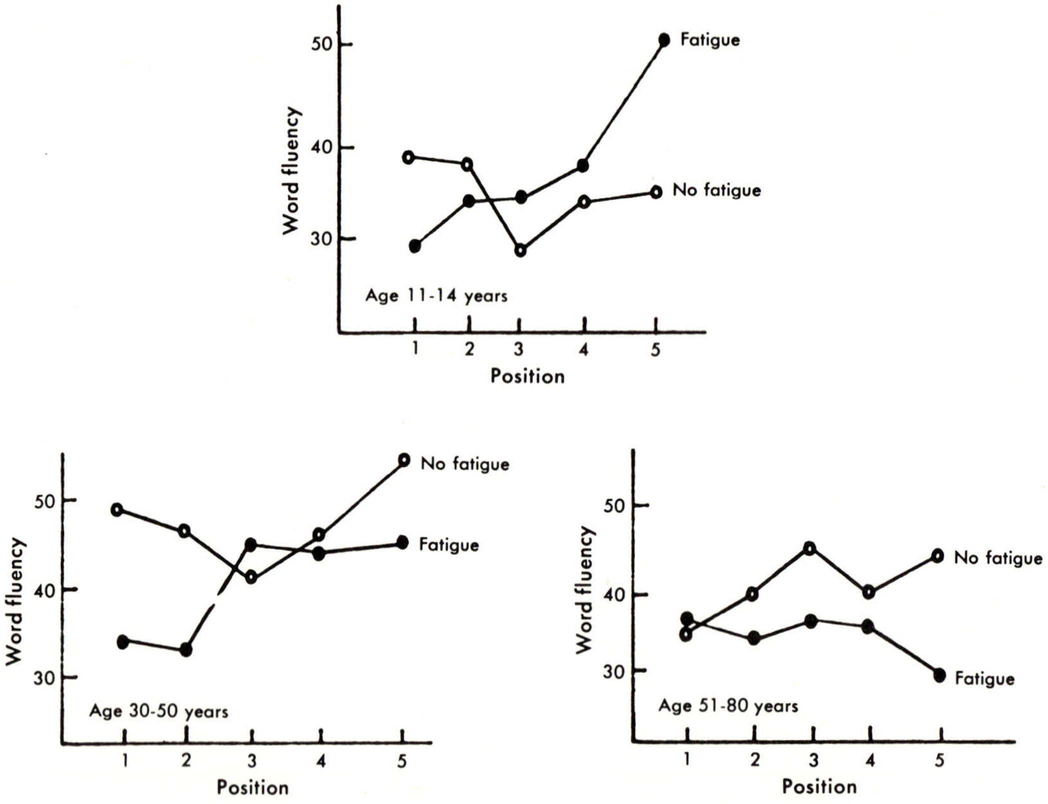

Fig. 6-12. The age-by-fatigue-by-position interaction for word fluency. Adults (30 to 50 years) and older adults (51 to 80 years) performed better under the no-fatigue (no pretest condition) than under the fatigue conditions when the test was positioned later in the series of tests, but adolescents exhibited the reverse trend. (From Furry, C. A., and Baltes, P. B. *Journal of Gerontology,* 1973, **28,** 73.)

adolescents exhibited the reverse trend. They showed higher performance under the fatigue condition when the test was positioned later in the sequence. The important generalization resulting from the Furry and Baltes study is that ability measures may be considerably less invariant from situation to situation than one might assume. Age differences on psychometric tests of ability may be influenced in an interactive manner by both ability and "ability-extraneous variables" (Furry and Baltes, 1973) that have direct and indirect effects on incentive to perform at an optimal level.

Just as there are problems with regard to the effective level of incentive provided by a given stimulus intensity used in animal studies of incentive, similar incentives may have different values for human beings of different ages by virtue of prior history and life experiences peculiar to a particular age-cohort. Data by Bellucci and Hoyer (1975) indicate that the incentive value of a reinforcing stimulus (i.e., S & H Green Stamps) may be different by virtue of age-associated differences in susceptibility to external feedback.

It is clear that age-associated decrements in performance may often be related to factors other than changes in neurophysiological substrates which are assumed to underlie adult developmental change. Alternative explanations (e.g., Baltes and Labouvie, 1973; Hoyer, 1974) deserve attention and *all performance studies must control for motivational differences among age groups if performance decrements are to be attributed to changes in the nervous system.*

SUMMARY

Several firm generalizations about motivation and aging may be gleaned from laboratory studies of human and animal motivation. Studies of hunger and thirst motivation with aging animals indicate that equal days of food or water deprivation may not be equally motivating for all age groups. One of the best ways to equate hunger- or thirst-induced drive for different age groups is to equate age groups in terms of weight loss. Activity level has been a popular index of the strength of hunger or thirst drive, but activity level itself varies among age groups, and it influences hunger drive in a feedback relationship, which leads to a confounding of the measure of drive strength (activity) with the drive-inducing aspects of activity. The hungry animal runs faster and explores more, but this activity results in increased hunger if no food is available. Eventually the animal weakens and motor activity decreases.

Animal research on aging and sex drives has concentrated on the identification of physiological bases of decline and the identification of hormonal correlates. Clearly, changes in androgen level and cellular structure in the accessory sex glands are important factors in the differential decline of different components of sexual behavior at different ages for various species and strains. However, evidence exists that early experience variables can affect various components of sexual activity with advancing age.

Aging research on sexual drive in humans has concentrated more on psychosocial factors than on hormonal factors. For many older persons, competence continues long after activity ceases. The best predictor of sexual activity and interest in old age is sexual activity and interest at a younger age. There are, of course, other determinants of continued sexual activities. Two of the most important predictors of continued activity for men are health and socioeconomic status; for women, marital status seems to be the best predictor. Often sexual activity falls drastically for women after their hubsands die. Limited choice of mates and society's attitudes toward sex among unmarried individuals, particularly elderly individuals, are among the factors that preclude the resumption of sexual activities for elderly widows.

Animal studies of exploratory behavior, emotionality, and locomotor activity in the open field suggest that these behaviors are not always related to each other in the same manner at different ages. Thus it is important to obtain separate measures of these variables, and all three should never be inferred from locomotion in the open field. The relationship of exploratory behavior and emotionality to aging is less clear than that for activity level per se. Decreased exploratory behavior has been reported in some strains of rats and mice but not in others. In some instances, confounding variables have not been carefully controlled, and the influence of locomotion per se on exploratory behavior has not been ruled out. Emotionality research with animals and humans has suffered from a lack of consistent research methods. Studies with both types of subjects have reported contradictory results, and no general conclusions may be reached regarding the traditional hypothesis that emotionality declines with advancing age.

In contrast to animal research, which has concentrated heavily on general decrease in psychomotor activity as a result of functional changes with age, human studies of activity have been concerned with the social-psychological factors involved in the substitution of some activities for others. At the animal level, concern centers about physical activity. At the human level, decline in physical activity appears to be an accepted fact. The major issue involves the qualitative and quantitative changes in social activities. Human studies of activity have not been discussed in this chapter but will be taken up in some detail in Chapter 7.

Perhaps the most notable advance in the experimental psychology of motivation at the human level has come in the area of laboratory task performance. Psychologists have learned that too much motivation can be as bad as too little and that overinvolvement or overarousal resulting in a heightened drive state may impair performance more for elderly persons than for young persons. Thus diminished intellectual ability does *not* necessarily account for age differences in laboratory performance. Older subjects may be more cautious or more threatened or more aroused by laboratory tasks. In some instances, laboratory tasks may have less meaning for elderly subjects, although laboratory studies do *not* provide consistent support for these propositions, and clearly they do not hold for all older subjects or in all situations. One difficulty encountered in manipulating the meaningfulness of stimulus materials is that task difficulty often varies with changes in stimulus materials. Caution is difficult to separate from decreased competence. Reduction in speed of task pacing in an effort to reduce task stress often makes the task less difficult. Thus further experiments are necessary to resolve issues of task difficulty and task meaningfulness, and many more studies need to be concentrated on individual differences in cautiousness behavior and their relationship to *functional* rather than chronological indices of age.

Animal investigations of the relationship between incentive and performance indicate that older animals may be less capable of responding to increased incentive to perform because of fatigue or diminished ability to respond to stressful stimuli. One problem with this research is that it is difficult to determine whether a given level of aversive stimulation (e.g., shock) is equally effective as a motivator across age groups. However, studies of the relationship between incentive and performance in aging animals are important because they indicate that performance decrements with advancing age can be related to factors other than decline in capacity to learn. It is difficult not to confound learning capacity and motivational factors in animal experiments because an animal must make some kind of motor response to indicate that it has learned the task. In some instances, these motor responses require rather strenuous activity for prolonged periods of time, for example, swimming from the start point to the choice point in a water maze, and thus age-associated differences in susceptibility to fatigue may affect performance.

Human studies of incentive indicate that a given social incentive may have different reinforcing value for subjects in different age groups because of age-associated differences in susceptibility to feedback. Human incentive manipulations often do not involve stress and fatigue, but fatigue plays an important role in the motivation of human subjects to perform at an optimal level. There is a growing body of evidence which suggests that in many instances apparent performance decrements in older adults may be related to nonintellectual variables, including incentive and drive level.

This chapter deals in some detail with animal studies of motivation. One may question the extent to which these studies are relevant to human motivation. Investigators of adult development and aging do not agree on this issue. Generally, infrahuman animals are used in psychological research and other areas of science when there are inherent dangers in conducting an experiment with humans and/or when the experimenter wishes to utilize a living animal model with a short life span. There is always a problem involved in generalizing from nonverbal animals to humans because of the complexities introduced by verbal communication.

Despite the difficulties involved in generalizing from lower to higher order animals with verbal skills, constraints on human research, imposed by ethical, moral, and legal considerations, have contributed to the necessity of research with animal subjects as models. This is no less true for other areas of science such as biology and medicine. Unfortunately, animal research to date has not taken full opportunity of the special advantages offered by animal models beyond the possibilities for manipulating life-history variables and the use of aversive and dangerous experimental manipulations. For example, one major advantage of the small animal model is that behavior genetic manipulations may be done. These manipulations enable a better understanding of the mode of inheritance and the nature of gene-environment interactions. The science of behavior genetics is rapidly growing. Today there are techniques available that permit links to be established between a particular chromosome segment and behavioral phenomenon that are controlled by physiological traits that intervene between a gene or genes and behavior (Elias, 1975a). Moreover, there are animal models for various nonneurological disease processes such as diabetes, obesity, cancer, and hypertension as well as neurological diseases (Russell and Sprott, 1975). Thus an animal model can be used to examine the extent to which disease processes may interfere with performance by way of their influence on motivation to perform.

Most motivational studies with aging animals have been done with rats and mice. Expansion of research to include other species may be of value in the construction of ontological models from the study of phylogenetic similarities and differences. Increased use of primates may constitute a critical step toward a better understanding of social-motivational factors as they influence sexual behavior, drive, fear, frustration, and social activities. The advantage of the primate is that it is close to man on the phylogenetic scale, and yet many potentially dangerous or stressful experiments can be done. Life span is limited, and life-history variables may be controlled and manipulated.

At present there is a hiatus between experimentally oriented motivational research featuring the manipulation of incentives and drive and more descriptive research that has been concerned with complex social motivators or, in Maslow's (1954) terms, higher order needs. Food deprivation may be important to the everyday life of the rat or mouse, and it may be much easier to manipulate shock intensity or stimulus pacing in humans than to manipulate complex social-motivating forces, which are influenced by language and higher order cognitive processes. However, socially complex motivators are important to the everyday life of adult persons. Thus descriptive research or research involving quasi-experimental designs is significant to the understanding of human motivation. Chapter 7 integrates the research on social motivation with the data on complex human social and work activities.

SELECTED READINGS

Botwinick, J. Drives, expectancies, and emotions. In J. E. Birren (Ed.), *Handbook of aging and the individual.* Chicago: University of Chicago Press, 1959, pp. 739-768.

Eisdorfer, C., Connor, J. F., and Wilkie, F. L. The effect of magnesium pemoline on cognition and behavior. *Journal of Gerontology,* 1968, **23,** 283-288.

Eisdorfer, C., Nowlin, J., and Wilkie, F. Improvement of learning in the aged by modification of autonomic nervous system activity. *Science,* 1970, **170,** 1327-1329.

Elias, M. F., and Elias, P. K. Drive, motivation, and activity. In J. E. Birren, and K. W. Schaie (Eds.), *Handbook of the psychology of aging.* New York: Van Nostrand-Reinhold Co., in press.

Elias, P. K., Elias, M. F., and Eleftheriou, B. E. Emotionality, exploratory behavior, and locomotion in aging, inbred strains of mice. *Gerontologia,* 1975, **21,** 46-55.

Furry, C. A., and Baltes, P. B. The effect of age differences in ability-extraneous performance variables on the assessment of intelligence in children, adults, and the elderly. *Journal of Gerontology,* 1973, **28,** 73-80.

Heron, A., and Craik, F. I. M. Age differences in cumulative learning of meaningful and meaningless material. *Scandinavian Journal of Psychology,* 1964, **5,** 209-217.

Kogan, N., and Wallach, M. A. The effect of anxiety on relations between subjective age and caution in an older sample. In P. H. Hoch, and J. Zubin (Eds.), *Psychopathology of aging.* New York: Grune & Stratton, Inc., 1961.

Leri, J. E., Lesswing, N. J., and Elias, M. F. Relation of mental ability to preference for varying rates of auditory stimulation. *Psychonomic Science,* 1969, **17,** 80-81.

Paré, W. P. Interaction of age and shock intensity on acquisition of a discriminated conditioned emotional response. *Journal of Comparative and Physiological Psychology,* 1969, **68,** 364-369.

Pfeiffer, E. Sexual behavior in old age. In E. W. Busse, and E. Pfeiffer (Eds.), *Behavior and adaptation in late life.* Boston: Little, Brown & Co., 1969, pp. 151-162.

Rees, J. N., and Botwinick, J. Detection and decision factors in auditory behavior of the elderly. *Journal of Gerontology,* 1971, **26,** 133-136.

Spence, K. W. A theory of emotionally based drive (D) and its relation to performance in simple learning situations. *American Psychologist,* 1958, **13,** 131-141.

Sprott, R. L., and Eleftheriou, B. E. Open field behavior in aging inbred strains of mice. *Gerontologia,* 1974, **20,** 155-162.

Troyer, W. G., Eisdorfer, C., Bogdonoff, M. D., and Wilkie, F. Experimental stress and learning in the aged. *Journal of Abnormal Psychology,* 1967, **72,** 65-70.

Troyer, W. G., Eisdorfer, C., Wilkie, F., and Bogdonoff, M. Free fatty acid responses in the aged individual during performance of learning tasks. *Journal of Gerontology,* 1966, **21,** 415-419.

Verwoerdt, A., Pfeiffer, E., and Wang, H. S. Sexual behavior in senescence. I. Changes in sexual activity and interest of aging men and women. *Journal of Geriatric Psychiatry,* 1969, **2,** 163-180.

Verwoerdt, A., Pfeiffer, E., and Wang, H. S. Sexual behavior in senescence. II. Patterns of sexual activity and interest. *Geriatrics,* 1969, **24,** 137-154.

Wittels, I. Age and stimulus meaningfulness in paired-associate learning. *Journal of Gerontology,* 1972, **27,** 372-375.

Wood, V. Age-appropriate behavior for older people. *Gerontologist,* 1971, **11,** 74-78.

CHAPTER 7

MOTIVATION—ACTIVITY AND DISENGAGEMENT IN WORK, RETIREMENT, AND LEISURE

Retirement—
Does two things
Motivates
Gives one wings.
MARTHA J. NEWTON (1974)

As a person ages in Western society, one of the most significant psychological transitions he must face involves the relationships among his work, retirement, and leisure activities. Beginning in childhood, each individual establishes attitudes and goals concerning work, retirement, and leisure. He develops patterns of work and leisure behaviors that are a function of his personal goals and the incentives made available to him by such sources as his family, educational background, and social class. By the time he reaches middle adulthood, these attitudes and behavior patterns are usually stable, although they may vary greatly between individuals. For example, the artist or novelist may recognize few constraints on the actual length of time that he engages in "work" each day, but the factory worker may be acutely aware of when his working day begins and ends. With regard to leisure, many persons may believe that "doing nothing" constitutes the best form of leisure behavior; others may think that leisure time must be spent "productively," for example, by engaging in home improvement projects.

WORK, RETIREMENT, AND LEISURE RELATIONSHIPS

The relationships among work, retirement, and leisure activities may be conceptualized in a number of ways. For example, first, the work *role* may be viewed as terminating with a retirement *event,* which is followed by a retirement *status* in which the individual's main *role* is leisure activity. Second, one may also view work and leisure as complementary activities in which a behavior that was once relegated to the realm of leisure during middle age becomes productive work for the retired person (e.g., a hobby such as carpentry may provide an additional source of income for the retired computer programmer). The latter view conceptualizes a certain behavior as being directed by changing incentives; that is, the initial incentive for engaging in carpentry may have been relaxation and pride in the finished product. With the advent of retirement, an additional incentive (income), which may or may not take priority over the previous incentives, emerges.

A third conceptualization of the work-leisure relationship has been proposed by

Kelly (1972). Kelly suggests that leisure may be characterized along two dimensions: (1) the extent to which an individual may freely choose to engage in leisure activity and (2) the type of relationship between leisure activity and an individual's occupation. Thus essentially four types of leisure are theoretically possible. Type 1 is labeled *unconditional leisure* and refers to any activity that is freely chosen and unrelated to one's occupation. The business executive who enjoys painting in his spare time merely for its own sake is engaging in type 1 leisure. Kelly refers to type 2 leisure as *coordinated activity,* in which the activity is freely chosen but is related to the individual's occupation in some manner. For example, taking a night course in accounting to improve his bookkeeping procedures might be type 2 leisure for the independent hardware store owner. Type 3 leisure is referred to as *complementary activity,* which is neither freely chosen nor directly related to one's work. However, it may be a consequence of the role expectations of a particular occupation, or it may be determined by goals indirectly related to that occupation. It is for these reasons that it is considered "complementary." In the first instance, a prominent attorney may be expected to accept certain speaking engagements such as commencement addresses. In the second instance, a junior level executive may be expected to become prominent in certain community activities if he desires to be promoted to a senior level position. The final category of leisure activity proposed by Kelly is type 4, *preparation and recuperation.* It is not freely chosen, and it is directly related to an individual's occupation, involving such activities as test evaluation after classroom hours for teachers or just relaxing in a comfortable chair for the tired waitress who has been on her feet all day.

Certainly as one grows older, the proportion of time spent in each of Kelly's four types of leisure may undergo both gradual and/or abrupt change. For example, the assistant professor must spend many more hours in classroom lecture preparation (type 4) than the veteran full professor who must only update his lecture notes from time to time. The most obvious abrupt change in leisure activities occurs at retirement. For many persons the leisure activities involved in types 2, 3, and 4 become totally unnecessary, and they are left with the opportunity for full-time engagement in type 1 activity. On the other hand, it is unlikely that the prominent attorney referred to earlier will cease receiving lecture requests, even when he has "officially" retired. In the following sections of this chapter we will explore the various work-leisure transitions that occur with increasing age and the psychological consequences of adaptation to these changes.

ACTIVITY AND DISENGAGEMENT THEORIES

One is not old
When one retires
Enjoy yourself
Light some fires!
It is too early
To sit and rock
Keep moving on
Don't watch that clock
MARTHA J. NEWTON (1974)

The major impetus for investigations describing motivational change associated with work, retirement, and leisure behaviors has come from two opposing theories: disengagement theory and activity theory. These theories have been a source of dispute among researchers for approximately fifteen years. Although both theories claim to encompass many aspects of the life situation, the changing patterns of work and leisure among older adults in American society has provided the clearest background for investigations of their validity.

Disengagement theory, first proposed by Cumming (1959), focuses on the social-psychological determinants of a hypothesized mutual withdrawal of society and the individual from each other with increasing age. The process of disengagement is viewed as developmental in nature rather than simply imposed by society. The individual is personally motivated to disengage. The objective for disengagement, a type of psychological equilibrium, is accomplished by decreasing emotional investments in former ties to persons and objects (goals) in the environment (Cumming and Henry, 1961). Disengagement theory is frequently contrasted with activity theory, which proposes essentially an opposite process. Activity theory suggests that older persons have the same psychological and social needs as younger persons. For the individual to find optimal satisfaction, reductions in activities such as employment must be accompanied by increases in other activities such as family interactions (Havighurst et al., 1964a). Thus disengagement theory suggests that there is motivation to decrease social interests and interactions, and activity theory suggests that there is motivation to substitute certain social interests and interactions for others while maintaining past levels of activity.

The extensive number of investigations that have been stimulated by disengagement and activity theories are characterized by contradictory results. The most common finding is that neither theory explains the goal-directed behavior of aging persons under all circumstances and all of the time. Rather, behavior patterns among elderly persons, such as those involved in work, retirement, and leisure, appear to be determined by multiple factors which are similar to those which influenced motivation throughout earlier portions of their lives. However, a number of theorists have proposed that there are, in fact, some more specific psychological (internal) and societal (external) forces which result in observable motivational changes. These may be particularly important during crisis periods of life, such as the work-retirement transition.

SPECIFIC THEORETICAL ISSUES INVOLVED IN THE RETIREMENT PROCESS

Kuhlen (1964) has suggested that many of the changes in motivation occurring with age may be brought about by the frustration of needs. In the context of the present chapter, the frustration may be more appropriately considered to affect goal achievement by means of the withdrawal of many of the incentives previously provided during the middle-adult years. Goals may be frustrated as a result of (1) the different status accorded to different age groups; (2) limitations of time and money, which become increasingly severe with advancing age; (3) physical changes, usually in the form of a decline in energy, resiliency, strength, and reaction time; (4) recent advances in technology (e.g., computers), which result in many deficits in the skills of the elderly; and (5) the increase in commitments, for example, to a specific job or to a marriage partner, which simultaneously decrease the options open to the individual. Kuhlen hypothesized that the life span is characterized by a curve of "needs" for expansion (e.g., achievement, creativity, and self-actualization) followed by "needs" for constriction (e.g., reduced activity and retirement). Unfortunately, although the reasons given by Kuhlen for need frustration are appropriate to the current situation of many older persons in American society, the expansion-constriction dimension does not appear to be an adequate description of the motivational changes that occur among the elderly. Rather, the changes that accompany the aging process may be more directly related to changes in the incentives offered to persons as they grow older.

Certainly the event of retirement may result in frustrations that, for many persons, are related to the imposed restrictions and withdrawal of incentives (e.g., money) mentioned by Kuhlen. Other theorists have hypothesized even more intrinsic problems with the concept of a work-retirement transition as it is viewed by this society. Back (1969) has suggested that one of the basic dilemmas faced by the elderly person is the "ambiguity of retirement." On the one hand, retirement is viewed as a privilege that is earned by virtue of contributing many years to the labor force. On the other hand, retirement is viewed as an obligation because it is increasingly anticipated as the "proper" *role* for the elderly. The result of this ambiguity, according to Back (1969:100), is that, "Retirement is regarded as an achievement in principle, but dreaded as a crisis when it actually occurs." Much of the dread of retirement stems from the fact that American society most often identifies an individual by his occupation. Thus retirement in many respects turns out to be the giving up of a previously respected status with little opportunity for acquiring an equally suitable status.

Closely related to Back's evaluation of retirement in American society is a theory proposed by Miller (1968), which focuses specifically on the relationship between work and leisure in the years following retirement. Basically, Miller proposes that the working person has no need to justify his leisure activities. Rather, he may view them as well-deserved recreational outlets. A retired person, who has lost his occupational identity, must legitimize his leisure activities. He is in a position where he must "establish the cultural value of his leisure which will act as a basis for a (new) social identity [Miller, 1968: 369]." Furthermore, he must choose activities in which his current capabilities allow him to live up to both his own and others' expectations. If he fails at his new avocation, the embarrassment caused both to himself and to those associated with him will result in mutual disengagement. Thus the retired carpenter, who boldly offers to build a new addition to his neighbor's house but who fails to complete it before winter because of poor health or failing physical strength, is a source of embarrassment to both himself and the neighbors. But the retired computer programmer, who had carpentry as a hobby, may successfully complete a playhouse for the neighbor's children, providing everyone concerned understands that he must do it at his own pace. Although both men were oriented toward specific goals and may have been induced to undertake their projects for specific incentives (e.g., monetary payment), one stood a good chance of success, whereas the other did not.

A number of the underlying assumptions made by both Back (1969) and Miller (1968) may be legitimately questioned (Atchley, 1972). For example, it may not be true that most persons derive their primary identity solely from occupational roles. Consequently, they may not feel the necessity of maintaining an achievement orientation with regard to their previous work status. Thus it is important to examine the distribution of attitudes and goals related to work and retirement currently present in American society.

THE DECISION TO RETIRE

A job long held
In such good grace
But now a Youth
Will take your place.
MARTHA J. NEWTON (1974)

Both disengagement and activity theories view retirement as a major turning point in the social situation of the older person. It represents the clearest example of mutual disengagement by society and the individual. But it may also offer opportunities for engagement in new activities that are more or less satisfying to the individual than his previous work role.

Perhaps one of the most pertinent aspects of retirement is whether it is forced or chosen. Many social and economic factors may enter into the decision to retire. Palmore (1971) analyzed data from the 1963 Social Security survey using a probability sample of persons aged 62 years and over. He found that age, independent of all other factors, had the most direct influence on the retirement of both men and women. When he controlled for age, poor health became the second most important factor for men. Marital status was the second most important factor for women; that is, married women were the most frequent retirees. Palmore concluded that, when all factors were considered, there appeared to be two main reasons for retirement: (1) inability to work, which included factors such as compulsory retirement at a given age, illness, and lower education; and (2) lower need for earnings, which included such factors as being a married female.

A report from the Cornell Study of Occupational Retirement (Streib and Schneider, 1971), a longitudinal study of persons nearing retirement age, indicated that men and women with higher incomes, education, and higher status occupations continued working longer than others. Furthermore, women were generally *less* willing to retire than men, although in this study the women had more education and a higher proportion of them were in professional occupations. Consequently, the results may not be indicative of a true sex difference. Further insights concerning the decision to retire have been provided by Barfield and Morgan (1969). They found that early retirees were more likely to have experienced recent changes in the nature of their jobs, to have found that commuting was a source of irritation, to have found it difficult to keep up with work demands, or to have had difficulty controlling the pace of their work. The major implications of these studies are that, with increasing age, the incentives for continued participation in the work force are actively withdrawn (e.g., compulsory retirement policies), passively cease to exist (e.g., a decrease in the need for income), or lose their reinforcing value (e.g., a disagreeable, forced change in work-related duties).

There are some current data which indicate that the effects of active withdrawal of incentives, such as compulsory retirement plans, may not be so universally pervasive as is commonly believed. For example, only 21% of the salaried workers who retired in 1963 did so because of mandatory retirement policies (Palmore, 1964). Furthermore, the general trend in retirement decisions between 1951 and 1963 appears to be in the direction of an increase in the proportion of persons who decide to retire on their own (1951—54%; 1963—61%). Six times as many people retired simply to enjoy leisure in 1963 compared with those doing so in 1961 (Palmore, 1964). However, as Kalish, (1975) points out, Palmore's survey applied only to salaried workers and did not include such categories as professionals, self-employed persons, or seasonal workers who are paid by the hour.

Generally, it may be concluded that factors such as educational level have a significant effect on the extent to which persons remain fully or partially employed beyond the age of 65 years. In 1960 one half of the male population over 65 years who had college degrees were still working, but only one fourth of those men with a fourth grade education or less were still working (Back, 1969). Thus a higher educational level, because of its direct effect on higher job status and independence, is more frequently associated with optional rather than compulsory retirement.

Regardless of whether retirement is forced or chosen, most people eventually do retire "officially." Thus it would seem likely that the older person would experience a significant change in aspirations and attitudes associated with achievement orientation and work activity. Certainly disengagement theory predicts that there are psychological as well as social sources of motivational change after retirement. However, current data suggest that, although some changes in incentives and goals may occur, the immediate effects of retirement are not as apparent as many psychologists once believed.

INCENTIVES AND GOALS DURING THE RETIREMENT PROCESS

How do incentives and goals associated with the work role affect the transition from work to retirement? Perhaps the most frequently tested hypothesis in the current literature is that an inverse relationship should exist between work satisfaction or commitment to work and attitudes toward retirement. Many recent studies do not support this hypothesis (e.g., Fillenbaum, 1971; Glamser, 1976; Goudy et al., 1975). Goudy and associates have suggested that a work satisfaction–retirement attitude typology represents a more realistic interpretation of current findings. Specifically, their data indicated that the population of workers nearing retirement is distributed among four categories in approximately equal proportions. Type A (high work satisfaction and positive attitudes toward retirement) and type B (low work satisfaction and positive attitudes toward retirement) should make the work-retirement-leisure transition with relative ease. Type C (high work satisfaction and negative attitudes toward retirement) and type D (low work satisfaction and negative attitudes toward retirement) should experience difficulty in making this transition. However, type C individuals can be helped through flexible retirement policies and/or assistance in finding a new career. On the other hand, Goudy and co-workers (1975: 197) find that type D individuals are prime candidates, "for entrance to what Kuypers and Bengtson (1973) describe as the 'social breakdown' syndrome, in which loss of age-appropriate norms, loss of roles, and loss of reference groups are seen as leading to a general 'susceptibility' on the part of the elderly to negatively evaluate their capabilities." Unfortunately, as Goudy and colleagues have noted, there are no longitudinal data currently available with regard to changes in work and retirement attitudes in the years following retirement. Thus psychologists do not know what specific steps need to be taken to prevent the type D individual from entering the "social breakdown syndrome."

There is some evidence to suggest that many persons fail to perceive adequately the actual nature of their postretirement status. For example, a cross-cultural study of the retirement process indicated that less than 8% of the retirees interviewed reported missing their work, itself; yet 19% of those persons still employed predicted that this loss would be paramount (Shanas et al., 1968). It is interesting that the status of a job may also be associated with preretirement and postretirement attitudes. Persons in high-prestige occupations, who are least enthusiastic about retirement while still working, tend to feel more positively about their new status once they have experienced it for a number of years. On the other hand, persons in low-prestige occupations are more likely to find retirement less attractive than they had predicted (Stokes and Maddox, 1967). This study presents evidence somewhat contrary to the theory proposed by Back (1969), which would predict that the status change undergone by persons retiring from high-prestige occupations would be more severe in terms of loss of satisfaction.

Data from other studies indicate that those persons who find retirement least satisfying are those for whom financial stress is a problem. Reichard and co-workers (1962) interviewed eighty-seven men 55 to 84 years of age, one half of whom were retired and one half of whom were still engaged in full- or part-time employment. They found that, although many of the employed subjects expressed anxiety concerning retirement, the most frequent complaint of retirees was reduced financial circumstances. Similarly, Shanas and associates (1968) reported that nearly one half of their retired subjects believed that money was the most serious retirement-related loss. It is apparent that financial circumstances in the postretirement years are substantially determined by the prestige and income of one's previous occupation. Thus, in many instances, the individual has little control over his perceptions of his financial situation, and for many persons retirement represents a severe loss of incentive (money). But it is also important to examine whether this loss of incentive is accompanied by changes in attitudes toward achievement and work activity.

It is clear that the value of work generally does not appear to be diminishing for middle-class adults in American society. Pfeiffer and Davis (1971) reported that 80% to 90% of the men and women in their middle-class sample, 46 to 71 years of age, would prefer to work even if they could maintain financial stability without working. Few of those subjects interviewed thought that they derived more satisfaction from leisure than from work activities. However, it may be that more specific work-related attitudes, such as achievement orientation, undergo change as persons approach and experience the retirement process. Current data appear to indicate that some changes occur, in fact, although these may be quite subtle.

Davis (1967) found that older men (66 to 85 years) maintained as high a level of aspiration for success as younger men (20 to 30 years) and middle-aged men (40 to 58 years) under experimentally induced social pressure. All subjects, regardless of age, responded to *failure* by setting higher achievement levels for performance on a level of aspiration test. However, the older men reacted to *success* by decreasing aspiration levels and the younger men by increasing aspiration levels. Davis interpreted this differential response to success in older and younger men in terms of an attempt on the part of the older men to conform more closely to a fictitious peer group norm introduced by the experimenter. When told that they were performing "better" than a peer group, the younger men apparently attempted to present themselves as superior to their peers. The older men did not respond with this push to "get ahead."

Streib (1958) reported some interesting indirect variations in achievement norms for employed as opposed to retired parents who were approximately 64 years of age at the time of their initial interview. The retired parents tended to place less importance on the upward mobility of their children than they had when they were employed. However, the retirees did not believe that the achievement norms of their children should be curtailed or that geographical mobility would impair cross-generational family relations. In other words, whereas there was a decrease in the extent to which retired parents thought achievement norms should dominate their children's lives, they did not expect the children to neglect a chance to "get ahead."

Although achievement norms may not be maintained into old age in all situations, the same cannot be said of all work-related attitudes. Distefano (1969) found that the attitudes of task orientation (concern about completing a job and doing the best job possible) and self-orientation (primary work emphasis placed on the direct rewards of the task) did not increase or decrease for male and female subjects ranging in age from 16 to 75 years. On the other hand, interaction orientation (extent to which an individual obtains satisfaction from the social aspects of his job) increased between the ages of 30 to 75 years for both males and females. It should be noted that males scored consistently higher than females in the attitudes of task orientation and self-orientation, although for interaction orientation, the opposite was true. However, the data from this study indicate that many work attitudes held by older persons do not differ from those held by younger persons, and it is likely that all age groups experience similar rewards and frustrations in work roles. In some cases (e.g., interaction orientation), work-related incentives actually may be amplified with increasing age.

It is possible that attitudes toward work may vary as a function of the capacity of the older person to maintain some involvement with his previous work role. A number of studies have explored the work-related attitudes of persons engaged in occupations that do not involve forced retirement or that allow some continuation of professional associations. Hearn (1972) used a semistructured interview to examine self-involvement and commitment in young and old artists. Career artists over 50 years of age appeared to maintain the same degree of self-involvement as did younger artists. In fact, older artists viewed increasing age as an aid to artistic maturity and skill.

Atchley (1971) found that there was a high potential for disengagement among college professors of all ages (20 to 70+ years) as measured by such variables as extent of tolerance for solitude and tendency toward passivity rather than active mastery of the environment. Yet work commitment remained high and preference for autonomous leisure remained low across all age groups. Atchley suggests that the conflict between the desire for disengagement and psychological commitment to work begins early in life, but for college professors the psychological commitment is stronger. Perhaps work roles that force retirement at a specific age and involve lesser degrees of commitment may invite more psychological disengagement and less conflict.

Why is it that certain occupational groups, such as university faculty, seem to experience a stronger psychological commitment to work than other occupational groups? We cannot fully answer this question because there is no information on occupational groups other than academicians. However, within this group there is evidence that those persons who continue to be involved in their profession view their work as a highly meaningful life experience. Fillenbaum and Maddox (1974) interviewed thirty-seven university faculty members, 65 to 70 years of age, who were in good health and who would not experience financial difficulties after retirement. Approximately three fourths of those persons interviewed continued to work for pay (e.g., writing books for royalties) after they had retired officially from their university positions. In spite of the attempt to control for initial health and financial status, the professors who continued to work tended to rate their health higher and had more financial responsibilities (e.g., they had more financial dependents) than those who did not. However, those who continued to work also perceived their work as a more meaningful life experience than those who did not, in terms of variables such as extent of involvement in curriculum development and membership in professional organizations.

Acuff and Allen (1970) collected questionnaire data on a group of retired emeritus professors (mean age = 73.3 years) to assess the degree to which these individuals experienced "purpose of life" and the association of purpose of life with the extent of their disengagement. Purpose in life was measured by a twenty-item scale consisting of items such as, "In life I have no goals or aims at all—In life I have very clear goals and aims." They found that maintenance of some type of professional activity and continued participation in professional organizations after retirement (indications of lack of complete disengagement) were positively related to purpose in life. Furthermore, those who believed that retirement resulted in a reduction in their sense of usefulness had higher purpose-in-life scores. Thus many of the postretirement behaviors and attitudes of persons involved in occupations that provide for some degree of continued engagement appear to be associated with more general attitudes toward the meaningfulness of their lives.

These findings lead to a further question. Is it possible for persons who cannot remain occupationally engaged, but who believe that their lives should contain "meaning," to find outlets in which to express their goal-directed behavior? We turn now to a potential answer to this question. Perhaps, as Miller (1968) has hypothesized, what was once considered "leisure" activity may become "productive" work activity for these persons during their postretirement years. The extent to which older persons engage in this type of substitution may also offer an indication of their desire for continued activity rather than psychological and social disengagement.

ACTIVITY AS OPPOSED TO DISENGAGEMENT IN WORK-RELATED BEHAVIOR

Confirmation of either disengagement or activity theory rests mainly on the determination of the actual maintenance or reduction of activity directed toward previously established goals or newly substituted goals. Assuming that retirement often brings about a loss of incentives for many persons, and therefore a loss of avenues for goal achievement, we must examine whether or not older persons maintain the motivation to find substitute means of goal achievement.

There is some evidence that disengagement from past work roles may be successfully replaced by engagement in new work roles that previously were considered to fall into Kelly's (1972) unconditional leisure category. To some extent this evidence supports Miller's (1968) hypothesis of the potential replacement of former work roles with new roles from which the individual may draw a social identity. However, the few studies available deal only with creative or artistic endeavors rather than substitute activities in general.

Hearn's (1972) survey of aging artists suggested that persons who chose art as a second career after retirement were just as "engaged" as first career artists. Specifically, they were interested in selling their work for economic gain, thought that recognition and prestige were important work goals, and expressed negative attitudes toward the concept of retirement. Dawson and Baller (1972) found that elderly persons (65 to 79 years) who were given the opportunity to attend art classes exceeded a college-aged student group in measures of satisfaction derived from art studies and in subjective ratings of their accomplishments. However, this study has a serious shortcoming because the elderly group of experimental subjects was self-selected; that is, they exhibited a higher degree of motivation to enroll in art classes than those subjects who refused the opportunity. Both the study by Dawson and Baller (1972) and the study by Hearn (1972) indicate that young, middle-aged, and elderly persons are equally capable of engagement in work activities that require some degree of creativity and, in fact, appear to succeed in achieving many of the same goals (e.g., self-satisfaction). These findings lend support to both activity theory and Miller's theory in that it does appear possible to provide substitute means of goal achievement, at least in specific situations.

At the present time it is not clear to what extent the successful substitution of avenues for goal achievement may be generalized to all work roles. If extensive retraining for a new role is necessary, it is unlikely to be an acceptable substitute for elderly persons. It is known, for example, that even middle-aged workers often are reluctant to engage in extensive retraining programs after the loss of their jobs. Belbin and Belbin (1968:343) report that, "Of 331 men rendered redundant by the closure of two British Railways Workshops, not one accepted opportunities for retraining." Furthermore, the opportunity to enter a training program for adult migrant workers in Arizona brought only seventy-five positive responses out of 900 families contacted. This lack of response to training opportunities may be partly attributable to an anxiety by the older worker to succeed in a new endeavor (see Chapter 6 for a review of anxiety and cautiousness). However, this hypothesis has not been tested adequately at the present time.

It must be kept in mind that many retirees, especially those for whom financial circumstances are not a problem, may not be motivated to enter a new work role. It was mentioned earlier that there appears to be a trend in American society in the direction of increasing numbers of persons whose decision to retire is based mainly on the desire to have and enjoy more leisure time (Palmore, 1964). Thus psychologists must determine whether or not the leisure activities of older persons actually are maintained or increased in the postretirement years. Proponents of disengagement theory would suggest that even many leisure activities, especially those involved in social interaction, would tend to become restricted with increasing age. Of course, proponents of activity theory would suggest the opposite; that is, for those leisure activities which are reduced in frequency (e.g., social interaction with job associates), substitute activities will be found.

ACTIVITY AS OPPOSED TO DISENGAGEMENT IN LEISURE-RELATED BEHAVIOR

To the extent that an individual, regardless of age, finds satisfaction in leisure activity, it may be assumed that he will attempt to maintain that activity unless conflicting goal situations arise. Thus it becomes important to determine if there are changes in the value placed on leisure activity with increasing age. Havighurst (1961) found that, between the ages of 40 and 70 years, there were no changes in the extent to which leisure activities were valued in terms of creativity, enjoyment, time killing, development of talent, physical energy input, relation of leisure to work, service, pleasure, vitality, and apathy. It would seem that most of the goals toward which leisure activity may be directed, as determined by the values attributed to such activity, do not show major changes with increasing age. Only one trend, change in range of interests, was apparent for different age groups, and this trend was different for various socioeconomic levels. Persons in higher socioeconomic levels tended to maintain an equivalent range of interests regardless of age. In contrast, persons in lower socioeconomic levels tended to restrict their range of leisure interests as they grew older. Thus one clue to the resolution of the conflict over disengagement as opposed to activity theory may lie in their application to the various social stratifications present in American society.

A significant proportion of leisure time for persons in all age groups involves some type of social interaction. Consequently, it is not surprising that this aspect of leisure has been studied most extensively by gerontological researchers. In a longitudinal study of the social environment of forty-seven elderly men (mean age = 71 years), Yarrow and associates (1963) raised questions concerning whether social activities were maintained at a constant rate. Findings suggested that a constant rate of activities was maintained. In

Fig. 7-1. Dr. Ewald ("Bud") Busse (Fig. 2-3) takes time from his busy schedule at Duke University to engage in some "leisurely activity."

fact, about one half of the men reported more social activities at the end of a five-year span of interviews than at the beginning. Lehr and Rudinger (1969) also conducted a longitudinal series of interviews and found that 78.8% of their sample of older men and women (60 to 75 years of age) did not make a significant number of social role changes over a four-year period. Only 7.9% reported a decrease in number of social roles, and 14.3% reported an increase in their number of social roles.

Youmans and Yarrow (1971) conducted an eleven-year longitudinal study of twenty-four men, 65 to 75 years of age, at the time of initial interviews. As a group, the men remained stable in the degree of complexity in daily behavior, feelings of satisfaction and contentment in living, degree of activity as opposed to passivity, and extent of social interactions. However, despite this basic continuity, a change did occur in the *interrelationships* of these measures. Correlations among the four sets of scores ranged from .24 to .64 at the time of the initial measurements. Eleven years later the range was from .58 to .78. The authors suggested that this greater interdependency reflects a growing all-or-none aspect of social functioning in the later years. In spite of the fact that a few subjects did appear to exhibit disengagement behavior, the lack of a general tendency for these men to withdraw from their social environments represents a failure to support some of the major tenets of disengagement theory.

Additional evidence for the maintenance of social activity toward the end of the life span has been provided by Palmore's (1968) longitudinal study of men ranging in age from 70 to 93 years. As a group, these men reported no decrease in activities relating to family and friends, economics, or religion over a ten-year period. A comparable group of women reported a significant, but small, decrease in activities relating to family, friends, and leisure but an increase in economic activities. No change in religious activities was observed. It should be noted that since a significantly higher proportion of women outlive their spouses than vice versa, the decrease in family interactions and increase in economic activity might be related to this factor.

Fig. 7-2. George L. Maddox, Ph.D. (Michigan State University, 1956). Dr. Maddox has contributed significantly to research in human activity and life-style but is probably best known for his work on alcohol and development. He has published many books and articles in these and other areas of sociology of life-span development. Presently Dr. Maddox is Director of the Center for the Study of Aging and Human Development and Professor of Sociology, Duke University. He has been honored many times for his professional contributions to adult developmental sociology and aging: Fellow of the Gerontological Society, Russell Sage Fellow in Medical Sociology, Duke University, and Kent Fellow, Danforth Foundation, elected in 1954. He has also served as Associate Editor for the *Journal of Health and Social Behavior* and as an Advisory Editor on the *Handbook of Aging and Social Sciences.*

For many years now, leaders in the field of social gerontological research have recognized the importance of gathering information on the life history of their subjects if they are to understand present behavior (Havighurst, 1968). For example, Maddox (1968) has suggested that one major determinant of the great variability in social activities among the elderly is persistence of individual differences in previous life-styles. Life-style may be defined as "the observable organization of an individual's activities in terms of his use of time, his investment of energy and his choice of interpersonal objects [Bengtson, 1973:37]." Maddox (1968) reported the results of a longitudinal study of 148 noninstitutionalized subjects who were 60 years of age and over. Activity, on the average, did decrease with age, but Maddox stressed that this finding must be interpreted in relation to the individual's own baseline; that is, the relative rank in activity among subjects remained stable. He argued that most persons (79% in his sample) exhibit a persistence of life-style with regard to extent of activity. This hypothesis may have more validity for some types of life-styles than for others. For example, Simpson and colleagues (1966) found that persons who had held jobs oriented toward people rather than toward symbols or things showed most continuity in style of activities from preretirement to post-retirement. Therefore, when quality rather than simply quantity of activities is considered, the persistence hypothesis may be valid in specific cases.

Other factors too have been implicated in the phenomenon of individual differences in social activities among the elderly. Taietz and Larson (1956) obtained evidence indicating that a sharp decline in participation in formal organizations does not occur until 80 years of age in rural communities. They also found that socioeconomic status and retirement have a greater effect on reduced participation than age. Youmans (1967) observed a reduction in family activities among women 75 years and over compared with women 60 to 64 years. However, this was true only for women living in rural rather than metropolitan areas. Factors such as lack of transportation facilities rather than desire for social disengagement might be responsible for the decline in activity among women in rural areas. It has also been shown that environmental situations, such as the type of retirement housing, may affect the extent of social activity among the elderly (Sherman, 1974). In most instances the relationship between retirement housing and social activity level may be explained by the facilities and programs that are made available to the residents at a particular location. Furthermore, the facilities and programs available often are dependent on the socioeconomic level of the residents.

It is clear that most studies have supported the contention that age, per se, is not causally related to either an overall decrease in activities or an overall decrease in the pleasure derived from work and leisure. To this extent they tend to support the tenets of activity theory and to refute those of disengagement theory. Nevertheless, it can be seen that, under some circumstances (e.g., living in a rural community), behaviors commonly viewed as disengagement phenomena do occur, although frequently they are associated with external factors correlated with the aging process rather than internal motivations. Based on a substantial amount of this type of evidence, many investigators seem to agree that some older individuals, for whatever reasons, do show a tendency to disengage (Atchley, 1971; Lehr and Rudinger, 1969; Streib, 1968; Youmans, 1966, 1967, 1969). A question then may be raised as to whether disengagement, when it occurs, is related to life satisfaction, morale, and other measures of "successful aging."

ACTIVITY AS OPPOSED TO DISENGAGEMENT: RELATIONSHIPS TO SUCCESSFUL AGING

Feelings of satisfaction with one's life often have been used as indices of successful aging (Erikson, 1964). Disengagement theory suggests that reductions in activity will result in increased feelings of satisfaction as one grows older. Activity theory suggests the opposite;

that is, a reduction in activities will result in feelings of dissatisfaction.

Before we present the evidence for and against these propositions in studies using postretirement subjects, mention should be made of an investigation dealing with factors related to life satisfaction among middle-aged adults (Palmore and Luikart, 1972). The subjects in this study were 45 to 69 years of age and were randomly chosen from membership lists of a health insurance association. Although most of the subjects were drawn from the middle and upper socioeconomic levels, there was some representation from lower socioeconomic levels. The results of the study indicated that self-rated health was the variable most strongly related to life satisfaction. The second most important variable was organizational activity. Those persons who engaged in greater amounts of organizational activity (e.g., clubs, unions, and religious groups) reported greater life satisfaction. Furthermore, it is interesting to note that in the Palmore and Luikart study, a number of variables, such as age, marital status, and total social contacts, which frequently are assumed to be related to life satisfaction, actually showed little or no relationship to it. Even a traumatic event, such as widowhood, does not appear to be associated with a decrease in life satisfaction during the middle-aged period (Noberini and Neugarten, 1975). In a later follow-up report of Palmore and Luikart's (1972) original sample, a longitudinal analysis revealed that past life satisfaction was the best predictor of current life satisfaction. For those individuals whose life satisfaction did change, self-rated health, sexual enjoyment, social contacts, and employment appeared to be the significant contributing factors (Palmore and Kivett, 1975). Thus amount of activity, per se, does not appear to be a good predictor of life satisfaction during middle age. With these data in mind, we will now examine the correlates of life satisfaction in the postretirement years.

Lemon and co-workers (1972) interviewed a sample of older persons (ages not reported) who were in the process of moving to a retirement community. Their data indicated that there was no relationship between life satisfaction and overall social activity. Furthermore, role loss (e.g., widowhood) was not inversely related to life satisfaction, as would be predicted by activity theory. Thus the authors found no support for the propositions that high frequency of activity is positively related to life satisfaction or that role loss is accompanied by decreases in life satisfaction. In a more recent study, Bull and Aucoin (1975) found no relationship between voluntary association participation and life satisfaction among noninstitutionalized adults 65 years and over, once health and socioeconomic status were controlled. However, not all studies have reported such optimistic results. The study by Palmore (1968), cited earlier, also involved measures of satisfaction with eight areas of life (e.g., economic security). A total life satisfaction score was obtained for each subject. Changes in amount of activity were significantly correlated with changes in satisfaction for both men and women. Specifically, reductions in activity were associated with a decrease in reports of satisfaction. Palmore viewed this finding as supportive of activity theory. Similarly, Havighurst and colleagues (1964b) found that high activity was associated with both positive affect and life satisfaction. These relationships did not show substantial change between the ages of 54 and 94 years, although it should be noted that the correlation between activity and affect regarding the *extent* of current activity was greater for those persons over 70 years than for those under 70 years. This finding is similar to the results of Youmans and Yarrow's (1971) study, which indicated that correlations between variables such as feelings of satisfaction and extent of social interaction became greater with increasing age.

Several investigators have considered the maintenance of an optimum level of morale as the criterion of successful aging. For example, Lipman and Smith (1968) investigated the question of general morale in a

Fig. 7-3. Bernice L. Neugarten, Ph.D. (University of Chicago, 1943). Dr. Neugarten is known for her work in many areas of adult developmental psychology, including studies of social development, personality, motivation, and retirement. Presently she is Professor of Human Development at the University of Chicago. An outstanding teacher and researcher, Dr. Neugarten has been honored frequently by the American Psychological Association and the Gerontological Society for her contributions. She has served as president of the Gerontological Society and is presently a member of the National Advisory Council on Aging. Among many other honors and awards, she has received the Kleemeier award for outstanding contributions to research on aging, and she was recently the recipient of the American Psychological Foundation Distinguished Teaching Award.

group of 281 elderly persons living in low-cost public housing. Disengagement indices included a tabulation of the number of social roles held by each person, a measure of interaction with voluntary organizations, frequency of contact among peer or primary group memberships, and a subjective evaluation of the perceived difference in interaction for the present year as opposed to former years. Using the concepts of disengagement, the investigators defined two *typical* groups: persons who were (1) under 75 years of age and engaged and (2) over 75 years of age and disengaged. *Atypical* groups were defined as persons who were (1) already disengaged although they had not yet reached 75 years and (2) not yet disengaged even though they were over 75 years. Results of the study indicated that higher morale was characteristic of persons who remained engaged regardless of age; that is, the "typical" younger group and the "atypical" older group had higher morale scores.

Not all investigators have measured the extent of disengagement among their subjects with direct indices such as frequency counts of social interactions. A more subtle, although equally interesting measure, is the extent to which persons remain oriented toward the future. Schonfield (1973) demonstrated a positive association between future commitments to planned activities, implying some degree of engagement, and "successful aging" in 100 females over the age of 65 years. Specifically, elderly women who were active with regard to future plans tended to receive higher scores for self-reported estimates of health, happiness, and usefulness.

However, the relationship of planning and satisfaction may not hold for some very old persons. Spence (1968) has presented evidence to this effect. He interviewed 226 subjects concerning the extent to which they made future plans and the extent to which they desired to make changes in their present life circumstances. The results of his study indicated that there was a decline in future orientation and an increase in the percentage of satisfied persons who do not make plans or desire change past the age of 75 years. These persons may be typically disengaged. However, the *most* satisfied persons at all ages over 65 years were those Spence called "composed planners." They planned ahead for future activities but did not desire to change their present circumstances. In terms of disengagement theory, these persons would certainly be atypical. They were anticipating future activity (an indication of desire to maintain activity), they apparently had no desire to change this life-style, and they reported high degrees of satisfaction. It would seem likely that both disengagement and activity maintenance may be considered successful styles of adaptation with increasing age, since a significant proportion of both disengagers and nondisengagers report average to high degrees of life satisfaction.

Successful adaptation for disengagers may be related to the ability to match current circumstances with psychological preparedness for disengagement. Tissue (1971) has presented evidence to this effect. He found that congruence between life space (monthly contacts with other persons) and disengagement potential (tendency toward passivity rather than active mastery of the environment, a high tolerance for solitude, an acceptance of one's ultimate death, and a lessening of emotional intensity) was associated with high morale in persons 65 to 88 years of age. Persons whose life space did not match their disengagement potential had lower morale scores.

On the other hand, it may be possible to disengage successfully from specific aspects of past involvement while remaining engaged in other areas of life. For example, Carp (1968a) reported that disengagement from family members correlated negatively with disengagement from other people and activities. Youmans (1966) administered a questionnaire designed to assess economic disengagement to rural and urban men who were 60 to 64 years of age and 75 years of age or over. Results of the study led Youmans to conclude that the older men had made a successful adjustment to their economic circumstances, even though they were less involved in work roles and had smaller incomes than the younger men. Thus it is possible that selected areas of life may be singled out for both social and psychological disengagement and that adaptation within these specific areas of disengagement may be successful.

SUMMARY AND IMPLICATIONS

Perhaps the only generalization that can be made with regard to disengagement and activity theories is that both may explain some situations for some persons some of the time. Henry (1965) has modified the original theory of disengagement (Cumming and Henry, 1961) in the direction of the persistence of life-styles' hypothesis. Specifically, Henry (1965:27) has suggested that a person's mode and style of disengagement may, "reside in the life style characteristic of the individual's life to that time, and the characteristic coping mechanisms of the personality."

It is clear that individual differences are the most pervasive phenomena reported in the current literature on disengagement and activity in the areas of work and leisure. It is also apparent that individual differences are determined by a wide variety of variables throughout the life history of the individual. For example, some persons with high educational levels, such as academicians, tend to continue work past the generally accepted retirement age of 65 years, despite a longstanding potential for disengagement that is in conflict with their commitment to their jobs. Persons who hold jobs that are people oriented tend to continue this style of activity into the postretirement years, although this particular continuation of style may be partially determined by the wider range of people-oriented activities available to the elderly (e.g., committee work within a church organization).

The importance of such personal history variables and current environment as determinants of activity maintenance or disengagement has been stressed by Carp (1968b: 185), who has stated:

> Engagement-disengagement probably is not an omnibus trait. Probably it is differently involved in various areas or types of engagement for different persons. Satisfaction and adjustment, then, depend upon congruence between person and situation not in a holistic, undifferentiated way, but in terms of specific needs or readiness in the person and the possibilities for their satisfaction by the environment.

Carp supported this hypothesis with evidence indicating that a knowledge of previous participation in community service and people-oriented leisure pursuits considerably improved the predictability of happiness, popularity, and adjustment of persons in a retirement community which offered an environment oriented toward social activity. However, knowledge of work status (whether or not these individuals were currently working) did *not* improve predictions, presumably because it was unrelated to the specific activity measures. Perhaps this situation-specific continuity of past history and current behavior offers the most important clue thus far to the explanation of individual differences in engagement-disengagement.

Many of the researchers who have explored the phenomena of general and/or specific disengagement in work and leisure have noted that disengagement occurs most often after the age of 75 or 80 years. A significant number of subjects are likely to be approaching death by the time they reach this age range. Some authors have suggested that total disengagement may not be inevitable except shortly before death (e.g., Palmore, 1969). In fact, there is some indirect evidence that young children, as well as elderly adults, who are dying exhibit disengagement behavior. Spinetta and associates (1974) studied a group of hospitalized children with leukemia and a group of hospitalized children with chronic, but nonfatal, illnesses. They presented the children with a scale model of a hospital room and five dolls representing a doctor, nurse, mother, father, and sick child in bed. The children were asked to (1) tell a story about a sick friend and put the figures in their usual places, and (2) put the figures where they (the subjects) would most like them to be. The fatally ill children consistently placed the doll figures farther from the toy bed than did the chronically ill children. Furthermore, when asked where they *wanted* the figures to be, the fatally ill children continued to put them farther away from the bed. The authors concluded that the dying children not only perceived a growing psychological distance from their relatives and the hospital personnel but also seemed to prefer to maintain this distance. It may be that disengagement is, in fact, a universal phenomenon but manifests itself most strongly among groups of elderly subjects, since a greater proportion of these persons are approaching and preparing for death. Another possibility is that many different types of disengagement may occur as each individual ages, but past history and current situation together determine which of these are predominant and which are latent. Once death is perceived as near, a more generalized disengagement may become evident.

Clearly a more comprehensive theory of social motivation across the life span that incorporates findings in the recent literature is needed. Some investigators (e.g., Neugarten et al., 1968; Youmans, 1969, 1973) have suggested that the focus of attention should include the study of individual differences, societal and generational change, and an integration of the physical, cognitive, and interpersonal factors which affect the social motivation of the elderly person. Glenwick (1975) has proposed a transactional model that stresses the importance of both past and present dynamic interactions between the individual and his environment. Martin (1975) has stressed the need for greater emphasis on the empirical evaluation of the contribution made by the social structure surrounding an individual. Others have opted for a more traditional developmental approach, which postulates a series of stages with unique tasks that must be accomplished if the individual is to adapt properly and move on to the next stage (e.g., Kurtz and Wolk, 1975). One such promising theory has been developed by Clark and Anderson (1967). These investigators have stressed the importance of accommodation to both an internal system of needs and external societal demands. The entire theory includes many aspects of the psychological forces impinging on the adult person. However, Clark and Anderson suggest that one of the five adaptive tasks unique to late adulthood is the substitution of alternate sources of need satisfaction. It is this adaptive task that has been the focus of the present chapter. Interestingly, Clark and Anderson (1967) found that, among a random sample of older people living in the community, 61% could be rated as adapted. However, among a hospital sample, only 12% could be considered to have adapted successfully. Of those persons rated as maladapted, 54% had difficulties finding alternate sources of need satisfaction. From the point of view espoused by Clark and Anderson, it is clear that motivational difficulties involving substitute avenues of need satisfaction present a major impediment to "successful aging."

Many psychologists who have been interested in social intervention have proposed policies and practices that might be successful in providing a wide range of sources of need gratifications to the older persons in American society. For example, Palmore (1972) has suggested compulsory retirement policies be discouraged through methods such as provision of tax incentives for companies who adhere to flexible retirement policies. Simpson (1973) has proposed that paid employment should be made available to those persons who have financial difficulties in their postretirement years. For those retirees who are financially satisfied, volunteer work, which is community based and *not* age segregated, should be available. Belbin and Belbin (1968:346) have noted the importance of peer participation in training programs aimed at providing the older worker with a new career and have stressed that society, as a whole, must reorient its "thinking toward acceptance of learning throughout life in a flexible pattern of work and study." Similarly, Sarason and co-workers (1975) found that many persons become dissatisfied with their careers at a fairly young age (25 to 30 years) and subsequently seek a career change. They have suggested that the problem stems from the fact that young college-aged adults are being forced to narrow their career choices and that their choice is currently expected to be final. These authors and many others (e.g., Birren and Woodruff, 1973) have expressed the opinion that preparation for lifelong education and relaxed attitudes toward career changes should begin in childhood. Certainly if such attitudes could be communicated to today's children and acceptable avenues for career substitution were available, some of the sources of need frustration would be alleviated for the adult facing retirement and "uselessness."

Perhaps the most important consideration for future studies of social motivation during the adult years is the use of a more sophisticated experimental method. Many of the studies cited in this chapter have utilized interviews and questionnaires rather than laboratory methods. Consequently, there is a great deal of information available concerning the frequency of engagement-disengagement behaviors in work and leisure and their association with demographic variables. However, there is little information about the causes, effects, and modification of activity and disengagement patterns of behavior for individuals with very different past histories and current situations. Until answers to these questions are found, it is unlikely that broad social policies will be widely successful or acceptable to the elderly person on an individual basis.

SELECTED READINGS

Back, K. W. The ambiguity of retirement. In E. W. Busse and E. Pfeiffer (Eds.), *Behavior and adaptation in late life.* Boston: Little, Brown, & Co., 1969, pp. 93-114.

Birren, J. E., and Woodruff, D. S. Human development over the life span through education. In P. B. Baltes and K. W. Schaie (Eds.), *Life-span developmental psychology: personality and socialization.* New York: Academic Press, Inc., 1973, pp. 305-337.

Carp, F. M. Some components of disengagement. *Journal of Gerontology,* 1968, **23**, 382-386.

Carp, F. M. Person-situation congruence in engagement. *Gerontologist,* 1968, **8**, 184-188.

Clark, M., and Anderson, B. G. *Culture and aging.* Springfield, Ill.: Charles C Thomas, Publisher, 1967.

Cumming, E., and Henry, W. E. *Growing old: the*

process of disengagement. New York: Basic Books, Inc., Publishers, 1961.

Henry, W. E. Engagement and disengagement: toward a theory of adult development. In R. Kastenbaum (Ed.), *Contributions to the psychobiology of aging.* New York: Springer Publishing Co., Inc., 1965, pp. 19-36.

Kuypers, J. A., and Bengtson, V. L. Social breakdown and competence: a model of normal aging. *Human Development,* 1973, **16,** 181-201.

Lipman, A., and Smith, K. J. Functionality of disengagement in old age. *Journal of Gerontology,* 1968, **23,** 517-521.

Maddox, G. L. Persistence of life style among the elderly: a longitudinal study of patterns of social activity in relation to life-satisfaction. In B. L. Neugarten (Ed.), *Middle age and aging.* Chicago: University of Chicago Press, 1968, pp. 181-183.

Miller, S. J. The social dilemma of the aging leisure participant. In B. L. Neugarten (Ed.), *Middle age and aging.* Chicago: University of Chicago Press, 1968, pp. 366-374.

Sarason, S. B., Sarason, E. K., and Cowden, P. Aging and the nature of work. *American Psychologist,* 1975, **30,** 584-592.

Simpson, I. H. Problems of the aging in work and retirement. In R. R. Boyd and C. G. Oakes (Eds.), *Foundations of practical gerontology.* Columbia, S.C.: University of South Carolina Press, 1973, pp. 157-172.

CHAPTER 8

LEARNING

In the 1959 *Handbook of Aging and the Individual* (Birren, 1959:655), Jerome clearly stated what has been the most popular notion of learning in late adulthood. Basically, he concluded that, in spite of the many individual differences found in studies of adult learning and in spite of the lack of knowledge concerning the physiological and psychological bases of these differences, it is commonly accepted that, "Every organism, as a result of persisting in time, sooner or later after maturity suffers a loss in its ability to learn." In the new *Handbook of the Psychology of Aging* (Birren and Schaie, in press), Arenberg and Robertson reported that the age differences found in most experimental studies of learning, in fact, do favor younger subjects. However, they also noted that most of the recent progress in research dealing with age differences in learning has concerned the identification of conditions which "improve or impair the learning performance of the older individual." In this chapter we will discuss many of those conditions in the context of both animal and human learning.

You may have noticed that Arenberg and Robertson referred not to the learning of older individuals but, rather, to the learning *performance* of older individuals. The distinction between learning (an internal process) and performance (an external act) has been extremely important for researchers interested in age-related variations in learning ability (Botwinick, 1973). Botwinick (1973:218) has summarized why this is so:

> Much of what in the past had been regarded as a deficiency in learning ability in later life has more recently been seen as a problem in the ability to express learned information. In other words, much of what had been thought of as a deficiency in the internal cognitive process is now seen as a difficulty older people have in adapting to the task and in demonstrating what they know.

In the sections that follow, it will be seen that much of both the human and animal literature has been devoted to teasing out what may be a decline in learning ability from what is most certainly a decline in performance.

We have chosen to discuss learning during the adult years in the context of traditional stimulus-response theory. In this context, research with humans has been limited almost exclusively to the study of verbal learning processes. Research with animal subjects has been more diverse, although the major portion of animal studies involve either maze or avoidance learning. Finally, we must point out that a discussion of the complete literature on age differences in learning would fill an entire volume. Consequently, we have chosen to cover those topics that we believe are most likely to provide a greater understanding of adult learning processes in the years to come.

VERBAL LEARNING

Current research in verbal learning has its theoretical roots in associationism as developed by the British empiricists. Simply stated, these philosophers believed that all knowledge was based on the formation of associations (Bourne et al., 1971). Today their theoretical orientation is reflected in stimulus-response (S-R) theories of learning. It is important to understand that verbal learning research, per se, is not directed toward the discovery of the laws that control linguistic behaviors (e.g., grammatical constructions) but, rather, toward the discovery of basic principles that underlie the formation of S-R associations (Bourne et al., 1971). In this respect, verbal behavior has provided a unique arena for the study of conditions under which humans, as opposed to lower mammals, learn.

Verbal learning theory has undergone many important changes since its initial conception. Many of these changes are very important when the learner's age is taken into consideration. For example, the classical theory included a view of the subject as a passive, rote learner whose associations were formed merely by virtue of the temporal relationships among a stimulus, a response, and a reinforcement (feedback concerning the "correctness" of a response). In contrast, current theories of verbal learning include a view of the subject as an active participant in the acquisition of associations. The participant transforms the verbal stimuli and responses in some manner that is meaningful. Furthermore, these transformations are based on generalized personal strategies that have been acquired throughout the life span (Arenberg and Robertson, in press). Thus many new research hypotheses are addressed to the important question of how these general strategies for the formation of learned associations change over the life span.

Most researchers who have investigated verbal learning processes among subjects of different ages have employed one of two types of tasks: paired-associate learning or serial learning. In *paired-associate learning* the subject must learn associations between pairs of verbal items (e.g., book/car) in such a way that he can spontaneously supply the correct responses to a set of verbal stimuli. Lists of stimuli are repeated, although most often with the stimulus pairs in a different order. Several performance measures may be used by the experimenter in the analysis of paired-associate verbal learning. The most common are number of trials to a specific criterion (e.g., one perfect recitation of the list) or number of errors per trial.

In *serial learning* a list of single verbal items is used. The subject must learn the list in the exact order in which it is presented; that is, he is presented with a single word and must recite the entire list using each successive word as a stimulus for the following word or response. Again, the experimenter may measure number of errors per trial or number of trials to one or more perfect recitation(s) of the list.

One early study is of special interest because it sets the stage for many of the later controversies concerning verbal learning and aging. In 1957 Korchin and Basowitz compared young (mean age = 26.8 years) and old (mean age = 78.1 years) subjects on three different paired-associate tasks. The tasks were designed to differ in the extent to which prior experience might facilitate or hinder learning. The tasks were (1) pairs of familiar words, (2) nonsense equations (e.g., $E \times Z = G$, where $E \times Z =$ is the stimulus and G is the response), and (3) false equations (e.g., $3 \times 5 = 6$). The old group performed more poorly than the young group on all three tasks, but their performance deficit increased substantially on the two tasks in which prior experience was least helpful, that is, the nonsense equations and false equations. In addition, Korchin and Basowitz noted that the older group was much more likely to omit responses than the young group. This experiment led many researchers to hypothesize two potential causes of the decrement in performance with age. First, older subjects exhibit the greatest learning deficits when they must deal with novel material or material for which typical learning strategies are not very useful. As might be expected, one avenue of subsequent research involved attempts to manipulate the learning strategies of older subjects. Second, older subjects may not be poorer *learners,* but, rather, they may exhibit a *performance* deficit in that most of their errors are omissions. In other words, they may *know* the correct response but be unable to respond within the appropriate time limits. During this period much evidence for a general slowing of response among the elderly was accumulating (Welford, 1958), and consequently, the latter hypothesis became highly popular among those who were concerned with separating real learning deficits from apparent decrements reflecting response slowing.

Pacing and age

The body of verbal learning literature dealing with the ability of older persons to respond within specific time limits generally involves studies that have manipulated the pacing of stimulus and stimulus-response presentations. There are two major time intervals in the typical verbal learning study, which may be manipulated in such a way as to affect the performance of young and/or elderly persons significantly. The first is the *anticipation* interval, the time in which the stimulus alone is presented and the subject is required to search his memory and supply the response. The second is the *inspection* interval, the time in which the stimulus and response are presented together and the subject is required to study and learn the appropriate S-R association.

Much of the initial work which followed Korchin and Basowitz's (1957) study was based on their observation that older subjects tended to omit responses during the anticipation interval, thus increasing substantially their overall error rate. For example, Canestrari (1963) varied the anticipation interval (1.5 seconds, 3.0 seconds, or self-paced) in a paired-associate task administered to old and young subjects whose mean ages were 65.4 and 23.9 years, respectively. The young subjects made fewer errors than the old subjects under all conditions, but the smallest age difference occurred under the self-paced schedule. Furthermore, when the error data were divided into omission and commission errors, it became clear that both groups made fewer omission errors under the 3.0-second schedule than under the 1.5-second schedule, but only the older subjects showed continued improvement with the self-paced schedule. Commission errors, which were more frequent among the old subjects, were not affected by increases in the anticipation interval. Eisdorfer and his colleagues (1963, 1965), using a serial learning task, confirmed Canestrari's results. They further demonstrated that old subjects (mean age = 66.2 years) continued to decrease their omission errors as the anticipation interval was extended to 10 seconds, but not beyond.

Eisdorfer (1968) continued to investigate the problem of omission errors among elderly subjects. He designed an experiment to find out exactly how much time elderly subjects would use to make a response if they were allowed at least 11 seconds. His subjects (mean age = 71.6 years) generally took only about 5 seconds to respond. Eisdorfer concluded that under slowly paced conditions old subjects are capable of responding rapidly. Eisdorfer and his colleagues then proceeded to investigate the possibility that elderly individuals are highly aroused under conditions of rapid stimulus pacing and that such high levels of arousal are the source of their omission errors. The results of their experiments are reported in detail in Chapter 6. Although the hypothesis appears plausible at the present time, Eisdorfer has not yet produced any evidence that decreasing arousal levels fails to benefit young subjects as well as older subjects. Thus his hypothesis has not been subjected to a critical test, and the contention that young subjects are performing under optimal levels of arousal remains an assumption.

At the present time it is generally accepted that older subjects make fewer errors in paired-associate and serial learning tasks as the length of time allowed for making a response (anticipation interval) increases. Arenberg and Robertson (in press) also have been investigating this problem for many

Fig. 8-1. David Arenberg, Ph.D. (Duke University, 1960). Dr. Arenberg is best known for his work in learning and problem solving in young, middle-aged, and elderly adults. Presently he is Chief of the Learning and Problem Solving Section of the Gerontology Research Center (National Institute on Aging, Baltimore, Maryland). He has published many articles and has been honored repeatedly for his professional contributions to psychology and aging. Dr. Arenberg is a Fellow in the Gerontological Society and the American Psychological Association and has served as Associate Editor for the *Journal of Gerontology.*

years and have reported both cross-sectional and longitudinal data from the Baltimore Longitudinal Study. Both types of analyses indicate that slower response pacing is beneficial to older subjects, especially after the age of 60 years. However, Arenberg (1965) carried out a critical investigation, which led a number of researchers to suspect that deficits in verbal learning among elderly subjects might be a result of more than lack of time to respond. In short, there may be a true learning deficit rather than simply a performance deficit with increasing age. Arenberg had young (mean age = 19.7 years) and old (mean age = 65.9 years) subjects learn a list of paired associates with anticipation intervals of either 1.9 or 3.7 seconds. However, he interspersed each of the paced trials with self-paced trials and made the following hypothesis: if the older subjects who receive the fast pace learn as much as the older subjects who receive the slow pace, but simply do not have enough response time, both groups should perform equally well when allowed to respond under the self-paced condition. This hypothesis was not confirmed. Under conditions of self-pacing the old group who had learned their list with the shorter anticipation interval made more errors than the old group who had learned their list with the longer anticipation interval. The younger subjects were superior under all conditions. Arenberg concluded that the older subjects' learning as well as their performance was impaired when the anticipation interval was short.

Canestrari (1968a) produced further support for this hypothesis. He presented a paired-associate task to old and young subjects (ages not reported) in a slightly different manner by varying the interitem interval. The paired-associate list was presented once in its entirety with both stimulus and response words occurring simultaneously. All pairs were presented for 1 second, but the intervals between pairs varied (0.0, 0.5, or 5.0 seconds). Following the study presentation, each stimulus word was presented alone, and the subjects were asked to supply the correct response. The response presentation was entirely self-paced. Young subjects, of course, performed at a higher level than older subjects under all conditions, but they also showed improvement when the interitem interval increased from 0.0 to 0.5 seconds. Older subjects continued to show substantial improvement with the 5.0-second interval. In view of the fact that the response intervals were all self-paced, Canestrari also concluded that something other than lack of time to respond must be affecting the older subjects' performance. In this study the only variable was length of interitem interval. Consequently, one might suspect that the older subjects benefited from the slow pace because they needed the additional time to rehearse the stimulus-response pairs.

There is, however, a more direct method for testing such a hypothesis. Recall for a moment that the inspection interval (i.e., the time in which the stimulus and response are presented together) is the most probable period for the subject to study and learn the appropriate association. Kinsbourne and Berryhill (1972) varied the inspection interval (2, 4, or 6 seconds) and held the anticipation interval constant at 2 seconds. Their young subjects (male undergraduates, ages not reported) learned the paired-associate list at a faster rate than their old subjects (mean age = 69.8 years), regardless of variations in the inspection interval. However, the most interesting analyses were performed only for the older subjects. If the rate of acquisition was calculated in terms of mean correct responses per trial, the learning curves suggest that the older subjects performed more poorly with the 2-second inspection interval than the 4- or 6-second intervals. If the rate of aquisition was calculated in terms of mean correct response per *total time* spent learning, the length of the inspection interval did *not* affect their performance. In other words, if total learning time (e.g., 384 seconds) is equated for groups with different inspection intervals, the rate of acquisition of these groups is similar. Encouraging though these results may be, interpretation is difficult because there is another variable that is inherently confounded with total time spent learning: feedback. Even when total learning time is held constant, subjects who learn under varying inspection intervals receive different amounts of feedback (i.e., a confirmation or disconfirmation of their response). For example, at 384 seconds into the paired-associate task, subjects who are learning with a 2-second interval have received 12 units of feedback per pair, compared with 8 and 6 units for subjects who are learning with 4- and 6-second intervals, respectively. In other words, even though the fast-paced subjects are spending less time studying the stimulus-response pairs, they are receiving proportionately more feedback information. This feedback might have the effect of enhancing their learning to the point where their performance equals or surpasses that of their slower paced counterparts.

No comprehensive study comparing the performance of young and old subjects with regard to number of feedback units per unit time has been performed. Consequently, it is not known if an analysis such as that performed by Kinsbourne and Berryhill would produce the same results with younger subjects. Certainly, analyses of the effects of feedback and the interaction of feedback with anticipation and inspection intervals are important topics for future investigations.

Currently there are three studies in the literature that represent a step in this direction. Although the authors have not directly explored the effects of different amounts of feedback, they have examined the consequences of various combinations of inspection and anticipation intervals. Hulicka and co-workers (1967) presented young (mean age = 15.5 years) and old (mean age = 70.2 years) subjects with paired-associate lists under four conditions: (1) LL—3-second (limited) inspection interval and 3-second (limited) anticipation interval; (2) LU—3-second inspection interval and unlimited anticipation interval; (3) UL—unlimited inspection interval and 3-second anticipation interval; and (4) UU—unlimited inspection and anticipation intervals. Performance for young subjects was superior to that for older subjects under all conditions. However, both young and old subjects were affected to the same degree by variations in the inspection interval. All subjects performed best under the UU condition, second best under the UL condition, and worst under either the LL or LU conditions. Hulicka and colleagues concluded that the inspection interval was most important with regard to the learning efficiency of both young and old subjects. The anticipation interval contributed to learning efficiency, but only if subjects had been allowed to pace themselves during combined stimulus-response presentations. One further point should be mentioned. When given unlimited anticipation intervals, the older subjects tended to take longer to respond than the younger subjects. Specifically, they used a mean response time of 4.7 seconds compared with 2.8 seconds for the younger group. The mean for the older group is in close agreement with Eisdorfer's (1968) data, which indicate that older subjects take about 5 seconds to respond.

Monge and Hultsch (1971) also covaried the inspection and anticipation intervals in a paired-associate learning task given to young and middle-aged subjects who were 28.3 and 49.4 years, respectively. They chose three anticipation and inspection intervals (2.2, 4.4, and 6.6 seconds) and presented all possible combinations. Again, the young subjects performed in an overall superior manner, although close inspection of the data revealed that this was not so when the longest inspection interval (6.6 seconds) was combined with the two longest anticipation intervals (4.4 and 6.6 seconds). Most probably the fact that middle-aged subjects rather than elderly subjects participated in this study accounts for the generally better performance of the older group. Monge and Hultsch confirmed the finding of Hulicka's group (1967) that increasing the length of the inspection interval has equally beneficial results for old and young subjects. However, contrary to the results of Hulicka and coworkers, the Monge-Hultsch data suggested that the anticipation interval interacted with age independently of the inspection interval. Specifically, the young subjects were not affected by the length of the anticipation interval, but the older subjects exhibited a large decrement in performance with the 2.2-second interval.

Recently, Winn and Elias (1975), using a concept similar to that suggested by Kinsbourne and Berryhill (1972), reanalyzed Monge and Hultsch's data. They suggested that the typical finding of poorer performance by elderly subjects when fast presentation rates are used may be explained by the total time principle (Bugelski, 1962; Murdock, 1960). Specifically, the presentation time multiplied by the number of trials will equal a constant (time to learn to a given criterion). For example, if the presentation time (inspection + anticipation intervals) is 4 seconds and it takes 30 trials to learn a list of paired associates, the total time to learn will be 120 seconds ($4 \times 30 = 120$). However, if the presentation time is 6 seconds, it should take approximately 20 trials to learn the list ($6 \times 20 = 120$). Winn and Elias demonstrated that the total time principle held for the old as well as the young subjects in the Monge and Hultsch study. Using a free-recall paradigm, Eisner and Kinsbourne (1975) also confirmed the total time principle for both old and young subjects. However, two essential points must be kept in mind. First, even though total time to learn may be a constant *within* specified age groups, it is likely that the specific constant will differ *between* various age groups. Second, the effect of number of feedback units has not been explored for any age group and, in fact, may be a prime determinant of the total time principle.

At the present time a number of conclusions may be gleaned from the verbal learning literature concerned with pacing and age. First, there is a definite performance deficit among elderly subjects, at least after the age of 60 years and under conditions of fast pacing. Second, slower response pacing allows elderly subjects to decrease their error rates but seldom allows them to perform at levels equal to those of younger subjects. Third, increasing the time for studying stimulus-response pairs (inspection interval) beneficially affects both young and old subjects to about the same degree. Fourth, several new hypotheses are suggested by the current literature. For example, age differences in verbal learning may be related to the amount of feedback inherent in a specific learning task rather than stimulus pacing, per se. Fifth, it might be more profitable to explore some of the original theories of verbal learning processes with respect to the recent findings regarding age differences.

Witte (1975) has proposed that researchers interested in the age variable might consider the utility of a stage analysis first proposed by Underwood and Schulz (1960). These authors suggested that paired-associate learning takes place in two stages: a response learning stage, in which independent responses are made available for recall, and an associative stage, in which pairs of stimuli and responses are recalled simultaneously. Currently, there are well-developed techniques available for separating the learning processes that occur at each stage. The obvious advantage of applying such analyses to adult developmental studies is, as Witte suggests, a unique opportunity to isolate the locus of well-established, age-related deficits in verbal learning. Clearly, the controversy over age and performance deficits associated with pacing is still very much alive, and many hypotheses (e.g., effects of arousal and feedback) await critical experimental tests.

Mediational strategies

In the last section we discussed the possibility that something other than simple response slowing and motivational changes (e.g. overarousal) may account for the poorer performance of elderly subjects on verbal learning tasks. We turn now to one frequently suggested factor influencing age-associated differences in performance: mediational strategies. Do mediational strategies contribute to the observed age-related decline in verbal learning?

Among young subjects, "mediators" are frequently used to provide links between the stimulus and response of a paired-associate item. These mediators may be visual images, verbal words, or verbal phrases. They may be shortened versions of each stimulus-response component brought together to form a single term. For young subjects there is evidence that visual mediators are more effective than verbal mediators (Pavio et al., 1966). Is this true for older subjects?

Hulicka and Rust (1964) reported that elderly subjects (mean age = 68.8 years) seemed to have difficulty in a paired-associate task using nonsense equations because they failed to convert the equations into meaningful units (e.g., K × U = T to KUT). Hulicka and Grossman (1967) provided even more direct evidence for mediational deficits among the elderly. They divided their young (mean age = 16.1 years) and old (mean age = 74.1 years) subjects into four groups, which received different instructions or no instructions as to the type of mediators that might be helpful in learning a list of paired associates. The results indicated that instructions to use mediators affected beneficially the performance of both young and old subjects. However, the elderly subjects demonstrated relatively greater improvement, even though they did not reach the high performance levels of the young subjects. Interestingly, the older group reported a more frequent use of verbal rather than visual mediators. Canestrari (1968b) has suggested that this tendency may decrease the facilitatory effect of mediational strategies for elderly persons because it had been demonstrated earlier that visual mediators are more effective for young subjects (Pavio et al., 1966).

Canestrari (1968b) reported a study by Knill (1966) in which an attempt was made to assist elderly subjects in developing visual mediators. Knill reasoned that, since visual mediators presumably are more effective than verbal ones, the performance of older subjects who are induced to use visual mediators might approach the levels exhibited by younger subjects. Knill's subjects were presented with either a black-and-white sketch that illustrated the stimulus and response of each pair (visual mediator) or a phrase that contained both words (verbal mediator). Again, the young subjects performed at a higher level regardless of the type of mediator used. Again, the older subjects showed relatively greater improvement when they were provided with mediators. However, both visual and verbal mediators were equally effective. The use of mediators sharply reduced omission errors, but it did not affect commission errors for elderly subjects. Since the task was entirely self-paced, the result suggests that omission errors may be further reduced by providing mediators rather than by simply slowing the anticipation or inspection intervals. Canestrari suggests that elderly subjects, particularly if they are instructed to use mediators, can reduce their error rates *under conditions of self-pacing.* However, their presumed loss of ability to produce spontaneous mediators may be attributed to experiential factors, for example, less frequent practice in mediation or physiological changes in the central nervous system that accompany the aging process.

Another approach to increasing the use of mediational strategies is to vary the extent of the abstract nature of the paired associates themselves. The more abstract a verbal item is the less is its image-arousing capacity. Studies with young subjects have demonstrated that paired-associate learning is facilitated by the use of high image–arousing items (Pavio, 1969). This finding is not surprising; young subjects tend to make greater use of visual mediators than verbal ones. Can the same effect be demonstrated with elderly subjects in spite of their preference for verbal mediators?

Rowe and Schnore (1971) presented either a highly concrete or highly abstract paired-associate task to young (mean age = 18.4 years), middle-aged (mean age = 50.4 years), and old (mean age = 72.8 years) subjects. After the learning task the subjects were asked to recall the strategies used in forming associations. As expected, all age groups received higher scores for concrete paired associates than for abstract paired associates. The young and middle-aged subjects performed at comparable levels on the concrete task, although the oldest group did show a decline in performance. However, performance on the abstract task declined progressively with increasing age. Rowe and Schnore performed one of the few verbal learning studies that employed more than two age groups. The results demonstrate the importance of investigating middle-aged as well as more extreme age groups. Rowe and Schnore also report that the oldest group used mediators less frequently, particularly for abstract paired associates.

Gordon and Slevin (1975) recently have extended the work on mediational strategies used by various age groups to include recall of entire sentences rather than single words. In their study the performance of young adults (mean age = 24.2 years) was superior to that of older adults (mean age = 68.3 years) for both concrete and abstract sentences. However, the older subjects reported using many more verbal mediators for both sentence types. The younger subjects reported an equal percent of verbal and imaginal (visual) mediators for concrete sentences and a tendency to process even abstract material with the aid of imaginal mediators. Gordon and Slevin suggest that this latter strategy may partially account for the finding of increasingly better performance over trials on abstract sentences by the younger subjects. The older group failed to improve their recall of abstract material over time.

All of the studies discussed indicate that older subjects fail to use mediational strategies, particularly of the visual type, as often or as effectively as younger subjects. When older subjects are instructed to use mediators or are overtly presented with suitable mediators, performance improves. However, it rarely reaches levels attained by younger subjects. Explanations for this age-related mediational deficiency are lacking, despite the fact that many potentially fruitful areas of inquiry exist. For example, one study has demonstrated that patients with *minimal* symptoms of arteriosclerosis used mediators less effectively than nonarteriosclerotic subjects (Rust, 1965). Perhaps early central nervous system changes, even those which remain undetected in otherwise healthy subjects, are partially responsible (see Canestrari, 1968b).

Associative strength and performance

Once it became clear that, even under optimal conditions (e.g., slow pacing, provision of mediators), older persons generally performed more poorly on verbal learning tasks, it was natural for investigators to turn to other factors which might influence performance. Some of these factors (e.g., arousal level, interest) will be discussed in Chapter 10. Researchers have shown interest in still other variables. In fact, several of them succeeded in improving the performance of their older subjects. For example, pretraining on a sorting task that provided information on how to organize later learning materials was more helpful to older subjects than to younger subjects (Hultsch, 1971). Supportive instructions, contrasted with challenging ones, were beneficial to elderly subjects but did not influence younger subjects in the learning of difficult paired associates (Ross, 1968). However, none of these conditions elevated the performance of elderly subjects to a level equal to that of younger subjects. At the present time only one variable, associative strength, has been shown to be critical in the achievement of this objective.

Associative strength is defined as the probability with which one word elicits another word during free association (Arenberg and Robertson, in press). For example, associative strength for the pair "light-dark" is high; for the pair "light-pen," it is low. It is apparent that high associative pairs should be learned with greater ease, since preexisting verbal habits may have a facilitatory effect.

Early studies (e.g., Canestrari, 1966; Kausler and Lair, 1966) seemed to indicate that older subjects performed better on tasks using pairs high in associative strength, although age-related declines were still observed. More recent evidence suggests that, under some circumstances, the age differences may disappear completely. For example, Zaretsky and Halberstam (1968) presented young (mean age = 23.4 years) and old (mean age = 69.7 years) subjects with lists composed of pairs which were high, medium, or low in preexisting associative strength. Their results indicated that age differences occurred only for items with low associative strength. Botwinick and Storandt (1974b) presented subjects ranging in age from 21 to 80 years with three paired-associate tasks: a high associative list, a low associative list, and a list in which the stimuli were two consonants and the responses were words (e.g., RU-sugar). The authors suggested that these lists represent varying degrees of difficulty in terms of associative strength and meaningfulness of the stimuli. The results of their experiment are presented in Fig. 8-2. There were no age differences for the high associative list, and there was a decline beginning around age 40 for the more difficult tasks. Furthermore, the decline was sharper after 50 years for the most difficult task.

It is interesting to note that Botwinick and Storandt used a medium-paced anticipation interval (5 seconds), whereas Zaretsky and Halberstam used a relatively long one (10 seconds). Yet the results of two studies are

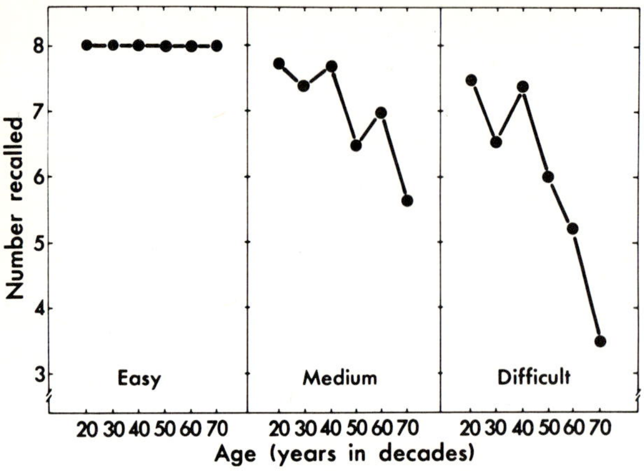

Fig. 8-2. Recall scores of paired-associate tasks as a function of age and difficulty (associative strength and meaningfulness of stimuli). (Modified from Botwinick, J., and Storandt, M. *Memory, related functions and age.* Springfield, Ill.: Charles C Thomas, Publisher.)

highly similar. Apparently, the debilitating effects of a medium-length anticipation interval can be modified by the associative strength of specific learning materials.

Interrelationships of learning, memory, and motivation: a digression

Our discussion of age variations in performance on verbal learning tasks deals selectively with only those studies emphasizing learning, per se, rather than memory or motivation. These closely related topics are discussed extensively in Chapters 6 and 9. However, verbal learning paradigms frequently have been used as tools to study other basic processes. For example, the concept of interference has provided the most popular theoretical framework for explanations of the decline in long-term memory observed in elderly persons. The basic argument is simply that older persons perform more poorly on tasks requiring memory because they are more susceptible to the effects of interference either from preexisting habits or extraneous laboratory variables. Interference effects are measured experimentally using typical verbal learning tasks, such as the retroaction paradigm. Even the simple verbal learning tasks we have discussed tap memory processes to some extent. Thus performance may be partially determined by susceptibility to interference, although such effects cannot be "teased out" using elementary paired-associate or serial learning tasks. Nonetheless, verbal learning researchers have devised many different experimental paradigms, which together with the newer information-processing models, offer promising research tools for the study of learning, memory, and motivation across the life span.

ANIMAL LEARNING

Animal research is considered by some to be intrinsically less interesting and of less importance to the understanding of human behavior than human research. This is an understandable attitude. Many questions involving behavioral changes in humans with advancing age have not been answered. Unfortunately, many research problems simply cannot be undertaken with human subjects, and the researcher interested in studies that fall into this category may turn to animal subjects. In this case it is important that full consideration be given to advantages and limitations of animal research.

There have been a number of traditional arguments offered in support of behavioral research with animals. Many of the basic laws governing animal and human behavior are similar. Ethical considerations demand the use of animals rather than humans in potentially dangerous or stressful studies. Many environmental and genetic variables that cannot be controlled with human subjects can be controlled, and even manipulated, with animal subjects. All of these arguments have validity. Moreover, there are a number of problems unique to adult developmental psychology that make animals attractive alternatives to human subjects as experimental participants.

One of the primary problems in human research is that the adult life span is virtually the same for psychologists and their subjects. Consequently, the researcher may either retire or, worse yet, expire before his longitudinal testing program is completed. Furthermore, his dropout rate is often high in human studies. The investigator often finds himself with a biased sample of superhealthy, well-educated, upper income level subjects, who tend to volunteer. In contrast, many animal species have a relatively short life span (a laboratory rat or mouse usually lives 2 to 3 years, depending on certain genetic variables and housing conditions). Furthermore, it has been our experience that few animal subjects drop out of our experiments because their employer transferred them to another town or because they simply have lost interest.

Another problem frequently encountered by the life-span developmental psychologist is the wide variety of past experiences brought to the experiment by the human subjects. It is not too unusual for data analysis to reveal almost as much variation among persons as among different age groups. Whereas no reasonably intelligent psychologist would deny the importance of individual differences, it is often extremely difficult to separate the effects of age, per se, from the effects of all the past history variables contributing to a given individual's performance. Consequently, genetic and environmental controls are important, and they become even more important to those researchers dealing with older subjects, who have had more experiences and more time for genetic predispositionary factors to unfold than have younger subjects. Moreover, humans are genetically heterozygous. Animal subjects permit control over genetic as well as environmental factors.

Finally, it is becoming increasingly apparent that there is a pressing need to explore the interrelationships among aging, disease processes, and behavior. For example, many researchers have become interested in the relationship between hypertension and learning deficits. Many aspects of this research problem may be carried out on the human level, but the complexities presented by the etiology of hypertension and the influence of genetic, endocrine, and environmental variables preclude many definitive studies of the relationship between hypertension and behavior in human subjects. However, there are genetically selected lines of mice and rats with high and low blood pressure available for interested researchers. These animals are being studied currently in terms of both behavioral and physiological changes and age-associated differences over the life span. For example, investigations have been carried out on the relationships of hypertension and aggression, early experience and adult stress reactions, and adult learning abilities. These studies will be discussed in Chapters 12 and 14. Mention of them is made here to give you a flavor of the unique opportunity offered by the animal model to explore the physiological and behavioral correlates of age-related disease processes.

In the sections that follow, we will acquaint the reader with four of the major issues most frequently explored by researchers interested in age changes and age differences in animal learning. These are task difficulty, genetic predispositions, perseveration, and early as opposed to later experience. We will not pursue a discussion of learning theories, per se, because research on age-related differences in learning has not been dealt with in terms of current controversies among stimulus-response theorists. Rather, the laboratory tasks and experimental designs of researchers embracing traditional stimulus-response theories have been adopted by researchers interested in how the age variable relates to learning processes.

Many of the studies concerned with animal learning over the life span have been devoted simply to establishing age differences for typical experimental tasks. In many respects this research is both practical and necessary. The development of elaborate animal models for the exploration of complex relationships, such as those involved in disease processes and behavior, often requires a knowledge of typical species behavior over the life span. However, it will become clear as we discuss this literature that the unique opportunities offered by animal models are just beginning to be realized by contemporary researchers.

Task difficulty

The dimension of task difficulty has been of major concern in both animal and human aging studies. Jakubczak (1973) reviewed the animal literature and concluded that age differences become increasingly apparent as task difficulty increases. Arenberg and Robertson (in press) have noted that, "There is a pervasive idea in aging and general cognitive performance that age differences are related to task difficulty or complexity; that is, the more difficult or complex the task, the more likely an age difference will be found." This "pervasive idea" extends to the area of human adult cognition, but the general hypothesis has its roots in the body of literature dealing with traditional animal learning paradigms.

"Difficulty" is usually defined in terms of the specific experimental task chosen by a researcher. Thus it is impossible to discuss a generalized concept of difficulty as it affects aging animals. For example, a task in which a rat must discriminate between different shapes is not directly analogous to a task in which the same subject must choose between two pathways in a maze. The latter task places fewer demands on the animal's innate response systems. Furthermore, some tasks (e.g., water-maze escape and shock avoidance) are tied more intrinsically to motivational processes by virtue of their direct effects on the subject's physiological systems. (See Chapter 6 for a discussion of these tasks from the viewpoint of age differences in motivation.)

Position discrimination. When task difficulty is defined in terms of choice points in a maze, the "difficulty-sensitivity" hypothesis (i.e., age differences become more prominent as difficulty increases) gains substantial support. Arenberg and Robertson (in press) recently reviewed the literature on maze learning and concluded that as the number of choice points in a maze increases from two to fourteen, progressively larger age differences are found. In tasks involving one or two choice points, age differences are virtually nonexistent. For example, Botwinick and colleagues (1962) reported no age decrement in initial learning of a single-choice Y-maze for Sprague-Dawley rats (age range = 3 to 27 months). Birren (1962) found essentially the same results with a simple, two-choice T-maze. In a later study with a four-choice maze, age differences favoring a young group (3 months) relative to an older group (23 to 25 months) clearly emerged (Botwinick et al., 1963). In fact, it had been known for some time that older rats had much more difficulty learning highly complex mazes (e.g., thirteen choice points) than younger rats (Stone, 1929a; Verzar-McDougall, 1957). Recently, Goodrick (1972) has confirmed the notion of general decline in performance with age for multiple-choice maze learning by rats (Wistar strain, ages 6 to 8 and 26 to 27 months). He systematically varied the number of choice points (one, four, and fourteen) and found that as the number of choice points increased, age differences became progressively larger.

Shape, pattern, and brightness discriminations. At this time it is certain that the ability to make simple (e.g., two choice) shape and pattern discriminations varies little for different age groups (Fields, 1953; Kay and Sime, 1962; Oldfield-Box, 1969; Stone, 1929b). There are, however, some interesting discrepancies in the literature. For example, Oldfield-Box (1969) noted that older Norway rats (18 months) made fewer correct responses early in training on a brightness discrimination problem than younger rats (3 to 4 months). However, this was true only if the subjects were given a height discrimination problem first. If they were given a width discrimination problem first, no age differences were found. Sprott (1975) reported that old (24 months) C57BL/6J and

DBA/2J mice made more errors in a simple brightness (black-white) discrimination than young mice (3 to 4 months). However, there were no age differences for a position discrimination task. Kay and Sime (1962) found no age difference in a shape discrimination problem. Yet in another study, Sime and Kay (1962) reported that an older group of male hooded rats (15 to 16 months) made more errors than a younger group (5 to 6 months) on a similar shape-discrimination problem. There was one major difference between these two studies. For the problem in which no age differences were found, the shapes were presented in a horizontal plane. For the other problem, shape was always confounded with height; that is, even though height was an irrelevant dimension for problem solution, one stimulus shape was always to the left and above or below the other.

Many explanations may be offered for these diverse findings (e.g., differences in visual acuity between old and young animals). Elias (1975c) points out a possible methodological artifact. Body size and weight are usually correlated with age. Thus it is possible that differently aged (and sized) animals might perform differently, depending on the position and dimensions of the stimuli. For example, it is known that height and area of stimulus patterns, as well as distance between patterns, affect discrimination learning in Long-Evans hooded rats (Elias, 1967; 1969a,b; Elias and Warner, 1970). It also is known that age differences in aversive conditioning tasks can be eliminated under some circumstances when the size of the entire apparatus is varied in proportion to the size of the subject (Feigley and Spear, 1970). It is likely that careful attention to such methodological considerations could do much to clarify many of the discrepant findings among aging studies using animal subjects.

More complex shape- and pattern-discrimination problems have been studied using subhuman primates. The results of these studies generally indicate that older subjects have greater difficulty with more complex tasks, although age differences are not uniformly obtained. For example, Medin (1969) reported that both an increase in complexity of stimuli and an increase in delay between stimulus offset and opportunity to respond more severely impaired the pattern discriminations of older rhesus monkeys (17 to 18 years) relative to younger subjects (mean age = 10 years). Medin and associates (1973) found no significant overall age effect for a concurrent discrimination problem presented to middle-aged (13 to 15 years) and older (20 to 21 years) rhesus monkeys. However, the pattern of errors between consecutive days of the experiment did reveal age differences. On the first day of training, both age groups performed equally well. On subsequent days the older monkeys made more errors on initial trials.

In a series of studies using chimpanzees ranging in age from 7 to 41 years (puberty to old age), Riopelle and Rogers (1963; 1965) reported results similar to those of Medin (1969). No age differences were noted for simple discriminations. Performance was inversely related to age for more complex discriminations, especially those involving delayed responses. The most difficult problem for older chimpanzees (over 20 years) was an oddity task in which the subject had to choose the "odd" or different stimulus from among a set of four stimuli.

Generally, it appears that older animal subjects perform more poorly than younger subjects on complex shape- and pattern-discrimination problems, especially if those problems involve more than two stimuli (Arenberg and Robertson, in press). Thus the difficulty hypothesis has received substantial support from studies using these tasks.

In difficult tasks that involve delayed responding, memory processes are tapped to a significant extent. However, in some situations, older subjects perform more poorly, regardless of whether or not they are forced to withhold their responses for a period of time. Riopelle and Rogers (1965) have suggested that older chimpanzees may experience deficits in attention rather than memory per se. Attentional processes have been studied extensively in human infants, both with regard to their physiological correlates and their relationship to learning (see Lipsitt, 1970). A similar approach might prove profitable in the study of primate learning processes during middle and late adulthood.

Avoidance behavior. There is some evidence that older animal subjects exhibit performance deficits even with simple avoidance tasks. The task most frequently employed to examine simple avoidance behavior involves a shuttle box with two compartments. The subject is placed in one compartment and must learn to avoid shock by moving to the opposite compartment when a cue (conditioned stimulus, or CS, usually a light or tone) is presented. Oliverio and Bovet (1966) found that very young DBA/2J mice (21 days) and older mice (6 and 12 months) performed more poorly on a simple avoidance task than 2-month-old mice. Freund and Walker (1971) reported a similar decline in aging C57BL/6J mice. Specifically, they found that 3- and 6-month-old mice exhibited superior performance in the shuttle box relative to 12- and 15-month-old mice. It is not entirely clear why the DBA/2J mice began declining at an earlier age than the C57BL/6J mice. One possible explanation involves the different life spans of these two strains. DBA/2J mice are reported to have a mean life span of 407 days (Russell, 1972). Freund and Walker (1971) reported that their C57BL/6J mice had a mean life span of 692 days. Apparently, a 6-month-old DBA/2J mouse and a 12-month-old C57BL/6J mouse both have lived approximately one half of their expected life spans and may be considered as "middle-aged mice." Thus the decline in avoidance performance may begin during this portion of the life span.

Doty (1966) has reported a comprehensive study that focused on the dimension of task difficulty in an avoidance learning situation. She used Long-Evans rats 1, 5, or 24 months old. The subjects were given one of three tasks: a simple avoidance task similar to those described previously, a discriminated avoidance task in which the subject had to make a correct brightness discrimination to avoid shock, and a delayed discriminated task in which the subject again had to make a correct brightness discrimination but was prevented from responding immediately. Doty also examined the effects of massed and spaced trials for each of these tasks. Trials were separated by 10 seconds, 1 hour, or 4 hours. The results of this study indicated that, for all age groups, peformance declined as problem difficulty increased, and in most cases, spacing of trials improved performance. However, the extent of decline with increasing difficulty was not the same for rats of different ages. Age differences in the simple avoidance task were eliminated by either 1- or 4-hour delays between trials. For the discriminated avoidance task, age differences were eliminated only with the 4-hour delay period. For the most difficult task, that of delayed discriminated avoidance, spacing of trials had no effect on the performance of the oldest subjects. They received lower scores than the other two age groups, even when trials were spaced 4 hours apart. Doty concluded that, except for very difficult problems, spacing does improve the performance of older animals on avoidance tasks. However, it appears that this improvement may be task specific. For example, Goodrick (1968) noted that massing rather than spacing of trials improved the performance of older subjects in a position-discrimination task.

In general, the hypothesis that task difficulty affects the older animal subject to a greater extent than the younger animal subject is supported by studies of discrimination and avoidance learning. The effects of task difficulty may be alleviated by varying the time between trials, but for very difficult tasks it appears that older animals perform more poorly regardless of massed or spaced trials.

Learning as opposed to performance: an issue revisited

A great deal of controversy has been generated by the learning as opposed to the performance distinction in studies of human verbal learning. The issue has been no less controversial in studies of learning that have employed animal subjects. For example, many investigators have demonstrated that motivational differences may exist among animal subjects of different ages. Motivational differences can severely affect performance level but should have no direct effect on learning abilities.

Occasionally, a specific experimental task is called into question with regard to its appropriateness for demonstrating true learning (as opposed to performance) deficits among aging animal subjects. One such task is the discriminated avoidance discussed in the previous section. Ray and Barrett (1973) noted that even though an age-related deficit in avoidance responses was observed for F_{344} rats ranging in age from 1 to 12 months, no deficit was observed for discrimination responses. All age groups made a similar number of correct discrimination choices, although the older animals often failed to avoid shock because they did not respond in time. You may recall that the inability to respond within certain time limits has been the major focus of controversy in studies of human learning and aging. Ray and Barrett concluded that avoidance responses are inappropriate as measures of true learning ability, although they may be indicative of age-related performance deficits.

Thompson and Fitzsimons (1976) decided to expand upon Ray and Barrett's (1973) results by using a wider age range of subjects. They used Sprague-Dawley rats aged 3, 6, 12, and 24 months and tested them in a discriminated avoidance situation. Avoidance responses were assumed to be inappropriate learning measures and were not recorded. However, Thompson and Fitzsimons found an age-related, linear decline in discrimination responses. The trend was significant even within the 3- to 12-month age range and thus called into question Ray and Barrett's (1973) original conclusion that no learning deficit occurs prior to 1 year of age.

Unfortunately, this conflict in findings cannot be resolved yet. The two studies used different strains of rats that previously have been observed to vary considerably in a number of behaviors over the life span (see Elias, 1975c). The experimental apparatuses were not identical (Y-maze as opposed to four-unit discrimination box). The response measures were not the same (number of correct responses as opposed to trials to criterion). Much to the dismay of many researchers, the current literature on age-related differences in learning abilities abounds with studies leading to contradictory conclusions. We suspect that careful attention to genetic control and experimental methodology might lead to a resolution of many of these controversies.

Genetic predispositions

A great deal of research has been devoted to the hypothesis that genetic factors play a significant role in the determination of learning abilities. Generally, this hypothesis is not considered to be highly controversial when one is dealing with animal subjects. In fact, it is highly unusual *not* to find that different strains of rats or mice behave in different ways when presented with the same experimental task (see Meier, 1964, and Meier and Foshee, 1963, for a discussion of strain differences in maze learning). Thus a simple demonstration of strain differences confirms the importance of genetic factors but provides little information about *how* genes and environment work together to influence a particular behavior. However, when age-related differences are a matter of concern, it is often important to know how various strains compare with regard to behavioral differences over the life span. This knowledge allows the investigator to choose the strains most suitable for his particular interests and to evaluate the interaction of genotype and age-associated factors.

In the previous section, it was noted that a decline in discriminated avoidance learning may not be observed at all for certain strains of rats, whereas it might be highly evident for other strains. The same situation exists for many other experimental tasks. Barrett and Ray (1970) tested four strains of rats aged either 2 months or 9 to 11 months. Their results were obtained for a variety of learning situations and were highly complex. Some of the important findings were as follows. In Holtzman albino and Zivic-Miller albino rats an age-related decline in simple shuttle-box avoidance responses occurred. The other two strains (Simonsen black-hooded and CDF albino rats) exhibited no decline. On the other hand, none of the strains showed a significant age effect for a Sidman avoidance problem in which the subjects had to learn to press a bar at least once every 20 seconds to avoid a shock. Sprott (1972), using a passive avoidance task, has demonstrated that strain differences favoring C57BL/6J mice over DBA/2J mice at low shock levels may be completely reversed at high shock levels. This reversal is more apparent in 5-month-old mice than in 5-week-old mice.

Studies such as Barrett and Ray's (1970) and Sprott's (1972) are important because they demonstrate that many of the discrepant findings in the literature on aging may be explained by the genotype of the subjects used. They emphasize the importance of making strain comparisons at more than one point during the life span before drawing conclusions such as, "strain X is inferior to strain Y" or "learning of Z appears to decline with increasing age."

Unfortunately, many of the studies reporting age and strain differences have used subjects of only two ages (e.g., Barrett and Ray, 1970). Often the age groups employed represent only immature and young mature animals (e.g., Sprott, 1972). It is encouraging to find that a few researchers are attempting to extend their initial studies by further investigations of age groups which represent a larger portion of the life span.

Stavnes and Sprott (1975) have continued to expand the information available with regard to age and strain differences in C57BL/6J and DBA/2J mice. They carried out a comprehensive study of simple active avoidance learning in mice ranging in age from 21 days (young immature) to approximately 19 months (old mature). Three behaviors were analyzed: avoidances, escapes (subjects received shock before making the appropriate response), and no response (subjects failed either to avoid or escape shock). The results of Stavnes and Sprott's experiment are shown in Figs. 8-3 and 8-4. Looking at Fig. 8-3, one can see that avoidance responses showed a similar trend for both C57BL/6J and DBA/2J mice. However, large age differences favoring the C57BL/6J strain occurred only at 1½ and 5 months of age (i.e., 45 and 145 days). Escape responses increased steadily with increasing age for the C57BL/6J mice. Stavnes and Sprott also were interested in the effects of shock intensity on the behavior of older subjects. They gave the 19-month-old mice 15 additional trials with 0.1 ma shock (the original intensity), 0.4 ma shock, or 1.0 ma shock. Fig. 8-4 shows that both additional trials and increasing intensity improved the avoidance behavior of old C57BL/6J mice but had little effect on the avoidance behavior of old DBA/2J mice. However, increasing shock intensity did produce even more escape responses and fewer failures to respond among the latter strain. Stavnes and Sprott have suggested that the strain differences found in their study may be related to differences in memory capacities between C57BL/6J and DBA/2J mice. They trained their subjects under conditions of distributed practice (1 trial a day). Perhaps, as these authors have noted, training with more closely spaced trials (massed practice) might result in yet another pattern of age and strain differences.

It is clear that many studies must be done before there is a body of information on typical strain and age variations for subjects which are well suited to aging research. Recently, a conference was conducted by the

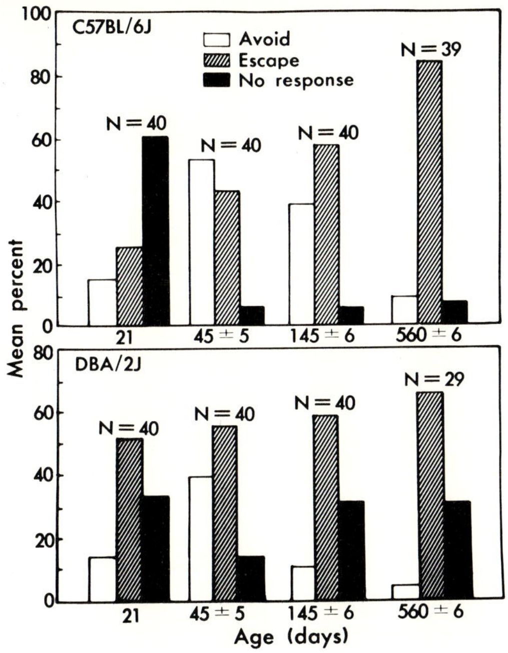

Fig. 8-3. Mean percentages (based on number of training trials) of avoidances, escapes, and no responses for C57BL/6J and DBA/2J mice of four ages. An active avoidance task was used, in which the subject had to jump from a grid floor to a shelf. (From Stavnes, K. L., and Sprott, R. L. *Developmental Psychobiology,* 1975, **8**, 437.)

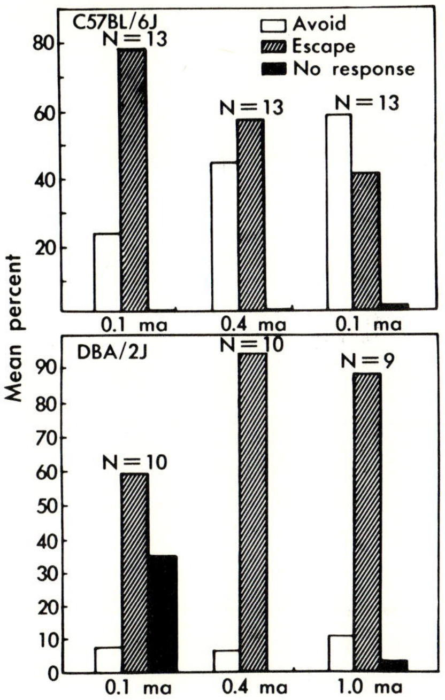

Fig. 8-4. Mean percentages (based on 15 trials) of avoidances, escapes, and no responses at three shock intensities for C57BL/6J and DBA/2J mice age 560 days. The trials were given after initial training at 0.1 ma shock intensity. (From Stavnes, K. L., and Sprott, R. L. *Developmental Psychobiology,* 1975, **8**, 437.)

National Institute on Aging (NIA), in which researchers from the biological and behavioral sciences were brought together to compile a comprehensive set of data on strains frequently employed by scientists interested in aging and development. Many of these researchers found that no systematic attempt had been made previously to evaluate age and strain differences for their particular area of interest (e.g., Elias, 1975c; Florini, 1975; Sprott, 1975). Conferences such as that conducted by NIA should provide valuable information with regard to scientific areas which must be investigated more fully prior to the development of useful animal models for life-span research.

Perseveration

On the human level, perseveration may be defined as "an abnormally persistent repetition or continuance in the expression of an idea [Kolb, 1968:96]." On the animal level, it is best defined in terms of behaviors exhibited in response to a specific experimental task. For example, in a maze learning situation, perseveration may be defined as "repetition of errors at specific choice points over many trials [Arenberg and Robertson, in press]."

The observation that older animals tend to exhibit more "perseverative" behaviors than younger animals had been made from time to time in the learning literature during the late 1950s and early 1960s. For example, Denenberg and Kline (1958) noted that older hooded rats (7 to 8 months) were slower to extinguish a simple avoidance response than younger hooded rats (1 and 2 months). The results could not be attributed to more practice for the older animals, since they learned the avoidance response at the same rate as the younger animals. Denenberg and Kline suggested that the increased resistance to extinction among the older subjects may have reflected a tendency to perseverate initially learned responses and that this tendency may be related to changes in the aging nervous system.

These early reports were not limited to extinction data. In 1964 Corke found that older rats (about 20 to 21 months) tended to repeat erroneous sequences more frequently than younger rats (about 3 to 4 months) in a task which required the subjects to press three bars in a specific order. Corke's results also could be interpreted in terms of perseveration (Arenberg and Robertson, in press).

Another measure of perseveration is the ease with which a subject learns to change his response when a previously unrewarded stimulus choice becomes the "correct" or rewarded choice. This behavior is generally referred to as reversal learning. Age differences in reversal learning have been found by some investigators (e.g., Stone, 1929b) but not by others (e.g., Birren, 1962). When age differences are found, it is frequently the case that older animals do more poorly only for initial reversals. As the number of reversals increases, the age differences disappear (Botwinick et al., 1962; 1963). Older animals may take a bit longer to learn the "concept" of reversal, but once they have learned it, they will perform as well as younger animals. At this point, psychologists do not have information on age differences in reversal learning for difficult tasks. With such tasks the poorer performance of older animals may be even more apparent.

In spite of these early studies, perseveration in aging subjects was not studied systematically until Goodrick began a series of investigations in 1968. He noted that 26-month-old Wistar rats, who failed to learn a difficult maze, tended to make many perseverative errors. Goodrick also found that older rats, who did master the maze, failed to extinguish as rapidly as 6-month-old rats; that is, the older animals continued to make correct choices although they were no longer reinforced for doing so (Goodrick, 1968). Later, he reported that perseverative errors during learning trials may be decreased somewhat under conditions of massed practice (Goodrick, 1972).

Goodrick (1975b) chose to attribute the perseverative errors of his older rats to "behavioral rigidity," a term generally employed to describe the lack of flexibility in problem-solving behavior among older human subjects. Recently, he has made an attempt to modify the perseverative tendencies of older rats (Goodrick, 1975b). He suggested that blocking all of the "wrong" choices (cul-de-sac) during early training in a fourteen-choice maze would reduce error rates for old animals during subsequent test trials. This hypothesis was tested using Wistar rats aged 5 and 25 months. Twenty training trials were given in which all incorrect choices were blocked. These were followed by 16 trials in which errors could be made. After the first 2 test trials few errors were made by either age group. Initially, however, the younger subjects made more errors. Goodrick attributed this finding to their greater tendency to engage in exploratory behavior. The older animals exhibited neither initial test trial variation nor improvement. Thus one cannot be certain whether they actually learned the maze during training or were simply perseverating previous responses that they had been forced to make.

On the human level, perseveration has been shown to be a correlate of certain types of organic brain damage and gross anatomical brain characteristics such as those present in senile dementia (Kolb, 1968). It is certainly possible to develop an animal model that would be useful in determining physiological and behavioral precursors of these diseases. Unfortunately, current research has not been directed toward the more important implications of recent findings with regard to perseveration and aging. Psychologists do not know the extent to which this behavior is a product of genotype (no strain by age interactions have been tested) or if any specific physiological correlates are related to age-associated perseveration in animals (no studies of even gross pathology have been reported). Psychologists do not know if the behavior has precursors during middle adulthood (only young-mature and senescent subjects have been tested). On the other hand, there is some evidence that the tendency of older subjects to make perseverative errors is subject to modification by various types of prior experience, such as environmental enrichment (see Doty, 1972). In general, however, a potentially important aging phenomenon has been identified, but few systematic attempts have been made to determine its implication for a more general model of changes in learning ability over the life span.

Early and late experience

The idea that early experience is important in determining the course of later development has provided a major impetus for the growth of child psychology (Chapter 2). In the context of adult developmental psychology, the idea has received much token recognition (see Baltes and Schaie, 1973); yet little research has been devoted to establishing exactly how early experience affects adult behavior throughout the life span. There are at least two major reasons for this lack of substantive research. First, interest in the area of early experience requires much patience on behalf of the investigator who, of necessity, must design highly complex experiments. Second, the concept of "critical periods" has stimulated research only for that early portion of the life span when physiological and behavioral changes are taking place at a rapid rate, that is, in infancy and early childhood.

Denenberg (1960:382) has provided a general statement of the critical period hypothesis as first proposed by Scott and Marston (1950): "The hypothesis states in part that stimulation administered during certain early developmental periods will have a more marked and longer lasting effect than will the same stimulation presented at other periods in the life of the organism." It is obvious that this hypothesis raises two important questions for the study of adult behavior. First, is the critical period hypothesis, as stated by Denenberg, correct for all types of stimulation and all behaviors; that is, are there other periods of the life span when equivalent forms of stimulation also affect later behavior? Second, assuming the hypothesis is correct for at least some types of stimulation and behavior, how long lasting is the effect of early stimulation?

A number of investigators have begun to provide some tentative answers to the first question. Initially, most work seemed to support the concept of a critical period for later learning (e.g., Denenberg, 1958; 1960). More recently, the critical period hypothesis has been seriously questioned (see Ader, 1975). There is now evidence that many types of stimulation presented during the adult portion of the life span have substantial effects on subsequent learning behavior.

The most prominent investigators in research studying "late experience" have been Doty and her colleagues. In 1966 Doty and O'Hare reported the results of a study that was designed to measure the effects of handling on two groups of Long-Evans rats aged 3 or 300 days at the beginning of the experiment. Handling during infancy (usually considered to be 0 to 21 days for the rat) previously had been shown to improve avoidance learning and reduce emotionality among adult rats (e.g., Denenberg and Kline, 1958; Denenberg and Smith, 1963). Doty and O'Hare's rats were handled for 20 consecutive days. All subjects were given a discriminated avoidance task, beginning 40 days after the last day of handling. Doty and O'Hare also varied the shock intensity used in their avoidance task because they were interested in evaluating the effects of handling on sensitivity to noxious stimulation. The results of this experiment indicated that handling was effective in improving the avoidance scores of both younger (preweaning) and older (middle-aged) rats. At both low (0.5 mA) and moderate (1.0 mA) shock intensities, age differences in avoidance behavior were eliminated by handling experiences. At the high (2.0 mA) shock intensity, the young, handled animals performed more poorly than their controls (no handling experience), and the old, handled animals did not differ from their controls. Doty and O'Hare interpreted their results in terms of altered (lowered) pain thresholds following the handling experience. Furthermore, they concluded that the critical period hypothesis was not supported by their data.

Doty (1972) conducted a further study to determine the effects of environmental enrichment at middle age on avoidance behavior at senescence. However, this study did not include a test of the critical period hypothesis because no young subjects were tested. The subjects were Sprague-Dawley rats aged 300 days at the start of the experiment. Half of the rats were exposed to an enriched environment (i.e., housed in plastic swimming pools and provided with dime-store toys) for 360 days. The other half served as controls and lived in standard wire laboratory cages. At the end of the enrichment of control experiences, all subjects were tested on a discriminated avoidance task, a discriminated avoidance reversal, and a passive avoidance task. The tasks were given in this order to all subjects. Environmental enrichment did not affect performance on the discriminated avoidance task, but it improved performance on the reversal and passive avoidance task. Doty (1972: 360) interpreted her results in terms of the impoverished environments of cage-reared rats, specifically suggesting the possibility that, "Rearing in laboratory cages impairs the rat's capacity to shift his behavior in recognition of new reinforcement contingencies." This interpretation makes sense in view of the fact that the reversal involved a response shift from a negative to a positive cue and the passive avoidance required the subjects to remain still in a situation where they had previously learned to run. Doty (Lowther, 1973) later interpreted these results as a reduction in perseverative errors on the part of the subjects that received the enriched experience. The interpretations are not mutually exclusive, but complementary. Certainly, they pose many interesting questions for further research. What happens if the enriched experience is given earlier in the life span? Will a shorter enrichment experience produce the same effect? Can the same effect be achieved for perseverative errors on other experimental tasks, for example, a difficult maze? How is the effect mediated on a physiological level? It is known that an increase in environmental complexity increases the brain weight and acetylcholinesterase activity in the brain of rats aged 1 to 6 months (Rosenzweig et al., 1964). Is this effect similar for older subjects and does it correlate with a reduction in perseverative errors?

The second question we asked at the beginning of this section concerned the long-range effects of early experience. Denenberg (1969a,b) has summarized early experience studies that were carried out further into adulthood than is typical for most investigations of the critical period hypothesis. From his summary one may conclude that many types of early experience affect later behavior, at least up to 7 months of age. However, none of the studies reviewed by Denenberg (1969a) dealt with aged subjects. Thus the effects of infantile experience on senescent behavior are virtually unknown for animal subjects.

Most research with human subjects has indicated that the effects of very early experience on later behavior are transitory at best (Wachs, 1973). However, Wachs (1973) has suggested that the reinstatement hypothesis first proposed by Campbell and Jaynes (1966) might account for the impermanent effects often found with human subjects. The reinstatement hypothesis may be summarized as follows. Young organisms

Table 8-1. Cross-sectional design for determining the effects of early and late enrichment experience on avoidance learning

Age (in months) at avoidance testing	Age (in months) at time of 1-month enrichment experience											
	3	3	3	3	3	3	12	12	12	12	24	24
4	A	A′										
13			B	B′			D	D′				
25					C	C′			E	E′	F	F′

1. Nonprimed groups received enrichment experiences; primed groups indicate controls.
2. To determine immediate effects of enrichment for different age groups, compare AA′, DD′, FF′.
3. To determine the effects of enrichment over extended periods of time, compare AA′, BB′, CC′, and DD′, EE′.
4. To determine immediate as opposed to delayed effects of enrichment at middle age and late adulthood, compare BB′, DD′, and CC′, EE′, FF′.

produce only unstable memory traces, and thus long-range effects of early experiences are unlikely to be found. However, if the experience is repeated periodically, the immediate effects of those experiences will be maintained over time. Wachs (1973) has proposed that an animal model for the reinstatement hypothesis is a useful starting point in testing its validity. He presented data which indicated that preweaning stimulus experiences given to Holtzman rats must be reinstated during the postweaning period to achieve improved performance on a brightness-discrimination problem at 2 months of age. However, it is not known if this effect was maintained into later adulthood because no older age groups were tested.

In Wachs' study, postweaning experience alone did not improve performance on the brightness-discrimination task. However, Desroches and co-workers (1964) presented evidence that bar-pressing experience at 3 months of age increased later operant responding at 15 months of age for Sprague-Dawley rats.

The paucity of research on long-range effects of experience during the early portion of the life span prevents us from drawing any general conclusions. It is likely that long-range effects will be found for some types of stimulation but not for others and that the extent of these effects will be correlated with more or less permanent changes in the central nervous system. Currently, a number of researchers are directing their efforts toward the potential relationships among early hormonal changes, central nervous system development, and adult learning (see Elias and Elias, 1975). However, none of this research has been extended to include middle and late adult age groups.

In reviewing the studies discussed in this section, we found that none employed even the most simple experimental design which might lead to significant conclusions regarding the effects of early and late experience over the life span. Table 8-1 presents an example of the type of design that would be useful for the study of enrichment effects on adult learning in mice or rats with a mean life span of about 26 months. The design requires only 120 subjects, assuming a minimum of ten subjects per group. If the experimenter employing this design wished to do strain comparisons (a wise decision), he would need an equal number of subjects from another strain for a total of 240 rats or mice. We have found that approximately 1,000 mice can be housed easily in a 10- by 12-foot colony room. Thus space requirements for such a design are far from overwhelming.

The primary advantage of the suggested

design is that it allows for the determination of both immediate and delayed effects of the enrichment experience at significant periods throughout the rodent life span. In Table 8-1 each primed letter represents a control group and each unprimed letter represents an experimental treatment (enriched) group. To determine the immediate effects of a 1-month enrichment experience on avoidance learning at different ages, one would compare groups A, D, and F (the enriched groups) with groups A′, D′, and F′ (the control groups). To determine whether or not the effect of enrichment extends over time, one would compare groups A, B, and C with A′, B′, and C′ and groups D and E with D′ and E′. Finally, to determine if immediate and delayed effects were equal during the middle-aged and senescent periods, one would compare groups B and D with B′ and D′ and groups C, E, and F with C′, E′, and F′.

Of course this design has a number of limitations. As presented, it is restricted to the adult portion of the life span, although it easily could be extended to include preweaning and postweaning age groups. It does not provide for a longitudinal assessment or a test of the reinstatement hypothesis. However, we have chosen to present a relatively simple experimental design that, although limited, would provide much more information than is currently available in the literature on early and late experience. As such, it represents a small beginning in the search for answers to what we consider are highly important questions for the adult developmental psychologist.

SUMMARY

Perhaps the most accurate statement that can be made about current research on adult learning is that behavioral scientists are finally beginning to understand some of the bases for the decline in performance usually seen with increasing age. For example, on the human level, mediational deficits and, on the animal level, perseverative tendencies have been shown to contribute to the general decline. Undoubtedly, a slowing of response and certain motivational factors also contribute to the decline. But even when these variables are controlled, the performance of older subjects seldom reaches the higher levels of younger subjects on difficult learning tasks.

Current research with animal subjects appears to be promising, especially for those investigators who are interested in how genetic factors may predispose individuals to different rates of decline. As researchers become more aware of genetic variables, it will be easier to uncover the physiological correlates that accompany a decline in learning ability. For example, certain strains of mice differ significantly in neurochemistry (see Stavnes, 1975), and these differences may be exaggerated with increasing age. Furthermore, they may correlate with strain differences in learning ability over the life span.

Another important area of animal research deals with the effects of early and late experience. Although this research is both relatively time consuming and expensive, it promises much in the way of information about potential modifiers of a general decline in learning ability among older individuals.

Both the animal and human literature on adult learning processes have been beset with methodological difficulties. Perhaps the toughest problems have centered around the learning as opposed to the performance distinction. Much progress has been made in this area (e.g., Arenberg, 1965), but much remains to be done. For example, few investigators have considered varying the size of their apparatus in accordance with the size of their animal subjects.

Finally, we believe that much is to be gained by studying learning abilities in middle and late adulthood in the context of disease processes which correlate with increasing age. It is likely that many of these diseases (e.g., atherosclerosis) have their beginnings early in life. Correlative changes in learning performance may occur long before clinical symptoms are evident. Most importantly, both animal and human studies are necessary if scientists are to understand the relationships among aging, disease processes, and learning. Thus we are hopeful that scientists engaged in animal research and those engaged in human research will find a common meeting ground as they begin to explore solutions for this highly significant problem.

SELECTED READINGS

Arenberg, D. Anticipation interval and age differences in verbal learning. *Journal of Abnormal Psychology,* 1965, **70,** 419-425.

Doty, B. A. The effects of cage environment upon avoidance responding of aged rats. *Journal of Gerontology,* 1972, **27,** 358-360.

Doty, B. A., and O'Hare, K. M. Interaction of shock intensity, age, and handling effects on avoidance conditioning. *Perceptual and Motor Skills,* 1966, **23,** 1311-1314.

Eisdorfer, C. Arousal and performance: experiments in verbal learning and a tentative theory. In G. A. Talland (Ed.), *Human aging and behavior.* New York: Academic Press, Inc., 1968.

Elias, M. F., and Elias, P. K. Hormones, aging, and behavior in infrahuman mammals. In B. E. Eleftheriou and R. L. Sprott (Eds.), *Hormonal correlates of behavior (Vol. 1). A lifespan view.* New York: Plenum Publishing Corp., 1975.

Jakubczak, L. F. Age and animal behavior. In C. Eisdorfer and M. P. Lawton (Eds.), *The psychology of adult development and aging.* Washington, D.C.: American Psychological Association, 1973.

Monge, R. H., and Hultsch, D. F. Paired-associate learning as a function of adult age and length of the anticipation and inspection intervals. *Journal of Gerontology,* 1971, **26,** 157-162.

Ray, O. S., and Barrett, R. J. Interaction of learning and memory with age in the rat. In C. Eisdorfer and W. E. Fann (Eds.), *Psychopharmacology and aging.* New York: Plenum Publishing Corp., 1973.

Russell, E. S. Genetic considerations in the selection of rodent species and strains for research in aging. In D. C. Gibson (Ed.), *Development of the rodent as a model system of aging* (DHEW Publication No. [NIH] 72-121). Washington, D.C.: U.S. Government Printing Office, 1972.

Sprott, R. L., and Stavnes, K. L. Avoidance learning, behavior genetics, and aging: a critical review and comment on methodology. *Experimental Aging Research,* 1975, **1,** 145-168.

Stavnes, K. L., and Sprott, R. L. Effects of age and genotype on acquisition of an active avoidance response in mice. *Developmental Psychobiology,* 1975, **8,** 437-445.

Thompson, C. I., and Fitzsimons, T. R. Age differences in aversively motivated visual discrimination learning and retention in male Sprague-Dawley rats. *Journal of Gerontology,* 1976, **31,** 47-52.

Witte, K. L. Paired-associate learning in young and elderly adults as related to presentation rate. *Psychological Bulletin,* 1975, **82,** 975-985.

CHAPTER 9

MEMORY

The study of memory is particularly important to the understanding of adult developmental processes because decline in memory is a frequent complaint by older adults, who are sometimes more objective about their assets and deficits than are the psychologists who study their behavior. It is true that complaints about "memory not being as good as it was" may reflect expectations that one's memory "will go" and that these expectations may be based on cultural and social stereotypes. On the other hand, it has been well documented that a decline in ability to remember does occur with age, although individual differences are as great as they are for other behavioral phenomena.

MODELS OF MEMORY

There are several ways of viewing the concept of memory and a number of models of how memory works. They all deal with the processes of *input, throughput,* and *output,* as defined in Chapter 4 (Fig. 4-1). The main difference between these models is the manner in which each deals with the concepts of time, space, and active and inactive memory processes. It is worth while to review some of these models briefly.

Multistore concept

Probably the most popular model for memory has been the multistore model (Herriot, 1974). This model, and closely related variants, suggest that information is processed and stored in temporal order, that is, (1) sensory register, (2) short-term store, and (3) long-term store. Information is seen as passing from one compartment to another, with decreasing amounts of information being passed at each point.

It is postulated that loss of information between the sensory store and short-term store is due to rapid decay of information in the sensory store and limited capacity of the short-term store. Whether information is really passed from store to store or merely copied from one store to another is not known.*

Sensory stores. Two sensory stores have been proposed: *iconic* and *echoic.* These terms refer to visual and auditory registration of stimuli, respectively. It is assumed than iconic and echoic storage (1) require anywhere from several hundred milliseconds to a few seconds, (2) involve a copy of the input, and (3) have a relatively large storage capacity (see Craik and Lockhart, 1972; Friedrich et al., 1973).

Short-term store. It has been hypothesized that information from these sensory stores is "read out" into *short-term* store and that the loss of information in the transfer process occurs as a result of the limited ability to read out quickly enough to avoid the erasure effect of incoming information not yet read out (Averbach and Coriell, 1961).

*The term *store,* as opposed to memory, is used to denote structures involved in memory because some investigators (Atkinson and Shiffrin, 1968; Craik and Lockhart, 1972) consider the terms *short-term memory* and *long-term memory* to refer more to the duration and number of trials in memory experiments than the processes involved in memory.

Because short-term store is presumed to have limited capacity, information must be passed along to long-term store if it is to be preserved (Craik and Lockhart, 1972). Loss of information during this "passing process" is not as neatly explained as it is for the sensory stores. Rehearsal allows information to be organized so that larger amounts of information can be retained and passed on to long-term storage. It is estimated that in the absence of rehearsal, the "memory trace" may be lost within 30 seconds because of interference with rehearsal or fading of the "memory trace" (Atkinson and Shiffrin, 1968).

Long-term store. Long-term storage may be distinguished from short-term storage in terms of capacity, which for all practical purposes is considered to be infinite (Craik and Lockhart, 1972; Spitz, 1973), and in terms of the "time course" of information processing, which is assumed to be long. However, the time course parameter, that is, length of time devoted to information processing, does not constitute a very important distinction between short- and long-term store in comparison with two other parameters: (1) maintenance of information at a conscious level and (2) the effect of diversion of attention and interference on maintenance of material at an active conscious level. Whereas information recalled to a conscious level from long-term storage may be interfered with if attention is diverted, the information is not lost to the system and may be retrieved at a subsequent time. Diversion of attention from short-term store may result in loss of information. Thus forgetting of material in long-term store is assumed to be more "cue dependent" than "trace dependent"; that is, the information is not lost to the system. It simply cannot be located and/or retrieved.

Before summarizing the aging research that has been done on memory, it will be helpful to discuss the concepts of active and inactive memory processes. A number of important aging studies are based on this notion.

Active and inactive memory processes

Several investigators have chosen to view memory in terms of its active and inactive processes (Broadbent, 1958; Posner, 1972). In this model, active memories can be generated from new experiences or can be withdrawn from long-term storage. The mechanism(s) controlling active storage appears to be the same regardless of the source of information. Active memories retrieved from long-term storage need not be rehearsed in the same manner as new input, but such memories do require attention. Information from long-term storage can be said to be differentially available in that some information is more easily retrieved from inactive to active states than other information. The ease with which information is retrieved is related, at least in part, to the number of times it has been retrieved previously. When one reviews the literature on aging, it will become clear how closely related the concepts of attention and retrieval are to memory. In a sense, individuals compartmentalize processes such as attention and memory, but only for purposes of study or model building. Essentially, attention is an important element in memory, just as memory is critical to learning.

Levels of processing

Levels of awareness or consciousness are considered to be important in the levels of processing approach to memory championed by Craik and Lockhart (1972). The emphasis in this approach is on the *encoding* operations that are necessary to organize information. Forgetting is considered to be a function of the type of information and the depth to which it is processed or encoded. As opposed to the traditional multistore concept of memory, the *levels of processing* system involves a *hierarchy* of information analysis; there is no need for information to flow in temporal order from one storage level to another. Level of processing depends on the degree of cognitive or semantic analysis that an input item receives; material that is more meaningful may proceed to a higher level of analysis more easily and, presumably, more quickly. Persistence of a memory trace is considered to be a function of depth of analysis. A deeper level of analysis produces a longer lasting and stronger trace.

Aging models

Although we have not presented the various models of memory in depth, we hope that you will recognize attention, rehearsal, retrieval, and short- and long-term store as important concepts in the literature on age comparisons. It will become apparent how difficult it is to test these models or to use them in aging experiments. Few, if any, of these theories have been constructed in an adult developmental context. If the reference sections of texts concerned with general memory theory can be said to reflect the degree of importance attached to studies of aging in the formulation of memory theory, one might conclude that the effects of age on memory processes are not very important or that memory ceases to exist somewhere between the ages of 26 and 30 years. J. W. Elias suggests that this absence of literature on aging within the literature dealing with learning and memory theories might be related to the desire to study so-called "normal" memory processes. However, there are studies of aging that are relevant to the theories and concepts that we have mentioned in the previous sections.

ICONIC MEMORY (VISUAL SENSORY REGISTER)

Iconic memory is not a new concept (see Sperling, 1960), yet it has not been studied extensively in older adults. You will recall that one hypothesis suggests that information taken into iconic memory (the sensory register) must be "read out" quickly into active short-term store for further processing. Obviously, any limitations in the "reading out" process would limit the amount of information taken into short-term store or passed on to a higher level of processing.

Kline and Birren (1975) and Kline and Szafran (1975) have completed two of the most recent aging studies in iconic memory, using what is referred to as the "backward masking" paradigm. Backward masking refers to the erasure or masking effect that incoming information has on information not yet "read out" from the sensory stores. This effect differs for the acoustic and visual stores in that the acoustic erasure effect is restricted to speech material (Herriot, 1974). A visual backward masking effect can occur to a flash of light as well as to more meaningful material (Sperling, 1960).

In the studies by Kline and co-workers, digits (targets) were followed at varying millisecond (msec) intervals by a masking stimulus: a 50% white–50% black random visual display composed of horizontal and vertical line segments. The variable of interest was the length of the interstimulus interval between target and masking stimuli that would allow the identification of 50% (or more) of the targets. Significantly longer intervals were needed for older (mean age = 68.2 years) than for younger (mean age = 23.3 years) adults to avoid the masking phenomenon. In other words, masking was more effective at short interstimulus intervals for the older than for the younger persons.

Kline and Szafran (1975) suggested that the nervous system of the older individuals required more time to clear incoming information out of the sensory registers, or, alternately, the presentation of the masking stimulus more readily interrupted or shifted attention from the processing of the target stimuli for the older adults. These data are consistent with the notion that, within the same time frame, older (as opposed to younger) adults have fewer bits of information "passed on" from sensory registers to memory stores. This phenomenon could constitute a limiting factor in the performance of older persons when they are forced to perform under conditions of rapid stimulus pacing.

SHORT-TERM STORAGE

How much

Many investigations of short-term storage processes have been concerned with estimating *storage capacity* (how much). One of the common experimental paradigms involves the presentation of a series of items in some specified order. Participants are then asked to recall either the entire series (in order, or irrespective of order) or to recall designated parts of the series. Typically, little decline with age is observed for tasks using this paradigm (Arenberg, 1973; Gilbert, 1941; Gilbert and Levee, 1971; Heron and Chown, 1967).

Coding and organization

A number of approaches to the study of short-term storage feature a concern for the processes involved in the organization of *input* and *output* rather than in how much adults of different ages can store. For example, there is some current interest in how adults of different ages transform the stimulus presented by the experimenter into a code that increases input capacity. The general method for testing "transformations-to-code" is to supply experimental participants with a method of organizing input and/or output; alternatively, it may be suggested to experimental participants that they supply their own input and/or output organization. Performance under one or more of these conditions is compared with conditions where no suggestions for input or output are given.

Whether or not the suggested organization of input stimuli and output operations proves to be relatively more beneficial to older adults (usually 60+ years of age) than to younger persons depends on the nature of the stimulus materials and the method of stimulus presentation. Generally, data from these studies have been interpreted as supportive of the notion that older adults are deficient in inputting or outputting information in "higher order units" (i.e., with elaborate coding or reductive coding) but that they can use these coding mechanisms to improve performance if they make a conscious effort. Such results are consistent with the levels of processing model for memory, and they suggest that older individuals typically do not process information at as high a level or as quickly as younger individuals, although conscious effort may improve their ability to some extent. However, even with conscious effort, older individuals as a group seldom reach the performance levels of younger individuals. Thus some of the deficiency in encoding involves more than organizational factors.

In an increasing number of studies, the objective is not merely to compare absolute levels of encoding performance between young and old persons; rather, emphasis is placed on observing and comparing relationships among input-output variables *within age groups*. In other words, the question asked refers to specific patterns within age groups. For example, in a study by Hultsch (1975), experimental participants were asked to recall and write down forty words from ten categories and to do so under conditions where category names either were or were not provided. Young (mean age = 20.24 years) participants recalled more words than older (mean age = 70.25 years) participants, but the main concern of the study was not the level of performance; rather, it was to compare the relative degree of improvement noted within age groups under cued (category names present) or uncued (category names absent) conditions. The older adults appeared to benefit more than young adults when the cues (higher order units, i.e., category names) were made available. These data suggest that age differences in memory are, at least partially, the result of differential use of higher order coding units.

Some interesting work on coding was stimulated by studies suggesting that reported age differences in the ability to use higher order codes might have been related to the use of subgroups of individuals of low ability

(Craik and Masani, 1967; Hultsch, 1969). Taub (1975) studied coding in older adults who exhibited different levels of ability on the visual version of the forward digit span subtest from the Wechsler Adult Intelligence Scale (WAIS). He used groups of subjects (mean age = 69.8 years) with digit span levels ranging from 4 to 7. These "span groups" did not differ with respect to age or education level. Stimuli consisted of eight letters arranged in either low-, medium-, or high-code sequences (levels of coding).

The low-code sequences were difficult to code (e.g., Q, N, P, I, R, M, D, V). Medium-code sequences were of medium difficulty (two meaningful three-letter words followed by two uncodable end letters). High-code sequences consisted of two complete four-letter words. Half of the participants in the experiment received coding instructions, were shown examples, and were given answer sheets with lines. The remaining participants received no information about coding or sequences and no other aids. Sequences were presented at a 1 sec/letter rate for both groups.

Results of the experiment indicated that span level (group) did not interact with knowledge of coding or with the combination of knowledge of coding (instructions) and level of coding (high, medium, and low). There was an interaction between span level and level of coding; performance on the medium- and high-code sequences varied directly with digit span. Thus *knowledge of the organization of the material, in terms of coding instructions, was not as important to these older adults as the ability to use the organized material.* It is possible that coding in the medium- and high-code conditions might have been so obvious that providing knowledge of coding could not produce any real advantage.

Imagery and verbal mediation

In addition to providing experimental participants with categories for organization, imagery and verbal mediation have also come to be considered important processing variables. Some studies indicate that older adults use mediational devices less often than younger adults (Hulicka and Grossman, 1967; Rowe and Schnore, 1971). However, performance in older and younger adults seems to be facilitated either by providing instructions to generate images or by providing stimuli that are high in imagery (Bruning et al., 1975; Hulicka and Grossman, 1967; Treat and Reese, 1974). You may recall that age-related changes in mediational strategies were discussed in Chapter 8. However, a number of studies within this body of research are related directly to the role of memory processes in experimental learning situations.

The most common experimental paradigm used in the study of mediational processes is a paired-associates task where pairs of stimuli (e.g., words) differ in the degree of imagery. Paired-associate studies in this context provide an example of the utilization of verbal learning paradigms to test hypotheses generated in terms of memory models rather than verbal learning theory. Researchers using such tasks must be extremely careful in interpreting their data in the absence of a knowledge of verbal learning theory (see Chapter 8). The most common method of presentation of stimuli is by way of the *method of anticipation.* During what is referred to as the *anticipation interval,* the stimulus member of a pair of associates is presented alone and the subject is required to supply the response member. This presentation is followed by a *joint presentation interval,* which is also known as the *inspection* or *study interval.* During this interval, the stimulus and response members of each paired-associate item are presented together. The joint presentation interval is then followed by an *intertrial interval* in which nothing is presented. A number of issues have been raised concerning the use of the method of anticipation in memory and aging studies. For example, this method may be biased in the direction of poorer performance for older adults because of the requirements for rapid alternation of demands on storage and retrieval processes. The result may be a response suppression for both older and younger adults, but greater suppression for older adults (Kanak and Neuner, 1970; Winn and Elias, 1976). An alternate method that avoids this problem is the *study-test* method in which all stimulus and response members of a paired-associate task are presented in succession; then all stimulus members are presented alone and the correct response is required for each.

In a study by Treat and Reese (1974), young (mean age = 29.7 years) and older (mean age = 69.9 years) adults were provided with three types of imagery instructions, and the anticipation interval, joint presentation interval, and intertrial interval were manipulated. Control groups were told only to learn the pairs of words. A second group was told to generate their own images, and a third group was provided verbally with an image to facilitate input and/or output. Stimuli consisted of ten pairs of highly concrete four-letter nouns presented by way of a memory drum. The experimenters intended trials-to-criterion to be the dependent variable; but, as often is the case in studies requiring older adults to reach a criterion of one or more perfect trials, a large number of older adults failed to reach criterion. Thus the investigators used the number of correct responses on the first trial as the dependent variable. For the younger adults the experimenter-generated imagery and the self-generated imagery instructions did not result in different levels of performance, but both resulted in superior performance when compared with the no-instruction condition. However, for the older adults there were no significant performance differences between experimenter-generated imagery and no-instruction conditions. Only self-generated imagery produced superior performance relative to the control (no-instruction condition) group. For both young and older subjects the length of the joint presentation interval (2 or 6 seconds) did not have a significant effect on performance. For older subjects the longer anticipation interval (6 seconds) resulted in more correct responses than the short anticipation interval (2 seconds). This result was interpreted as indicating that performance decline with age on timed paired-associates tasks may be due more to a greater amount of time needed to output information rather than a longer period of time to learn the association. However, in Chapter 8, we pointed out that several studies of verbal learning (e.g., Arenberg, 1965) resulted in data which are not entirely consistent with this interpretation. The Treat and Reese study does point out the complex interaction of variables involved in memory processes. For example, for the younger adults, imagery instructions seemed to be effective, but only when there was a short time to respond. For the older adults, self-generated imagery was helpful, but only when there was a longer time to respond. Therefore, in evaluating the effectiveness of imagery, one must take into account the time allowed to make a response.

Another group of investigators studied age differences in imagery by measuring memory by way of delayed recall and recognition paradigms. Bruning and associates (1975) asked young adults (mean age = 21.9 years), older adults (mean age = 73.5 years) and very old adults (mean age = 83.3 years) to make pictures of words in their minds to help them remember word lists that were high or low in imagery. Examples of stimuli that are high in imagery are "automobile" and "elephant." Stimuli that are low in imagery are words such as "thought." The same experimental participants were asked to recall the lists either 0 or 20 seconds after presentation. To prevent rehearsal during the 20-second interval, participants were asked to read aloud a string of single digit numbers. The second phase of the experiment required these same participants to recall and then recognize the words 24 hours later. Performance declined with increasing age under all experimental conditions. Imagery had a positive effect on recognition and recall but did not interact with age except in the 24-hour condition. In this condition no significant differences were noted for the old and very old adults, but the young adults recognized a greater number of both high and low imagery words than did the other age groups. Thus age differences were brought out in the longest delay condition, which placed the greatest demands on memory in terms of length of time that stimuli had to be remembered. However, these results did not indicate that the young have any specific advantage over the old in their ability to use imagery under conditions in which they are instructed to do so.

Recall as opposed to recognition memory

In general, studies employing recall strategies show greater age-related memory decline than studies requiring recognition of stimuli (Drachman and Leavitt, 1972). These findings have prompted much discussion as to whether *storage mechanisms are deficient in the elderly adult or whether information is available but not as readily accessible as it is in the younger adult.* Schonfield and Robertson (1966) reported the results of a simply designed study that showed a consistent decline with age for recall and no significant decline with age in recognition scores. In this study, Schonfield and Robertson required adults (ages 20 to 60 years as opposed to 60 to 75 years) either to recognize or recall word lists of twenty-four items presented in counterbalanced order. No decline with age was noted for recognition, but a decline with age of almost 50% was noted on recall scores. This result was interpreted as indicating that *accessibility* of stored information, not the storage process per se, was impaired in old age.

In response to the Schonfield and Robertson study, McNulty and Caird (1966) suggested that amounts learned (synonymous with amounts stored) may decrease with age but that a recognition task may not be sensitive to this decline. This argument was based on McNulty's (1965) finding that only part of a stimulus (e.g., two or three letters) need be stored to produce correct recognition. Thus, whereas young adults may store whole items and old adults may only be able to store parts of items, recognition level would be the same because storage of part items is sufficient for recognition. On the other hand, recall would be poorer for the older participants, since it depends on storage of the whole item (e.g., word, nonsense syllable).

McNulty and Caird (1966) also suggested that older adults will exhibit poorer recognition performance than younger adults if "foil" stimuli in recognition tasks are similar to the "target" words. *Foil stimuli* are those which are not to be responded to, whereas *target stimuli* are those for which a recognition response is correct. If "happy" is in the list, but it was not one of the words memorized for later recall or recognition, "happy" is a foil word. In response to this suggestion, Schonfield and his colleagues (1972) designed a study in which one to six pairs of words were presented simultaneously to the left and right ears (*dichotic presentation*). Participants from three age groups (20 to 29, 30 to 59, and over 60 years) were asked to recognize the words from among three distractor vowels (foils). The distractors were either difficult (resembled target word in sound) or easy (no resemblance to the target word in sound or meaning). Prior to each presentation of stimuli, participants were informed as to which ear stimuli were to be recalled from first. Surprisingly, there was no greater decline in recognition with age from the ear in which stimuli were recalled second as opposed to the ear in which stimuli were recalled first. In recall studies the second set of recall scores (second ear in this case) are expected to be lower, since this information must be stored for a longer period of time. However, in this study, distractors were *less* effective in impairing performance with increasing age. In fact, the distractor effect almost disappeared in the over 60-year age group. In contrast to the Schonfield and Robertson (1966) study, recognition scores did *not* decline significantly with age. Schonfield and co-workers (1972) suggested that this finding may be due to age differences in acquisition of the list rather than differences in retrieval. Unfortunately, age differences in initial acquisition were not equated for the three age groups, and thus the conclusion must be considered tentative. Schonfield and his colleagues also suggested that age differences in their study may have been related to the fact that they used a dichotic listening paradigm, which not only involves rapid pacing but the shifting of attention from ear to ear, an activity which becomes increasingly difficult with increasing age. Thus it can be seen that the studies discussed so far do not provide a consistent answer to the question as to whether short-term memory decline in old age is a matter of limited accessibility (information is available but cannot be produced), availability (information was never stored), or both.

Studies by Craik (1971a) and Wickelgren (1975) tend to support the contention that short-term memory decline with age is a problem of accessibility, not availability. Both of these investigators used a "recognition paradigm," which required participants to recognize stimuli that had been presented at different times earlier in the experimental session. The emphasis in these studies was placed on estimating and separating initial memory acquisition from rate of decay using a signal detection theory. "Hit" and "false alarm" rates were used to calculate d′ as an index of memory trace strength. We will not go into the details of calculating d′; it is sufficient to say that both studies reported substantial age differences in learning and a decline in initial learning with increasing age but no age differences in rate of forgetting. Both studies also stress that the specifics of the research paradigm in terms of mode of output can produce age differences in forgetting related to *output interference*; that is, the methods used to output information in the act of verbal recall can interfere with information still waiting for output.

Drachman and Leavitt (1972) have proposed a "stimulus threshold" theory. The idea is that information is simply not learned and stored in an all-or-none fashion. Rather, in cases of impaired retrieval, the signal threshold required to achieve recall may be raised above normal by a cue (e.g., part of a word). If poor storage is the problem, the threshold necessary for retrieval may again be below normal, and the cue would raise it above threshold level. However, function of the cue cannot be specified, since only output can be measured. An interesting question that might be answered within the context of research designed to test this hypothesis is whether older adults are less capable than younger adults in raising inactive memories above the threshold level needed to bring information to an active, conscious level.

Interference

In the context of studies of memory and attention, the term *interference* has been defined in many ways. One useful definition describes interference as resulting from competition within "information processing channels" for time and space. Interference can be tested by using an experimental paradigm in which a paired-associates list is presented and performance is analyzed in terms of failure to recall words in different serial positions in the list. In one such study by Smith (1975), retroactive interference was examined for three age groups of adults; 20 to 39, 40 to 59, and 60 to 80 years. *Retroactive interference* is interference with memory that is created by tasks imposed *between* input and output. In this case the concern is with interference as it affects output, since input is unaffected.

Smith (1975) presented word lists by the study-test method mentioned earlier. There were eight words in each list that were paired with a digit, which served as the stimulus cue for recall. Fewer words were recalled with increasing age, but no interaction was observed for age and output position. In other words, interference occurred at similar points in the word lists for each age group, although fewer words were recalled as chronological age increased. The conclusion which may be drawn is that these data indicate no differential effects of retroactive interference for different age groups.

In another study, Fozard and Waugh (1969) examined proactive interference. *Proactive interference* refers to interference with memory for material that is caused by previously memorized material. Two age groups were involved in this study: 25 to 43 years and 47 to 65 years. The older group showed about 50% greater deficit in recall than the younger group, and all groups exhibited proactive interference. Again, however, the pattern of recall indicated that each age group had difficulty at similar points in the list of words to be recalled. As with the Smith (1975) study, Fozard and Waugh's data indicated that the serial effects of interference are the same, although fewer words are recalled by older groups. However, there was a wide range of ages in the two groups compared, and there was only a 4-year difference between the oldest person in the young group and the youngest person in the old group. It would be useful to repeat the study with more than two age groups and to utilize homogeneous age grouping.

A study by Hulicka (1967a) was stimulated by her observation that in many nonlaboratory situations, individuals are given equal opportunity to learn new materials but are not required to learn (memorize) information to some established criterion. Consequently, she designed a study in which two groups of subjects (mean ages = 15.5 and 70 years) either were given a set number of trials in which to learn a seven-pair list of names and occupations or were required to memorize to a criterion of no errors on one trial of the list. Following list 1, participants in the experiment were presented with list 2. List 2 was to be memorized to criterion before list 1 was recalled. When recall performance on list 1 was measured, there were no age-associated increases in interference effects (retroactive interference) under the condition in which list 1 had to be learned to criterion before list 2 was presented. However, more errors were observed for older adults (greater interference effects) on list 1 recall under the condition in which list 1 was originally exposed for a fixed number of trials rather than memorized to some criterion. The latter outcome was attributed to a lower level of original learning by the older group. Thus Hulicka suggested that *susceptibility to retroactive interference with increasing age is more directly related to deficits in original learning than to attention or retrieval deficits.*

Rabbitt (1965) was concerned with the possibility that interference effects with increasing age may be due to inability to ignore stimuli that are not relevant. Young (mean age = 20 years) and older (mean age = 65 years) adults were required to search a visual display for relevant stimuli, which were mixed among irrelevant stimuli. Participants also were asked to sort cards for which the ratio of relevant and irrelevant stimuli differed. The number of relevant stimuli was either two or eight letters; irrelevant stimuli were one, four, or eight letters. Sorting time was similar for the two age groups regardless of the number of relevant stimuli. However, as the number of irrelevant stimuli increased, older participants exhibited increasingly slower sorting times compared with those of the younger participants. It is not clear whether the results of Rabbitt's study can be interpreted, in the strictest sense, as indicating age differences in ability to ignore irrelevant information, since participants in the experiment were not required to ignore stimuli but, rather, to process and reject stimuli that were not relevant.

Rabbitt suggested that these data indicate that when older adults are required to process increased amounts of information, they experience a greater decline in their "perceptual sampling" space than do younger adults. Consequently, the number of stimuli that can be simultaneously processed are fewer. These studies would seem to have particularly important implications for the everyday functioning of older adults, especially in the area of driving skills and for tasks requiring discrimination between irrelevant and relevant stimulus materials. Additional studies with different sensory modalities and modes of stimulation are important to determine the extent to which decreased ability to ignore or reject irrelevant stimuli in older adults is characteristic of all modalities and how it relates to other age-associated phenomena such as perceptual closure.

SPECIAL PROBLEMS IN MEMORY RESEARCH WITH OLDER ADULTS

Just as "learning" performance reflects many variables other than learning ability, per se, performance on memory tasks can reflect many variables aside from what are defined as memory processes. In some cases a research task that is accepted without question by a younger group of experimental participants, who have been accustomed to psychologists and their tests from early childhood, may be rejected by an older age-cohort as silly or irrelevant to the real world. Hulicka (1967a) described a paired-associate task in which there was an 80% attrition rate for older subjects (age range = 60 to 72 years) who refused to learn "such nonsense" (Gladis and Braun, 1958). Hulicka solved the problem by changing the task so that it had more face validity. She paired occupations with persons' names and explained the study as an attempt to discover why people have trouble remembering names, a rather practical aspect of adaptation to the environment. Unfortunately, as we noted in the chapters on intelligence and motivation, attempts to make tasks more meaningful can also make them less difficult if the experimenter does not alter stimulus materials with great care.

Equalizing levels of learning among age groups is an important consideration if age differences are to be attributed to "memory" processes rather than initial level of learning ability. The point at which a process is labeled "memory" rather than "learning" is determined by operational definition. It is exceedingly difficult to separate learning from memory, since memory is involved in the learning process and vice versa. As Botwinick (1967) points out, without memory there is no sign of learning, and without learning there is nothing to remember. We have already discussed Hulicka's (1967a) data, which indicated that the way in which stimuli are learned (fixed number of trials or trials-to-criterion) can have differential effects in terms of retroactive interference for different age groups. Goulet (1972) has demonstrated that there are "learning-how-to-learn" aspects of experimental research, in which older adults are more likely to learn *how* to go about learning a task at a slower rate than younger adults; and, as a consequence, various age groups show improvement in performance at different points of the experiment.

Monge (1975) has pointed out that an inadequate learning set can have a "snowball" effect in terms of producing confusion and anxiety, which further handicap performance, especially among the elderly. In previous chapters we have discussed the importance of pacing in experimental tasks. In many cases where the experimental procedure permits the older adult to control pacing, better performance has resulted and anxiety is less evident. Self-pacing can produce problems as well as solving them; for example, the variance between and within experimental participants in the pacing variable is likely to be greater within older than younger samples. Many experimental paradigms that test short-term memory processes demand few errors and constant pacing of stimulus events to permit assessment of ongoing processes. Thus, whereas the subject can select the pace for trials, timing of stimulus events within trials must be fixed.

Equating of experimental participants in

Fig. 9-1. Irene Mackintosh Hulicka, Ph.D. (University of Nebraska, 1954). Dr. Hulicka is presently Professor of Psychology at the State University of New York College at Buffalo and Dean of the Faculty of Natural and Social Sciences. She has published many papers in the areas of memory, clinical psychology, learning perception, health, motivation, and social psychology. In fact, her numerous publications represent almost all areas of adult developmental psychology. Her greatest contribution to aging and developmental psychology has been published literature, much of which is summarized in this book and other books on life-span developmental psychology and aging. Dr. Hulicka's many positions, her varied and broad background in psychology, experimental and clinical, her many consultantships and services would take pages to summarize properly. Among these she has served as author, co-author, and editor of a number of books and reviews, and currently she serves as Editorial Consultant for the *Journal of Gerontology, Experimental Aging Research, Archives of Rehabilitation Therapy, International Journal of Behavioral Sciences,* and a variety of textbook firms. Dr. Hulicka is known for her readiness to help students and colleagues whenever they require professional assistance or personal encouragement.

terms of health status and education level is no less important in memory studies than it is in learning or intelligence studies. This principle was demonstrated well in an experiment by Keevil-Rogers and Schnore (1969), who matched different age groups (17 to 25, 40 to 50, and 65 to 78 years) on the WAIS vocabulary subtest and digit span. All participants (nurses and teachers) were of above-average intelligence and described as active and in good health. They were tested on three tasks involving (1) increasing delay intervals between presentation and recall; (2) varying retention intervals filled with unrelated activity; and (3) exceeding of immediate memory span by varying amounts. No age-related decrements were found on any of the tasks. Of course, the tasks on which the subjects were matched all included memory components, and thus the results are not altogether surprising.

Hulicka (1967b) was one of the first investigators to call attention to possible confounding by what might be referred to as "memory extraneous" variables. When scores were statistically adjusted for health status (defined in terms of number of diagnoses and months of hospitalization), no differences among age groups were observed for tests of recognition of faces, recall of names and matching to faces, memory for names and activities, and paired-associate learning.

These data are consistent with arguments raised by Abrahams and associates (1975) with regard to inadequate control of health status in many aging studies. However, the exact nature of the relationship between health variables and performance is not known for many diseases and symptoms. Often diagnoses emphasize cardiovascular status, and probably more literature has been directed toward cardiovascular diseases than any others. There is a tendency to emphasize studies that demonstrate a relationship between health status and performance, but there are studies that fail to find any such relationship. For example, Hertzog and coworkers (1975) found no relationship between cardiovascular status and stability of performance on the Primary Mental Abilities Test and the Test of Behavioral Rigidity. Many important variables such as geographical area have not been investigated. This variable may influence health status and many other variables indirectly.

Matching should be done with great care

in aging studies, and when one adjusts for variables such as education and health, it is well to remember that a more limited population of old than young subjects will be tested. In some instances, matching with respect to one variable may result in the introduction of other confounding variables. For example, one may match for education level in terms of years of schooling, but this may serve to systematically unmatch with regard to age-cohort differences in motivation to achieve higher levels of education. In other words, an eighth grade education in the early 1900s may represent the same degree of motivation for education as a twelfth grade education in the late 1900s (see Elias and Wright, 1976; Neale and Liebert, 1973). Furthermore, matching in an attempt to reduce "error variance" in experiments may restrict the variance attributable to the effects of experimental conditions if it is not done properly (Boneau and Pennypacker, 1961). Prior to matching, the experimenter should have a solid knowledge of the relationship between the dependent variable and the matching variable. This is absolutely critical in aging studies because the correlation between these variables may not be the same for different age groups (see Elias and Wright, 1976). These arguments can become complex. Perhaps it is sufficient to say that one should never automatically match with regard to a variable without understanding its relationship to the variable of interest in the sample tested.

Herriot (1974) makes an interesting argument that can be applied to future directions in aging research. In most studies, experimental participants are required to use the organization of material to be recalled provided by the experimenter, and/or they are asked to respond in an organizational format defined by the experimenter. To the extent that they fail to do this, they may be considered deficient in memory. However, organizational processes for the *input* or *output* of information may be different for different age groups, quite aside from memory ability per se. If *input* and *output* organization is fixed by the experimenter, the result may be a built-in age bias, which suggests poor memory but really reflects difficulty in getting information to be remembered into the system and/or a failure to demonstrate by response that it is, in fact, available. Perhaps a useful method for studying memory processes would be to examine the way in which subjects of different ages organize material to be remembered and organize responses to that material when given the opportunity to use any strategy. This approach seems to be emerging as somewhat more popular among investigators who are currently interested in aging and memory processes.

SUMMARY

Of all the processes that decline with age, perhaps one of the most feared is that of memory loss. This fact helps to explain the copious amount of research that has been conducted concerning memory change or loss with age. Despite the great amount of research in memory and aging, it would seem that little has been taken from the literature on aging in an attempt to understand and build general models of memory. Hopefully, this will change in the future, since the investigation of memory seems to be becoming more involved with arousal mechanisms and the role of neurotransmitters. The study of changes in these mechanisms with age could provide a valuable insight into memory processes.

Some of the earlier studies involving memory and aging were concerned with estimating the storage capacity of individuals in different age groups. These studies were mostly concerned with short-term retention, since long-term stores were considered to be infinite or at least very large. Typically, individuals were asked to store and recall a series of items either in order or irrespective of order. Such studies did not show large differences with age and did not seem to provide much insight into the process of memory itself. More recent studies of memory have been concerned with the exploration of the memory input process (e.g., iconic or echoic memory), the throughput process (e.g., encoding and organization of stimuli), and the output process (e.g., retrieval of stored information). These approaches to the study of memory reflect a general trend toward the investigation of process mechanisms in all aspects of psychology.

Studies of iconic memory and aging have been done through the use of what has come to be termed *backward masking* paradigms. Backward masking refers to the erasure or masking effect that incoming information has on information in the "sensory stores," that is, information that has not been "read out" into the short-term store or elevated to some higher level of encoding or processing. In general, it appears that as one grows older, more time is required to clear and pass on information from the sensory stores. Thus, with rapid input of information, there is a greater potential for the loss of information.

Recent investigations of short-term storage processes have centered around the study of the transformation of a stimulus which has been inputted to the form of that stimulus which will be retained and outputted at some future time. Although the question of *how much* can be stored is still being investigated, a question of more central importance in aging studies at present seems to be *how* information is stored. Thus the question of differences in memory capacity between age groups is less important than the question of how age groups differ in their organization of input. Most researchers who are interested in this question have provided several test conditions in which (1) some type of organization has been supplied for the participants, and (2) material must be organized by the individuals themselves. Not surprisingly, older individuals usually tend to benefit more from experimenter-provided organization than younger individuals but, in many cases, still do not reach or surpass the performance of younger participants. It must be remembered, however, that age differences in the use of experimenter-provided organization may simply reflect age differences in organizational strategies rather than changes in memory ability, per se.

One organizational strategy that has become of more recent interest to researchers is the use of imagery. In many cases a paired-associate task is borrowed from verbal learning methodology, and results are interpreted in terms of memory processes rather than verbal learning theory. A between- or within-subjects design is used, in which subjects are either provided with instructions to generate images, are given images, or are provided with stimuli that are high in imagery-producing potential. The results of these studies are very similar to those of other studies of organizational strategy. Imagery is often useful to older subjects and may produce greater proportionate improvement within older age groups, but generally older groups do not perform at the level of younger groups. The word *perform* is an important one because it connotes not only the memory process itself but also those factors which are involved in any kind of output (e.g., motivation, health, anxiety, prior familiarity with stimuli and experimental situations), all of which most certainly change with age along with memory processes. In fact, research has been directed toward the study of the interaction of variables such as health and prior learning with memory processes. The results frequently indicate that older subjects improve greatly in performance relative to younger subjects when extraneous memory variables are controlled and/or equated across age groups.

In terms of output processes, the central question for some time seems to have been, "Is failure to output (respond correctly) a problem of availability or accessibility?" Put another way, "Is forgetting a 'trace-dependent process' (loss or nonformation of a neural trace) or a 'cue-dependent process' (information cannot be raised to the threshold of consciousness or be located)?" The most popular research paradigms used to investigate this process have been recall and recognition paradigms, in which subjects are required either to recall or recognize prior inputted information. Not surprisingly, individuals are often able to recognize more than they can recall, and older subjects seem to do proportionately better in a recognition than a recall situation. Such outcomes cannot be said to support a "stimulus accessibility" position readily, however. It has been suggested that, in a recognition paradigm, only part of a stimulus need be stored to produce correct recognition. Therefore younger persons may store more of the stimulus, whereas older persons will store only part of the stimulus, but enough for recognition in a short-term memory task. Perhaps the most clearly stated outcome of this line of research is that *information is simply not learned and stored in an all-or-none fashion.*

Another important concept that has been investigated in relationship to memory is that of interference. Interference can occur during *input, throughput,* or *output,* and it appears to be more detrimental to older than younger persons. Some investigators have suggested that interference has more severe effects with increasing age because older individuals are more likely to suffer from diversions or shifts of attention.

Although most people will eventually suffer some memory decline, in most cases the loss will not be severe and may never become recognizable except in a laboratory situation. Perhaps more importantly, memory loss should not be confused with "loss of contact" with reality or disorientation because of the inability to organize one's thoughts in a coherent fashion. These latter processes most likely represent much more severe underlying physiological problems.

SELECTED READINGS

Craik, F. I. M., and Lockhart, R. S. Levels of processing: a framework for memory research. *Journal of Verbal Learning and Verbal Behavior,* 1972, **11,** 671-684.

Elias, J. W., and Wright, L. L. Matching, the null hypothesis and the aging variable: Would the real age variable please stand up? *Experimental Aging Research,* 1976, **2,** 261-269.

Herriot, P. *Attributes of memory.* London: Methuen & Co., Ltd., 1974.

Hulicka, I. Short-term learning and memory efficiency as a function of age and health. *Journal of the American Geriatrics Society,* 1967, **15,** 285-294.

Kline, D. W., and Birren, J. E. Age differences in dichoptic masking. *Experimental Aging Research,* 1975, **1,** 17-25.

McNulty, J. A., and Caird, W. Memory loss with age: retrieval or storage? *Psychological Reports,* 1966, **19,** 229-230.

Monge, R. Learning in the adult years: set or rigidity. In D. B. Lumsden and R. H. Sherron (Eds.), *Experimental studies in adult learning and memory.* Washington, D.C.: Hemisphere Publishing Corp., 1975.

Schonfield, D., Trueman, V, and Kline, D. Recognition tests of dichotic listening and the age variable. *Journal of Gerontology,* 1972, **27,** 487-493.

Winn, F. J., Jr., and Elias, J. W. The total time principle as a substitute for the pacing variable in paired-associate tasks with the aged. *Experimental Aging Research,* 1975, **1,** 307-312.

CHAPTER 10

PERCEPTION AND PSYCHOMOTOR RESPONSE

Research on perception and aging is not nearly as well integrated as are other areas of aging research. In some cases the same research papers are repeatedly cited as representative of progress in the area. One also tends to find researchers of diverse scientific backgrounds working on problems in perception, a factor that leads to communication difficulties. Hopefully, the study of perceptual processes across the life span will serve as a catalyst for the integration of what now appear to be largely isolated findings.

It is clear that, with advancing age, there is a decline in the functioning of all sensory systems. The important question is how *input* (peripheral processes) and *throughput* (central processes) interact to produce behavioral change. You will recall that this is an extremely difficult question to answer because one can only observe *output* as the result of manipulations of stimulus parameters. Thus one must make inferences about the interaction of *input* and *throughput* processes.

VISION

The visual and auditory systems are the two most investigated sensory systems in humans. Some of the visual problems that are associated with growing old can be eliminated, or at least reduced, by means of prosthetic devices, such as glasses, or by simply raising levels of illumination. It is more difficult to compensate for other types of problems, such as thickening of the lens.

The lens

Changes in the lens are primarily responsible for a number of visual problems that are commonly associated with increasing age in the adult years. The two main functions of the lens are to transmit and refract light. Changes in the structure and functioning of the lens account for a large portion of the decline in fidelity of visual input in older persons. The lens not only loses its transparent properties with advancing age, but there is also a loss of fluid and a compression of the nuclei and cell membranes of inert tissue at the center of the lens. The lens also thickens and loses its elasticity with age, a phenomenon that results in farsightedness (presbyopia) (McFarland, 1968). Moreover, the pliable cortex of the lens occupies a smaller and smaller portion of the total lens with advancing age. Since the pliable cortex is involved in accommodation to near and far objects, there is a corresponding loss of lens flexibility (Corso, 1971). Visual acuity, the ability to see small details, shows its greatest decline after 40 years of age, when many aspects of visual functioning begin to decline more rapidly than at younger ages (Bischof, 1976; Hirsch, 1960).

Illumination levels

Generally there is an increased demand for higher levels of illumination as persons grow older. This demand is related to peripheral processes, such as decreasing pupil diameter, which allow less light to reach the

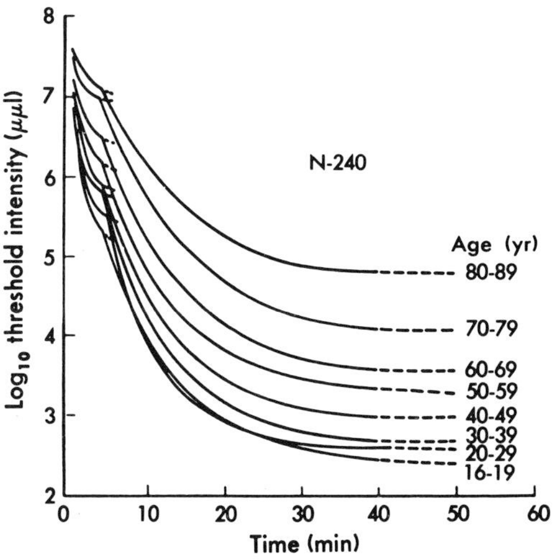

Fig. 10-1. Dark adaptation as a function of age (range 16 to 89 years). (From McFarland, R. A. The sensory and perceptual process in aging. In K. W. Schaie [Ed.], *Theory and method of research on aging.* Morgantown, W.Va.: West Virginia University Press, 1968.)

retina. However, it may also be related to more central processes, such as metabolic effects on central nervous system functioning (McFarland, 1968).

With age, adaptation to *changing* levels of illumination is also affected. There seems to be less sensitivity or adaptability to changing levels of illumination at the higher illumination levels. This finding is best illustrated by an examination of Fig. 10-1, which shows a dark adaptation curve constructed from data by McFarland and associates (1960). In a dark adaptation study, subjects are exposed to a known intensity of light and then allowed to remain in total darkness for a set period of time; then sensitivity to light sources of different intensities is measured by psychophysical procedures. It may be noted that all subjects in Fig. 10-1 showed the classical "dark adaptation" curve, but at 2 minutes of dark adaptation, the very young subjects were five times more sensitive than the very old subjects. At 40 minutes they were as much as 240 times more sensitive. (Note that sensitivity increases with *decreasing* height of the curves.) Moreover, the *rate* of adaptation to darkness is slower with increasing age.

Fusion of flicker

Just as dark adaptation may prove to be a valuable indicator of sensory processing efficiency with advancing age, so may critical flicker frequency (CFF). The dependent variable in studies of flicker fusion is the frequency at which a flickering light source appears to fuse into one light source. A decrease in CFF is typically observed with increasing age. CFF has also been found to be lower for groups with brain pathology. For persons with presumably normal brains, it has been related to several tests of intellectual functioning (Loranger and Misiak, 1959).

On the surface, CFF seems to be a useful index of central nervous system efficiency. However, it is not as useful as it may seem. Reitan (personal communication, 1976) reports that it has not been particularly useful as a measure of brain damage. The relationship between scores on tests of mental ability and CFF seems to be more reliable in the older age ranges than in the younger age ranges.

It is important to note that whether or not one finds relationships between chronological age or intellectual functioning and CFF depends heavily on a number of factors identified by Coppinger (1955) and McFarland and co-workers (1958): (1) the characteristics of the light, (2) the level of brightness, and (3) the ratio of light-to-dark time. Weale (1965) has suggested that a considerable proportion of the variance in CFF with advancing age is due to *peripheral* factors involving the pupil and lens rather than more central factors involving the cerebral cortex. Keep in mind that the eye is a part of the brain but that the pupil, the lens, and the retina are considered peripheral structures. Weale has pointed out that when more light reaches the retina (when the pupil is dilated), there is much less decline in CFF with advancing age. We have already noted that as persons grow older, pupil diameter decreases. Thus, at lower levels of illumination, the relationship between age and CFF may be an artifact of a peripheral factor (pupil diameter) rather than a reflection of changes in the functioning of more centralized portions of the brain. However, it is difficult to evaluate the extent to which amount of light on the retina, as determined by pupil size, may interact with central processing factors. Actually, arguments with regard to the peripheral as opposed to the central nature of CFF have existed ever since the phenomenon was first discovered. If nothing else, they illustrate the kinds of difficulties involved in perceptual research with different age groups of adults and the dangers involved in assuming that age changes or age differences in CFF are centrally mediated or somehow reflect structurally based intellectual changes with age.

Peripheral as opposed to foveal vision

One consequence of increased opaqueness of the lens and decreased pupil diameter is a shrinking of the visual field size with increasing age. Thus task performance requiring peripheral vision would be expected to decline more sharply with age than task performance requiring foveal vision. In the absence of such knowledge, the investigator may well attribute decline in peripheral vision or decline on tasks demanding peripheral vision as indicative of brain damage or as decline in central processing factors, such as those involved in intellectual functioning and learning.

Diet

It has been noted that the investigator must be very careful to separate what may be termed "primary" mental decline with age from factors such as changes in the lens, pupil, and retina which may affect performance. Similarly, general health and diet are important considerations when one makes inferences about the fidelity of the visual system. For example, decreased sensitivity to light could be exaggerated by vitamin A deficiency (McFarland, 1968). Many elderly persons live alone and either do not or cannot provide well-balanced meals for themselves. Thus it is possible that some elderly subjects in perception experiments may do less well because of dietary deficiency. Just as health status must be taken into consideration when working with elderly persons in the laboratory, adequacy of diet must be taken into consideration. This is particularly true of patients with a history of alcoholism.

Retina

Many textbooks ignore the role of the retina in visual decline with advancing age. The adequate functioning of the retina is influenced by the vascular system. Changes in the vascular system may lead to conditions such as sclerosis of the retinal and choroidal vessels of the eye and possibly to atrophy of the retina and the optic nerve. Glaucoma may have serious detrimental effects on the retina and the optic nerves because of the buildup of fluid within the eye. It may result in loss of certain fields of vision or in total loss of vision if it is not detected and treated. In some instances these problems are not detected, and they can most certainly have profound effects on visual input processes and performance.

Visual illusions

A number of aging studies have been concerned with visual illusions rather than basic visual processes. Research on age differences in visual illusion perception gives credence to the notion that visual perceptual abilities are altered with age, not only in terms of input factors but also in terms of the *organization* of perceptions as well. Organization of perceptions depends on the fidelity of input processes and the structural integrity of the eye, but it also depends on central factors, such as intelligence, motivation, and past experience.

Beyond these rather general statements, it is most difficult to make general statements about the illusion studies. The most recent period of interest in illusions was between the late 1950s and the early 1960s. Interest may have waned because of the great distance between actual experimental results and theoretical rationale for performing the experiments. Nevertheless, these studies provide some interesting data that stimulate thinking about the qualitative changes in perception that may occur with advancing age.

Concealed figures. The concealed figures test has been popular in aging studies. In this test a simple geometrical design appears at the left of a row of four more complex designs. The experimental participant's task is to identify the complex figures in which the simple figure is hidden. Because the complex figures have what is known as "good gestalt," their properties impell the person who views them to "closure." In other words, the participant tends to see them as unified wholes. This tendency toward closure must be resisted to search successfully for the simple figure that is hidden within the complex figures.

Using this task, Basowitz and Korchin (1957) tested old (mean age = 78 years) and young (mean age = 27 years) persons. They also tested them on the Gestalt Completion Test, which demands the identification of seventy-two ambiguous drawings and requires the fusion of disorganized percepts into one, single, unified percept. For the concealed figures task, the younger participants completed more of the items of greater difficulty than did the older participants. The experimenters suggested that the latter group had poorer resistance to closure than the younger subjects. For the Gestalt Completion Test, which required the organization of smaller perceptions into a whole, the number of drawings attempted by the young and old participants was the same, but the younger group perceived many more drawings correctly. The response styles of the older subjects were characterized as perseverative and loosely organized with a tendency to fixate on detail.

Visual as opposed to tactile concealed figures. Axelrod and Cohen (1961) compared young (mean age = 26.5 years) and older (mean age = 68.9 years) participants on both a visual and tactile hidden figures task. The visual task was the embedded figures test and the tactile task consisted of wooden figures (similar to the embedded figures) raised in relief against a plywood background.

The older participants performed less adequately than the younger participants on both tasks. The fact that both the visual and tactile tasks showed similar decline with age was interpreted as ruling out the possibility that the results from the visual concealed figures tests are biased by a "peripheral" visual deterioration. It is interesting to note that both young and old participants reported relying heavily on visualization of the tactile tasks.

Muller-Lyer Illusion and Titchener Circles Illusion. The Muller-Lyer Illusion and the Titchener Circles Illusion also test the perception of part-whole relationships. Wapner and colleagues (1960) have suggested that the perceptions of these illusions across the life span should be consonant with the law of development, which implies that there is an increasing differentiation and integration with development. Fig. 10-2 provides an example of the Muller-Lyer Illusion, which is thought to involve the assimilation of parts in such a way that the horizontal lines are assimilated to the total figure.

Results indicated a *decrease* in susceptibility to the Muller-Lyer Illusion from young (age range = 20 to 24 years) to middle (age range = 35 to 39 years) age. The investigators suggested that this finding indicated a decrease in global perception as persons grow older. However, the effectiveness of

Fig. 10-2. Response to the Muller-Lyer Illusion as a function of age. Subjects ranged in age from 20 to 80 years. (From Wapner, S., Werner, H., and Comalli, P. E., Jr. *Journal of Gerontology,* 1960, **15,** 412.)

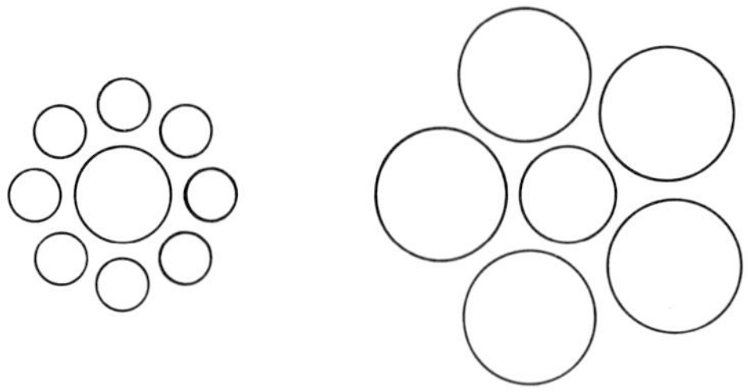

Fig. 10-3. Titchener Circles Illusion. (From Wapner, S., Werner, H., and Comalli, P. E., Jr. *Journal of Gerontology,* 1960, **15,** 412.)

the illusion *increased* from middle to old (age range = 65 to 80 years) age. This result was interpreted as indicating an increase in global perception (ability to assimilate parts to the whole).

The second test used by Wapner's group, the Titchener Circles Illusion (Fig. 10-3), is thought to be related to greater or lesser ability to contrast the parts of the figure. If older persons show an increase in global perception with age, as was suggested by the results of tests with the Muller-Lyer Illusion, there should be less contrasting of parts by elderly subjects and greater susceptibility to the illusion. The greater susceptibility would be due to an assimilation of the outer circles to the inner circle. Findings were opposite to the predictions. There was a *decrease* in susceptibility to the illusion from middle to old age. However, this decrease in susceptibility was interpreted by Wapner and associates (1960) to be in agreement with the notion of an increase in global perception in old age. Perhaps the safest conclusion is that the trends for the Muller-Lyer and Titchener Circles Illusions were not consistent for the age span studied (20 to 80 years). It is very difficult, indeed, to interpret the results of illusion studies because they involve so many factors other than the central processing mechanisms, per se.

Eisner and Schaie (1971) have reported a study by Gajo (1966) in which susceptibility to the Titchener Circles Illusion did increase with age. In view of the fact that these data were inconsistent with the finding of a decrease in susceptibility by Wapner and colleagues (1960), Eisner and Schaie (1971) performed yet another experiment with the Muller-Lyer and Titchener Circles Illusions. They tested men, ranging in age from 55 to 77 years, twice over a six-month period. Longitudinal estimates of the effects of the illusions showed an increase in susceptibility to the Muller-Lyer Illusion with age and a decrease in susceptibility to the Titchener Circles Illusion. However, more refined analyses indicated that cohort differences accounted for part of the increase in susceptibility to the Muller-Lyer Illusion with age, and time-of-measurement effects provided at least a partial explanation of the decrement in susceptibility to the Titchener Circles Illusion.

AUDITORY SYSTEM

The term for loss of auditory acuity with age is *presbycusis.* Four kinds of presbycusis have been identified (Rupp, 1970): (1) sensory presbycusis, produced by atrophy of cells at the basal end of the organ of Corti, which produces abrupt hearing loss for high-pitched tones; (2) neural presbycusis, which involves neuronal loss in the pathways from the ear to the auditory cortex, producing speech discrimination loss; (3) metabolic presbycusis, which involves atrophy of the stria vascularis and results in pure tone hearing loss; and (4) mechanical presbycusis, which involves loss of flexibility of the basilar membrane and results in hearing loss for high-frequency tones.

Hearing losses can be further identified in terms of *conductive* and *sensorineural functions.* The conductive losses are those which occur in the transmission of sound from the outer through the middle ear, where the ossicles are located (malleus, incus, stapes). These are usually losses of amplitude and do not involve distortion of sound. Sensorineural loss involves the functioning of the inner ear (cochlea) or the transmission of the electrical signals from the inner ear along the cochlear nerve to the brain. A loss of function here can involve not only a loss in amplitude but a distortion of sound as well.

In terms of communication and information input, loss of speech perception is most likely to have a great personal as well as social impact. Sataloff and Vassallo (1966) have pointed out that with the greatest loss of discriminability occurring at high frequencies, those consonants which are low in acoustic power and have high-frequency characteristics (e.g., f, g, s, t, z, or th and sh), are the most likely to be misperceived by the aged. Speech perception involves not only peripheral processing but central processing mechanisms as well so that changes in speech perception cannot be attributed to sensory decline alone.

Auditory illusions

The verbal transformation effect is an auditory illusion that has been studied across the life span (Warren, 1961). This effect occurs when an auditory stimulus is repeated over and over and produces illusory changes in the perceived word or sound. The simpler the repeated stimulus is the greater the number of transformations that will occur (Lass and Golden, 1971). Children at the age of 6 years are reported to hear few or no transformations of repeated stimuli. Most children hear verbal transformations by the age of 8 years. The rate of transformations of illusory changes remains constant into the twenties and then declines through middle age. Older adults, like children, report fewer transformations than young or middle-aged persons. There are qualitative differences between the transformations of children and older adults. The transformations of children are sounds in the English language, but they may not be recognizable words. Older individuals tend to report only meaningful transformations. Younger adults make transformations that include the sounds of the language used in the proper order, but they may be nonsense words, such as changing "stress" to "stresh." The loss of susceptibility to this illusion is thought to represent a loss of organizational skills. Whenever older adults do make transformations, they tend to be of a gradual nature, whereas those of younger persons are more abrupt without transitional states. In one sense, such a lack of transformations in older subjects might represent the combination of a more cautious, accuracy-seeking approach to stimulus input as a result of declining sensory processes. The lack of transformations does not seem to be related, however, to the loss of auditory acuity, and this is one task where elderly persons are actually more accurate than younger persons (Warren and Warren, 1971).

OLFACTION AND GUSTATION

Olfaction and gustation are often grouped together for purposes of discussion. This may be related to the fact that they are interdependent in terms of the qualitative aspects of food preference and enjoyment. There is little to discuss when they are considered separately. These senses are difficult to study, and this may be a contributing factor to the absence of knowledge about them. In terms of behavior, neither olfaction nor gustation appears to have the same importance to social and cognitive functioning that sight and hearing do. Of course, no one is certain of the extent of this lack of importance. Perhaps as scientists learn more about the relationship of gustation and olfaction to the aging process, they will be better able to evaluate their significance for successful adaptation among elderly persons.

Much of the research in taste and olfaction must, of necessity, rely on self-reports. Both taste and olfactory stimuli are difficult to control and manipulate. The olfactory system frustrates even the most patient investigator because experimental participants adapt to smells very quickly. There appears to be little agreement on the number or nature of the basic types of odors. Furthermore, difficulties involved in studying taste arise from the fact that many of the qualitative aspects of taste are due to stimulation of the olfactory system (Thompson, 1967). Thus it would seem that taste and olfaction are senses which have not been thoroughly investigated for any age group. However, research in this area may be very important in terms of improving the quality of life for older persons who suffer taste and olfactory losses. Many of these same persons must cope with increasing restriction to the home, hospitalization, institutionalization, and reduced mobility. Thus they are particularly likely to value pleasant surroundings and good food in terms of overall life satisfaction. These aspects of the environment may be even more important for older persons who also suffer from failing vision and hearing or who are restricted to bed.

Olfaction

There is only limited information available with regard to the rate of adaptation or sensitivity to odors as a function of age. Liss and Gomez (1958) have provided some evidence for an age-associated atrophy of olfactory fibers, although the correlation between age and fiber loss was not high. Schiffman (1975) found that older persons (mean age = 76 years) were less sensitive to odors than college students (mean age = 19 years). She also found that amplification of odors in foods by means of artificial food flavors greatly improved the ability of the older subjects to recognize foods. Thus there is some evidence of functional decline in odor detection that supports the notion that olfactory fibers may atrophy with age. It is interesting to note that obese subjects were able to identify foods better than normal-weight college students.

In view of the difficulty in studying olfaction with humans, one might give some thought to the possible value of animal models, particularly models provided by animals with highly developed olfactory systems. It is interesting to note that a great number of experiments with rodents have concentrated on visual discrimination and spatial discrimination, but there are few studies of olfactory changes in aging rodents. Of course, the advantage of the small animal model lies with the possibility for surgical manipulations, genetic studies, and acquisition of data that may be of help in relating functional changes to structural alterations with age. Most competent comparative psychologists are well aware of the difficulties in controlling olfactory cues in visual and spatial experiments with rodents, and yet few have taken advantage of the possibilities to study olfaction offered by this well-developed "smell brain."

Taste

In terms of quality of sensation, more is known about taste than about olfaction. Taste can be fairly reliably divided into four different qualities: sweet, sour, salty, and bitter. Most reviews of studies on taste indicate that there is a decline in taste sensitivity in old age as demonstrated by a higher threshold for taste discrimination. For example, the threshold for discrimination of salt appears to be much higher in old age for men than for women. A study by Cooper and associates (1959) is cited frequently. They found that sensitivity to the four qualities of taste is fairly constant and unimpaired until about the late fifties, after which a sharp decline in taste sensitivity begins.

Experimentation in taste preference is further complicated by the great amount of variance between individuals. For example, Desor and co-workers (1975) reported considerable individual differences in preference for sweetness or saltiness, and these preferences seemed to persist over a considerable period of time. Many factors influence taste preferences, including culture, state of hunger, expectations, dietary history, and genotype (Moscowitz et al., 1975). It is not clear what the role of these factors is in taste discrimination, but they should be considered as potential sources of variance in the design of experiments. In one study, which did include different age groups, Desor and colleagues (1975) found sex and race differences in preference for sweetness and saltiness for 9- to 15-year-old persons but not for 18- to 64-year-old persons. Younger males showed a greater preference for sucrose than young females; a similar trend was observed in the older group, but it was statistically nonsignificant. In contrast, no sex differences were observed for salt preference. Younger blacks showed a greater preference for stronger sucrose and salt solutions than younger whites. These race differences in preference were absent in adults, although there was a tendency within the adult groups for blacks to select the more concentrated solutions. Investigators should be aware of these preferences, especially when they conduct experiments with subjects whose age range extends from childhood through adulthood.

PSYCHOMOTOR RESPONSE AND REACTION TIME

The most cursory review of the literature on aging leaves little doubt as to the popularity of reaction time (RT) as an index of performance. Actually RT studies have been more helpful in providing descriptions of relationships among variables than they have been in providing explanations. In many aging studies the rationale for using RT as a measure is the idea that it can be viewed as representing the functional capacity of the nervous system. Although this is true in some cases, there are clearly many instances in which RT may be affected by motivation, affect (e.g., depression), response strategies, response style, caution, anxiety, and many other variables that are not directly associated with structural integrity of nervous system tissue or neurophysiological events. Considerable evidence exists that, in those instances where age-associated changes in the nervous system do affect RT, the changes are the result of *throughput* processes rather than impaired *input* or slowing of neurophysiological transmission involved in motor response *(output)*. Whereas this may be true in many cases, it is not necessarily true in all cases. Many diseases that increase in incidence with old age affect both perception and motor output rather severely. For example, severe auditory or visual impairment may slow RT to visual or auditory stimuli in the absence of decrements in central mediating processes *(throughput)*.

Simple reaction time as opposed to complex reaction time

Simple RT (a discrete response to onset or offset of a stimulus) and choice (discriminative or disjunctive) RT increase with age beyond young adulthood. In many studies with presumably healthy subjects, simple RT increases only slightly with age (Elias and Elias, 1976; Elias and Kinsbourne, 1974). In healthy persons these increases are often so slight as to be of little practical significance. On the other hand, considerable increase in RT (slowing of response) is seen for RT tasks that involve one of the following characteristics: (1) a discrimination involving withholding of a response; (2) a discrimination in which one response must be made while another is withheld; (3) a series of responses; and (4) matching stimuli to determine a correct response. These increases in RT are not just seen in very old persons but also in middle-aged persons and may begin as early as the late teens.

Task difficulty

Fig. 10-4 illustrates the relationship between simple and complex RT of the matching stimuli-discrimination variety. This figure summarizes a study by Elias and Elias (1976) in which subjects were asked to respond to the onset of a tone as quickly as possible (simple RT) and, in another portion of the experiment, to identify what were defined as successive verbal and nonverbal stimuli in terms of being identical (same) or different. The stimuli were defined as "verbal" (words) and "nonverbal" (tones) because the experimenters were interested in the interaction of the type of stimuli with age

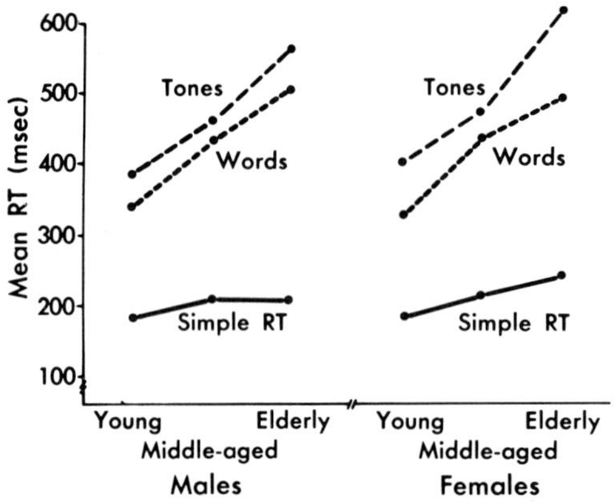

Fig. 10-4. Mean RT for a simple RT task and a matching RT task for men and women in three age groups. In the simple RT task, subjects were asked to respond to a tone as quickly as possible. In the matching RT task, subjects were asked to identify a pair of stimuli (nonverbal or verbal) as "same" or "different" as quickly as possible. (From Elias, J. W., and Elias, M. F. *Journal of Gerontology,* 1976, **31**, 164.)

differences in RT on the complex RT task. It may be seen that age differences in simple RT were slight. Furthermore, there was no significant correlation between RTs for the simple and complex tasks. When statistical covariance techniques were used to adjust the complex RT scores for the simple RT scores, the latter had no effect on the complex scores. The conclusion was that simple slowing of motor response did not account for the age differences observed for the complex task because notable age differences were observed only when rather complex decisions were superimposed on the need to respond rapidly.

Reaction time may show greater or lesser decrement with age depending on the type of stimuli, practice, health, and other factors. In addition, as task difficulty increases, RT increases to a greater extent in older than in younger adults. There have been exceptions to the finding of proportionately greater increases in complex as opposed to simple RT scores for older than for younger persons (Simon and Wolf, 1963), but in most studies this relationship holds. No one explanation can account for these relatively consistent findings. It has been suggested that older persons require increased amounts of time to (1) initiate responses, (2) input and/or identify stimuli, (3) maintain stimuli in memory, and (4) retrieve stimuli from "short-term store" (Canestrari, 1968b; Rabbitt, 1965; Surwillo, 1968; Talland, 1965; Welford, 1969).

A question of major importance in relation to age and RT concerns the "locus" of slowing. Stated somewhat differently, how much of the variance in RT at different points in the adult life span can be attributed to sensory receptors, afferent input neuronal pathways, central processing mechanisms, or motor-efferent pathways and muscle movement? Just as in studies of intelligence, psychologists find that they are back to the old problem of separating *input, throughput,* and *output* mechanisms to explain decline in efficiency of performance with age. There is considerable support for the notion that peripheral *(input)* mechanisms account for only a very small portion of the decline in speed of response with advancing age (Botwinick, 1965; Magladerly, 1959). A study by Norris and colleagues (1953) is representative of research in this area. These investigators measured speed of neuronal impulse conduction in the peripheral nerve component of muscles involved in reflexive and voluntary motor behavior. Their subjects ranged in age from 30 to 90 years. There was a slowing in the conduction velocity of neuronal transmission, but this slowing only accounted for about 4% of the variance in RT. In other words, speed of neuronal transmission in the strictly motor component of RT accounted for only a small proportion of the variance in RT among the various individuals in the study.

Botwinick and Thompson (1966) elaborated on a method used by Weiss (1965), which allowed the partitioning of RT into two components: premotor RT and motor RT. Participants in their experiment were required to respond to simple auditory stimuli (1,000 cps tones), and electromyograms (records of muscle activity) were recorded from the extensor muscle of the forearm during the sequence of movements involved in reacting to the stimulus. *Premotor RT* was defined as the time between stimulus onset and the occurrence of increased muscle neuron firing. *Motor RT* was defined as follows: Total RT − Premotor RT = Motor RT. Older subjects (median age of men = 78 years; median age of women = 76 years) were slower than younger subjects (median age of men and women = 20 years) on both components of RT. However, premotor time consumed 84% of total RT for both age groups, whereas motor time consumed the remaining 16%. It is particularly important to note that (1) premotor time accounted for the greatest proportion of total RT, and (2) although total RT (premotor RT + motor RT) was greater for the older subjects, the premotor time and the motor time occupied roughly the *same* percentage of response time for both age groups. Thus it would seem that "nonmotor" factors represent the largest portion of the difference in RT between young and old subjects, but older subjects do not show a disproportionately greater slowing in nonmotor factors.

Set and attentiveness

As we noted in the chapters on motivation, variables such as the biological state of the person, set to respond, attentiveness, and arousal have important influences on RT. Botwinick and his colleagues have devoted considerable time to research on the effect of "set" on RT for different age groups (e.g., Botwinick, 1965; 1971; Botwinick and Storandt, 1973a).

Set refers to expectancies that develop in anticipation of the onset of a stimulus. It is defined operationally in the studies by Botwinick and co-workers as the relationship that develops between speed of response and a preparatory interval. The *preparatory interval* (PI) is the time between a warning (preparatory) signal and the onset of the stimulus. Generally, age differences in RT are greater when the PIs are short (e.g., 1 second) rather than long (e.g., 60 seconds) (Botwinick et al., 1957). However, the effect of length of PI is more dramatic for older men than for older women, a finding that has not been well explained (Botwinick and Brinley, 1962).

It has also been established that the louder the stimulus the faster the RT will be, and as stimulus loudness decreases, expectancy and set become even more important (Botwinick and Storandt, 1972). One logical question is whether differences in RT between younger and older adults may reflect the fact that loudness is not the same for older and younger persons. You may recall that *intensity* of sound is physical, but *loudness* is psychological. Thus "effective" loudness may be different for younger and older subjects and thus account for RT differences. Botwinick (1971) not only made this suggestion but tested the possibility that it might be true. He varied both time of the PI (0.5 and 6.0 seconds) and stimulus intensity. An attempt was made to equate for stimulus intensity across age groups (17 to 22 years as opposed to 64 to 79 years) by allowing experimental participants to select 75% and 100% threshold intensities; that is, by using psychophysical techniques, intensities perceived with this degree of accuracy were determined. Surprisingly, age differences persisted regardless of attempts to maximize the stimulus intensities or PIs in favor of elderly subjects. Again, age differences were greater for men than for women. Botwinick suggested that the extremely low-intensity stimuli used in this study may have placed extreme demands on the attentive abilities of the older subjects. He also noted that the use of suprathreshold stimuli may have produced a very different effect on his results.

Arousal and attention

The observation that RT, especially complex RT, increases with age stimulated a search for timing mechanisms in the nervous system that may subserve attention and arousal. The electroencephalographic alpha rhythm has played a role in that search because it slows notably with age (Surwillo, 1968). The *alpha rhythm* is the most prominent rhythm of the waking electroencephalogram. It has a frequency of 8 to 13 cps and originates as a sequence of waves predominantly in the occipital cortex.

Because of slowing of the alpha rhythm, it has been suggested that the alpha period increases at the rate of 4 msec. a decade. The *alpha period* is the period of time relative to total waking electroencephalogram time that alpha waves are seen. Surwillo (1960; 1961) found a rank order correlation of 0.81 between RT and alpha period for thirteen adult subjects, ranging in age from 18 to 72 years. In a subsequent investigation (Surwillo, 1963) the correlation was 0.72, and the correlation between RT and age was 0.19. Surwillo reasoned that if the slowed alpha rhythm was responsible for the slowing of RT, the positive correlation between RT and age (0.19) should disappear when alpha scores were partialled out of the correlation. When alpha rhythm period was partialled out, the positive correlation did disappear as predicted. However, keep in mind that a simple RT task was used and the correlation between age and RT was not large to begin with because of individual variability. When a more complex task (discrimination RT) was used, the correlation between age and RT was 0.26 (Surwillo, 1964). This correlation disappeared when alpha period was partialled out. However, it is important to remember that, whereas alpha period and alpha rhythm are electrophysiological correlates of brain activity and may predict slowing with age, the correlation between alpha period and RT does not *explain* slowing with age. In fact, alpha is not unlike RT to the extent that it is a gross reflection of a more highly organized process *(throughput)*.

For the most part the idea that central processes account for the largest portion of age-associated differences in RT has been arrived at in a de facto manner; that is, peripheral processes (motor components) do not seem to contribute much to the total variance in RT, and thus it is assumed that central processing factors must be responsible. This seems logical, but as we have stated before: Logic is often a systematic way of going wrong with reason.

Despite the fact that RT, as a variable, tends to be more descriptive than explicative, slowing with age is one of the most replicated findings in the literature. It is particularly sensitive to pathology (Timiras, 1972) and is affected by hypertension and cardiovascular disease (see Abrahams and Birren, 1973), even to the point of predicting individuals who are predisposed to coronary heart disease by virtue of their RT behavior. Since these diseases increase in incidence with age, RT becomes an exceedingly important dependent variable.

Reaction time and information processing

Aside from comparisons of simple as opposed to complex RT tasks, RT studies can be useful in determining the efficiency with which different age groups can respond to different kinds of stimulus information. Space does not permit summaries of all the studies falling into this category, but several examples may provide an indication of how RT studies may be used in this context and the nature of the problems encountered.

You may recall from the chapters on intelligence testing that a general assumption frequently made is that so-called nonverbal skills are less resistant to effects of aging than are verbal skills. However, the kinds of questions that are used on psychometric tests, such as the Wechsler Adult Intelligence Scale (WAIS), do not really permit the investigator to compare the subject's ability to process "verbal" as opposed to "nonverbal" stimulus materials. This is because the nonverbal components of psychometric tests require individuals to deal with information that they have not been acquainted with previously, and to do so under time constraints. On the other hand, verbal components of many psychometric tests (e.g., WAIS) do not have time requirements, and much of the material is familiar to the individual being tested. Thus there is a confounding of tasks demands and stimulus characteristics. This confounding does not alter the value of the WAIS and other psychometric tests as indicators of the general level of intellectual functioning, or does it suggest that comparisons of verbal and performance (nonverbal) portions are not useful in terms of clinical evaluation. Rather, it means that, from an experimental perspective, there is a confounding of task demands with stimulus characteristics. Thus one does not know whether it is the dimension of specific tasks demands that causes subjects to perform differently on the verbal and performance subtests or whether it is the nature of the stimuli presented. Most likely it is both, but it is very difficult to determine which aspect is most important when a psychometric test is used.

One solution to this problem is to use an information-processing paradigm involving RT. Elias and Kinsbourne (1974:162) have defined information processing as follows:

> The processing of information is defined as those sets of activities which have been identified with short-term attention and memory processes. Previous studies indicate that these short-term processes involve detection, encoding, storage, re-

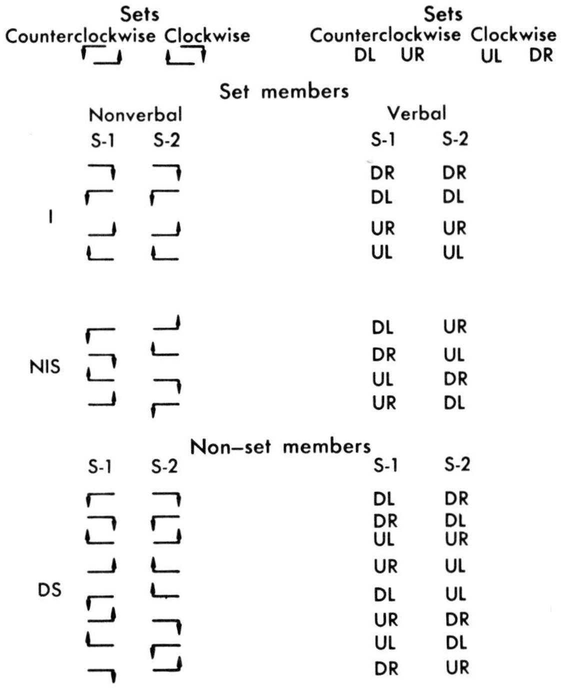

Fig. 10-5. Stimuli used in the Elias and Kinsbourne (1974) reaction time study. "Stimulus combinations labeled I and NIS are in the same set or category by virtue of the fact that S-1 and S-2 rotate in a common direction. The I stimulus combinations are not only in the same set but they are either spatially identical (arrows) or physically identical (letters). The DS stimulus combinations are members of different sets. All stimulus combinations in the same set (I and NIS) require a 'same' response, and all stimuli in a different set (DS) require a 'different' response." (From Elias, M. F., and Kinsbourne, M. *Journal of Gerontology,* 1974, **29,** 162.)

hearsal, and retrieval of information which is briefly presented and must be acted upon quickly (Norman, 1969; Posner and Boies, 1971; Waugh and Norman, 1965).

Several studies have been done with information-processing paradigms in an effort to maintain constant task demands while manipulating the nature of the stimulus materials. One such study involved the matching of stimuli that were presented rapidly and in temporal succession. Elias and Kinsbourne (1974) compared male and female elderly (age range = 63 to 77 years) and young (age range = 23 to 33 years) adults on their ability to match successive "verbal" and "nonverbal" stimuli on the basis of their membership in one of two binary sets that were defined to the subjects prior to testing. The nonverbal stimuli were arrows, indicating a direction of rotation (e.g., ¯¯↓ ↑__); the verbal stimuli were verbal analogs of the nonverbal stimuli. For example, DR (standing for "down-right") followed by UR (standing for "up-right") was the verbal analog of ¯¯↓ __↑. A complete set of these stimuli is presented in Fig. 10-5. Subjects were asked to respond with one hand if the sets of two stimuli were the same and with another hand if they were different. The rule was to respond "same" if the direction of rotation indicated by the arrows was the same (e.g., __↑ ↓¯¯) and respond "different" if it was not (e.g., __↑ ¯¯↓). The hands, right or left, used to respond "same" or "different" were counterbalanced such that one half of the subjects responded "same" with the left hand and one half responded "same" with the right hand. In short, there were verbal analogs for each of the combinations of arrows indicating direction of rotation; the subjects matched either on the basis of the orientation of the arrows or the letter analogs of the arrows. Since rotation in space was the basis for making the match, it is accurate to say that there was a visual-spatial matching task (arrows) and a verbal-spatial matching task (letter analogs of arrows).

Results of this study are shown in Figs. 10-6 and 10-7. From Fig. 10-6 one can see that elderly females were slower to match the visual-spatial stimuli than were elderly males. However, the elderly females exhibited faster matching times than the elderly males on the verbal-spatial matching task. In addition,

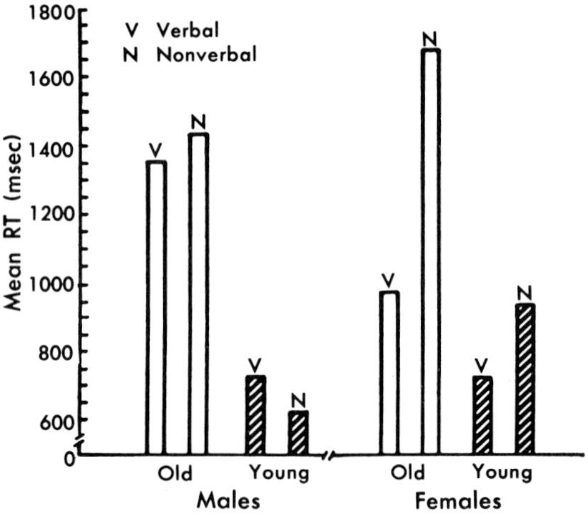

Fig. 10-6. Matching RT as a function of age, sex, and verbal as opposed to nonverbal stimuli. (From Elias, M. F., and Kinsbourne, M. *Journal of Gerontology,* 1974, **29,** 162.)

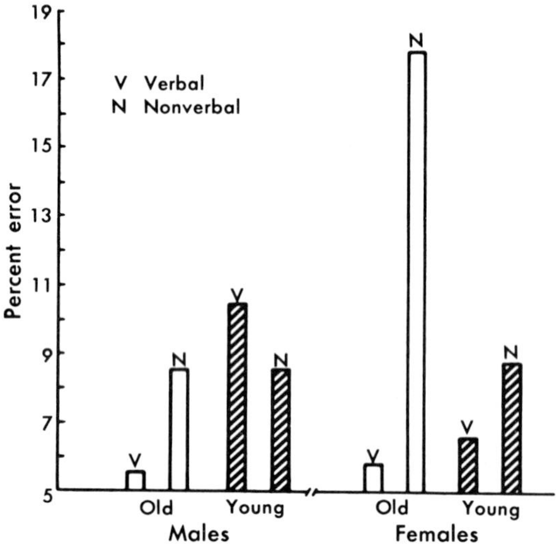

Fig. 10-7. Percent error on a matching RT task as a function of age, sex, and verbal as opposed to nonverbal stimuli. (From Elias, M. F., and Kinsbourne, M. *Journal of Gerontology,* 1974, **29,** 162.)

examination of Fig. 10-7 makes it clear that the older women not only required a greater amount of time to match the nonverbal stimuli than did the older men but they made more errors as well. Thus longer times were not a compensation for increased accuracy. It should also be noted that the verbal-nonverbal discrepancy in RT occurred for younger women, although to a much lesser extent than for the older women.

Results of the Elias and Kinsbourne study were consistent with results of a number of studies that have shown men to perform in a superior fashion to women on some spatial tasks (Hutt, 1972; Maccoby, 1966; McGlone and Davidson, 1973). However, Elias and Kinsbourne (1974) were careful to point out that any distinction between verbal and nonverbal stimuli is one of degree. Elias, Wright, and Winn (1976) have shown superior performance for young females (18 to 21 years) over young males (18 to 21 years) on a spatial matching task that involved matching by concept, not merely physical appearance. The arrows used in the Elias and Kinsbourne study could have been given a verbal label by the subjects. On the other hand, the letter analogs of the arrows could have been mentally transformed to arrows indicating direction of rotation. In other words, one can present stimuli that are "more verbal" than other stimuli, but the subject may apply his own coding strategy. Also, a word may be considered a verbal stimulus but not necessarily a language stimulus. The point is that it takes time to convert letters to arrows and arrows to letters, and when stimuli are presented rapidly, these strategies are not very efficient. Thus one may find that nonverbal stimuli are processed less efficiently (longer RT) because an encoding strategy (conversion to letters) which is not particularly efficient is used. Such strategies may be culturally determined or may be built up as a result of habits used over a number of years.

Elias and Elias (1976) questioned the notion that the longer RT of older women for nonverbal stimuli really reflected a general finding that would apply to other sensory modalities. Consequently, these investigators compared verbal and nonverbal, stimuli-matching times using an auditory mode of presentation. The stimuli were rather complex, but basically subjects were asked to match tone stimuli according to rules and were given a set of word analogs that were to be matched by the same rules. In contrast to the Elias and Kinsbourne (1974) study, no sex differences were found and no sex by age interaction was observed. Matching RT times increased with age, but simple RT showed only a slight increase across age groups. Word stimuli were matched more rapidly than tone stimuli. This did not indicate that verbal stimuli were matched more efficiently than nonverbal stimuli. Closer examination of the RT scores indicated that the subjects matched in terms of the physical properties of the word and tone stimuli rather than in terms of a verbal-nonverbal dimension. Stated somewhat differently, the subjects found it more efficient to process the word stimuli in terms of their physical characteristics than in terms of their verbal meaning, and the differences in time required to match tone and word stimuli most likely represented differences in task difficulty.

We have stated that Elias and Elias (1976) attempted to test the generality of the verbal-nonverbal by age interaction reported by Elias and Kinsbourne (1974) by employing the same matching paradigm with auditory stimuli. The basic problem with this strategy is that changing sensory modalities altered task difficulty, despite the fact that the experimental paradigm was the same. This problem also exists when one changes stimulus dimensions to more verbal or less verbal within a single sensory modality. The subject may be instructed to respond according to the same set of rules for different types of stimuli, but the stimuli themselves place different demands on short-term memory, retrieval, and other dimensions of information *throughput*. Consequently, task difficulty is altered.

Difficulties encountered in comparing auditory and visual modalities while maintaining equal task difficulty are partially related to the complexity of the two systems. Some investigators argue that the auditory system is much more complex than the visual system and appears to be geared to analyzing more complex, abstract stimulus input (Worden, 1971). Clear support for this hypothesis may be obtained by analyzing speech components presented visually by means of a sonograph. The auditory system appears to be designed to input information on an immediate, successive, nonrepetitive basis. In contrast, visual stimuli can normally be viewed for some period of time. Thus a task that requires a rapid, one-time input of information may place the visual system at more of a disadvantage than the auditory system.

It has been suggested that one reason for a differential decline in the ability to process nonverbal as opposed to verbal stimuli with increasing age may be related to age-associated changes in the relative efficiency with which the cerebral hemispheres process verbal as opposed to nonverbal information. A number of studies with young adults indicate that words and letters are more efficiently processed in the left cerebral hemisphere, whereas geometric forms and other nonverbal stimuli are more efficiently processed in the right hemisphere (Kimura, 1973). Several investigators have used reaction time paradigms to determine whether this "hemisphere asymmetry" is (1) maintained across the adult life span, (2) declines, or (3) becomes even more pronounced with advancing age. Reaction time studies of asymmetry make use of known structural relationships between the visual half fields and the visual cortex and the fact that the auditory portions of each cerebral hemisphere receive auditory information primarily from the contralateral ear. The studies are complex, and thus we will not discuss them in detail. Generally, no evidence of hemisphere asymmetry has been obtained, and thus an adequate test of the age by hemisphere interaction was not possible (Elias and Elias, 1976). Elias, Wright, and Winn (1976) have obtained data which suggest that laterality or asymmetry effects are obtained only when a task requires competing processes in the left hemisphere or right hemisphere. Watson and co-workers (1975) have suggested that the hand contralateral to the hemisphere which supposedly processes verbal and nonverbal stimuli can be used to produce or enhance laterality effects in a reaction time study if the subject is required to respond with that hand. Generally, it would seem that much more data need to be collected and several methodological problems overcome before researchers can say with any conviction that the elderly are more or less efficient in processing verbal or nonverbal stimuli and that this phenomenon is somehow related to changing relationships between the cerebral hemispheres with advancing age. Electrophysiological studies combined with the reaction time paradigms may eventually lead to answers to these questions.

PHYSIOLOGIZING ABOUT PERCEPTION

Psychologists have been no less tempted to suggest physiological bases for perceptual changes with age than they have to "physiologize" about the brain. Clearly, many, many behavioral changes reflect alterations in underlying physiology. The problem is that it is difficult to test hypotheses about the physiological bases of age-related changes in behavior because behavioral scientists are just beginning to develop the kinds of experimental and physiological approaches that will allow them to relate specific behaviors to specific neuronal events. This approach is really in its infancy at the present time, and unfortunately, much in the way of theory is not substantiated by hard empirical data. Nevertheless, it is interesting, and perhaps profitable, to consider some hypotheses that have been advanced to account for perceptual changes with age. Most of these hypotheses have been concerned with *throughput* mechanisms. Welford (1965) has presented a more detailed summary of many of these theories and hypotheses.

Signal-to-noise ratio

Proponents of the signal-to-noise ratio hypothesis suggest that there is a reduction of signal strength from the sense organs to the brain. This reduction is accompanied by "neural noise," which is produced by increasing random neural activity in the brain. One factor which has been proposed in the context of this general idea is that there is a reduction in the total number of functional brain cells with age. Loss of functional cells is seen as resulting in longer neuronal recovery time following neuronal firing, less responsive cells, or irregular, weak signals (see Welford, 1965).

Crossman and Szafran (1956) are generally credited with suggesting increased random neural activity in the brain as a second factor influencing signal-to-noise ratio. A third factor that has been proposed has its origins in the observation that the electroencephalographic records of older adults exhibit longer lasting aftereffects during increased cerebral activity. The idea is that neural aftereffects could have a detrimental effect on subsequent incoming signals and serve to distort, or reduce, signal strength.

A fourth factor in the signal-to-noise ratio concept involves arousal and activation in the nervous system. The hypothesis is that heightened arousal increases cell sensitivity, that is, lowers thresholds to firing and results in an increased sensitivity to incoming signals, but an increased probability of random, spontaneous firing. This hypothetical phenomenon is analogous to an attempt to increase the volume of a radio message, only to discover that such an action also increased the amount of static.

These are, indeed, interesting hypotheses which really suggest that the operation of *throughput* and *output* mechanisms follows the same logic as that of computers, radios, or television sets. Although current analogies may eventually be proved or refuted, there is at present not much direct evidence to support them. For example, there is little evidence to support the notion that whatever cell loss does occur in so-called "normal aging" affects behavior to any significant extent (Chapter 12). Many physiologists, such as Timiras and Bignami (1976), believe that there is so much redundancy built into the neuronal systems that what relatively minimal cell loss does occur with age cannot account for much in the way of functional decline in *throughput* processes. Moreover, scientists are beginning to learn that many other functional units of the nervous system may exist in addition to neuronal cells and that they may subserve different functions. Thus ideas such as the signal-to-noise ratio hypothesis, although helping to organize the thoughts of researchers, may be an oversimplification.

Perceptual noise

Layton (1975) has suggested that a large part of the perceptual decline which occurs with advancing age is caused by the inability to ignore irrelevant stimuli in the environment. This "perceptual noise" theory is more concerned with changes in dealing with environmental stimuli effectively as opposed to changes in neural structure. To this extent it offers a much more practical and testable hypothesis than the signal-to-noise ratio notion. Many perceptual phenomena can be explained either by the signal-to-noise concepts or by the perceptual noise hypothesis. However, the latter makes possible an experimental testing of the hypothesis because the experimenter can manipulate perceptual noise. Environmental manipulations, coupled with evoked cortical potential research, may eventually lead to a relating of changes in physiological structure to changes in behavior.

Overdominance

Another suggestion from the field of perception research is that there is a potential for changes in the direction of overdominance of some sensory modalities relative to others. In humans the dominant sensory modality appears to be the visual system. Posner and co-workers (1976) have recently discussed several instances of the visual mode showing dominance over other sensory systems. However, this theory has not been investigated in terms of changes that might occur with age.

With the exception of the perceptual noise theory, the basic problem with these hypothetical notions about physiological bases of age changes in perception is that they are difficult to test. It is probably best to think of them as interesting, but oversimplistic, notions about how physiology relates to perception. Before they can really be tested, much more is needed in the way of well-designed, fundamental perceptual studies involving interactions among the sensory modalities.

SUMMARY

There is accumulating evidence to suggest that there are age-associated perceptual decrements on a peripheral level which can give the appearance of more centrally located decrements. This is not to say that psychologists know all there is about the *input, throughput,* and *output* mechanisms involved in the ability to perceive and act on the environment. There may be many age-associated changes in central and peripheral processes that have not yet been characterized. For example, the senses of taste and smell have been largely overlooked. Hearing, although very important to adaptation and social interaction, has not even come close to being fully explored in terms of age changes. Certainly, there is a loss of hearing sensitivity, particularly with regard to high-frequency tones, but more subtle aspects of hearing loss with age have only begun to be studied to any significant extent. For example, the study of aphasic symptoms, receptive or expressive, which may accompany even normal aging, has barely been touched on.

A number of studies have been done with perceptual illusions, particularly visual and auditory illusions. Qualitative changes have been documented with increasing age, but they remain largely unexplained, and often one illusionary phenomenon can be used to explain more than one theory of perception or information processing.

Clearly, reaction time (RT) slows in response to pathological states of the nervous system and thus becomes useful as a predictor or indicator of structural change in the nervous system that is associated with age. Simple RT increases with age and increases in RT can be exaggerated when older adults have suffered brain impairment, strokes, heart attacks, and a number of other diseases. Complex RT is usually much more influenced by disease and other age-correlated variables than simple RT, but this is because discrimination or matching RT usually involves more complex decision-making processes. However, the usefulness of complex RT studies extends beyond comparisons of age groups with regard to level of performance on complex decision-making tasks that require a rapid response. Their real usefulness is for the determination of *how* age groups differ in the way in which they process information.

In this context there have been attempts to relate chronological age to ability to process stimuli varying along a verbal-nonverbal continuum and to relate this ability to "laterality" of brain function. There is some evidence that, for some tasks, age by sex interactions occur with respect to the ability to rapidly match verbal as opposed to nonverbal stimuli. Generally, however, these results do not hold across sensory modalities. In fact, the concept of verbal as opposed to nonverbal dimensioning of stimuli is probably highly oversimplified. There are many artifacts of test procedure influencing these studies, not the least of which are observations that (1) subjects use different strategies to approach problems regardless of stimulus parameters, (2) strategies vary with age, and (3) differences in task difficulty accompany differences in stimulus dimension and sensory modality. Moreover, once level of performance begins to decline appreciably in senescence, one cannot perform refined discrimination RT experiments that require sustained attention, memory for complex rules, and performance under conditions of rapid pacing. Perhaps the greatest problem with the comparison of verbal or nonverbal information-processing ability is that the right and left half cerebral hemispheres are not specialized in such an oversimplified way.

Psychologists must remember that there are ever-present feedback relationships between perceived and real loss of sensory functioning, and these influence cautiousness and other response strategies that may be different for different age groups. Thus response slowing is not always an indicator of changes in the nervous system or extensive pathology. Considerable "physiologizing" has been done with regard to the underlying bases for changes in perceptual functioning and speed of responding with advancing age. Unfortunately, behavioral scientists have not advanced far enough in the development of techniques used to study behavior-physiology relationships that these hypotheses can be tested adequately.

If students of aging are searching for an area much in need of basic experimental studies, they might well profit from turning their attention to the field of perception. Furthermore, it appears that little of the perceptual literature in aging has been applied for practical purposes outside of the traditional compensation for sensory loss. However, there appears to be an increasing number of ingenious perceptual experiments relating input to behavior. Thus we can predict that the special problems of the aged will eventually lead to a more coherent organization of the general perception literature in the field of psychology.

SELECTED READINGS

Abrahams, J. P., and Birren, J. E. Reaction time as a function of age and behavioral predisposition to coronary heart disease. *Journal of Gerontology,* 1973, **28,** 471-478.

Basowitz, H., and Korchin, S. J. Age differences in the perception of closure. *Journal of Abnormal and Social Psychology,* 1957, **54,** 93-97.

Botwinick, J., and Thompson, L. W. Premotor and motor components of reaction time. *Journal of Experimental Psychology,* 1966, **71,** 9-15.

Corso, J. F. Sensory processes and age effects in normal adults. *Journal of Gerontology,* 1971, **26,** 90-105.

Desor, J. A., Greene, L. S., and Maller, D. Preferences for sweet and salty in 9- to 15-year-old and adult humans. *Science,* 1975, **190,** 686-687.

Eisner, D. A., and Schaie, K. W. Age changes in response to visual illusions from middle to old age. *Journal of Gerontology,* 1971, **26,** 146-150.

Kimura, D. The asymmetry of the human brain. *Scientific American,* 1973, **3,** 70-78.

Layton, B. Perceptual noise and aging. *Psychological Bulletin,* 1975, **82,** 875-883.

McFarland, R. A. The sensory and perceptual processes in aging. In K. W. Schaie (Ed.), *Theory and methods of research on aging.* Morgantown, W.Va.: West Virginia University Press, 1968.

Timiras, P. S. *Developmental physiology and aging.* New York: The Macmillan Co., 1972.

Wapner, S., Werner, H., and Comalli, P. E., Jr. Perception of part-whole relationships in middle and old age. *Journal of Gerontology,* 1960, **15,** 412-416.

Warren, R. M. Illusory changes in repeated words: differences between young adults and the aged. *American Journal of Psychology,* 1961, **74,** 506-516.

Warren, R. M., and Warren, R. P. Some age differences in auditory perception. *Bulletin of the New York Academy of Medicine,* 1971, **47,** 1365-1377.

Welford, A. T. Performance, biological mechanisms and age: a theoretical sketch. In A. T. Welford and J. E. Birren (Eds.), *Behavior, aging, and the nervous system.* Springfield, Ill.: Charles C Thomas, Publisher, 1965.

CHAPTER 11

HORMONES elixirs of youth?

As a student I sat at the great master's feet in the late seventies; saw him again surprisingly rejuvenated after his tests with orchitic extracts.

FREEMAN (1967) QUOTING SAJOUS

It is a well-established fact that hormones influence behavior (Levine, 1972) and that changes in the endocrine system are correlated with age (Eleftheriou and Sprott, 1975). It is thus surprising to find that relatively few studies have been concerned with the relationship between hormonal changes with age and behavior. Although animal models are very important for this kind of research, relatively few animal studies have been concerned with behavioral correlates of changes in the endocrine system with increasing age (see Elias and Elias, 1975). The evidence that comes from human research is mostly based on studies of mental and physical abnormalities (Eisdorfer and Raskind, 1975).

One of the major problems in studying behavioral correlates of hormone changes with advancing age is that research on hormones and aging per se is not conclusive in this respect. Does the apparent decline in capability of the older person to adapt to environmental stress relate to alterations in neuroendocrine control systems that ensure homeostasis in the face of deviation from steady states? This is an interesting question, but evidence is still inconclusive because it is not clear to what extent hormone deficiencies influence the aging process (Timiras and Bignami, 1976).

EARLY INTERESTS

Aging was actually a stimulus for the field of endocrinology. There has long been an interest in chemical methods for improving the quality and increasing the length of life. One historian points out that the observation of death in animals after the adrenals were removed stimulated a concern for a possible association between hormones and long life (Freeman, 1967). Brown-Séquard, one of the earliest endocrinologists, became convinced that "vital energy" could be preserved by stimulating the nervous system with testicular material. At the age of 72 years, he reported the results of self-treatment with injections of Pasteur-filtered aqueous, dog testes suspension. It seems that he was unsuccessful in reversing the aging processes, since he died five years later, but his students were convinced that the treatments resulted in a change in his behavior. Brown-Séquard's treatments may not have prolonged his life, but they did stimulate a rash of research activity designed to isolate a hormone, or combination of hormones that would successfully retard aging. Brown-

Séquard's ideas were not without merit, nor was the attempt to retard aging illogical.

Today scientists know that treatment with exogenous testosterone may have beneficial effects on the alleviation of behavioral symptoms related to the male climacteric, for example, nervousness, irritability, decreased memory and concentration, somatic complaints, depression, and sometimes psychosis (see Eisdorfer and Raskind, 1975). Furthermore, several theories of aging emphasize the failure of endocrine homeostatic mechanisms in response to stress as a key factor in aging and eventual death. However, endocrine treatments generally have been applied to supplement hormones in situations where there are specific hormone deficiencies accompanied by notable behavioral manifestations of these deficiencies. Clinical data from these treatments do not answer questions about the "beneficial" effects of hormone supplements for "healthy" aging adults.

Freeman (1967) notes that many pseudoscientific attempts to find an "elixir of life" resulted from an interest in prolonging human life with hormone treatments. In fact, this emphasis challenged the scientific respectability of endocrinology for some period of time. Eventually, however, a concern for scientific respectability developed, and research was directed toward the treatment of diseases with hormones. This research led to theories of aging that viewed the aging process as a pathological condition of the endocrine system.

The assumption that a single hormone or combination of hormones could actually alter the aging process was oversimplified, as was the idea that degeneration of the endocrine system per se was responsible for aging. *Aging of the endocrine glands is not a simple process of wear and tear in which all endocrine structures and functions are equally affected. Rather, it is a selective process in which some hormonal substances act in different ways at different periods of the life span.* Furthermore, endocrine changes are highly influenced by neuroregulator mechanisms and by a wide variety of behavioral and physiological changes that occur with age. Thus there is a very complex, reciprocal endocrine-behavior feedback system such that the endocrines affect behavior; but behavior affects the endocrines, and both are influenced by life events associated with aging.

In the following sections it will become clear just how complex these feedback relations are and how difficult it is to separate cause and effect. Some of the endocrinological terms may not be familiar to you; thus we have provided a list of terms and definitions for quick reference (pp. 202 and 203).

AGE, SEX, AND GONADAL FUNCTION

We discussed the role of sex hormones in Chapter 6. Some additional discussion is appropriate here because a portion of the research on hormones has been concerned with changes in sexual activity and mating behavior as a function of age and the effects of the cessation of sexual activity on aging.

There are data for a variety of species which suggest that sexual activity can shorten life (Bilewicz, 1953). The possibility of lengthening life through sexual activity has received less attention, although sex provides an attractive alternative to Brown-Séquard's dog-testes solution. The difficulty of separating the beneficial (or detrimental) effects of sexual activity from the sets of behaviors accompanying sexual activity complicates this type of research. When one examines the practice of shunamitism, one can see a good example of the problem. Shunamitism is an ancient theory about the beneficial effects of the proximity of young females on old males. Comfort (1956) points out that the medieval Indian kings of Chandell are said to have pursued longevity through ritual coition with well-trained maids and that in the 1700s a Dutch physician named Boerhave (1668-1738) advised an elderly patient to renew his strength by

ENDOCRINOLOGICAL TERMS AND DEFINITIONS

ACTH The hypothalamus secretes corticotropin-releasing factor (CRF), which induces the pituitary to secrete adrenocorticotropic hormone (ACTH). In response to ACTH, the adrenal cortex synthesizes and releases its hormones, for example, cortisol in the human and corticosterone in the rodent.

adrenal insufficiency A condition in which the adrenal gland is not performing its job normally.

adrenergic Describes an epinephrine-type effect at the synapse of the end organs or target organs; it refers to epinephrine-mediated transmission between the postganglionic neurons and the effector target organs.

adrenergic receptors Receptors that are primarily concerned with inhibitory functions.

adrenocortical hormones Hormones secreted by the adrenal cortex of the adrenal gland.

affective Pertaining to mood or affect, for example, depression, euphoria.

anabolic Describes a drug or hormone that is purported to have a constructive role rather than a "breaking-down" role in the nervous system.

androgen Chemical substances that possess activities that lead to masculinization; testosterone is a good example.

blocker (blocking agent) A drug that antagonizes the action of another drug or blocks nerve transmission at the neuroeffector synapses.

catecholamines Chemical substances that are formed and released by the adrenal gland and in the brain. Epinephrine and norepinephrine are the two principal catecholamines in the class released by the adrenal gland. Adrenal gland catecholamines serve as "circulating hormones" and affect areas of the body other than the brain. Catecholamines formed in the brain act as neurotransmitters substances. Serotonin provides a good example; it is believed to be involved in learning and memory.

climacteric A particular epoch of the life span in which the body is believed to undergo a radical change, for example, the time of puberty and the menopause.

cortex The outer layer of an organ as distinguished from its inner substance. The adrenal cortex is the cortical portion of the adrenal gland that secretes the steroid hormones.

corticosterone A crystalline steroid that is found in the adrenal cortex. It represents a major steroid in rodents.

cortisol The hormone of the adrenal cortex that represents a major steroid in the human. It provides an indication of response to a stressor (see steroid response).

Cushing's syndrome A disease that results from adrenocortical hyperfunction. It is accompanied by a diversity of associated personality disturbances such as depression in response to endocrine imbalance and disfiguration. An attractive young woman may become an obese bearded woman.

desoxycorticosterone A synthetic compound with the activity of the adrenocortical hormone (cortin).

double blind A drug or hormone experiment in which neither the patient nor the physician (or investigator) knows which patient has been given the treatment and which patient has been given the placebo.

epithelium The covering of the skin and mucous membranes consisting of cells in varying forms and arrangements.

estrogen A generic term for the estrus-producing compounds and commonly used for the female sex hormones.

estrus, or oestrus The period of mating activity in female mammals that is marked by intense sexual urge. The term is also used for specific genital changes induced in laboratory animals by the injection of ovarian substances.

euphoria Feelings of well-being and the absence of pain. The term is sometimes used to connote abnormal feelings of well-being.

exogenous Refers to a substance outside the body or a substance that may be introduced to the body but originates outside the body, for example, exogeneous testosterone.

5-hydroxytryptamine (serotonin) A brain catecholamine believed to be related to learning and/or memory.

free fatty acids (FFA) Acids that are released into the circulation from adipose tissue in response to catecholamine stimulation and the glucocorticoids of the adrenal cortex. Thus their presence has been used as an indication of sympathetic nervous system activity and response to stress.

hallucination A perception not based on what is believed by most persons to be physical reality.

hypochondria A state of anxiety about health beyond normal. It is often accompanied by simulated disease.

insulin A hormone secreted by the islands of Langerhans that helps in the regulation of blood glucose levels.

nihilistic A form of delusion in which, to the patient, nothing exists. It sometimes refers to extreme denial or skepticism.

plasma The fluid portion of the blood before clotting has occurred.

propranolol A drug used in the treatment of hypertension and other medical problems. It is an adrenergic blocker.

serum The clear portion of any animal liquid separated from its more solid elements. The term is commonly used in connection with blood.

steroids Substances that are secreted by the adrenal cortex. This involves the biosynthetic pathways leading from cholesterol through progesterone and 17-OH-progesterone to the major adrenal steroids. Cortisol is the major steroid of primates and certain other species such as sheep, cows, cats, and dogs. Corticosterone is a predominant steroid in rodents.

steroid response Mechanism by which the body responds to stress. Central nervous system mechanisms promote the release of large quantities of various hormones from the pituitary gland when faced with a stressor. The principal hormone is the adrenocorticotropic hormone (ACTH). Stimulation by ACTH causes the outer layer (cortex) of the adrenal gland to increase its release of steroids, which provide an indication of how stressed the person or animal is. Plasma corticosterone is commonly used as a stress index in animals, and plasma cortisol is used for humans.

stroke Simply stated, a generalized or localized paralysis resulting from a cerebrovascular accident (a "blowout" in the vasculature).

testosterone A crystalline, androgenic steroid. It is a male testicular hormone that functions in the induction and maintenance of male secondary sex characteristics and influences male sex drive.

testosterone propionate A form of testosterone most widely used in therapy for impotence, senility, sterility, etc.

thromboembolic Describes a disease that is an embolism of the blood vessels.

thyroxine A hormone that was isolated from the thyroid gland. It is not only secreted by the thyroid but can be prepared synthetically and used to treat defective thyroid functioning.

vaginitis Inflammation of the vagina marked by pain and discharge.

vasomotor instability A lack of stability in the expansion and contraction of the walls of the blood vessels. It may result in flushing symptoms typical of menopause.

vulvar Pertaining to the vulva, which is the external part of the female reproductive organs.

lying between two young girls. Apparently he was not too concerned about the effects of this treatment on the young girls, and we do not know whether he was motivated to give elderly women similar advice with regard to young men. Perhaps we will never know, but we do know that it has not been established that such a treatment will lengthen life. Perhaps it only seems longer.

Several studies with animals suggest that sexual intercourse may prolong life, although it is difficult to separate the effects of social contact from sexual intercourse. Early reports indicated longer life in old male rats if one young female was introduced to groom them (e.g., Muhlbock, 1959). Several studies indicate that regular mating improves the physical condition and longevity of the male rat, and still other reports indicate the opposite effect (see Elias and Elias, 1975). The latter studies have been better controlled than the former, but it is probably safe to say that clear evidence does not exist for the hypothesis that sexual activity either prolongs or shortens life.

Sexual intercourse may have a beneficial effect on health by providing stimulation to the heart and other organs, although the presence of disease processes, such as severe cardiovascular or cerebrovascular disease, may contraindicate sex as a therapeutic treatment. Clearly, extramarital sex can abruptly shorten life if it involves a jealous mate. The student will forgive our attempts at humor if they serve to underscore the importance and difficulty of separating social factors from hormonal factors when one attempts to evaluate the influence of sexual behavior on life span. Several good examples come from the animal literature. Plasma testosterone (the male sex hormone) levels are increased in rabbits, bulls, and elephants following copulation with receptive females, but visual access to these females has the same effect. The male rat exhibits a decrease in reproductive system atrophy as a result of the opportunity to copulate, but ejaculations appear to be more effective than intromission in preventing reproductive system atrophy (see Elias and Elias, 1975:400).

Sex, longevity, and disease

Wexler (1964a,b) has conducted some of the better controlled studies with regard to effects of copulatory behavior on the development of disease. Although it does not speak directly to the effects of sex on long life or the effects of hormones on behavior with advancing age, his work has important implications for these issues. Wexler found that frequent sexual activity resulted in premature development of pathological conditions such as obesity, hypertension, and arteriosclerosis. Furthermore, it was associated with premature death in male and female breeders of the Sprague-Dawley strain of rats. Effects were more pronounced for males than for females. In a later study, Lewis and Wexler (1974) found that higher corticosterone levels and free fatty acid levels were present in middle-aged animals with breeding activity. Thus the maxim that "sex is good for you" may have to be qualified if the results of studies with other strains of rats and other animal species show similar relationships. However, it should be kept in mind that these studies involved only one strain (homozygous genotype) of rats, and thus the implications of the study are more relevant to the use of this particular strain of rat than they are to the general question of pathology induced by sexual activity. Moreover, it is not clear to what extent behaviors of a social nature that accompanied the sexual activity may have influenced physiology. At most, this study indicates that behavioral findings in aging studies which compare young virgin animals with retired breeders, a relatively common procedure, may be confounded by pathology which is correlated with breeding history.

Reproductive functioning and age

Rather than ask the general question concerning how sexual activity influences aging, many investigators have been concerned with the relationship between decline in sexual vigor and physiological changes that accompany growing old (see Timiras and Meisami, 1971). Decrements in the production of sex hormones and decline in sexual vigor in old age are common to males and females of many species. However, decline in sexual activity is related to social, motivational, and learning factors as well as the action of sex hormones. Cognitive and emotional changes influence sex hormones and vice versa. Both factors influence sexual behavior, and sexual behavior, in turn, influences these factors.

There is a growing emphasis in the human literature on the notion that the general decrease in sexual activity for the nonsenile elderly adult is related, in no small part, to psychosocial factors (Verwoerdt et al., 1969a, b). Changes in housing patterns and social isolation are two major environmental events in the lives of elderly adults that may well bring about changes in sexual behavior by way of their influence on the social parameters of sexual activity. Animal studies, particularly with primates, may be helpful in separating and identifying various psychosocial and hormonal factors that directly and indirectly influence sexual activity at different ages.

Physiological bases of decline. Despite the potential of animal models, particularly primate models, for examining psychosocial factors involved in the reduction in sexual activities with advancing age, research with animals has concentrated on the hormonal basis of this decline. There is no question that deficits in the sex hormones are related to decline in sexual activity with advancing age. This is partially related to changes in the sexual organs themselves, but changes in sexual organs are brought about by changes in the cells of the accessory glands, and these changes are similar to those which occur in many other tissues of the body. Moreover, deficits in sex hormones are sufficient, but not necessary, for the observation of a decline in sexual activity.

The important question from a life-span developmental point of view concerns the nature of the events that precede sex hormone deficiency. Evidence from a number of sources indicates that decrements in the neural mechanisms which mediate the summation of neuronal impulses leading to ejaculation occur earlier in life than changes in sex hormone levels (Jakubczak, 1964).

Early experience studies may relate to the "neural mediation" explanations of decline in sexual activity in a very important way. Early experiences, particularly those of a stressful nature, influence neurohumors (brain hormones); in some cases these influences may last a lifetime (Levine, 1972) and may not only influence endocrine response to stress but also sexual activity by way of neural mediating mechanisms, that is, mechanisms which stimulate the release of neurohumors, which in turn affect hormones involved in sex drive and sexual intercourse.

Testosterone. Human studies have not been particularly enlightening in terms of the question of psychosocial as opposed to hormonal influences on the decline in sexual activity with age. Is decreased sexual activity related to a decline in sex hormones, or does it work the other way? Again, it probably differs from individual to individual and may be best described as a symbiotic relationship between behavior and hormones. Summaries of the earlier literature (e.g., Catt, 1971) suggest that testosterone secretion remains fairly constant with advancing age in humans. However, Eisdorfer and Raskind (1975) point to the fact that more sensitive assays for urine and serum testosterone have been developed within the past six years. They summarize data by Vermeulen and associates (1972), which indicate that free plasma testosterone concentration and testosterone levels "remain within the same range from adolescence through the fifth decade, but from the sixth decade on," there is a decrease in mean plasma levels. They also state that there is a wide range of individual variation; in the eighth and ninth decades, individual plasma testosterone levels *can* be in a high normal range similar to that of younger adults (Eisdorfer and Raskind, 1975). However, the question remains as to whether these changes *cause* a loss in sexual vigor or result from a loss of sexual vigor.

Treatment with testosterone in androgen-deficient men seems to result in an improvement in sexual drive, but when androgen levels are normal, testosterone treatments seem to have little effect (Catt, 1971). Estrogen administration to men results in a marked decline in sexual drive and reduction in potency, which is related, in part, to reduced testosterone secretion. In general, treatment with testosterone seems to be more beneficial for men who are "sex hormone" deficient to begin with, although there may be some placebo effect in men who are low in sexual drive or activity by virtue of social motivational factors.

Ismail and Harkness (1967) compared basal levels of testosterone in two normal men during and after a period of abstinence and found that plasma testosterone levels increased to a significant extent when sexual activity was resumed. Fox and co-workers (1972) compared resting testosterone levels with testosterone levels during and after sexual intercourse and found that they were higher during and after sexual intercourse than they were during the resting period. However, masturbation had no significant effect on these levels. Eisdorfer and Raskind (1975:386) have summarized the current state of the literature well:

> It remains unclear whether testosterone induces or is a consequence of sexual behavior in man; and the lower testosterone levels in the elderly may be a function of decreased sexual activity itself, which in turn may be dependent on a host of social and psychological factors.

Estrogen. Reliable physiological indices of estrogen activity seem to have been developed earlier than those for testosterone (Eisdorfer and Raskind, 1975). It is clear that decreased estrogen production accompanies the cessation of the cyclical ovarian function in women. The process begins in the fifth decade of life and continues until the sixth decade (Eisdorfer and Raskind, 1975). Decreased estrogen in menopausal and postmenopausal women results in genital atrophy and vasomotor instability (Ross and Vande Wiele, 1974). These physiological phenomena, in turn, predispose menopausal and postmenopausal women to painful vaginitis, and atrophy itself can impede sexual intercourse, Eisdorfer and Raskind have noted. They point out that secondary behavioral effects occur in such instances, although the pattern varies according to past history, personality, and other factors influencing a person's immediate life situation.

Eisdorfer and Raskind (1975) make the important point that, whereas genital atrophy and vasomotor instability are distressing in their own right, they also often symbolize the end of young adulthood to many women. Therefore the anxiety and depression that are sometimes observed in menopausal and postmenopausal women may be a reaction to the process of aging as well as a response to the secondary and primary effects of sex hormone deficiency. Thus, as in men, the extent to which decreased sexual activity may be related to decreased sex hormone production per se is difficult to determine.

The psychological and physical discomfort that accompanies the menopausal period for many women has prompted investigations of ways in which to alleviate symptoms. Vaginal and vulvar epithelium may be rapidly restored to the premenopausal condition by means of exogenous estrogen (Eisdorfer and Raskind, 1975). Similarly, the behavioral manifestations of vasomotor instability, that is, hot flashes and sweats, can be alleviated by exogenous estrogen. For some women, exogenous estrogen seems to relieve anxiety and/or depression. However, there are some relatively serious complications that accompany estrogen therapy.

These complications have been identified in the context of clinical studies of oral contraceptive preparations. Eisdorfer and Raskind (1975) point to the relationship between oral contraceptive use and thrombophlebitis and pulmonary embolism. The highest risk is observed for the preparations that are highest in estrogen. There also seems to be an increased risk of occlusive cerebrovascular disease in oral contraceptive users. Eisdorfer and Raskind (1975:382) have summarized the work of a Collaborative Group for the Study of Stroke in Young Women (1973).

> This large collaborative study found the relative risk of cerebral ischemia or stroke to be almost nine times greater for women who use oral contraceptives than for those who do not. Comparable studies have not been done for postmenopausal women on estrogen replacement therapy. Arterial hypertension has been linked to oral contraceptive use (Smith, 1972), and one careful study (Crane et al., 1971) found arterial hypertension related to conjugated estrogen administration.*

The possibility of a relationship between estrogen supplementation and hypertension is a cause for concern from a medical point of view. In Chapter 12 we discuss the evidence that cognitive functioning suffers in cases of severe hypertension. Thus estrogen supplementation may result in impaired cognitive functioning by way of its influence on blood pressure (Eisdorfer and Raskind, 1975).

Heart disease and estrogen. At one time it was believed that estrogens prevented coronary heart disease. This generalization was based on the observation that premenopausal women seem to have a significantly lower incidence of coronary heart disease than do men of a similar age but that the incidence rises in women after menopause. In general, there does not appear to be substantial support for this "estrogen-protection hypothesis." It appears that the decrease in the ratio of male-to-female mortality related to coronary artery disease, beginning in the fifth decade, is primarily due to a diminished rate of acceleration in male mortality (Eisdorfer and Raskind, 1975). Moreover, it appears that lower coronary heart disease mortality rates in females are limited to white women who are free of complicating disorders such as diabetes and whose lives are associated with affluent life-styles (Furman, 1971). Thus there seems to be little hard evidence indicating that coronary heart disease is a result of postmenopausal estrogen deficiency, and, in fact, estrogen supplementation may have harmful effects.

MENTAL HEALTH AND HORMONES

Aside from interest in the influence of sex hormones on sexual activity in old age, there has been a long-standing interest in the use of androgen therapy to retard the physical symptoms that accompany aging. In general, *these treatments have had some effect on physical correlates of aging, but they do not prolong life; and they are more important in those instances where sex hormone deficiency has been a part of the clinical picture.* The importance of sex hormone extracts with regard to the maintenance of youth has been greatly diminished by a failure to demonstrate their efficacy, although many thousands of dollars are spent each year by persons in quest of age-retarding hormone treatments. A number of physicians, many in Europe, make a good living off these latter-day Ponce de Leóns.

Perhaps the most important aspect of sex hormone therapy, other than treatment of hormone deficiencies, has been in the treatment of those emotional and mental disorders which occur with higher frequency in older than in younger adults.

Depression

Isolation of testosterone (1935) stimulated work directed toward the treatment of involutional melancholia. Involutional melancholia is an early clinical term that is used to describe symptoms characterized by psychotic behavior with depression as the cen-

*From Eisdorfer, C., and Raskind, M.: Aging; hormones and human behavior. In B. E. Eleftheriou and R. L. Sprott, (Eds.), Hormonal correlates of behavior. Vol. 1. *A lifespan view.* New York: Plenum Press, 1975, p. 382.

tral behavioral manifestation of the problem. The involutional psychoses occur most frequently in women in their forties and men in their fifties (Kolb, 1968:326). The term *involutional* derives from the fact that this is the period when the endocrine and reproductive glands begin to decrease in functional activity (the involutional period).

Danziger and his colleagues (cited in Eisdorfer and Raskind, 1975:384) reviewed data on eighty-three case histories and found that, "Androgen therapy shortened the course of illness for some patients whose depression was (presumably) secondary to androgen deficiency of later life." However, the success rate was lower than that obtained with electroconvulsive shock and not higher than that which occurred with no treatment whatsoever (spontaneous remissions). A number of other studies in which testosterone replacement therapy was attempted do not provide support for the hypothesis that testosterone is a good antidepressant agent. Two well-controlled studies were cited by Eisdorfer and Raskind (1975). Wilson and co-workers (1974) treated depressed middle-aged men with testosterone and obtained no significant antidepressant effect. In fact, a paranoid reaction occurred in several patients. Sachar and associates (1973) obtained measures of both plasma and urinary testosterone levels in a group of depressed older adults (46 to 78 years) and found no significant differences between the illness and recovery periods. Moreover, absolute concentrations of testosterone were similar to those reported for normal persons of the same age range. No correlations were found between testosterone levels and measures of aggressiveness, emotional arousal, or sexual drive.

Male climacteric

Eisdorfer and Raskind (1975:384) point out that isolation of testosterone and its use in clinical practice prompted the discovery of the male climacteric by Werner in 1944. Werner claimed that "many men experienced a climacteric secondary to decreased gonadal hormone production," which was associated with nervousness, irritability, inability to concentrate, decreased memory, somatic complaints, depression, and sometimes psychosis. Werner recommended testosterone replacement therapy, but the reports of successful hormonal treatment of the male climacteric are sporadic.

Eisdorfer and Raskind (1975:384) summarize studies that "claimed improvement of impotence, depression, urinary disturbance, headache, irritability, tremor and palpitations" after the implantation of crystalline testosterone supplemented with estrogen. They comment on the significance of the estrogen to the treatment regimen in view of the "significant, though often ignored, decrease in estrogen production in the aging male." However, they point out that, until recently, examination of testosterone-behavior relationships in aging men has been hindered by the lack of accurate assays for serum testosterone and urine testosterone as well as a lack of a physiological marker analogous to that available for estrogen.

Menopausal behavioral syndrome

The relationship between estrogen and behavioral change with advancing age has been most frequently addressed within the context of the so-called "menopausal behavioral syndrome." Some investigators question whether such a syndrome really exists. Eisdorfer and Raskind (1975) have summarized a number of studies that challenge the traditional notion of a menopausal syndrome.

In one study, in which a self-administered symptom check list was used (Neugarten and Kraines, 1965), menopausal women (45 to 54 years of age) reported a higher incidence of physical complaints than other age groups, but adolescent women (14 to 19 years) reported more psychological complaints. Common menopausal symptoms such as irritability, nervousness, insomnia, depression, and crying spells were reported with a frequency which was equal to, or lower than, that reported by the premenopausal and postmenopausal groups. Presumably, the postmenopausal group (55 to 64 years) had the lowest estrogen production levels, yet they reported the lowest incidence of tired feelings, headaches, dizzy spells, irritability, difficulty in concentrating, nervousness, and depression (see Eisdorfer and Raskind, 1975: 380).

Other studies of estrogen and behavioral change, summarized by Eisdorfer and Raskind, cast serious doubt on the proposition that estrogen deficiency per se causes psychological symptoms in older menopausal and postmenopausal women (Donovan, 1951; Rybo, 1971; Thompson et al., 1973; Utian, 1972). Donovan (1951) suggests that the menopausal syndrome may be an artifact of the traditional methods of clinical case history taking because patients emphasize symptoms that have been directed to their attention by the physician.

Despite the recent emphasis on the "myth of the menopausal syndrome," there still seems to be a widespread belief among physicians and their patients that there are behavioral correlates of menopause and that exogenous estrogens can relieve symptomatology (Eisdorfer and Raskind, 1975). There are data which support the notion that estrogens may have a mood-elevating effect, regardless of whether or not estrogen deficiency is actually present, although opposite effects have been reported for some oral contraceptives (Eisdorfer and Raskind, 1975).

Depression in women

Treatment of involutional melancholia (serious depression of psychotic proportions) with estrogen therapy does not seem to be particularly successful. Eisdorfer and Raskind (1975) point out that a large number of case reports which appeared in the late 1930s and the early 1940s suggested variable success with estrogen therapy and that the average cure rate of 50% was not notably different from the natural remission rates reported at that time. They cite a carefully controlled psychiatric study (Ripley et al., 1940), in which estrogen therapy had little apparent effect on serious depression accompanied by feelings of unreality, agitation, suspiciousness, hypochondriacal and nihilistic delusions, negativism, abusiveness, and combativeness. However, milder depression did seem to be favorably influenced by estrogen therapy.

Data collected in a relatively recent study (Michael, 1970) have been interpreted as indicating that estrogen therapy might play a useful role in the treatment of aged, female nursing home patients in terms of improved communication, interpersonal relationships, self-care, social responsibility, and recreation as rated by physicians and nurses. However, rating studies of this nature have methodological limitations, and there was no rigorous assessment of cognitive functioning with standardized measures, or was there a careful assessment of possible deleterious "side effects" mentioned earlier in this chapter (i.e., thromboembolic disease, hypertension, and stroke).

The preceding data suggest that although there have been more reliable markers for estrogen deficiency in women than testosterone deficiency in men, it is no less difficult to separate the many behavioral correlates of growing old (which are related to general health, attitude, motivation, economic conditions, etc.) from those which may be related to estrogen deficiency, per se. Furthermore, it seems that the role of estrogen deficiency in behavioral change among middle-aged and older women is questionable. One of the most promising applications of estrogen therapy was for the treatment of depression, although data were controversial. Now it appears that improved antidepressant medication and electroconvulsive shock treatment obviate the need for estrogen therapy in the treatment of severe depression.

It is clear that hormones other than testosterone and estrogen can affect behavior with advancing age. We can only summarize some of the highlights of Eisdorfer and

Raskind's (1975) and Elias and Elias's (1975) reviews of the studies in this area. The student should bear in mind that these authors cite a number of experiments reported in the literature in support of these generalizations.

Thyroxine

The thyroid gland plays a crucial role in the early stages of physiological growth and maturation of the brain. It seems that early clinicians attributed part of the aging processes to failure of the thyroid gland because *hypothyroid* patients exhibited many behavioral and physiological symptoms of senility: slowed responding and speech, lowered motor activity, drying and coarsening of skin, graying of hair, cold intolerance, and constipation. However, the "thyroid failure hypothesis" has not been supported by clinical and experimental studies. The thyroid gland does undergo some degenerative histological changes with advancing age, but from a functional point of view these changes seem to be of little significance; plasma thyroxine (T_4) levels do not seem to show much change with age in humans, and although T_4 secretion rate is somewhat reduced, it seems to be reduced as a compensatory response to decreased T_4 disposal.

There are conflicting reports in the animal literature with regard to changes in thyroid activity with advancing age. However, decrease in thyroxine secretion, if any, seems to be offset by increased tissue responsiveness. Thus it appears that the role of thyroxine in the genesis of senescence and concomitant behavioral changes remains a subject for further investigation.

The adrenals

The human adrenal cortex appears to show no striking changes in anatomical features with increasing age, although changes of a microscopical nature and with unknown significance are noted. Functional changes appear to be minor. Serum cortisol concentrations remain relatively unaltered with increasing age, and the small decline in cortisol secretion rate may be representative of a response to slowed metabolic disposal. Many psychiatric symptoms are seen in cases of adrenal insufficiency and in a disease called Cushing's syndrome, but they occur most frequently in early and middle life and are not commonly observed in elderly adults. There does seem to be a significant fall in adrenal androgens with advancing age, but the behavioral implications of this decline have not been thoroughly investigated. Eisdorfer and Raskind (1975) cite a double-blind study by Marie (1963) in which elderly women who received an "anabolic" steroid over a six-month period were rated higher on "mental attitude, general interest, activity, appetite, and good health" in a nursing home. Cognitive functioning was not measured, and no comparisons were made with younger persons. Thus, on the human level, the role of adrenal androgens in behavioral changes with age remains a question that must be answered with further research.

There has been some suggestion that end organs in the autonomic nervous system may become increasingly sensitive to catecholamines with advancing age. One investigator (Eisdorfer, 1972) has proposed that "end-organ hypersensitivity" may explain the cautiousness found in the behavior of older persons in novel laboratory situations. So far there is no strong evidence in support of this hypothesis, although elevated free fatty acid response of the older persons in Eisdorfer and co-workers' (1970) study with propranolol (a beta-adrenergic blocker) has been cited as evidence for a greater degree of arousal in the target organs of the elderly (Chapter 9).

The preceding data suggest that psychologists need to learn more about changes with age in hormone activity and their implications for behavior before hormone treatments for "aging" become a widespread practice. Eisdorfer and Raskind (1975) point out the important fact that the therapeutic use of hormones to treat disease can produce behavioral symptoms of an adverse nature, including psychotic reactions. For example, cortisone and ACTH have given rise to euphoria, joviality, hallucinations, paranoid delusions, and affective disturbances such as depression, apathy, and panic. These symptoms may be related to side effects and/or to the reaction to sudden physiological changes that occur when hormone imbalance is suddenly corrected. Of course, individual differences in reactions to these hormones do occur, and they are most likely related to life history and genetic factors.

HORMONES, AGING, AND STRESS

The study of hormone influences on behavioral differences among age groups is intimately tied to the study of stress. This is true because hormone responses (e.g., corticosterone response in rodents and cortisol response in primates, sheep, cats, dogs, cows, and humans) have been used to evaluate stressor effects, and because one of the major roles of the neuroendocrine system is to maintain homeostasis in the face of deviations from environmental steady-state conditions, and such deviations constitute a stressor stimulus. Age-associated differences in behavior and endocrine response are often brought out under conditions of stress. In fact, a number of theories of aging define aging as the accumulation of stress experiences (e.g., Comfort, 1956; Jones, 1956; Selye and Prioreschi, 1960). The stress theories of aging have not received wide support from experimental and clinical findings, but it seems clear that capacity to adapt to stressors varies as a function of age (Timiras, 1972).

Few investigations have been concerned with the interaction of age and stressors as reflected in the responses of the pituitary and adrenal hormones, although data on the pituitary-adrenal axis have been obtained for a variety of species (see Elias and Elias, 1975). Generally, there have been inconsistent findings with regard to age-associated changes in levels of adrenocortical hormones. Differences in findings from study to study reflect species specificity in corticosteroid concentrations with advancing age, use of different age groups in various studies, differences in techniques used for measurements, time of day of sampling, wide variation in handling and maintenance of laboratory animals, and differences in genotype.

Human studies have not advanced far because of sheer complexity of brain-pituitary-adrenal relationships. Adrenocorticoid hormones in the blood of older persons are increased, but this increase may be complementary to a decrease in secretion and utilization. Moreover, the pituitary adrenal axis is influenced by the brain hormones or neurohumors, and it is not clear at this time whether or not brain-endocrine relationships change in old age. One current hypothesis is that decrements in brain function in the absence of brain disease and loss of neurons might be related to the reduction in the number of brain hormone receptors (Timiras and Bignami, 1976). Thus one of the major problems encountered in the study of behavioral correlates of stressor effects on pituitary and adrenal hormones with advancing age is that the basic groundwork of endocrinological studies has not advanced to a point where baseline data are available. There are also methodological problems. For example, plasma hormone levels are used as an index of hormone response to stress in many studies, but plasma hormone concentration is not an entirely reliable index of the concentration of a particular hormone that is *active physiologically*. This lack of one-to-one correspondence between actual hormone activity and experimental measurement is related to the complexity of relationships between secretion, reception, and utilization just noted. Thus technically accurate studies of aging, stress-hormonal relationships, and behavior are not easily accomplished. Nevertheless, a number of studies have provided practical implications for the housing, care, and maintenance of laboratory animals used in experiments. (If you are not familiar with the pituitary-adrenal axis and its role in response to a stressor stimulus, you may find a chapter by Brush and Froehlich [1975] most helpful as a review or as an introductory presentation.)

Early experience

Behavioral effects of early and "late" experience were discussed in Chapters 6 and 8. Much of the early experience research in endocrinology was concerned with ACTH secretion and adrenocortical responsivity in aging animals. These studies are important because they may provide insight as to why behavioral responses are influenced by early or late experiences. In a study using plasma corticosterone levels as an index of stress response, rats that were not handled as infants responded more slowly to a stressor as adults, and stress responses were observed over a longer period of time than they were for nonhandled controls (e.g., Haltmeyer et al., 1967). In another study, animals handled as infants, when compared with nonhandled controls, exhibited lower steroid responses when they were exposed to novel environmental stimuli (Levine and Brush, 1967).

Although there is a limited amount of direct evidence tying the effects of early experience (handling, etc.) to adrenocortical responses and their behavioral correlates, it is clear that behavior is influenced by adrenocortical activity. Animals with significantly greater adrenocortical activity exhibit less rapid extinction of passive avoidance responses; there is a significant, positive correlation between the corticosterone response to stressors and active avoidance conditioning; and performance on a variety of tasks is influenced by hormones that are normally released from the adrenal cortex (Elias and Elias, 1975; Levine, 1972).

Unfortunately, none of the early experience-stress-hormone studies involved follow-up of behavioral observations on old or senile animals. In most cases the "older" animals tested in these early experience studies were very young adults. Nevertheless, early experience studies have important implications for aging studies. First, they suggest that many behavioral differences among young, middle-aged, and old animals may be related to differential handling schedules, or other rearing procedures, at a young age. Second, they suggest that these age differences may be dictated by changes in endocrine response to stress in adulthood. Third, they suggest the importance of studies that not only follow the effects of early environmental conditions across the entire life span but also explore effects of experiences later in life. Is there really a critical period very early in life that results in profound behavioral and endocrine changes that cannot be affected so dramatically at any other period of the life cycle? Can experiences in late or middle life have qualitatively different effects that are no less dramatic?

Late experience

There have been a number of studies of behavioral effects of late experience (Chapter 8), but few have examined hormonal correlates of behavior such as pituitary-adrenal responsiveness at different ages. There are some studies in this area. Elias and Redgate (1975) compared C57BL/6J mice that were immobilized for 10 seconds (stressor) with control C57BL/6J mice that were handled in the same way but not immobilized. These procedures were done for animals that were 2.2, 6.2, 12.0, and 23.3 months of age. The immobilization procedure was identical to that used to obtain blood pressure measurements in studies of blood pressure changes with age.

Open-field behavior was observed before and after immobilization or handling, and plasma corticosterone levels were assessed 11 days after these treatments. No differences in open-field activity were observed for immobilized animals as opposed to controls, but 11 days after the immobilization treatments, elevated plasma corticosterone levels were observed for all but the 12-month-old animals. The greatest differences between immobilized animals and their handled controls occurred for the youngest and oldest animals, with the greatest difference for the youngest group. Thus a simple linear age effect was not observed; the extreme age groups were most affected. It seems clear that the immobilization procedure influences corticosterone response to a stressor and that the immobilization response itself may influence blood pressure by way of the influence of corticosterone precursors on blood pressure.

In another study dealing with stressor effects on corticosterone levels in different age groups of C57BL/6J mice, Elias, Elias, Zolovick, and Eleftheriou (1975) examined open-field activity before and after preparation for the recording of electroencephalographic (EEG) sleep patterns. In addition, they obtained plasma corticosterone levels 11 days after surgery for electrode implantation. Four age groups were used: 3.0, 6.3, 12.5, and 23.5 months.

All animals in this study exhibited a decrease in activity level when they were tested for a second time (after surgery or control handling); however, activity levels were lower for the surgery group, with the most notable lowering in activity for the youngest animals. Significant elevations in corticosterone levels were observed for the surgery group, with the greatest differences occurring between posthandling and postsurgery conditions at 6.3 and 23.5 months of age. The oldest group exhibited almost twice the plasma corticosterone level exhibited by the 6.3-month-old group.

The implications of the study by Elias and associates are fairly clear. Surgery is a necessity to implant electrodes for EEG recording; surgical stress effects are seen 11 days after surgery. Effects of surgical stress on endocrine response may, in turn, influence EEG recordings by virtue of the connections between electrophysiological responses and neuroendocrine responses as influenced by hormone balance anywhere in the body.

General implications of stress studies

Frequently, experimenters argue that the absence of struggling and activity in an immobilized animal is evidence that it is no longer stressed (has been habituated) to a laboratory procedure. Such arguments must be viewed with caution, since a quiet animal may be extremely stressed as indicated by hormone reactivity. Stress reactions can take the form of increased mobility or extreme immobility (freezing), depending on the severity and length of exposure to the stressor. It is very important to remember this fact because differential stressor effects on young and old animals may influence activity levels and learning performance, but they may not be immediately apparent from standard behavioral measures of stress response such as increased or decreased mobility, vocalization, and defecation. Thus pituitary-adrenal response becomes an important tool in the repertoire of the researcher who would make careful use of animal models in aging studies.

In general, psychologists have used open-field activity and defecation as indices of response to stress. Serious questions have been raised as to the sensitivity and appropriateness of these measures as stress-response indices (see Elias, 1975a). Use of endocrine response as an index of stress response and recovery from stress provides a more sensitive index of the stress effects induced by various laboratory procedures at different ages. Hormone indices of stress response are highly important to aging studies because very often young and old groups of animals are shipped to the laboratory for experimentation. Frequently older animals are exposed to accumulated laboratory stressors for a longer period than younger animals. In these contexts, behavioral-endocrine studies become an important methodological step in the direction of understanding why age differences are observed for some kinds of behaviors.

Implications of early experience and hormone-response studies for careful control of handling and housing conditions are obvious. However, many studies with aging animals do not provide information regarding handling and housing procedures, and often, reported handling controls are inadequate. Lovely and associates (1972) and Hatch and co-workers (1965) have summarized the consequences of long-term individual or group housing of rats. Briefly, rats housed in isolation for extended periods exhibit heavier adrenal, thyroid, and pituitary glands, lighter spleens and thymuses, and hypersecretion of adrenocorticoids. Behaviorally, they are less active in the open field, more likely to make startle responses, more likely to vocalize when handled, and generally more aggressive. In another study, Lovely and associates (1972) reported that rats housed individually (30 to 50 days) learned a shuttle-box avoidance task more rapidly and exhibited a significant elevation in baseline levels of plasma corticosterone relative to group-housed rats. Thus it seems that differential periods of group or individual housing between age groups within studies, or between studies, may lead to conflicting findings for animal research done in different laboratories.

It is very important that students planning to do research with animals, or to evaluate the animal literature in aging, realize that hormones are greatly influenced by laboratory environment and that, in turn, hormones influence behavior. The problems of environmental control are intensified in aging studies because important environmental factors (noise level, diet, temperature, humidity, day-night cycle) accumulate over time and thus produce exaggerated effects in older animals. Use of pituitary-adrenal indices of stress is beginning to reveal just how much the hormonal response to these environmental conditions may influence behavioral differences between young and old animals—differences that may not be related to learning ability of activity level per se.

LIFE-SPAN DEVELOPMENTAL STUDIES

Hormones are not just important because they may be used as indices of stress or aging but because they can be used as tools to manipulate growth and development. The effect of "hormone-precipitated early development" on behavior in later life is possibly the most important life-span developmental question that can be answered using animals and the tools of the behavioral endocrinologist. It is clear that hormone-stimulated advancement (or retardation) of development is possible. The question remains concerning the effects of early hormone treatment on behavior across the entire life span. In rats, cortisol administration on postnatal day 1 causes delayed development of (1) the startle reflex, (2) swimming behavior, and (3) evoked electrical potentials to light and sound; however, at 30 days of age, maze performance and light-dark discrimination in these "delayed animals" is improved relative to controls (Schapiro, 1968, 1971; Schapiro and Hupperty, 1967). These data were interpreted as evidence for a facilitating effect on adult learning brought about by delayed central nervous system development. However, it should be noted that the 30-day-old rat is not really a mature adult in terms of behavioral development.

Schapiro and his colleagues (see Elias and Elias, 1975:417) examined the effects of thyroxine administered on postnatal days 2, 3, and 4. The thyroxine treatment caused an accelerated development of the startle reflex, swimming behavior, and evoked potentials. Furthermore, the rats that received thyroxine treatment acquired a conditioned avoidance response more rapidly than saline-treated controls at 16 days of age; but at 35 to 45 days of age the hormone-treated animals performed less well than the saline-treated controls. Apparently, thyroxine administration resulted in advanced central nervous system development but had debilitating effects on later learning ability (or performance). Eayrs (1964) has presented data indicating that either hormone-induced acceleration or delay in development results in impairment of learning in the adult rat.

There is a very important implication of these findings for the life-span developmental approach to the understanding of behavioral changes with advancing age. *Appropriately timed hormonal events are necessary for optimal brain development; the hormone environment influences the developmental timetable in such a way that unduly rapid or slow progression in development results in impaired learning and performance later in life.* However, it is important that studies be extended to a variety of species, particularly primates, and that testing be done for truly mature animals of various ages. In the studies by Schapiro and coworkers and by Eayrs, "later" learning and performance were observed at a very early age in relationship to the total life span of the rat. An important question is the extent to which these hormonal-influenced accelerations or delays in development influence learning performance for middle-aged and aged adult animals. Does the performance decrement (or improvement) continue to accelerate with advancing age, or does it remain constant after maturity has been reached? We have been unable to find any studies in which this question has been raised; we hope some of the readers of this book will pursue the answer.

ANIMAL MODELS

The many studies dealing with the influence of hormones on disease processes are beyond the scope of this chapter. They are important because, as we will emphasize in Chapter 12, disease processes may have deleterious effects on behavior in old age. We have noted that serious questions are being raised with regard to the extent that performance declines with age may be associated with cardiovascular disease, with cerebrovascular disease, and with severe untreated hypertension. We will briefly mention a few studies involving hypertension as an example of the relationship between endocrine function, disease processes, and behavior, and by way of introduction to the material on genetics in Chapter 13.

In some studies, hypertension has been linked with impaired performance. Hypertension (high blood pressure) is not a disease but a symptom of a pathological condition. It does not have a direct influence on behavior but influences behavior by way of blood pressure effects on physiology or changes in physiology resulting from high blood pressure. Of course, the possibility exists that correlates of high blood pressure, such as anxiety or life stress (for some individuals), may also influence behavior independently of physiological cause-effect relationships.

Adrenocortical function and catecholamines influence learning and memory (see Levine, 1972). They have also been implicated in the genesis of hypertension (Streeten et al., 1969). (In Chapter 12 you will see that Light's [1975] study of hypertensive patients at Upstate Medical Center in Syracuse revealed a very different relationship between nonmedicated and medicated hypertensives and controls when plasma renin activity levels were taken into account.) Thus it is not illogical to suggest that performance decrements relating to essential hypertension in the absence of clinical signs may be due, at least in some cases, to alterations in neurohumors or peripherally acting hormones that indirectly influence central nervous system activity by way of feedback mechanisms. Is it possible that hormone factors may account for performance decrements in middle-aged hypertensive patients? Is it possible that performance decrements in senility may be related to hormone factors and the physiological correlates of sustained high blood pressure? Do genetic factors interact with stressor effects over a lifetime? Animal studies provide a unique opportunity to answer these questions because the natural course of a disease or symptom of disease can be studied and hormone correlates of behavioral changes can be investigated; that is, animal subjects may be allowed to remain in an untreated state to observe the natural progression of the disease.

Light's (1975) findings were difficult to interpret because patients had been treated with different antihypertensive drugs for varying periods of time. The drug factor can be controlled in animal studies. Moreover, studies of endocrine response, biochemistry, physiology, and pathology that simply are not possible with humans for ethical reasons can be done with animals. This does not imply that animal data can be substituted for data obtained with human research participants; rather, studies with animals can lead to more refined and goal-directed questions at the human level by providing focus and reasonable hypotheses. An important element in the development of good animal models to study hypertension and behavior is to determine whether blood pressure elevations in hypertensive animals are related to the same physiological or endocrine factors as the different categories of hypertension in humans. Thus it is important to collect physiological, anatomical, endocrinological, and behavioral data in parallel and to do so over the entire life span.

To our knowledge no life-span developmental studies of animals combining hormonal, behavioral, and blood pressure parameters have been done. However, several experiments with adult animals have been concerned with blood pressure and catecholamines.

Griew (1966) found that rats from a colony of animals with hypertension exhibited less spontaneous activity, slower swimming times, and reduced learning ability in comparison with "normotensive" rats from the same colony. The hypertensive rats exhibited *increased levels of catecholamines* in tissue samples of the entire brain (Robertson and Laverty, 1967). In another study, Laverty (1968) observed decreased home cage activity at night and decreased Y-runway exploration in white hypertensive rats as opposed to white normotensive rats from the same colony. When compared with normotensive rats, the hypertensive rats exhibited *increased levels of norepinephrine* (noradrenaline) in the cerebral cortex, cerebellum, and thalamic regions of the brain. Contradictory findings are reported for comparisons of spontaneously hypertensive male rats (SHR) developed by Okamoto and Aoki (1963) and control rats (NIH Wistar and Sprague-Dawley, 5 to 20 days old). Yamori and associates (1970) reported a *reduction in norepinephrine* for the SHR rat in the hypothalamus, lower brainstem, and whole brain. One possible reason for the contradiction is that different parts of the brain were sampled and that the genotypes of the hypertensive animals used by Griew, Robertson and colleagues, and Yamori and associates were different. Although an animal may be hypertensive, neurohumor levels may still be influenced by his unique genotype. It is frequently true that different inbred strains of mice and rats show differences in norepinephrine in the same parts of the brain, even though they are not hypertensive.

Studies such as those by Griew and by Robertson's and Yamori's groups are on the right track in terms of understanding behavior-hormonal-disease relationships, and they should be expanded to include old animals. However, there are some major problems that must be solved before much more effort is invested. One major problem is the lack of appropriate biochemical controls for the hypertensive rats. Generally, the NIH Wistar strain is considered to be an appropriate biochemical control animal for the Aoki spontaneously hypertensive strain. Recently, however, the appropriateness of the NIH Wistar strain as a normotensive control has been challenged (Eichelman et al., 1973).

A more serious and related problem has been the lack of appropriate genetic control groups. You will understand this point more fully after you read Chapter 15. However,

Table 11-1. Summary of statistical comparisons of a hypertensive group of white rats with a normotensive group of black rats and a normotensive group of white rats*

All comparisons	
Noradrenaline:	W-Hyp. = Bl-Norm. > W-Norm.
Activity†:	W-Hyp. = Bl-Norm. < W-Norm.
Comparisons with white normotensives	
Noradrenaline:	W-Hyp. > W-Norm.
Activity:	W-Hyp. < W-Norm.
Comparisons with black normotensives	
Noradrenaline:	W-Hyp. = B-Norm.
Activity:	W-Hyp. = B-Norm.

*These comparisons were done as part of a more comprehensive study by Laverty (1968). Actual data are presented in Laverty, R. *Psychonomic Science,* 1968, **10,** 25-26.

†Animals were 3 to 4 months of age in this portion of the study.

an example provided by a study by Laverty (1968) may serve to introduce the concept of a genetic control group and the problems involved when one is not used.

Table 11-1 summarizes the statistical results of Laverty's comparisons of white hypertensive (W-Hyp.), white normotensive (W-Norm.), and black normotensive rats (Bl-Norm.). Assume for the moment that only the white hypertensive and normotensive rats had been compared. Table 11-1 shows that noradrenaline levels were significantly higher in the thalamus for the white hypertensive than for the white normotensive rats but that activity level was lower. One might become somewhat enthused about the possibility that hypertensive rats exhibit lower levels of activity and higher levels of noradrenaline in the thalamus and question the relationship between activity and noradrenaline in relation to hypertension, if it were not for the fact that nonsignificant differences were obtained when the hypertensive white and the normotensive black rats were compared. The fact that Laverty used two normotensive groups of rats makes apparent what would have been an erroneous conclusion about causal relationships among the variables studied. These data illustrate something very important in addition to the obvious fact that noradrenaline levels, blood pressure, and behavior cannot be linked causally based on comparisons of only two strains, one hypertensive and one normotensive. It illustrates the fact that apparent behavior–blood pressure relationships based on comparisons of a strain or stock of animals with high blood pressure with other strains or stocks of animals with low blood pressure may be an accident of the fact that extremes of these two phenotypes are present in one strain and not another. In other words, strain A may show *low* noradrenaline in the thalamus, hypertension, and high activity, but only because these three phenotypic traits happen to be present in strain A by virtue of its unique genetic characteristics relative to strain B and other strains. Similarly, strain B can show normal blood pressure levels, low activity, and high values of noradrenaline in the thalamus, but only because the three phenotypic traits happen to be present in strain B. Thus comparisons of strains A and B signify nothing with regard to cause-effect relationships between these two phenotypic traits. Sounds logical doesn't it? This principle holds for any endocrine or physiological phenomenon one may wish to compare and relate to behavior. Unfortunately, many investigators are unaware of the dangers in making cause-effect interpretations based on comparisons of one high and one low blood pressure stock or strain derived from very different genetic backgrounds. To avoid this problem one may compare a number of hypertensive and normotensive strains or, even better, use animals for high and low blood pressure lines and random control lines derived from a common foundation stock by genetic selection. In Chapter 14 we will describe how selection experiments may be used to create physiological and biochemical phenotypes, which may then be related to behavior.

SUMMARY

Despite the fact that hormones can have a dramatic influence on behavior and the earliest work on hormones was stimulated by a concern for "treating" the aging process, little has been done with regard to investigations of hormone-age-behavior relationships. This is partly because it is very difficult to separate the effects of hormones on behavior from the effects of behavior on hormones. Behavioral investigations are made difficult by the fact that the basic groundwork has not yet been laid by the "aging endocrinologists."

To be sure, there have been a number of clinical studies and some experimental studies, but much remains to be done in this new area called behavioral endocrinology and aging. It does seem clear that aging of the endocrine glands is not a simple process of wear and tear in which all endocrine structures and functions are equally affected. Rather, it is a selective process in which some hormonal substances act in different ways at different periods of the life span. Moreover, endocrine changes are highly influenced by neuroregulator mechanisms and by many behavioral and physiological changes that occur as one grows old. Thus there exist highly complex reciprocal endocrine-behavior feedback systems, such that endocrines influence behavior and behavior influences endocrines, and both are influenced by life events and physiological changes associated with aging.

Decrements in the production of sex hormones and decline in sexual vigor with old age are common to males and females of many species. In humans, and in some infrahuman species, the decline in sexual activity is related to social, motivational, and learning factors as well as to the activity of sex hormones. Cognitive and emotional changes influence sex hormones; these factors also influence sexual behavior independently of direct effects of sex hormones. The general decrease in sexual activity for the nonsenile elderly adult is related, in no small part, to psychosocial factors. Thus decline in sex hormones has been given less emphasis in the recent literature, although they still play an important role in sexual behavior. Hormones influence sexual behavior in a variety of ways, including their effects on the cells of the accessory glands. However, the changes which occur in the cells of the accessory sex glands are not unlike those which occur in many other tissues of the body. Hormones and social factors do not tell the whole story. For example, evidence from the animal literature indicates that age may bring with it decrements in the neural mechanisms which lead to ejaculation.

Testosterone levels appear to remain within the same range from adolescence through the fifth decade of life, but from the sixth decade on there is a decrease in mean plasma levels. As would be expected, there is a wide range of individual variation. For example, in the eighth and ninth decades, individual plasma testosterone levels can be in a high normal range similar to that of younger adults. Treatment with testosterone in androgen-deficient men seems to result in improvement in sexual drive, but generally only when androgen levels are below normal.

It is clear that decreased estrogen production accompanies the cessation of the cyclical ovarian functioning in women. The process begins in the fifth decade of life and ends in the sixth decade. Decreased estrogen in menopausal and postmenopausal women results in genital atrophy and vasomotor instability. Not only can this impede sexual activity but it sometimes results in discomfort as well, and the symptoms can be traumatic psychologically. For many women they mark the end of young adulthood. Anxiety and depression often accompany menopause and postmenopause, but these symptoms can be a reaction to the social implications of growing old as well as to sex hormone deficiency. However, there are wide individual differences in both the physical and psychological reactions to menopause.

Exogenous estrogen treatments have been used to relieve anxiety, depression, and other symptoms that are observed in menopausal and postmenopausal women, but there are a number of risks involved, including occlusive cerebrovascular disease, stroke, cerebral ischemia, and hypertension. It was once believed that estrogens prevented coronary heart disease, but there seems to be little evidence that this is true.

There has been a long-standing interest in the use of androgen therapy to retard the physical symptoms that accompany aging. In general, these treatments have had some beneficial effect on physical correlates of aging, but they do not seem to prolong life, and they are more useful in those instances where androgen deficiency has been part of the clinical picture.

The most important use of sex hormone therapy, other than the treatment of hormone deficiencies, has been in the treatment of those emotional and mental disorders that occur with higher frequency in older than in younger adults. Some successes have been reported with testosterone and estrogen, but in many cases the success rate has not exceeded the spontaneous cure rate. More important, new developments in drug therapy lessen the need to treat depression and other affective disorders with hormones.

Hypothyroid patients exhibit many behavioral and physiological symptoms of senility. However, there is not much support for the idea that aging results from thyroid failure. The thyroid gland does undergo some degenerative changes with advancing age, but from a functional point of view, they seem of little significance. The human adrenal cortex shows no striking changes in anatomical features with advancing age, although there are microscopical changes of unknown significance. Functional changes are minor in healthy persons, and the small decline in cortisol secretion rate may be representative of a response to slowed metabolic disposal.

Many psychiatric symptoms are observed in cases of adrenal insufficiency, but they occur most frequently in early and middle life and are seldom observed in elderly adults. There does seem to be a considerable fall in adrenal androgen with advancing age, but the behavioral implications of this decline have not been revealed at this point in time. There have been reports of improvement in interest, activity, appetite, and good health in nursing home patients as a result of steroid treatment, but these studies were not carefully done and need to be replicated. Before hormone treatment of behavioral correlates of aging becomes a widespread practice, scientists need to learn a great deal more about changes with age in hormone functions and their implications for behavior. Some hormones, used for the treatment of disease, have deleterious effects on behavior and result in psychotic symptoms when used in high doses or for a prolonged time, for example, cortisone and ACTH.

Hormone-behavior-aging studies do not lend much support to the stress theories of aging, but it is clear that endocrine response to stress varies across the life span and may affect other behaviors. Much more in the way of long-term evaluations of early experience effects on endocrine response need to be done if psychologists are to understand fully the effects of early experience on behavior at different points in the life span and the ability to cope with stress at different ages. Moreover, psychologists need to know if the same stressors take on a different meaning for different age groups. Increased understanding of the effects of laboratory stress on endocrine response will help researchers to design experiments that more carefully evaluate learning ability, drive, and performance for different age groups. Keep in mind that individual differences can be greater than differences between age groups, since endocrine response to stress is determined by past experience and genetic predisposition.

Hormones have been used to advance or retard development in rodents. These studies have not followed behavioral consequences into middle and late adulthood. Such studies may provide important hypotheses with regard to the behavioral consequences of precocious or delayed development. Within the area of behavioral endocrinology, these developmental studies may contribute most to life-span psychology because they allow a direct manipulation of developmental time schedules.

Hormones are involved in many diseases and symptoms of disease, for example, hypertension. These diseases, in turn, influence behavior in a deleterious manner. More sophisticated use of laboratory animal models and greater attention to endocrine variables at the human level may help psychologists to learn more about how diseases influence behavior by way of intermediate hormonal and physiological variables. They may also allow a more sophisticated evaluation of the role of genotype in disease-hormone-behavior relationships at different points in the life cycle.

SELECTED READINGS

Brush, F. R., and Froehlich, J. C. Motivational effects of the pituitary and adrenal hormones. In B. E. Eleftheriou and R. L. Sprott (Eds.), *Hormonal correlates of behavior.* (Vol. 2). *An organismic view.* New York: Plenum Publishing Corp., 1975.

Catt, K. J. *An ABC of endocrinology.* Boston: Little, Brown, & Co., 1971.

Collaborative Group for the Study of Stroke in Young Women. Oral contraception and increased risk of cerebral ischemia or thrombosis. *New England Journal of Medicine,* 1973, **288,** 871-877.

Eayrs, J. T. Endocrine influences on cerebral development. *Archives of Biology,* 1964, **75,** 529-565.

Eisdorfer, C., and Raskind, M. Aging, hormones and human behavior. In B. E. Eleftheriou and R. L. Sprott (Eds.), *Hormonal correlates of behavior.* (Vol. 1). *A lifespan view.* New York: Plenum Publishing Corp., 1975.

Elias, M. F., and Elias, P. K. Hormones, aging and behavior in infrahuman mammals. In B. E. Eleftheriou and R. L. Sprott (Eds.), *Hormonal correlates of behavior.* (Vol. 1). *A lifespan view.* New York: Plenum Publishing Corp., 1975.

Freeman, J. T. Endocrinology in geriatrics: historical background. In L. Gitman (Ed.), *Endocrines and behavior.* Springfield, Ill.: Charles C Thomas, Publisher, 1967.

Schapiro, S., and Hupperty, M. H. Neonatal cortisol administration and immunological impairment in the adult rat. *Proceedings of the Society for Experimental Biology and Medicine,* 1967, **124,** 744-746.

Selye H., and Prioreschi, P. Stress theory of aging. In N. W. Shock (Eds.), *Aging—some social and biological aspects.* Washington, D.C.: American Association for the Advancement of Science, 1960.

Verwoerdt, A., Pfeiffer, E., and Wang, H. S. Sexual behavior in senescence. *Geriatrics,* 1969, **24,** 137-154.

CHAPTER 12

HEALTH AND BEHAVIOR

Few gerontological researchers disagree with the general statement that aging and disease processes are highly correlated and that, as a consequence, it is often very difficult to separate the effects of changing physiology from social and psychological variables. In actual practice, however, many of these same researchers fail to consider physical and mental health as important factors in their behavioral studies. In a recent review of research reports published in the *Journal of Gerontology,* Abrahams and associates (1975) found that the percent of studies concerned with health status, controlling for health status, or even mentioning the health of subjects declined in recent years (1963 to 1968 versus 1969 to 1974). Abrahams and associates (1975:671) considered this to be a disturbing situation, since many researchers "have clearly demonstrated the negative effect of the presence of even mild chronic disease or sensory impairment on a variety of psychological measures, particularly psychomotor performance and intellectual functioning."

The extent of physical impairment among community-dwelling older persons may vary widely, depending on geographical area, socioeconomic level, and other demographic variables. In one study, conducted on a random stratified probability sample of persons over 65 years of age who resided in Durham County, North Carolina, Pfeiffer (1973) reported that 25% suffered significant physical impairment. Thus an aging study based on random sampling in this geographical location might be expected to include one fourth of physically impaired subjects. Abrahams (1976b:69) has elaborated on the argument for more complete and comprehensive consideration of health status in aging studies.

> By using samples of subjects unselected for health, experimental-manipulative researchers have implied an inherent homogeneity within a given aged sample. This however ignores much research which has indicated a greater heterogeneity, not only of abilities and performance levels, but also of health status among older adults than among young adults. It is this heterogeneity which may obscure important treatment effects.

The issue of health status is intrinsically related to definitions of aging. There has been a long-standing debate among gerontological researchers over whether or not "normal" aging processes can or should be distinguished from "pathological" aging processes. Busse (1969) has pointed out that the argument is usually described in terms of *primary aging* (inherited biological processes which are time related and detrimental but are independent of stress, trauma, or disease) and *secondary aging* (declines in functioning which are a result of trauma or chronic disease). The latter processes are not related to aging in a direct, causative manner, although they are often correlated with age by virtue of the increasing incidence of chronic disease and accidents among elderly persons. Currently, the issue of normal (primary) as opposed to pathological (secondary) aging processes is expressed most clearly in the terminal drop hypothesis, that is, the question of whether significant decline in functioning occurs progressively with

You won't be able to play in the T-maze today.

increasing age or is not particularly significant until shortly before death, when disease plays a substantial role in behavioral decrements. Thus the first section of this chapter is devoted to the more recent evidence for and against the terminal drop hypothesis. Subsequent sections discuss the behavioral effects of selected disease processes that are common among aging persons. We have limited our discussion to those diseases which have been investigated most extensively in recent years. However, we believe that even these limited areas of research are sufficient to stress the importance of a more adequate consideration of the health variable by contemporary researchers.

TERMINAL DROP HYPOTHESIS

In previous chapters we pointed out that "nonintellective" variables can influence performance on intelligence tests, learning tasks, and other measures of cognitive ability. These nonintellective variables (e.g., physical health, motivation) sometimes are associated closely with the passage of time from birth to death. We can say, without doubt, that the passage of time itself has no effect on behavior. Rather, it is the events that take place within time that are important. It is not necessary to understand the terminal drop hypothesis to appreciate this intuitively obvious view. The contribution of the terminal drop hypothesis is that it has facilitated understanding of critical events which take place over time in at least two ways: (1) It has called attention to the controversy over so-called "normal" aging changes as opposed to those changes which are related to pathological processes, and (2) it has stimulated research efforts aimed at examining time-correlated phenomena that influence changes in intellectual performance. For the most part the terminal drop hypothesis deals with the question of modifiers of intellectual performance with an emphasis on health factors. Theoretically, it could include more variables than intellectual performance; however, only a few investigators have studied terminal drop effects for behaviors other than those measured by standardized intelligence tests.

Simply stated, the terminal drop hypothesis suggests that health factors which bring an individual closer to death are related to a decline in intellectual performance. Thus the onset of decline should not be observable until a point in time relatively near to death, that is, "near to death" in terms of the total life span.

Kleemeier (1962:294) has presented the following argument with regard to the terminal drop hypothesis.

> Great individual differences in intelligence performance are found as age increases in the senium. These differences may be accounted for to a substantial degree by the presence of a terminal drop or decline in performance associated with the death of the subject, but are not directly related to age in the senium. The presence of this death factor tends to associate intellectual decline to adverse changes in health or organic integrity of the person rather than so-called "normal" age change. It suggests that any decline in performance not accounted for by terminal drop cannot simply be attributed to the passage of time or age alone, but must be explained in more explicit terms.

Kleemeier uses the phrase "so-called" normal aging processes because there is by no means general agreement that some physiological changes which occur with age are normal. Perhaps aging is nothing more than the accumulation of abnormal physiological processes (diseases) that eventually lead to the destruction of the organism. Alternatively, some processes leading to death may be normal, whereas others may be abnormal. This theoretical argument has not been resolved and, in one sense, is irrelevant to the terminal drop hypothesis because physiological changes, normal or abnormal, do take place with the passage of time. The terminal drop hypothesis calls attention to the role of these physiological changes at the end of life as modifiers of intellectual functioning.

Aside from its emphasis on disease rather than time as a causal variable, Siegler (1975) has noted several important issues. The terminal drop hypothesis (1) promises a life associated with only minor intellectual decline until the end; (2) attempts to explain increased variability in performance for old, as opposed to young, persons based on the notion that each person reaches his terminal drop state at a different time; (3) suggests that it might make more sense to establish age-cohorts on the basis of time to death rather than age from birth; (4) holds out a promise that psychological measures may provide useful indices of impending death due to disease phenomena which might be prevented, and (5) has important implications for data collection strategies (e.g., Riegel and Riegel, 1972). Thus it is important theoretically, practically, and methodologically to determine whether the terminal drop hypothesis is supported by the literature.

Data collection strategies

If the terminal drop hypothesis is correct with respect to the debilitating effect of disease in late life, health becomes an important and potentially biasing factor in cross-sectional designs because health care has become better over several generations, and as a result, the average life span has been lengthened. Just as one may partition subjects in cross-sectional designs into high and low education groups, one may also partition subjects into suvivors as opposed to nonsurvivors based on a post hoc analysis (after the fact). In other words, one group may be formed from persons who live ten years beyond initial testing (IT), and another group may include persons who live only one year beyond IT. Alternatively, the researcher may calculate distance-from-death at IT and adjust performance scores for distance-from-death scores by covariance analysis.

These cross-sectional designs provide information concerning the importance of distance-from-death as a way of classifying subjects in aging studies, and they provide information about physiological correlates of survival. However, they do not provide information about change over time because subject groups are compared only with regard to performance at IT. Thus cross-sectional designs cannot be used as sensitive tests of the terminal drop hypothesis because testing of the hypothesis requires examination of two, or preferably several or many, sets of scores for the same persons at different points in time (see Siegler, 1975).

On the other hand, longitudinal designs are themselves affected by "terminal drop" if the phenomenon, in fact, does exist. Siegler (1975:170) points out that older age groups represent an "increasingly elite group and may mask declines that exist in the population." Survivors tend to perform at a higher level than those who do not survive (Riegel and Riegel, 1972). Moreover, refusal rates are often higher for older persons, and frequently poor health is given as the reason for refusing (Siegler, 1975). The importance of the longitudinal design lies in the fact that *trends* in performance may be analyzed, and thus the terminal drop hypothesis can be tested directly. For example, the Wechsler Adult Intelligence Scale (WAIS) may be given to a group of older perons two or three times, for example, at ages 60, 65, and 70 years. Trends in scores between the ages of 60 and 70 years may be compared, for example, for those subjects who die before their seventy-fifth birthday and those who

Table 12-1. Descriptive characteristics of terminal drop studies*

Study	Ages	IQ range	Average health	Analytic strategy	
				Cross-sectional	Longitudinal
Moosehaven	65-79	94-104	Below	No	Yes
NYS Twins	69-76	100-106	Average	Yes	Yes
Bath VA	50-84	100	Below	Yes	Yes
Chicago	65-91	100-104	Below	Yes	Yes
Hamburg	55-75+	100-104	Average	Yes	Yes
NIH	65-91	108-120	Above	Yes	No
Newcastle	60-75+	100	Average	Yes	No
Duke	60-94	100-104	Average	Yes	Yes

*Modified from Siegler, I. C. *Experimental Aging Research,* 1975, **1**, 169. Reprinted by permission of the author and publishers of *Experimental Aging Research.* © EAR, Inc., 1975.

live on into their eighties. Siegler points to the fact that the problem of bias can be minimized if the objective of the study is to describe surviving individuals. In other words, for longitudinal data analysis the number of subjects at each measurement point (age) should be limited to the survivors who share all data points, and nonsurvivor data should be analyzed separately and compared with survivor data.

In a comprehensive review of the literature, Siegler (1975) examined eight extensive studies, which included either a cross-sectional analysis (i.e., tested the relationships between performance and survival or distance-from-death) and/or a longitudinal analysis (i.e., tested the terminal drop hypothesis directly). A summary of the subject characteristics and analytic strategies employed in these studies is presented in Table 12-1.

Survivors as opposed to nonsurvivors

Siegler (1975) concluded that five of the eight studies supported a *positive relationship between survivorship and a high level of cognitive performance at a given measurement point* (i.e., cross-sectional data analysis). The remaining three studies, which did not support this positive relationship, dealt with institutionalized subjects. These studies were characterized by participants in poor physical health relative to the other studies (see Berkowitz, 1953; Berkowitz and Green, 1963; 1965; Remains and Green, 1971, for an evaluation of Wechsler-Bellevue (W-B) scores in the Bath VA studies). One important investigation, in terms of physiological correlates of behavior (the Moosehaven studies), demonstrated a relationship between slowing of brain wave frequencies, measured by electroencephalographic (EEG) recordings and decline in intellectual performance with greater slowing for nonsurvivors than for survivors (e.g., Obrist et al., 1962). Moreover, when the performance of less healthy subjects in three studies (Moosehaven, Bath VA, and Chicago) was compared with the performance of above-average healthy subjects in the National Institutes of Health (NIH) study, it became clear that *physical health was not only important for survival but for maintenance of many cognitive abilities* (see Siegler, 1975).

In her review, Siegler (1975) noted that the Newcastle studies were designed to examine the relationship between intellectual performance and several psychiatric diagnostic categories. None of the patients diagnosed as brain damaged on initial testing was alive when retesting was conducted three and one-half years later. A similar relationship between psychiatric diagnosis and survivorship was found in a study by Hall and co-workers (1972). Of thirty-five subjects who were diagnosed as having either senile or arteriosclerotic dementia (types of organic brain damage), only one subject survived four years after initial testing. Moreover, in the Newcastle studies, 40% of the patients with functional psychiatric disorders (i.e., those presumably unrelated to brain damage) did not survive to be retested. When the subjects with functional psychiatric disorders and brain damage were removed from the analysis and scores at initial testing were adjusted for age differences at initial testing, only the comprehension subtest and the full-scale score on the WAIS discriminated between survivors and nonsurvivors. These results, summarized by Siegler (1975), emphasize the relationship between both mental and physical health and cognitive performance. Most importantly, they demonstrate the necessity of controlling for health factors in studies designed to assess cognitive changes with increasing age.

It is interesting to note that survivorship may not be related to all varieties of psychological change over time. For example, Powers and Bultena (1972) found no differences between survivors and nonsurvivors (those who died within eleven years after initial testing) in terms of self-reported satisfaction with life. However, we cannot conclude that survivorship is related solely to cognitive change, since far too few studies have examined other behavioral variables.

Distance-from-death

What implications do the survivor as opposed to nonsurvivor data have with regard to distance-from-death as an index of importance in aging studies? Do persons perform more poorly with nearness to death? Siegler (1975) states that in every cross-sectional analysis reporting a relationship between high levels of performance and survival, the survivors were further from death than the nonsurvivors at any specific point in time, but she argues that these studies do not provide a direct test of the relationship between peformance and distance-from-death because subjects were grouped only into survivors and nonsurvivors rather than groups based on distance-from-death. An alternative way of directly assessing the issue is to give each subject a score based on the number of years between initial testing and death (distance-from-death) and to correlate these scores with performance scores at initial testing. Siegler (1975) cites studies by Wilkie and Eisdorfer (1974, the Duke longitudinal studies) and Berkowitz (1965, the Bath VA studies) as indicating no significant correlation between distance-from-death and WAIS or W-B measures, and a study by Lieberman (1965) in which change scores, not absolute level of performance, were related to distance-from-death. Riegel and Riegel (1972) have presented data from the Hamburg studies, which suggest that distance-from-death was an important variable with regard to five verbal tests. However, Siegler views these data as only "tentative evidence" because statistical analyses were not performed.

In Siegler's (1975) estimation the Newcastle studies represent a very careful examination of distance-from-death and WAIS performance (see Savage et al., 1973). Survivors (persons who lived at least seven years past the first time of measurement) and those who died between four and seven years after initial testing were not different from each other when WAIS scores were adjusted statistically for initial age differences by covariance analysis. However, these survivors and nonsurvivors were significantly different from a group who survived even less time after the examination with respect to verbal, performance, and total scaled scores. This latter group included persons who died *within* four years of the initial examination.

Siegler (1975) has also summarized data from the Duke longitudinal studies, in which the distance-from-death variable was evaluated over a twenty-year period. These data indicated that distance-from-death on total WAIS scores and performance on individual subtests were positively related. In this case the same results were observed when scores obtained on initial testing were adjusted for age.

Two important points emerge from Siegler's review: (1) *When distance-from-death is correlated with performance scores, the correlations are usually not significant when the range of times prior to death* (initial testing to time of death) *are restricted* (narrow range) *or when the samples contain persons with some kind of functional or organic disorder;* and (2) *when studies are done within a broad range of times before death and with initially healthy subjects, distance-from-death is an important predictor of performance.*

Direct tests of the terminal drop hypothesis

Of the studies listed in Table 12-1, Siegler (1975) noted that six studies included data relevant to the terminal drop hypothesis (longitudinal analysis) and that five of the six studies supported the terminal drop hypothesis. For example, in the Moosehaven study thirty-seven subjects who survived at least six years past the second time of measurement were compared with thirty-three subjects who died within six years of the second time of measurement. The subjects were equal in age at the first and second times of measurement (73 and 79 years). Survivors declined 0.98 point per year on the Wechsler-Bellevue test, but nonsurvivors dropped 1.99 points per year (see Obrist, Henry, and Justiss, 1961).

The NYS Twin studies involved a unique approach to evaluation of the terminal drop hypothesis. Siegler (1975:180-181) has elaborated on the method used.

> In the NYS Twin studies, the concept of critical loss was used to assess changes in performance over an eight year period. The highest and lowest of the three examinations were any two of the three following: any loss in vocabulary, annual rate of decline of 10% in similarities, and annual rate of decline of 2% in digit symbol substitution. Thus, all subjects participated for a minimum of eight years. Then subjects who died within five years were compared with those who survived an additional five years after T_3.
>
> In 1960, 29 of 24 subjects were correctly classified. In 1973, 53 of 62 subjects were correctly classified. That is, survival was related to no critical loss, or critical loss on only 1 of the three subtests, and death was related to critical loss on two or three of the subtests. In evaluating 26 surviving co-twin pairs, critical loss correctly predicted death within pairs (the twin with critical loss died first) (Jarvik and Blum, 1971).

In the Duke studies, Wilkie and Eisdorfer (1974) compared thirty-seven nonsurvivors with sixty-six survivors and matched these groups so that everyone had participated in the study for fifteen years. Performance was evaluated at 74, 77, and 80 years of age. Survivors were defined as those alive more than four years after the final testing at 80 years of age. The data provide partial support for the terminal drop hypothesis. First, only those who died between thirteen and thirty-two months exhibited significant losses on verbal, performance, and total WAIS scores over the period of testing. Those who survived did not change significantly over the six-year period. However, those who died within one year did not change significantly either. Thus the group who survived for the least number of years and the group who survived for the greatest number of years did not show change.

A more recent and sophisticated analysis of the Duke longitudinal data (Palmore and Cleveland, 1976) has led to the notion that three conceptually different time-related performance curves are important and should be distinguished from each other. The first curve would indicate gradual changes, which are a product of the aging process, per se. The second curve would relate to *terminal decline,* that is, a steady, *linear* decline beginning at some point prior to death and continuing to shortly before death. The third curve would refer to the process of *terminal drop,* that is, a *curvilinear* or accelerating decline occurring shortly before death. Palmore and Cleveland (1976) applied a series of multiple regression analyses to the Duke longitudinal data (physical, psychological, and social measures), which allowed them to separate the effects of aging decline, terminal decline, and terminal drop statistically. Their results are summarized as follows (Palmore and Cleveland, 1976:80-81).

> These analyses found: (1) there was no substantial terminal drop, (2) all the health measures showed substantial aging declines, and physical function showed an additional substantial terminal decline, (3) intelligence had a large aging decline and a small but significant terminal decline, (4) several activities had strong aging declines, but none had significant terminal decline, and (5) most of the attitudes and adjustment measures had small or insignificant aging declines and little or no terminal decline.

Thus what may have been interpreted as evidence for the terminal drop hypothesis in previous studies may be described more accurately as terminal decline, a process which itself is relatively independent of gradual patterns of decline with increasing age but, in all probability, is related to either subclinical or observable declines in general health.

Both Palmore and Cleveland (1976) and Siegler (1975) point out that there are large individual differences in patterns of intellectual growth and decline in various studies and note that these patterns are impossible to isolate when large sample statistics are applied. Furthermore, these authors indicate that some intervening disease process can usually be identified when individuals show a sharp decline in performance between testings (e.g., 10 or more points on WAIS full-scale performance).

In summary, the literature regarding terminal drop does not suggest a clear and unqualified support for this hypothesis. Siegler (1975) notes that questions still remain concerning the extent to which "terminal drop" data reflect artifacts of measurement as opposed to changes in underlying function of the brain as a person approaches the end of life. She suggests that the question is complicated by the fact that there are changes in the brain which may be viewed as normal to the aging process, whereas others reflect disease processes which increase in incidence with increasing age, for example, cardiovascular disease, cerebrovascular disease, hypertension, and organic damage of a diffuse nature. Clearly, it is important that persons in poor health initially be removed from samples and that health variables be continually assessed in the remaining subjects if the terminal drop hypothesis is to be tested adequately.

The question psychologists may ask, then, is what has the terminal drop hypothesis contributed to an understanding of the process of aging? The answer is straightforward. It has caused attention to be directed to the effects of health on cognitive performance and several interrelated relationships of importance: (1) High levels of intellectual performance are positively related to survival; (2) the higher the level of performance is the greater is distance-from-death, the better is physical health, and the less likely it is that organic brain damage or functional psychiatric disorders will be present. These relationships are so important that we devote the remaining portions of this chapter to them.

CARDIOVASCULAR DISEASE

The general term *cardiovascular disease* includes a number of diseases commonly found among middle-aged and elderly persons. In this section we are primarily concerned with chronic coronary and peripheral artery disease (arteriosclerosis and atherosclerosis), coronary heart disease (e.g., "heart attack"), and hypertension. These diseases are distinguished from similar degenerative diseases that involve cerebral functioning (e.g., cerebral arteriosclerosis and stroke). The latter diseases are discussed in the section on organic brain damage.

Before beginning the discussion of the various behavioral effects of cardiovascular disease, a few definitions are appropriate. The term *arteriosclerosis* refers to "a group of vascular diseases characterized morphologically by hardening of the vessel wall [Kolb, 1968:243]." The term *atherosclerosis,* generally considered a more serious disease, refers to a condition ". . . characterized by the narrowing or obliteration of the lumen. It is an occlusive disease that affects the nutrient vessels of the brain, heart, or kidney, and by progressively choking off the flow of blood, leads to functional alteration and even to disability or death [Kolb, 1968:243]." Arteriosclerosis occurs almost inevitably with advancing age (Kolb, 1968), but it may be relatively insignificant if it produces little interference with blood flow. Many authors appear to use both terms, arteriosclerosis and atherosclerosis, to refer to an occlusive process within the blood vessels. A few authors prefer to use the term *atherothrombosis* when referring to the most common form of peripheral vascular disease. It includes the processes of atherosclerosis and thrombosis (i.e., development of a blood clot that blocks a blood vessel) (Wright, 1970).

Hypertension refers to a chronic condition characterized by abnormally high blood pressure. Frequently, the etiology of hypertensive disease is unknown and cannot be determined by the physician. In this case the disease is commonly referred to as *essential hypertension.* Blood pressure is "a function of the *amount* of blood pumped by the heart per unit time and the *diameters* of the vessels through which the blood must pass [Grossman, 1967:509]." *Diastolic blood pressure* refers to the minimum pressure occurring during the diastole (relaxation) phase of the cardiac cycle. *Systolic blood pressure* refers to the maximum pressure occurring during the systole (contraction) phase of the cardiac cycle. Most readers are probably aware that normal blood pressure, taken at rest, is approximately 120 (systolic)/80 (diastolic) mm Hg (millimeters of mercury). However, the definition of hypertension may vary from study to study. Light (1975) classified subjects whose blood pressure exceeded 140 mm Hg systolic or 90 mm Hg diastolic as hypertensive. Future studies in our laboratory will employ a measure known as *mean arterial pressure* (systolic – diastolic/3 + diastolic). This measure is particularly useful if one wishes to assess the severity of hypertension (e.g., mean arterial pressure = 107 – 110, mild; 115 – 125, moderate; 133+, severe). In classifying hypertensive and normotensive subjects, it is important to take the average of many readings (e.g., 40 measurements), since rather extreme fluctuations are not uncommon.

The most widely investigated psychological variables that are thought to be affected by the various types of cardiovascular disease are intellectual functioning (e.g., WAIS performance) and psychomotor performance (slowing of response). Abrahams (1976a) has noted that these effects have been found for both young and old subjects and may even occur when the diseases are mild or asymptomatic (e.g., Birren, Butler, Greenhouse, Sokoloff, and Yarrow, 1963; Spieth, 1964; 1965). However, much more research needs to be done before it can be concluded that asymptomatic (benign) hypertension has a deleterious effect on performance.

The relationship between cardiovascular disease and behavior has also been studied in "reverse" fashion; that is, a number of authors have attempted to define behavioral precursors of cardiovascular disease (e.g., Henry and Cassel, 1969; Rosenman, 1974; Torgersen and Kringlen, 1971). Thus, as will be seen in the sections that follow, it is likely that behavior and disease (or behavior and health) stand in a reciprocal cause-and-effect relationship to each other.

Behavioral predispositions to cardiovascular disease

One major concern within the fields of geriatrics and gerontology is the identification of early predictors of disease in order that appropriate preventive measures may be taken. Thus many investigators have attempted to identify potential behavioral precursors of cardiovascular disease (e.g., Brown and Ritzman, 1967; Nowlin et al., 1973). Eisdorfer and Wilkie (in press) have presented an excellent review of the literature concerned with the relationship between various premorbid personality factors and the development of cardiovascular disease.

Hypertension. Eisdorfer and Wilkie (in press) state that the findings with regard to premorbid behavioral characteristics and hypertension have been contradictory, "depending in part upon the population studied, techniques used to assess behavior, whether the study was prospective or retrospective and the operational definitions of disease categories used." For example, the results of one study, which focused on monozygotic twins (age range = 33 to 65 years), suggested that the twin who had higher systolic blood pressure as an adult had been more submissive, quiet, withdrawn, obedient, and insecure during childhood (Torgersen and Kringlen, 1971). In this study the assessment technique for determination of childhood behavior was an interview during the adult years. On the other hand, Harris and Singer (1967) conducted an eleven-year longitudinal study in an attempt to identify the behavioral precursors of essential hypertension. Their prehypertensive, college-aged women were characterized as having more abrasive, hostile, and tense interactions with other persons relative to a normotensive control group.

Eisdorfer and Wilkie (in press) have pointed out that hypertensive persons are commonly thought to have exaggerated blood pressure responses to environmental stressors. These responses are often transient during the early stages of the disease, but they have a cumulative effect such that continuous stressful events lead to sustained hypertension. In this context, state Eisdorfer and Wilkie (in press), stressful events consist of situations "where aspirations are blocked, meaningful human interactions are restricted, and the outcome of events is uncertain." A further hypothesis suggests that, among aged persons, hypertension may be the result of failure to adapt to ambiguous situations presented by rapidly occurring cultural change (Eisdorfer and Wilkie, in press). However, at present there are little adequate data to support either of these hypotheses.

Moreover, it is probably wise to explore physiologically based causes of hypertension (yet unknown) before generalizing too readily about psychological and sociocultural factors. There is no doubt that these social-behavioral factors can sometimes influence dramatic increases in blood pressure in persons who show blood pressure lability. However, one must examine carefully the physiological basis of lability and the predisposition to exhibit a rise in blood pressure in response to a stressor. Sustained high blood pressure may be conditioned in some cases, but there must be a physiological basis to the unconditionable variable (rise in blood pressure) that occurs in response to a stressor or to a threat stimulus (conditionable stimulus).

Coronary heart disease. As is true for hypertension, the literature on behavioral predispositions to coronary heart disease (e.g., myocardial infarct) has led to contradictory conclusions regarding behavior (Eisdorfer and Wilkie, in press). For example, several researchers found that middle-aged and older individuals who develop coronary disease tend to report high levels of anxiety prior to the onset of their illnesses (Bakker, 1968; Nowlin et al., 1973). On the other hand, many persons who develop coronary diseases fail to exhibit these high levels of anxiety (Caffrey, 1969; Rosenman, 1974). Eisdorfer and Wilkie (in press) have suggested that part of the problem with current data may be related to different definitions attributed to the concept of anxiety; specifically, "We may confuse 'trait' anxiety to represent neuroticism, as measured by psychological tests, with 'state' anxiety, as measured specific to the situation or with arousal, as measured by neuroendocrine activity."

Perhaps the most popular and comprehensive description of the behavioral precursors of coronary disease has been the "Type A" pattern conceptualized by Rosenman and his colleagues (see Rosenman, 1974; Rosenman and Friedman, 1971). Eisdorfer and Wilkie (in press) have summarized the cluster of behaviors typical of the Type A individual.

> The Type A pattern has been defined as a style of living characterized by excesses of competitiveness, striving for achievement, aggressiveness, time urgency, restlessness, acceleration of common activities (e.g., walking, eating), hostility, hyperalertness, explosiveness of speech amplitude, tenseness of facial musculature, and feelings of struggling against the limitations of time and insensitivity of the environment. The Type A person is punctual and greatly annoyed if kept waiting. In his impatience, he anticipates what others will say and frequently interrupts to answer questions before they are fully asked. The Type A behavior pattern is not a personality trait (Jenkins, et al., 1974), but is associated with traits which emerge when certain challenges or conditions of the milieu arise in susceptible individuals (Rosenman, 1974).

Those persons whose typical behavior is characterized by an absence of the Type A pattern are referred to as "Type B" individuals. It is fairly obvious that only a small percentage of the population (about 10%) will exhibit a complete Type A or Type B pattern (Rosenman and Friedman, 1971). Nonetheless, Rosenman and his colleagues have conducted an extensive longitudinal investigation of Type A and Type B men, aged 39 to 59 years. All subjects were without clinical signs of coronary heart disease at the beginning of the study and were classified as Type A or Type B individuals at that time. Subsequent data were collected two and one-half, four and one-half, and eight and one-half years after the initial evaluations. Rosenman (1974) has reported that those individuals who manifested the Type A pattern were about twice as likely to develop coronary disease when compared with the Type B men. In addition to the increased probability of coronary problems, the Type A behavior pattern was associated with several physiological indices (e.g., elevated serum cholesterol levels), which themselves are related to coronary heart disease.

Interestingly, the Type A behavior pattern is a rather poor predictor of coronary heart disease in older individuals; that is, it is a statistically significant predictor between the ages of 35 and 49 years, but after 50 years of age Type A and Type B individuals no longer have a differential risk for coronary disease (Rosenman et al., 1970). Abrahams (in press) has suggested that this lack of predictive power for older age groups may be due to selective dropout of about-to-be-diseased Type A persons who are over 50 years of age. On the other hand, there is some evidence that the physiological correlates of the Type A pattern may also be less predictive among older individuals. For example, Thompson and colleagues (1965) found that serum cholesterol levels are not related to clinical symptoms of cardiovascular disease for persons between the ages of 60 and 93 years. Unfortunately, little work has been done with Type A or B women. Consequently, one cannot be sure that the behavioral and physiological manifestations of the Type A pattern are unrelated to coronary heart disease among older women.

In addition to the usual characteristics associated with the Type A pattern, there is some evidence that behaviors which are present in individuals subsequent to the development of coronary disease are also present in healthy individuals who manifest Type A behavior. For example, Abrahams and Birren (1973) evaluated the psychomotor performance of Type A and B men 40 to 60 years of age. Abrahams (1976a:335) has summarized the results of this study as follows.

> The Type A subjects exhibited significant response slowing in both simple and 3-choice RT tasks when compared to noncoronary-prone (Type B) subjects of the same age. Additionally, the Type A subjects were disproportionately slower than the Type B subjects on the choice RT task (relative to the simple RT task). Thus, even in the absence of clinical cardiovascular disease, males who were behaviorally predisposed to coro-

nary disease manifested significant slowing of psychomotor performance similar to that reported to occur in subjects with clinical cardiovascular disease.

It appears that the exploration of Type A and B behavior patterns has been profitable, at least with regard to middle-aged men. At this point, however, behavioral scientists need to know much more. Why does the predictive power of the Type A pattern diminish with age? Are the patterns typical of women as well as men? Can Type A behavior be modified (e.g., environmental challenges and conflicts removed; see Rosenman, 1974), and if so, is the risk factor for coronary heart disease reduced? Clearly, this area of research has led to a number of important findings, and many interesting questions remain to be answered.

Slowing of response

In previous chapters, we have noted that a general slowing of response appears to be characteristic of most older subjects, especially when task requirements involve complex decision making. Thus, for all practical purposes, this psychomotor slowing is considered to be part of the "normal" aging process. We turn now to the issue of a possible relationship between impaired physical health and exaggerated psychomotor slowing. Birren (1965:199) has suggested that at least two factors contribute to the speed of behavior: "a primary age factor of subcortical basis reflected in all or most processes mediated by the central nervous system, and a factor of cortical integrity influenced by disease, particularly those resulting in local cell loss and interference with circulation and ischemia." Regardless of whether or not one accepts the specific physiological bases (e.g., cell loss) suggested by Birren's statement, his view succinctly raises the question of an additional slowing of response that may be superimposed on the "normal" aging curve of decline in speed for those older adults suffering from diseases such as hypertension and arteriosclerosis.

The first intensive investigation of the relationship between psychomotor slowing and cardiovascular disease was conducted by Spieth (1964; 1965). His subjects (all men; age range = 35 to 69 years) were drawn from a population of military or civil airplane pilots, air traffic controllers, and outside volunteers. All subjects were of above-average intelligence and socioeconomic level. Spieth divided his subjects into a number of groups based on their specific physical diagnoses (e.g., arteriosclerosis, hypertension), whether or not they were taking medication, and whether or not they were under certification stress, that is, possible revocation of their medical certification to fly or control air traffic. All subjects were given a ten-choice serial reaction time task (adapted from the Psychomet test; Birren et al., 1962), the WAIS Digit-Symbol Substitution Test (Wechsler, 1955), and the Trail Making Test (Reitan, 1958). Scores from these three tests were combined into a "composite speed score."

Results indicated that arteriosclerotic subjects performed more poorly than healthy subjects. The findings for hypertensive subjects were less clear because certification stress was confounded with the taking of antihypertensive medication. Basically, subjects who were stressed and were not taking medication exhibited very slow performance, whereas the nonstressed, medicated group performed equally as well as the healthy subjects.

Abrahams (1976a) has noted that a number of more recent studies have corroborated Spieth's results. For example, Botwinick and Storandt (1974a) found that self-reported cardiovascular symptoms (Cornell Medical Index) were significantly related to slower reaction times regardless of age (subjects ranged in age from 20 to 28 and 64 to 74 years). In this study there was also a significant positive relationship between cardiovascular status and depression (SDS scale; Zung, 1967), a situation that might have been expected, since cardiovascular status was based on self-report. Since reaction time was significantly related to depression, Botwinick and Storandt (1974a) suggested that cardiovascular symptoms (at least as determined by self-report), depression, and reaction time may, in fact, be interdependent.

Other studies have led to the suggestion that the relationship between cardiovascular status and psychomotor response may be more complex than Spieth's results suggested. In comparing the reaction time performance of a group of very healthy older men (65+ years) and a group of men (65+ years) suffering from mild, asymptomatic, or subclinical disease (generally arteriosclerosis), Birren, Butler, Greenhouse, Sokoloff, and Yarrow (1963) reported similar declines for both groups relative to healthy, young subjects. However, Abrahams (1976a) noted that subclinical disease probably did have adverse effects on reaction time, since "significant correlations were found between mean arterial blood pressure, systolic blood pressure, diastolic blood pressure, and a factor component of speed and timing of behavior . . ." in the less healthy group. However, keep in mind that most of these subjects showed evidence of arteriosclerosis in addition to elevations in blood pressure.

Recently, Light (1975) elaborated on Spieth's (1964; 1965) results using a larger sample of hypertensive and normotensive subjects (age range = 18 to 59 years). In addition to examining the relationships among blood pressure, age, and reaction time, she was interested in the effects of various levels of plasma renin activity (PRA) on the reaction time (RT) performance of medicated and unmedicated hypertensive subjects. Plasma renin activity is currently used as one of several classificatory variables for persons suffering from essential hypertension. Light (1975:210) has explained the physiological action of renin as follows.

> Renin is a substance (hormone) normally produced by the kidney when a fall in blood pressure occurs and threatens the kidney's perfusion. It has no pressor properties in itself, but one of its products, angiotensin, acts on arteriolar smooth muscle to produce contraction. This contraction increases vascular resistance and thus raises blood pressure so that adequate blood flow through the kidney and other vital organs is maintained (Berman and Vertes, 1973).

Light (1975) noted that hypersecretion of renin usually occurs when hypertension is caused by, or results in, kidney damage. However, among persons with essential hypertension, most have normal PRA levels and approximately 25% have low PRA levels. Furthermore, she reported the results of a longitudinal study in which 11% of normal PRA and 14% of high PRA hypertensive subjects suffered either cardiovascular or cerebrovascular infarcts over a period of four and one-half years. However, none of the subjects with low PRA levels experienced infarction during this time (Brunner et al., 1972). Light (1975:211) reasoned that, "If the variable of renin level is prognostically important, it may also be related to early changes in function, such as RT slowing, which may precede more drastic complications."

The subjects in Light's study were divided into three age groups: 18 to 31, 32 to 45, and 46 to 59 years. Hypertensive subjects were further classified into groups based on PRA levels and whether or not they were receiving antihypertensive medication. However, there was a complicating factor in this study, which occurred because of the screening procedure used to determine the source of hypertension; that is, all hypertensive subjects who had been taking medication discontinued its use 3 to 21 days prior to testing, and regardless of previous medication record, all hypertensive subjects were given a potent diuretic just prior to behavioral testing so that their blood pressures fell within the normal range. The behavioral test battery consisted of twelve serial reaction time tasks similar to those described by Spieth (1964; 1965).

The results of Light's study showed that serial reaction time, as expected, increased with age, especially for the more complex tasks. Interestingly, only the *medicated* hypertensive subjects exhibited slower reaction times than the normotensive group. This finding stands in direct contradiction to Spieth's results, in which *unmedicated* hypertensive subjects were significantly slower than normotensive subjects. Keep in mind, however, that Light's subjects had discontinued taking their antihypertensive medication prior to testing, and thus it is not known how they might have performed had they been receiving drugs at the time the test battery was given, or is it possible to evaluate the effect that the diuretic might have had on either the medicated or the unmedicated group. Spieth's unmedicated subjects were tested with elevated blood pressures, although his medicated group had normal blood pressures because of the antihypertensive drugs they were taking. In both studies the blood pressure by age interaction was not significant.

The relationship of PRA and reaction time (RT) performance of hypertensive subjects

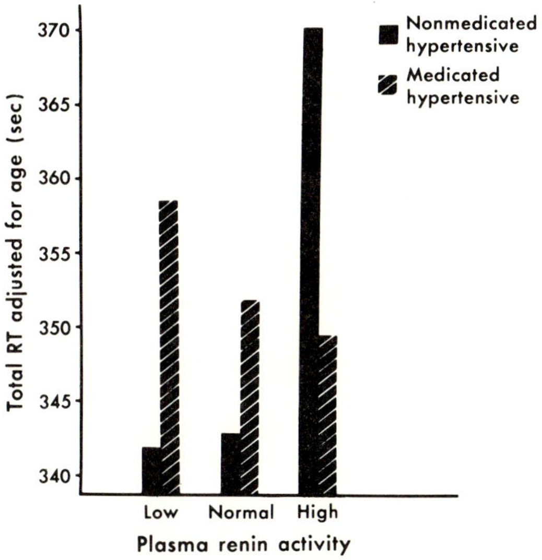

Fig. 12-1. Reaction time (RT) performance of hypertensive subjects as a function of medication and plasma renin activity (PRA). (From Light, K. C. *Experimental Aging Research,* 1975, **1**, 209. By permission of author and editor. © EAR, Inc., 1975.)

proved to be highly complex. Fig. 12-1 depicts the results of the significant drug treatment by renin level interaction. Essentially, medicated hypertensive subjects with low PRA levels exhibited slower reaction times than those with normal or high PRA levels. For unmedicated hypertensive subjects, the opposite trend was found: high PRA levels were associated with slower reaction times.

Light (1975) interpreted these results in terms of the different etiologies for hypertension associated with high, normal, and low levels of plasma renin activity. As noted earlier, high renin hypertension is associated with renal arterial insufficiency. It is most common among younger adults and produces overt symptoms, such as headache. Thus it is likely to be diagnosed and treated before severe and irreversible vascular changes occur. The result of treatment is the maintenance of good cerebral circulation and, consequently, better reaction time performance. Low renin hypertensive subjects tend to have greater blood volume expansion and less vasoconstriction than normal or high PRA subjects. The low PRA subjects in this study were older than the subjects with normal and high PRA levels and thus had more time to develop sclerotic vascular damage, which has been shown to be associated with impaired cerebral blood flow autoregulation. Light further postulated that taking of medication may have increased the inefficiency of cerebral autoregulation. (Remember, only the medicated, low PRA subjects had excessively slow reaction times relative to the normal and high PRA subjects.) Specifically, she suggested that, since maintenance of cerebral blood flow is difficult when blood pressure is lowered in these subjects (see Bentson et al., 1975), the use of medication to lower blood pressure might actually increase the risk of cerebral ischemia and thus result in poorer performance. Light's interpretation is extremely complex and involves a considerable degree of speculation. However, she is currently engaged in examining the relationship of cerebral blood flow and performance among hypertensive subjects, and hopefully, supportive evidence for her hypotheses will be forthcoming.

In a study employing the same patients that had participated in Light's study at Upstate Medical Center in Syracuse, Watson (unpublished master's thesis, Syracuse University, 1976) compared medicated, middle-aged hypertensive subjects with normotensive controls. He used an information-processing paradigm in which the subjects were asked to match stimulus 1 with stimulus 2 on the basis of some defined set of rules. The shorter the time was between the two stimuli (SOA) the less time the subjects had to encode the stimuli.

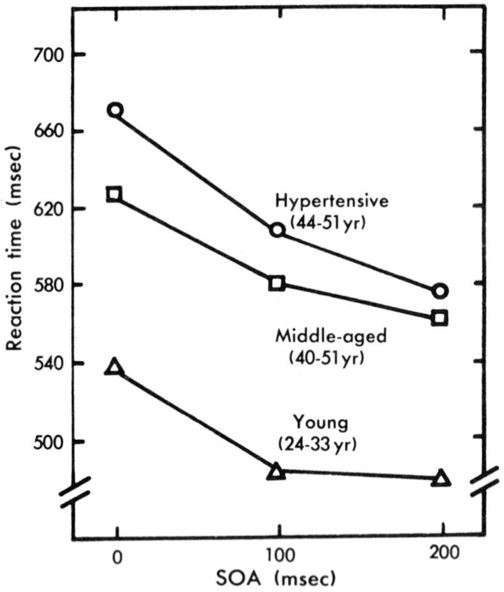

Fig. 12-2. Reaction time performance of young and middle-aged normotensive subjects and middle-aged hypertensive subjects as a function of interstimulus interval (SOA). (From Watson, W. E. Unpublished master's thesis, Syracuse University, Syracuse, N.Y., 1976; by permission of the author.)

There were no statistically significant differences between the middle-aged, blood pressure groups in reaction time performance using this information-processing paradigm. More important, Watson found that the time required to encode the stimuli was no greater for the hypertensive than for the normotensive subjects. Fig. 12-2 shows Watson's curves for the middle-aged control group, the medicated hypertensive group, and a young, nonhypertensive group. The latter group differed from the two former groups in absolute level of performance (height of the curves) but not in the slopes of the curves. Any differences in the slopes of the curves would have indicated a difference in the encoding of stimulus 1 to match it with stimulus 2.

Watson's data are consistent with the literature, which shows no reaction time differences between medicated hypertensive subjects and normotensive subjects (e.g., Spieth, 1964; 1965) and do not agree with Light's (1975) findings. Remember, Light found that medicated hypertensive subjects exhibited longer reaction times than nonmedicated hypertensive and control subjects. It should be noted, however, that Watson used a different task and fewer subjects, and his subjects were not under the influence of a potent diuretic as they were when Light performed her reaction time tests. It is possible that, with an increased number of subjects and a nonmedicated hypertensive group, Watson would have found differences between medicated and nonmedicated subjects in his study. Nevertheless, the magnitude of the effect and percent variance accounted for has been consistently small in reaction time studies. Even in Light's study, significant differences in reaction time between medicated hypertensive subjects and controls were so small as to be of little practical significance. Thus these studies may tell researchers something about how the brain is potentially influenced by hypertension (i.e., since the brain influences test performance), but they reveal little of a practical nature about hypertension. Studies of WAIS performance and clinical tests of brain damage address themselves to the issue of the practical significance of hypertension. Generally, it has a practical impact on the life of the individual if it is no longer asymptomatic, but it has caused changes in cerebral blood flow and end organs, such as the heart and cerebral vasculature of the brain. In these cases, hypertension is a symptom, and the causes and results of the hypertension exert a deleterious influence on behavior; that is, they begin to affect important intellectual abilities adversely.

Cognitive decline

During the past ten years, gerontological researchers have shown a considerable amount of interest in the potential relationships among cardiovascular disease, cognitive performance, and age. Early reports (Apter et al., 1951; Reitan, 1954) suggested that essential hypertension was associated with rather extensive intellectual impairment. However, Abrahams (1976a) has pointed out that these results are not typical of later investigations; that is, more recent studies suggest that, whereas some amount of intellectual deficit is common with cardiovascular disease, it is not nearly as severe as previously thought. Nonetheless, Abrahams (1976a:345) concluded the following:

> The vast weight of evidence has supported the hypothesis that cardiovascular diseases (coronary artery disease and arterial hypertension) are associated with intellectual decline. This relationship has been found among subjects of all ages, but has been reported to be particularly important in the elderly.

However, as we discuss the current literature, you will find that there are some important qualifications to this generalization.

The hypothesis of a recognizable decline in intellectual abilities in persons suffering from cardiovascular disease became increasingly popular after Spieth (1964; 1965) reported supporting evidence. He gave his subjects two "cognitive" tests (Halstead Tactual Performance Test and WAIS Block Design Test) in addition to the speed tests mentioned earlier. The Halstead test is of particular interest, since it involves the matching of geometrical forms and an untimed recall test for these forms. His combined pathology group (subjects with arteriosclerosis, coronary disease, and hypertension) performed more poorly than his healthy group on these tests. The greatest differences were for the more complex tasks. Spieth concluded that impairment in the pathology group occurred not in the "doing" but in the "deciding what to do" phase of the problem-solving process. None of Spieth's subjects was receiving medication at the time of testing, and many had suffered myocardial infarctions six months to several years prior to the study.

Many of the drugs currently in use for treatment of cardiovascular diseases, such as hypertension, had not been developed in the early 1960s. Recognition of the clinical importance of hypertension and other cardiovascular symptoms and related improvements in treatment and drug therapy partly account for the differences in results of early and later studies. In fact, Abrahams (1976a) has noted that those studies reporting no differences between diseased and healthy groups (Hertzog et al., 1975; Thompson et al., 1970) involved subjects who were receiving repeated health assessments (e.g., belonged to a health maintenance program). Thus these subjects were likely to receive early diagnosis and treatment.

Several important investigations of the relationship between cognitive decline and hypertension have emerged from the Duke longitudinal study (see the section on terminal drop). Wilkie and Eisdorfer (1971) reported the results of a ten-year longitudinal study concerned with blood pressure and WAIS performance. Their subjects were divided into two age groups (60 to 69 years and 70 to 79 years at initial testing) and three blood pressure groups based on diastolic pressures (normal BP = 66 to 95 mm Hg; borderline elevated BP = 96 to 105 mm Hg; high BP = 105+ mm Hg). Wilkie and Eisdorfer (1971:960) found that most of the subjects in the high blood pressure group showed evidence of end-organ change, that is, "a cardiac-thoracic ratio of more than 50 percent on the basis of actual measurements taken from x-ray photographs and clinical signs of eyeground changes of grade II or III." The borderline elevated and normotensive groups had significantly fewer end-organ changes than the hypertensive group. End-organ changes are indicative of prolonged and severe hypertension and are considered predictive of more serious cardiovascular disease and stroke. However, none of the subjects in this study showed clinical evidence of cerebrovascular disease. Unfortunately, the use of antihypertensive medication could not be controlled.

The results of Wilkie and Eisdorfer's (1971) study are summarized in Fig. 12-3 (WAIS performance scores). There was some intellectual decline over the ten-year period among the normotensive (*N*) subjects, especially for those aged 70 to 79 years. On the other hand, the 60- to 69-year-old borderline elevated group (*B*) exhibited an increase in scores. The 70- to 79-year-old borderline elevated subjects showed considerable decline, as did the 60- to 69-year-old hypertensive group (*H*). Unfortunately, all of the hypertensive subjects in the older group failed to return for the ten-year follow-up and, in fact, nonreturning hypertensive subjects in both age groups had the lowest, initial WAIS scores. Interestingly, verbal ability, as measured by the WAIS, did not decline for any of the blood pressure groups. Thus all full-scale score changes were a reflection of loss in performance scores (Fig. 12-3).

Wilkie and Eisdorfer (1971) concluded that high elevations in blood pressure are associated with intellectual loss, and among older subjects even mild elevations appear to be detrimental. Borderline elevations in blood pressure appeared to be beneficial among 60- to 69-year-olds, and the authors suggested that these mild elevations might be necessary to maintain cerebral circulation.

In a more recent longitudinal investigation, Wilkie and co-workers (1976) examined the relationship between hypertension and memory. Subjects were the same 60- to 69-

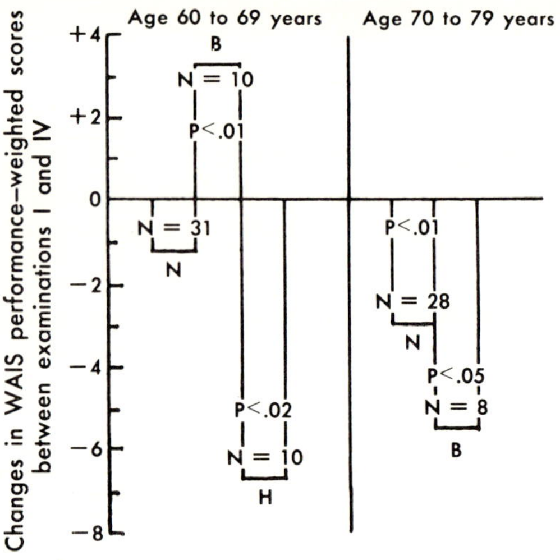

Fig. 12-3. Changes in WAIS performance scores over a ten-year period for two age groups of subjects with normal *(N)*, borderline elevated *(B)*, or heightened *(H)* blood pressures. (From Wilkie, F., and Eisdorfer, C. *Science,* 1971, **172,** 959. Copyright 1971 by the American Association for the Advancement of Science.)

year-old group employed in their previous study. They were given the Wechsler Memory Scale (Stone and Wechsler, 1945; Wechsler, 1945), which comprises three tasks: (1) logical memory (immediate and delayed recall of meaningful material), (2) paired-associate learning (six "easy" association pairs plus four "difficult" association pairs), and (3) visual reproductions (geometrical designs that must be reproduced from memory). These tests were administered on two occasions separated by about six and one-half years. Blood pressure groups were the same as those used in the earlier study, that is, normal, borderline elevated, and high.

Results indicated that initial performance on the Wechsler Memory Scale was similar for all blood pressure groups. On retesting, the high blood pressure group suffered a significant loss on the immediate recall task of the logical memory test and the visual reproductions test relative to the borderline elevated and normal blood pressure groups.

Wilkie and associates (1976) also examined group differences for each of the subtask items from logical memory and visual reproductions tests. They found that the high blood pressure group performed more poorly only on the first item of the logical memory test and the second design of visual reproductions test. In the latter test the initial design has one figure and the second and third designs both have two figures.

Wilkie and associates (1976:13) interpreted these results as follows:

> These findings suggest that the hypertensives' poorer performance on some memory tasks on the follow-up evaluation may be related more to performance factors than to memory deficits. Thus, their poor performance on the visual reproductions total score was primarily reflected in poor performance on one design (involving two figures). Their performance was not different from the remaining BP groups on the initial design (involving one figure) or on the third design (which also involved two figures). On the logical memory task, the hypertensives at the follow-up evaluation had difficulty recalling the first, but not the second passage read to them. These findings tend to suggest that their difficulty was not due to memory impairment or item difficulty but instead performance factors such as 'learning to learn', a change in set, or to state anxiety associated with the testing situation.

The authors also pointed out that their results are in accordance with a suggestion put forth by Spieth (1965); that is, his pathology group appeared to have more difficulty in "deciding what to do" rather than in "doing." Thus the poorer performance of hypertensive subjects may be related to factors such as test instructions, strategy, or anxiety rather than cognitive ability, per se.

A number of other investigators have focused on cognitive performance as measured by various tests from the Halstead Reitan Neuropsychological Test Battery for Adults. This battery was originally designed for assessment of the intactness of cerebral functions and has been shown to be highly sensitive to cognitive impairment resulting from brain damage (e.g., Reed and Reitan, 1962; Reitan, 1955).

Goldman and associates (1974) administered the Halstead Category Test to fourteen male subjects (mean age = 47.6 years; mean systolic pressure = 173 mm Hg; mean diastolic pressure = 118 mm Hg) who were diagnosed as having essential hypertension. This test is particularly sensitive to the ability to form concepts and change mental sets. The mean error score for these subjects was in the range suggestive of cerebral impairment and error scores correlated positively with diastolic pressures ($r = .52$). The correlation remained significant ($r = .48$) even after the effects of IQ were controlled. Goldman and associates (1974:572) concluded that, "Hypertension has neuropsychological as well as cardiovascular consequences." Remember, however, that the subjects in the study by Goldman's group had very high blood pressures, and none had been previously diagnosed or treated for hypertension. Thus the length of time they were suffering from this disease is not known; nor is it known if improvement in cognitive abilities might be demonstrated once their blood pressure was controlled by medication.

All of the human studies to date have had one problem or another with regard to the control of important variables that may influence poor performance as well as hypertension. Part of the problem in establishing a relationship between hypertension and behavior is that hypertension is a symptom, not a disease. Moreover, it has multiple causes, and there are as many different kinds of hypertension as there are causes. Remember, hypertension is a term that has been used to refer to any elevation in blood pressure of unknown or questionable etiology and that asymptomatic (benign) hypertension or essential hypertension is distinct from hypertension secondary to kidney damage, kidney tumor, etc. The many different syndromes that have been suggested for essential hypertension include (1) errors in sodium metabolism, (2) neurogenic hypertension involving epinephrine and norepinephrine and other biogenic amines, (3) adjustment of the threshold of vagal receptors, (4) renin (endocrine) hypertension, and (5) conditioning based on stress objects and predisposition to lability in blood pressure (D. H. P. Streeten, personal communication).* Some, but not all, types of hypertension may be associated with adverse influences on behavior because the physiological causes and the physiological results of a particular "type of hypertension" have the potential to influence behavior. Remember, an elevation in blood pressure has no direct effect on behavior itself. Studies to date have not come close to categorizing subjects into all the different classes of causative factors that potentially exist for hypertension.

In addition to hypertension, another symptom of impending cardiovascular disease is elevated serum cholesterol. Control of cholesterol levels, especially among middle-aged adults, has been stressed increasingly over the past several years by physicians and other health professionals. Reitan and Shipley (1963) conducted an investigation of the relationship between reduction of serum cholesterol levels and the maintenance of cognitive abilities, as measured by several tests from the Halstead Reitan Battery. Their subjects (age range = 25 to 65 years) received baseline determinations of serum cholesterol levels over a six-month period. Subjects who had average levels of 240 mg/100 ml were offered a one-year treatment program to control their cholesterol, either by dietary means or drugs. The Halstead-Reitan tests were administered before, during, and after the treatment phase of the study, and summary scores from the test battery were calculated for each time of testing.

The most important results from the Reitan and Shipley (1963) study are summarized in Fig. 12-4. Basically, reductions in serum cholesterol (by 10% or more) did not seem to make much difference prior to age 55. All subjects, 25 to 54 years of age, showed improvement relative to their initial test scores, a finding that may be attributed to practice effects. Among the older age groups, reduction in cholesterol levels was associated with maintenance of abilities. However, those subjects 60 to 64 years old who failed to reduce their cholesterol levels actually showed a decline in performance relative to their initial scores. Reitan and Shipley (1963) concluded that reduction in serum cholesterol levels is beneficial to the maintenance of cognitive abilities, especially for older men. It is interesting that serum cholesterol level has not been a particularly good predictor of coronary disease among older subjects (Thompson et al., 1965). The Reitan and Shipley study suggests that those individuals with high serum cholesterol levels who do survive into their sixties without developing coronary disease may be vulnerable to other detri-

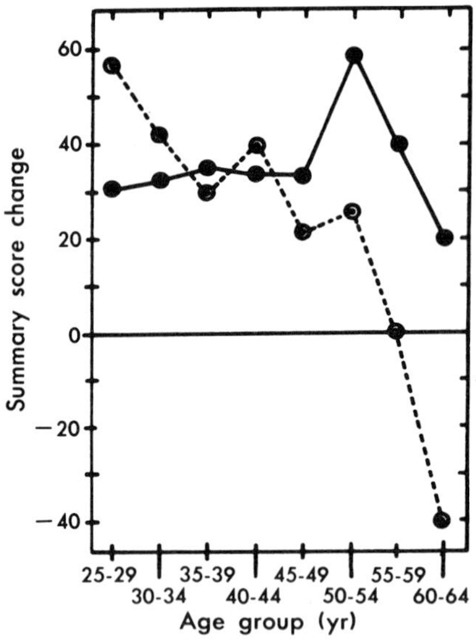

Fig. 12-4. Mean change scores (mean change for combined scores from eleven psychological tests) for performance on Halstead and Reitan tests as a function of age and serum cholesterol levels. Black (●——●) circles indicate scores for subjects whose serum cholesterol levels were lowered by 10% or more over a one-year period. Dotted (⊙——⊙) circles indicate scores for subjects whose serum cholesterol levels were lowered by less than 10%. (From Reitan, R. M., and Shipley, R. E. *Journal of Gerontology,* 1963, **18,** 350.)

*Dr. Streeten is Director of a hypertension clinic in the Department of Medicine at Upstate Medical Center (S.U.N.Y.), Syracuse, N.Y.

mental changes more closely associated with cerebral functioning.

Electroencephalographic correlates of cardiovascular disease

Most researchers agree that prolonged cardiovascular disease has the potential to impair cognitive performance eventually. Exactly why this effect occurs cannot always be determined. A number of authors have suggested that a reduction in cerebral blood flow may be the predominant physiological basis (e.g., Light, 1975). Other researchers have explored electroencephalograhic (EEG) changes in an attempt to describe the type of physiological change accompanying cardiovascular disease. Remember, however, that the EEG cannot explain *why* certain changes are occurring. It is merely a record of electrical brain activity, and abnormal activity can have a wide variety of different causes (e.g., atherosclerosis, stroke, or injury from external sources).

The most frequently studied aspect of the EEG is the alpha rhythm, which Thompson and Marsh (1973) have defined as "waves in the range of 8 to 13 cycles per second (cps)." Alpha rhythm has been shown to decrease as a function of age among healthy adults (mean frequency = 10.2 to 10.5 cps for young adults and 8.0 to 9.7 cps for elderly adults), and additional decreases have been found to be typical of patients with senile dementia and other forms of organic brain damage (Thompson and Marsh, 1973).

Alpha rhythm has also been observed to be slower for patients with arteriosclerosis, even when the symptoms appear to be mild or asymptomatic (Obrist, 1963; Obrist and Bissell, 1955). The basic argument proposed by many researchers is that a slowing of alpha rhythm is associated with vascular insufficiency and reduced cerebral blood flow (Obrist and Busse, 1965). Thus there are likely to be at least two factors (age and pathology) contributing to EEG changes among elderly adults.

Few studies have been done that involve measures of cognitive abilities in addition to EEG changes for persons with cardiovascular disease. However, Obrist and co-workers (1962) collected both WAIS and EEG data on a group of psychiatric patients, residents in a home for the elderly, and community volunteers. The obtained correlations ranged from .20 to .45 between alpha slowing and performance subtests. However, Thompson and Marsh (1973:118) interpreted their results as follows:

> When patients were grouped according to the presence or absence of arteriosclerosis, it became evident that this variable was contributing heavily to the relationship between EEG and test scores. Patients without arteriosclerosis showed no relationship between the two measures. The authors speculated that cardiovascular pathology is chiefly responsible for the observed results in this and other studies with similar findings.

You may recall that Wilkie and Eisdorfer (1971) suggested that borderline elevated blood pressure might be beneficial to the maintenance of cerebral circulation and, consequently, the maintenance of intellectual abilities. In this regard, Obrist, Busse, and Henry (1961) found that low blood pressure was associated with more diffuse EEG slowing than mildly elevated blood pressure among elderly psychiatric patients. To our knowledge, no conclusive tests of the relationships among age, EEG slowing, blood pressure, and cognitive abilities have been carried out, or have EEG changes and intellectual performance been simultaneously studied for borderline hypertensive subjects. However, this is an interesting and potentially profitable area of research, which hopefully, will provide answers to some of the many questions concerning cardiovascular disease and brain-behavior relationships.

Animal models for hypertension and behavior

Animals have been used in studies of hypertension and behavior to avoid the problems involved in experimental control. Studies of aggression, learning performance, activity, and alcohol consumption have been done. Some of these studies will be discussed in

Chapters 13 and 14 (behavior genetics), but some discussion is of value at this point.

Despite the fact that it is commonly assumed that hypertension is associated with increased aggressiveness and irritability (Sapira et al., 1971), evidence from the clinical literature indicates that subjects with hypertension exhibit less social aggression than do normal control subjects (Gressel et al., 1949). As with most clinical studies, many of the studies of aggressiveness and nonaggressiveness in hypertensive persons have not been able to control many important and potentially confounding factors. Unfortunately, the animal literature has not produced results that are as clear as one might hope.

Ben-Ishay and Welner (1969) have reported that rats susceptible to hypertension associated with high salt intake (Brookhaven sensitive) were *less* aggressive than a matched strain of rats that were hypertension resistant (Brookhaven resistant). However, Henry and colleagues (1967) found that the intensity of fighting for mice placed in social situations was not directly proportional to blood pressure values. Eichelman and co-workers (1973) replicated findings by Ben-Ishay and Welner (1969) but found that surgically induced hypertension failed to alter aggressive reactions to foot shock. In general, it may be seen that different results are obtained when hypertension is produced in different ways.

In a behavior-genetic study, Elias, Elias, and Schlager (1975) compared aggressive social behavior for mice selected genetically for blood pressure extremes. "Aggressor mice" from the high and low blood pressure lines (BP I lines) were pitted against mice that were also either from the high or the low blood pressure lines. These mice were referred to as "target mice" because they were secured to the "arena" in such a way as to place them in a defensive position. The low blood pressure mice exhibited the higher social aggression scores when the blood pressure group of the target was ignored in the statistical analysis. However, a blood pressure aggressor by blood pressure target interaction was observed. Essentially, the highest aggression scores were observed for the *low* blood pressure aggressors when they were pitted against the high blood pressure targets. Casual interpretation might suggest that low blood pressure causes increased aggression, which is exhibited more readily against an animal with high blood pressure. However, when high blood pressure mice from an entirely different stock (BP II) were tested, they were much more aggressive than the high blood pressure BP I mice. This makes the possibility doubtful that the relationship between aggression and blood pressure was causal. In fact, genetic manipulations (of a nature explained more fully in Chapter 14) suggested that the relationship may be explained by a linked-gene effect or a pleiotropic effect rather than a cause-effect relationship between blood pressure extremes and aggressive social behavior. We will define pleiotropic and linked-gene effects in Chapters 13 and 14. For now it is sufficient to say that correlations between behavior and a physiological phenotype, such as hypertension, may have a basis in genotype, and this possibility has been largely overlooked in animal studies.

In a series of studies with the BP I mice, Elias and Schlager (1974) found that the high blood pressure mice performed a water-maze discrimination task more poorly than the low blood pressure mice. In this instance, however, there was no age by blood pressure genotype interaction, and further genetic tests indicated that the blood pressure–behavior relationship was an accident of selection rather than a causal relationship, a linked-gene effect, or a pleiotropic effect.

Wood and Elias (reported in Elias, Wood, and Pentz, 1976) found that the high blood pressure mice of the BP I stock consumed more alcohol and were less active than low blood pressure mice. However, there was no age by blood pressure interaction over a broad range of ages studied, and genetic studies with an F_2 generation from an initial high BP I by low BP I cross indicated that the relationships between these behaviors and hypertension were merely accidents of the selection procedures used to develop the high and low lines. Accidents of selection, as shall be seen in Chapter 14, are not the fault of the person who develops the lines by breeding; rather, they are "fortuitous" in nature. Nevertheless, they can create correlations between phenotypes such as high blood pressure and behavior, which can be erroneously interpreted as causal if great care is not taken and adequate genetic manipulations are not performed.

With a few exceptions, animal studies of hypertension and behavior have not taken the steps necessary to separate genetic effects (e.g., linked genes, pleiotropy) from those which are related to the deleterious effects of high blood pressure on the nervous system and corresponding influences on behavior. Thus, whereas the animal model has an important potential for answering gene-environment questions concerning behavior and disease processes, one must be aware that it is not always applied in methodologically sound ways, and careful evaluations of the experimental literature must be done before researchers can make firm statements about cause-effect relationships between animal behavior and hypertension.

BRAIN DAMAGE

As was mentioned previously, there is by no means agreement that there is such a phenomenon as "normal aging." Some investigators view aging as a disease process or at least as highly similar to a disease process. Although this view has lost popularity in recent years, its influence is apparent on investigators and physicians who believe that changes in the brain accompanying senile dementia are similar to those accompanying old age. Generally, we do not accept this definition but prefer to think of senile dementia as one type of abnormal deterioration of the brain in old age.

Some investigators express the view that what has been termed *presenile dementia* (early deterioration of the brain with accompanying behavioral symptoms) reflects the early onset of true senile dementia. Again, we do not ascribe to the view that presenile dementia and senile dementia reflect similar processes at different stages of the life cycle.

Aside from the correctness or incorrectness of views about dementia, the topic of brain damage is extremely important for adult developmental psychology. It is important because, as a person grows older, he becomes more susceptible to heart attacks, infections, accidents, strokes, and other events that increase susceptibility to brain damage. As we explore the topic of brain damage, it will become clear that it is *not* always impossible to help a person with brain damage and that brain damage is not a unitary phenomenon. Furthermore, the diagnosis of "organic brain syndrome" is no more definitive than the diagnosis of "mentally ill."

Organic brain syndrome

There really is no such thing as organic brain syndrome. In reality there are many different organic brain syndromes. Yet, if one were to enter a state mental hospital in many parts of the United States and glance at patients' charts in the geriatric unit, one would surely find the diagnosis of organic brain syndrome (OBS) in a significant number of patients. The term *OBS* is very general and is often assigned in response to symptoms that involve impairment of orientation, defective memory, decreased intellectual ability and judgment, as well as highly variable emotional behavior (emotional lability) and shallowness. These symptoms are frequently accompanied by disorders of affect and loss of acceptable social interactions with others. Organic brain syndrome can be acute or chronic. Some authors refer to acute OBS as that which is reversible and chronic OBS as that which is irreversible (e.g., Verwoerdt, 1976). We prefer not to make the distinction between acute and chronic brain syndrome

Fig. 12-5. Robert N. Butler, M.D. (Columbia University, 1953). Dr. Butler is Director of the National Institute on Aging, National Institutes of Health. Physician, psychiatrist, gerontologist, and author, Dr. Butler has contributed significantly to the field of adult developmental psychology and aging. His many professional memberships and contributions are too numerous to summarize here. Briefly, he has published many books and over a hundred research and clinical papers in the area of aging, psychotherapy, drugs, creativity, professional issues, and so on. Dr. Butler received the Pulitzer Prize in 1976 for his book *Why Survive: Being Old in America* and serves on the editorial board of the *International Journal of Aging and Human Development* as well as other journals relevant to his many professional interests.

in this way because many acute brain syndromes are not reversible, and, in some instances, symptoms of chronic brain syndrome can be alleviated with proper treatment.

Verwoerdt (1976) points out that the rate of OBS of moderate to severe degree is estimated at about 2.3% in the elderly population. It is much higher for psychiatric hospitals and extended care facilities. He refers to a survey which showed that, among old patients admitted to a mental hospital, almost 80% received a diagnosis of OBS.

Intelligence. Frequently persons with organic brain damage present a clinical picture characterized by decreased intelligence test performance. However, severity of brain damage and intellectual deterioration are not associated in a one-to-one manner. In a study cited by Verwoerdt (1976), about 20% of the patients diagnosed as senile psychotic (OBD) had few, if any, senile plaques as revealed by autopsy examination (Corsellis, 1962). In another study no behavioral evidence of dementia was reported in 25% of individuals who revealed severe brain atrophy (Willanger et al., 1968). Demented patients may have EEG records in the normal range, whereas aged individuals in apparently good psychological condition can exhibit gross abnormalities in the EEG (Busse and Wang, 1965). This is partly related to the fact that "one-time" measures of behavior do not reflect change from a previously higher level of functioning, and it is partly related to the fact that previous personality patterns and stress determine the extent to which symptoms of brain damage will be slight or severe. For example, highly verbal persons can often conceal symptoms of brain impairment that might otherwise become apparent on careful testing by a skilled neuropsychologist.

Irreversibility

Structural damage to the brain tends not to repair itself because neurons do not reproduce and have a limited capacity to recuperate from trauma. However, the symptoms of brain damage may be reduced in magnitude by a variety of treatment regimens. Often older persons admitted to general hospitals or mental hospitals exhibit symptoms of organic damage that are much reduced in magnitude after they have been in the hospital for a while and steps have been taken to reduce situational stress. Thus it is important to remember that it is simply not the case that, "Nothing can be done for an elderly person with behavioral and intellectual impairments resulting from brain damage." Attenuation of the symptoms of brain damage does not mean that the underlying cause has disappeared; rather, it means that reduction of stress leading to increased feelings of security, self-worth, and self-confidence has resulted in a diminution of the symptoms. For this reason the good neuropsychologist is concerned with assessing those abilities which are spared as well as those which are not.

Causes of brain damage

To understand and diagnose brain damage, one must be thoroughly familiar with the causes of brain damage. Verwoerdt (1976) has suggested that the causes of brain damage may be broken down into two major categories: organic-cerebral factors and extracerebral-somatic factors. Organic-cerebral factors include all those having a direct influence on brain tissue (e.g., neoplasm), whereas extracerebral-somatic factors include diseases that occur with high frequency in the late adult years and can have an adverse effect on the brain (e.g., cardiovascular and pulmonary disease). It should be noted that metabolic processes are included under both organic-cerebral and extracerebral-somatic categories. This is because metabolic disturbances can eventually lead to direct brain damage if they are not diagnosed quickly.

Personality factors

It has been noted that increased stress in a person's life can "bring out" behavioral symptoms of brain damage which might otherwise be so minimal as to go unnoticed for some period of time. Similarly, personality traits prior to brain damage can influence the behavioral symptoms that accompany brain damage. As might be expected, patients who were characterized as hostile prior to brain damage tend to behave in a hostile manner. Patients whose behavior can be characterized as versatile tend to be better able to adjust to or compensate for brain damage by modification of habits and approaches to problem solving. Frequently, the stress caused by awareness of intellectual decline acts to potentiate other behavioral responses to brain damage that are not directly influenced by the specific brain lesion involved in deterioration; for example, a compulsive person may become even more compulsive in response to loss of memory, whereas an aggressive person may become more aggressive in an attempt to cope with the problem. This indirect correlation of physical symptoms and psychosocial behavioral responses provides difficulties in terms of diagnoses because frequently what appears to be a learned or social behavior (e.g., depression, compulsion, paranoia) can instead be a reflection of a specific brain lesion.

Differential diagnosis

The term *differential diagnosis* has been used to describe diagnostic procedures that attempt to discriminate between patients who are "brain damaged" and those who are "psychogenic." Very often psychogenic factors interact with organic factors to produce behavioral changes. For example, depression, ranging from mild to psychotic, frequently accompanies cardiovascular and cerebrovascular disease (see Schuckit et al., 1975). This makes sense because the patient is most often aware of his loss of intellectual prowess and reacts to his cognitive changes with feelings of depression. Psychotic symptoms are often seen with chronic brain syndrome, for example, paranoid states and depression with and without agitated behavior (Verwoerdt, 1976).

It is difficult to separate depression secondary to atherosclerosis from depression of a purely nonorganic origin because depression in response to changing life situations in old age is common. Often depression in the elderly is misdiagnosed as brain damage because the symptoms are dissimilar to those observed in young persons and frequently are the same symptoms suggestive of brain damage. The young person's depression is characterized by affective manifestations, such as sad feelings, crying, self-depreciation, and reluctance to talk. These same affective manifestations of depression are observed in older persons, but often symptoms such as loss of attention, impaired memory, and decreased energy are more prominent (Verwoerdt, 1976). It is easy to misdiagnose these symptoms in the older person as organic in origin. Often the diagnostician feels vindicated in his diagnosis because the elderly person's behavior shows increasing characteristics of brain damage with the passage of time. The validity of the original diagnosis is verified by "more brain damaged–like behavior" because patients tend to conform to their environment. This is not to say that brain damage and depression are not simultaneous problems for some patients. Often they are. The point is that careful diagnosis requires an understanding of differences in symptoms in older and younger persons and an evaluation of the older person's ability to function in a supportive environment once situational stress precipitating behavioral manifestations of organic and/or psychogenically based disorders has been removed or minimized.

Localization of lesions

Although space does not permit us to discuss the many tests and approaches to neuropsychological diagnosis that have been developed, it should be pointed out that the sophistication of neuropsychological diagnosis has increased significantly in recent years (see Reitan and Davison, 1974). It is now recognized that it is not sufficient to diagnose a person as brain damaged because there are many kinds of brain damage with many different symptoms, depending on the nature of the damage, its location in the brain, and its magnitude in terms of brain area. Thus there really is no such thing as an organic brain syndrome; rather, there are many syndromes associated with different kinds of lesions in different parts of the brain. One important goal of the neuropsychological examination once the diagnosis of brain damage has been made is to determine where the lesion is, how large it is, what kind it is, and whether it is rapidly or slowly developing. To accomplish these diagnostic objectives, the neuropsychologist makes use of tests that allow comparisons of the left and right side of the body in terms of strength of grip, tapping speed, reaction time, tactile perception, sensitivity to touch, and others. These tests and tests of language skills, abstract reasoning, etc. provide information concerning which side of the brain and which specific area (e.g., left parietal) are involved. Reitan and his colleagues (see Reitan, 1967; Reitan and Davison, 1974; Reitan and Fitzhugh, 1971) have developed a battery of neuropsychological tests based on known brain-behavior relationships, and through comparisons of results for different tests within the battery, it is possible to localize brain lesions with a substantial degree of accuracy.

Of course, the neurological examination is a vital part of the diagnostic procedure when brain damage is suspected. The neurological examination done routinely in the physician's office includes rough indices of memory and orientation for time and space as well as a rather thorough evaluation of the cranial nerves and what may be referred to as extrapyramidal symptoms, paresis, etc. Often a patient is referred for more refined neurological diagnostic techniques, including pneumoencephalography, echoencephalography, and static and dynamic brain scanning. None of these diagnostic techniques is infallible, although when used together they lead to many accurate diagnoses. Ultimately, the brain biopsy is the only procedure that permits a direct examination of the living brain. However, even these techniques sometimes fail to provide conclusive information (Smith et al., 1966).

The electroencephalograph (EEG) has been very popular as part of the diagnostic equipment of the neurologist, and many psychologists have invested much time in establishing correlations between EEG patterns and behavior. EEGs are somewhat helpful in differential diagnosis because the incidence of abnormal EEGs (e.g., diffuse slowing) is higher in elderly persons diagnosed as brain damaged than in those with psychogenic disorders (Obrist, 1965; Obrist and Henry, 1958). Verwoerdt (1976) has pointed out some important facts about the elderly and EEG data. Patients with "diffuse (nonlocalized) slowing" in the EEG are more likely to remain in the hospital and have a shorter life expectancy than those with normal EEGs (McAdam and Robinson, 1962; Obrist and Müller et al., 1975; Obrist and Henry, 1958). This slowing may well be attributable to reduced metabolic activity (e.g., reduced cerebral oxygen uptake) and is fairly well correlated with severity of intellectual deterioration (Lassen, 1966; Lassen et al., 1957; Obrist et al., 1963). However, as we have stated before and as Verwoerdt (1976:40) has emphasized, "The EEG may be normal in patients with definite organic brain syndrome, and old persons apparently in good psychological health may show abnormalities in their EEG."

Focal disturbances in the EEG are useful in the diagnosis of the lesion's location. They are disturbances in a specific area of the recording from the surface of the skull. With increasing age the incidence of focal disturbances also increases, most commonly as slow wave activity in the left anterior temporal region of the brain (Verwoerdt, 1976). Verwoerdt points out that focal disturbances are not uncommon in organic brain syndromes (reflecting neoplasms or arteriosclerosis): in fact, they may be present for several years in the absence of readily recognizable symptomatology. However, aged persons with such foci seem to undergo a faster rate of decline in intelligence than those without such foci. For most persons the temporal region of the left cerebral hemisphere plays an important role in language skills. Since the right cerebral hemisphere, particularly the parietal-occipital area plays an important role in many of the performance abilities tested on the WAIS, it is not surprising to learn that diffuse slowing in the occipital rhythm or decreased blood flow in the left parietal cortex is accompanied by a decline in performance abilities (Busse and Wang, 1965; Obrist et al., 1963).

Because EEG changes are not pathognomonic (predictive of brain damage) and because of wide variations among older persons of comparable age and health, one EEG tracing is not of great value. On the other hand, repeated EEGs are useful in following the course of patients suspected of brain damage. Moreover, healthy old persons with normal EEGs over several years do not seem to exhibit a decline in intellectual performance during this time (Wang et al., 1970).

Neuropsychology and aging

Although it may seem that available techniques for neuropsychological examination provide a means for evaluating older persons in terms of questions concerning level of functioning and, if appropriate, locus of brain lesion, this is not entirely true. Neuropsychological studies used to develop data for clinical practice have been done largely with children and young and middle-aged adults. Thus the neuropsychologist who wishes to work with adults over the age of 65 years does not have the advantage of normative data for persons who are psychologically and physically healthy. Normative data are much less critical where there is clear evidence of asymmetry of function; that is, psychological tests reveal unmistakable differences in functioning of one side of the brain or the other. In these cases of "left-right asymmetry of function," it may be possible to localize a specific kind of lesion and refer a patient for treatments, including speech therapy, surgery, or supportive environments designed to reduce stress. Early diagnosis of this nature can prevent misreferral and a long hospitalization under inappropriate conditions. However, it is often the case that symptoms may reflect diffuse and widespread damage, which is not localized, and an initial screening may be necessary to determine if level of functioning warrants further testing. Is the person functioning at a level that would be considered as reflective or brain damage? To answer this question, one must have normative data for older control subjects who do not have brain damage so that normal changes beyond the age of 65 years can be compared with changes associated with organic brain syndromes. Many neuropsychologists argue that the development of a battery designed to answer this question would require careful studies of normal aging populations in the same geographical location as the hospital or clinic which plans to develop the neuropsychological service for older persons. These studies involve the selection of tests which do not correlate with each other but, rather, measure independent aspects of behavior and the elimination of those tests which fail to discriminate between known brain-damaged persons and known healthy persons. The approach is tedious and involves statistical techniques such as factor analysis, multiple discriminant analysis, and stepwise regression. Thus much more in the way of normative data needs to be collected for normal, older persons for a variety of tests that are useful in neuropsychological diagnosis with younger adults and tests that may ultimately be useful specifically with older adults. It may be expected that some tests which are useful for differential diagnoses with young adults may not be useful with elderly adults. Conversely, tests that do not discriminate at a younger age may discriminate well in old age. The point is that psychologists cannot expect to apply neuropsychological tests with elderly adults in exactly the same way as with young and middle-aged adults. Much needs to be done in terms of research with elderly, normal populations if psychologists are to be able to perform "level of functioning" analyses to enable differentiation between normal and brain-damaged older persons.

Some brain syndromes associated with aging

Some diseases of the brain occur with such high frequency in older persons that a number of behavioral symptoms and anatomical changes can be identified. Verwoerdt (1976) has prepared a comprehensive table that lists distinguishing features (factors) of these various diseases and compares them with the diagnosis, "depressive psychosis" (Table 12-2). There is no need to memorize the distinguishing features, but you should examine the table to develop a full appreciation for the fact that frequently the diseases cannot be distinguished from each other or from depressive psychosis on the basis of knowledge of a single factor. For example, it is assumed that depressive psychosis involves no brain damage, and yet some of the behavioral symptoms are similar to those seen in various organic brain syndromes, for example, psychomotor retardation, depressive stupor, transient memory problems, personality changes, and transient memory loss. Of course, examination of other factors reveals differences between depressive psychosis and the organically based diseases. Similarly, discrimination of Pick's from Alzheimer's disease requires knowledge of the age of onset, the rate of development, and so on. Frequently, factors do not emerge in a clear-cut manner, and misdiagnoses are made. Moreover, there are individual differences in the effect that these diseases have on the ability to function at any given time during the progression of the disease. As we examine these disease categories, it becomes clear that there are diseases of the brain which are clearly abnormal and represent an accelerated deterioration, very dissimilar to that which occurs over a much longer time in the normal aging brain. Thus it is probably not proper to think of *pre*senile dementia (Alzheimer's disease) as a case of senile dementia with an earlier onset or to think of senile dementia as an extreme case of behavioral and physiological changes occurring in the normal aging brain. There are those who might take issue with these statements. Hopefully, further research with the aging and diseased brain will explain what specific changes are reflective of a disease process as opposed to those which are "normal" for all living organisms. One thing is certain: not all abnormal aging brains are alike, and these dissimilarities in "brain profiles" partly contribute to differences in pat-

Text continued on p. 251.

Table 12-2. Differential diagnosis of organic brain syndromes*

Factors	Depressive psychosis	Cerebral arteriosclerosis	Senile dementia	Alzheimer's disease	Pick's disease
Usual age of onset	Any age	55-70 Average: 65	70+ Average: 75	50-60 Average: 56	45-55 Average: 50
Sex distribution	Early life: more women Late life: more men	Men-women = 3:1	Men-women = 2:3	Men-women = 2:3	Men-women = 2:3
Duration	Varies from weeks to years	Varies from days to many years Average: 4 yr	Varies from months to years Average: 5 yr	Average: 4 yr	Average: 4 yr
Mode of onset	Gradual or sudden; precipitating stress often apparent	Gradual or acute	Insidious	More sudden and less gradual than S.D.	Slow and insidious
Course	Self-limited, but with tendency to recur	Intermittent, fluctuating	Slowly or rapidly progressive	Rapidly progressive	Progressive and fatal
Prognosis	Responsive to drugs or ECT	Varies depending on multiple factors	Poor (in moderate or severe cases)	Very poor	Very poor
Outcome	Usually recovery; sometimes suicide or regression to paranoid level	Death from CVA, heart disease, or infection	Death from general organismic failure, or infection		
Hereditary and precipitating factors	Involuton; previous history of depression	Some familial tendency	Multiple genetically determined factors	Multifactorial inheritance, genetic factors causing premature aging	Heredodegenerative process
Signs of brain damage	None	Diffuse or focal	Diffuse, generalized	Diffuse, generalized more severe than in S.D.	Circumscribed atrophy; frontal, temporal, or parietal lobes
Impairment of higher cortical functions	No structural impairment	Some isolated impairments, e.g., aphasia, apraxia, agnosia	Progressive dementia	Involvement of cerebral associative areas; transcortical aphasia, apraxia, agnosia, etc.	Focal cortical impairments, e.g., motor or sensory aphasia

*From Verwoerdt, A. *Clinical geropsychiatry.* Baltimore: The Williams & Wilkins Co., 1976.

Continued.

Table 12-2. Differential diagnosis of organic brain syndromes—cont'd

Factors	Depressive psychosis	Cerebral arteriosclerosis	Senile dementia	Alzheimer's disease	Pick's disease
Neuro-muscular	Psychomotor retardation or agitation	Paralyses; minor extra-pyramidal signs	Tremors, uncertain gait, variable muscular rigidity	Transient or progressive paresis; unsteady gait; increased muscle tone; occasional tremors	Primitive reflexes; extra-pyramidal signs; attacks of muscular hypotonia
			Incontinence	Incontinence	Incontinence
Seizures	None	Epileptiform attacks	Rare	Occasional	Rare
Medical	Physiological concomitants of depression (sleep, appetite, weight, energy)	Common history of CVA; headaches, dizziness and syncope (in 50%); "little strokes"; arteriosclerosis in heart, kidney, legs, etc.	Infections, contractures, fractures, decubitus	Infections, contractures; fractures, decubitus	Infections, contractures, fractures, decubitus

Neuro-pathology	Depressive psychosis	Cerebral arteriosclerosis	Senile dementia	Alzheimer's disease	Pick's disease
Macroscopic	None characteristic	Large or small areas of softening and hemorrhage	Diffuse generalized shrinkage of brain, especially gray matter; dilated ventricles; internal hydrocephalus	General cerebral atrophy; dilated ventricles; internal hydrocephalus	Circumscribed lobar atrophy, mostly orbito-frontal and temporal
Microscopic	None characteristic	Granular atrophy of cortex diffusely with hypertensive cardiovascular disease	Neuronal degeneration and shrinking; most damage in upper layers of cortex	Diffuse loss of neurons, especially in cortex layers 3 and 5; disturbed cortical layers	Progressive atrophy of neurons; no predilection for cortical layers
		Destruction of neurons, nerve fibers and glia; focal neuronal and	Deposition of lipofuscin and intracellular fibrils	Neuron degeneration: pyknosis, granulovacuolar, Alzheimer's	Neuron degeneration, increased pigment, pyknosis Swollen cells

Table 12-2. Differential diagnosis of organic brain syndromes—cont'd

Neuropathology	Depressive psychosis	Cerebral arteriosclerosis	Senile dementia	Alzheimer's disease	Pick's disease
		selective cortical degeneration		neurofibrillary change	Argyrophilic cytoplasmic inclusions
		Secondary gliosis	Moderate gliosis, especially in outer layer of cortex	Gliosis more severe than in S.D.	Gliosis prominent
		Senile plaques not typical	Senile plaques	Senile plaques throughout cortex	Senile plaques rare
Vascular	None characteristic	Vascular: Large arteries: atherosclerosis; Small vessels: endothelial proliferation; medial hypertrophy; intima hyalinization	Endothelial degeneration; media fibrosis; adventitial proliferation; vascular loops	Degenerative changes of endothelial and adventitial cells	Endothelial proliferation; hyaline degeneration

Psychiatric symptomatology (I)	Depressive psychosis	Cerebral arteriosclerosis	Senile dementia	Alzheimer's disease	Pick's disease
Orientation	Intact, except in depressive stupor	Episodes of acute confusion; lucid intervals	Progressive disorientation in all spheres; loss of time perspective	Progressive disorientation in all spheres; loss of time perspective	Progressive disorientation in all spheres; loss of time perspective
Perception	Occasional auditory hallucinations	Auditory and visual hallucinations during acute exacerbations	Various types of hallucinations in advanced stages	Occasional hallucinations	Occasional hallucinations
Intellect and thought	No mental impairment	Lacunar types of intellectual deficit	Progressive, generalized dementia	Progressive dementia and loss of abstraction	*Frontal lobe* syndrome: progressive loss of abstraction
	Delusions consistent with affect	Delusions rare	Delusions depend on degree of regression and premorbid personality	Aphasia, alexia, agnosia, asymbolia, agraphia, apraxia	*Aphasic* syndrome: aphasia, alexia, etc. *Alogic* syndrome: agnosia, apraxia, etc.

Continued.

Table 12-2. Differential diagnosis of organic brain syndromes—cont'd

Psychiatric symptomatology (I)	Depressive psychosis	Cerebral arteriosclerosis	Senile dementia	Alzheimer's disease	Pick's disease
	Insight varies	Insight present in early stages	No insight	No insight	No insight
Memory	Transient memory problems due to C.N.S. slowing	Varying deficits of recent and remote memory, of retention and recall	Progressive impairment of all memory functions	Progressive impairment of all memory functions	Progressive impairment of all memory functions
		Confabulations rare	Confabulations in presbyophrenic type	Confabulations rare	Confabulations common

Psychiatric symptomatology (II)	Depressive psychosis	Cerebral arteriosclerosis	Senile dementia	Alzheimer's disease	Pick's disease
Affect	Depression; guilt; low self-esteem	Emotional lability; anxiety and depression; later, blunting of affect	Depends on subtype Simple: apathy Depressed: agitation Delirious: anxiety Paranoid: hostility Presbyophrenic: shallow euphoria	Variable at first; later, apathy	Apathy and indifference
Psychomotor	Retardation; sometimes, agitation	Hypoactive or hyperactive or restless agitation	Hyperactive or hypoactive, or restless agitation	Hyperactive; repetitive, primitive motor behavior; extrapyramidal signs	Hypo- or hyperkinetic; primitive reflexes; stereotyped activity: perseveration; echolalia; logoklony
Personality changes	Transient regressive changes	Regressive changes are intermittent or slowly progressive	Progressive deterioration of social behavior and personal habits		

terns of behavior observed on tests of mental, perceptual, and psychomotor functioning. Furthermore, even "nondiseased" brains have their unique physiological, biochemical, and structural characteristics that contribute to individual differences in behavior.

CELLULAR CHANGES, AGING, AND BEHAVIOR

Up to this point, we have said little about the relationship between so-called "normal aging" and behavior as related to microscopic anatomy and changes in biochemistry at the cellular level. This is because the bulk of the work in psychobiology and aging has been more concerned with gross changes in anatomy and physiology as they relate to behavior.

In view of the obvious importance of the brain to mental functioning, it has been tempting for investigators to speculate about the relationship of neurons, neurochemical events in the cell, and neurotransmission to changes in mental functioning, activity, and motivation with advancing age. Loss of neurons has long been proposed as a reason for the apparent decline in learning, performance, and intellectual functioning in very old age. However, there is really little evidence for the importance of numerical neuronal cell loss. Timiras and Bignami (1976) have pointed out that, "Neurons represent a numerically small component of the CNS, and functionally, the neuronal composition of central pathways is so highly redundant that no serious performance deficiency would be expected to arise even after a considerable decrease in neuronal number (Eccles, 1973)." Moreover, studies with infrahuman animals do not reveal significant changes in neuron *number* with advancing age (see Feldman and Peters, 1975).

Cell size and properties

There may be changes in cell size and constituents with advancing age, but data are contradictory. There do seem to be age-related changes in the structure, functions, and chemistry of the synapse. One "working hypothesis" is that impaired neurotransmission results in deficits in mental functioning with advancing age. For example, Timiras and Bignami (1976) review some interesting studies suggesting that the horizontally oriented dendrites from the pyramidal cell bodies may be the location for information processing and storage of "central programs." They cite findings that suggest a "characteristic sequence of events associated with age which, in some respects, retraces the path followed by the maturing cell during early phases of development, but is reversed in sequence." These dendrites have synapses within the cortex that transport information from one part of the cortex to the other. The loss of horizontal dendrites has been interpreted as removing the subtle, modulatory (possibly inhibitory) aspects of cerebral cortical activity (Scheibel and Scheibel, 1975) with a consequent functional impairment characterized by symptoms of senility (e.g., decreased muscular strength, lack of dexterity and agility, failing cognitive performance, and deficits in association, retrieval, and recall of information). However, these relationships are highly speculative at the present time, and much more needs to be done in the way of providing hard data that relate to *specific* decrements in intellectual functioning as opposed to motor performance or vigor.

Neurotransmission and neurohumors

Neurohumors act to "excite" and stimulate the brain. Similarly, they transport information that may be particularly important to memory and learning. An area of investigation that deserves much more attention is the relationship of age-related changes in neurotransmitter (neurohumor) levels to behavioral changes with age.

There is some evidence that levels of norepinephrine decrease with advancing age, but serotonin levels remain the same (Robinson, 1975). Serotonin and norepinephrine have long been implicated in learning, memory, and motivation. Unfortunately, the precise nature of this relationship is elusive because it is extremely difficult to hold all physiological changes constant except for changes in a single neurohumor. The nervous system and the endocrine system are so complex with regard to compensatory-feedback relationships that it is almost impossible to separate multiple neurohumoral effects which occur in response to attempted drug manipulations of a single neurohumor. Moreover, as we have seen, it is difficult to separate behavioral parameters, such as attention, learning, activity, and motivation. These difficulties are multiplied enormously in the context of aging studies because of the absence of noncontradictory baseline data concerning changes in neurohumors with advancing age. Researchers are just beginning to scratch the surface in this area.

Despite the absence of studies that firmly establish a relationship between brain neurohumors and changes in specific behaviors with advancing age, Timiras and Bignami (1976) have advanced an interesting and exciting hypothesis that researchers may be able to test some day when behavioral and biological technology is improved. The interesting thing about this hypothesis by Timiras and Bignami (1976:365) is that it stresses the *balance* of neurohumoral events rather than deficit or excess.

> Another consequence of the differential effects of aging on neuronal elements may involve preferential decrements in some neurotransmitter systems while others remain unaffected. In this case, excess or deficit of a specific neurotransmitter would result not only in functional alterations ascribable to that single loss or decrease, but, more importantly, in imbalances among several neurotransmitters. We know that normal brain function depends on the delicate tuning of inhibitory and excitatory impulses and that a disequilibrium of this balance—such as may occur during aging—will have severe and widespread functional repercussions . . . this hypothesis is supported by the changes which occur with old age in several free amino acids considered to be putative neurotransmitters.

Certainly, there are many exciting possibilities for relating mental function to neurochemistry and neurotransmission that go beyond simple hypotheses about neuronal cell loss. However, researchers need to improve their capability for clearly separating motivation, activity, attention, learning, and memory aspects of task performance before they can pursue these hypotheses. Furthermore, researchers must overcome difficulties encountered in attempting to hold one dimension of biochemistry or structural change constant while manipulating others.

Up to the present time, scientists have been more successful in establishing relationships between behavior and well-defined diseases or injuries of the brain than they have been in linking specific behaviors to specific molecular events in the brain and other parts of the nervous system. Here we are referring to so-called normal aging changes rather than clear-cut pathological conditions of the brain. One of the most exciting challenges to the investigator in aging is to establish links between age-related behavioral changes and neurochemical and structural changes in the cells of the brain. Until investigators can accomplish this objective, they should be wary of *physiologizing* beyond their data; that is, they must separate exciting hypotheses from fact and they should not let too little knowledge of current data in cell physiology prompt naive hypotheses and meaningless experiments.

SUMMARY

There has been a proliferation of research concerned with specific disease processes (e.g., cardiovascular disease), aging, and behavior. In spite of this upsurge of interest in the debilitating effects of disease, little attention has been paid to the health status of subjects in most adult developmental studies. This is a highly unfortunate situation, since there is much evidence to support the notion that even asymptomatic disease processes may have adverse effects on many of the behaviors commonly examined by gerontological researchers.

Current debate over primary ("normal") as opposed to secondary ("pathological") aging declines has centered around the terminal drop hypothesis (i.e., a sudden loss in level of functioning shortly before death). Many researchers have not tested this hypothesis directly but instead have examined the relationship of survival or distance-from-death to measures of cognitive abilities (cross-sectional analyses). Most of these investigations have led to the conclusion that survivorship and distance-from-death are positively related to higher levels of intellectual functioning. Studies not supporting this finding have failed to include a wide range of times before death and/or have tested subjects who were not initially in good health.

Direct tests of the terminal drop hypothesis must involve a longitudinal analysis, that is, a measure of trends in performance as the time before death grows shorter. Among studies utilizing this approach, the evidence for terminal drop has been somewhat contradictory. Recently, it has been suggested that there may be at least three time-related processes operating to produce decrements in functioning: (1) aging decline, per se; (2) terminal drop (an accelerating decline occurring shortly before death); and (3) terminal decline (a slower, linear rate of decline which is probably related to insidious disease processes, such as hypertension and arteriosclerosis). In any case, most researchers agree that individual differences play a significant role in the extent to which older adults are susceptible to behavioral declines.

Of the many diseases that increase in incidence among older populations, cardiovascular disease has received the most attention, at least with regard to its effects on behavior. Behavioral predictors of cardiovascular disease have been of special concern because of the recent emphasis on prevention. However, early suggestions that neuroticism, stress, and anxiety may be good predictors of hypertensive disease have received only meager support, and few methodologically sophisticated studies have been conducted. The evidence is contradictory and, in many cases, misleading because investigators often differ with regard to definitions of terms and methodological approaches. Little research has been directed toward changes in the behavioral predictors of hypertension with advancing age.

A more sophisticated effort has been made with regard to behavioral predictors of coronary heart disease, specifically "Type A" as opposed to "Type B" patterns of behavior. Type A individuals are twice as likely as Type B individuals to develop coronary disease, although these behavioral patterns apparently lose their predictive power for persons over the age of 50 years. In addition to behavioral differences, the Type A pattern is associated with a number of physiological precursors of coronary disease (e.g., elevated serum cholesterol levels). Furthermore, Type A subjects exhibit some behaviors (e.g., slowing of response) that are typical of persons who have suffered from coronary disease for a number of years. Much work remains to be done before scientists fully understand the implications of Type A and B behavior. For example, investigators know very little about Type A and B patterns among women and have virtually no data on potential modifiers of Type A behavior.

The relationship between psychomotor slowing and cardiovascular disease has been of concern because slowing, per se, is widely regarded as the most prominent behavioral trend among aging adults. Although most evidence supports the notion that exaggerated slowing of response is characteristic of persons suffering from hypertension and arteriosclerosis, recent data suggest that this relationship is highly complex and involves many factors, including specific etiology of the disease in question, history of medication, and situational variables associated with the testing milieu. Furthermore, one may question the practical significance of the additional slowing of response accompanying cardiovascular disease, since the magnitude of the effect and percent variance accounted for is usually small.

Evidence for a general intellectual decline, over and above that associated with aging, among persons suffering from cardiovascular disease is perhaps of more practical importance than is similar evidence for a slowing of response. Again, however, the behavior-disease relationship is far from straightforward. For example, investigators have reason to believe that mild elevations in blood pressure might actually be beneficial for the maintenance of cognitive abilities, at least for persons in their sixties and early seventies. On the other hand, severe elevations in blood pressure accompanied by end-organ changes are detrimental. Other evidence suggests that at least some of the intellectual decline seen among hypertensive subjects may be related to performance factors, such as test instructions or anxiety rather than cognitive ability, per se.

Most researchers who have studied cardiovascular disease and intellectual performance have found that declines occur regardless of age. However, one study concerned with the positive effects of serum cholesterol reduction demonstrated that age was, in fact, an important variable. Reduction of serum cholesterol was associated with the maintenance of cognitive abilities past the age of 60 years. Reductions did not seem to make much difference among younger subjects, none of whom suffered a loss in ability, regardless of serum cholesterol levels.

There has been a great deal of speculation with regard to the physiological bases for slowing of response and decline in intellectual performance among persons suffering from cardiovascular disease. Some researchers have thought that declines are related to reduced cerebral blood flow associated with hypertension and arteriosclerosis. Although a number of researchers are currently engaged in exploring this hypothesis, there is no firm evidence for it at the present time. Although many studies have produced results suggesting that EEG slowing accompanies cardiovascular disease, EEG changes, taken by themselves, are only indices of a symptom and not measures of underlying physical causes.

Animal models for disease processes and aging are just beginning to be developed, although they offer a promising research tool for studying the relationships among disease, aging, and behavior. For example, one study has led to the suggestion that a relationship between hypertension and socially aggressive behavior may have a genetic basis (linked-gene or pleiotropic effect). At this point, however, psychologists must be very cautious in their interpretations drawn from the animal literature on genetics and aging because this area of research abounds with methodologically questionable generalizations.

Perhaps nowhere has the debate over normal as opposed to pathological aging processes been more evident than among investigators engaged in research on brain damage and aging. There are those who believe that aging is analogous to, if not isomorphic with, progressive diseases of the brain characterized by deteriorating intellectual and social behavior (e.g., presenile and senile dementia). Other researchers believe that these disease processes are qualitatively different from brain changes accompanying "normal" aging. In either case it is becoming increasingly clear that there are many, many types of debilitating diseases which may affect the brain as one grows older. A number of researchers are directing much effort toward the development of neuropsychological test batteries that will discriminate between these various diseases. This area of research is particularly important because many of the diseases affecting the brain as one grows older are very difficult to diagnose properly; that is, the gross behavioral manifestations (e.g., depression) are similar and often lead to misdiagnosis and ineffectual treatment regimens.

Adequate methods for assessment of brain damage and recommendations for treatment have been especially lacking for elderly patients. At this point in time, little normative data exist on "normal" elderly populations that can be compared with data on brain-damaged elderly populations. It is time consuming and tedious to collect these data, but researchers cannot expect to reduce the number of misdiagnoses for elderly patients unless they invest the time and energy needed. Psychologists simply cannot continue to administer neuropsychological tests that have been standardized for young populations to elderly persons and "hope for the best." In the past this habit has led to many ineffective and even harmful diagnoses and treatment (or lack of treatment) regimens.

On the cellular level the traditional hypothesis of neuronal loss as the precipitating biological cause underlying aging declines in learning, memory, and other cognitive abilities has not received much support in recent years. A number of exciting new hypothesis (e.g., involving balance among neurotransmitters) have been advanced. However, until researchers improve methods for accurately measuring both behavioral and biological variables, they must be wary of "physiologizing" beyond current data. All too often, the simplest and most obvious explanations of physiology-behavior relationships are far from adequate. Perhaps this is because man has tended to use a simple machine model for the central nervous system.

It is tempting as psychologists to overlook or deny the importance of good health and the integrity of underlying biological mechanisms as they influence behavior. We have seen in this chapter that poor health can have a deleterious effect on learning, thinking, and performing. Moreover, as difficult as it may be to accept, there is much to be said for the notion that all behavior is ultimately influenced by and itself influences physiology. In the search for the nature of this mutual influence, psychologists have often tended to oversimplify complex relationships. Nevertheless, Benjamin Franklin's observation that "Early to bed, early to rise, makes a man healthy, wealthy, and *wise*" was most insightful in its recognition of the three most important factors for a long and happy life: health, income, and maintenance of intellectual capacity.

SELECTED READINGS

Abrahams, J. P. Health status as a variable in aging research. *Experimental Aging Research,* 1976, **2,** 63-71.

Light, K. C. Slowing of response time in young and middle-aged hypertensive patients. *Experimental Aging Research,* 1975, **1,** 209-228.

Müller, H. F., Grad, B., and Engelsmann, F. Biological and psychological predictors of survival in a psychogeriatric population. *Journal of Gerontology,* 1975, **30,** 47-52.

Obrist, W. D. Electroencephalographic approach to age changes in response speed. In A. T. Welford and J. E. Birren (Eds.), *Behavior, aging, and the nervous system.* Springfield, Ill.: Charles C Thomas, Publisher, 1965.

Palmore, E., and Cleveland, W. Aging, terminal decline, and terminal drop. *Journal of Gerontology,* 1976, **31,** 76-81.

Reitan, R. M. Psychological changes associated with aging and with cerebral damage. *Mayo Clinic Proceedings,* 1967, **42,** 653-673.

Reitan, R. M., and Davison, L. A. *Clinical neuropsychology: current status and applications.* New York: John Wiley & Sons, Inc., 1974.

Siegler, I. S. The terminal drop hypothesis: fact or artifact? *Experimental Aging Research,* 1975, **1,** 169-185.

Thompson, L. W., and Marsh, G. R. Psychophysiological studies of aging. In C. Eisdorfer and M. P. Lawton (Eds.), *The psychology of adult development and aging.* Washington, D.C.: American Psychological Association, 1973.

Verwoerdt, A. *Clinical geropsychiatry.* Baltimore: The Williams & Wilkins Co., 1976.

Wilkie, F., and Eisdorfer, C. Intelligence and blood pressure in the aged. *Science,* 1971, **172,** 959-962.

Wilkie, F. L., Eisdorfer, C., and Nowlin, J. B. Memory and blood pressure in the aged. *Experimental Aging Research,* 1976, **2,** 3-16.

CHAPTER 13

GENOTYPE-ENVIRONMENT INTERACTIONS

The sociological aversion to social biology, however, is based on more than a routine rejection of faulty evidence. It is also fortified by the lingering suspicion that an explanatory sequence that begins with the organism inevitably ends with predatory ethics.
BRESSLER (1968:179)

Traditionally, behavioral and social scientists have been reluctant to embrace genetic approaches to the study of behavior. Life-span psychologists have not been an exception. Many conferences on life-span psychology have not included behavior genetics as a topic; few, if any, life-span developmental textbooks provide a chapter that discusses behavior genetics. Only very recently, K. Warner Schaie organized a two-day workshop on behavior genetics and adult developmental psychology, the purposes of which were to inform psychologists about the value of behavior genetics approaches and to familiarize them with behavioral genetic techniques (see Schaie et al., 1975).

Resistance to behavior genetics on the part of behavioral and social scientists is partially related to a vested interest in a strong environmentalist approach (Bressler, 1968; Eckland, 1967; Haller, 1968). However, this resistance is not based on an environmental ideology entirely. Haller, pointing to the lack of really respectable behavior genetics research before 1920, notes that the nation's most influential geneticist in the early 1900s, Davenport (1912), argued that many character traits could be explained with simple Mendelian genetics. Traits such as insanity, feeblemindedness, shyness, love of alcohol, shiftlessness, and mechanical ability were considered to be recessive, whereas violent temper and laziness were viewed as dominant.

It would be unfair to single out geneticists for criticism. McDougall (1908), a famous social psychologist, acknowledged concepts of genetics in his book *Introduction to Social Psychology*. Unfortunately, he confused the concepts of instinct and genetic predisposition, and thus he may have contributed more to intellectual rejection of behavior genetics than any of the overenthusiastic biologists of the early 1900s. McDougall developed the thesis that individuals and races differ in the strengths of different instincts and inherited tendencies (Elias, 1973). Boring (1950:217) points out that there is no limit to the number of instincts which can be developed to explain behavioral phenomena and that McDougall's social psychology lost popularity when behaviorists discovered that anyone can make up a list of instincts and that there is no way to provide evidence that one list is more valid than another.

HEREDITARIAN EXTREMISM

The rather uncritical writings about genetics, exemplified by Davenport and McDougall, were not inconsistent with a hereditarian extremism that seemed to exist in the United States in the early 1900s. Haller (1968:271) noted that the use of the Binet intelligence test in an uncritical manner reinforced hereditarian extremism by providing "conclusive proof that, except for Jews, those races that were believed to be inferior were in fact inferior," and that "most criminals, prostitutes, tramps, and other undesirables were hereditary morons." There was widespread concern for "hereditary reform," which seems to have climaxed in the 1920s, when Congress enacted a law restricting immigration of groups that were assumed to be racially inferior (Higham, 1955). Haller (1968) points out that even some prestigious biologists and social scientists drew socially conservative conclusions from hereditarian interpretations of human behavior. For example, (Elias, 1973:121):

> Davenport (1912, p. 281) advised a national conference of social workers that social reform was futile and the only way to secure innate capacity is by breeding it. McDougall (1912) called for the replacement of democracy by a caste system based on biological capacity with legal restrictions upon breeding by the lower castes and upon breeding between the castes.

Heredity and politics

Aversion to the hereditary extremism expressed in the views of some scientists of the early 1900s was intensified by some unfortunate ideological associations of genetics and politics. In fact, these politically motivated, pseudogenetic arguments may well have resulted in an aversion to the phrase *behavior genetics.* For example, the Nazis incorporated pseudogenetic arguments into their doctrines of the 1930s. The International Genetic Congress took an official stand against these doctrines in terms of their scientific validity (Benedict, 1940:259), but the fact that a concept of genetics, misinformed as it was, was associated with a repugnant political/social ideology served to reinforce a strong environmentalist position on the part of the social scientists of the 1940s. This aversion is summed up well by the quotation from Bressler (1968) at the beginning of this chapter.

It is extremely important for the student to realize how much these unfortunate associations of genetics and questionable ideology have created an emotional reaction to the topic of behavior genetics when it is introduced into the classroom or the textbook. It is important to understand that aversion to genetics is often based on the notion that it is antienvironmental in its emphasis, a notion which is far from the truth. In fact, the study of behavior genetics emphasizes just how important the environment is in terms of promoting the fullest expression of behavior at different points in the life-span. Unfortunately, associations of the concepts of genetics and political ideology are not restricted to the distant past. There are scientists who see a social breakdown, which is presumably related to spiritual decay and insufficient intelligence to keep pace with the progressively increasing complexities of modern life. One such individual, McConnell (1970:903), argues for a selective breeding program for intelligence as an important aspect of "genetic fitness."

Putting emotional feelings aside, one might raise the question as to why it might not be possible to breed humans selectively for longer life and freedom from debilitating and killing diseases of old age, middle age, and youth. Why not breed only the most intelligent humans? The very thought of these kinds of programs is repulsive to most social and behavioral scientists because it is far too easy for such programs to infringe on basic rights of human beings and to be grossly distorted for political purposes. Aside from politics, knowledge of human genetics has not reached a point where objective decisions can be made with regard to those qualities which a well-adjusted, intelligent adult should possess. If anything, there is evidence that a diversity of characteristics, rather than extremes of specific characteristics, has survival value for humans and that those sets of traits which do have survival value will evolve naturally (Dobzhansky, 1967). Furthermore, eugenics programs which emphasize planned alteration of human breeding patterns ignore the growing behavioral genetics literature, which indicates that genetically influenced traits or characteristics are influenced in no small way by the environment in which they exist. Genotypes define a range of possibilities for the development of a trait or skill, but often the range is very large and development with that range is greatly influenced by environment. Thus improving environmental conditions, that is, education, income, nutrition, for all persons, becomes a legitimate approach to helping persons to survive longer, to remain in good health, to maximize intellectual capacity, and to adapt and function adequately well into old age.

Our emphasis on the importance of environment does not mean that genetics is unimportant. If students who read this chapter gain nothing else, they should come away with the understanding that demonstration of the importance of environment does not deny the importance of genetics and that the reverse is true. Environmental and genetic factors work together from birth to death. By understanding genetics, we understand the operation of environment in developmental processes better than if we only concerned ourselves with the role of learning and environment as they influence behavior.

Environmental extremism: a backlash

Unfortunately, the response to hereditary extremism of the early 1900s was an environmental backlash, which lasted in one form or another until the middle 1900s and, in fact, still exists among some social scientists. The end result has been that many students of psychology, sociology, and human development are denied the opportunity to learn basic genetic principles which would help them to better understand the developmental processes.

The earliest opposition to hereditary extremism came from a sociologist named Ward (1903), who maintained that the progress and dissemination of technology and culture rather than biological selection explained the evolution of human society. Another sociologist, Boas (1911), argued that biological inheritance did not determine the difference between the lower and upper classes; rather, access to social heritage contributes to this difference. Although there is truth to these positions, they are not entirely accurate. Contemporary sociologists and anthropologists (e.g., Haller, 1968) note that biological selection interacts with cultural and technological evolution. In human beings, assortative mating can come about by marriages between phenotypically similar, and presumably genotypically similar, persons. Thus, although upward social mobility can be restricted by environmental factors, it can also be limited by genetic factors when the individual finds himself in a "closed environment" that imposes a restricted breeding pattern.

Sociologists were not alone in their somewhat blind enthusiasm for environmental determinants of development and evolution. Psychologist J. B. Watson's *behaviorism* is often cited as an example of an extreme environmentalist point of view. Behaviorism was much more than a reaction against hereditary extremism, but Watson's feelings about the importance of environment were strong, as is evident in his famous statement about child development (Watson, 1930: 104).

> I should like to go one step further now and say, give me a dozen healthy infants, well formed, and my own specified world to bring them up in and I'll guarantee to take any one at random and train him to become any type of specialist I might

select—doctor, lawyer, artist, merchant-chief and, yes even beggerman and thief, regardless of his talents, penchants, tendencies, abilities, vocations and the race of his ancestors.

It is important to note that Watson specifies that the infants should be well formed. How well the infant is formed is in no small part determined by genetic factors. Assuming that this qualifying word represents a concession to the importance of genetic constitution, Watson's statement still remains as an extreme example of environmentalism. Watson (1930) and later Skinner (1968) pointed out that this particular statement goes beyond the facts in an effort to counteract extreme hereditarian views that existed for centuries and to emphasize what could be done despite genetic limitations. These are good motives, and it is unfortunate that Watson's behaviorism and the extreme environmentalist views of Boas and Ward resulted in such an overemphasis on environment that the importance of genetic factors has been ignored in American psychology.

THE ARGUMENT OVER HOW MUCH

Many controversies stimulated by human behavior genetics research have resulted from attempts to determine the proportional contribution of environment and heredity to a given behavioral trait. We are all aware of the controversy generated by Jensen's (1969; 1970) studies of the inheritance of intelligence in blacks and whites. Many highly emotional criticisms have been leveled against Jensen, but the fundamental weakness in his argument is that high heritability of intelligence within the white population indicates that genetic factors are strongly implicated in mean differences in IQ between blacks and whites. Aside from the issue of culture-fair tests, one cannot really compare heritability coefficients for two populations unless environmental conditions are identical. Heritability is estimated by constructing a ratio between the amount of variance attributable to genotype and the amount attributable to environment (E) + genotype (G) + GE interaction. Another way to define heritability is the ratio of genotypic variance over phenotypic variance. For comparisons of heritability values to make sense, one must be able to control environment in the populations for which comparisons are made and one must make certain assumptions about GE interactions that are difficult to test. For this reason a number of contemporary behavior geneticists argue that attempts to determine the proportional contribution of heredity and environment to a behavioral characteristic at different points in the life span or for different racial groups are futile because heredity and environment rarely combine in a static, additive manner. In short, the proportional contribution of heredity to a given phenotype is not the same under different environmental conditions. Similarly, given different hereditary predispositions, the relative contribution of various environments differs. The interaction of environment and heredity in the context of growth and development is not unlike the emphasis on the organism and the environment as an active process of change in dialectic psychology (Payne, 1968).

Range of reaction

The relationship between environment and genotype is nicely stated in Gottesman's "reaction range" concept. According to this concept, as environment increases in richness or favorableness, the degree to which genotype is expressed in a behavior is increased. Presumably, this is true in terms of the variance of the behavior and its heritability. In other words, an enriched environment allows the effects of genotype to be expressed more fully than would be possible in an impoverished environment. This concept of reaction range is demonstrated in an animal study by Henderson (1975:9). Henderson compared behaviors for mice reared in standard labo-

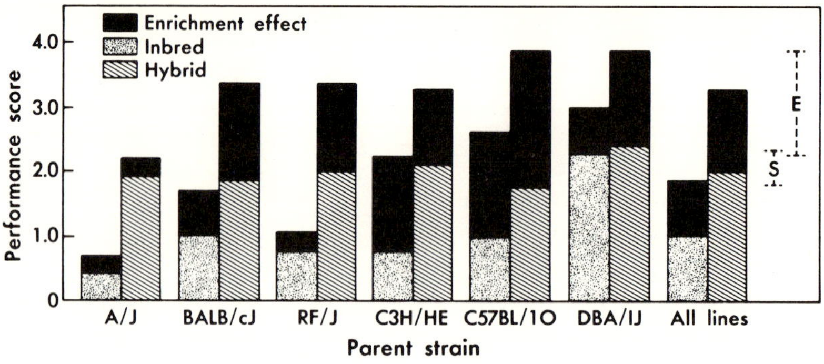

Fig. 13-1. Example of the way in which different environments can modify behavior that is influenced by genotype. Each inbred strain represents a unique genotype relative to each other strain. (From Henderson, N. D. *Journal of Comparative and Physiological Psychology,* 1970, **72,** 505-511. Copyright 1970 by the American Psychological Association. Reprinted by permission.)

ratory cages and mice reared in cages allowing considerably more exploration and contact with stimulus objects than the standard cages. Different strains of mice and hybrids were utilized and may be looked on as representing different genotypes. The mice were tested in a simple food-seeking task after six weeks in one or the other of these environments. A hungry mouse was placed in a large enclosure and was given a score in terms of length of time required to find its way to food located on the upper part of one wall of the enclosure.

Data analyses revealed that this behavior was influenced to only a small degree by genetic factors (about 10%). In contrast, animals that spent the first six weeks of their lives in the more complex cages not only performed better but much more variability among strains and stocks (genotypes) was observed. Heritability for these animals was 40%.

Fig. 13-1 shows the results of Henderson's study. Keep in mind that each strain and hybrid stock represents a different genotype. Some of the genotypes exhibited almost no difference in performance as a result of rearing under the two different environmental conditions, whereas others exhibited a substantial increase in performance when reared in the more complex environment. One can also see (Fig. 13-1) the relatively narrow range of performance scores obtained by the different hybrids raised in standard cages as opposed to those raised in the more complex cages.

Often it is assumed that whereas behavioral traits are influenced by environment, biological characteristics are basically influenced by genotype. However, biological traits are affected by genotype by environment interactions just as are behavioral traits. Eleftheriou and co-workers (1975) compared inbred strains and hybrids in terms of brain weight, body weight, and brain/body weight ratio. Mice from each strain and stock were reared in a laboratory in Italy and in one in the United States. Care was taken to control such factors as the way in which the brains were taken out. In fact, the Italian investigators learned and repeated the procedure many times in the United States laboratory so that they would take the same amount of brain and excise the brain in the same way. However, laboratory handling practices and activities were allowed to vary as they would naturally for the Italian and United States laboratories.

Table 13-1 shows brain/body ratios for the two laboratories (identified as *Laboratory A* and *Laboratory B*). Table 13-2 shows statistical tests of differences in brain weight between the two laboratories. It may be seen in Table 13-1 that the rank ordering of

Table 13-1. Means and standard deviations for brain/body ratios*†

Laboratory A‡ brain/body ratio				Laboratory B§ brain/body ratio			
Group	Mean		SEM	Group	Mean		SEM
C	12.64	±	0.13	D	12.51	±	0.09
G	11.95	±	0.22	G	12.23	±	0.12
B6	11.17	±	0.23	H	12.17	±	0.15
D	11.15	±	0.18	B6	11.80	±	0.09
H	11.07	±	0.31	E	11.73	±	0.09
E	10.73	±	0.30	J	11.57	±	0.09
J	10.71	±	0.16	BCF_1	11.56	±	0.11
K	10.32	±	0.15	C	11.31	±	0.07
BCF_1	10.09	±	0.17	K	11.23	±	0.14
I	09.35	±	0.17	I	10.62	±	0.10
CBF_1	09.25	±	0.17	CBF_1	10.48	±	0.12

*From Eleftheriou, B. E., Elias, M. F., Castellano, C., and Oliverio, A. *Journal of Heredity,* 1975, **66,** 207-212. Copyright 1975 by The American Genetic Association.
†Each strain and hybrid represents a unique genotype. Straight lines connect nonsignificant differences between strains and hybrids. Note that the pattern of significant differences ($p < .05$) is different for the two laboratories and the rank order of means is different.
‡The Laboratorio di Psicofisiologia e Psicobiologia, Rome, Italy.
§The Hamilton Station, The Jackson Laboratory, Bar Harbor, Maine.

Table 13-2. Summary of the statistical tests of the differences between means for brain/body ratios for Laboratory A and for Laboratory B (Lab. A – Lab. B)*†

Group	C	B6	BCF_1	CBF_1	D	E	G	H	I	J	K
Difference	–	+	+	+	+	+	0	+	+	+	+
P values	.01	.01	.01	.01	.01	.01	NS	.01	.05	.01	.01

*From Eleftheriou, B. E., Elias, M. F., Castellano, C., and Oliverio, A. *Journal of Heredity,* 1975, **66,** 207-212. Copyright 1975 by The American Genetic Association.
†– refers to a significant difference in the negative direction. + refers to a significant difference in the positive direction. 0 refers to no significant difference. Note that some differences are in the positive direction, some are in the negative direction, and in some cases no differences existed.

brain/body ratios is different for the animals reared in Laboratory A and those reared in Laboratory B, although some of the genotypes (strains) maintained about the same rank position in both laboratories. It may be seen in Table 13-2 that significant differences between laboratories were observed for some genotypes but not all genotypes. Brain/body weight ratios were used because brain weight and body weight are correlated, and body weight was also influenced by rearing in the two different laboratories. However, the rank orderings of body weight were not the same as those for brain weight, and brain weight ordering was still different between laboratories when brain weights were statistically adjusted for their correlation with body weight. Thus a trait that is often thought of as primarily influenced by genotype, brain size, can be altered by virtue of the laboratory environment. In Chapter 6 we reviewed a study by Sprott and Eleftheriou (Table 6-1) in which activity level was modified by rearing animals in laboratories only a few miles apart, and we have provided many other examples of genotype by environment interactions in the various chapters in this book.

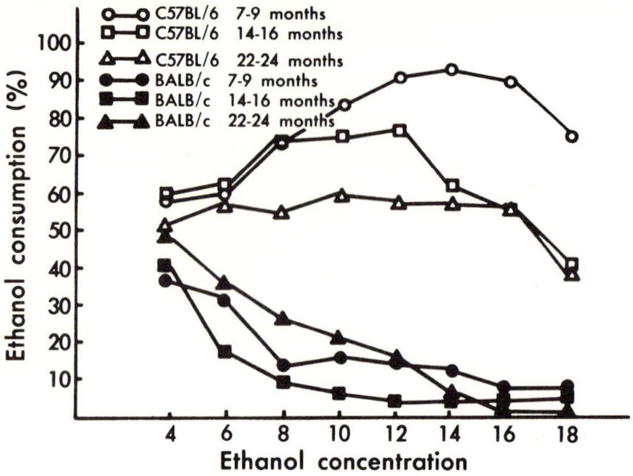

Fig. 13-2. Percent ethanol consumed for two strains of mice of three different ages in an alcohol study. (From Wood, W. G. *Experimental Aging Research,* 1976, **2,** 425-434. By permission of the authors and editors. © EAR, Inc., 1976.)

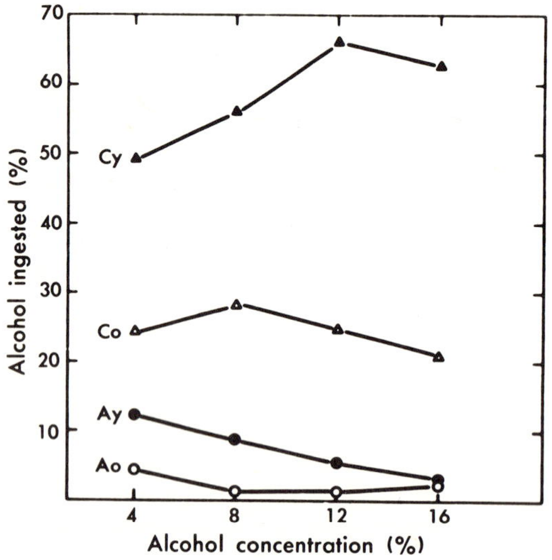

Fig. 13-3. Results of an alcohol preference study. (From Goodrick, C. L. *Experimental Aging Research,* 1975, **1,** 191-207. By permission of the authors and editors. © EAR, Inc., 1975.)

Often the rank ordering of various strains is maintained across a range of ages, but differences among strains increase and decrease at different ages. A study of alcohol preference (see Elias, Wood, and Pentz, 1976) by Wood (1976) provides a good example of the differences among strains that occur at different ages. Animals used in the study were male mice of the C57BL/6 and the BALB/c strains, which were generously provided by the National Institute on Aging (National Institutes of Health). Age groups were as follows: 7 to 9 months, 14 to 16 months, and 22 to 24 months. Ethanol and tap water were presented for a number of days. Beginning at a concentration of 4% ethanol (v/v prepared from 95% ethanol), the mice were presented with ethanol concentrations ranging from 4% to 18%, and drinking at each concentration was measured for 2 days at the same time each day. Each day fresh solutions were placed in the tubes, and the positions of the tubes were altered.

Fig. 13-2 summarizes the results of this experiment in terms of fluid consumption for each strain and age group at each concentration. It may be seen that age differences were rather slight for the C57BL/6J strain at the low concentration, but they become more pronounced with increasing concentrations, with the youngest animals exhibiting the largest percentage of fluid consumption. On the other hand, the BALB/c mice differed much less in terms of the age variable and showed a general trend of decline with increasing concentrations.

An interaction of age by genotype was reported in another alcohol study done by Goodrick (1975a). The nature of this interaction, involving C57BL/6J and A/J strains of mice is clear from inspection of Fig. 13-3.

Genotype by age interactions are not always observed. Sometimes the rank order of two genotypes is maintained across age groups. In a study by Elias and Pentz (unpublished), high and low blood pressure stocks of mice differed at each age group in terms of open-field activity (Fig. 13-4), but they exhibited an age by genotype interaction for number of boluses dropped in the open field (Fig. 13-5). Often increased open-field activity and decreased number of boluses are interpreted as reflecting a decreased stress response to the open-field test situ-

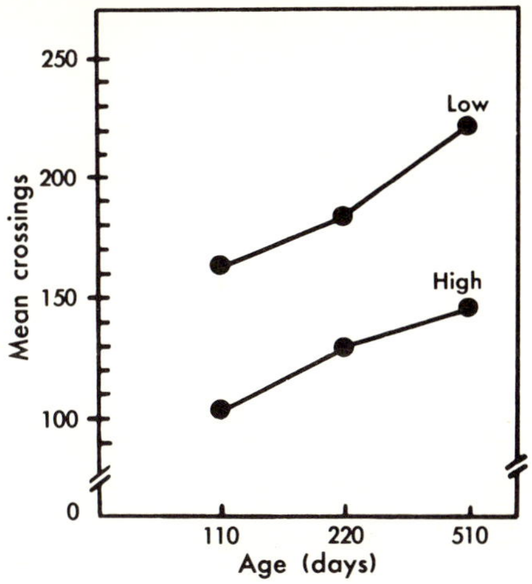

Fig. 13-4. Age and blood pressure main effects with a nonsignificant interaction for age and blood pressure. (From Elias, M. F., and Pentz, C. A., III. *Activity level in high and low blood pressure mice.* Unpublished manuscript, Syracuse University, Syracuse, N.Y. By permission of the authors.)

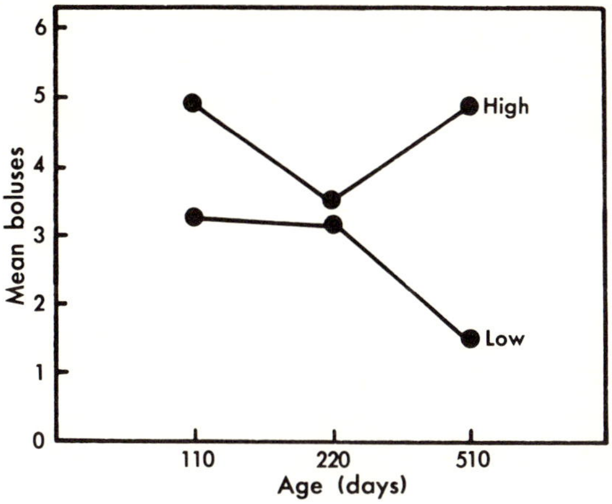

Fig. 13-5. Age by blood pressure interaction for defecation in the open field. (From Elias, M. F., and Pentz, C. A., III. *Activity level in high and low blood pressure mice.* Unpublished manuscript, Syracuse University, Syracuse, N.Y. By permission of the authors.)

ation. What would you conclude about stress response for the 220-day-old animals based on an examination of Figs. 13-4 and 13-5?

Interpretations of the results of the studies summarized in Figs. 13-1 to 13-5 are unimportant in the present context. The point that we wish to make is that differences between genotype are the rule rather than the exception and that any aging experiment with only one strain is gathering rather restricted information about the effect of treatments and the age variable on a single genotype. Just as one would never perform a drug experiment without more than one drug dose level, one really should include more than a single inbred strain in aging or developmental studies to gain the full power of the animal model for testing genotype by treatment by age interactions. Remember that all individuals within a strain are identical. Thus a single strain study allows *control* over the variation in behavior due to genotype; it neither allows one to examine genotype by treatment by age interactions, nor does it produce data that permit generalizations to the species as a whole.

Perhaps one more illustration of this important principle will serve as a good reminder about the confidence with which investigators may make generalizations from single strain studies. We have been advised on many occasions, by colleagues in comparative psychology, that brain lesioning studies with a single strain of rat or mouse are on fairly safe grounds because, after all, "a brain is a brain," and brains within a species are pretty similar with regard to their influence on behavior. Is this true? Elias and colleagues (1973) asked this question in a study in which the amygdala (a small structure in the brain near the hypothalamus) was lesioned in five different areas with tiny electrodes, and the effects on behavior of lesioning in these five very small brain areas was observed for two different strains of mice. It may be seen in Fig. 13-6 that the influence of the various lesions on reversal learning were very different for the two strains of mice. What would you conclude about the effects of these lesions on the "mouse brain"? Clearly, it depends on genotype. Yes, it is true that the baseline levels of performance (performance for the nonlesioned control strains) differ. This is precisely why one

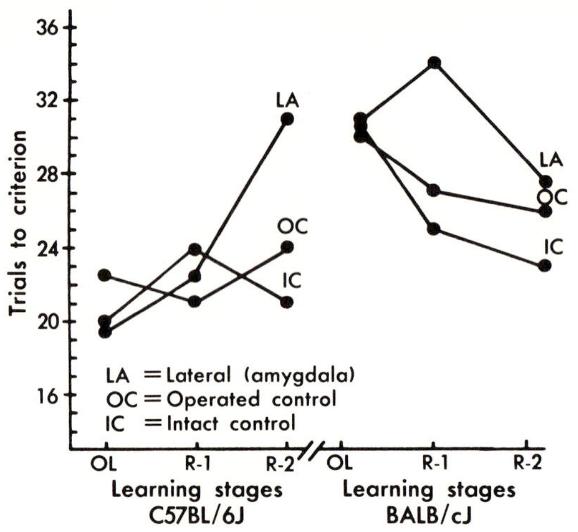

Fig. 13-6. Strain by site of lesion interaction for two inbred strains of mice. (From Elias, M. F., Dupree, M., and Eleftheriou, B. E. *Journal of Comparative and Physiological Psychology,* 1973, **83,** 149-156. Copyright 1973 by the American Psychological Association. Reprinted by permission.)

should use more than one inbred strain of mice for a lesioning study, particularly in developmental or aging studies where interactions with age may also occur.

The diallel cross

Of course, the more inbred strains and hybrids one has in an aging experiment or developmental study the greater is the possibility of observing age by genotype interactions. In fact, if a sufficient number of strains are used, a breeding design that allows the investigator to analyze data in such a way as to estimate a number of important genetic parameters may be used, that is, the *diallel cross* procedure. The diallel cross allows the investigator to obtain information regarding maternal effects, sex-linked effects, additive genetic variance, and several sources of nonadditive variance. This procedure, and other genetic tools, may be reviewed in an excellent methods text by Manosevitz and co-workers (1969). Briefly, the diallel cross involves crossing a number of inbred strains in all possible combinations (N^2, where $N = $ number of strains). The method is laborious and requires large numbers of animals, but many behavior geneticists believe that it provides useful information about genotype by environment interactions and the influence of genotype on behavior.

Heterozygous stocks

In the interest of generalizing to the species as a whole, the investigator may wish to create heterozygous stocks for experimentation. This is not as simple as it appears and is time consuming, since it involves the intercrossing of inbred strains. Techniques have been worked out and are described in a paper by Henderson (1969). The paper is well worth reading for the student who is interested in working with an animal stock that represents a heterozygous genotype rather than the homozygous genotype represented by inbred strains; that is, phenotype variability results from genotypic as well as environmental variability. The procedure described by Henderson (1969) seems to be a useful alternative to the suggestion by one investigator that wild mice be used.

Genotype by environment interactions in humans

It is, of course, impossible to find studies on the human level that are strictly analogous to genotype by treatment by age studies in animals. There are no inbred strains of humans; monozygotic twins are not present in large numbers; and there are no F_1 hybrid stocks that have resulted from a cross between two inbred strains of humans. Thus it is necessary to resort to estimates of heritability and to use various correlational techniques to tease out genotype and environment components of behavior. Even with some relatively new and sophisticated statistical techniques, enormous numbers of subjects are necessary to generate meaningful designs.

Henderson (1975) points out that Scarr-Salapatek (1971) encountered difficulties in comparing heritability estimates for black children and white children in Philadelphia using standard procedures with monozygotic (MZ) twins and dizygotic (DZ) twins who lived together. It is significant to note that her total of nearly a thousand pairs was not sufficient for these kinds of comparisons (Henderson, 1975). Keep in mind that this study was done within a given environment (did not compare environments) and was not a life-span study. Even a greater number of subjects would have been necessary to fill in the cells of a longitudinal/cross-sectional design of the variety suggested by K. W. Schaie (Chapter 3).

Generally, twin studies predominate in the literature about adult development, but they are not without methodological problems, which have been described by Henderson (1975:10). Part of the problem is related to the large number of subjects needed to compare twins reared together as opposed to twins reared apart. Henderson points out that some investigators have been able to obtain moderately large samples of MZ twins reared apart and that the correlation between MZ twins reared apart and examined in the context of estimates of parent-offspring correlations and correlations between parents' scores allows a partitioning of genetic variance into additive genetic, dominance and assortative mating effects, and environmental effects. However, despite the fact that large samples can be obtained with great effort, there is a fundamental problem, according to Henderson (1975: 10): The correlational approach depends "on the assumption that phenotypic variance between individuals is a simple sum of genetic and environmental variances and that both GE interactions and the covariance or correlation between genotype and environment are negligible."

Henderson has described some rather complex statistical methods designed to correct for these problems and to test assumptions that must be made. One of these techniques is referred to as multiple abstract variance analyses (MAVA). MAVA is extremely useful, but it requires large numbers of subjects. More limited approaches with MAVA have been used, but there are problems with these approaches, including the fact that the investigator must assume that environment for identical and fraternal twins reared together is the same.

Recognizing these limitations, we can now consider some of the data on the magnitude of genotype by environment interactions for studies using MZ and DZ twin comparisons and correlational statistics. Jinks and Fulker (see Henderson, 1975) found that neuroticism, as measured by a modified Maudsley Personality Inventory, was not characterized by a genotype by environment interaction. A simple genetic model could be used to explain the data. A similar finding evolved from Jinks and Fulker's analysis of Schields' twin data (see Henderson, 1975:13) for two tests of cognitive ability: a vocabulary test and a Dominoes intelligence test involving perceptual-cognitive materials like those on the Raven Progressive Matrices test.

> The analysis of the vocabulary test indicated that a small degree of G $\times$ E interaction, again involving within-family environment was present. Individuals with lowest scores appeared more influenced by their environment than those with higher scores. Again, however, only a small percentage, in this case 8 percent, of the phenotypic variance could be attributed to an environmental interaction with genotype. The nonverbal Dominoes test, which would probably be regarded as a "culture fair" intelligence test, indicated no significant GE interaction, either between or within families. Thus, in Shields' data it was found that on the personality measure and the aptitude measure on which one would expect strong environmental influences, low magnitude genotype $\times$ within-family environmental interactions were found.*

At first thought these failures to obtain genotype-environment interactions seem surpris-

*Reprinted by permission of the publisher, from Henderson, N. D. In K. Warner Schaie, V. Elving Anderson, Gerald E. McClearn, and John Money (Eds.), *Developmental human behavior genetics.* Lexington, Mass.: Lexington Books, D. C. Heath & Co., 1975.

ing, but Henderson (1975:13-14) offers some interesting hypotheses in way of explanation.

> The reasons for the relatively negligible GE interactions for these populations might be more appropriately attributed to a nature of the measurements themselves. Most good measuring instruments or tests of personality or intelligence are generally constructed in such a way as to maximize test-retest reliability. In other words, most test makers have gone to great efforts to choose items that are relatively buffered from the short-term influence of minor environmental fluctuations that individuals are subject to. This conscious effort to provide stability of measures has most likely resulted in minimizing short-term environmental or GE interaction effects. As a result, analysis of data from such tests is less likely to indicate a complex mode of inheritance including genotype-environmental interactions than one might find on behavioral measures other than these standardized tests.*

Thus it can be seen, through the foregoing discussion, that many problems are encountered when one performs biometric analyses on human behavior genetics data and that these problems are related to (1) the way in which behaviors are measured, (2) the large samples needed, and (3) the need to make assumptions about genotype by environment interactions which may not be met. These problems are magnified when studies are placed in a life-span framework or a developmental context. Consequently, there have been relatively few life-span or age-comparison studies using human behavior genetic methods. (Some of the terms used in the short section to follow and in the remainder of the text may not be familiar to the student without review. Consequently a glossary of terms may be found in the boxed material.)

In one study of older adults, Jarvik and her associates (1972) obtained data leading to the conclusion that the genetic components of intellectual ability are fairly consistent into old age. The pattern of abilities and concordances of twins (N = 19 sets, 77 to 88 years of age) was still similar to that found twenty years earlier. The identical twins were still more similar to each other than were the fraternal twins for most of the measures used.

Other than studies by Jarvik and her colleagues (discussed later), there have been few efforts to perform behavior genetic studies with elderly adults.

EARLY EXPERIENCE AND GENOTYPE

Early experience studies have provided considerable support for the range of reaction model with a developmental context. This research, including studies of child-rearing practices, has been reviewed by Anastasi (1958) and others. A chapter by Denenberg (1969a) is particularly worth reading because he has taken a species comparison approach to the study of variables with a strong genetic component. He reviews, in a single paper, studies in which early experience treatments for dogs, mice, rats, monkeys, and humans involved the nature of mothering, maternal deprivation, peer deprivation, stress, and restricted environment. Not all of these treatments were applied to each of the species compared, and the behavioral measures differed among the species (aggression, pain perception, problem solving, sexual behavior, maternal behavior, physical height, onset of menarche). However, an early experience manipulation was the common theme in all studies, and the behaviors all had a strong genetic basis or adaptive value in the evolutionary sense of facilitating survival of the species.

For each of the studies (species) reviewed, behavior was rather drastically modified by manipulation of postnatal experience. Moreover, for all species studied, modifications in behavior lasted well into maturity. For rats, effects not only lasted into old age but were

---

*Reprinted by permission of the publisher, from Henderson, N. D. In K. Warner Schaie, V. Elving Anderson, Gerald E. McClearn, and John Money (Eds.), *Developmental human behavior genetics.* Lexington, Mass.: Lexington Books, D. C. Heath & Co., 1975.

DEFINITIONS FOR SOME TERMS USED IN CHAPTERS 13 AND 14

allele One of two or more alternative forms of a gene that occupies a common locus on a chromosme.

assortative mating Nonrandom mating in which members of a population mate with others of a similar or dissimilar phenotype.

autosome Any chromosome except the sex chromosomes.

backcross Mating between a hybrid and one of the two parental strains (progenitor strains). It usually involves a backcross of an F to the progenitor strain carrying the recessive alleles (or presumably carrying the recessive alleles).

concordance Presence of a condition in both members of a pair of twins.

congenic Describes a line of animals differing from an inbred strain only at one locus.

co-twin control Application of a specific treatment to one member of a monozygotic twin pair.

Down's syndrome A classification of mental retardation that is due to chromosome abnormality. The patients have all or most of chromosome 21 represented three times instead of only twice. Clinical features are mental retardation and abnormalities in the eyelid fold, stubby hands and feet, and short stature.

dominant Describes an allele that produces the phenotype in question regardless of whether it is heterozygous or homozygous.

eugenics The study of methods of improving the genetic quality of the human species.

F_1 First filial generation resulting from the crossing of parental strains or stocks.

F_2 Second filial generation resulting from crossing of F_1 hybrids.

full sibs Individuals who have both parents in common.

gene A unit of genetic material that is localized in the chromosome. The gene has been operationally defined as a specific sequence of nucleotides in DNA or RNA that acts as a functional unit.

gene pool Genetic information that is represented (encoded) in all of the genes in a breeding population.

genetic drift Changes in gene frequencies because of random fluctuations.

genotype "Genetic baggage"; the genetic makeup of an individual.

heritability Ratio of genetic variance to variance due to phenotype. Variance phenotype $= (G + E) + GE$.

homologous Describes chromosomes having the same sequence of genes.

Huntington's chorea A dominant condition that becomes apparent at different ages. It is characterized by impaired motor control, progressive dementia, and severe mental impairment.

hybrid Any offspring of a cross between two genetically dissimilar strains.

inborn error of metabolism Genetically determined biochemical disorder in which there is an enzyme defect producing a metabolic block.

inbred strain Homozygous stock of mice derived from repeated full-sib mating for twenty consecutive generations.

inbreeding The mating of relatives.

karyotype An individual's complement of chromosomes.

Lesch-Nyhan syndrome An X-linked deficiency of the enzyme hypoxanthine-guanine phosphoribosyltransferase. The syndrome includes self-mutilation, mental retardation, and hyperuricemia.

linkage Nonrandom assortment of genes that results from their location on the same chromosome.

Continued.

DEFINITIONS FOR SOME TERMS USED IN CHAPTERS 13 AND 14—cont'd

locus Fixed position of a gene on the chromosome.

MAVA Multiple abstract variance analysis. A statistical technique developed to estimate the relative importance of genetic and environmental factors within a family or a culture.

Mendelian inheritance The mode of inheritance of chromosomal genes as opposed to cytoplasmic hereditary determinants.

metachromatic leukodystrophy Severe disorder transmitted genetically as an autosomal recessive trait. It is characterized by an accumulation of sulfatide in neural and nonneural tissue and a diffuse loss of myelin in the central nervous system.

mutant An organism possessing one or more genes that have undergone mutation.

mutation A change in genetic material that can be passed on from generation to generation.

phenotype Anatomical, physiological, or behavioral characteristic of an animal.

phenylketonuria (PKU) A defect in metabolism resulting in mental retardation. The metabolic block involves the conversion of phenylalanine to tyrosine.

pleiotropy The influence of one gene on two or more phenotypes.

polygenic Describes multiple genetic factors.

recessive Refers to an allele that produces a phenotypic effect only when it is homozygous. A trait or phenotype that results when one mates animals carrying two recessive alleles at the same locus.

recombination A combination of alleles in progeny that is different from the combination in the parents. This phenomenon results from an exchange of chromosomal material between homologous chromosomes.

recombinant inbred strains A battery of inbred strains developed on the basis of recombination and serving as a genetic tool in the search for specific chromosome loci that influence specific phenotypes.

sex chromosomes Chromosomes that are nonhomologous in one sex (X and Y in human beings).

sex linked Describes a form of inheritance determined by a gene located on the X chromosomes.

observed for children and grandchildren of the experimental subjects. For each species the number of behaviors influenced by early experience manipulations or naturally occurring early experience events was altered by the age of the animal at which these experiences occurred.

The interaction of genotype and environment begins at conception, and this is why it is so difficult to assume that genotype and environment are additive effects, even when they can be carefully controlled in studies performed on postnatal animals. Joffe (1969) has presented an extensive review of research on prenatal determinants of behavior. Most studies have been done with animals because of the difficulties in obtaining sufficient control over genetic and prenatal environmental variables with human subjects. These animal studies revealed that exposure to x rays, drugs, sex hormones, and stress during pregnancy has seriously detrimental effects on the emotional and/or cognitive behavior of offspring. Some of these stressors not only influence the prenatal environment, per se, but may influence the chromosomes and genes. Thus the gene environment is influenced as well as the environment of the fetus.

Aside from clinical studies, Joffe uncovered only a limited number of experimental-type manipulative studies with humans. It is clear that malnutrition during pregnancy has damaging effects on the developing nervous system. However, Joffe reports finding only one experimental investigation of the effects of maternal nutrition on the behavior of children. Harrell and associates (1955) found that the mean IQ of children of three groups of mothers given different vitamin supplements was significantly higher (statistically) than the mean IQ of the children of mothers who received a placebo. However, this result was observed in one clinic and not another. In a Virginia clinic the mean IQ of the progeny of the three vitamin supplement–mother groups was 3.7 points higher when the groups were combined and compared with the placebo group. This result was obtained when the children were 3 years of age. At 4 years of age the combined treatment group mean was 5.2 points higher than the placebo mean. However, these results were not replicated in a Kentucky clinic. The investigators argue that the nutrition of the mothers in the Kentucky clinic was adequate without vitamin supplement. If we can ignore the many potentially confounding variables introduced by comparisons of the two clinics, these data seem to indicate that the positive behavioral effects of a vitamin supplement during pregnancy are small and may be beneficial only when there are inadequate diets to begin with. Much more work is needed in this area, and observations need to be carried over a large segment of the life span.

Early experience studies provide evidence that traits influenced by genes and environment are modifiable by training and manipulation of the environment. However, it is unsafe to conclude that they are infinitely modifiable or that they demonstrate the fact that genotype is unimportant. Such conclusions perpetuate the nature-nurture controversy. It makes no sense to argue that intelligence is not influenced by genotype. The evidence is very strong for the high heritability of intelligence within given populations (Burt, 1972; Erlenmeyer-Kimling and Jarvik, 1963; Schull and Neel, 1969). Conversely, it makes no sense to argue that since there is such a high heritability coefficient, attempts to enhance intelligent behavior through adequate prenatal care and postnatal treatments are futile.

Many behavioral genetic studies have focused on cognitive abilities and intelligence, possibly because they are more easily measured than personality variables and other human qualities and possibly because they are highly regarded in competitive Western society. Attempts to compare heritability coefficients for different measures of personality with those for intelligence are interesting but probably of limited value. High heritability for a trait does not necessarily mean that it has had more adaptive value than a trait with low heritability. In fact, the reverse may be true because natural selection over many years can reduce or exhaust genetic variability for a trait. If all persons must exhibit a trait to survive and to reproduce, they will become alike with regard to that trait and genetic variability will become zero.

It should be clear by now that there are those who are critical of studies which compare heritability coefficients for different behaviors or for different groups of persons. There are also those who are critical of tests of gene by environment interactions. At best, a study in which one demonstrates an age by genotype by environment interaction indicates that both genotype and environment interact differently at different ages. The really important question, in the opinion of many investigators (see Anastasi, 1958; Elias, 1973), is not *how much* does genotype contribute to behavior but *how* does genotype contribute to behavior. Just how does one go about answering the *how question?*

HOW: GOING BEYOND GENOTYPE BY ENVIRONMENT INTERACTIONS

Before we discuss approaches to the *how* question, the student must be reminded that *only genes can be inherited. Behaviors are*

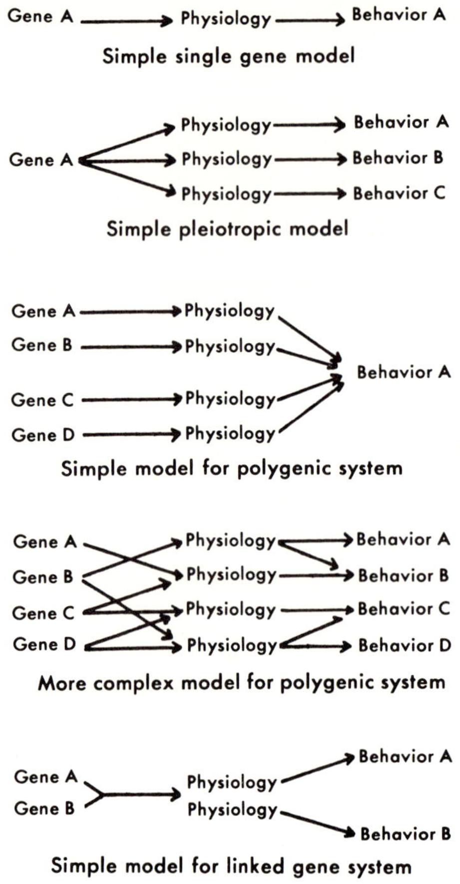

Fig. 13-7. Oversimplified set of models for the different ways in which a gene or genes might influence one or more behaviors via one or more intervening physiological variables.

not inherited. Behaviors are influenced by genes by way of physiological phenomena that intervene between genes and behavior. Schematic drawings of these relationships are shown in Fig. 13-7. The social scientist may concentrate on the question of how environment influences behavior by searching for variables that intervene between a macroscopic environmental condition and a given behavior. These may be physiological variables or microscopical environmental variables. The behavior geneticist engages in a search for variables that intervene between genes or a single gene and behavior. The search is very difficult because, just as environment can influence behavior in many ways, genes can influence behavior in many ways. These different possibilities are summarized in Fig. 13-7.

Let us define a single gene as a unit of genetic material localized at a segment of a chromosome, that is, found at a single *locus.* A single gene may influence a given behavior by way of an intervening variable or variables. We can refer to this as a single gene effect or a single locus effect. Sometimes a single gene involves a major effect on a behavior, but other genes influence the behavior as well. This is often referred to as a *major gene* or major locus effect. Alternatively, a single gene may influence a variety of behaviors by virtue of diffuse physiological effects, which is referred to as a *pleiotropic effect,* or *pleiotropy.* Of course, a number of genes can influence a number of behaviors or a single behavior *(polygenic effect).* Sometimes genes on the same chromosome that are in close proximity to each other influence two or more behaviors *(linked-gene effect).* They may also influence physiological phenomena and a behavior or behaviors.

Animal research: path markers

Obviously, when many environmental factors influence a behavior, or when many behaviors are influenced by a single environmental variable, it is difficult to sort them out and to establish causal relationships. The same is true of genotype and genetic studies. When many genes influence a behavior (polygenic system) or when many behaviors are influenced by a gene (pleiotropic system), it is difficult to track down and to isolate intervening variables so as to answer the question *how.*

In those rare instances when one or several genes influence a behavior, it is sometimes possible to answer *how* by tracing pathways of expression between these genes and behavior by using a *path marker,* for example, a neurohumor or hormone that is controlled by a gene and influences behavior. Many different kinds of path markers can be used. Research in this area has concentrated on seizure susceptibility, alcohol preference and aversion, avoidance conditioning, drug response, emotionality, and open-field behavior (see Eleftheriou, 1975; Fuller, 1956; Lindzey et al., 1971; McClearn, 1971).

At the human level some amount of path-marker research has focused on metabolic disorders, particularly those associated with mental retardation. These studies have led to the understanding and treatment of phenylketonuria, cleft palate, and other metabolic disorders and may eventually lead to enzyme replacement therapy for a number of birth defects that are related to defects or mutations in one or few genes. It is suspected that some debilitating diseases of old age may be influenced by one or two genes, but little progress has been made in this direction, although some progress has been made in terms of the relationship between chromosomes, behavior, and aging.

Jarvik and her colleagues have been concerned with the relationship between the chromosome abnormalities, psychopathology, and senile dementia. We will discuss this literature in the section to follow, which deals with answering *how* in human behavior genetics.

Fig. 13-8. Elizabeth S. Russell, Ph.D. (University of Chicago, 1937). Affectionately known as "Tibby" by her friends, colleagues, and students, Dr. Russell has contributed significantly to the field of genetics. She is well known for her work in mammalian genetics and, more recently, mammalian genetics and aging. Although she is not a behavior geneticist, her work has paved the way for new approaches in behavior genetics. She has stimulated many students to go on to scientific careers in genetics. Presently Dr. Russell is a Senior Staff Scientist at The Jackson Laboratory, Bar Harbor, Maine, where she has been for many years. She is a member of the American Academy of Arts and Sciences, the National Academy of Sciences, a Past President of the Genetic Society of America and a trustee of the University of Maine.

Human behavior genetics of how

Just as the question of *how much* (proportion due to genotype as opposed to environment) is more difficult to answer with humans than animals, so is the question of *how* more difficult to answer with human subjects. Some "how type" research with humans has focused on metabolic disorders. Diseases of metabolism resulting in mental retardation have been of particular concern to developmental behavior geneticists. It has been established that chromosomal anomalies, for example, trisomy 21 (Down's syndrome) and deletion of the short arm of one of the B group of chromosomes (cri-du-chat syndrome), result in impaired initial development of the nervous system. Similarly, it has been established that homozygosity for genes causing enzyme defects result in diseases that impair neural functioning severely, for example, phenylketonuria. In a chapter which deals with these diseases, Russell and Sprott (1975:24) point out that it is easier to prove genetic bases for diseases which appear early in life than those which appear late in life. They note that at least one disease which appears in adulthood, Huntington's chorea, is inherited as a unit dominant and that, "We can suspect but not prove that genetic factors contribute to the development of Alzheimer's disease."

As was noted before, the basic difficulty

concerning late-appearing diseases is the ability to distinguish between genotype and environment as causative factors because no two humans have the same genotype, with the exception of identical twins. Consequently, not much progress has been made with regard to identifying single loci that result in neurological and other types of diseases that have deleterious effects on behavior in middle and late life. Moreover, many behaviors of importance to humans who do not suffer from debilitating diseases are influenced by many, many genes. It may be for these reasons that most of the progress toward answering the question *how* in human behavior genetics of aging has focused on the chromosome rather than the gene.

Chromosome hypodiploidy. Studies relating chromosome loss *(hypodiploidy)* and aging have been under way for a number of years. They may well have been stimulated by a report that increased frequency of aneuploidy (cells with more or less than forty-six chromosomes) are seen more frequently in old age (Jacobs et al., 1961). In summaries of this literature, Yen and coworkers (1976) and Cohen (1976) note that many independent studies since the one by Jacobs and associates have confirmed the fact that there is a higher frequency of hypodiploid cells (cells with less than forty-six chromosomes) in older compared with younger women. A number of studies have indicated that, for women, the C-group chromosomes (containing the X chromosome) are lost more frequently in older than in younger persons, although one study (Jarvik and Kato, 1970) did not report significant C-group loss for women.

Increased hypodiploidy has not been observed for older men, although there are data that indicate a loss of G-group chromosomes (probably containing the Y chromosome) as men grow older (Yen et al., 1976).

The variability in reported levels of hypodiploidy has been large, although most studies seem to agree that there is greater loss in older women than in younger women. Cohen (1976) points out that this variability is related to the fact that different investigators have modified cell culture techniques and that different populations from different parts of the world have been studied. Thus it has been difficult to match studies in terms of drug use, radiation, pollution, health, medical history, and other nongenetical factors. Not only do these factors have a potential influence on length of life and behavior but they may also influence the integrity of chromosomes. One might postulate that longer exposure to these agents may explain greater chromosome loss in older persons. Of course, one needs to explain why men seem to be protected from this loss.

It is important to note that the bulk of the data in favor of hypodiploidy as an age-associated phenomenon are cross-sectional data. Cohen (1976) points out that Jarvik and her associates (in press) have reported the first longitudinal data on chromosome loss. Seventeen older persons (eleven women and six men) were examined at mean ages of 83 and 89 years. Women showed a significant increase in hypodiploidy and monosomy (loss of one of a pair of chromosomes). These results are important because they indicate that women of advanced age do lose chromosomes as they grow older. However, Cohen (1976) cautions about drawing conclusions relating to age changes in chromosome frequency from these longitudinal data because, she argues, health status has not been stated and previous studies indicate the clear possibility that disease processes influence chromosome loss. Jarvik and associates did examine drug use patterns and reached the conclusion that increased use of drugs with increasing age did not seem to account for the increase in chromosome loss.

Hypodiploidy, sex differences, and survival. Sex differences in the frequency of chromosome loss lead to some interesting speculations concerning the longer lives of women and the fact that more women than men are found with diagnoses of organic brain syndrome (Chapter 12). However, several studies indicate that the frequencies of hypodiploidy, monosomy G, and monosomy C do not differ for those who die earlier (decedents) and those who live longer (survivors) (see Yen et al., 1976).

Hypodiploidy: in vivo studies. Cohen (1976) points out that few studies have demonstrated chromosome loss in vivo compared with those which have demonstrated in vitro loss. Cadotte and Fraser (1970) examined blood cultures and bone marrow preparations for older men and women and found no significant differences in the proportion of hypodiploid cells in groups that were younger than 60 years of age when compared with groups that were older than 60 years.

Hypodiploidy and cognitive changes. Although the question of whether or not hypodiploidy is a reliable age-associated phenomenon has an important bearing on behavioral studies, the literature on correlations between behavior and hypodiploidy in persons of advanced age may be of greater interest to behavioral scientists than the question of survival, per se. Jarvik (1963; 1967) may have been the first experimenter to hypothesize that an increased frequency of hypodiploidy cells in older adults is related to cognitive functioning (see Cohen, 1976). Apparently this hypothesis was stimulated by the notion that hypodiploidy (demonstrated in cultures of peripheral lymphocytes) might also occur in cells that divide and affect cognitive processes (e.g., intellect, memory, and learning). Since glial cells have been implicated as functional units of the nervous system (they were once believed to serve only a support role), they have been cited as potential victims of hypodiploidy. However, Cohen (1976) points out that there have been no studies of hypodiploidy for glial cells, and thus much rests on the assumption that hypodiploidy which occurs in lymphocytes also occurs in glial cells. Absence of data suggesting that it does weakens the hypothesis that intellectual loss results from hypodiploidy.

A second major problem with studies which correlate hypodiploidy with behavior at different ages is that karyotype abnormalities may represent only one of many age-associated biological and health changes which take place as one grows old. We have already discussed changes in health, drug use, endocrine balance, and many other factors, including the possibility that neuronal transmission is altered in some manner as one grows older.

A major methodological problem is introduced by the fact that many of these age-correlated phenomena simply cannot be controlled. However, one must start somewhere, and the data about hypodiploidy and behavior represent an interesting and provocative beginning. They may some day represent important baseline data for studies devised to eliminate confounding variables. What are the current data regarding hypodiploidy and behavior? What are the confounding variables? We draw heavily on Cohen's excellent review for our discussion (Cohen, 1976).

The evidence for a relationship between chromosome loss and mental performance is not strong. One of the first studies reported a significant correlation ($r = 0.81$) between chromosome loss and scores on the Grahm-Kendall Memory for Designs Test in ten healthy persons (Jarvik and Kato, 1969). The subjects were aged twins who were part of a larger group of female twins who were examined in the context of a continuing longitudinal study conducted at the New York State Psychiatric Institute. In a subsequent study, Grahm-Kendall scores and percent hypodiploidy were examined for male and female twins separately. Hypodiploidy was higher in the men than in the women.

Nielsen (1970) has reported a higher level of C-group loss in women diagnosed as senile demented than in age-matched control subjects. Although senile dementia results in impaired memory and poor performance on tests of mental ability, these data do not necessarily provide support for the relation-

Table 13-3. Hypodiploidy in aged men and women with and without organic brain syndrome*†

	Women			Men		
	N	Age	Hypo-diploidy (%)	N	Age	Hypo-diploidy (%)
Nielsen (1970)‡						
Old	33	65-89		33	65-89	
Controls	10		10.1	10		6.1
Arteriosclerotic dementia	10		9.4	10		5.9
Senile dementia	10		18.0	10		6.6
Presenile dementia	3		10.2	3		5.9
Young	10	19-39	3.6	10	20-39	4.3
Jarvik, Altshuler, Kato, and Blumner (1971)§						
Old	23	77-93	16.8	13	79-91	16.5
No OBS	15		12.4	7		17.7
Mild/moderate OBS	8		21.8	6		15.1
Young	15	17-35	12.0	15	20-39	14.8

*From Cohen, D. A behavioral-chromosome relationship in the elderly: a critical review of a biobehavioral hypothesis. *Experimental Aging Research,* 1976, **2,** 271-287.
†Hypodiploidy levels of young men and women are included for comparison with the levels reported for older persons.
‡48-hour cultures.
§72-hour cultures.

ship between impaired mental ability and chromosome loss. At most, they suggest a relationship between chromosome loss and the specific disease processes that characterize senile dementia.

In a study by Bettner and colleagues (1971), a significant relationship was observed for hypodiploidy and one measure on the Stroop Color Word Test. The test was given to thirty-eight survivors from the New York Psychiatric Institute longitudinal study (fourteen diagnosed as brain damaged and twenty-four without any sign of brain damage). The only significant correlation reported was between chromosome loss and a score on card 3 of the test, and this correlation was computed from a mixed sample of twenty-nine men and women, some of whom were diagnosed as brain damaged. Cohen (1976) points out that patients diagnosed as arteriosclerotic were eliminated from the Stroop analysis but that they were not eliminated from the analysis of the Grahm-Kendall scores. This is unfortunate because advanced arteriosclerosis can itself result in cognitive deficit and represents a potential influence on chromosome loss as well. For this same study, significant correlations between chromosome loss and behavior were not observed for a number of other tests, that is, vocabulary, tapping, similarities, digits forward and backward, digit symbol substitution, and block design.

In studies by Nielsen (1968; 1970) a higher proportion of women with a diagnosis of organic brain syndrome exhibited chromosome loss than women of comparable age who were not diagnosed as brain damaged and did not fall in the following diagnostic categories: senile demented, arteriosclerotic, presenile demented. Similarly, Jarvik and coworkers (1971) have reported that older women who functioned well enough to live in the community rather than an institution (but showing sufficient memory loss and other symptoms of cognitive decline so as to be diagnosed as mildly or moderately brain damaged) did exhibit chromosome loss.

Cohen has prepared a table that summarizes these studies and data concerning the relationship between senile dementia and hypodiploidy (Table 13-3). It may be seen in Table 13-3 that the sample sizes were relatively small. Nielsen's study shows different levels of hypodiploidy for men and women. Cohen points out that the few women and the men who fell in the presenile dementia category in Nielsen's study exhibited hypodiploidy levels which were comparable with the healthy controls and the arteriosclerotic sample. It may be seen that for women, hypodiploidy is considerably higher than for men. It was considerably higher for older women of all categories than for younger women. Moreover, there is a somewhat noteworthy difference between the women classified as presenile demented and those classified as senile demented.

In the study by Jarvik and colleagues (1971), summarized in Table 13-3, the eight women with the diagnosis of brain damage without arteriosclerosis exhibited a significantly higher percentage of hypodiploidy than the fifteen women diagnosed as free from brain damage. These differences were not observed for the male sample. However, the older men with no diagnosis of organic brain syndrome (OBS) exhibited levels of hypodiploidy that were similar to the women with the diagnosis of OBS. At present there seems to be no explanation for the high frequency of hypodiploidy in men in the absence of a diagnosis of OBS. One of the major problems confronting studies such as these is that the diagnosis of OBS is very general and can include different kinds of brain damage with effects more pronounced in one sphere of mental functioning than another. Furthermore, misclassification of patients in diagnostic categories can and does occur. As anyone knows who has performed diagnoses on older patients, one cannot really diagnose with 100% accuracy in the absence of histological studies of the brain, and the correlation between structural damage and behavioral impairment is simply far from perfect. Thus considerable variability in performance may be expected among persons placed in these diagnostic categories.

In a study by Cohen and Jarvik (1973), seventy-eight women (mean age = 82.8 years) were given medical, psychiatric, psychological, and chromosome examinations. The range of hypodiploidy for women with no diagnosis of OBS was 5% to 24%; those with moderate OBS, 2% to 29%; and those with severe OBS, 7% to 24%. Mean hypodiploidy for forty-two subjects with a diagnosis of no OBS or mild OBS was 14.3%, compared with 15.7% for the thirty-six women with moderate and severe OBS. It is clear that these mean levels of hypodiploidy were not significantly different and that the averages are lower than those reported for older women diagnosed as mild or moderate OBS in the study by Jarvik and associates (1971). In fact, they are similar to the percentage hypodiploidy figures for older men.

There were no significant correlations between hypodiploidy and any of the psychological tests. Seventy-eight women completed chromosome examinations, but many of the women *did not* complete the cognitive test battery because of health or motivation or because the test was too difficult. Correlations between hypodiploidy and tests administered to the twin sample (including the Stroop Color Word and the Grahm-Kendall Memory for Designs Tests) were not particularly meaningful because sample sizes ranged from five to fifty-six. Furthermore, all of the women were in some type of an institution, many were not mobile, and many had chronic diseases that could affect motivation level and performance adversely as well as representing potential influences on chromosome integrity.

What exactly can we conclude from these data on hypodiploidy. First, it seems that there is no solid evidence at present that survivors and nonsurvivors differ with regard to hypodiploidy. This may be related to the fact that sample sizes were relatively small (it is extremely difficult to obtain subjects). Thus it is probably best to say that the hypothesis of differences between surviving and nonsurviving men and women must be tested further and provides an interesting line of further research.

Second, there is meager evidence for a correlation between hypodiploidy and impaired performance, but samples were small and many tests did not show significant correlations with hypodiploidy. A longitudinal study seems to confirm the findings of many cross-sectional studies that hypodiploidy in women does increase with age, but other studies need to be done with careful control of health factors. This is not easily accomplished because of the great difficulties in obtaining sufficient numbers of subjects meeting experiment requirements.

There are some problems with the notion of age-behavior-chromosome loss correlations on theoretical grounds. There is an underlying assumption that changes in peripheral lymphocytes (hypodiploidy in lymphocytes) are reflective of the same phenomenon in some functional unit of the nervous system (e.g., neural cells), but there are no data to support or refute the assumption.

Third, incidence of hypodiploidy differs between senile-demented and nondemented controls, but these data indicate only that disease processes which are associated with aging may influence both cognitive functioning and hypodiploidy. They do not provide strong evidence for impaired cognitive decline as a *result* of hypodiploidy. Furthermore, so many biological changes are taking place which have a potential for influencing cognitive and emotional behaviors that it is difficult to design a study which will reveal cause-effect relationships or uncontaminated correlations between chromosome loss and behavior. It would seem, then, that the hypodiploidy-behavior correlation hypothesis, as it relates to aging, remains an interesting hypothesis for further exploration. Perhaps the control possible at the animal level of research would dictate a strategy of well-designed and carefully controlled animal studies to be followed by human studies.

Animal behavior genetics of how

Laboratory animals, particularly small animals such as the mouse and rat, show great promise as tools for the emerging area of life-span developmental behavior genetics. Their obvious advantage is that their life span is relatively limited, and they may be reared in large numbers under controlled environmental conditions. Thus the many, many animals that must be used in developmental studies are available to the researcher. Moreover, he may very carefully control both genotype and environment or manipulate one or the other. The obvious disadvantage of animal models is that animals do not exhibit many of the behaviors which are important to humans. Nevertheless, some phenomena, for example, drug response, alcohol preference, diseases, and neurological disorders may be studied with animals, and these studies may produce animal models with which to develop hypotheses for study at the human level. In some instances, discovery of a single gene-behavior relationship at the animal level can lead the way to the discovery of a path marker that may be used with humans.

Before one uses an animal model to trace the relationship between a single gene and a behavior, one must find a behavior that is influenced in a major way by a single gene. These behaviors are "few and far between," and thus some investigators believe that the probability of discovering one does not justify the search for "a needle in the haystack." On the other hand, the importance of finding a single gene-behavior relationship is such that many investigators persist in this effort, and recently they have turned their attention to aging studies.

How does an investigator go about searching for a single gene effect? There are several approaches, which we review in Chapter 14, and as you read about these tools of the animal behavior geneticist, keep in mind that the literature about the application of these tools in aging studies is sparse. The reason for presenting methods of the animal behavior geneticist in Chapter 14 is that they represent a new and potentially very important area of research in life-span developmental psychology. Comparative psychologists can contribute to this area enormously if they become familiar with the available tools. Moreover, students may better understand some of the methods employed in human behavior genetics if they understand methods employed in animal behavior genetics and how they can be applied to developmental studies.

SUMMARY

In this chapter we described briefly the history of behavior genetics with special emphasis on the applications of this important area of psychology to developmental studies, particularly life-span developmental studies. It was noted that hereditary extremism resulted from the association of pseudogenetic arguments with repugnant political ideologies and early attempts to explain complex social behavior in terms of simple Mendelian genetic principles. The response to hereditary extremism was an environmentalist backlash, which lasted in the United States for many years, and it still influences behavioral and social scientists to the point that studies involving behavior genetics, particularly human behavior genetics, are often the subject of emotional responses rather than informed arguments and questioning. The history of environmental extremism in the United States has been as unfortunate as the history of hereditarian extremism because it is only through an understanding of genetic influences on behavior through the life span, starting with conception, that the developmental psychologist can obtain a real understanding of all the forces which determine growth and development. In fact, the importance of environment becomes very clear when one learns more about genetics and genetic studies.

The influence of genotype can only be revealed in an environment, and behavioral differences among individuals or among individuals (lower animals) with a given genotype become most clear in enriched environments.

For years scientists and lay persons have perpetuated the nature-nurture controversy by asking *how much* is contributed by environment and *how much* is contributed by heredity. The question is often difficult, sometimes impossible, to answer because most traits and behavioral characteristics are products of genotype (G) by environment (E) interactions. As one grows older and develops both socially and biologically, the manner in which genotype and environment interact changes. Actually, different points in the life span represent different environments as the organism is both acted on and, in turn, acts on his surroundings to change them. These interactions, involving a dynamic and ever-changing organism, make it difficult to use statistics to estimate heritability for given behaviors because the underlying assumption for application of these procedures is that genotype and environment are additive, but not interactive. For this reason many investigators believe that it is futile to go on asking how much but believe that it makes a lot of sense to ask *how*. How do genes influence behavior?

The question about how genes influence behavior is not easily answered with humans either. With the exception of identical twins, no two persons are alike genetically, and unfortunately there never seem to be enough identical twins around to meet the needs for the enormous numbers of subjects necessary to test genetic hypotheses in a life-span context.

Despite difficulties with human behavior genetic research, particularly with regard to the question of how genes influence behavior, there have been efforts to answer *how*. For the most part these studies have concentrated on genetically based inborn errors of metabolism that result in birth defects and gross behavioral disorders in their unfortunate child victims. It is much more difficult to perform these kinds of studies with elderly and middle-aged persons. They have lived longer, and thus genotype and environment influences have had a longer time to interact and become entangled, one with another. There are those who believe that some diseases of middle and old age, such as presenile dementia, senile dementia, and arteriosclerosis, have a genetic basis. There is reasonably good evidence that genotype plays a role, but it has not been possible to determine how genes influence these diseases, that is, to discover the mechanism(s) that intervenes between genes and disease.

Perhaps the greatest progress in terms of answering the question of "how" genes influence behavior has been made with respect to studies of the relationship between chromosome loss and aging. Older women seem to exhibit more chromosome loss than older men; chromosome loss appears to increase with age in women; and there is some evidence that chromosome loss is greater for institutionalized patients with diagnoses such as organic brain syndrome, senile dementia, and presenile dementia. These same studies suggest a relationship between mental performance and chromosome loss with increasing age, but much more work needs to be done to establish the validity of chromosome loss–impaired behavior hypotheses. First, there is no evidence thta chromosome loss with age which appears in lymphocytes also characterizes those functional cells in the nervous system which divide (e.g., neural cells). Second, the evidence for relationships between poor performance and chromosome loss is not impressive. Studies have been confounded by the fact that it is extremely difficult to control the incidence of many age-associated variables other than chromosome loss, for example, drug use, endocrine system changes, cardiovascular disease, and hypertension.

In general, behavior genetics research is difficult with humans, even when one concentrates on the most elementary kind of information, for example, heritability coefficients and descriptions of genotype by environment by age interactions. For this reason some researchers believe that the control and the model for short life made available by small animals, in combination with the behavior genetic tools for answering how, may make animal behavior genetics a valuable approach to understanding developmental processes. Because it is easier to answer the question of how genes influence behavior by using behavior genetic tools with animal models, mutants, inbred strains, and congenic lines, etc., many researchers advocate a strategy of initial work at the animal level to be followed by work at the human level once critical parameters, for example, likely hypotheses or useful path markers, have been defined. Alternatively, there are investigators who believe that one must move quickly, if not immediately, to research at the human level to answer important questions. As in all areas of research, this disagreement will continue to exist in behavior genetics research. Meanwhile, developmental psychologists will continue to obtain data on the human and animal level that will lead them closer and closer to understanding how genes influence behavior.

SELECTED READINGS

Anastasi, A. Heredity, environment, and the question "how"? *Psychological Review,* 1958, **65,** 197-208.

Bressler, M. Sociology, biology, and ideology. In D. C. Glass (Ed.), *Genetics.* New York: Rockefeller University Press, 1968.

Cohen, D. A behavioral-chromosome relationship in the elderly: a critical review of a biobehavioral hypothesis. *Experimental Aging Research,* 1976, **2,** 271-287.

Dobzhansky, T. Of flies and men. *American Psychologist,* 1967, **22,** 41-48.

Elias, M. F. Disciplinary barriers to progress in behavior genetics: defensive reactions to bits and pieces. *Human Development,* 1973, **16,** 119-132.

Erlenmeyer-Kimling, L., and Jarvik, L. F. Genetics and intelligence. A review. *Science,* 1963, **142,** 1477-1479.

Fuller, J. L. The path between genes and behavior characteristics. *Eugenics Quarterly,* 1956, **3,** 209-212.

Fuller, J. L., and Thompson, W. R. *Behavior genetics.* New York: John Wiley & Sons, Inc., 1960.

Goodenough, U., and Levine, R. P. *Genetics.* New York: Holt, Rinehart, & Winston, Inc., 1974.

Gottesman, I. I. Beyond the fringe—personality and psychopathology. In D. C. Glass (Ed.), *Genetics.* New York: Rockefeller University Press, 1968.

Haller, M. H. Social sciences and genetics. A historical perspective. In D. C. Glass (Ed.), *Genetics.* New York: Rockefeller University Press, 1968.

Henderson, N. D. Gene-environment interaction in human behavioral development. In K. W. Schaie, V. E. Anderson, G. E. McClearn, and J. Money (Eds.), *Developmental human behavior genetics: nature-nurture redefined.* Lexington, Mass.: Lexington Books, D. C. Heath & Co., 1975.

Jarvik, L. F., Kallmann, F. J., and Falek, A. Psychiatric genetics and aging. *Gerontologist,* 1962, **2,** 164-166.

Jarvik, L. F., and Kato, T. Chromosome examinations in aged twins. *American Journal of Human Genetics,* 1970, **22,** 562-573.

Joffe, J. M. *Prenatal determinants of behavior.* New York: Pergamon Press, Inc., 1969.

Schaie, K. W., Anderson, V. E., McClearn, G. E., and Money, J. (Eds.). *Developmental human behavior genetics: nature-nurture redefined.* Lexington, Mass.: Lexington Books, D. C. Heath & Co., 1975.

CHAPTER 14

TOOLS OF THE COMPARATIVE BEHAVIOR GENETICIST

answering how in developmental studies

A hen is an egg's way of making another egg.

In Chapter 3 the concept of genetic control was introduced. We have already noted that it is difficult, if not impossible, to answer the question concerning how much environmental factors contribute to a given behavior in humans because it is impossible to *control* genotype. This is true because, with the exception of identical twins, individuals differ widely in terms of their unique genetic constitution (genotype). In this sense the study of *human behavior genetics* is the study of individual differences. Any differences among individuals on a given task may be related to differences in genotype as well as differences in learning and environmental backgrounds.

One can control genotype by comparing identical twins in two different treatment conditions, but there are so few identical twins that it is difficult to find the many, many persons necessary to construct a life-span study or even to compare several different age groups of adults.

INBRED STRAINS

Inbred strains and genetically well-defined stocks provide control over genotype and provide the large numbers of laboratory animals that are needed to do life-span research. Inbred strains, for example, mice that are identical genetically with the exception of some small, insignificant amount of residual genetic variation, are produced by at least twenty generations of full-sib mating. When one compares different treatment conditions for different age groups of mice of the *same* inbred strain, one is comparing genetically identical individuals and thus has achieved genetic control. Behavioral differences among the animals within the strain must be related to treatment conditions, age, and any uncontrolled influence of the microenvironment or macroenvironment. Individual differences simply cannot be attributed to the influence of genotype. The disadvantage of this kind of a single strain study is that there may be little generalization of the findings to other inbred strains of mice, and one learns nothing about genotype by environment interactions. Thus a much more useful and powerful model is made possible when more than a single inbred strain is used in an aging experiment.

GENOTYPE BY ENVIRONMENT BY AGE INTERACTIONS

When two or more inbred strains are used, one has a model for differences among genotypes and may also study genotype by environment by age (G × E × Age) interactions. The model becomes more useful when a number of inbred strains and hybrids are used. However, at best, strain comparison studies indicate that genotype influences behavior, and strain by treatment by age interactions indicate that genotype, age, and treatment conditions interact. This is not really a surprising finding. The important question, from the standpoint of behavior genetics, is *how* (by what intervening mechanism) does genotype influence behavior at a given age in response to specific experimental treatments or environmental manipulations.

As a first step in answering the question *how,* one must go beyond the simple description of G × E × Age interactions. To do this, the investigator must employ the tools of the behavior geneticist. Inbred strains represent an important component of these tools, but when used alone, they cannot answer the really important questions that lead to answers to the *how* question. Used in the absence of physiological and biochemical studies of the mechanisms that intervene between a gene (or genes) and behavior, the tools of the behavior geneticist cannot answer the *how* question either, but they constitute an important first step in this direction; they ask questions about how many genes are involved in a phenomenon (more correctly, they test the hypothesis that one is involved); they make it possible to determine which genetic model might best explain a genotype-behavior relationship (e.g., pleiotropy or linked genes); and they allow the investigator to create a physiological or behavioral phenotype of interest in his own animal model. These tools include the *test cross, recombinant inbred strains, mutants, congenic lines,* and *selected lines.*

The test cross

The test cross procedure is as old as the study of genetics. Often mice are the animal of choice in test cross studies with animal subjects. There is a considerable amount of genetic knowledge about the mouse, and previous studies involving strain comparisons provide hypotheses for testing with the test cross procedure.

A simple example. To understand how the test cross is used and how it might be applied in aging studies, it is necessary to review some basic principles of Mendelian genetics. Suppose you were to plant what you knew to be two kinds of purebred corn. Let us call them tall-beautiful and short-beautiful. Since they are purebred, all the corn within the tall-beautiful genotype are genetically the same and all the corn within the short-beautiful genotype are the same. Suppose that you generate a hypothesis: The difference between the two phenotypes (tall-beautiful and short-beautiful) is a result of a difference between the two kinds of corn at a single locus. (The terms *single gene* effect and *single locus effect* are often used interchangeably.) We are only concerned with the tall versus short phenotypes because the two strains of corn are identical in every other respect.

Keep in mind that there is absolutely no reason why a single locus hypothesis must be correct. You could be wrong; you might find that the F_1 hybrid is intermediate in height to the tall-beautiful and short-beautiful corn. You might then reject your single locus hypothesis and postulate an intermediate mode of inheritance with several or many loci involved. On the other hand, you may find that the hybrid corn (formed of a cross between the tall and short parents) is as tall as the tall parent. It might even be taller (heterosis). *Heterosis* is a new term for hybrid vigor. Basically, this means that the values for the F_1 hybrid are actually outside (usually greater than) the values of both progenitor strains. A finding of heterosis would not necessarily eliminate the possibility of a single locus effect because alleles may carry different weights in terms of their relationship to phenotype.

Let us assume, for purposes of our example, that the F_1 corn looks just like the short-beautiful corn. It is all short and beautiful. First, it would be necessary to reject the hypothesis that the tall-beautiful corn is carrying the dominant alleles for tallness. If it were, the hybrid corn would be tall and

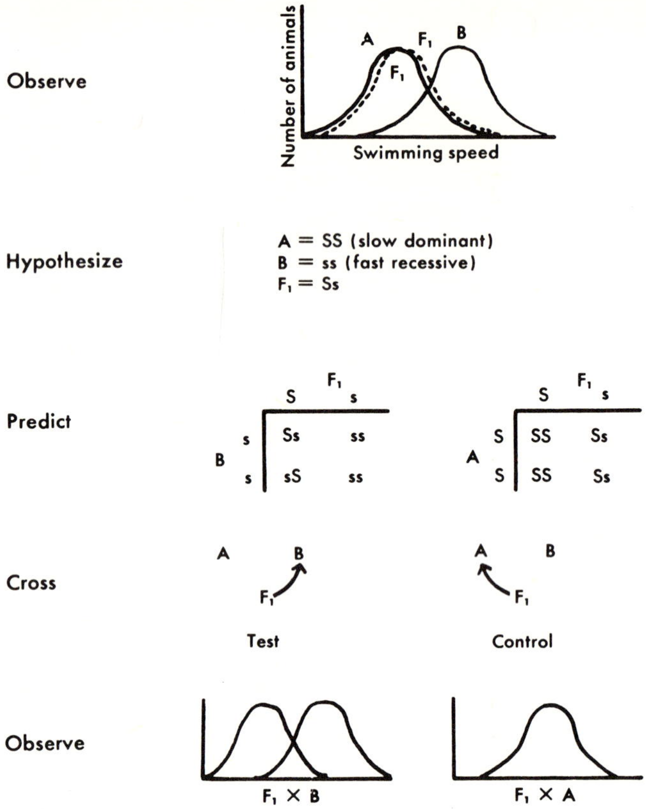

Fig. 14-1. Schematic diagram of the test cross procedure. The measure of performance is speed of swimming in a T-maze. Performance (slow to fast) is on the abscissa, and the ordinate contains information on the number of animals obtaining a given score. The investigator postulated that strain *A* was carrying two dominant alleles for slowness based on the fact that the distribution of scores for the F_1 hybrid was similar to strain *A*. He also postulated that strain *B* was carrying two recessive alleles resulting in rapid swimming. Predictions were made on the basis of this simple single locus model, and a test cross was performed. The outcome was consistent with the prediction in this hypothetical example.

beautiful because it must carry a dominant and recessive allele, and the dominant allele determines the phenotype. This hybrid corn is short and beautiful; the simplest hypothesis is that the short-beautiful corn is carrying two dominant alleles for shortness and that the tall-beautiful corn is carrying two recessive alleles. Our hypothesis might be stated as follows: tall-beautiful (*s/s*) ; short-beautiful (*S/S*) ; F_1 (*S/s*).

To test the hypothesis we make a test cross (backcross) to the recessive genotype (tall-beautiful phenotype) and a control cross back to the dominant genotype (short-beautiful phenotype). It turns out that the corn produced by the test cross–to–recessive genotype is approximately one half tall and one half short. The control cross to the dominant genotype results in all short corn. The critical test was the F_1 hybrid back to the recessive genotype, and it resulted in data that are consistent with a single locus hypothesis. As an additional test, we might want to cross the product of our F_1 × Tall-beautiful cross to members of the recessive genotype again. The expected outcome would be one fourth short corn and three fourths tall corn (remember, short is dominant). Other test crosses could be performed with expected outcomes under a single locus model compared with actual outcomes.

If each of our test and control crosses turns out in the expected direction, we may wish to give the locus a tentative name and gene symbols. Then we might wish to employ more complicated genetic techniques to identify the locus on a given chromosome. The steps involved in the test cross procedure that we have just reviewed are summarized in Fig. 14-1, but in the example we are using, a phenotype may be influenced by environmental variation and early experience, and thus we do not have discrete values. The curves seen when one generates frequency distributions are related to individual differences among animals or plants within a strain. These individual differences are related not only to early experience factors but to error of measurement as well. Thus we do not have a nice, neat, discrete phenotype (tall versus short) to work with, and frequently we must rely on statistical techniques to determine whether there are one or two distributions when we perform a test cross.

A more complicated example. By now you will have realized that the last section was simply a review of the simple Mendelian genetics that you learned in high school biology. Now we shall take a more complicated example from the literature.

Sprott (1972) conducted a series of systematic studies (with mice) that were designed to examine the effects of genotype, age, and stimulus conditions on the acquisition of a passive avoidance response. One thousand ninety-six mice were used in the study, the ages of which were 5 weeks, 4 to 5 months, and 18 months at the beginning of passive avoidance testing. Two popular inbred strains for behavior genetic studies and aging studies were used: DBA/2J and C57BL/6J. Keep in mind that the two strains are different in terms of genotype, but for all practical purposes each mouse within a strain is genetically identical to each other mouse. If the mice in the parental strains were heterozygous stocks (i.e., littermates that differed genetically), the test cross procedure would make no sense.

To date, Sprott has reported the data dealing with the 5-week and the 5-month-old mice, and most importantly, he has presented frequency distributions for the F_1 hybrids and for each of the parental strains. As might be expected, Sprott observed an age by shock intensity by strain interaction. Fig. 14-2 shows frequency distributions for the trials-to-criterion data for the two strains and the F_1 hybrids at 0.1 mA shock, and Fig. 14-3 shows the same data for 0.4 mA shock. Keep in mind that the fewer trials-to-criterion there are the better the performance is. Now examine the inbred strain data of Fig. 14-2 very carefully. It can be seen that at 5 weeks the C57BL/6J mice reached criterion more quickly than did the DBA/2J mice. The same relationship between C57BL/6J mice and the DBA/2J mice was observed at 5 months, but it was less clear. When you examine Fig. 14-3 (0.4 mA shock), you will see that the 5-week-old C57BL/6J mice performed slightly less well than did the 5-week-old DBA/2J mice, and at 5 months of age the poorer performance of the C57BL/6J mice became even more apparent.

Now it is time to glance back at Fig. 14-2. This time, examine the frequency distributions for the F_1 mice. These are labeled B6D2F_1, a shorthand way of saying that C57BL/6J males were crossed with DBA/2J females to produce the F_1 hybrid. At 5 weeks of age these F_1 hybrids resemble the parental strain C57BL/6J. The similarity of the F_1 hybrids to the C57BL/6J mice is much less clear at 5 months. Now look at Fig. 14-3 again. You can see that the B6D2F_1 mice (the F_1 hybrids) at 5 weeks of age are similar to the C57BL/6J strain, but the relationship is not as clear as it was for the 0.1 mA shock condition at 5 weeks (Fig. 14-2). Examine the F_1 hybrids (Fig. 14-3) at 5 months of age, and you will see that the F_1 distribution of scores looks similar to the C57BL/6J parental strain.

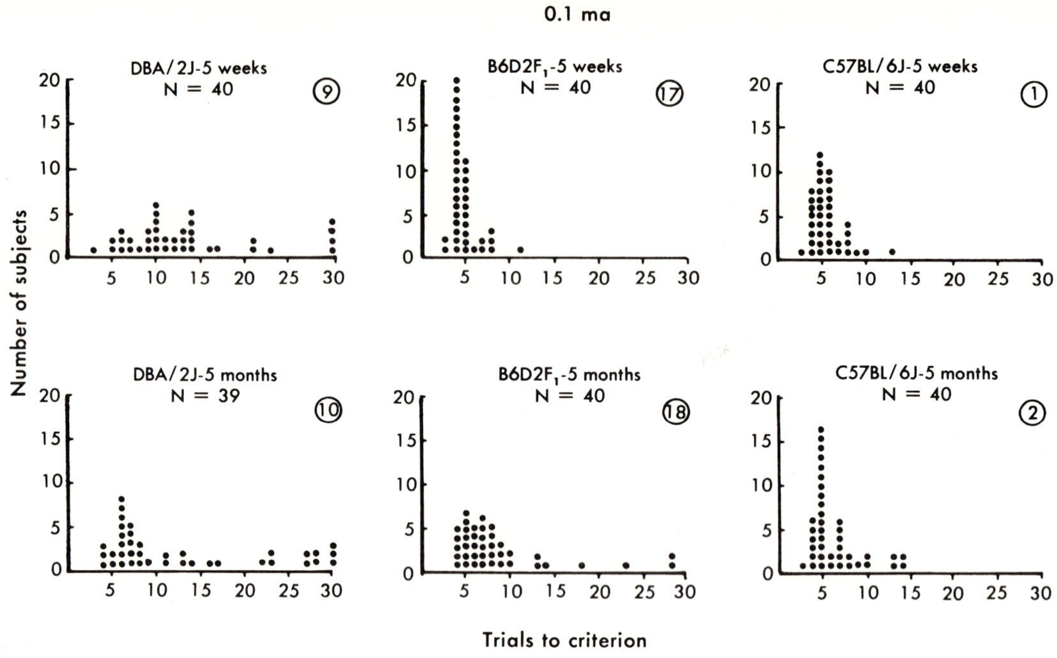

Fig. 14-2. Frequency distributions arranged so as to show the effects of age and genotype on performance when mice were tested at the 0.1 mA shock level. (From Sprott, R. L. *Journal of Comparative and Physiological Psychology,* 1972, **80**, 327-334. Copyright 1972 by the American Psychological Association. Reprinted by permission.)

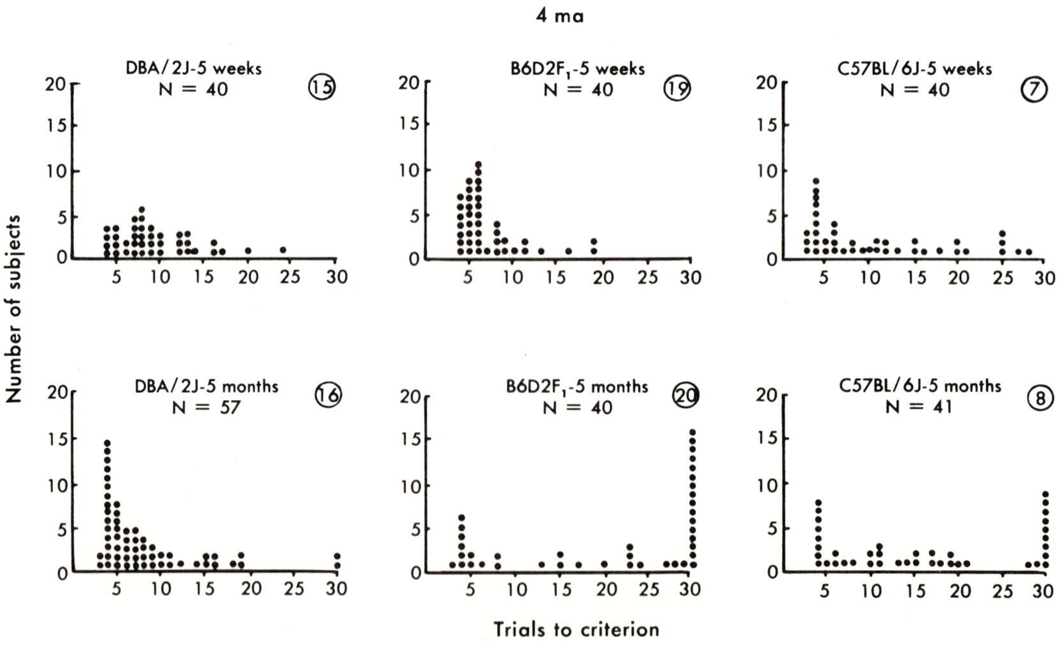

Fig. 14-3. Frequency distributions arranged so as to illustrate the effects of age and genotype on performance when mice were tested at the 0.4 mA level of footshock. (From Sprott, R. L. *Journal of Comparative and Physiological Psychology,* 1972, **80**, 327-334. Copyright 1972 by the American Psychological Association. Reprinted by permission.)

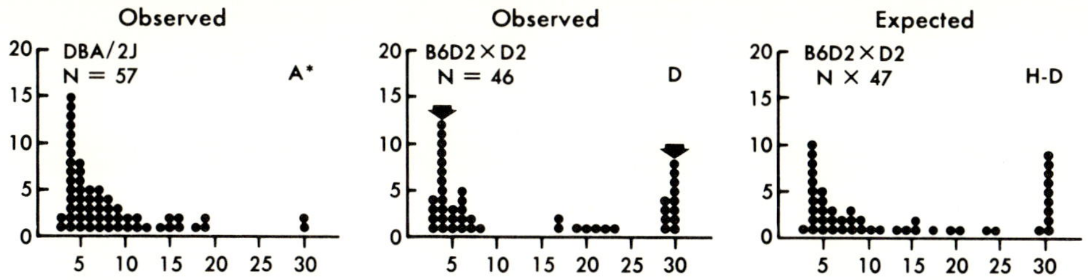

Fig. 14-4. Results of Sprott's (1974) test cross experiment. The F_1 hybrid was crossed with strain DBA/2J. Left panel shows the frequency distribution for strain DBA/2J; right panel shows the expected frequency distribution for the test cross; and center panel shows the observed outcome of the test cross. (From Sprott, R. L. *Behavioral Biology,* 1974, **11,** 231-237.)

In general, the clearest similarity of distributions between the hybrid mice and the C57BL/6J mice is observed at 0.1 mA shock at 5 weeks of age and at 0.4 mA shock at 5 months of age. These results are not inconsistent with the hypothesis that passive avoidance performance, as measured by Sprott, is influenced in a major way by a single locus. However, it should be apparent that it is no simple matter to determine whether the F_1 hybrid resembles one parent strain or another when one compares distributions based on continuous variables. Thus it was necessary for Sprott (1972) to use some statistical tests to help determine whether the hybrids were more similar to one parent than another.

So far in this illustration, results for comparisons of F_1s with parent strains are not inconsistent with a single locus hypothesis. However, it was necessary for Sprott to test this hypothesis with the traditional test cross methods. He did so, and the results were presented in a second report (Sprott, 1974). Several of the frequency distributions published in Sprott's article are summarized in Fig. 14-4. Before we discuss the meaning of the distributions, we must point out that these curves represent only a few of the test crosses that Sprott performed. He performed several other crosses and replications which provided evidence for his conclusion that a single locus is involved in passive avoidance performance. We present only one set of critical distributions to provide the student with a general idea as to the strategy employed in testing a single locus hypothesis with mice.

The curve on the left represents the *observed* distribution of scores (trials-to-criterion) for the mice. Essentially, the frequency distribution of the DBA/2J mice at 0.4 mA shock is highly similar to the one obtained under 0.4 mA shock in the study summarized in Figs. 14-2 and 14-3. Note that at 5 months of age and 0.4 mA shock, the DBA/2J mice are good passive avoidance performers relative to the C57BL/6J mice. The hybrid distribution is more similar to that of the C57BL/6J strain. Thus it appears that the C57BL/6J strain is carrying two recessive alleles (poor performance phenotype), and two dominant alleles at the locus in question are carried by DBA/2J mice (good performance). If this is true, a test cross of F_1 to DBA/2J should yield a distribution which is bimodal in nature; that is, it should have two lumps representing poor and good performers. What did Sprott find when he performed this particular cross? Fig. 14-4 shows the result in the central panel labeled *B6D2* × *D2*. This is a shorthand way of saying that the F_1 (C57BL/6J × DBA/2J) was crossed with DBA/2J. You can see that the observed and expected distributions are similar. Both are bimodal in form. Again it was necessary for Sprott to test the bimodality of the distribution with statistics, which help to determine whether the points on the distribution might represent a chance disper-

Is this his idea of fun?

sion of data points or a nonbimodal distribution.

In general, Sprott's data are consistent with a single locus hypothesis, and he performed additional tests to support this finding. We will not discuss the additional crosses, but basically they consist of predicting the outcome of a variety of crosses based on a single locus hypothesis and then comparing the expected outcomes (under that hypothesis) with observed outcomes. However, it should be remembered that even when the data are consistent with a single locus hypothesis, a more complex explanation might be valid. The single locus model is the simplest explanation of the data. As such, it is parsimonious and consistent with good model-building practices.

Implications. At this point the reader may be somewhat puzzled about what implications test cross experiments have for developmental research. Although Sprott tested several age groups, he only reported the data for one age and one shock level. Sprott's studies are continuing, and he may well provide data on test cross procedures that include other age groups. Hopefully, other investigators will use this test procedure in studies with different age groups of mice and rats. Such studies constitute behavior genetics studies in the strictest sense of the words. Strain comparisons tell little more than the relatively obvious fact that genotype by environment by age interactions exist. The test cross procedure represents a follow-through study that can demonstrate whether a single gene is exerting a predominant influence on a given behavior at one age(s) and not another. It does not mean that the gene has disappeared at the age for which no major effect is exhibited. Rather, it means that other genes may begin to influence that same behavior by way of a variety of intervening mechanisms. Genes may "turn on" and "turn off" at different ages, but this is not a necessary condition for an age by genotype interaction. Remember that different ages represent different environments in terms of social and physical correlates of maturing and growing old. Moreover, genes do not come and go away; rather, the physiological variables that intervene between genes and behavior may be altered as a function of maturity and old age.

The student will be quick to point out that one limitation to test cross procedures is that beyond a certain breeding age, animals cannot be crossed to produce F_1 hybrids and that crosses with mature and immature animals can obscure experimental designs involving different age groups. Fortunately, one does not need actually to use the parents of the F_1 hybrids in test cross experiments. The beauty of inbred strains is that if great care has been taken and inbreeding procedures have not been violated, ancestors of the parent strains are genetically identical to the parent strains. Thus new batteries of crosses and hybrids can be developed at any time and can be aged as necessary for developmental experiments. When batteries are developed, it is a good idea to produce reciprocal F_1 hybrids. This means that the fathers and mothers of each strain are balanced, for example, male C57BL/6J × female BALB/cJ, and vice versa. If two reciprocal stocks of hybrids are used and they are found to differ significantly behaviorally, the investigator begins to suspect that behavior has been influenced by the specific mothering or fathering environment or is sex linked in a genetic sense. Designs to separate these factors then may be employed. It is particularly important for the investigator to compare both hybrids (the reciprocals) if he plans to generate and test single gene hypotheses or make statements about mode of inheritance (e.g., intermediate, dominant, over dominant).

Sometimes F_1 hybrids live longer than their parent (progenitor) strains. This heterosis for long life provides a useful model for studying long life in mice and for comparing physiological and behavioral correlates in long-lived parents as opposed to short-lived or shorter-lived progenitors. The same approach can be used in an inbred strain comparison design, but often strains live longer or shorter periods than others because of rather obvious diseases that accompany old age. Moreover, there are the problems of comparing inbred strains with differences at many, many loci. This will be described in more detail when we discuss selection as a genetic tool for life-span studies.

Large N designs. It becomes clear, as we consider the genetic tools for comparative developmental studies, that a lot of animals are needed to combine genetic tests and incorporate these in a developmental study. These are long studies, and final publications of the results are few and far between. However, to answer genetic and behavior genetic questions, the investigator must be willing to produce and maintain large numbers of animals and take the time to perform studies that are characteristic of population genetics investigations. You will remember that a finding of strain differences only tells you that genotype is important with respect to the behavior in question.

Keep in mind that the test cross tests a hypothesis that a single locus plays a major role with respect to a behavioral phenotype; it does not locate the gene on the chromosome. Neurological mutants and congenic lines have been very useful in this respect. Unfortunately, they have been overlooked by developmental psychologists because there has been more interest in behaviors that are influenced by many genes (e.g., intelligence and many aspects of cognitive functioning, motivation, emotionality, and performance). However, single gene defects resulting from mutations may have a drastic effect on behavior, and although the numbers of children and adults who may be affected are small, the impact on the individual, his family, and society is enormous. There are investigators who postulate that one or a few genes may be responsible for some adult diseases which result in degeneration of the nervous system (e.g., Alzheimer's disease or Huntington's chorea), but it is almost impossible to locate the responsible genes when investigators must work with humans. There is much greater potential with the animal model, and neurological mutants have been most helpful with respect to diseases of the central nervous system.

Neurological mutants

Neurological mutants should hold great fascination for the comparative developmental psychologist who wishes to have a model for relating neurological disease to behavior. Physiological psychology studies in these areas are most important; not only is behavior influenced by physiology but long life is influenced by the integrity of the nervous system, and behavior provides an excellent index of structural integrity.

In previous chapters we have discussed a number of yet unproved "neural hypotheses" about increases in random neuronal firing or decreases in neuronal firing as one grows older. One model advances the idea that increases in random firing of neurons take place with advancing age. Consequently, incoming signals must be discriminated against high background noise levels. The hypothesized mechanism for high background noise produced by random firing is increased irritability of cells and longer aftereffects of neuronal stimulation (Crossman and Szafran, 1956). In contrast, the activation hypothesis suggests that the nervous system becomes less excitable as the individual grows older (Birren, 1970). Thus input to the nervous system is weak, and responses to this input are slowed. These are contradictory hypotheses; both explain behavioral decrements with advancing age and both are extremely difficult to prove or disprove with human subjects because it is almost, if not completely, impossible to trace slowing of response back to its physiological basis in neuron firing. However, if there was a more elementary model for the nervous system, and one in which a behavior could be related to a gene or few genes, it might be possible to make some progress in the testing of neural hypotheses. This is where the model provided by the neurological mutant mouse becomes important.

Mutations occur all the time. Often the investigator must be very familiar with the behavior or physiology of a mouse strain to become aware of a phenotypic expression of a mutation from its genotype. Usually, mutations involve a small portion of the chromosome, and in fact the difference genotypically between a mutant and its littermate may reside in the fact that the mutant is carrying two recessive alleles, which results in the neurological deficit. Mutant genes that do not kill the young animal in utero or prevent conception are referred to as postnatal lethals; the affected mice are born alive but die before they reach adulthood (see Russell and Sprott, 1975:31).

Many experimental psychologists believe that even though mutants differ from their normal littermates by a single gene, the findings of differences in behavior between mutants and littermate controls is relatively uninteresting and unimportant because the defect in the nervous system is so pronounced in the mutant. In a way this is unfortunate because these mutants have not been extensively studied by psychologists as a result of this kind of thinking. The important question is not whether behavior differs for a mutant and its normal littermate but the nature of the deficit and, particularly, what behavioral performances are relatively unimpaired. Elias and Eleftheriou (1972) found that a severely impaired neurological mutant, quaking, could swim well and could master a simple spatial discrimination learning problem in the water maze as well as its normal littermate, but it could not learn a reversal problem. It is interesting to note that reversal learning is often more sensitive than original learning to deficits in the nervous system in animals and humans.

In terms of life-span development, these mutants may provide models for changes in the nervous system that are observed in adults with central nervous system diseases, for example, demyelination of the brain and spinal cord. However, in many cases the diseases do not parallel human neurological diseases, and thus the search for good parallels to the human situation goes on. (It would be interesting to find a mutant with a hyperexcitability of cells or a slowing of neuronal activity.) Table 14-1 contains a brief description of some of the outstanding characteristics of the developmental defects that are characteristic of different neurological mutant mice. These mutants, and others that will be discovered in the future, may provide important material for comparative developmental psychologists who wish to use an animal model to characterize the consequences

Table 14-1. Common characteristics of some neurological mutant mice*

Neurological mutant	Outstanding characteristic
Dystonia musculorum (dt/dt)	Progressive incoordination 6 to 10 days after birth Degeneration of neural fibers in peripheral nerves, spinal and cranial nerves, spinal cord, and brainstem
Reeler (rl/rl)	Instability of posture and gait; recognizable 18 days after birth Abnormal distribution of cerebral cortical cells before birth
Quaking (qk/qk)	Quaking tremor as early as 10 days after birth; adults show tonic seizures; can swim and learn a water-maze discrimination task, but take longer to learn reversals than do controls Myelin synthesis begins but is not completed
Leaner (tg^{ia}/tg^{ia})	Ataxia, retarded motor activity, and stiffness beginning at about 10 days Cerebellum is much reduced in size with proliferation of glial cells and loss of Purkinje and granule cell bodies; white matter of cerebellum exhibits moderate loss of myelin fibers secondary to neuron loss
Ataxia (ax/ax)	Smaller than littermates and show weakness in extremities and trunk; difficulty in righting at 3 weeks of age progresses to paralysis of the hind limbs Abnormalities in many parts of the nervous system, including deficiency of the corpus callosum
Lipofuscin depositing†	Early locomotor difficulties and premature death Premature depositing of lipofuscin granules

*Information about the neurological mutants from Russell, E. S., and Sprott, R. L. In G. J. Maletta (Ed.), *Survey report on the aging nervous system* (Public Health Service Publication No. [NIH] 74-296). Washington, D.C.: U.S. Government Printing Office, 1975.
Information about discrimination learning in the quaking mutant mouse from Elias, M. F., and Eleftheriou, B. E. *Physiology and Behavior,* 1972, **9**, 27-34.
†A promising model for aging studies. Accumulation of lipofuscin is one of the most reliable neurocytological changes that takes place with aging.

of severe neurological impairment of central nervous system functioning and structure. The student who is interested in learning more about these mutants and finding out about available mutants for research should consult the following sources: Elias and Eleftheriou (1972); Russell and Sprott (1975); Sidman and associates (1975).

"Normal mutants" and "congenic lines"

Many investigators are not particularly interested in models for severe neurological deficit and neuronal diseases of old age. However, many mutations involving a single locus do not result in readily apparent biological disturbances and alterations in metabolic processes (Russell and Sprott, 1975). These "normal" mutants may be of particular value to the experimental developmental psychologist if, in addition to the absence of grossly apparent behavioral and biological impairment, the single mutant allele is the only genetic difference between an inbred strain and a mutant. This model makes it possible to relate subtle behavioral differences to differences in physiology which are *not* so terribly destructive that behavioral impairment is inevitable and profound.

Often a mutant gene will be placed on a genetic background which is different from the one represented by the normal littermates of the strain in which the mutation originally occurred. Thus a commonly used mouse strain, such as C57BL/6J, might have a number of *congenic lines* associated with it. Actually, a small chromosome segment is placed on a new background (inbred strain), and it is assumed that only a single locus is involved. This model becomes very useful to the investigator because a strain that has been thoroughly studied behaviorally can be compared behaviorally to a congenic line which differs from it by virtue of a single locus (the segment of the chromosome placed on the background of the inbred strain to develop congenic lines). A battery of congenic lines can be developed, each differing from an inbred strain by a single locus, and the loci may be identified. If the investigator finds that a given locus is responsible for a behavioral difference between a congenic line and an inbred strain, he may then search for physiological differences which are related to this single locus. In this way it is possible to discover physiological variables that are related to the behavior and that may be the link between the gene and behavior or between behavior and a physiological event that is closer to the gene.

One of the main objections to research with congenic lines is that it is somewhat like spending a research career looking for a needle in a haystack. There are many congenic lines. Where does one begin? How does one pick a congenic line that will yield an interesting behavioral difference from its inbred strain background and provide interesting data with regard to physiological correlates of that behavior? These are legitimate questions, and the difficulties in answering them in an encouraging manner have probably discouraged behavioral research with congenic lines. Fortunately, a recently revived genetic tool permits a systematic selection of appropriate congenic lines within the context of inbred strain comparisons. To employ this method one may make use of Bailey's (1971) recombinant inbred strains. Although they have not been used extensively in aging studies, they provide a powerful tool for the comparative developmental psychologist. However, they require much patience and large numbers of animals, as do all genetic studies. This method employs recombinant inbred strains, and it is probably worthwhile to describe it briefly.

Recombinant inbred (RI) strains

The recombinant inbred (RI) strains represent a genetic tool that may be used (1) to determine whether a single locus exerts a major influence on a given behavior or behaviors and (2) under appropriate circumstances to identify the specific locus involved. RI strains are developed from two genetically divergent inbred strains. Donald Bailey of The Jackson Laboratory, Bar Harbor, Maine, has developed a battery of RI strains that have been used for behavioral and physiological studies. The breeding scheme employed for Bailey's RI strains is shown in Fig. 14-5.

It may be seen in Fig. 14-5 that two strains of mice were crossed to produce reciprocal F_1 hybrids and the hybrids were crossed to produce an F_2 generation. Males and females from the F_2 generation were then paired off and inbred. Inbreeding for these selected pairs of males and females (designated with letters of the alphabet) was continued for the twenty plus generations that were necessary to produce new sets of inbred strains. These new inbred strains are shown in Fig. 14-5 and are designated with letters. Some of the letters are missing because, as the result of inbreeding, some of the strains failed to reproduce and survive. The remaining inbred strains (the RI strains with the letters) contain recombinations of the genes contained in the original parent strains (progenitor strains C57BL/6By and BALB/cBy). Russell and Sprott (1975:41) state this in a precise manner as they point out that for each of the new strains, the allele carried at each genetic locus for which the original parent strains differed must be identical with the allele in one of the parent

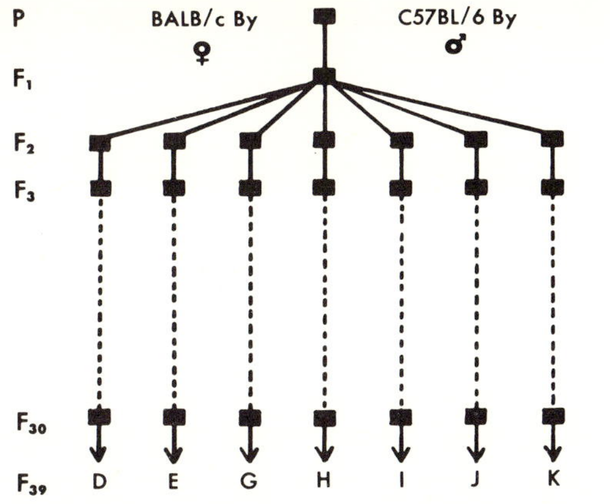

Fig. 14-5. Schematic diagram of the derivation of the RI strains by Bailey. (Modified from B. E. Eleftheriou and D. W. Bailey, *Journal of Endocrinology,* 1972, 55, 415-420.)

strains or the other; consequently, "A new homozygous combination of genes carried by the two strains has been produced and can be replicated indefinitely simply by continuing brother-sister inbreeding."

Generally, the entire battery of strains and the hybrids (including the progenitor strains) are tested in the same time period. Thus, of course, descendants from the original parent strains are used. New F_1 hybrids can be produced at any time from a progenitor strain cross. Thus a battery of animals can be produced and aged as necessary. Cross-sectional and/or longitudinal studies can be carried out with the entire battery of animals.

Strain distribution pattern (SDP). We cannot go into the details as to why, but when the entire battery of mice are tested with the same performance task, it is possible to generate what is called a strain distribution pattern, or *SDP.* Since in behavioral studies the strains and hybrids rarely group themselves neatly and clearly, it is necessary to do statistical tests of the differences between the different strains and the reciprocal F_1 hybrids in the battery. Generally, when the RI strains can be classified into two groups with regard to performance, one which resembles one progenitor and one, the other, and both reciprocal F_1 hybrids perform in a similar manner to one of the progenitor strains, a single locus effect may be postulated and a hypothetical genetic model can be developed. A hypothetical example is shown in Table 14-2. It may be seen that D, E, G, BCF_1, CBF_1, and B (C57BL/6By) perform in a similar manner and differ significantly from the other strains, including progenitor strain BALB/cBy. Thus we assigned hypothetical gene symbols to these animals based on a hypothesis of a single locus effect.

We can test this hypothesis by a series of crosses, but methods exist that shortcut the process. They are complicated, but briefly,

Table 14-2. Hypothetical example of an RI strain distribution pattern*

Battery of genotypes and rank order	Mean and SEM (loss of reflexes)	Hypothetical symbols
C57BL/6By (B)	30.9 ± 0.54	*A/A*
D	29.8 ± 0.43	*A/A*
E	28.7 ± 0.44	*A/A*
G	28.6 ± 0.48	*A/A*
BCF_1	28.0 ± 0.32	*A/a*
CBF_1	27.9 ± 0.33	*A/a*
H	12.2 ± 0.34	*a/a*
I	11.9 ± 0.33	*a/a*
J	11.6 ± 0.22	*a/a*
BALB/cBy (C)	10.9 ± 0.36	*a/a*
K	10.7 ± 0.18	*a/a*

*In this hypothetical example, *nonsignificant* differences among means for the different strains and the hybrids are connected with straight lines. Means represent time taken to lose the righting reflexes in response to halothane anesthesia. Note that the battery of "genotypes" has broken into two discrete groups. One group does not differ significantly from the reciprocal F_1 hybrids and progenitor strain C57BL/6By. Consequently, under a single locus model it is assigned gene symbols A/A for resistance to effects of the anesthetic. One group shows short times to loss of righting reflexes and is not significantly different from progenitor strain BALB/cBy; hence it is assigned gene symbols a/a. The gene symbols are tentatively assigned and are based on the hypothesis of a single locus effect of the anesthesia on righting reflexes.

they consist of determining the exact pattern of behavioral differences in terms of whether or not an RI strain behaved similarly to one or the other of the progenitor strains. This, in turn, leads to selection of congenic lines for testing. We cannot explain how one gets from a strain distribution pattern to a particular congenic line without going into highly sophisticated genetics and risking inaccuracy in presentation. It is sufficient to say that there are congenic lines associated with the battery of strains. They represent specific loci that have been identified and marked by using skin grafting techniques (see Bailey, 1971). The congenic lines differ from one of the progenitor strains by virtue of this single segment. Conversely, they are identical to the other progenitor strain. (They differ from C57BL/6By and they are identical to BALB/cBy.) The investigator selects a congenic line by virtue of the strain distribution pattern and then compares that congenic line with both progenitor strains. (The investigator may wish to replicate the original study with the battery of strains at the same time he tests the congenic lines, or it may be possible to test only the progenitor strains again because of limitations on the number of naive animals available.) If the congenic line differs from progenitor strain C57BL/6By and is similar to strain BALB/cBy with respect to the behavior under investigation, the researcher has identified the chromosome segment that is responsible for the difference between the progenitor strains in the behavior. Remember that each congenic line represents a specific chromosome segment.

Sometimes investigators will give a name to this chromosome segment and assign gene symbols. However, before doing so it is wise to see if other behaviors are related to the same chromosome segment (locus). Of course, the investigator would want to relate physiological phenomena to this same chromosome segment as the beginning step in the tracing of pathways between gene expression and the behavior of interest. It is not unusual to find that a single major locus may exert pleiotropic effects (effects on several behaviors and several aspects of physiology). Thus a finding that the same locus is related to a given behavior and a given aspect of physiology does not necessarily indicate a direct cause-effect relationship. One must perform other tests to determine whether direct cause and effect, pleiotropy, or close linkage explain a behavior-physiology correlation.

If you do not have a fairly extensive background in population genetics, you may not understand much of our description of the RI strains and their relationship to congenic lines. Do not be discouraged. The details are unimportant. They can be learned if you plan to use this tool for behavior genetic studies. The important thing to remember is that if you plan to do behavior genetic–aging studies or behavior genetic–developmental studies, sophisticated research tools are available and you should become familiar with them.

Our explanation has been too simple and too cryptic, and for that reason it may suffer from lack of accuracy or clarity. If you wish to learn more about the RI strains, read a paper by Bailey (1971) and a brief description by Russell and Sprott (1975). Several articles and papers provide bibliographies on the use of RI strains to test single locus hypotheses (see Bailey and Hoste, 1971; Elias, 1975a; Oliverio et al., 1973a,b).

In the next section we discuss a behavior genetic tool that does not have as its rationale the search for a single gene-behavior relationship. Rather, the investigator attempts to manipulate genotype in such a way as to create a phenotype of interest from a heterozygous gene pool. The developmental psychologist can study the effects of that phenotype on behavioral change over the entire life span.

Genetic selection

Genetic selection has been used to manipulate and study neuroanatomical traits (see

Roderick et al., 1975), including brain size (Elias, 1969b; 1970; Fuller and Geils, 1973; Fuller et al., 1973). Not only can researchers selectively breed for neuroanatomical characteristics and other biological phenotypes but breeding for behavioral characteristics in animals (e.g., emotionality, activity level, learning ability) is one of the oldest approaches in animal behavioral genetics.

Selective breeding has a long history in behavior genetics. The first attempts were not too successful because investigators applied too much *pressure* for selection. As a result, animals failed to reproduce after several generations of selection. Moreover, many early selection experiments did not employ a randomly bred genetic control group, and they often selected only in one direction (for one behavioral extreme). We will discuss two-way selection and appropriate genetic controls in some detail, since selective breeding represents a powerful tool for the physiological psychologist who is interested in contributing his or her unique skills and interests to the field of developmental psychology.

Selection is often confused with inbreeding designed to create an inbred strain. Often selected lines are referred to incorrectly as inbred strains. The student should not confuse selected lines and inbred strains. Some degree of inbreeding is involved in producing a selected line because a closed breeding system is employed, but the stocks that result from selection are not inbred strains because full-sib mating is not employed.

To select genetically for a trait (e.g., high or low brain weight), there must be a substantial amount of genetic variation associated with that trait. Thus one cannot begin selecting from a homozygous gene pool such as that represented by an inbred strain; neither can one select for a trait that has close to zero genetic variability. For example, suppose we decide to select for blood pressure extremes. We want to select for animals with both higher than average and lower than average systolic blood pressure values (two-way selection). To begin selection we must have a *foundation stock,* that is, a group of animals (usually rats or mice) which show a wide range of blood pressure values which are a reflection of genetic variability in the genes which influence blood pressure values. Suppose we search for a stock of animals that is heterozygous with regard to blood pressure genotype but cannot find one with a large enough range of blood pressure values within the stock. We might then wish to create a foundation stock with a wide range of blood pressures and considerable variability in blood pressure values. We could do this by starting with inbred strains and outbreeding in a systematic manner; that is, we could mix homozygous gene pools to obtain a heterozygous foundation stock. Of course, the foundation stock will be heterozygous with respect to its total genetic constitution, and we could select for a number of traits from this foundation stock, providing that the trait shows genetic variability for the foundation. Thus, although we cannot select for blood pressure extremes from a single inbred strain (zero genetic variability), we can cross a number of inbred strains and produce a foundation stock.

If we crossed eight inbred strains, which vary along a continuum of blood pressure values, most likely we could produce a single stock that contains a gene pool with considerable genetic variability. Obviously, we would want to choose inbred strains that vary from very low blood pressure values to very high blood pressure values. Fig. 14-6 shows the kind of breeding scheme we might use. The strains are crossed in pairs, and then the four-way cross is crossed again to produce a gene pool that has the same genes as represented in the inbred strains. The only difference is that each animal in the foundation stock is unlike every other animal in the foundation stock in terms of genotype; that is, animals within the stock are variable in terms of blood pressure phenotypes. If we have been successful in producing the foun-

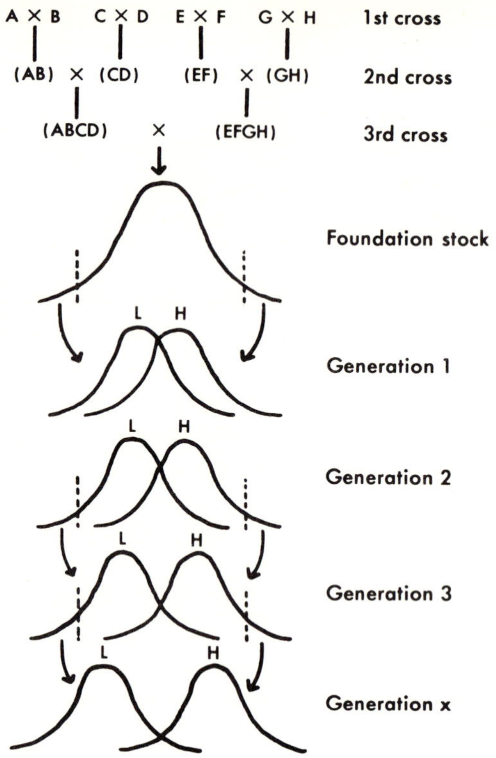

Fig. 14-6. Schematic diagram for the formation of the foundation stock for the selection of high and low blood pressure mice. Once the foundation stock is formed, selection is begun by mating animals from extremes of the distribution of blood pressures found in the foundation stock, that is, high males and females are mated with low males and females, and the procedure is repeated for each generation of selection. A randomly mated control line (not shown here) should be maintained for each generation of selection. If possible, two control lines should be utilized. *The foundation stock is randomly mated for several generations prior to selection.*

dation stock, it will exhibit a range of blood pressure values and variability in blood pressure values. Once we have a foundation stock, we can begin to select for blood pressure extremes.

Selection is started by mating the highest blood pressure males with the highest blood pressure females and the lowest blood pressure males with the lowest blood pressure females. Some arbitrary percentage of the upper and lower ends of the distributions of blood pressure in the foundation stock may be chosen. The idea is to avoid rapid inbreeding. Thus brother-sister matings are avoided. Remember that we are trying to breed selectively for blood pressure extremes, but we are not trying to create inbred strains. Moreover, if we attempt to inbreed a selected trait rapidly, it is most likely that the animals will fail to reproduce after several generations. When we select, some inbreeding is taking place, and we can quantify the extent to which this is true. However, the objective is not inbred strains; the objective is selected lines.

For each generation of selection, we continue to breed animals from the highest and lowest ends of the distribution, never crossing animals from one end of the distribution with those from the other. Animals born as a result of the first pairs of matings from the foundation stock are born to high and low lines. The highest blood pressure animals within the high line and the lowest blood pressure animals within the low line are mated (high × high and low × low) to create the next generation. This process continues generation after generation.

As might be expected, the mean values for blood pressure for the high and low lines become increasingly divergent as generations of selection continue, and gradually the distributions of blood pressure values in the high and low lines will begin to overlap less and less. The extent to which the two distributions move away from each other from generation to generation provides an index of heritability. If the trait being selected is highly heritable, the high and low distributions will "move away from each other" rapidly, and it will not take many generations to produce high and low blood pressure means that differ significantly.

A genetic control group is necessary to ensure that the two selected lines, high and low, did not occur as a result of a chance divergence of means for high and low blood pressure groups over successive generations of mating or as a result of factors unrelated to selection. Moreover, to know how extreme the values are, the investigator needs some reference point that is related to the original foundation stock. In short, a genetic control group is necessary. This is easily accomplished. For every generation of selection, the investigator engages in random mating of animals. Starting with the foundation stock and continuing each generation, animals are randomly mated, and random mating continues in parallel with each generation of selection for blood pressure extremes. It is important that random matings are not restricted to the animals which remain after extremes have been mated. Since more than one litter of animals is born to each set of parents each generation, the investigator can randomly mate animals from the entire distribution of blood pressure values as well as selecting for extremes.

If selection is successful, the mean value for the randomly mated genetic control group should be positioned somewhere between the means for the high and low lines. If the investigator really wishes to be elegant, it is possible to utilize two control groups; this allows him to spot any unusual changes in one control group. If the random mating procedure is truly random, the two control groups should maintain similar means over the generations of selection. Sometimes the randomly mated control group is used as a control group in experiments in which the high and low lines are compared. This kind of design requires a considerable number of control animals, since blood pressure values vary considerably for animals in the random control group. Thus it may be more convenient to compare high and low lines with inbred strains that are widely used in behavioral research. These strains provide a reference point against which to compare the performance of selected lines.

Selection can be continued for many generations, but once the means of the high and low lines are significantly different and

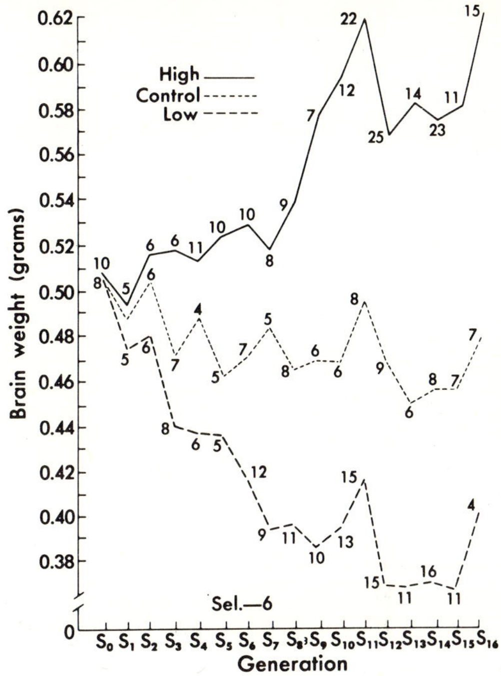

Fig. 14-7. Curves for brain weight (grams) over sixteen generations of selection for high and low brain weight. Note that the curves for the high and low lines differ significantly from those of the low line and control group after several generations of selection. Numbers at each data point refer to the number of mating pairs used to compute the mean for that generation. (From Roderick, T. H., Wimer, R. E., and Wimer, C. C. In L. Petrinovich and J. L. McGaugh [Eds.], *Knowing, thinking, and believing: a Festshrift for Professor David Krech.* New York: Plenum Publishing Corp., 1975.)

show considerable absence of overlap concerning their respective distributions of blood pressure values, behavioral testing can begin. This technique has been used to create stocks with divergent neurological characteristics, differing brain weights, and differing blood pressures. Remember that the selected lines which result are not inbred strains, although some amount of inbreeding does take place.

Fig. 14-7 shows curves for brain weights for mice selected genetically for many generations. Note that the curves for the high and low lines become increasingly divergent from the curve for the randomly mated control group as selection is carried out from generation to generation. A number of studies have been done with brain weight at one age, and some age comparisons have been done at the lower end of the life cycle, but we could find no examples of a life-span study or cross-sectional age comparisons at the upper end of the life cycle. A review of this literature is provided by Roderick and associates (1975).

Why bother? At just about this time in our discussion of selected lines, you are asking the question about why we should bother to go to all this trouble to create selected lines for high and low blood pressure when we started out with inbred strains that differed widely in blood pressure values. If you understand the answer to this question, and many sophisticated biologists and psychologists do not, you will understand why it is dangerous to make generalizations about physiology-behavior relationships based on nothing more than comparisons of inbred strains that happen to differ with respect to some physiological characteristic, for example, blood pressure or brain weight.

In Chapter 11 we pointed out that it really was not too meaningful to compare inbred strains with respect to blood pressure and norepinephrine levels in the brain and behavior and then attempt to draw conclusions about causal relationships among these variables.

Why is this true? Consider, for a moment, the fact that one inbred strain may have high blood pressure and another low blood pressure but may differ with respect to loci other than those related to blood pressure. Some of the genes (different at the same loci for the different strains) may influence behavior, and others (at different loci) may influence norepinephrine levels. All of these genes may be relatively independent except for the fact that genes resulting in high blood pressure, aggressive behavior, and high norepinephrine values may be found in one strain and genes for low values for these three variables may be found in the other strain. Thus there is no guarantee that the three variables are related in a causal manner because the two strains differ with regard to all three. There could be a cause-and-effect relationship; on the other hand, behavior, blood pressure, and endocrine relationships in one strain may reflect pleiotropy or linkage relationships among genes. Unfortunately, strain comparisons alone cannot provide this information, which is why investigators select for traits when they are interested in developing a maximally useful physiological model.

The ideal goal of selection is to achieve a random distribution of genes other than those involved in the selected trait. Unfortunately, this ideal is rarely achieved because segments of chromosomes are transmitted during breeding and segments carry more than one gene. Moreover, some genes have pleiotropic effects (influence a number of traits). Thus, inevitably, there are "correlated traits" that begin to emerge as one selects for the trait of interest. For example, increases in body weight generally accompany increases in brain weight. It is not inconceivable that increases in blood pressure are accompanied by increases in another physiological parameter or some specific aspect of behavior, for example, activity level. Fortunately, when researchers employ selection as a behavior genetic tool, they have ways of finding out whether or not this has happened, which is the real beauty of selection as a genetic tool relative to simple comparisons of inbred strains. A secondary advantage is that the values which are obtained with selected lines may be considerably more extreme than those which may be compared when inbred strains are utilized. Blood pressure values in the selected lines may be much higher and lower than those observed for the highest and lowest inbred strains.

Enough of the explanation about how selected lines are created and how the research strategy differs from that employed with inbred strains; it is time to give a specific example. The student should keep in mind that we are not criticizing the use of inbred strains. Rather, the objective is to discuss the advantages and disadvantages of different genetic tools and to make the student aware of the limitations of each and the kind of generalizations that various research strategies permit.

Animal models for hypertension. Perhaps a personal example will best serve as an explanation of how selection may be employed in a life-span behavioral project. In Chapter 12 we discussed the fact that abnormally high blood pressure can limit the length of life because it increases the probability of stroke and heart disease and that it may also exert a deleterious influence on various aspects of cognitive performance.

When the senior author of this text was somewhat younger than he is now, or at least felt younger, he became interested in finding an animal model with which to study the relationships among behavior, hypertension, and physiological correlates of hypertension. The small animal model offered a short life span and the opportunity for the kind of control over environment and genotype that is not possible with human subjects. Rat models for hypertension were available, but somewhat less was known in general about the genetics of the rat when compared with the mouse, and there were some problems with the way in which rat models had been employed in studies of hypertension and behavior. (Since then there have been some good studies of behavior and hypertension with the rat.)

Given these facts, and the fact that aging studies were being started with mice (and everyone knows that mice are really much nicer little creatures than rats), we set out in search for a good mouse model for hypertension. There were, of course, inbred strains of mice that exhibited higher levels of systolic blood pressure than other inbred strains of mice. But the use of inbred strain comparisons as a research strategy was discarded because of the problems involved in comparing inbred strains (for purposes of relating a physiological phenotype to a behavioral phenotype), which have been noted previously. For one thing, the highest blood pressures observed in inbred strains (relatively free from obvious diseases resulting in hypertension) were not very extreme. Those mice which did show extreme blood pressures could be characterized as having severe problems with the kidney. Kidney disease could have adverse effects on behavior quite separately from the effects of the high blood pressure produced by the kidney disease.

The search for a model came to an end one evening at the Asticou Inn in Northeast Harbor, Maine, when we met Dr. Jack Schlager and discovered that he had produced lines of high and low blood pressure mice from the foundation stock that had been used to develop the high and low brain weight mice. This foundation stock had been derived from an eight-way cross of eight inbred strains: LP/J, SJL/J, BALB/cJ, C57BL/6J, 129J, CBA/J, RF/J, and BDP/J. A schematic diagram of the cross is presented in a paper by Fuller and Geils (1973). After three generations of random mating from the foundation stock, Schlager began selecting for high and low blood pressure extremes. For each generation of selection, he maintained a genetic control line by random mating from the foundation stock. At seven generations of selection, the means for the population of high and low lines differed by 40 mm Hg systolic pressure, and both high and low lines differed significantly from the randomly mated genetic control group. Schlager had done the job of selection properly, blood pressure was heritable, and consequently, an appropriate mouse model for hypertension and low blood pressure was available.

As evidence that the two lines of mice do, in fact, differ with regard to blood pressure, we can examine the relationship between systolic blood pressure values and diastolic values in these mice. Schlager (personal communication) has reported correlations in

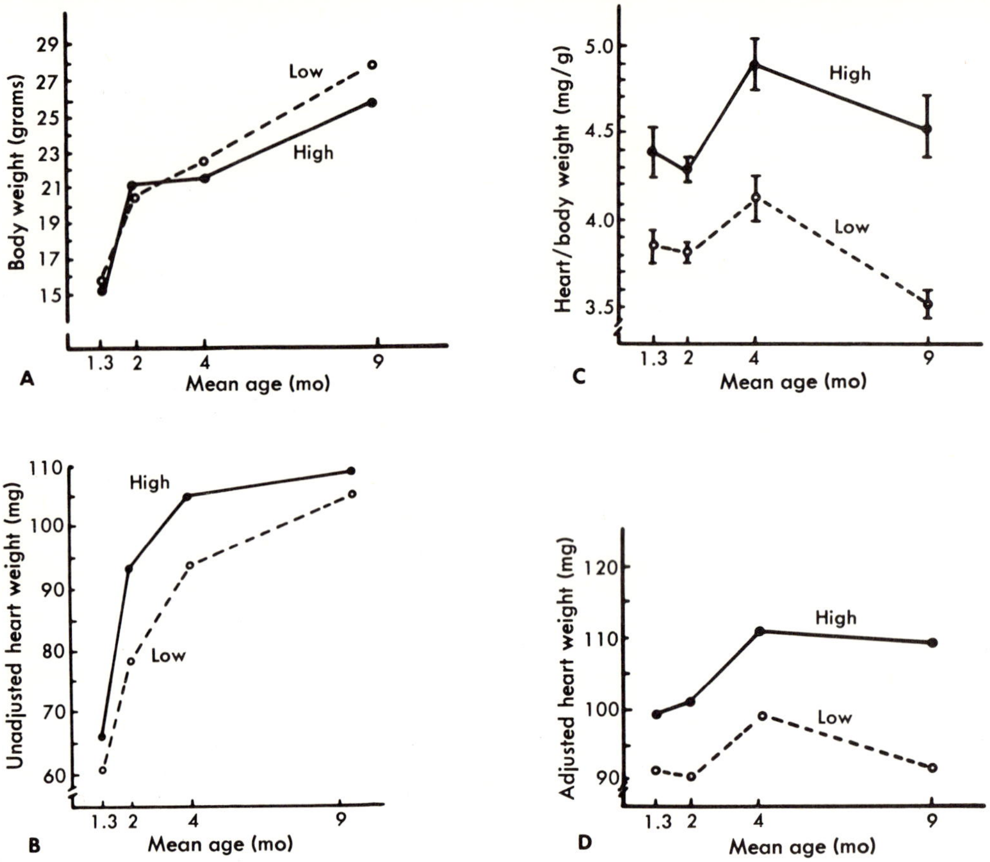

Fig. 14-8. A, Body weight in relationship to age. **B** to **D,** Unadjusted heart weight (mg), heart/body weight ratios (mg/g), and heart weights adjusted for body weight by means of covariance analysis. (From Elias, M. F., Sorrentino, R., Pentz, C. A., III, Florini, J. L., and Schlager, G. S. *Experimental Aging Research,* 1975, **1,** 251. Taken by permission of the authors and editors. © EAR, Inc., 1975.)

excess of 0.90 between systolic and direct diastolic blood pressure values for both the low and high lines. Elias, Sorrentino, Pentz, Florini, and Schlager (1975) found that high blood pressure mice exhibited higher heart/body weight ratios than low blood pressure mice. The heart/body weight ratios from this study are shown in Fig. 14-8 and Table 14-3. It is interesting to note that heart size and heart/body weight ratios were greater for the high blood pressure line than for the low line at 1.2 months of age. At present, we cannot be sure that the high blood pressure values actually produced the greater heart/body weight ratios because the appropriate follow-through studies with the F_2 progeny of a $HLF_1 \times HLF_1$ cross have not been done. However, increased heart/body weight ratios have been reported for hypertensive rats (see Elias et al., 1975) and are commonly observed for humans who have experienced sustained, untreated elevations in blood pressure.

The first study in our series of behavioral investigations was designed to determine whether Schlager's high and low blood pressure mice differed from each other and from the random controls in terms of swimming ability and spatial reversal learning ability. A spatial learning task was used because a

Table 14-3. Summary of means (± SEM) for heart/body weight ratios (H/B) and adjusted heart weights for high and low blood pressure mice*

Value	Group	11-12 months	14-15 months	17-18 months	20-23 months
H/B	High BP (mg/g)	4.45 ± 0.14	5.00 ± 0.26	4.86 ± 0.18	5.23 ± 0.76
	Low BP (mg/g)	3.87 ± 0.32	4.45 ± 0.23	4.35 ± 0.07	4.73 ± 0.39
Adjusted heart weight	High BP (mg)	106.28	143.69	152.69	154.48
	Low BP (mg)	90.72	132.71	130.42	126.90

*Modified from Elias, M. F., Sorrentino, R., Pentz, C. A., III, Florini, J. R., and Schlager, G. S. *Experimental Aging Research,* 1975, **1**, 251.

condition of retinal degeneration was discovered in one of the inbred strains used to formulate the foundation stock. In addition to the effects of hypertension, we were concerned with possible interactions between blood pressure genotype and performance at different ages varying from 250 to 686 days of age (Elias et al., 1972). There was a low significant correlation between age and the number of trials required to reach criterion ($r = 0.21$), but correlations between age and trials to criterion with the high and low lines were nonsignificant. Similarly, when subjects were placed into three discrete age groups, differences were nonsignificant for age within each blood pressure line. We were disappointed to find that there was no significant blood pressure by genotype interaction, but we were interested to note that at all ages the mice with high blood pressure performed more poorly on the discrimination task than the mice with low blood pressure, and high blood pressure mice performed more poorly than the mice in the randomly mated control line. Absence of an age by blood pressure interaction may have been related to the fact that the oldest animals were not old enough.

The important question concerned the difference between the high and low blood pressure mice. Why did they differ in performance? The human literature suggested a number of physiologically based hypotheses without much evidence to support them. We were not certain that the relationship between blood pressure values and behavior was really a cause-effect relationship. Thus we tested a group of mice from an entirely different foundation stock (produced by one-way selection for high blood pressure) and compared the data with data obtained on Schlager's high and low blood pressure mice. These "very high blood pressure" mice performed as well as the low blood pressure mice (Table 14-4). Thus one could not conclude that high blood pressure, per se, was responsible for inferior learning for the high blood pressure mice from the two-way selection. It could be that there was something unique about the high line mice produced by two-way selection. But what? There were several possibilities: The relationship between blood pressure and learning in the high and low line mice from two-way selection was (1) an accident of selection; (2) due to a pleiotropic effect of a gene influencing behavior and blood pressure; or (3) related to a linked-gene effect such that during selection for high blood pressure, genes for high blood pressure and genes influencing poor performance "traveled together" by virtue of their location on the same segment of a chromosome. (Remember that chromosome segments tend to be transmitted as a unit, and sometimes chromosome segments contain several genes which influence more than one phenotype.) These three possibilities were cast in the form of three hypotheses:

1. Pleiotropic effects of a gene
2. A linked-gene effect
3. An accident of selection

Table 14-4. Comparisons of discrimination learning performance (trials-to-criterion) for high and low blood pressure mice from Schlager's two-way selection experiment with high blood pressure mice from Schlager's one-way selection experiment. Selections employed entirely different foundation stocks.*†

BP phenotype	Blood pressure mean	Systolic range (mm Hg)	Trials-to-criterion	
			Mean	SEM
High (two-way)	139	117-154	60	10.3
Low (two-way)	71	63- 79	25	3.4
High (one-way)‡	134	124-138	25	1.0

*Modified from Elias, M. F., and Schlager, G. S. *Physiology and Behavior,* 1974, **13,** 261-267.
†Note that the high blood pressure mice from one-way selection perform as well as the low blood pressure mice, thus casting doubt on the hypothesis that blood pressure extremes, per se, have a deleterious influence on behavior.
‡Sometimes referred to as "very high blood pressure," or BP II, line. In the present study, animals were taken from the high end of the two-way selection high line so that mean blood pressures would be approximately the same for the high one-way and high two-way animals in the high blood pressure groups.

A pleiotropic effect (a gene influences more than one trait) and a linked gene effect are true genetic effects. (If the investigator can be reasonably sure that many genes influence the selected trait in question, hypothesis 2 need not be considered, since the probability of a linked gene effect is close to zero.) An accident of selection is a spurious finding that does not reflect a true genetic relationship between the selected trait and the correlated trait and would not be repeatedly observed if selection were repeated several times. If the behavior–blood pressure relationship was observed, no matter how many times selection for blood pressure was repeated, we could eliminate hypothesis 3. However, repeating a selection experiment requires an enormous amount of time. The investigator might wish to follow the relationship between blood pressure and behavior over the entire course of selection to determine whether increasingly extreme blood pressure values are accompanied by increasingly large behavioral differences (evidence for a true genetic effect), but again this procedure can be as time consuming as repeated selection experiments. Fortunately, there are procedures that permit the testing of the hypothesis without the necessity of repeating the selection experiment or collecting data for many generations.

To test hypothesis 3, high and low lines are crossed to produce an F_1 (high × low) hybrid, and the hybrids are crossed to produce an F_2.* A range of blood pressure values may be expected for the F_2 mice because the gene pool for blood pressure has been mixed just as it was in the foundation. Hypothesis 3 is *rejected* if the correlation between blood pressure values and the behavior of interest is high, positive, and in the same direction as that obtained for the original comparison of high and low lines. Rather than compute a correlation, one may compare animals with extreme high and low blood pressures, that is, very high as opposed to very low animals from the F_2 stock. Hypothesis 3 is *rejected* if the extremes differ in the same direction as the high and low lines of the original experiment.

We compared extremes of an F_2 distribution for the spatial discrimination learning task. Table 14-5 summarizes the results for F_2 extremes, and here it may be seen that high and low blood pressure mice of the F_2 distribution did not differ significantly. Thus we accepted hypothesis 3. We did not pro-

*One may also compare extreme high and low blood pressure animals from the randomly mated control line.

Table 14-5. Comparisons of animals from the high, low, and very low portions of the distribution of blood pressure values obtained for the F_2 generation formed from a cross of high × low F_1 hybrids.*†

F_2 group	Blood pressure mean	Systolic range (mm Hg)	Trials-to-criterion	
			Mean	SEM
High	131	123-147	36	4.5
Low	95	70-118	32	2.5
Very low	78	70-85	40	7.4

*Modified from Elias, M. F., and Schlager, G. S. *Physiology and Behavior,* 1974, **13,** 261-267.
†Note that animals do not differ significantly, indicating that the original differences between the high and low lines from the two-way selection were due to an accident of selection rather than a linked-gene or pleiotropic effect.

vide data for or against hypothesis 1 or 2, but clearly we could not rule out hypothesis 3 based on the F_2 data. This is a disappointing finding, but it emphasizes how very important the additional genetic test procedures were. We would have been incorrect to suggest a causal relationship between blood pressure and spatial discrimination learning. We would have been just as incorrect to suggest that the relationship might reflect pleiotropy or a linked-gene phenomenon. We have not ruled out these possibilities, but we have absolutely no basis for suggesting them.

If you are having trouble understanding the logic of the test with the extreme F_2 groups, consider the following analogy. Suppose you have some blocks of wood that are painted white or black on one side and red or green on the other side. You cannot see the side painted red or green. Your job is to place the white blocks in one pile and the black blocks in another. You generate separate piles of black and white blocks, but in so doing you discover (when you turn them over) that all the red blocks are in one pile and all the green blocks are in one pile. You could not help but separate red and green when you were separating black and white because, as it turns out, the colors were linked together—red with white and black with green. No matter how many times you separated the blocks into black and white piles you would get a correlation of red with white and green with black. This is analogous to a linked-gene effect. If genes influencing two different phenotypes (e.g., a specific behavior and blood pressure) are located on the same segment of a chromosome that is transmitted as an intact segment, the two phenotypes are correlated as a result of genetic linkage; thus what may appear to be a cause-effect relationship may reflect a linked-gene relationship. The further apart the genes are on a chromosome the less likely this is to occur because of a phenomenon referred to as *crossing-over* (see Goodenough and Levine, 1974:451).

A pleiotropic effect is much more easily understood. The simplest model is the case where one gene influences a number of traits so that when one selects for trait A, selection for other traits is inevitable if those other traits are influenced in a major way by the gene influencing trait A.

Even if you do not understand the logic of the behavior genetic tests described, it is important that you become aware of the necessity of withholding judgments regarding cause-effect relationships based on comparisons of selected lines in the absence of other tests.

Comparisons of F_2 distributions do not always reveal that initial findings were an accident of selection. Elias, Elias, and Schlager (1975) found that high blood pressure mice were generally less "socially aggressive" than low blood pressure mice, and the same relationship was observed for the extreme blood pressure groups of the F_2 distribution. Thus the student should not conclude that accidents of selection are inevitable. Similarly, the student should not conclude that absence of blood pressure by genotype by age interactions are inevitable. In a recent study in our laboratory, Elias and Pentz (unpublished manuscript) reported an age by blood pressure interaction for one aspect of open-field behavior (number of boluses) but not for another.

We have used blood pressure phenotype as an example of the kind of studies that may be done using selection techniques. However, selection for many different physiological phenotypes and behavioral phenotypes is possible. The major problem encountered in selection experiments is that correlated traits (traits correlated with the selected trait) are inevitable. Thus investigators must be sensitive to possible confounding of design caused by correlated traits (e.g., body weight in brain weight experiments), and they must be aware that correlated traits may lead to erroneous conclusions about direct physiology-behavior relationships when, in fact, genes influencing a specific behavior are linked to genes influencing a selected trait.

Pleiotropic and/or linked-gene effects provide interesting models for the study of gene by age interactions. There are obvious correlations among traits such as brain size and body size. The developmentalist may be interested in less obvious correlates, for example, selection for a behavior along with a physiological phenotype. The relationship between blood pressure and learning performance may provide a good example. We have reasonably good evidence that the relationship between spatial discrimination learning and blood pressure for Schlager's lines is due to an accident of selection, but senile high blood pressure mice may show a more pronounced decrement in performance than animals in the low blood pressure group. In other words, at a point in time representing extreme old age, the physiological phenotype may exert an effect on behavior that is directly related to impairment in the central or peripheral nervous system rather than by virtue of an accidental relationship.

We know that blood pressure and aggression in Schlager's lines are related by way of either pleiotropy or close linkage, but we do not know how the presence of both high blood pressure and low levels of aggression influence the development of other behavioral characteristics. Heart/body size is different for the high and low lines. Is this due to pleiotropy or close linkage? Is the relationship an accident of selection? Do relationships between heart/body ratio and blood pressure genotype emerge in later life, and how are they related to behavior at various ages? These represent challenging areas of investigation that permit the investigator to combine the tools of selection and developmental designs.

SUMMARY

This chapter differs from the others in that it does not represent a discussion of the literature in a particular area of aging and life-span developmental psychology. Rather, the objective was to introduce some genetic tools for research that may be of practical value to the comparative developmental psychologist. The tools reviewed included: (1) the test cross technique; (2) neurological mutants; (3) normal mutants and congenic lines; (4) recombinant inbred (RI) strains and congenic lines; and (5) selection. The student cannot hope to understand these techniques from the brief descriptions and examples given, but he should know that they are available and where to get additional information.

There is little aging or developmental literature based on studies with these techniques. Thus they represent an area of research that is both challenging and necessary if psychologists are to learn more about the influence of genes on behavior and if they are to do so in the context of dynamic, developmental studies. The techniques described are useful to the experimental comparative psychologist because they permit a controlled, manipulative experimental design and creative use of animals in aging research. Hopefully, the next ten years of research in life-span developmental psychology will see contributions from the students who used this text and were encouraged to employ new techniques that go beyond the mere description of genotype by age by treatment interactions.

SELECTED READINGS

Bailey, D. W. Recombinant inbred strains: an aid to finding identity, linkage, and function of histocompatibility and other genes. *Transplantation,* 1971, **11,** 325-327.

Elias, M. F., and Eleftheriou, B. E. Reversal learning and RNA labeling in neurological mutant mice and normal littermates. *Physiology and Behavior,* 1972, **9,** 27-34.

Elias, M. F., and Eleftheriou, B. E. Genetic analysis of simple water escape behavior: test of a major-gene hypothesis. *Physiology and Behavior,* 1975, **15,** 732-740.

Elias, M. F., and Schlager, G. S. Discrimination learning in mice genetically selected for high and low blood pressure: initial findings and methodological implications. *Physiology and Behavior,* 1974, **13,** 261-267.

Elias, M. F. Commentary II. In K. W. Schaie, V. E. Anderson, G. E. McClearn, and J. Money (Eds.), *Developmental human behavior genetics: nature-nurture redefined.* Lexington, Mass.: Lexington Books, D. C. Heath & Co., 1975.

Fuller, J., and Geils, H. Brain growth in mice selected for high and low brain weight. *Developmental Psychobiology,* 1973, **5,** 307-317.

Gibson, D. G. *Development of the rodent as a model system of aging.* (U.S. Public Health Service Publication No. [NIH] 72-121). Washington, D.C.: U.S. Government Printing Office, 1972.

Harlow, H. F., Gluck, J. P., and Sumi, S. J. Generalization of behavioral data between nonhuman and human animals. *American Psychologist,* 1972, **27,** 709-716.

Manosevitz, M., Lindzey, G., and Thiessen, D. (Eds.), *Behavioral genetics: method and research.* New York: Appleton-Century-Crofts, 1969.

Oliverio, A., Eleftheriou, B. E., and Bailey, D. W. A gene influencing active avoidance performance in mice. *Physiology and Behavior,* 1973, **11,** 497-501.

Roderick, T. H., Wimer, R. E., and Wimer, C. C. Genetic manipulation of neuroanatomical traits. In L. Petrinovich, and J. L. McGaugh (Eds.), *Knowing, thinking, and believing: a Festschrift for Professor David Krech.* New York: Plenum Publishing Corp., 1975.

Russell, E. S., and Sprott, R. L. Mice, genetics and the aging nervous system. In G. J. Maletta (Ed.), *Survey report on the aging nervous system* (U. S. Public Health Service Publication No. [NIH] 74-296). Washington, D.C.: U. S. Government Printing Office, 1975.

Schlager, G. S. Selection for blood pressure levels in mice. *Genetics,* 1974, **76,** 537-549.

Sidman, R. L., Green, M. C., and Appel, S. H. *Catalog of the neurological mutants of the mouse.* Cambridge, Mass.: Harvard University Press, 1975.

Sprott, R. L. Passive avoidance conditioning in inbred mice: effects of shock intensity, age, and genotype. *Journal of Comparative and Physiological Psychology,* 1972, **80,** 327-334.

Sprott, R. L. Passive-avoidance performance in mice: evidence for single-locus inheritance. *Behavioral Biology,* 1974, **11,** 231-237.

Thiessen, D. D. Reply to Wilcock on gene action and behavior. *Psychological Bulletin,* 1971, **75,** 103-105.

Wahlsten, D. *Genetic experiments with animal learning: a critical review,* Research Report No. 26, 1971. (Available by writing to Department of Psychology, University of Waterloo, Waterloo, Ontario, Canada.)

Wilcock, J. Gene action and behavior: an evaluation of major gene pleiotropism. *Psychological Bulletin,* 1969, **72,** 1-29.

REFERENCES

Abrahams, J. P. Psychological correlates of cardiovascular diseases. In M. F. Elias and B. E. Eleftheriou (Eds.), *Special review of experimental aging research: progress in biology.* Bar Harbor, Maine: EAR, Inc., 1976a.

Abrahams, J. P. Health status as a variable in aging research. *Experimental Aging Research,* 1976b, **2,** 63.

Abrahams, J. P., and Birren, J. E. Reaction time as a function of age and behavioral predisposition to coronary heart disease. *Journal of Gerontology,* 1973, **28,** 471.

Abrahams, J. P., Hoyer, W. J., Elias, M. F. and Bradigan, B. Gerontological research in psychology published in the *Journal of Gerontology,* 1963-1974: Perspectives and progress. *Journal of Gerontology,* 1975, **30,** 668.

Acuff, G., and Allen, D. Hiatus in "meaning": disengagement for retired professors. *Journal of Gerontology,* 1970, **25,** 126.

Ader, R. Early experience and hormones: emotional behavior and the adrenocortical function. In B. E. Eleftheriou and R. L. Sprott (Eds.), *Hormonal correlates of behavior* (Vol. 1). *A lifespan view.* New York: Plenum Publishing Corp., 1975.

Adkins, D. The simple structure of the A.P.A. *American Psychologist,* 1954, **9,** 175.

Anastasi, A. Heredity, environment, and the question "how"? *Psychological Review,* 1958, **65,** 197.

Apter, N. S., Halstead, W. C., and Heimburger, R. F. Impaired cerebral functions in essential hypertension. *American Journal of Psychiatry,* 1951, **107,** 808.

Arenberg, D. Anticipation interval and age differences in verbal learning. *Journal of Abnormal Psychology,* 1965, **70,** 419.

Arenberg, D.: Concept problem solving in young and old adults, *Journal of Gerontology,* 1968, **23,** 279.

Arenberg, D. Cognition and aging: verbal learning, memory, problem solving, and aging. In C. Eisdorfer and M. P. Lawton (Eds.), *The psychology of adult development and aging.* Washington, D.C.: American Psychological Association, 1973.

Arenberg, D., and Robertson, E. A. Learning. In J. E. Birren and K. W. Schaie (Eds.), *Handbook of the psychology of aging.* New York: Van Nostrand-Reinhold Co., in press.

Atchley, R. C. Respondents versus refusers in an interview study of retired women: an analysis of selected characteristics. *Journal of Gerontology,* 1969, **24,** 42.

Atchley, R. C. Disengagement among professors. *Journal of Gerontology,* 1971, **26,** 476.

Atchley, R. C. *The social forces in later life.* Belmont, Calif.: Wadsworth Publishing Co., Inc., 1972.

Atkinson, R. C., and Shiffrin, R. M. Human memory: a proposed system and its control processes. In K. W. Spence and J. T. Spence (Eds.), *The psychology of learning and motivation.* New York: Academic Press, Inc., 1968.

Averbach, E., and Coriell, A. S. Short-term memory in vision. *The Bell System Technical Journal,* 1961, **60,** 309.

Axelrod, S., and Cohen, L. D. Senescence and embedded-figure performance in vision and touch. *Perceptual and Motor Skills,* 1961, **12,** 283.

Back, K. W. The ambiguity of retirement. In E. W. Busse and E. Pfeiffer (Eds.), *Behavior and adaptation in late life.* Boston: Little, Brown & Co., Inc., 1969.

Bailey, D. W. Recombinant inbred strains: an aid to finding identity, linkage, and function of histocompatibility and other genes. *Transplantation,* 1971, **11,** 325.

Bailey, D. W., and Hoste, J. A gene governing the

female immune response to the male antigen in mice. *Transplantation,* 1971, **11**, 159.

Bakker, C. B. Psychosocial factors in angina pectoris. *Psychosomatics,* 1968, **8**, 43.

Baltes, P. B., and Goulet, L. R. Status and issues of a life-span developmental psychology. In L. R. Goulet and P. B. Baltes (Eds.), *Life-span developmental psychology: research and theory.* New York: Academic Press, Inc., 1970.

Baltes, P. B., and Labouvie, G. V. Adult development of intellectual performance: description, explanation, modification. In C. Eisdorfer and M. P. Lawton (Eds.), *The psychology of adult development and aging.* Washington, D.C.: American Psychological Association, 1973.

Baltes, P. B., and Schaie, K. W. On life-span developmental research paradigms: retrospects and prospects. In P. B. Baltes and K. W. Schaie (Eds.), *Life-span developmental psychology: personality and socialization.* New York: Academic Press, Inc., 1973.

Baltes, P. B., and Schaie, K. W. Aging and IQ: the myth of the twilight years, *Psychology Today,* 1974, **70**, 419.

Baltes, P. B., Schaie, K. W., and Nardi, A. H. Age and experimental mortality in a seven-year longitudinal study of cognitive behavior. *Developmental Psychology,* 1971, **5**, 18.

Baltes, P. B., Schmidt, L. R., and Boesch, E. E. Preference for different stimulus sequences in children, adolescents, and young adults. *Psychonomic Science,* 1968, **11**, 271.

Barchaas, J. D., Ciaranello, R. D., Stolk, J. J., Brodie, H., and Hamberg, D. A. Biogenic amines and behavior. In S. Levine (Ed.), *Hormones and behavior.* New York. Academic Press, Inc., 1972.

Barfield, R., and Morgan, J. N. *Early retirement; the decision and the experience.* Michigan University Survey Research Center publication. Ann Arbor: University of Michigan Institute for Social Research, 1969.

Barrett, R. J., and Ray, O. S. Behavior in the open field, Lashley III maze, shuttle-box, and Sidman avoidance as a function of strain, sex and age. *Developmental Psychology,* 1970, **3**, 73.

Bartko, J. J., Patterson, R. D., and Butler, R. N. Biomedical and behavioral predictors of survival among normal aged men: a multivariate analysis. In E. Palmore and A. C. Jeffers (Eds.), *Prediction of life span.* Lexington, Mass.: Lexington Books, D. C. Heath & Co., 1971.

Basowitz, H., and Korchin, S. J. Age differences in the perception of closure. *Journal of Abnormal and Social Psychology,* 1957, **54**, 93.

Beattie, W. M., Jr. Mobilizing community resources for older persons, Public Welfare, *The Journal of the American Public Welfare Association,* 1961, **19**, 97.

Beattie, W. M., Jr. *The plight of older people in urban areas.* Presented at the 94th Annual Forum, National Conference on Social Welfare, Dallas, May, 1967.

Beattie, W. M., Jr. The design of supportive environments for the life-span. *Gerontologist,* 1970, **10**, 190.

Belbin, E., and Belbin, R. M. New careers in middle age. In B. L. Neugarten (Ed.), *Middle age and aging.* Chicago: University of Chicago Press, 1968.

Bellucci, G. B., and Hoyer, W. J. Feedback effects on performance and self-reinforcing behavior of elderly and young adult women. *Journal of Gerontology,* 1975, **12**, 66.

Bender, I. E. Changes in religious interest: a retest after 15 years. *Journal of Abnormal and Social Psychology,* 1958, **57**, 41.

Benedict, R. F. *Race: science and politics.* New York: Modern Age Books, 1940.

Bengtson, V. L. *The social psychology of aging.* New York: Bobbs-Merrill Co., Inc., 1973.

Ben-Ishay, D., and Welner, A. Sensitivity to experimental hypertension and aggressive reactions in rats. *Proceedings of the Society for Experimental Biology and Medicine,* 1969, **132**, 1170.

Bennett, E. L., Diamond, M., Krech, D., and Rosenzweig, M. R. Chemical and anatomical plasticity of the brain. *Science,* 1964, **146**, 610.

Bentson, N., Larsen, B., and Strandgaard, S. *Chronic impairment of CBF autoregulation in man: Observations in hypertensive and diabetic patients.* Presented at the International Conference on Cerebral Blood Flow and Metabolism, Aviemore, Scotland, June, 1975.

Berezin, M. A. Sex and old age: a review of the literature. *Journal of Geriatric Psychiatry,* 1969, **2**, 131.

Berkowitz, B. The Wechsler-Bellevue performance of white males past 50. *Journal of Gerontology,* 1953, **8**, 76.

Berkowitz, B. Changes in intellect with age. IV. Changes in achievement and survival in older people. *Journal of Genetic Psychology,* 1965, **107**, 3.

Berkowitz, B., and Green, R. F. Changes in intellect with age. I. Longitudinal study of Wechsler-Bellevue scores. *Journal of Genetic Psychology,* 1963, **103**, 3.

Berkowitz, B., and Green, R. F. Changes in intellect with age. V. Differential change as functions of time interval and original score. *Journal of Genetic Psychology,* 1965, **107**, 179.

Berlyne, D. E. *Conflict, arousal, and curiosity.* New York: McGraw-Hill Book Co., 1960.

Berman, L. B., and Vertes, V. Serum renin—black and white. *New England Journal of Medicine,* 1973, **288.** 216.

Bernstein, S., and Mason, W. A. The effects of age and stimulus conditions on the emotional responses of rhesus monkeys: responses to complex stimuli. *Journal of Genetic Psychology,* 1962, **101,** 279.

Bettner, L. G., Jarvik, L. F., and Blum, J. E. Stroop Color-Word Test, non-psychotic organic brain syndrome in chromosome loss in aged twins. *Journal of Gerontology,* 1971, **26,** 458.

Bilash, I., and Zubek, J. P. The effects of age on factorially "pure" mental abilities. *Journal of Gerontology,* 1960, **15,** 175.

Bilewicz, S. Influence of mating on the longevity of Drosophila Melanogaster. *Folia Biologica (Warsaw),* 1953, **1,** 175.

Binet, A., and Simon, T. Methodes nouvelles pour le diagnostic du nouveau intellectuel des anomaux. *Annẽe Psychologique,* 1905, **11,** 191.

Binet, A., and Simon, T. Le developpement de l'intelligence chez les enfants. *Annẽe Psychologique,* 1908, **14,** 1.

Birkhill, W. R., and Schaie, K. W. The effect of differential reinforcement of cautiousness in intellectual performance among the elderly. *Journal of Gerontology,* 1975, **30,** 578.

Birren, J. E. A factorial analysis of the Wechsler-Bellevue Scale given to an elderly population. *Journal of Consulting Psychology,* 1952, **16,** 399.

Birren, J. E. (Ed.). *Handbook of aging and the individual.* Chicago: University of Chicago Press, 1959.

Birren, J. E. A brief history of the psychology of aging. I. *Gerontologist,* 1961a, **1,** 69.

Birren, J. E. A brief history of the psychology of aging. II. *Gerontologist,* 1961b, **1,** 127.

Birren, J. E. Age differences in learning a two-choice water maze by rats. *Journal of Gerontology,* 1962, **17,** 207.

Birren, J. E. *The psychology of aging.* Englewood Cliffs, N.J.: Prentice-Hall, Inc., 1964.

Birren, J. E. Age changes in speed of behavior: its central nature and physiological correlates. In A. T. Welford and J. E. Birren (Eds.), *Behavior, aging, and the nervous system.* Springfield, Ill.: Charles C Thomas, Publisher, 1965.

Birren, J. E. Increment and decrement in the intellectual status of the aged. *Psychiatric Research Reports,* 1968, **23,** 207.

Birren, J. E. Toward an experimental psychology of aging. *American Psychologist,* 1970, **25,** 124.

Birren, J. E., Botwinick, J., Weiss, A., and Morrison, D. F. Interrelations of mental and perceptual tests given to healthy elderly men. In J. E. Birren, R. N. Butler, S. W. Greenhouse, L. Sokoloff, and M. Yarrow (Eds.), *Human aging: A biological and behavioral study* (National Institute of Mental Health, U.S. Public Health Service Publication No. 986). Washington, D.C.: U.S. Government Printing Office, 1963.

Birren, J. E., Butler, R. N., Greenhouse, S. W., Sokoloff, L., and Yarrow, M. Human aging: a biological and behavioral study (National Institute of Mental Health, U.S. Public Health Service Publication No. 986). Washington, D.C.: U.S. Government Printing Office, 1963.

Birren, J. E., and Kay, H. Swimming speed of the albino rat I. Age and sex differences. *Journal of Gerontology,* 1958, **13,** 374.

Birren, J. E., and Morrison, D. F. Analysis of the WAIS subtests in relation to age and education. *Journal of Gerontology,* 1961, **16,** 363.

Birren, J. E., Riegel, K. F., and Morrison, D. F. Age differences in response speed as a function of controlled variations of stimulus conditions: evidence of a general speed factor. *Gerontologia,* 1962, **6,** 1.

Birren, J. E., and Schaie, K. W. (Eds.). *Handbook of the psychology of aging.* New York: Van Nostrand-Reinhold Co., in press.

Birren, J. E., and Szafran, J. Behavior, aging, and the nervous system. In J. E. Birren (Ed.), *Contemporary gerontology: issues and concepts.* Los Angeles: University of Southern California Gerontology Center, 1970.

Birren, J. E., and Woodruff, D. S. Human development over the life span through education. In P. B. Baltes and K. W. Schaie (Eds.), *Life-span developmental psychology: personality and socialization.* New York: Academic Press, Inc., 1973.

Bischof, L. J. *Adult psychology.* New York: Harper & Row, Publishers, 1976.

Boas, F. *The mind of primitive man.* New York: The Macmillan Co., 1911.

Boesch, E. E., Baltes, P. B., and Schmidt, L. R. Preferences for different auditory stimulus sequences in various age groups. *Psychonomic Science,* 1968, **10,** 205.

Boneau, C. A., and Pennypacker, H. S. Group matching as a research strategy: how not to get significant results. *Psychological Reports,* 1961, **8,** 143.

Boring, E. G. *A history of experimental psychology.* New York: Appleton-Century-Crofts, 1950.

Botwinick, J. Drives, expectancies and emotions. In J. E. Birren (Ed.), *Handbook of aging and the individual.* Chicago: University of Chicago Press, 1959.

Botwinick, J. Theories of antecedent conditions of speed of response. In A. T. Welford and J. E. Birren (Eds.), *Behavior, aging, and the nervous system.* Springfield, Ill.: Charles C Thomas, Publisher, 1965.

Botwinick, J. Cautiousness in advanced age. *Journal of Gerontology,* 1966a, **21,** 347.

Botwinick, J. Disinclination to venture response versus cautiousness in responding: age differences. *Journal of Gerontology,* 1966b, **115,** 55.

Botwinick, J. *Cognitive processes in maturity and old age.* New York: Springer Publishing Co., Inc., 1967.

Botwinick, J. Sensory-set factors in age differences in reaction time. *Journal of Genetic Psychology,* 1971, **119,** 24.

Botwinick, J. *Aging and behavior.* New York: Springer Publishing Co., Inc., 1973.

Botwinick, J. Behavioral processes. In S. Gershon and A. Raskind (Eds.), *Aging* (Vol. 2). *Genesis and treatment of psychologic disorders in the elderly.* New York: Raven Press, 1975.

Botwinick, J., and Birren, J. E. Differential decline in the Wechsler-Bellevue subtests in the senile psychoses. *Journal of Gerontology,* 1951a, **6,** 365.

Botwinick, J., and Birren, J. E. The measurement of intellectual decline in the senile psychoses. *Journal of Consulting Psychology,* 1951b, **15,** 145.

Botwinick, J., and Brinley, J. F. Aspects of RT set during brief intervals in relation to age and sex. *Journal of Gerontology,* 1962, **17,** 295.

Botwinick, J., Brinley, J. F., and Birren, J. E. Set in relation to age. *Journal of Gerontology,* 1957, **12,** 300.

Botwinick, J., Brinley, J. F., and Robbin, J. S. The interaction effects of perceptual difficulty and stimulus exposure time on age differences in speed and accuracy of response. *Gerontologia,* 1958, **2,** 1.

Botwinick, J., Brinley, J. F., and Robbin, J. S. Learning a position discrimination and position reversals by Sprague-Dawley rats of different ages. *Journal of Gerontology,* 1962, **17,** 315.

Botwinick, J., Brinley, J. F., and Robbin, J. S. Learning and reversing a four-choice multiple Y-maze by rats of three ages. *Journal of Gerontology,* 1963, **18,** 279.

Botwinick, J., and Kornetsky, C. Age differences in the acquisition and extinction of the GSR. *Journal of Gerontology,* 1960, **15,** 83.

Botwinick, J., and Storandt, M. Sensation and set in reaction time. *Perceptual and Motor Skills,* 1972, **34,** 103.

Botwinick, J., and Storandt, M. Age differences in reaction time as a function of experience, stimulus intensity, and preparatory interval. *Journal of Genetic Psychology,* 1973a, **123,** 209.

Botwinick, J., and Storandt, M. Speed functions, vocabulary ability, and age. *Perceptual and Motor Skills,* 1973b, **36,** 1123.

Botwinick, J., and Storandt, M. Cardiovascular status, depressive affect and other factors in reaction time. *Journal of Gerontology,* 1974a, **29,** 543.

Botwinick, J., and Storandt, M. *Memory, related functions and age.* Springfield, Ill.: Charles C Thomas, Publisher, 1974b.

Botwinick, J., and Storandt, M. Vocabulary ability in later life. *Journal of Genetic Psychology,* 1974c, **125,** 303.

Botwinick, J., and Thompson, L. W. Premotor and motor components of reaction time. *Journal of Experimental Psychology,* 1966, **71,** 9.

Botwinick, J., West, R., and Storandt, M. Qualitative vocabulary test responses and age. *Journal of Gerontology,* 1975, **30,** 574.

Bourne, L. E., Ekstrand, B. R., and Dominowski, R. L. *The psychology of thinking.* Englewood Cliffs, N.J.: Prentice-Hall, Inc., 1971.

Brackbill, Y. (Ed.). *Division of developmental psychology* (Division 7) *Newsletter,* Winter, 1971.

Braun, H. W., and Geiselhart, R. Age differences in the acquisition and extinction of the conditioned eyelid response. *Journal of Experimental Psychology,* 1959, **57,** 386.

Bressler, M. Sociology, biology, and ideology. In D. C. Glass (Ed.), *Genetics.* New York: Rockefeller University Press, 1968.

Broadbent, D. E. *Perception and communication.* Oxford, England: Pergamon Press, 1958.

Broadhurst, P. L. Analysis of maternal effects in the inheritance of behavior. *Animal Behavior,* 1961, **9,** 129.

Brotman, H. B. Analytical section. In Aging (U. S. Department of Health, Education and Welfare, Publication No. 187. Washington, D.C.: U.S. Government Printing Office, 1970.

Brown, R. C., and Ritzman, S. Some factors associated with absence of coronary heart disease. *Journal of the American Geriatrics Society,* 1967, **15,** 239.

Bruning, R. H., Holzbauer, I., and Kimberlin, C. Age, word imagery, and delay interval: effects on short-term and long-term retention. *Journal of Gerontology,* 1975, **30,** 312.

Brunner, H. R., Laragh, J. H., Baer, L., Newton, M. E., Goodwin, F. T., Krakoff, L. R., Bard, R. H., and Buhler, F. R. Essential hypertension: renin and aldosterone, heart attack and stroke. *New England Journal of Medicine,* 1972, **286,** 441.

Brush, F. R., and Froehlich, J. C. Motivational effects of the pituitary and adrenal hormones. In B. E. Eleftheriou and R. L. Sprott (Eds.), *Hor-*

monal correlates of behavior (Vol. 2). *An organismic view.* New York: Plenum Publishing Corp., 1975.

Bugelski, B. R. Presentation time, total time, and mediation in paired-associate learning. *Journal of Experimental Psychology,* 1962, **63,** 409.

Bull, C. N., and Aucoin, J. B. Voluntary association participation and life satisfaction: a replication note. *Journal of Gerontology,* 1975, **30,** 73.

Burt, C. Inheritance of general intelligence. *American Psychologist,* 1972, **27,** 175.

Busse, E. W. Theories of aging. In E. W. Busse and E. Pfeiffer (Eds.), *Behavior and adaptation in late life.* Boston: Little, Brown & Co., 1969.

Busse, E. W., and Wang, H. S. The value of electroencephalography in geriatrics. *Geriatrics,* 1965, **20,** 906.

Butler, R. N. Research and clinical observation on the psychologic reactions to physical change with age. *Mayo Clinic Proceedings,* 1967, **42,** 596.

Cadotte, M., and Fraser, D. Étude de l'aneuploidie observée dans les cultures de sang et de moelle en fonction du nombre et de la longeur des chromosomes de chaque groups et de l'age et du sexe des sujets. *Union Medicale du Canada,* 1970, **99,** 2003.

Caffrey, B. Behavior patterns and personality characteristics related to prevalence rates of coronary heart disease in American monks. *Journal of Chronic Diseases,* 1969, **22,** 93.

Cameron, P. The affective-instinctual level and age. *Aging and Human Development,* 1971, **2,** 73.

Cameron, P., and Biber, H. Sexual thought throughout the life-span. *Gerontologist,* 1973, **13,** 144.

Campbell, B. A., and Cicala, G. A. Studies of water deprivation in rats as a function of age. *Journal of Comparative and Physiological Psychology,* 1962, **55,** 763.

Campbell, B. A., and Jaynes, J. Reinstatement. *Psychological Review,* 1966, **73,** 478.

Canestrari, R. E., Jr. Paced and self-paced learning in young and elderly adults. *Journal of Gerontology,* 1963, **18,** 165.

Canestrari, R. E., Jr. The effects of commonality of paired associate learning in two age groups. *Journal of Genetic Psychology,* 1966, **108,** 3.

Canestrari, R. E., Jr. Age changes in acquisition. In G. A. Talland (Eds.), *Human aging and behavior.* New York: Academic Press, Inc., 1968a.

Canestrari, R. E., Jr. Age differences in verbal learning and verbal behavior. In S. M. Chown and K. F. Riegel (Eds.), *Interdisciplinary topics in gerontology* (Vol. 1). *Psychological functioning in the normal aging and senile aged.* Basel: S. Karger, 1968b.

Carp, F. M. Person-situation congruence in engagement. *Gerontologist,* 1968a, **8,** 184.

Carp, F. M. Some components of disengagement. *Journal of Gerontology,* 1968b, **23,** 382.

Catt, K. J. *An ABC of endocrinology.* Boston: Little, Brown & Co., 1971.

Charles, D. C. Historical antecedents of life-span developmental psychology. In L. R. Goulet and P. B. Baltes (Eds.), *Life-span developmental psychology: research and theory,* New York: Academic Press, Inc., 1970.

Chown, S. M. Age and the rigidities. *Journal of Gerontology,* 1961, **16,** 353.

Christenson, C. V., and Gagon, J. H. Sexual behavior in a group of older women. *Journal of Gerontology,* 1965, **20,** 351.

Clark, L., and Knowles, J. B. Age differences in dichotic listening performance. *Journal of Gerontology,* 1973, **28,** 173.

Clark, M., and Anderson, B. G. *Culture and aging.* Springfield, Ill.: Charles C Thomas, Publisher, 1967.

Cohen, D. A. A behavioral-chromosome relationship in the elderly: a critical review of a biobehavioral hypothesis. *Experimental Aging Research,* 1976, **2,** 271.

Cohen, D., and Jarvik, L. F. *Cognitive deficits and chromosome loss in aged institutionalized women.* Presented at the 26th Annual Meetings of the Gerontological Society, Miami, 1973.

Collaborative Group for the Study of Stroke in Young Women: oral contraception and increased risk of cerebral ischemia or thrombosis. *New England Journal of Medicine,* 1973, **288,** 871.

Comfort, A. *The biology of senescence.* London: Routledge & Kegan Paul, Ltd., 1956.

Cooper, R. M., Bilash, I., and Zubek, J. P. The effect of age on taste sensitivity. *Journal of Gerontology,* 1959, **14,** 56.

Coppinger, N. W. The relationship between critical flicker frequency and chronological age for varying levels of stimulus brightness. *Journal of Gerontology,* 1955, **10,** 48.

Corke, P. P. Complex behavior in "old" and "young" rats. *Psychological Reports,* 1964, **15,** 371.

Corsellis, J. A. N. *Mental illness and the ageing brain; the distribution of pathological change in a mental hospital population,* London: Oxford University Press, 1962.

Corso, J. F. Sensory processes and age effects in normal adults. *Journal of Gerontology,* 1971, **26,** 90.

Cowdry, E. V. (Ed.). *Problems of aging.* Baltimore: The Williams & Wilkins Co., 1939.

Craik, F. I. M. *Age differences in confidence and decision processes.* Doctoral dissertation, University of Liverpool, 1965.

Craik, F. I. M. Age differences in recognition memory. *Quarterly Journal of Experimental Psychology,* 1971a, **23,** 316.

Craik, F. I. M. Primary memory. *British Medical Bulletin,* 1971b, **27,** 232.

Craik, F. I., and Lockhart, R. S. Levels of processing: a framework for memory research. *Journal of Verbal Learning and Verbal Behavior,* 1972, **11,** 671.

Craik, F. I., and Masani, P. A. Age differences in the temporal integration of language. *British Journal of Psychology,* 1967, **58,** 291.

Crane, M. G., Harris, J. J., and Winson, W. Hypertension, oral contraceptives, and conjugated estrogens. *Annals of Internal Medicine,* 1971, **74,** 13.

Crossman, E. R. F. W., and Szafran, J. Changes with age in the speed of information intake and discrimination. *Experientia* (supp.), 1956, **4,** 128.

Cumming, E. *Disengagement—a tentative theory of aging.* Presented at Symposium on Developmental Theories of Aging at the Annual Meetings of the American Psychological Association, 1959.

Cumming, E., and Henry, W. E. *Growing old: the process of disengagement.* New York: Basic Books, Inc., Publishers, 1961.

Davenport, C. B. Eugenics and charity. *Proceedings of the 39th National Conference on Charities and Corrections, 1912.* Cited by Haller, 1968.

Davies, D. R. Age differences in paced inspection tasks. In G. A. Talland (Ed.), *Human aging and behavior.* New York: Academic Press, Inc., 1968.

Davis, R. M. Social influences on the aspiration tendency of older people. *Journal of Gerontology,* 1967, **22,** 510.

Dawson, A. M., and Baller, W. R. Relationship between creative activity and the health of elderly persons. *Journal of Psychology,* 1972, **82,** 49.

Dean, L. R. Aging and the decline of affect. *Journal of Gerontology,* 1962, **17,** 440.

Demming, J. A., and Pressey, S. L. Tests indigenous to the adult and older years. *Journal of Counseling Psychology,* 1957, **4,** 144.

Denenberg, V. H. Effects of age and early experience upon conditioning in the C57BL/10 mouse. *Journal of Psychology,* 1958, **46,** 211.

Denenberg, V. H. A test of the critical period hypothesis and a further study of the relationship between age and conditioning in the C57BL/10 mouse. *Journal of Genetic Psychology,* 1960, **97,** 379.

Denenberg, V. H. Animal studies of early experience: some principles which have implications for human development. In J. Hill (Ed.), *Minnesota symposia on child psychology.* Minneapolis: University of Minnesota Press, 1969a.

Denenberg, V. H. Experimental programming of life-histories in the rat. In A. Ambrose (Ed.), *Stimulation in early infancy.* New York: Academic Press, Inc., 1969b.

Denenberg, V. H., and Kline, N. J. The relationship between age and avoidance learning in the hooded rat. *Journal of Comparative and Physiological Psychology,* 1958, **51,** 488.

Denenberg, V. H., and Smith, S. A. Effects of infantile stimulation and age upon behavior. *Journal of Comparative and Physiological Psychology,* 1963, **56,** 307.

Desor, J. A., Greene, L. S., and Maller, D. Preferences for sweet and salty in 9- to 15-year-old and adult humans. *Science,* 1975, **190,** 686.

Desroches, H. F., Kimbrell, G. M., and Allison, J. T. Effect of age and experience on bar pressing and activitiy in the rat. *Journal of Gerontology,* 1964, **19,** 168.

Distefano, M. K. Changes in work related attitudes with age. *Journal of Genetic Psychology,* 1969, **114,** 127.

Dobzhansky, T. Of flies and men. *American Psychologist,* 1967, **22,** 41.

Doll, E. A. The average mental age of adults. *Journal of Applied Psychology,* 1919, **3,** 317.

Donovan, J. E. Menopausal syndrome: a study of case histories. *American Journal of Obstetrics and Gynecology,* 1951, **62,** 1281.

Doppelt, J. E., and Wallace, W. L. Standardization of the Wechsler Adult Intelligence Scale for older persons. *Journal of Abnormal and Social Psychology,* 1955, **51,** 312.

Doty, B. A. Age differences in avoidance conditioning as a function of distribution of trials and task difficulty. *Journal of Genetic Psychology,* 1966, **109,** 249.

Doty, B. A. The effects of cage environment upon avoidance responding of aged rats. *Journal of Gerontology,* 1972, **27,** 358.

Doty, B. A., and O'Hare, K. M. Interaction of shock intensity, age, and handling effects on avoidance conditioning. *Perceptual and Motor Skills,* 1966, **23,** 1311.

Drachman, D. A., and Leavitt, J. Memory impairment in the aged: storage versus retrieval deficit. *Journal of Experimental Psychology,* 1972, **93,** 302.

Duffy, E. The psychological significance of the concept of "arousal" or "activation." *Psychological Review,* 1964, **61,** 129.

Eayrs, J. T. Endocrine influence on cerebral development. *Archives of Biology,* 1964, **75,** 529.

Eccles, J. C. Tropic influences in the mammalian central nervous system. In M. Rockstein (Ed.), *Development and aging in the nervous system.* New York: Academic Press, Inc., 1973.

Eckland, B. K. Genetics and sociology: a reconsideration. *American Sociological Review,* 1967, **32,** 173.

Edwards, A. E., and Wine, D. B. Personality changes with age: their dependency on concomitant intellectual decline. *Journal of Gerontology,* 1963, **18,** 182.

Eichelman, B., Dejong, W., and Williams, R. Aggressive behavior in hypertensive and normotensive rat strains. *Physiology and Behavior,* 1973, **10,** 301.

Eisdorfer, C. Autonomic changes in aging. In C. M. Gaitz (Ed.), *Aging and the brain.* New York: Plenum Publishing Corp., 1962.

Eisdorfer, C. Verbal learning response time in the aged. *Journal of Genetic Psychology,* 1965, **107,** 15.

Eisdorfer, C. Arousal and performance: experiments in verbal learning and a tentative theory. In G. A. Talland (Ed.), *Human aging and behavior.* New York: Academic Press, Inc., 1968.

Eisdorfer, C., Axelrod, S., and Wilkie, F. L. Stimulus exposure time as a factor in serial learning in an aged sample. *Journal of Abnormal and Social Psychology,* 1963, **67,** 594.

Eisdorfer, C., Connor, J. F., and Wilkie, F. L. The effect of magnesium pemoline on cognition and behavior. *Journal of Gerontology,* 1968, **23,** 283.

Eisdorfer, C., Nowlin, J., and Wilkie, F. Improvement of learning in the aged by modification of autonomic nervous system activity. *Science,* 1970, **170,** 1327.

Eisdorfer, C., and Raskind, M. Aging, hormones and human behavior. In B. E. Eleftheriou and R. L. Sprott (Eds.), *Hormonal correlates of behavior* (Vol. 1). *A lifespan view.* New York: Plenum Publishing Corp., 1975.

Eisdorfer, C., and Wilkie, F. Intellectual changes with advancing age. In L. F. Jarvik, C. Eisdorfer, and J. E. Blum (Eds.), *Intellectual functioning in adults.* New York, Springer Publishing Co., Inc., 1973.

Eisdorfer, C., and Wilkie, F. Stress, disease, aging, and behavior. In J. E. Birren and K. W. Schaie (Eds.), *Handbook of the psychology of aging.* New York: Van Nostrand-Reinhold Co., in press.

Eisner, D. A., and Schaie, K. W. Age changes in response to visual illusions from middle to old age. *Journal of Gerontology,* 1971, **26,** 146.

Eisner, H. C., and Kinsbourne, M. *Age and presentation time effects on free recall.* Presented at the 28th Annual Meetings of the Gerontological Society, Louisville, Oct., 1975.

Eleftheriou, B. E. Hormones and behavior: a genetic approach. In B. E. Eleftheriou and R. L. Sprott (Eds.), *Hormonal correlates of behavior.* (Vol. 2). *An organismic view.* New York: Plenum Publishing Corp., 1975.

Eleftheriou, B. E., and Bailey, D. W. Genetic analysis of plasma corticosterone in two inbred strains of mice. *Journal of Endocrinology,* 1972, **55,** 415.

Eleftheriou, B. E., Elias, M. F., Castellano, C., and Oliverio, A. Cortex weight: a genetic analysis in the mouse. *Journal of Heredity,* 1975, **66,** 207.

Eleftheriou, B. E., and Sprott, R. L. (Eds.). *Hormonal correlates of behavior* (Vol. 1). *A lifespan view.* New York: Plenum Publishing Corp., 1975.

Elias, J. W., and Elias, M. F. *Information processing: age and laterality effects.* Presented at the 27th Annual Meetings of the Gerontological Society, Portland, Ore., 1974.

Elias, J. W., and Elias, M. F. Matching of successive auditory stimuli as a function of age and ear of presentation. *Journal of Gerontology,* 1976, **31,** 164.

Elias, J. W., Elias, M. F., and Schlager, G. Aggressive social interaction in mice genetically selected for blood pressure extremes. *Behavioral Biology,* 1975, **13,** 155.

Elias, J. W., and Wright, L. L. Matching, the null hypothesis and the aging variable: Would the real age variable please stand up? *Experimental Aging Research,* 1976, **2,** 261.

Elias, J. W., Wright, L., and Winn, F. *Sex differences and laterality of brain function.* Presented at the 23rd Annual Meetings of the Southwestern Psychological Association, Albuquerque, N. Mex., April, 1976.

Elias, M. F. Relation of stimulus size to pattern discrimination training for the hooded rat. *Perceptual and Motor Skills,* 1967, **26,** 613.

Elias, M. F. Background area, pattern height, and discrimination learning for the hooded rat: preliminary findings and methodological comments. *Perceptual and Motor Skills,* 1969a, **28,** 615.

Elias, M. F. Differences in spatial discrimination reversal learning for mice genetically selected for high brain weight and unselected controls. *Perceptual and Motor Skills,* 1969b, **28,** 707.

Elias, M. F. Pattern area and discrimination learning with pattern spacing, pattern height, pattern-border contiguity, and pattern manipulation controlled. *Perceptual and Motor Skills,* 1969c, **28,** 407.

Elias, M. F. Discrimination reversal learning for mice genetically selected for different brain sizes. *Perceptual and Motor Skills,* 1970, **30,** 149.

Elias, M. F. Disciplinary barriers to progress in behavior genetics: Defensive reactions to bits and pieces. *Human Development,* 1973, **16** (1-2), 119.

Elias, M. F. Commentary II, in response to a paper by N. D. Henderson, Gene-environment interaction in human behavioral development. In K. W. Schaie, V. E. Anderson, G. E. McClearn, and J. Money (Eds.), *Developmental* human behavior genetics: nature-nurture redefined. Lexington, Mass.: Lexington Books, D. C. Heath & Co., 1975a.

Elias, M. F. Potential applications of multivariate analysis of variance to psychopharmacogenetics research. In B. E. Eleftheriou (Ed.), *Psychopharmacogenetics.* New York: Plenum Publishing Corp., 1975b.

Elias, M. F. *Age studies of behavior with $Fischer_{344}$, Sprague-Dawley, and Long-Evans rats.* Presented at the Workshop on Information and Data on Animal Models for Aging Research. Adult Development and Aging Branch, National Institute of Child Health and Human Development, San Antonio, Texas, May, 1975c.

Elias, M. F., Dupree, M., and Eleftheriou, B. E. Differences in spatial discrimination reversal learning between two inbred mouse strains following specific amygdaloid lesions. *Journal of Comparative and Physiological Psychology,* 1973, **83,** 149.

Elias, M. F., and Eleftheriou, B. E. Reversal learning and RNA labeling in neurological mutant mice and normal littermates. *Physiology and Behavior,* 1972, **9,** 27.

Elias, M. F., and Eleftheriou, B. E. Separating measures of learning and incentive in water maze experiments with aging inbred strains of mice. *Psychological Reports,* 1975, **36,** 343.

Elias, M. F., and Elias, P. K. Hormones, aging, and behavior in infrahuman mammals. In B. E. Eleftheriou and R. L. Sprott (Eds.), *Hormonal correlates of behavior* (Vol. 1). *A lifespan view.* New York: Plenum Publishing Corp., 1975.

Elias, M. F., and Elias, P. K. Drive, motivation, and activity. In J. E. Birren and K. W. Schaie (Eds.), *Handbook of the psychology of aging.* New York: Van Nostrand-Reinhold Co., in press.

Elias, M. F., Elias, P. K., Zolovick, A. J., and Eleftheriou, B. E. Methodological problems in age comparisons of EEG sleep patterns for C57BL/6J mice. *Experimental Aging Research,* 1975, **1,** 107.

Elias, M. F., and Kinsbourne, M. Age and sex differences in the processing of verbal and nonverbal stimuli. *Journal of Gerontology,* 1974, **29,** 162.

Elias, M. F., and Pentz, C. A., III. *Activity level in high and low blood pressure mice.* Unpublished manuscript. May be obtained by writing to the authors at Department of Psychology, Syracuse University, Syracuse, N.Y. 13210.

Elias, M. F., Prinz, P. A., and Schlager, G. S. Hypertension and learning in aging mice. Presented at the 25th Annual Meetings of the Gerontological Society, San Juan, Puerto Rico, Dec., 1972.

Elias, M. F., and Schlager, G. S. Discrimination learning in mice genetically selected for high and low blood pressure: initial findings and methodological implications. *Physiology and Behavior,* 1974, **13,** 261.

Elias, M. F., Sorrentino, R., Pentz, C. A., III, Florini, J. F., and Schlager, G. S. "Spontaneously" hypertensive mice: a potential genetic model for the study of the relationship between heart size and blood pressure. *Experimental Aging Research,* 1975, **1,** 251.

Elias, M. F., and Warner, L. Effect of pattern configuration on the relation between pattern area and pattern discrimination. *Perceptual and Motor Skills,* 1970, **30,** 919.

Elias, M. F., Wood, W. G., and Pentz, C. A., III. *Contributions of Mus musculus to the study of behavioral correlates of hypertension at various periods of the life span.* Presented at the Conference on Genetic Effects on Aging, sponsored by the National Foundation March of Dimes, The Jackson Laboratory, Bar Harbor, Maine, Sept., 1976. (To be published by the National Foundation March of Dimes, White Plains, N.Y. 10605.)

Elias, P. K., Elias, M. F., and Eleftheriou, B. E. Emotionality, exploratory behavior, and locomotion in aging inbred strains of mice. *Gerontologia,* 1975, **21,** 46.

Elias, P. K., and Redgate, E. S. Effects of immobilization stress on open field behavior and plasma corticosterone levels of aging C57BL/6J mice. *Experimental Aging Research,* 1975, **1,** 127.

Erikson, E. H. Generativity and ego integrity. In J. E. Birren (Ed.), *Relations of development and aging.* Springfield, Ill.: Charles C Thomas, Publisher, 1964.

Erlenmeyer-Kimling, L., and Jarvik, L. F. Genetics

and intelligence: a review. *Science,* 1963, **142,** 1477.

Feigley, D. A., and Spear, N. E. Effect of age and punishment condition on long term retention by the rat of active and passive avoidance learning. *Journal of Comparative and Physiological Psychology,* 1970, **73,** 515.

Feldman, M. L., and Peters, A. Morphological changes in the aging brain. In G. J. Maletta (Ed.), *Survey report on the aging nervous system* (U.S. Department of Health, Education and Welfare Publication No. [NIH] 74-296). Washington, D.C.: U.S. Government Printing Office, 1975.

Fields, P. E. The age factor in multiple discrimination learning by white rats. *Journal of Comparative and Physiological Psychology,* 1953, **46,** 387.

Fillenbaum, G. G. On the relation between attitude to work and attitude to retirement. *Journal of Gerontology,* 1971, **26,** 244.

Fillenbaum, G. G., and Maddox, G. L. Work after retirement: an investigation into some psychologically relevant variables. *Gerontologist,* 1974, **14,** 418.

Finkle, A. L., Tobenkin, M. I., and Karg, S. J. Sexual potency in aging males. I. Frequency of coitus among clinic patients. *Journal of the American Medical Association,* 1959, **170,** 113.

Fisher, J. Competence, effectiveness, intellectual functioning and aging. *Gerontologist,* 1973, **13,** 61.

Florini, J. R. Differences in enzyme levels and physiological processes and some enzyme levels in mice of various ages: a review. *Experimental Aging Research,* 1975, **1,** 137.

Foulds, G. A. Variations in the intellectual activities of adults. *American Journal of Psychology,* 1949, **62,** 238.

Foulds, G. A., and Raven, J. C. Normal changes in mental abilities of adults as age advances. *Journal of Mental Science,* 1948, **94,** 1133.

Fox, C. A., Ismail, A. A. A., Love, D. N., Kirkham, K. E., and Loraine, J. A. Studies on the relationship between plasma testosterone levels and human sexual activity. *Journal of Endocrinology,* 1972, **52,** 51.

Fozard, J. L., and Waugh, N. C. Proactive inhibition of prompted items. *Psychonomic Science,* 1969, **17,** 67.

Freeman, J. T. Endocrinology in geriatrics: historical background. In L. Gitman (Ed.), *Endocrines and behavior.* Springfield, Ill.: Charles C Thomas, Publisher, 1967.

Freund, G., and Walker, D. W. The effect of aging on acquisition and retention of shuttle box avoidance in mice. *Life Sciences,* 1971, **10,** 1343.

Friedrich, D., Libkuman, T., Craig, E., and Winn, F. *Read-out times from iconic memory in normal and retarded adolescents.* Presented at the 6th Annual Meetings of the Gatlinburg Conference on Research and Theory in Mental Retardation, Gatlinburg, Tenn., March, 1973.

Fuller, J. L. The path between genes and behavioral characteristics. *Eugenics Quarterly,* 1956, **3,** 209.

Fuller, J. L., Brady-Wood, S., and Elias, M. F. Effects of retinal degeneration and brain size upon spatial reversal learning in mice. *Perceptual and Motor Skills,* 1973, **36,** 947.

Fuller, J. L., and Geils, H. D. Brain growth in mice selected for high and low brain weight. *Developmental Psychobiology,* 1973, **5,** 307.

Fuller, J. L., and Thompson, W. R. *Behavior genetics.* New York: John Wiley & Sons, Inc., 1960.

Furman, R. H. Coronary heart disease and the menopause. In K. J. Ryan and D. C. Gigson (Eds.), *Menopause and aging.* Bethesda, Md., U.S. Department of Health, Education and Welfare, 1971.

Furry, C. A., and Baltes, P. B. The effect of age differences in ability-extraneous performance variables on the assessment of intelligence in children, adults, and the elderly. *Journal of Gerontology,* 1973, **28,** 73.

Gajo, F. D. Adult age differences in the perception of visual illusions. Doctoral dissertation, Washington University, Ann Arbor, 1966. (University Microfilms No. 62-7036).

Galton, F. *Inquiries into human faculty and its development.* London: Collier-Macmillan Ltd., 1883.

Gilbert, J. A. Researchers on mental and physical development of school children. *Studies of the Yale Psychological Laboratory,* 1894, **2,** 40.

Gilbert, J. G. Memory loss in senescence. *Journal of Abnormal and Social Psychology,* 1941, **36,** 73.

Gilbert, J. G., and Levee, R. F. Patterns of declining memory, *Journal of Gerontology,* 1971, **26,** 70.

Gladis, M., and Braun, H. Age differences in transfer and retroaction as a function of intertask similarity. *Journal of Experimental Psychology,* 1958, **55,** 25.

Glamser, F. D. Determinants of a positive attitude toward retirement. *Journal of Gerontology,* 1976, **31,** 104.

Glenwick, D. S. *Beyond despair and disengagement: a transactional model of personality.* Presented at the 28th Annual Meetings of the Gerontological Society, Louisville, Oct., 1975.

Goddard, H. H. A measuring scale for intelligence. *Training School Bulletin,* 1910, **6,** 146.

Goldman, H., Kleinman, K. M., Snow, M. Y., Bidus, D. R., and Korol, B. Correlation of diastolic blood pressure and signs of cognitive dysfunction in essential hypertension. *Diseases of the Nervous System,* 1974, **35,** 571.

Goodenough, U., and Levine, R. P. *Genetics.* New York: Holt, Rinehart, & Winston, Inc., 1974.

Goodrick, C. L. Social interactions and exploration of young, mature, and senescent male rats. *Journal of Gerontology,* 1965, **20,** 215.

Goodrick, C. L. Activity and exploration as a function of age and deprivation. *Journal of Genetic Psychology,* 1966, **108,** 239.

Goodrick, C. L. Exploration of non-deprived male Sprague-Dawley rats as a function of age. *Psychological Reports,* 1967, **20,** 159.

Goodrick, C. L. Learning, retention, and extinction of a complex maze habit for mature-young and senescent Wistar albino rats. *Journal of Gerontology,* 1968, **23,** 298.

Goodrick, C. L. Light and dark-contingent bar pressing in the rat as a function of age and motivation. *Journal of Comparative and Physiological Psychology,* 1970, **73,** 100.

Goodrick, C. L. Variables affecting free exploration responses of male and female Wistar rats as a function of age. *Developmental Psychology,* 1971, **4,** 440.

Goodrick, C. L. Learning by mature-young and aged Wistar albino rats as a function of test complexity. *Journal of Gerontology,* 1972, **27,** 353.

Goodrick, C. L. Behavioral differences in young and aged mice: strain differences for activity measures, operant learning, sensory discrimination, and alcohol preference. *Experimental Aging Research,* 1975a, **1,** 191.

Goodrick, C. L. Behavioral rigidity as a mechanism for facilitation of problem solving for aged rats. *Journal of Gerontology,* 1975b, **30,** 181.

Gordon, S. K., and Slevin, A. E. Imagery and sentence retention in elderly and young adults. Presented at the 28th Annual Meetings of the Gerontological Society, Louisville, Oct., 1975.

Gottesman, I. I. Beyond the fringe—personality and psychopathology. In D. C. Glass (Ed.), *Genetics.* New York: Rockefeller University Press, 1968.

Goudy, W. J., Powers, E. A., and Keith, P. Work and retirement: a test of attitudinal relationships. *Journal of Gerontology,* 1975, **30,** 193.

Goulet, L. R. New directions for research on aging and retention. *Journal of Gerontology,* 1972, **27,** 52.

Goulet, L. R., and Baltes, P. B. (Eds.). *Life-span developmental psychology: research and theory.* New York: Academic Press, Inc., 1970.

Gressel, G. C., Shobe, F. O., Saslow, G., Dubois, P. H., and Schroeder, H. A. Personality factors in arterial hypertension. *Journal of the American Medical Association,* 1949, **140,** 265.

Griew, S. Ageing and behavior in genetically-hypertensive rats. *Proceedings of the 7th International Congress on Gerontology* (Vienna), 1966.

Groffman, K. J. Life-span developmental psychology in Europe: past and present. In L. R. Goulet and P. B. Baltes (Eds.), *Life-span developmental psychology: Research and theory.* New York: Academic Press, Inc., 1970.

Grossman, S. P. *A textbook of physiological psychology.* New York: John Wiley & Sons, Inc., 1967.

Gurin, G., Veroff, J., and Feld, S. *Americans view their mental health* (Joint Commission on Mental Illness and Health, Monograph Series No. 4). New York: Basic Books, Inc., Publishers, 1960.

Hall, E. H., Savage, D., Bolton, N., Pidwell, D. M., and Blessed, G. Intellect, mental illness, and survival in the aged: a longitudinal investigation. *Journal of Gerontology,* 1972, **27,** 237.

Hall, G. S. *Adolescence* (2 vols.) New York: D. Appleton & Co., 1904.

Hall, G. S. *Educational problems.* New York: D. Appleton & Co., 1911.

Hall, G. S. *Senescence, the last half of life.* New York, D. Appleton & Co., 1922.

Haller, M. H. Social sciences and genetics: a historical perspective. In D. C. Glass (Ed.), *Genetics,* New York: Rockefeller University Press, 1968.

Haltmeyer, G. C., Denenberg, V. H., and Zarrow, M. X. Modification of the plasma corticosteroid response as a function of infantile stimulation and electric shock parameters. *Physiology and Behavior,* 1967, **2,** 61.

Hankins, F. H. *Adolphe Quetelet as statistician.* Doctoral dissertation, Columbia University, New York, 1908.

Harlow, H. F., Gluck, J. P., and Sumi, S. J. Generalization of behavioral data between nonhuman and human animals. *American Psychologist,* 1972, **27,** 709-716.

Harrell, R. F., Woodyard, E., and Gates, A. E. *The effects of mothers' diets on the intelligence of offspring: a study of the influence of vitamin supplementation on the diets of pregnant and lactating women on the intelligence of their children.* New York: Teachers College Press, 1955.

Harris, R. E., and Singer, M. T. Interaction of personality and stress in the pathogenesis of essential hypertension. *Hypertension, Proceedings of the Council on High Blood Pressure Research,* 1967, **16,** 104-115.

Hatch, A. M., Wiberg, G. S., Zawidzka, Z., Cann, M., Airth, J. M., and Grice, H. C. Isolation syndrome in the rat. *Toxicology and Applied Pharmacology,* 1965, **7,** 737.

Havighurst, R. J. The nature and value of meaningful free-time activity. In R. W. Kleemeier (Ed.), *Aging and leisure.* London: Oxford University Press, 1961.

Havighurst, R. J. A social-psychological perspective on aging. *Gerontologist,* 1968, **8,** 67.

Havighurst, R. J., Neugarten, B. L., and Tobin, S. S. Disengagement and patterns of aging. In J. E. Birren (Ed.), *Relations of development and aging.* Springfield, Ill.: Charles C Thomas, Publisher, 1964a.

Havighurst, R. J., Neugarten, B. L., and Tobin, S. S. Disengagement, personality and life satisfaction in the later years. In P. From Hansen (Ed.), *Age with a future,* Copenhagen: Einar Munksgaard, 1964b.

Hearn, H. L. Aging and the artistic career. *Gerontologist,* 1972, **12,** 357.

Henderson, N. D. Prior treatment effects on open field behavior of mice—a genetic analysis. In M. Manosevitz, G. Lindzey, and D. Thiessen (Eds.), *Behavioral genetics: method and research.* New York: Appleton-Century-Crofts, 1969.

Henderson, N. D. Gene-environment interaction in human behavioral development. In K. W. Schaie, V. E. Anderson, G. E. McClearn, and J. Money (Eds.), *Developmental human behavior genetics: nature-nurture redefined.* Lexington, Mass.: Lexington Books, D. C. Heath & Co., 1975.

Henry, J. P., and Cassel, J. C. Psychosocial factors in essential hypertension: recent epidemiological and animal experimental evidence. *American Journal of Epidemiology,* 1969, **90,** 171.

Henry, J. P., Meehan, J., and Stephens, P. M. The use of psychosocial stimuli to induce prolonged systolic hypertension in mice. *Psychosomatic Medicine,* 1967, **29,** 408.

Henry, W. E. Engagement and disengagement: toward a theory of adult development. In R. Kastenbaum (Ed.), *Contributions to the psychobiology of aging.* New York: Springer Publishing Co., Inc., 1965.

Heron, A., and Chown, S. *Age and function.* London: J. & A. Churchill, Ltd., 1967.

Heron, A., and Craik, F. I. M. Age differences in cumulative learning of meaningful and meaningless material. *Scandinavian Journal of Psychology,* 1964, **5,** 209.

Herriot, P. *Attributes of memory.* London: Methuen & Co., Ltd., 1974.

Hertzog, C., Gribben, K., and Schaie, K. W. The influence of cardiovascular disease and hypertension on intellectual stability. Presented at the 28th Annual Meetings of the Gerontological Society, Louisville, Oct., 1975.

Hicks, L. H., and Birren, J. E. Aging, brain damage, and psychomotor slowing. *Psychological Bulletin,* 1970, **74,** 377.

Higham, J. *Strangers in the land: patterns of American nativism,* 1860-1925. New Brunswick, N.J.: Rutgers University Press, 1955.

Hirsch, M. J. Data cited by Weymouth, F. W. Effects of age on visual acuity. In M. J. Hirsch (Ed.), *Vision of the aging patient.* Philadelphia: Chilton Book Co., 1960.

Hollander, E. P., and Hunt, R. G. *Current perspectives in social psychology.* New York: Oxford University Press, 1967.

Horn, J. L. Organization of data on life-span development of human abilities. In L. R. Goulet and P. B. Baltes (Eds.), *Life-span developmental psychology: research and theory.* New York: Academic Press, Inc., 1970.

Horn, J. L. Psychometric studies of aging and intelligence. In S. Gershon and A. Raskind (Eds.), *Aging* (Vol. 2). *Genesis and treatment of psychologic disorders in the elderly.* New York: Raven Press, 1975.

Horn, J. L., and Cattell, R. B. Age differences in fluid and crystallized intelligence. *Acta Psychologica,* 1967, **26,** 107.

Hoyer, W. J. Application of operant techniques to the modification of elderly behavior. In P. B. Baltes (Ed.), *Strategies for psychological intervention in old age: a symposium. Gerontologist,* 1973, **13,** 18.

Hoyer, W. J. Aging as intraindividual change. *Developmental Psychology,* 1974, **10,** 821.

Hoyer, W. J., Labouvie, G. V., and Baltes, P. B. Modification of response speed deficits and intellectual performance in the elderly. *Human Development,* 1973, **16,** 233.

Hoyt, D. P. *The relationship between college grades and adult achievement: a review of the literature* (ACT Research Reports, No. 7). Iowa City: American College Testing Program, 1965.

Hulicka, I. Age differences in retention as a function of interference. *Journal of Gerontology,* 1967a, **22,** 180.

Hulicka, I. Short-term learning and memory efficiency as a function of age and health. *Journal of the American Geriatrics Society,* 1967b, **15,** 285.

Hulicka, I. M., and Grossman, J. L. Age-group comparisons for the use of mediators in paired-associate learning. *Journal of Gerontology,* 1967, **22,** 46.

Hulicka, I. M., and Rust, L. D. Age-related retention deficit as a function of learning. *Journal of the American Geriatrics Society,* 1964, **12,** 1061.

Hulicka, I. M., Sterns, H., and Grossman, J. Age-group comparisons of paired-associate learning as a function of paced and self-paced association and response time. *Journal of Gerontology,* 1967, **22,** 274.

Hultsch, D. F. Adult age differences in the organization of free recall. *Developmental Psychology,* 1969, **1,** 763.

Hultsch, D. F. Adult age differences in free classification and free recall. *Developmental Psychology,* 1971, **4,** 338.

Hultsch, D. F. Adult age differences in retrieval: trace dependent and cue dependent forgetting. *Developmental Psychology,* 1975, **11,** 197.

Hutt, C. *Males and females.* Middlesex, England: Penguin Books, Ltd., 1972.

Ismail, A. A. A., and Harkness, R. A. Urinary testosterone excretion in men in normal and pathological conditions. *Acta Endocrinologica,* 1967, **56,** 469.

Jacobs, F. A., Court-Brown, W. M., and Doll, A. Distribution of human chromosome count in relation to age. *Nature,* 1961, **191,** 1178.

Jakubczak, L. F. Effects of testosterone propionate on age differences in mating behavior. *Journal of Gerontology,* 1964, **19,** 458.

Jakubczak, L. F. Age differences in the effects of terminal food deprivation (starvation) on activity, weight loss, and survival of rats. *Journal of Gerontology,* 1967, **22,** 421.

Jakubczak, L. F. Effects of age and activity restriction on body weight loss of rats. *American Journal of Physiology,* 1969, **216,** 1081.

Jakubczak, L. F. Age differences in the effects of water deprivation on activity, water loss, and survival of rats. *Life Sciences,* 1970, **9,** 771.

Jakubczak, L. F. Age and animal behavior. In C. Eisdorfer and M. P. Lawton (Eds.), *The psychology of adult development and aging.* Washington, D.C.: American Psychological Association, 1973.

Jarvik, L. F. Senescence and chromosomal changes. *Lancet,* 1963, **1,** 114.

Jarvik, L. F. Survival and psychological aspects of aging in man. In H. W. Woolhouse (Ed.), *Aspects of the biology of aging* (Vol. 21). *Symposia of the Society for Experimental Biology.* Cambridge: Cambridge University Press, 1967.

Jarvik, L. F., Altshuler, K. Z., Kato, T., and Blummer, B. Organic brain syndrome and chromosome loss in aged twins. *Diseases of the Nervous System,* 1971, **32,** 159.

Jarvik, L. F., and Blum, J. E. Cognitive decline as predictor of mortality in twin pairs: a twenty-year long study of aging. In E. Palmore and F. C. Jeffers (Eds.), *Prediction of life-span.* Lexington, Mass.: Lexington Books, D. C. Heath & Co., 1971.

Jarvik, L. F., Blum, J. E., and Varma, A. O. Genetic components and intellectual functioning during senescence: a twenty-year study of aging twins. *Behavior Genetics,* 1972, **2,** 159.

Jarvik, L. F., and Cohen, D. A biobehavioral approach to intellectual changes with aging. In C. Eisdorfer and M. P. Lawton (Eds.), *The psychology of adult development and aging.* Washington, D.C.: American Psychological Association, 1973.

Jarvik, L. F., Kallmann, F. J., and Falek, A. Psychiatric genetics and aging. *Gerontologist,* 1962, **2,** 164-166.

Jarvik, L. F., and Kato, T. Chromosomes and mental changes in octogenarians. *British Journal of Psychiatry,* 1969, **115,** 1193.

Jarvik, L. F., and Kato, T. Chromosome examinations in aged twins. *American Journal of Human Genetics,* 1970, **22,** 562.

Jarvik, L. F., Yen, F-S, Fu, T. K., and Matsuyama, S. S. Chromosomes in old age: a six-year longitudinal study. *Humangenetik,* in press.

Jenkins, C. D., Rosenman, R. H., and Zyzanski, S. J. Prediction of clinical coronary heart disease by a test for the coronary-prone behavior pattern. *New England Journal of Medicine,* 1974, **290,** 1271.

Jensen, A. R. How much can we boost IQ and scholastic achievement? *Harvard Educational Review,* 1969, **39,** 1.

Jensen, A. R. Race and the genetics of intelligence: a reply to Lewontin. *Bulletin of the Atomic Scientists,* 1970, **26,** 17.

Jerome, E. A. Age and learning—experimental studies. In J. E. Birren (Ed.), *Handbook of aging and the individual.* Chicago: University of Chicago Press, 1959.

Joffe, J. M. *Prenatal determinants of behavior.* New York: Pergamon Press, Inc., 1969.

Johnson, D. F., and Mihal, W. L. Performance of blacks and whites in computerized versus manual testing environments. *American Psychologist,* 1973, **28,** 694.

Jones, H. B. A special consideration of the aging process, disease, and life expectancy. In J. H. Lawrence and C. A. Tobias (Eds.), *Advances in biological medical physics* (Vol. 4). New York: Academic Press, Inc., 1956.

Jones, H. E., and Conrad, H. S. The growth and decline of intelligence: a study of homogeneous populations between the ages of ten and sixty. *Genetic Psychology Monographs,* 1933, **13,** 233.

Kaack, B., Ordy, J. M., and Trapp, B. Changes in limbic, neuroendocrine, and anatomic systems, adaptation, homeostasis during aging. In J. M. Ordy and K. R. Brizzee (Eds.), *Neurobiology of aging: an interdisciplinary life-span approach.* New York: Plenum Publishing Corp., 1975.

Kagan, J., and Moss, H. A. *Birth to maturity: a study in psychological development.* New York: John Wiley & Sons, Inc., 1962.

Kahn, E., and Fisher, C. REM sleep and sexuality in the aged. *Journal of Geriatric Psychiatry,* 1969, **2,** 181.

Kalish, R. A. *Late adulthood: perspectives on human development.* Monterey, Calif.: Brooks/Cole Publishing Co., 1975.

Kamin, L. J. Differential changes in the mental ability in old age. *Journal of Gerontology,* 1957, **12,** 66.

Kanak, N. J., and Nuener, S. D. Associative symmetry and item availability as a function of five methods of paired-associate acquisition. *Journal of Experimental Psychology,* 1970, **86,** 288.

Kangas, J., and Bradway, K. Intelligence at middle age: a thirty-eight year follow up. *Developmental Psychology,* 1971, **5,** 333.

Kausler, D. H., and Lair, C. V. Associative strength and paired-associate learning in elderly subjects. *Journal of Gerontology,* 1966, **21,** 278.

Kay, H., and Birren, J. E. Swimming speed of the albino rat. II. Fatigue, practice, and drug effects on age and sex differences. *Journal of Gerontology,* 1958, **13,** 378.

Kay, H., and Sime, M. E. Discrimination learning with old and young rats. *Journal of Gerontology,* 1962, **17,** 75.

Keevil-Rogers, P., and Schnore, M. M. Short-term memory as a function of age in persons of above average intelligence. *Journal of Gerontology,* 1969, **24,** 184.

Kelly, J. R. Work and leisure: a simplified paradigm. *Journal of Leisure Research,* 1972, **4,** 50.

Kessel, F. The philosophy of science as proclaimed and science as practiced: identity or dualism? *American Psychologist,* 1969, **24,** 999.

Kimble, G. A., and Pennypacker, H. S. Eyelid conditioning in young and aged subjects. *Journal of Genetic Psychology,* 1963, **103,** 283.

Kimura, D. The asymmetry of the human brain. *Scientific American,* 1973, **3,** 70.

Kinsbourne, M., and Berryhill, J. L. The nature of the interaction between pacing and the age decrement in learning. *Journal of Gerontology,* 1972, **27,** 471.

Kleemeier, R. W. Intellectual changes in the senium. *Proceedings of the American Statistical Association,* 1962, **1,** 290.

Kleiber, M. A., Smith, A. H., and Chernikoff, H. N. Metabolic rate of female rats as a function of age and body size. *American Journal of Physiology,* 1956, **186,** 9.

Kline, D. W., and Birren, J. E. Age differences in dichoptic masking. *Experimental Aging Research,* 1975, **1,** 17.

Kline, D. W., and Szafran, J. Age differences in backward monoptic visual noise masking. *Journal of Gerontology,* 1975, **30,** 307.

Klodin, V. M. The relationship of scoring treatment and age in perceptual-integrative performance. *Experimental Aging Research,* 1976, **2,** 303.

Knill, F. P. The effect of visual and verbal mnemonic devices on the paired associate learning of an aged population. Masters thesis, University of Richmond, Richmond, Va., 1966.

Kogan, N., and Wallach, M. A. The effect of anxiety on relations between subjective age and caution in an older sample. In P. H. Hoch and J. Zubin (Eds.), *Psychopathology of aging.* New York: Grune & Stratton, Inc., 1961.

Kogan, Y., and Morant, G. M. On the degree of association between reaction times in the case of different senses. *Biometrika,* 1923, **15,** 346.

Kolb, L. C. *Noyes' modern clinical psychiatry.* Philadelphia: W. B. Saunders Co., 1968.

Korchin, S. J., and Basowitz, H. Age differences in verbal learning. *Journal of Abnormal and Social Psychology,* 1957, **54,** 64.

Kuhlen, R. G. Age and intelligence: the significance of cultural change in longitudinal versus cross-sectional findings. *Vita Humana,* 1963, **6,** 113.

Kuhlen, R. G. Developmental changes in motivation during the adult years. In J. E. Birren (Ed.), *Relations of development and aging.* Springfield, Ill.: Charles C Thomas, Publisher, 1964.

Kuhn, T. S. *The structure of scientific revolutions.* Chicago: University of Chicago Press, 1962.

Kurtz, J., and Wolk, S. Continued growth and life satisfaction. *Gerontologist,* 1975, **15,** 129.

Kuypers, J. A., and Bengtson, V. L. Social breakdown and competence: a model of normal aging. *Human Development,* 1973, **16,** 181.

Lacey, J. I., and Van Lehn, R. Differential emphasis and somatic responding to stress: an experimental study. *Psychosomatic Medicine,* 1952, **14,** 71.

Langer, J. *Theories of development.* New York: Holt, Rinehart, & Winston, Inc., 1969.

Larsson, K. *Conditioning and sexual behavior in the male albino rat.* Stockholm: Almqvist & Wiksell, 1956.

Larsson, K., and Esslerg, L. Effect of age on the

sexual behavior of the male rat. *Gerontologia,* 1962, **6,** 133.

Lass, N. J., and Golden, S. S. The use of isolated vowels as auditory stimuli in eliciting the verbal transformation effect. *Canadian Journal of Psychology,* 1971, **25,** 349.

Lassen, N. A. Cerebral blood flow and metabolism in health and disease. In C. H. Millikan (Ed.), *Cerebrovascular disease.* Baltimore: The Williams & Wilkins Co., 1966.

Lassen, N. A., Munck, O., and Tottey, E. R. T. Mental function and cerebral oxygen consumption in organic dementia. *Archives of Neurology and Psychiatry,* 1957, **77,** 126.

Laverty, R. Activity and brain amine metabolism in strains of normotensive and hypertensive rats. *Psychonomic Science,* 1968, **10,** 25.

Layton, B. Perceptual noise and aging. *Psychological Bulletin,* 1975, **82,** 875.

Lehr, U., and Rudinger, G. Consistency and change of social participation in old age. *Human Development,* 1969, **12,** 255.

Lemon, B. W., Bengtson, V. L., and Peterson, J. A. Activity types and life satisfaction in a retirement community. *Journal of Gerontology,* 1972, **27,** 511.

Leri, J. E., Lesswing, N. J., and Elias, M. F. Relation of mental ability to preference for varying rates of auditory stimulation. *Psychonomic Science,* 1969, **17,** 80.

Levine, S. (Ed.). *Hormones and behavior.* New York: Academic Press, Inc., 1972.

Levine, S., and Brush, F. R. Adrenocortical activity and avoidance learning as a function of time after avoidance training. *Physiology and Behavior,* 1967, **2,** 385.

Lewis, B. K., and Wexler, B. C. Serum insulin changes in male rats associated with age and reproductive activity. *Journal of Gerontology,* 1974, **29,** 139.

Lieberman, M. A. Psychological correlates of impending death: some preliminary observations. *Journal of Gerontology,* 1965, **20,** 181.

Light, K. C. Slowing of response time in young and middle-aged hypertensive patients. *Experimental Aging Research,* 1975, **1,** 209.

Lindzey, G., Loehlin, J., Manosevitz, M., and Thiessen, D. Behavioral genetics, *Annual Review of Psychology,* 1971, **22,** 39.

Lipman, A., and Smith, K. J. Functionality of disengagement in old age. *Journal of Gerontology,* 1968, **23,** 517.

Lipsitt, L. P. The experiential origins of human behavior. In L. R. Goulet and P. B. Baltes (Eds.), *Life-span developmental psychology: research and theory.* New York: Academic Press, Inc., 1970.

Liss, L., and Gomez, F. The nature of senile changes of the human olfactory bulb and tract. *Archives of Otolaryngology,* 1958, **67,** 167.

Livson, N. Developmental dimensions of personality: a life-span formulation. In P. B. Baltes and K. W. Schaie (Eds.), *Life-span developmental psychology: personality and socialization.* New York: Academic Press, Inc., 1973.

Lockhard, R. Some effects of light on the behavior of rodents. *Psychological Bulletin,* 1963, **60,** 509.

Looft, W. R. Conceptions of human nature, educational practice, and individual development. *Human Development,* 1973, **16,** 21.

Loranger, A. W., and Misiak, H. Critical flicker frequency and some intellectual functions in old age. *Journal of Gerontology,* 1959, **14,** 323.

Lorge, I. The influence of test upon the nature of mental decline as a function of age. *Journal of Educational Psychology,* 1936, **27,** 100.

Lovely, R. H., Pagano, R. R., and Paolino, R. M. Shuttle-box avoidance performance and basal corticosterone levels as a function of duration of individual housing in rats. *Journal of Comparative and Physiological Psychology,* 1972, **81,** 331.

Lowenthal, M. F. Social isolation and mental illness in old age. In B. L. Neugarten (Ed.), *Middle age and aging.* Chicago: University of Chicago Press, 1968.

Lowther, B. D. *Environmentally-induced behavioral changes in aged animals.* Presented as part of a symposium, "The Role of the Rat and Mouse in Life-Span Research" at the annual meeting of the American Psychological Association, Montreal and Quebec, Sept., 1973.

Maccoby, E. E. (Ed.). *The development of sex differences.* Stanford, Calif.: Stanford University Press, 1966.

Maddox, G. L. A longitudinal multidisciplinary study of human aging: selected methodological issues. *Proceedings of the Social Statistics Section of the American Statistical Association.* Washington, D.C.: American Statistical Association, 1962.

Maddox, G. L. Persistence of life style among the elderly: a longitudinal study of patterns of social activity in relation to life-satisfaction. In B. L. Neugarten (Ed.), *Middle age and aging.* Chicago: University of Chicago Press, 1968.

Magladerly, J. W. Neurophysiology of aging. In J. E. Birren (Ed.), *Handbook of aging and the individual.* Chicago: University of Chicago Press, 1959.

Manosevitz, M., Lindzey, G., and Thiessen, D. (Eds.). *Behavioral genetics: method and research.* New York: Appleton-Century-Crofts, 1969.

Marie, M. A new anabolic agent (stanozolol):

clinical evaluation in the aged. *Journal of the American Geriatrics Society,* 1963, **11,** 540.

Martin, W. C. *A social structural conceptualization and operationalization of disengagement.* Presented at the 28th Annual Meetings of the Gerontological Society, Louisville, Oct., 1975.

Maslow, A. H. *Motivation and personality.* New York: Harper & Row, Publishers, 1954.

Masters, W. H., and Johnson, V. E. *Human sexual response.* Boston: Little, Brown & Co., 1966.

McAdam, W., and Robinson, R. A. Diagnostic and prognostic value of the electroencephalogram in geriatric psychiatry. In H. T. Blumenthal (Ed.), *Medical and clinical aspects of aging.* New York: Columbia University Press, 1962.

McCall, R. B. The use of multivariate procedures in developmental psychology. In P. H. Mussen (Ed.), *Carmichael's manual of child psychology* (Vol. I). New York: John Wiley & Sons, Inc., 1970.

McCall, R. B., and Appelbaum, M. I. Bias in the analysis of repeated-measures designs: some alternative approaches. *Child Development,* 1973, **44,** 401.

McClearn, G. E. Behavioral genetics. *Behavioral Science,* 1971, **16,** 64.

McConnell, R. A. The future revisited. *Biological Science,* 1970, **20,** 903.

McDougall, W. *Introduction to social psychology.* Boston: John W. Luce, 1908.

McFarland, R. A. The sensory and perceptual processes in aging. In K. W. Schaie (Ed.), *Theory and methods of research on aging.* Morgantown, W.Va.: West Virginia University Press, 1968.

McFarland, R. A., Domey, R. G., Warren, A. B., and Ward, D. C. Dark adaptation as a function of age. I. A statistical analysis. *Journal of Gerontology,* 1960, **15,** 149.

McFarland, R. A., Warren, A. B., and Karis, C. Alterations in critical flicker frequency as a function of age and light:dark ratio. *Journal of Experimental Psychology,* 1958, **56,** 529.

McGlone, J., and Davidson, W. The relation between cerebral speech laterality and spatial ability. *Neuropsychologia,* 1973, **11,** 105.

McNulty, J. A. An analysis of recall and recognition processes in verbal learning. *Journal of Verbal Learning and Verbal Behavior,* 1965, **4,** 430.

McNulty, J. A., and Caird, W. Memory loss with age: retrieval or storage? *Psychological Reports,* 1966, **19,** 229.

Medin, D. L. Form perception and pattern reproduction by monkeys. *Journal of Comparative and Physiological Psychology,* 1969, **68,** 412.

Medin, D. L., O'Neil, P., Smeltz, E., and Davis, R. T. Age differences in retention of concurrent discrimination problems in monkeys. *Journal of Gerontology,* 1973, **28,** 63.

Meier, G. W. Differences in maze performances as a function of age and strain of housemice. *Journal of Comparative and Physiological Psychology,* 1964, **58,** 418.

Meier, G. W., and Foshee, D. P. Genetics, age, and the variability of learning performances. *Journal of Genetic Psychology,* 1963, **102,** 267.

Michael, C. M. Further psychometric evaluation of older women—the effect of estrogen administration. *Journal of Gerontology,* 1970, **25,** 337.

Miles, C. C. The influence of speed and age on intelligence scores of adults. *Journal of General Psychology,* 1934, **10,** 208.

Miles, C. C., and Miles, W. R. The correlations of intelligence scores and chronological age from early to late maturity. *American Journal of Psychology,* 1932, **44,** 44.

Miles, W. R. Age and human ability. *Psychological Review,* 1933, **40,** 99.

Miller, S. J. The social dilemma of the aging leisure participant. In B. L. Neugarten (Ed.), *Middle age and aging.* Chicago: University of Chicago Press, 1968.

Minnick, R. S., Warden, C. J., and Arieti, S. The effect of sex hormones on the copulatory behavior of senile white rats. *Science,* 1946, **103,** 749.

Monge, R. H. Learning in the adult years: set or rigidity. In D. B. Lumsden and R. H. Sherron (Eds.), *Experimental studies in adult learning and memory.* Washington, D.C.: Hemisphere Publishing Corp., 1975.

Monge, R. H., and Gardner, E. F. *A program of research in adult differences in cognitive performance and learning: backgrounds for adult education and vocational retraining.* Final Report (Project No. 6-1963, Grant No. OEG 1-706193-0149), 1972.

Monge, R., and Gardner, E. F. Education as an aid to adaptation in the adult years. In K. F. Riegel and J. A. Meacham (Eds.), *The developing individual in a changing world* (Vol. II). *Social and environmental issues.* The Hague: Mouton & Co., Publishers, 1976.

Monge, R. H., and Hultsch, D. F. Paired-associate learning as a function of adult age and length of the anticipation and inspection intervals. *Journal of Gerontology,* 1971, **26,** 157.

Moscowitz, H. W., Kumaraith, U., Sharma, K. N., Jacobs, H. L., and Sharma, S. D. Cross-cultural differences in simple taste preferences. *Science,* 1975, **190,** 1217.

Muhlbock, O. Factors influencing the life span of inbred mice. *Gerontologia,* 1959, **3,** 177.

Müller, H. F., Grad, B., and Engelsmann, F. Biological and psychological predictors of survival in a psychogeriatric population. *Journal of Gerontology,* 1975, **30,** 47.

Murdock, B. B., Jr. The immediate retention of unrelated words. *Journal of Experimental Psychology,* 1960, **60,** 222.

Neale, J. M., and Liebert, R. M. *Science and behavior: an introduction to methods of research.* Englewood Cliffs, N.J.: Prentice-Hall, Inc., 1973.

Nelson, E. N. P. Persistence of attitudes of college students fourteen years later. *Psychological Monographs,* 1954, **68,** 1.

Nesselroade, J. R. Application of multivariate strategies to problems of measuring and structuring long-term change. In L. R. Goulet and P. B. Baltes (Eds.), *Life-span developmental psychology: research and theory.* New York: Academic Press, Inc., 1970.

Neugarten, B. L., Havighurst, R. J., and Tobin, S. S. Personality and patterns of aging. In B. L. Neugarten (Ed.), *Middle age and aging,* Chicago: University of Chicago Press, 1968.

Neugarten, B. L., and Kraines, R. J. Menopausal symptoms in women of various ages. *Psychosomatic Medicine,* 1965, **27,** 266.

Newman, G., and Nichols, C. R. Sexual activities and attitudes in older persons. *Journal of the American Medical Association,* 1960, **173,** 33.

Newton, M. J. A salute to retirement. *Gerontologist,* 1974, **14,** 413.

Nielsen, J. Chromosomes in senile dementia. *British Journal of Psychiatry,* 1968, **114,** 303.

Nielsen, J. Chromosomes in senile, presenile, and arteriosclerotic dementia. *Journal of Gerontology,* 1970, **25,** 312.

Noberini, M., and Neuarten, B. *A follow-up study* of *adaptation in middle-aged women.* Presented at the 28th Annual Meetings of the Gerontological Society, Louisville, Oct., 1975.

Norman, D. L. *Memory and attention.* New York: John Wiley & Sons, Inc., 1969.

Norris, A. H., Shock, N. W., and Wagman, G. H. Age changes in the maximum conduction velocity of motor fibers of human ulnar nerves. *Journal of Applied Physiology,* 1953, **5,** 589.

Nowlin, J. B., Williams, R., and Wilkie, F. Prospective study of physical and psychological factors in elderly men who subsequently suffer acute myocardial infarction (AMI). *Clinical Research,* 1973, **21,** 465.

Obrist, W. D. The electroencephalogram of healthy aged males. In J. E. Birren, R. N. Butler, S. W. Greenhouse, L. Sokoloff, and M. Yarrow (Eds.), *Human aging: a biological and behavioral study* (National Institute of Mental Health, Public Health Service Publication No. 986). Washington, D.C.: U.S. Government Printing Office, 1963.

Obrist, W. D. Electroencephalographic approach to age changes in response speed. In A. T. Welford and J. E. Birren (Eds.), *Behavior, aging, and the nervous system.* Springfield, Ill.: Charles C Thomas, Publisher, 1965.

Obrist, W. D., and Bissell, L. F. The electroencephalogram of aged patients with cardiac and cerebral vascular disease. *Journal of Gerontology,* 1955, **10,** 315.

Obrist, W. D., and Busse, E. W. The electroencephalogram in old age. In W. P. Wilson (Ed.), *Applications of electroencephalography in psychiatry: a symposium.* Durham, N.C.: Duke University Press, 1965.

Obrist, W. D., Busse, E. W., Eisdorfer, C., and Kleemeier, R. W. Relation of the EEG to intellectual function in senescence. *Journal of Gerontology,* 1962, **17,** 197.

Obrist, W. D., Busse, E. W., and Henry, C. E. Relation of electroencephalogram to blood pressure in elderly persons. *Neurology,* 1961, **11,** 151.

Obrist, W. D., and Henry, C. E. Electroencephalographic findings in aged psychiatric patients. *Journal of Nervous and Mental Diseases,* 1958a, **126,** 254.

Obrist, W. D., and Henry, C. E. Electroencephalographic frequency analysis of aged psychiatric patients. *Electroencephalography and Clinical Neurophysiology,* 1958b, **10,** 621.

Obrist, W. D., Henry, C. E., and Justiss, W. A. *Longitudinal study of EEG in old age.* Presented at the Fifth International Congress of Electroencephalography and Clinical Neurophysiology, Rome, Italy, Sept., 1961.

Obrist, W. D., Sokoloff, L., Lassen, N. A., Lane, M. H., Butler R. N., and Feinberg, I. Relation of EEG to cerebral blood flow and metabolism in old age. *Electroencephalography and Clinical Neurophysiology,* 1963, **15,** 610.

Okamoto, K., and Aoki, K. Development of a strain of spontaneously hypertensive rats. *Japanese Circulation Journal,* 1963, **27,** 282.

Oldfield-Box, H. Age differences in performance between rats in two experimental social organizations. *Journal of Gerontology,* 1969, **24,** 18.

Oliverio, A., and Bovet, D. Effects of age on maze learning and avoidance conditioning of mice. *Life Sciences,* 1966, **5,** 1317.

Oliverio, A. B., Eleftheriou, B. E., and Bailey, D. W. Exploratory activity: genetic analysis of its modification by scopolamine and amphetamine. *Physiology and Behavior,* 1973a, **10,** 893.

Oliverio, A., Eleftheriou, B. E., and Bailey, D. W. A gene influencing active avoidance performance in mice. *Physiology and Behavior,* 1973b, **11,** 497.

Olsen, I. A., and Elder, J. H. A word-association test of emotional disturbance in older women. *Journal of Gerontology,* 1958, **13,** 305.

Overton, W. F., and Reese, H. W. Models of development: methodological implications. In J. R. Nesselroade and H. W. Reese (Eds.), *Life-span developmental psychology: methodological issues.* New York: Academic Press, Inc., 1973.

Palmore, E. B. Retirement patterns among aged men: findings of the 1963 survey of the aged. *Social Security Bulletin,* 1964, **27,** 3.

Palmore, E. B. The effects of aging on activities and attitudes. *Gerontologist,* 1968, **8,** 259.

Palmore, E. B. Sociological aspects of aging. In E. W. Busse and E. Pfeiffer (Eds.), *Behavior and adaptation in late life.* Boston: Little, Brown & Co., 1969.

Palmore, E. B. Why do people retire? *Aging and Human Development,* 1971, **2,** 269.

Palmore, E. B. Compulsory versus flexible retirement: issues and facts. *Gerontologist,* 1972, **12,** 343.

Palmore, E. B., and Cleveland, W. Aging, terminal decline, and terminal drop. *Journal of Gerontology,* 1976, **31,** 76.

Palmore, E. B., and Kivett, V. R. *Change in life satisfaction among the middle-aged.* Presented at the 28th Annual Meetings of the Gerontological Society, Louisville, Oct., 1975.

Palmore, E. B., and Luikart, C. Health and social factors related to life satisfaction. *Journal of Health and Social Behavior,* 1972, **13,** 68.

Paré, W. P. Interaction of age and shock intensity on acquisition of a discriminated conditioned emotional response. *Journal of Comparative and Physiological Psychology,* 1969, **68,** 364.

Pavio, A. Mental imagery in associative learning and memory. *Psychological Review,* 1969, **76,** 241.

Pavio, A., Yuille, J. C., and Smythe, P. C. Stimulus and response abstractness, imagery, and meaningfulness, and reported mediators in paired associate learning. *Canadian Journal of Psychology,* 1966, **20,** 362.

Payne, T. R. *S. L. Rubinstein and the philosophical foundations of Soviet psychology.* New York: Humanities Press, Inc., 1968.

Pfeiffer, E. Sexual behavior in old age. In E. W. Busse and E. Pfeiffer (Eds.), *Behavior and adaptation in late life.* Boston: Little, Brown & Co., 1969.

Pfeiffer, E. *Multidimensional qualitative assessment of three populations of elderly.* Presented at the 26th Annual Meetings of the Gerontological Society, Miami Beach, Nov., 1973.

Pfeiffer, E. *Sexuality in the aging individual.* Presented at the 31st Annual Meetings of the American Geriatric Society, Toronto, Canada, 1974.

Pfeiffer, E., and Davis, G. C. The use of leisure time in middle life. *Gerontologist,* 1971, **11,** 187.

Pfeiffer, E., and Davis, G. C. Determinants of sexual behavior in middle and old age. *Journal of the American Geriatrics Society,* 1972, **20,** 151.

Posner, M. I. *Cognition: an introduction.* Glenview, Ill.: Scott, Foresman & Co., 1972.

Posner, M. I., and Boies, S. J. Components of attention. *Psychological Review,* 1971, **78,** 319.

Posner, M. I., Nissen, M. J., and Klein, R. M. Visual dominance: an information processing account of its origins and significance. *Psychological Review,* 1976, **83,** 157.

Powell, A. H., Jr., Eisdorfer, C., and Bogdonoff, M.D. Physiologic response patterns observed in a learning task. *Archives of General Psychiatry,* 1964, **10,** 192.

Powell, D. A., Buchanan, S. L., and Milligan, W. L. *Relationships between learning, performance and arousal in aged versus younger VA patients.* Presented at the 28th Annual Meetings of the Gerontological Society, Louisville, Oct., 1975.

Powell, M., and Ferraro, C. D. Sources of tension in married and single women teachers of different ages. *Journal of Educational Psychology,* 1960, **51,** 92.

Powers, E. A., and Bultena, G. L. Characteristics of deceased dropouts in longitudinal research. *Journal of Gerontology,* 1972, **27,** 530.

Pressey, S. L. The new division on maturity and old age: its history and potential services. *American Psychologist,* 1948, **3,** 107.

Pressey, S. L., Janney, J. E., and Kuhlen, J. E. *Life: a psychological survey.* New York: Harper & Row, Publishers, 1939.

Pressey, S. L., and Kuhlen, R. G. *Psychological development through the life-span.* New York: Harper & Row, Publishers, 1957.

Rabbitt, P. M. A. An age decrement in the ability to ignore irrelevant information. *Journal of Gerontology,* 1965, **20,** 233.

Ransom, D. An index of future growth for divisions of A.P.A. *American Psychologist,* 1956, **11,** 14.

Ray, O. S., and Barrett, R. J. Interaction of learning and memory with age in the rat. In C. Eisdorfer and W. E. Fann (Eds.), *Psychopharmacology and aging.* New York: Plenum Publishing Corp., 1973.

Reed, H. B. C., and Reitan, R. M. The significance of age in the performance of a complex psychomotor task by brain-damaged and non-brain-damaged subjects. *Journal of Gerontology,* 1962, **17,** 193.

Reed, H. B. C., Jr., and Reitan, R. M. Changes in psychological test performance associated with the normal aging process. *Journal of Gerontology,* 1963, **18,** 271.

Rees, J. N., and Botwinick, J. Detection and decision factors in auditory behavior of the elderly. *Journal of Gerontology,* 1971, **26,** 133.

Reese, H. W., and Overton, W. F. Models of development and theories of development. In L. R. Goulet and P. B. Baltes (Eds.), *Life-span developmental psychology: research and theory.* New York: Academic Press, Inc., 1970.

Reichard, S., Livson, F., and Peterson, P. G. *Aging and personality: a study of eighty-seven older men.* New York: John Wiley & Sons, Inc., 1962.

Reinert, G. Comparative factor analytic studies of intelligence throughout the human life-span. In L. R. Goulet and P. B. Baltes (Eds.), *Life-span developmental psychology: research and theory.* New York: Academic Press, Inc., 1970.

Reitan, R. M. Intellectual and affective changes in essential hypertension. *American Journal of Psychiatry,* 1954, **110,** 817.

Reitan, R. M. The distribution according to age of a psychologic measure dependent upon organic brain damage. *Journal of Gerontology,* 1955, **10,** 338.

Reitan, R. M. Validity of the Trail Making Test as an indication of organic brain damage. *Perceptual and Motor Skills,* 1958, **8,** 271.

Reitan, R. M. Psychological changes associated with aging and with cerebral damage. *Mayo Clinic Proceedings,* 1967, **42,** 653.

Reitan, R. M., and Davison, L. A. *Clinical neuropsychology: current status and applications.* New York: John Wiley & Sons, Inc., 1974.

Reitan, R. M., and Fitzhugh, K. B. Behavioral deficits in groups with cerebral vascular lesions. *Journal of Consulting and Clinical Psychology,* 1971, **37,** 215.

Reitan, R. M., and Shipley, R. E. The relationship of serum cholesterol changes to psychological abilities. *Journal of Gerontology,* 1963, **18,** 350.

Remains, G., and Green, R. F. Imminence of death and intellectual functioning in the aged. *Developmental Psychology,* 1971, **5,** 270.

Riegel, K. F. On the history of psychological gerontology. In C. Eisdorfer and M. P. Lawton (Eds.), *Psychology of adult development and aging.* Washington, D.C.: American Psychological Association, 1973a.

Riegel, K. F. An epitaph for a paradigm: introduction for a symposium. *Human Development,* 1973b, **16,** Nos. 1-2, 1.

Riegel, K. F., and Riegel, R. M. A study of changes of attitudes and interests during later years of life. *Vita Humama,* 1960, **3,** 177.

Riegel, K. F., and Riegel, R. M. Development, drop, and death. *Developmental Psychology,* 1972, **6,** 309.

Riegel, K. F., Riegel, R. M., and Meyer, G. A study of the dropout rates in longitudinal research on aging and the prediction of death. *Journal of Personality and Social Psychology,* 1967, **5,** 342.

Riegel, K. F., Riegel, R. M., and Meyer, G. The prediction of retest-resistance in longitudinal research. *Journal of Gerontology,* 1968, **23,** 370.

Riopelle, A. J., and Rogers, C. M. Behavior of chimpanzees of differing ages. *Activitas Nervosa Superior,* 1963, **5,** 260.

Riopelle, A. J., and Rogers, C. M. Age changes in chimpanzees. In A. M. Schrier, H. F. Harlow, and F. Stollnitz (Eds.), *Behavior of nonhuman primates.* New York: Academic Press, Inc., 1965.

Ripley, H. S., Shorr, E., and Papanicolaou, G. N. The effect of treatment of depression in the menopause with estrogenic hormones. *American Journal of Psychiatry,* 1940, **96,** 905.

Robertson, A., and Laverty, R. Brain catecholamines in normotensive and hypertensive rats. *Proceedings of the University of Otago Medical School,* 1967, **45,** 1.

Robinson, D. S. Changes in monoamine oxidase and monoamines with human development and aging. *Federation Proceedings,* 1975, **34,** 103.

Roderick, T. H., Wimer, R. E., and Wimer, C. C. Genetic manipulation of neuroanatomical traits. In L. Petrinovich and J. L. McGaugh (Eds.), *Knowing, thinking, and believing: a Festschrift for Professor David Krech.* New York: Plenum Publishing Corp., 1975.

Rose, R. M., Gordon, T. P., and Bernstein, I. S. Plasma testosterone levels in the male rhesus: influences of sexual and social stimuli. *Science,* 1972, **178,** 643.

Rosen, J. L., and Neugarten, B. L. Ego functions in the middle and later years: a thematic apperception study of normal adults. *Journal of Gerontology,* 1960, **15,** 62.

Rosenman, R. H. The role of behavior patterns and neurogenic factors in the pathogenesis of coronary heart disease. In R. S. Eliot (Ed.), *Stress and the heart.* Mt. Kisco, N.Y.: Futura Publishing Co., 1974.

Rosenman, R. H., and Friedman, M. The central nervous system and coronary heart disease. *Hospital Practice,* 1971, **6,** 87.

Rosenman, R. H., Friedman, M., Straus, R., Jenkins, C. D., Zyzanski, S., Jr., Wurm M., and Kositchek R. Coronary heart disease in the Western Collaborative Group Study: a follow-up experience of four and one-half years. *Journal of Chronic Diseases,* 1970, **23,** 173.

Rosenzweig, M. R., Bennett, E. L., and Krech, D. Cerebral effects of environmental complexity and training among rats. *Journal of Comparative and Physiological Psychology,* 1964, **57,** 438.

Rosow, I. Housing and local ties of the aged. In B. L. Neugarten (Ed.), *Middle age and aging.* Chicago: University of Chicago Press, 1968.

Ross, E. Effects of challenging and supportive instructions in verbal learning in older persons. *Journal of Educationl Psychology,* 1968, **59,** 261.

Ross, G. T., and Vande Weile, R. L. The ovaries. In R. H. Williams (Ed.), *Textbook of endocrinology.* Philadelphia: W. B. Saunders Co., 1974.

Rowe, E. J., and Schnore, M. M. Item concreteness and reported strategies in paired-associate learning as a function of age. *Journal of Gerontology,* 1971, **26,** 470.

Rupp, R. R. Understanding the problems of presbycusis: an overview of hearing loss associated with aging. *Geriatrics,* 1970, **25,** 100.

Rusin, M. J., and Siegler, I. C. *Personality differences between participants and drop-outs in a longitudinal aging study.* Presented at the 28th Annual Meetings of the Gerontological Society, Louisville, Oct., 1975.

Russell, E. S. Genetic considerations in the selection of rodent species and strains for research in aging. In D. C. Gibson (Ed.), *Development of the rodent as a model system of aging* (U.S. Department of Health, Education and Welfare Publication No. [NIH]) 72-121). Washington, D.C.: U.S. Government Printing Office, 1972.

Russell, E. S., and Sprott, R. L. Genetics and the aging nervous system. In G. J. Maletta (Ed.), *Survey report on the aging nervous system* (U.S. Public Health Service Publication No. [NIH] 74-296). Washington, D.C.: U.S. Government Printing Office, 1975.

Rust, L. D. *The performance of arteriosclerotic and non-arteriosclerotic subjects on a mediation-interference task.* Doctoral dissertation, State University of New York, Buffalo, N.Y., 1965.

Rybo, L. Symptoms of the climacterium. *Acta Obstetricia et Gynecologica Scandanavica* [supp.], 1971, **9,** 25.

Sachar, E. J., Halpern, F., Rosenfeld, R. S., Gallager, T. F., and Hellman, L. Plasma urinary testosterone levels in depressed men. *Archives of General Psychiatry,* 1973, **28,** 15.

Sapira, J. D., Scheib, E. T., Moriarity, R., and Shapiro, A. P. Differences in perception between hypertensive and normotensive populations. *Psychosomatic Medicine,* 1971, **33,** 239.

Sarason, S. B., Sarason, E. K., and Cowden, P. Aging and the nature of work. *American Psychologist,* 1975, **30,** 584.

Sataloff, J., and Vassallo, L. Hard-of-hearing senior citizens and the physician. *Geriatrics,* 1966, **21,** 182.

Savage, R. D., Britton, P. G., Bolton, N., and Hall, E. H. *Intellectual function in the aged.* London: Methuen & Co., Ltd., 1973.

Scarr-Salapatek, S. Race, social class and IQ. *Science,* 1971, **174,** 1285.

Schaie, K. W. Rigidity-flexibility and intelligence: a cross sectional study of the adult life span from 20 to 70 years. *Psychological Monographs,* 1958, **72,** 1.

Schaie, K. W. A general model for the study of developmental problems. *Psychological Bulletin,* 1965, **64,** 92.

Schaie, K. W. Age changes and age differences. *Gerontologist,* 1967, **7,** 128 .

Schaie, K. W. A reinterpretation of age-related changes in cognitive structure and functioning. In L. R. Goulet and P. B. Baltes (Eds.), *Life-span developmental psychology: research and theory.* New York: Academic Press, Inc., 1970.

Schaie, K. W. Translations in gerontology—from lab to life: intellectual functioning. *American Psychologist,* 1974, **29,** 802.

Schaie, K. W. Research strategy in developmental human behavior genetics. In K. W. Schaie, V. E. Anderson, G. E. McClearn, and J. Money (Eds.), *Developmental human behavior genetics: nature-nurture redefined.* Lexington, Mass. Lexington Books, D. C. Heath & Co., 1975.

Schaie, K. W., Anderson, E. V., McClearn, G. E., and Money, J. (Eds.), *Developmental human behavior genetics: nature-nurture redefined.* Lexington, Mass.: Lexington Books, D. C. Heath & Co., 1975.

Schaie, K. W., Labouvie, G. V., and Buech, B. U. Generational and cohort-specific differences in adult cognitive functioning: a fourteen year study of independent samples. *Developmental Psychobiology,* 1973, **79,** 18.

Schaie, K. W., Rosenthal, F., and Perlman, R. M. Differential mental deterioration of factorially "pure" functions in later maturity. *Journal of Gerontology,* 1953, **8,** 191.

Schapiro, S. Influence of hormones and environmental stimulation on brain development. In D. H. Ford (Ed.), Influence of hormones on the nervous system. *Proceedings of the International Society of Psychoneuroendocrinology.* Basel: S. Karger, 1971.

Schapiro, S. Some physiological, biochemical and behavioral consequences of neonatal hormone administration: cortisol and thyroxine. *General and Comparative Endocrinology,* 1968, **10,** 214.

Schapiro, S., and Hupperty, M. H. Neonatal cortisol administration and immunological impairment in the adult rat. *Proceedings of the Society for Experimental Biology and Medicine,* 1967, **124,** 744.

Scheibel, M. E., and Scheibel, A. B. Structural changes in the aging brain. In H. Brody, D. Harman, and J. Ordy (Eds.), *Aging* (Vol. 1). *Clinical, morphologic, and neurochemical aspects in the aging central nervous system.* New York: Raven Press, 1975.

Schiffman, S. *Taste and smell changes of foods during the aging process.* Presented at the 28th Annual Meetings of the Gerontological Society, Louisville, 1975.

Schlager, G. S. Selection for blood pressure levels in mice, *Genetics,* 1974, **76,** 537-549.

Schonfield, D. Future commitments and successful aging. I. The random sample. *Journal of Gerontology,* 1973, **28,** 189.

Schonfield, D., and Robertson, B. Memory storage and aging. *Canadian Journal of Psychology,* 1966, **20,** 228.

Schonfield, D., Trueman, V., and Kline, D. Recognition tests of dichotic listening and the age variable. *Journal of Gerontology,* 1972, **27,** 487.

Schuckit, M. A., Miller, P. L., and Hahlbohm, D. Unrecognized psychiatric illness in elderly medical-surgical patients. *Journal of Gerontology,* 1975, **30,** 655.

Schull, W. J., and Neel, J. V. *The effects of inbreeding on Japanese children.* New York: Harper & Row, Publishers, 1969.

Scott, J. P., and Marston, M. V. Critical periods affecting the development of normal and maladjustive social behavior in puppies. *Journal of Genetic Psychology,* 1950, **77,** 25.

Selye, H., and Prioreschi, P. Stress theory of aging. In N. W. Shock (Ed.), *Aging—some social and biological aspects.* Washington, D.C.: American Association for the Advancement of Science, 1960.

Shanas, E., Townsend, P., Wedderburn, D., Friis, H., Milhoj, P., and Stehouwer, J. (Eds.), *Old people in three industrial societies.* New York: Atherton Press, 1968.

Sherman, S. R. Leisure activities in retirement housing. *Journal of Gerontology,* 1974, **29,** 325.

Sidman, R. L., Green, M. C., and Appel, S. H. *Catalog of the neurological mutants of the mouse.* Cambridge, Mass.: Harvard University Press, 1975.

Siegler, I. C. Threats to external validity: the effects of selective drop-out on health, morale, social relations and environmental circumstances in the elderly. Doctoral dissertation, Syracuse University, Syracuse, N.Y., 1971.

Siegler, I. C. The terminal drop hypothesis: fact or artifact? *Experimental Aging Research,* 1975, **1,** 169.

Siegler, I. C., Roseman, J., and Harkins, S. W. *Complexities in the terminal drop hypothesis.* Presented at the Meetings of the 10th International Congress of Gerontology, Jerusalem, Israel, June, 1975.

Sime, M. E., and Kay, H. Inter-problem interference and age. *Journal of Gerontology,* 1962, **17,** 81.

Simon, J. R. Ear preference in a simple reaction time task. *Journal of Experimental Psychology,* 1967, **75,** 49.

Simon, J. R., and Wolf, J. D. Choice reaction time as a function of angular stimulus-response correspondence and age. *Ergonomics,* 1963, **6,** 99.

Simpson, I. H. Problems of the aging in work and retirement. In R. R. Boyd and C. G. Oakes (Eds.), *Foundations of practical gerontology.* Columbia, S.C.: University of South Carolina Press, 1973.

Simpson, I. H., Back, K. W., and McKinney J. C. Continuity of work and retirement activities. In I. H. Simpson and J. C. McKinney (Eds.), *Social aspects of aging.* Durham, N.C.: Duke University Press, 1966.

Skinner, B. F. The phylogeny and ontogeny of behavior. In N. S. Endler, L. R. Boulter, and H. Ossler (Eds.), *Contemporary issues in developmental psychology.* New York: Holt, Rinehart, & Winston, Inc., 1968.

Smith, A. D. Aging and interference with memory. *Journal of Gerontology,* 1975, **30,** 319.

Smith, R. S. Hypertension and oral contraception. *American Journal of Obstetrics and Gynecology,* 1972, **113,** 482.

Smith, W. T., Turner, E., and Sim, M. Cerebral biopsy in the investigation of presenile dementia. *British Journal of Psychiatry,* 1966, **112,** 127.

Spence, D. L. The role of futurity in aging adaptation. *Gerontologist,* 1968, **8,** 180.

Spence, K. W. A theory of emotionally based drive (D) and its relation to performance in simple learning situations. *American Psychologist,* 1958, **13,** 131.

Spence, K. W. Anxiety level and performance in eyelid conditioning, *Psychological Bulletin,* 1964, **61,** 129.

Sperling, G. The information available in brief visual presentations. *Psychological Monographs,* 1960, **74,** 11.

Spieth, W. Cardiovascular health status, age, and psychological performance. *Journal of Gerontology,* 1964, **19,** 277.

Spieth, W. Slowness of task performance and cardiovascular diseases. In A. T. Welford and J. E. Birren (Eds.), *Behavior, aging, and the ner-*

vous system. Springfield, Ill.: Charles C Thomas, Publisher, 1965.

Spinetta, J., Rigler, D., and Karon, M. Personal space as a measure of a dying child's sense of isolation. *Journal of Consulting and Clinical Psychology,* 1974, **42,** 751.

Spitz, H. H. Consolidating facts into the schematized learning and memory system of educable retardates. In N. R. Ellis (Ed.), *International review of research in mental retardation* (Vol. 6). New York: Academic Press, Inc., 1973.

Sprott, R. L. Passive-avoidance conditioning in inbred mice: effects of shock intensity, age, and genotype. *Journal of Comparative and Physiological Psychology,* 1972, **80,** 327.

Sprott, R. L. Passive avoidance performance in mice: evidence for single-locus inheritance. *Behavioral Biology,* 1974, **11,** 231.

Sprott, R. L. Behavioral characterisitcs of C57BL/6J, DBA/2J, and B6D2F1 mice which are potentially useful for gerontological research. *Special Review of Experimental Aging Research: Progress in Biology,* 1975, **1,** 313.

Sprott, R. L. Behavior genetics in aging rodents. In M. F. Elias, and B. E. Eleftheriou (Eds.), *Special review of experimental aging research: progress in biology.* Bar Harbor, Maine: EAR, Inc., 1976.

Sprott, R. L., and Eleftheriou, B. E. Open field behavior in aging inbred strains of mice. *Gerontologia,* 1974, **20,** 155.

Sprott, R. L., and Stavnes, K. L. Avoidance learning, behavior genetics, and aging: a critical review and comment on methodology, *Experimental Aging Research,* 1975, **1,** 145.

Stavnes, K. L. Biogenic amines and behavior: activity and avoidance learning. In P E. Eleftheriou and R. L. Sprott (Eds.), *Hormonal correlates of behavior* (Vol. 2). *An organismic view.* New York: Plenum Publishing Corp., 1975.

Stavnes, K. L., and Sprott, R. L. Effects of age and gentoype on acquisition of an active avoidance response in mice. *Developmental Psychobiology,* 1975, **8,** 437.

Stokes, R. G., and Maddox, G. L. Some social factors in retirement adaptation. *Journal of Gerontology,* 1967, **22,** 329.

Stone, C. P. The age factor in animal learning. I. Rats in the problem box and the maze. *Genetic Psychology Monographs,* 1929a, **5,** 1.

Stone, C. P. The age factor in animal learning. II. Rats in a multiple light discrimination box and a difficult maze. *Genetic Psychology Monographs,* 1929b, **6,** 125.

Stone, C. P., and Wechsler, D. *Wechsler Memory Scale Form II.* New York: The Psychological Corporation, 1945.

Storandt, M., and Hudson, W. Misuse of analysis of covariance in aging research and some partial solutions: a methodological note. *Experimental Aging Research,* 1975, **1,** 121.

Streeten, D., Schletter, F., Clift, G., Stevenson, C., and Dalakos, T. Studies of the renin-angiotensin-aldosterone system in patients with hypertension and in normal subjects. *American Journal of Medicine,* 1969, **46,** 844.

Streib, G. F. Family patterns in retirement. *Journal of Social Issues,* 1958, **14,** 46.

Streib, G. F. Participants and drop-outs in a longitudinal study. *Journal of Gerontology,* 1966, **21,** 200.

Streib, G. F. Disengagement theory in socio-cultural perspective. *International Journal of Psychiatry,* 1968, **6,** 69.

Streib, G. F., and Schneider, C. J. *Retirement in American society: impact and process.* Ithaca, N.Y.: Cornell University Press, 1971.

Strong, E. K. *Change of interests with age.* Stanford, Calif., Stanford University Press, 1931.

Strother, C. R., Schaie, K. W., and Horst, P. The relationship between advanced age and mental abilities. *Journal of Abnormal and Social Psychology,* 1957, **55,** 166.

Surwillo, W. W. Central nervous system factors in simple reaction time. *American Psychologist,* 1960, **15,** 419.

Surwillo, W. W. Frequency of the "alpha" rhythm, reaction time, and age. *Nature,* 1961, **191,** 823.

Surwillo, W. W. The relation of simple response time to brain-wave frequency and the effects of age. *Electroencephalography and Clinical Neurophysiology,* 1963, **15,** 1029.

Surwillo, W. W. The relation of decision time to brain wave frequency and to age. *Electroencephalography and Clinical Neurophysiology,* 1964, **16,** 510.

Surwillo, W. W. Timing of behavior in senescence and the role of the central nervous system. In G. A. Talland (Ed.), *Human aging and behavior.* New York: Academic Press, Inc., 1968.

Taietz, P., and Larson, O. F. Social participation and old age. *Rural Sociology,* 1956, **21,** 229.

Talland, G. A. Initiation of response and reaction time in aging and with brain damage. In A. T. Welford and J. E. Birren (Eds.), *Behavior, aging and the nervous system.* Springfield, Ill.: Charles C Thomas, Publisher, 1965.

Taub, H. A. Effects of coding cues upon short-term memory of aged subjects. *Developmental Psychology,* 1975, **11,** 254.

Taylor, J. A. A personality scale of manifest anxiety. *Journal of Abnormal and Social Psychology,* 1953, **48,** 285.

Tepperman, J. *Metabolic and endocrine physiol-*

ogy. Chicago: Year Book Medical Publishers, Inc., 1973.

Terman, L. M. *The measurement of intelligence.* Boston: Houghton Mifflin Co., 1916.

Tetens, J. N. *Philosophische Versuche über die menschliche Natur und ihre Entwicklung,* (2 vols.). Leipzig: Weidmanns Erben & Reich, 1777.

Thiessen, D. D. Reply to Wilcock on gene action and behavior. *Psychological Bulletin,* 1971, **75,** 103.

Thompson, B., Hart, S. A., and Durno, D. Menopausal age and symptomatology in a general practice. *Journal of Biosocial Science,* 1973, **5,** 71.

Thompson, C. I., and Fitzsimons, T. R. Age differences in aversively motivated visual discrimination learning and retention in male Sprague-Dawley rats. *Journal of Gerontology,* 1976, **31,** 47.

Thompson, L. W., Eisdorfer, C., and Estes, E. H. Cardiovascular disease and behavioral changes in the elderly. In E. Palmore (Ed.), *Normal aging.* Durham, N.C.: Duke University Press, 1970.

Thompson, L. W., and Marsh, G. R. Psychophysiological studies of aging. In C. Eisdorfer and M. P. Lawton (Eds.), *The psychology of adult development and aging.* Washington, D.C.: American Psychological Association, 1973.

Thompson, L. W., Nichols, C. R., and Obrist, W. D. Relation of serum cholesterol to age, sex, and race in an elderly community group. *Journal of Gerontology,* 1965, **20,** 160.

Thompson, R. F. *Foundations of physiological psychology.* New York: Harper & Row, Publishers, 1967.

Thorndike, E. L. *Animal intelligence.* New York: The Macmillan Co., 1898.

Thorndike, E. L. On the improvement in intelligence scores from 14 to 18. *Journal of Educational Psychology,* 1923, **14,** 513.

Thorndike, E. L. *Adult learning.* New York: The Macmillan Co., 1928.

Thorndike, E. L. *Adult interests.* New York: The Macmillan Co., 1935.

Thumin, F. J. Ability scores as related to age among male job applicants. *Journal of Gerontology,* 1970, **25,** 390.

Thumin, F. J., and Boernke, C. Ability scores as related to age among female job applicants. *Journal of Gerontology,* 1966, **21,** 369.

Timiras, P. S. *Developmental physiology and aging.* New York: The Macmillan Co., 1972.

Timiras, P. S., and Bignami, A. Pathophysiology of the aging brain. In M. F. Elias and B. E. Eleftheriou (Eds.), *Special review of experimental aging research: progress in biology.* Bar Harbor, Maine: EAR, Inc., 1976.

Timiras, P. S., and Meisami, E. Changes in gonadal function. In P. S Timiras (Ed.), *Developmental physiology and aging.* New York: The Macmillan Co., 1972.

Tissue, T. Disengagement potential: replication and use as an explanatory variable. *Journal of Gerontology,* 1971, **26,** 76.

Torgersen, S., and Kringlen, E. Blood pressure and personality: a study of the relationship between intrapair differences in systolic blood pressure and personality in monozygotic twins. *Journal of Psychosomatic Research,* 1971, **15,** 183.

Treat, N., and Reese, H. Age, imagery, and pacing in paired-associate learning. Presented at the 27th Annual Meetings of the Gerontological Society, Portland, Ore., Nov., 1974.

Troyer, W. G., Eisdorfer, C., Bogdonoff, M. D., and Wilkie, F. Experimental stress and learning in the aged. *Journal of Abnormal Psychology,* 1967, **72,** 65.

Troyer, W. G., Eisdorfer, C., Wilkie, F., and Bogdonoff, M. D. Free fatty acid responses in the aged individual during performance of learning tasks. *Journal of Gerontology,* 1966, **21,** 415.

Underwood, B. J., and Schulz, R. W. *Meaningfulness and verbal learning.* Philadelphia: J. B. Lippincott Co., 1960.

Utian, W. H. The true clinical features of postmenopause and oophorectomy, and their response to oestrogen therapy. *South African Medical Journal,* 1972, **46,** 732.

Vermeulen, A., Rubens, R., and Verdonck, L. Testosterone secretion and metabolism in male senescence. *Journal of Clinical Endocrinology and Metabolism,* 1972, **34,** 730.

Vernon, P. E. The variation of intelligence with occupation, age, and locality. *British Journal of Psychology,* 1947, **1,** 52.

Verwoerdt, A. *Clinical geropsychiatry.* Baltimore: The Williams & Wilkins Co., 1976.

Verwoerdt, A., Pfeiffer, E., and Wang, H. S. Sexual behavior in senescence. I. Changes in sexual activity and interest of aging men and women. *Journal of Geriatric Psychiatry,* 1969a, **2,** 163.

Verwoerdt, A., Pfeiffer, E., and Wang, H. S. Sexual behavior in senescence. II. Patterns of sexual activity and interest. *Geriatrics,* 1969b, **24,** 137.

Verzar-McDougall, E. J. Studies in learning and memory in aging rats. *Gerontologia,* 1957, **1,** 65.

Wachs, T. O. Reinstatement of early experiences and later learning: an animal analogue for human development. *Developmental Psychobiology,* 1973, **6,** 437.

Wahlsten, D. *Genetic experiments with animal learning: a critical review,* Research Report No. 26, 1971. (Available by writing to Department of Psychology, University of Waterloo, Waterloo, Ontario, Canada.)

Wallach, M. A., and Kogan, N. Aspects of judgment and decision making: interrelationships and changes with age. *Behavioral Science,* 1961, **6,** 23.

Wang, H. S., Obrist, W. D., and Busse, E. W. Neurophysiological correlates of the intellectual function of elderly persons living in the community. *American Journal of Psychiatry,* 1970, **126,** 1205.

Wapner, S., Werner, H., and Comalli, P. E., Jr. Perception of part-whole relationships in middle and old age. *Journal of Gerontology,* 1960, **15,** 412.

Ward, L. F. *Pure sociology.* New York: The Macmillan Co., 1903.

Warren, R. M. Illusory changes in repeated words: differences between young adults and the aged. *American Journal of Psychology,* 1961, **74,** 506.

Warren, R. M., and Warren, R. P. Some age differences in auditory perception. *Bulletin of the New York Academy of Medicine,* 1971, **47,** 1365.

Watson, J. B. *Psychology from the standpoint of a behaviorist.* Philadelphia: J. B. Lippincott Co., 1919.

Watson, J. B. *Behaviorism.* New York: W. W. Norton & Co., Inc., 1930.

Watson, J. B., and Raynor, R. Conditional emotional reactions. *Journal of Experimental Psychology,* 1920, **3,** 1.

Watson, W. E. *Components of reaction time slowing with aging and with hypertension.* Unpublished master's thesis, Syracuse University, Syracuse, N.Y., 1976.

Watson, W. E., Elias, M. F., and Pentz, C. A., III. Hemisphere-hand interactions for the matching of letters. *Experimental Aging Research,* 1975, **1,** 293.

Waugh, N. C., and Norman, D. A. Primary memory. *Psychological Review,* 1965, **72,** 92.

Weale, R. A. On the eye. In A. T. Welford and J. E. Birren (Eds.), *Behavior, aging and the nervous system.* Springfield, Ill.: Charles C Thomas, Publisher, 1965.

Wechsler, D. *The measurement of adult intelligence.* Baltimore: The Williams & Wilkins Co., 1939.

Wechsler, D. A standardized memory scale for clinical use. *Journal of Psychology,* 1945, **19,** 87.

Wechsler, D. *Manual for the Wechsler Adult Intelligence Scale.* New York: The Psychological Corporation, 1955.

Wechsler, D. *The measurement and appraisal of adult intelligence.* Baltimore: The Williams & Wilkins Co., 1958.

Weiner, B. From each according to his abilities: the role of effort in a moral society. *Human Development,* 1973, **16,** 53.

Weiner, B., and Rundquist, W. *Discovering psychology.* Palo Alto, Calif.: Science Research Associates, Inc., 1977.

Weisenburg, T., Roe, A., and McBride, K. E. *Adult intelligence.* New York: The Commonwealth Fund, 1936.

Weiss, A. D. The locus of reaction time change with set, motivation, and age. *Journal of Gerontology,* 1965, **20,** 60.

Welford, A. T. *Ageing and human skill.* Westport, Conn.: Greenwood Press, Inc., 1958.

Welford, A. T. Psychomotor performance. In J. E. Birren (Ed.), *Handbook of aging and the individual.* Chicago: University of Chicago Press, 1959.

Welford, A. T. Performance, biological mechanisms and age: a theoretical sketch. In A. T. Welford and J. E. Birren (Eds.), *Behavior, aging and the nervous system.* Springfield, Ill.: Charles C Thomas, Publisher, 1965.

Welford, A. T. Age changes in discrimination choice and the control of movement: nine years on. *Proceedings of the Eighth International Congress of Gerontology* (Vol. 1). Washington, D.C.: International Association of Gerontology, 1969.

Werboff, J., and Havlena, J. Effects of aging on open field behavior. *Psychological Reports,* 1962, **10,** 395.

Werboff, J. Reply to "comment on effects of aging on open field behavior." *Psychological Reports,* 1962, **10,** 862.

Werner, A. A. Male climacteric. *Journal of the American Medical Association,* 1944, **112,** 1441.

Werner, H. *Comparative psychology of mental development.* New York: International Universities Press, 1948.

Werner, H. The concept of development from a comparative and organismic point of view. In D. B. Harris (Ed.), *The concept of development.* Minneapolis: University of Minnesota Press, 1957.

Wexler, B. C. Correlation of adrenal cortical histopathology with arteriosclerosis in breeder rats. *Acta Endocrinologica,* 1964a, **45,** 613.

Wexler, B. C. Spontaneous arteriosclerosis in repeatedly bred male and female rats. *Journal of Atherosclerosis Research,* 1964b, **4,** 57.

White, C. B., and Johnson, D. F. *Computerized assessment of intelligence: its differential effects on aged and young individuals.* Presented at the

28th Annual Meetings of the Gerontological Society, Louisville, Oct., 1975.

Wickelgren, W. A. Age and storage dynamics in continuous recognition memory. *Developmental Psychology,* 1975, **11,** 165.

Wilcock, J. Gene action and behavior: an evaluation of major gene pleiotropism. *Psychological Bulletin,* 1969, **72,** 1-29.

Wilkie, F. L., and Eisdorfer, C. Intelligence and blood pressure in the aged. *Science,* 1971, **172,** 959.

Wilkie, F. L., and Eisdorfer, C. Terminal changes in intelligence. In E. Palmore (Ed.), *Normal aging II.* Durham, N.C.: Duke University Press, 1974.

Wilkie, F. L., Eisdorfer, C., and Nowlin, J. B. Memory and blood pressure in the aged. *Experimental Aging Research,* 1976, **2,** 3.

Willanger, R. Thygesen, P., Nielsen, R., and Petersen, O. Intellectual impairment and cerebral atrophy—a psychological, neurological, and radiological investigation. *Danish Medical Bulletin,* 1968, **15,** 65.

Willoughby, R. R. Family similarities in mental-test abilities (with a note on the growth and decline of these abilities). *Genetic Psychology Monographs,* 1927, **2,** 235.

Wilson, I. C., Prange, A. J., and Lara, P. P. Methyltestosterone with imipramine in men: conversion of depression to paranoid reaction. *American Journal of Psychiatry,* 1974, **131,** 21.

Winn, F. J., Jr., and Elias, J. W. The total time principle as a substitute for the pacing variable in paired-associate tasks with the aged. *Experimental Aging Research,* 1975, **1,** 307.

Wissler, C. Correlation of mental and physical tests. *Psychological Monographs,* 1901, **16.**

Witte, K. L. Paired-associate learning in young and elderly adults as related to presentation rate. *Psychological Bulletin,* 1975, **82,** 975.

Wittels, I. Age and stimulus meaningfulness in paired-associate learning. *Journal of Gerontology,* 1972, **27,** 372.

Wohlwill, J. F. Methodology and research strategy in the study of developmental change. In L. R. Goulet and P. B. Baltes (Eds.), *Life-span developmental psychology: research and theory.* New York: Academic Press, Inc., 1970.

Wood, V. Age-appropriate behavior for older people. *Gerontologist,* 1971, **11,** 74.

Wood, W. G. Effects of age on ethanol consumption in C57BL/6 and BALB/C mice. *Experimental Aging Research,* 1976, **2,** 425.

Worden, F. G. Hearing and the neural detection of acoustic patterns. *Behavioral Science,* 1971, **16,** 20.

Wright, I. S. Peripheral vascular disease problems in the aged—considerations regarding prevention. *Journal of the American Geriatrics Society,* 1970, **18,** 193.

Wright, W. E., Werboff, J., and Haggett, B. N. Aging and water submersion in C57BL/6J mice: initial performance and retest as a function of recovery and water temperature. *Developmental Psychobiology,* 1971, **4,** 363.

Yamori, Y., Lovenberg, W., and Sjoerdsma, A. Norepinephrine metabolism in brainstem of spontaneously hypertensive rats. *Science,* 1970, **170,** 544.

Yarrow, M. R., Blank, P., Quinn, Q. W., Youmans, E. G., and Stein, J. Social psychological characteristics of old age. In J. E. Birren, R. N. Butler, S. W. Greenhouse, L. Sokoloff, and M. R. Yarrow (Eds.), *Human aging: a biological and behavioral study* (National Institute of Mental Health, U.S. Public Health Service Publication No. 986). Washington, D.C.: U.S. Government Printing Office, 1963.

Yen, F-S, Matsuyama, S. S., and Jarvik, L. F. Survival of octogenarians: six years after initial chromosome examination. *Experimental Aging Research,* 1976, **2,** 17.

Yerkes, R. M. (Ed.) Psychological examining in the United States Army. *Memoirs of the National Academy of Sciences,* 1921, **15,** 1.

Youmans, E. G. Objective and subjective economic disengagement among older rural and urban men. *Journal of Gerontology,* 1966, **21,** 439.

Youmans, E. G. Family disengagement among older urban and rural women. *Journal of Gerontology,* 1967, **22,** 209.

Youmans, E. G. Some perspectives on disengagement theory. *Gerontologist,* 1969, **9,** 254.

Youmans, E. G. Age stratification and value orientations. *International Journal of Aging and Human Development,* 1973, **4,** 53.

Youmans, E. G., and Yarrow, M. Aging and social adaptation: a longitudinal study of healthy old men. In S. Granick and R. D. Patterson (Eds.), *Human aging II: an eleven-year follow-up biomedical and behavioral study* (U.S. Department of Health, Education and Welfare Publication No. [HSM] 71-9037). Washington, D.C.: U.S. Government Printing Office, 1971.

Young, W. C. The hormones and mating behavior. In W. C. Young (Ed.), *Sex and internal secretions.* Baltimore: The Williams & Wilkins Co., 1961.

Zaretsky, H. H., and Halberstam, J. L. Age differences in paired-associate learning. *Journal of Gerontology,* 1968, **23,** 165.

Zung, W. W. K. The measurement of depression. Milwaukee: Lakeside Laboratories, 1967.

INDEX